Petroleum Characterization and Bioprocesses: Numerical and Experimental Investigation

Petroleum Characterization and Bioprocesses: Numerical and Experimental Investigation

Guest Editors

Dicho Stratiev
Dobromir Yordanov
Aijun Guo

Basel • Beijing • Wuhan • Barcelona • Belgrade • Novi Sad • Cluj • Manchester

Guest Editors

Dicho Stratiev
Institute of Biophysics and
Biomedical Engineering
Bulgarian Academy of Sciences
Acad. Georgi Bonchev Str.
Sofia
Bulgaria

Dobromir Yordanov
Industrial Technologies and
Management
Professor Dr. Assen Zlatarov
Burgas
Bulgaria

Aijun Guo
Department of Applied
Chemistry
China University of
Petroleum (East China)
Qingdao
China

Editorial Office
MDPI AG
Grosspeteranlage 5
4052 Basel, Switzerland

This is a reprint of the Special Issue, published open access by the journal *Processes* (ISSN 2227-9717), freely accessible at: www.mdpi.com/journal/processes/special_issues/B58S4E3VUG.

For citation purposes, cite each article independently as indicated on the article page online and as indicated below:

Lastname, A.A.; Lastname, B.B. Article Title. *Journal Name* **Year**, *Volume Number*, Page Range.

ISBN 978-3-7258-3736-6 (Hbk)
ISBN 978-3-7258-3735-9 (PDF)
https://doi.org/10.3390/books978-3-7258-3735-9

© 2025 by the authors. Articles in this book are Open Access and distributed under the Creative Commons Attribution (CC BY) license. The book as a whole is distributed by MDPI under the terms and conditions of the Creative Commons Attribution-NonCommercial-NoDerivs (CC BY-NC-ND) license (https://creativecommons.org/licenses/by-nc-nd/4.0/).

Contents

About the Editors vii

Preface ix

Dicho Stratiev, Dobromir Yordanov and Aijun Guo
Special Issue: "Petroleum Characterization and Bioprocesses: Numerical and Experimental Investigation"
Reprinted from: *Processes* 2024, 12, 2876, https://doi.org/10.3390/pr12122876 1

Jorge Ancheyta
The Handicap of New Technologies: Nobody Wants to Be the First for Commercial Application
Reprinted from: *Processes* 2024, 12, 467, https://doi.org/10.3390/pr12030467 6

Walaa S. Osman, Asmaa E. Fadel, Shazly M. Salem, Abeer M. Shoaib, Abdelrahman G. Gadallah and Ahmed A. Bhran
Optimum Design of Naphtha Recycle Isomerization Unit with Modification by Adding De-Isopentanizer
Reprinted from: *Processes* 2023, 11, 3406, https://doi.org/10.3390/pr11123406 16

Xiaofeng Chang, Quande Wang, Jiale Hu, Yan Sun, Shijun Chen, Xuefan Gu and Gang Chen
Preparation and Application of New Polyhydroxy Ammonium Shale Hydration Inhibitor
Reprinted from: *Processes* 2023, 11, 3102, https://doi.org/10.3390/pr11113102 33

Ye Yang, Zongguang Sun, Yanhai Yang, Chonghua Wang and Lin Qi
Research on the Damage Model of Cold Recycled Mixtures with Asphalt Emulsion under Freeze-Thaw Cycles
Reprinted from: *Processes* 2023, 11, 3031, https://doi.org/10.3390/pr11103031 50

Weijun Ni, Guohao Yang, Jie Dong, Yansong Pan, Gang Chen and Xuefan Gu
Research and Evaluation of Foam-Drainage Corrosion-Inhibition Hydrate Anti-Aggregation Integrated Agent
Reprinted from: *Processes* 2023, 11, 2745, https://doi.org/10.3390/pr11092745 65

Yunlei Zang, Huaizhu Liu, Dong Chen, Shu Zhang, Shanjian Li and Gang Chen
Synergistic Catalysis of Reservoir Minerals and Exogenous Catalysts on Aquathermolysis of Heavy Oil
Reprinted from: *Processes* 2023, 11, 2635, https://doi.org/10.3390/pr11092635 81

Dianfa Du, Peng Liu, Lichuan Ren, Yuan Li, Yujie Tang and Fanghui Hao
A Volume Fracturing Percolation Model for Tight Reservoir Vertical Wells
Reprinted from: *Processes* 2023, 11, 2575, https://doi.org/10.3390/pr11092575 95

Lina M. Yañez Jaramillo, Joy H. Tannous and Arno de Klerk
Persistent Free Radicals in Petroleum
Reprinted from: *Processes* 2023, 11, 2067, https://doi.org/10.3390/pr11072067 116

Montserrat Cerón Ferrusca, Rubi Romero, Sandra Luz Martínez, Armando Ramírez-Serrano and Reyna Natividad
Biodiesel Production from Waste Cooking Oil: A Perspective on Catalytic Processes
Reprinted from: *Processes* 2023, 11, 1952, https://doi.org/10.3390/pr11071952 134

Shuai Ma, Yunyun Li, Rigu Su, Jianxun Wu, Lingyuan Xie, Junshi Tang, et al.
Ketones in Low-Temperature Oxidation Products of Crude Oil
Reprinted from: *Processes* 2023, 11, 1664, https://doi.org/10.3390/pr11061664 174

Sofia M. Kosolapova, Makar S. Smal, Viacheslav A. Rudko and Igor N. Pyagay
A New Approach for Synthesizing Fatty Acid Esters from Linoleic-Type Vegetable Oil
Reprinted from: *Processes* **2023**, *11*, 1534, https://doi.org/10.3390/pr11051534 185

Jeramie J. Adams, Joseph F. Rovani, Jean-Pascal Planche, Jenny Loveridge, Alex Literati, Ivelina Shishkova, et al.
SAR-AD Method to Characterize Eight SARA Fractions in Various Vacuum Residues and Follow Their Transformations Occurring during Hydrocracking and Pyrolysis
Reprinted from: *Processes* **2023**, *11*, 1220, https://doi.org/10.3390/pr11041220 203

Hugo Kittel, Jiří Horský and Pavel Šimáček
Properties of Selected Alternative Petroleum Fractions and Sustainable Aviation Fuels
Reprinted from: *Processes* **2023**, *11*, 935, https://doi.org/10.3390/pr11030935 241

A. Qubian, A. S. Abbas, N. Al-Khedhair, J. F. Peres, D. Stratiev, I. Shishkova, et al.
Screening and Investigation on Inhibition of Sediment Formation in a Kuwait Light Crude Oil by Commercial Additives with Some Guidelines for Field Applications
Reprinted from: *Processes* **2023**, *11*, 818, https://doi.org/10.3390/pr11030818 255

Esaú A. Hernández, Carlos Lira-Galeana and Jorge Ancheyta
Analysis of Asphaltene Precipitation Models from Solubility and Thermodynamic-Colloidal Theories
Reprinted from: *Processes* **2023**, *11*, 765, https://doi.org/10.3390/pr11030765 280

Dicho Stratiev, Sotir Sotirov, Evdokia Sotirova, Svetoslav Nenov, Rosen Dinkov, Ivelina Shishkova, et al.
Prediction of Molecular Weight of Petroleum Fluids by Empirical Correlations and Artificial Neuron Networks
Reprinted from: *Processes* **2023**, *11*, 426, https://doi.org/10.3390/pr11020426 303

Dicho Stratiev, Rosen Dinkov, Mariana Tavlieva, Ivelina Shishkova, Georgi Nikolov Palichev, Simeon Ribagin, et al.
Correlations of HTSD to TBP and Bulk Properties to Saturate Content of a Wide Variety of Crude Oils
Reprinted from: *Processes* **2023**, *11*, 420, https://doi.org/10.3390/pr11020420 319

About the Editors

Dicho Stratiev

Dicho Stratiev is the chief process engineer in the LUKOIL Neftohim Burgas, Bulgaria (LNB). During his 35 years with LNB, he has held several positions as a process engineer in the Institute for Oil Refining and Petrochemistry (IORP), a unit manager on the Visbreaker, Vacuum distillation, and FCC units, director of IORP, and chief process engineer. He holds Ph.D. and D.Sc. degrees and is the author of more than 300 papers and 3 books and has 1700 citations. Professor Dicho Stratiev has been the supervisor of fourteen successfully defended Ph.D. theses.

Dobromir Yordanov

Dobromir Yordanov is a full professor at the Burgas University "Professor Dr. Assen Zlatarov". He teaches at the Industrial Technologies and Management Department in the field of the technology of fossil and synthetic fuels and quality management. Professor Dobromir Yordanov is the author of more than 120 articles and has more than 250 citations.

Aijun Guo

Aijun Guo is a professor at the State Key Laboratory of Heavy Oil Processing, Department of Applied Chemistry, College of Chemical Engineering China University of Petroleum (East China), Qingdao. He has an H-index of 20, is an author of 155 papers, and has over 1500 citations.

Preface

Petroleum is a valuable mineral source rich in hydrocarbons, which, after refining, can be used either as components for the production of internal combustion engine fuels or as feeds for the production of chemicals. As the quality of crude oil is the single factor that most affects oil refining performance, its characterization has a pivotal importance for refining process performance optimization. Bioprocesses, due to their versatile nature, can be employed in the processes of production of sustainable energy sources and find applications in many areas of human activity. Petroleum characterization and bioprocesses can be modeled by the use of different numerical techniques. Nonlinear least squares methods and metaheuristic methods like artificial neural networks, genetic algorithms, colony optimization, least square support vector machines (LSSVMs), radial basis function (RBF) neural networks, multilayer perceptrons (MLPs), support vector regression (SVR), adaptive neuro-fuzzy inference systems (ANFIS), decision trees (DTs), random forests (RF), and simulated annealing programming find application in research of petroleum characterization and bioprocesses. This Special Issue addresses researchers in the fields of petroleum fluid characterization and bioprocesses. It aims to collect current work in the field of "numerical modeling and experimental investigation in characterization of petroleum and its derivatives and bioprocesses". The scope of this Special Issue includes cases of investigations on petroleum property relations, modeling of petroleum properties, application of different methods for characterization of petroleum and its derivatives, sustainable fuels, biofuels, petroleum refining process performance optimization, and bioprocesses.

Dicho Stratiev, Dobromir Yordanov, and Aijun Guo
Guest Editors

Editorial

Special Issue: "Petroleum Characterization and Bioprocesses: Numerical and Experimental Investigation"

Dicho Stratiev [1,2,*], Dobromir Yordanov [3] and Aijun Guo [4]

[1] LUKOIL Neftohim Burgas, 8104 Burgas, Bulgaria
[2] Institute of Biophysics and Biomedical Engineering, Bulgarian Academy of Sciences, Georgi Bonchev 105, 1113 Sofia, Bulgaria
[3] Department Industrial Technologies and Management, University Prof. Dr. Assen Zlatarov, Professor Yakimov 1, 8010 Burgas, Bulgaria; dobromirj@abv.bg
[4] State Key Laboratory of Heavy Oil Processing, Department of Applied Chemistry, College of Chemical Engineering, China University of Petroleum (East China), 66 Changjiang West Road, Qingdao 266580, China; ajguo@upc.edu.cn
* Correspondence: stratiev.dicho@neftochim.bg

Petroleum is a valuable mineral source rich in hydrocarbons, which, after refining, can be used either as components in the production of internal combustion engine fuels, or in feeds for the production of chemicals. While the use of petroleum hydrocarbons as components for internal combustion engine fuels is expected to decrease due to efficiency improvements, advances in clean energy generation, and stricter environmental regulations, along with stricter policies, the use of petroleum as a feedstock for chemical production is expected to increase. Many studies dedicated to the effect that feed quality has on the petroleum-refining process performance have reported that the petroleum feedstock is the single variable that most affects the performance of oil-refining processes. Therefore, petroleum characterization has pivotal importance where oil-refining process performance optimization is concerned. Bioprocesses, due to their versatile nature, can be employed in the production of sustainable energy sources and find applications in many areas of human activity.

Petroleum characterization and bioprocesses can be modeled via different numerical techniques. Nonlinear least-squared methods and meta-heuristic methods such as artificial neural networks, genetic algorithms, and ant-colony optimization, least-square support vector machine (LSSVM), radial basis function (RBF) neural network, multilayer perceptron (MLP), support vector regression (SVR), adaptive neuro-fuzzy inference system (ANFIS), decision trees (DTs), random forest (RF), and simulated annealing programming find application in research on petroleum characterization and bioprocesses.

This Special Issue aims to showcase cutting-edge research on numerical modeling and experimental investigation in the characterization of petroleum and its derivatives, and bioprocesses. The scope includes cases of investigations on petroleum property relationships, the modeling of petroleum properties, the application of different methods for the characterization of petroleum and its derivatives, sustainable fuels, biofuels, petroleum-refining process performance optimization, and bioprocesses. Included in this Special Issue are seventeen contributions from researchers across the globe in the fields of petroleum fluid characterization and bioprocesses.

Osman et al. [1] present an investigation dedicated to a light naphtha isomerization process where they employ Aspen HYSYS version 12.1 to simulate the operation of commercial once-through isomerization unit with the aim to find the best design that efficiently raises octane number at the lowest cost. They discovered that the optimum unit configuration can enhance the isomerate octane number by 7% and decrease operation costs by 13%.

Chang et al. [2] discuss the wellbore instability caused by the hydration of shale formations during drilling and how the shale formation can be inhibited by using polyhydroxy-alkanolamine by employing an anti-swelling test, linear swelling test, wash-durable test, and montmorillonite hydration and dispersion experiment. The explored inhibition mechanism disclosed that the polyhydroxy-alkanolamine can permeate and adsorb on the surface of montmorillonite, thus considerably decreasing the dispersion ability of water to easily hydrated shale. The obtained results indicate that the stability of a wellbore can be saved by employing the approach used in this study.

Yang et al. [3] examine the performance of the destroy and damage model of cold recycled mixtures with asphalt emulsion (CRME), which suffer the majority of damage from freezing and thawing cycles in seasonally frozen regions. The extent of the damage is investigated at 60 °C and −10 °C, the mechanical properties are analyzed in a laboratory, and the damage evolution models based on macroscopic properties, reliability, and damage theory are then developed. The study clearly indicates that the freezing and thawing cycles accelerated the damage caused by CRME, especially under complete water saturation conditions.

Ni et al. [4] communicate that during the conventional operations in natural gas exploitation, it has been found that the different chemicals used to separately control foam drainage, corrosion inhibition, and hydrate inhibition are frequently ineffective when applied together. For that reason, the authors investigate the application of integrated formulation of multiple chemical agents (0.1% sodium alpha-olefin sulfonate (AOST) + 0.3% dodecyl dimethyl betaine (BS-12) + 0.3% sodium lignosulfonate + 0.5% hydrazine hydrate) to simultaneously control foam drainage, corrosion inhibition, and hydrate inhibition of wellbore fluid in natural gas exploitation. They discovered that this formulation is capable of effective control of the processes mentioned above.

Zang et al. [5] explore the feasibility of viscosity reduction in heavy oil in the existing heavy oil extraction technology by employment of the synergistic catalytic effect of reservoir minerals and exogenous catalysts under the reaction system of a hydrogen-rich environment. They reveal that the sodium montmorillonite within the reservoir minerals exhibits an optimal catalytic effect, and its combination with catalyst C-Fe (catechol iron) results in a viscosity reduction rate of about 60%. Following the addition of ethanol as a hydrogen donor under the optimal reaction conditions, the viscosity decrease reaches 75%. It is observed that the synergistic catalytic aquathermolysis of heavy oil with an exogenous catalyst and minerals promotes the breaking of the C-C, C-N, and C-S bonds.

Du et al. [6] demonstrate the development of a seven-area percolation model for volume fracturing vertical wells in tight reservoirs based on the nonlinear seepage characteristics of tight reservoirs and the reconstruction mode of vertical wells with actual volume fracturing. After the verification of the model, the impact of the fracture network parameters on the pressure and production is studied. The Results Of The Study Show The Leading Importance Of For The Design Of Vertical Well Volume Fracturing Design In Tight Reservoirs.

Jaramillo et al. [7] provide a review of the field of persistent free radicals in petroleum with the aim of addressing and explaining apparent inconsistencies between free radical persistence and reactivity. It is shown that the persistent free radical content in petroleum is of the order 1018 spins/g (1 µmol/g), with higher and lower values found depending on origin and in different distillation fractions. The straight-run petroleum and converted petroleum demonstrate different levels of persistent free radicals, and the differences are due to straight-run petroleum being an equilibrated mixture, but converted petroleum is not at equilibrium, and the free radical concentration can change over time. Persistent free radical species are partitioned during the solvent classification of whole oil, with the asphaltene (n-alkane insoluble) fraction having a higher concentration of persistent free radicals than that of maltenes (n-alkane soluble). However, attempts to relate persistent free radical concentration to petroleum composition were inconclusive.

Ma et al. [8] investigate ketone compounds as oxidation products of crude oil in the in situ combustion (ISC) process. Low-temperature oxidation (LTO) experiments at 170 °C, 220 °C, 270 °C, and 320 °C are carried out, and the obtained thermally oxidized oils are analyzed for the molecular composition of different kinds of ketones (fatty ketones, naphthenic ketones, and aromatic ketones). The concentrations of ketones peak at 170 °C and decrease at high temperatures due to over-oxidation. The nitrogen-containing compounds are more easily oxidized to ketone compounds than their hydrocarbon counterparts in the LTO process.

Kosolapova et al. [9] synthesize fatty acid esters from linoleic-type oil and ethanol via transesterification reactions in different ranges of volumetric ratios of the ethanol to the linoleic-type oil with the aim being to magnify the kinetics of the process. The synthesis is carried out in the presence of a homogeneous alkaline catalyst. Optimal process conditions have been determined to shorten the reaction time from 2.5 h to 5 min while keeping a high conversion level. The obtained results show the possibility to produce fatty acid esters from linoleic raw materials containing up to 16% of free fatty acids.

Adams et al. [10] show how the use of model compounds can provide some chemical boundaries for the eight-fraction SAR-AD^{TM} characterization method for heavy oils. It is revealed that the saturates fraction consists of linear and highly cyclic alkanes; the Aro-1 fraction consists of molecules with a single aromatic ring; the Aro-2 fraction consists of mostly two- and three-ring fused aromatic molecules, the pericondensed four-ring molecule pyrene, and molecules with 3–5 rings that are not fused; and the Aro-3 fraction consists of four-membered linear and catacondensed aromatics, larger pericondensed aromatics, and large polycyclic aromatic hydrocarbons. The resins fraction consists of mostly fused aromatic ring systems containing polar functional groups and metallated polar vanadium oxide porphyrin compounds, and the asphaltene fraction consists of both island- and archipelago-type structures with a broad range of molecular weight variation, aromaticity, and heteroatom contents. The behavior of the eight SAR-AD^{TM} fractions during hydrocracking and pyrolysis was investigated, and quantitative relations were established.

Kittel et al. [11] employ six alternative jet fuel samples of different origins to investigate their jet fuel-specific properties, i.e., aromatics, smoke point, freezing point, and net specific energy, and these properties were compared to standard hydrotreated straight-run Jet A-1 kerosene. Although the properties of six jet fuel samples substantially diverge, they could be well correlated, which provides an opportunity to study possible synergies in blending these components. The current methods and instruments used do not always allow a precise determination of the smoke point (>50 mm) and freezing point (<80 °C).

Qubian et al. [12] test a light crude bottom hole fluid sample from a deep well with an asphaltene deposition problem in a laboratory. Density, viscosity, bubble point, GOR, and asphaltene onset pressure are examined at a PVT laboratory. Asphaltene characterization is performed by using asphaltene phase diagrams generated from two developed software programs in both Matlab and Excel codes. Eleven chemical inhibitors from five global companies were tested to inhibit the precipitation. The optimum concentration and the amount of reduction in precipitation were determined for all of these chemicals to identify the most suitable ones.

Hernández et al. [13] analyze the action of twenty-five models based on the equation-of-state (EoS), polymer solution, and thermodynamic-colloidal theories to predict the thermodynamic conditions under which asphaltenes precipitate by matching the literature experimental data of precipitated asphaltene mass fractions. The analysis recognizes the necessity for further model elaboration for general applications over wide pressure, temperature, and composition intervals.

Stratiev et al. [14] verify which of the correlations (proposed in the literature) to predict petroleum fluid molecular weight in the range of 70 to 1685 g/mol are the most appropriate. A total of 430 data points for the boiling point, specific gravity, and molecular weight of petroleum fluids and individual hydrocarbons were extracted from the literature. Twelve empirical correlations taken from the literature, and two additional different techniques, nonlinear regression and artificial neural networks (ANNs), were used to model the molecular weight of the 430 petroleum fluid samples. The ANN model demonstrates the best accuracy of prediction with a relative standard error (RSE) of 7.2%, followed by the newly developed nonlinear regression correlation with a RSE of 10.9%.

Stratiev et al. [15] study forty-eight crude oils pertaining to the five crude oil groups (extra light, light, medium, heavy, and extra heavy) via HTSD, TBP, and SARA analyses. A modified SARA analysis of petroleum facilitating the attainment of a mass balance $\geq$97 wt.% for light crude oils was proposed; a procedure for the simulation of petroleum TBP curves from HTSD data using nonlinear regression and Riazi's distribution model was developed; and a new correlation to predict petroleum saturate content from specific gravity and pour point with an average absolute deviation of 2.5 wt.%, maximum absolute deviation of 6.6 wt.%, and bias of 0.01 wt.% was established.

Ferrusca et al. [16] present a review of the classification of the lipidic feedstocks and the catalysts for biodiesel production. The different processes and feedstocks through which biodiesel is obtained are reviewed, and their pros and cons are discussed. Ferrusca et al. also investigate the advances in the study of bifunctional catalysts, which are capable of simultaneously carrying out the esterification of free fatty acids (FFAs) and the triglycerides present in biodiesel feedstocks. For a better understanding of biodiesel production, flow diagrams and the mechanisms implied by each type of process (enzymatic, homogenous, and heterogeneous) are provided.

Ancheyta [17] discusses the difficulties researchers face when trying to convince decision makers in industries to apply a new technology that has been established in a small-scale laboratory. He gives an example of a moderate-reaction-severity process for hydrotreating of heavy crude oil (HIDRO-IMP technology) in fixed-bed reactors, in which despite the positive technical and economical results, the decision makers in petroleum refining ask for previous commercial applications of the process developed. The different stages of development of the HIDRO-IMP technology are remarked upon, and some results that affirm its feasibility for commercial application are discussed.

The Guest Editors thank all the authors who submitted their contributions to this Special Issue.

Conflicts of Interest: Author Dicho Stratiev was employed by LUKOIL Neftohim Burgas. The remaining authors declare that the research was conducted in the absence of any commercial or financial relationships that could be construed as a potential conflict of interest.

References

1. Osman, W.S.; Fadel, A.E.; Salem, S.M.; Shoaib, A.M.; Gadallah, A.G.; Bhran, A.A. Optimum Design of Naphtha Recycle Isomerization Unit with Modification by Adding De-Isopentanizer. *Processes* **2023**, *11*, 3406. [CrossRef]
2. Chang, X.; Wang, Q.; Hu, J.; Sun, Y.; Chen, S.; Gu, X.; Chen, G. Preparation and Application of New Polyhydroxy Ammonium Shale Hydration Inhibitor. *Processes* **2023**, *11*, 3102. [CrossRef]
3. Yang, Y.; Sun, Z.; Yang, Y.; Wang, C.; Qi, L. Research on the Damage Model of Cold Recycled Mixtures with Asphalt Emulsion under Freeze-Thaw Cycles. *Processes* **2023**, *11*, 3031. [CrossRef]
4. Ni, W.; Yang, G.; Dong, J.; Pan, Y.; Chen, G.; Gu, X. Research and Evaluation of Foam-Drainage Corrosion-Inhibition Hydrate Anti-Aggregation Integrated Agent. *Processes* **2023**, *11*, 2745. [CrossRef]
5. Zang, Y.; Liu, H.; Chen, D.; Zhang, S.; Li, S.; Chen, G. Synergistic Catalysis of Reservoir Minerals and Exogenous Catalysts on Aquathermolysis of Heavy Oil. *Processes* **2023**, *11*, 2635. [CrossRef]
6. Du, D.; Liu, P.; Ren, L.; Li, Y.; Tang, Y.; Hao, F. A Volume Fracturing Percolation Model for Tight Reservoir Vertical Wells. *Processes* **2023**, *11*, 2575. [CrossRef]
7. Yañez Jaramillo, L.M.; Tannous, J.H.; de Klerk, A. Persistent Free Radicals in Petroleum. *Processes* **2023**, *11*, 2067. [CrossRef]
8. Ma, S.; Li, Y.; Su, R.; Wu, J.; Xie, L.; Tang, J.; Wang, X.; Pan, J.; Wang, Y.; Shi, Q.; et al. Ketones in Low-Temperature Oxidation Products of Crude Oil. *Processes* **2023**, *11*, 1664. [CrossRef]
9. Kosolapova, S.M.; Smal, M.S.; Rudko, V.A.; Pyagay, I.N. A New Approach for Synthesizing Fatty Acid Esters from Linoleic-Type Vegetable Oil. *Processes* **2023**, *11*, 1534. [CrossRef]
10. Adams, J.J.; Rovani, J.F.; Planche, J.-P.; Loveridge, J.; Literati, A.; Shishkova, I.; Palichev, G.; Kolev, I.; Atanassov, K.; Nenov, S.; et al. SAR-AD Method to Characterize Eight SARA Fractions in Various Vacuum Residues and Follow Their Transformations Occurring during Hydrocracking and Pyrolysis. *Processes* **2023**, *11*, 1220. [CrossRef]
11. Kittel, H.; Horský, J.; Šimáček, P. Properties of Selected Alternative Petroleum Fractions and Sustainable Aviation Fuels. *Processes* **2023**, *11*, 935. [CrossRef]
12. Qubian, A.; Abbas, A.S.; Al-Khedhair, N.; Peres, J.F.; Stratiev, D.; Shishkova, I.; Nikolova, R.; Toteva, V.; Riazi, M.R. Screening and Investigation on Inhibition of Sediment Formation in a Kuwait Light Crude Oil by Commercial Additives with Some Guidelines for Field Applications. *Processes* **2023**, *11*, 818. [CrossRef]

13. Hernández, E.A.; Lira-Galeana, C.; Ancheyta, J. Analysis of Asphaltene Precipitation Models from Solubility and Thermodynamic-Colloidal Theories. *Processes* **2023**, *11*, 765. [CrossRef]
14. Stratiev, D.; Sotirov, S.; Sotirova, E.; Nenov, S.; Dinkov, R.; Shishkova, I.; Kolev, I.V.; Yordanov, D.; Vasilev, S.; Atanassov, K.; et al. Prediction of Molecular Weight of Petroleum Fluids by Empirical Correlations and Artificial Neuron Networks. *Processes* **2023**, *11*, 426. [CrossRef]
15. Stratiev, D.; Dinkov, R.; Tavlieva, M.; Shishkova, I.; Nikolov Palichev, G.; Ribagin, S.; Atanassov, K.; Stratiev, D.D.; Nenov, S.; Pilev, D.; et al. Correlations of HTSD to TBP and Bulk Properties to Saturate Content of a Wide Variety of Crude Oils. *Processes* **2023**, *11*, 420. [CrossRef]
16. Cerón Ferrusca, M.; Romero, R.; Martínez, S.L.; Ramírez-Serrano, A.; Natividad, R. Biodiesel Production from Waste Cooking Oil: A Perspective on Catalytic Processes. *Processes* **2023**, *11*, 1952. [CrossRef]
17. Ancheyta, J. The Handicap of New Technologies: Nobody Wants to Be the First for Commercial Application. *Processes* **2024**, *12*, 467. [CrossRef]

Disclaimer/Publisher's Note: The statements, opinions and data contained in all publications are solely those of the individual author(s) and contributor(s) and not of MDPI and/or the editor(s). MDPI and/or the editor(s) disclaim responsibility for any injury to people or property resulting from any ideas, methods, instructions or products referred to in the content.

Opinion

The Handicap of New Technologies: Nobody Wants to Be the First for Commercial Application

Jorge Ancheyta [1,2]

[1] Instituto Mexicano del Petróleo, Eje Central Lázaro Cárdenas No. 152, Ciudad de México C.P. 07730, Mexico; jancheyt@imp.mx

[2] Instituto Politécnico Nacional, ESIQIE-IPN, Unidad Profesional "Adolfo López Mateos", Ciudad de México C.O. 07730, Mexico

Abstract: This work highlights the frustration that a researcher may face when trying to convince people in industries to use a new technology that has been developed in a small-scale laboratory. A moderate-reaction-severity process for hydrotreating of heavy crude oil (HIDRO-IMP technology) in fixed-bed reactors is used as an example. Although the development of such a technology has been scaled-up from bench and pilot-plant scales to a semi-commercial level with positive technical and economical results, the people in petroleum refinery who make decisions on the suitability of technologies for commercial implementation always ask for previous applications of the process developed. The different stages of development of the HIDRO-IMP technology are commented on, and some results that corroborate its feasibility for commercial application are discussed.

Keywords: technology development; semi-commercial level; commercial application; HIDRO-IMP

Citation: Ancheyta, J. The Handicap of New Technologies: Nobody Wants to Be the First for Commercial Application. *Processes* **2024**, *12*, 467. https://doi.org/10.3390/pr12030467

Academic Editors: Aijun Guo, Dicho Stratiev and Dobromir Yordanov

Received: 5 February 2024
Revised: 20 February 2024
Accepted: 21 February 2024
Published: 25 February 2024

Copyright: © 2024 by the author. Licensee MDPI, Basel, Switzerland. This article is an open access article distributed under the terms and conditions of the Creative Commons Attribution (CC BY) license (https:// creativecommons.org/licenses/by/ 4.0/).

1. Introduction

The main wish of a scientific researcher is to see the results of their laboratory investigation in commercial application. Most of the time, research is conducted to obtain more knowledge on certain phenomena without a clear objective for possible commercial application. This mostly happens in universities, although recently, these have been receiving funding from the industrial sector and are needing to focus more on providing solutions to industries. Achieving the goal of the commercial application of a technology can sometimes be frustrating, depending on various factors such as the following: (1) Competitors, which typically dominate the market with old, mature, and well-established technologies that are preferred by those in the industry—not exactly by being the best option but due to their long experience working with them. Even if the new technology proposed shows better economic benefits (lower investment and operating costs, with the consequent higher internal rate of return and payback period) and superior performance (higher yields and better-quality products), those in the industry still prefer the processes that are already in use. This preference may be influenced by other non-technical factors, which will not be commented on here. (2) Market needs: there is no global solution to all problems—one technology can be attractive for some clients but not for others. For instance, European refineries mostly use catalytic hydrocracking processes to produce low-sulfur diesel, whereas in refineries in America (the continent), catalytic hydrotreating process is preferred. Thus, it would be complicated to compete in one of these markets with technologies different from those that they use. (3) Investment costs: currently, some industries are facing problems related to investing in installing new technologies, and they choose to revamp the old processes available. Even if there is an investment group that proposes a service with a fee in return, with zero investment cost, they are sometimes not interested in such a business model.

If the technology is new, the most commonly asked question when trying to convince end users to install a plant in their facilities is, where has this technology been used before? It is fully understandable that the end user is concerned about the potential risks associated with the commercial application of new technologies. However, it is also true that successful technological developments need to be scaled up for commercial application.

In the case of the petroleum refining industry, and surely in other industries as well, some large companies have their own research centers, and, once a technology is developed, access to industrial application is relatively easy. Unfortunately, this is not the case for many universities and research institutions, which need to demonstrate that a developed technology is indeed better than commercially available ones and that it is economically attractive to be interested in it. In any case, decision-making people always ask for previous commercial applications of a new technology. Can you imagine the face of researchers when they are asked for this? The common answer of a technology developer is, how can I have my technology commercialized if there is no chance to demonstrate it at the industrial level? This seems to be the same controversy as when a recently graduated engineer looks for a job, with employers asking for previous experience from young engineers who have never worked.

Even if a semi-commercial demonstration test of a technology has been performed, sometimes, this is not enough to obtain the authorization for its industrial implementation, which is worst if the testing level is only at the laboratory scale. In summary, nobody wants to be the first for the commercial application of new technologies. This situation motivated me to share my own experience of technology development with the scientific community, as well as my frustration for not achieving my scientific wish—at least, so far.

2. The HIDRO-IMP Technology

The technology that I am referring to is HIDRO-IMP. The word "HIDRO" refers to hydrogen in Spanish (hidrógeno). It is a fixed-bed catalytic process for the hydrotreating of heavy and extra-heavy crude oils and residua that works at moderate reaction severity (under mild conditions of temperature and pressure). The HIDRO-IMP technology was developed by the Mexican Institute of Petroleum (IMP). Figure 1 shows a simplified flow process diagram of the HIDRO-IMP technology. As can be observed, the plant configuration is a typical one, found in other hydrotreating processes. That is, it includes feed conditioning, fixed-bed reactors, separation products, and hydrogen recycling as main sections. The equipment involved in each section is the same as in other commercial hydrotreating plants, e.g., fixed-bed reactors, pumps, heaters, compressors, and separators; mainly, there is no complex equipment, and there is therefore no need for a big plant to demonstrate the performance of this technology.

The initial step involves splitting full boiling-range heavy crude oil into a light fraction and a heavy fraction (typically, a sort of atmospheric residue). The heavy fraction is subjected to hydrotreating conditions in a first fixed-bed reactor, where substantial metal and asphaltene removal is achieved and at least a portion of sulfur and nitrogen is eliminated. The partially converted products from this stage enter a second fixed-bed reactor to achieve substantial removal of sulfur and nitrogen and a moderate level of hydrocracking. The reactor effluent is sent to a high-pressure separator where the liquid products are recovered from the gases. The liquid stream from the high-pressure separator is provided with additional stripping to remove the remaining dissolved hydrogen sulfide. The gas mixture from the high-pressure separator is fed to the scrubbing unit to remove hydrogen sulfide and ammonia, and the resulting high hydrogen purity stream is recompressed and recycled to the reaction system. Finally, the liquid stream is either mixed with the light fraction to obtain upgraded oil, or both streams (the product from the reactors and light fraction from fractionation) can be sent to be utilized in the distillation of crude oil. The first option aims to produce better-quality upgraded oil for commercialization purposes (upstream sector), and the objective of the second option is to serve as a means of pretreating the crude oil before it enters the atmospheric distillation column in a refinery.

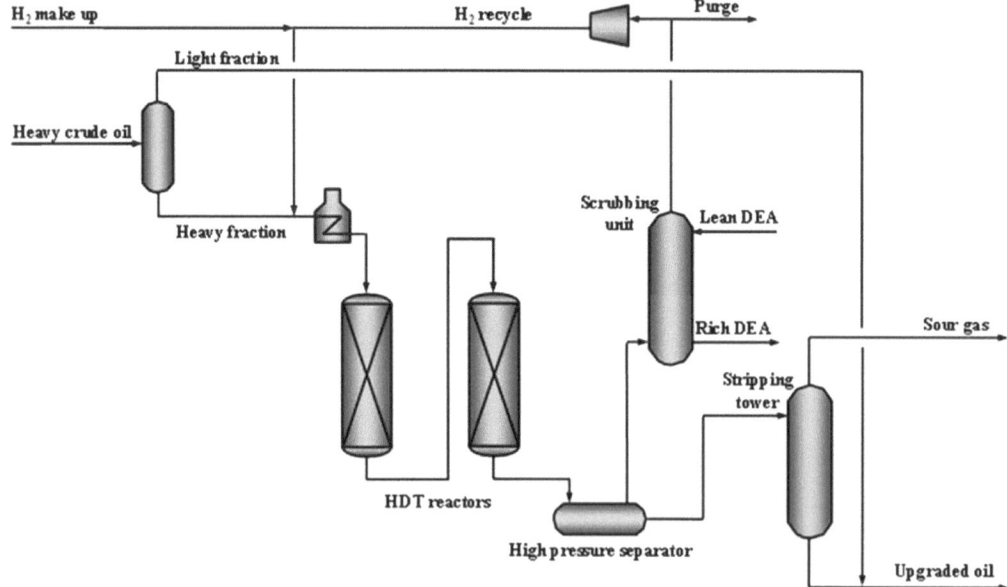

Figure 1. Simplified flow process diagram of HIDRO-IMP technology.

By working under moderate-reaction-severity conditions at mild conversion, the HIDRO-IMP technology can upgrade heavy and extra-heavy crude oils so that they can be transported and processed in conventional refineries, as well as sold at a higher price. The main characteristics of HIDRO-IMP, which make it different from other technologies, are as follows: operation at mild pressure and temperature; its use of in-series fixed-bed reactors with proprietary selective catalysts for the removal of metals (mainly nickel and vanadium) and sulfur; the hydrocracking of asphaltenes; mild conversion of vacuum residue fraction into valuable distillates with a volumetric expansion of 104–108%, depending on the heavy crude oil processed; low sediment formation; high removal of impurities present in the heavy oil feed (sulfur, nitrogen, metals, asphaltenes); low investment and operating costs; the upgrading of the heavy crude oil by increasing the yield of distillates; reduced viscosity; and the production of an upgraded oil with low acidity, corrosivity, and tendency to form coke. More detailed information about the HIDRO-IMP technology can be found in a recently published book [1].

The development of the HIDRO-IMP technology officially started in the year 1999. Some previous small projects for catalyst and process development were executed in the years 1990–1995, from which two Mexican patents were granted [2,3]. A timeline of all the stages of HIDRO-IMP technology development is shown in Figure 2. This can be considered the beginning of worldwide research on upgrading heavy crude oils, since before this date, nothing can be found in the literature regarding the processing of whole heavy crude oil via hydrotreating. There are, indeed, other commercial technologies already in use, but they are aimed at either the removal of sulfur or high-severity hydrocracking of the bottom of the barrel, i.e., atmospheric or vacuum residue.

Research and development stages were conducted during the years 1999–2003. Many short-term bench-scale tests were carried out with different heavy crude oils and hydrotreating catalysts. The catalysts were developed in our laboratories. The results obtained were presented to different authorities of the Mexican Oil company. At that time (~2004), petroleum production in Mexico was mainly composed of heavy crude oils (>50%), and the idea of converting them into light crude oil was of high interest. However, the level of experimentation (bench-scale) was questioned in terms of scaling-up the results, and a larger unit to conduct a semi-commercial demonstration test was recommended. Fortunately, we received a budget from the oil company to perform the requested semi-commercial test. Prior to this, a long-term experimental evaluation (~6 months) in a two fixed-bed bench-scale unit with crude oil having a 13°API was carried out. The main conclusions derived from this test latter were as follows:

- ✓ The activity and stability of the proprietary catalysts used for the hydrotreating of heavy crude oils with the HIDRO-IMP technology were successfully tested and demonstrated.
- ✓ The three-catalyst system allowed the hydrotreating reactions to remove the high content of metals in the first bed of reactor 1, and the other two catalysts were consequently protected from premature catalyst deactivation.
- ✓ The moderate-reaction-severity conditions used in the test (total pressure of 100 kg/cm^2, hydrogen-to-oil ratio of 5000 ft^3/Bbl of heavy oil entering the reactor, liquid hourly space velocity (LHSV) of 0.5 h^{-1}, and start-of-run temperature of 380 °C) were properly used. These reaction conditions are lower than other commercially available technologies and ensure the production of a constant API gravity in upgraded oil, with reduced contents of sulfur, asphaltenes, and metals.
- ✓ Working at such conditions also limits the residue conversion at values lower than 50%, thus keeping sediment formation low (<0.4 wt.%) and ensuring the continuous operation of the unit.

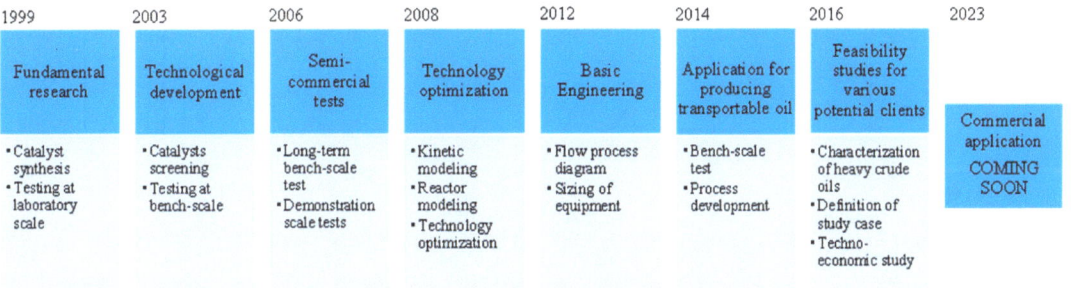

Figure 2. Stages of HIDRO-IMP process development.

Figure 3 depicts the relevant results of the long-term experiments. According to Figure 1, the feedstock for the HIDRO-IMP plant is heavy crude oil, and the feedstock for the first reactor is its atmospheric residue (AR). Figure 3 shows the API gravity values considering the two feedstocks, the heavy crude oil, and the AR.

Various patents related to the process [4–7] and catalysts [8–12] were granted, which include the use of the HIDRO-IMP technology for upgrading the fluidity properties of heavy crude oils for transportation via pipeline (HIDRO-IMP-T), the upgrading of heavy crude oils to produce light crude oils (HIDRO-IMP-U), the conversion of residue in a petroleum refinery (HIDRO-IMP-C), and catalysts for hydrodemetallization, hydrodesulfurization, and hydrocracking.

Once this long-term bench-scale test was properly developed and confirmed to be successful, a couple of demonstration tests in a 10 BPD unit were conducted (2006–2008). Figure 4 shows the main results of this demonstration scale test, from which the following main conclusions were obtained:

- ✓ The HIDRO-IMP-C technology was successfully demonstrated at the semi-commercial level.
- ✓ The API gravity of the heavy crude oil increased from 12.93 to 23.28°, while reductions in sulfur and metals contents were 77.8% (from 5.19 wt.% to 1.15 wt.%) and 83.2% (from 584 ppm to 98 ppm), respectively.

✓ Sediment formation was kept at low values while the continuous operation of the commercial plant was guaranteed.
✓ The catalysts demonstrated their high metal retention capacity and high selectivity towards hydrodesulfurization and hydrocracking reactions, thus producing a constant-quality upgraded oil, and ensuring acceptable runs of operation.

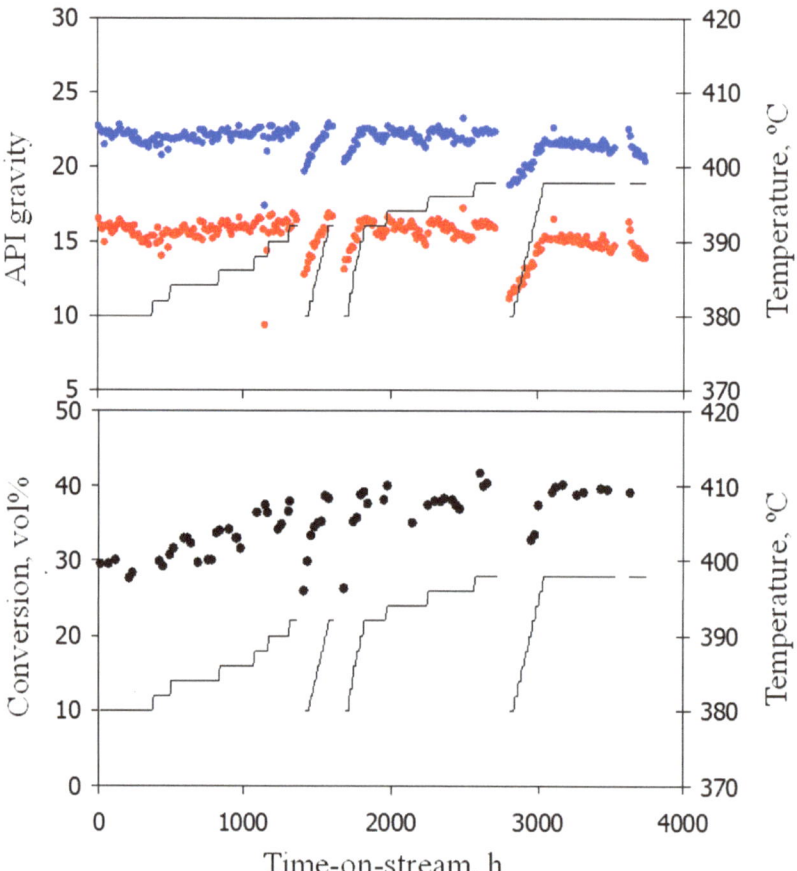

Figure 3. API gravity and conversion during the long-term test. (•) Upgraded oil (crude oil feed = 12.7° API), (•) Hydrotreated product (AR feed = 3.2° API), (•) Conversion, (—) reactor temperature.

The results of the semi-commercial test were presented and discussed again with the individuals in the oil company, but at that time (~2008), the situation of oil production in Mexico was more favorable, and the need to convert heavy crude oils into light crude oils was not as urgent as in previous years.

In the following years (2008–2012), the development of the HIDRO-IMP technology continued with some optimization studies and a basic engineering design. Some additional studies focused on reducing the viscosity of heavy crude oils to produce transportable oil, and experimental evaluations with different Mexican heavy crude oils were also conducted (2012–2015).

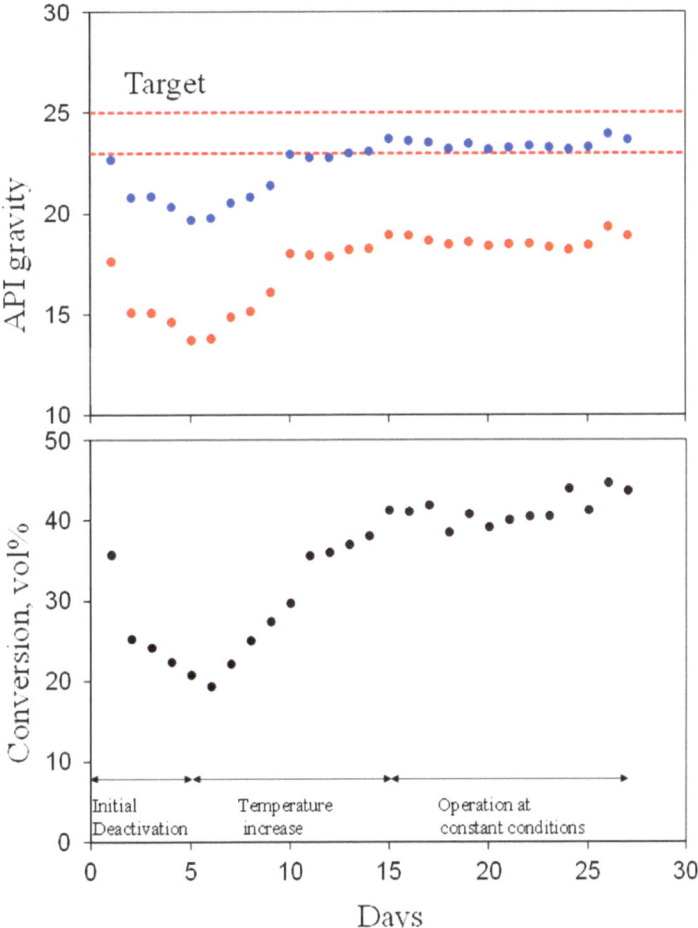

Figure 4. API gravity and conversion during the semi-commercial test (●) Upgraded oil (crude oil feed = 12.9° API), (●) Hydrotreated product (AR feed = 5.4° API), (●) Conversion.

Other clients outside Mexico were also identified, and techno-economic studies were conducted via simulation (2016–2018). It should be highlighted that with all the experimental information generated at different scales, operating conditions, and feedstocks, robust kinetic and reactor models were developed. The application of the HIDRO-IMP technology was clearly demonstrated to be an excellent alternative for the partial upgrading of heavy crude oils. The differences with other commercially available technologies that work at full conversion (ebullated-bed- and slurry-bed-based technologies) were clearly established, and no direct competition with them was identified. The HIDRO-IMP technology focuses on partial upgrading (around 50% conversion) at moderate-reaction-severity conditions, whereas others are based on full upgrading (70–95% conversion) at high-reaction-severity conditions. These differences make HIDRO-IMP a low-operating- and investment-cost technology, as is indicated in Figure 5. It was observed that producing high-quality upgraded oil (full upgrading) also requires high investment and operating costs, but this option does not yield the highest return of investment. On the contrary, partial upgrading, although not producing an oil with the high quality of full conversion technologies, gives the highest return of investment. To achieve this target, during HIDRO-IMP technology development, the main objective function was economics. In other words, every experimental study was accompanied by an economic analysis so that the optimal operating conditions, process scheme, and even the cut boiling point of the heavy oil sent to the first reactor were defined to minimize the investment and operating cost of the unit. It should be noted that Figure 5 remains the same regardless of the changes in prices of crude oil over time, since the economic analysis considers both the price of the crude oil and the price of the upgraded oil, and the differences between the two prices is kept more or less constant over the years; therefore, the economical parameters are not affected to a great extent.

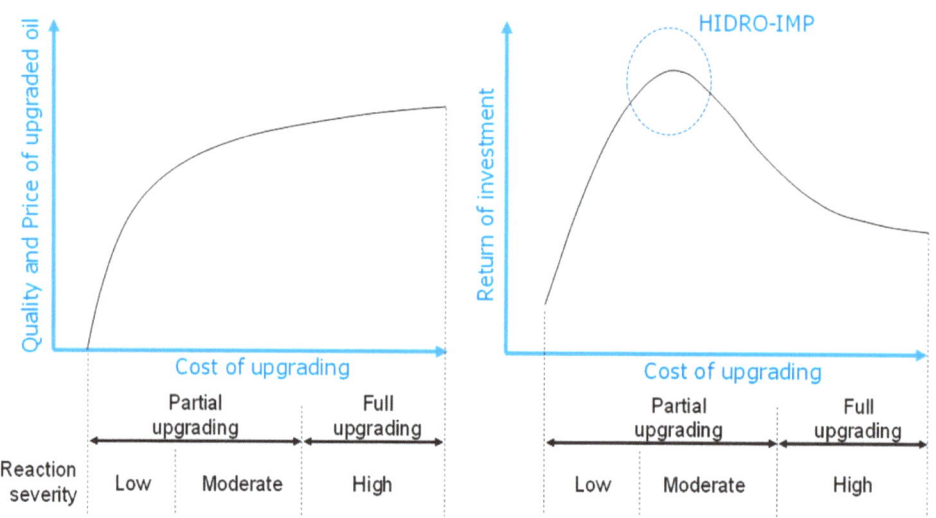

Figure 5. Economics of partial upgrading versus full upgrading of heavy crude oils.

Other companies (Genoil Inc. (Calgary, AB, Canada), Rigby Refining LLC (Houston, TX, USA), Gazprom Neft (Saint Petersburg, Russia)) and the University of Bradford developed similar technologies and were granted patents or published scientific papers after the publication of the HIDRO-IMP patent. Except for the Rigby process, which was designed to produce a marine fuel oil product, the other technologies have the same objective as HIDRO-IMP. The Ribby patents were granted in 2019 ("Heavy marine fuel oil composition") and in 2020 ("Process and device for treating high sulfur heavy marine fuel oil for use as feedstock in a subsequent refinery unit"). The Genoil patent was granted in 2014 ("Process for treating crude oil using hydrogen in a special unit"). These patents were granted by the US patent office. Gazprom Neft is promoting a hydroconversion technology ("Hydroprocessing of heavy residues"), but the associated patent was not found; surely it was granted in Russia. In the case of the University of Bradford, the researchers published a series of papers dating back to 2011 as part of a PhD thesis. It was confirmed with them that no patents were granted. In one of their papers, they stated that the hydrotreating of whole crude oil was reported for the first time, which is obviously an erroneous statement, since our first Mexican patent ("Procedure for hydrotreating of heavy crude oils to produce synthetic oil") was granted in 1995 and our first US patent was granted in 2010 ("Process for the catalytic hydrotreatment of heavy hydrocarbons of petroleum"). Both HIDRO-IMP technology patents were granted before this academic group published their papers.

This clearly indicates that the Mexican Institute of Petroleum has been a pioneer in the area of the upgrading of heavy and extra-heavy crude oils. Like us, these other developments have not been introduced at a commercial level yet. To do so, apart from the corresponding questions of intellectual property, hydrotreating catalysts must be tested at different conditions to define the operating window in which the process can operate without sediment formation problems. In addition, long-term experiments are mandatory to verify the metal retention capacity of the catalyst, particularly the front-end catalyst, which is designed with optimized pore size distribution to maximize the accumulation of metals (vanadium and nickel) and protect the following catalyst from premature deactivation. And, not only this, but the experimentation must also be scaled-up to a semi-commercial level in order to confirm the laboratory experimental results; techno-economic studies must be developed as well in order to keep the economics of the technology as attractive as possible. To offer a technology for possible commercial applications, basic engineering is necessary at least, and the cost of all the unit components must be determined. All these steps have already been developed for the HIDRO-IMP technology. In other words, it is already available for commercial application.

3. Combination of HIDRO-IMP with Delayed Coking

Given that the commercial application of the HIDRO-IMP technology on its own was delayed longer than expected, its combination with a delayed coking process was evaluated for partial bottom-of-the-barrel conversion, and the remaining unconverted residue was then processed in a coker unit [13]. The main idea for this combination was that many current refineries around the world have a delayed coking unit as a bottom-of-the-barrel conversion process. However, when processing heavier crude oils in a refinery, the amount of produced vacuum residue is high, and it exhibits a high content of sulfur and metals, which reduces the quality of the coke. Also, the high content of Conradson carbon residue increases the production of coke. For instance, for a 22° API crude oil, the liquid product yield is about 90 vol.%, and the yield of coke is 12 wt.%, whereas for a 16° API crude oil, they are 80 vol.% and 22 wt.%, respectively. This means that the heavier the crude oil, the higher the production of coke and the lower the volumetric liquid product yield. Using the HIDRO-IMP technology before a delayed coker unit can yield better performance. For example, the hydrotreated residue would exhibit lower amounts of metals and sulfur, so that the feed to the delayed coker would be of higher quality, and all the coker products, i.e., coker naphtha and gas oil, would exhibit reduced concentrations of sulfur and would have less of an aromatic nature, which would allow them to become better feed components for producing low sulfur gasoline and diesel. Also, the coke would be lower in sulfur and metals and could be used to produce better products.

From the study of the combination of HIDRO-IMP technology with delayed coker units, the main results were as follows:

- ✓ HIDRO-IMP plus delayed coking yields the highest economic benefits.
- ✓ The results of HIDRO-IMP alone were better than from delayed coking alone.
- ✓ Other advantages of combined HIDRO-IMP plus delayed coking are zero production of fuel oil, high-quality feed and products that would require null or less-severe further hydrotreating (coker naphtha and gas oil), lower production of coke, and the production of coke with reduced metal and sulfur content.
- ✓ It proved evident that the combination of HIDRO-IMP plus delayed coking presents advantages for refineries that do not have a process for bottom-of-the-barrel conversion or those that only have a delayed coker unit.

The technical and economic benefits that have been previously commented on are only for the HIDRO-IMP technology itself; however, the upgraded oil produced when processed in a refinery can yield the following additional benefits in different conversion processes compared with a typical refinery feed without hydrotreating:

- ✓ The hydrodesulfurization of gas oil: Gas oil coming from the distillation unit would have a reduced concentration of sulfur and other impurities. It would also be partially hydrogenated so that the required operating conditions to achieve the ultra-low sulfur specification would be less severe (lower start-of-run temperature, higher space velocity). This would increase the life of the catalyst; i.e., the starting operation at a low reaction temperature would increment the operating temperature window and reduce energy consumption in order to heat up the feed, with a consequent reduction in operating costs.

✓ Fluid catalytic cracking of vacuum gas oils: The same benefits of better-quality feed would be obtained in catalytic cracking, i.e., reduced amount of sulfur, nitrogen, and metals, as well as less aromatic content. These better properties would positively influence the catalytic cracking unit. For instance, low amount of metals would produce low amount of gases, and, as the compressor could work at more capacity so could the catalytic cracking unit. It would also reduce the catalyst deactivation rate and fresh catalyst addition; catalytic gasoline and light cycle oil would be better feed components for naphtha and gas oil hydrodesulfurization units, and heavy cycle oil could be used as better-quality diluents for producing low sulfur fuel oil.

The spent catalysts from the HIDRO-IMP technology, which would be highly concentrated in metals such as vanadium and nickel, could be used for further rejuvenation or metal recovery. There are plenty of companies that would benefit from these used catalyst samples. In fact, when I was looking for a catalyst manufacturer, a company offered me fresh catalysts for free if, after finishing the operation of the plant, I gave the spent samples back to them.

It should also be highlighted that the HIDRO-IMP technology is focused on the use of hydrotreating technology for the upgrading of heavy crude oils. These heavy crude oils are characterized by having a low H/C ratio; that is, they are deficient in hydrogen and highly concentrated in carbon. To decarbonize the refining industry, this type of technology is necessary so that the carbon fingerprint can be reduced to achieve net zero emissions.

In summary, the HIDRO-IMP technology has been subject to all the possible experimental tests and studies that could guarantee its commercial application, which I expect could be soon.

4. Conclusions

Although the HIDRO-IMP technology has been tested at different experimentation scales, including two semi-commercial tests, has been evaluated for the upgrading of various heavy and extra-heavy crude oils, has had various positive techno-economic studies performed on its benefits, has robust kinetic and reactor models developed for the prediction of the process's performance, and indicates that preliminary basic engineering is already available, its commercial application is still under negotiation. The main reason for such an indecision of people in refinery is that they feel more comfortable with already-proven technologies. To overcome this situation, it is recommended that people in refinery be involved in a technology's development from early research stages so that they can provide not only information but also guidance to adjust the technology to real-life requirements. There should also be a compromise between the research center and the end user to apply the developments at the commercial scale. This is why, from a research point of view, nobody wants to be the first for the commercial application of new technologies.

Funding: This research was funded by the Mexican Institute of Petroleum.

Conflicts of Interest: Author Jorge Ancheyta was employed by the company Instituto Mexicano del Petróleo. The remaining authors declare that the research was conducted in the absence of any commercial or financial relationships that could be construed as a potential conflict of interest.

References

1. Ancheyta, J. *Upgrading of Heavy and Extra-Heavy Crude Oils by Catalytic Hydrotreating: The History of HIDRO-IMP Technology*; CRC Press Taylor and Francis Group: Boca Raton, FL, USA, 2013.
2. Ancheyta, J.; Nares, H.R.; Moreno, A. Procedure for Hydrotreating of Heavy Crude Oils to Produce Synthetic Oil. Mexican Patent 9200929, 25 August 1995.
3. Betancourt, G.; Ancheyta, J.; Gómez, M.T.; Cortez, M.T.; Marroquín, G. Catalytic Composition for Hydrotreating of Heavy Crude Oils. Mexican Patent 271346, 29 October 2009.
4. Ancheyta, J.; Betancourt, G.; Marroquín, G.; Centeno, G.; Muñoz, J.A.D.; Alonso, F. Process for the Catalytic Hydrotreatment of Heavy Hydrocarbons of Petroleum. US Patent 7651604 B2, 26 January 2010.

5. Ancheyta, J.; Alvarez, A.; Marroquín, G.; Centeno, G. Hydroprocessing of Heavy Hydrocarbons Using Liquid Quench Streams. US Patent 9,771,528 B2, 26 September 2017.
6. Ancheyta, J.; Muñoz, J.A.D.; Castañeda, L.C.; Ramírez, S.; Marroquín, G.; Centeno, G.; Alonso, F.; Aguilar, R. Hydroconversion-distillation of Heavy and extra-Heavy Crude Oils. US Patent 9,920,264 B2, 20 March 2018.
7. Ancheyta, J.; Castañeda, L.C.; Muñoz, J.A.D.; Centeno, G.; Marroquín, G.; Ramírez, S.; Alonso, F. Process for Partial Upgrading of Heavy and Extra-Heavy Crude Oils for Transportation. US Patent No. 9,969,945 B2, 15 May 2018.
8. Rayo, P.; Ancheyta, J.; Ramírez, J.; Maity, S.K.; Singh, M.; Alonso, F. Catalyst, Its Preparation, and Use for Hydrodesulfurization of Residua and Heavy Crudes. US Patent No. 7,968,069 B2, 28 June 2011.
9. Rana, M.S.; Ancheyta, J.; Maity, S.K. Catalyst for the First Hydrodemetallization Step in a Hydroprocessing System with Multiple Reactors for Improvement of Heavy and Extra-Heavy Crudes. US Patent No. 9,133,401 B2, 15 September 2015.
10. Maity, S.K.; Ancheyta, J.; Alonso, F.; Terai, H.F.S.; Uchida, M. Carbon Supported Catalyst for Hydrodemetallization of Heavy Crude Oils and Residue. US Patent No. 8,431,018 B2, 30 April 2013.
11. Singh, M.; Ancheyta, J.; Leyva, Z.C.; Maity, S.K.; Torres, L.P. Mild Acidic Catalyst for Hydroprocessing of Heavy Crude Oils and Residue and Its Synthesis Procedure. US Patent No. 9,387,466 B2, 12 July 2016.
12. Rayo, P.; Ancheyta, J.; Marroquín, G.; Centeno, G.; Ramírez, J.F. Mesoporous Composite of Molecular Sieves for Hydrocracking of Heavy Crude Oils and Residue. US Patent No. 9,896,628 B2, 20 February 2018.
13. Muñoz, J.A.D.; Páez, G.; Ancheyta, J. Combination of hydrotreating and delayed coking technologies for conversion of residue. *Chin. J. Chem. Eng.* **2023**, *63*, 209–219. [CrossRef]

Disclaimer/Publisher's Note: The statements, opinions and data contained in all publications are solely those of the individual author(s) and contributor(s) and not of MDPI and/or the editor(s). MDPI and/or the editor(s) disclaim responsibility for any injury to people or property resulting from any ideas, methods, instructions or products referred to in the content.

Article

Optimum Design of Naphtha Recycle Isomerization Unit with Modification by Adding De-Isopentanizer

Walaa S. Osman [1], Asmaa E. Fadel [1], Shazly M. Salem [1], Abeer M. Shoaib [1], Abdelrahman G. Gadallah [2,3] and Ahmed A. Bhran [2,*]

[1] Petroleum Refining and Petrochemical Engineering Department, Faculty of Petroleum and Mining Engineering, Suez University, Suez 43512, Egypt; walaa.osman@pme.suezuni.edu.eg (W.S.O.); asmaa.faah@pme.suezuni.edu.eg (A.E.F.); shazly.nasrallah@pme.suezuni.edu.eg (S.M.S.); a.shoaib@suezuni.edu.eg (A.M.S.)

[2] Chemical Engineering Department, College of Engineering, Imam Mohammad Ibn Saud Islamic University (IMSIU), Riyadh 11432, Saudi Arabia; agadallah@imamu.edu.sa

[3] Chemical Engineering Department, National Research Center, Cairo 11241, Egypt

* Correspondence: aabahran@imamu.edu.sa; Tel.: +966-580772698

Abstract: Environmental standards have recently imposed very rigorous limitations on the amounts of benzene, aromatics, and olefins, which can be found in finished gasoline. Reduction of these components could negatively affect the octane number of gasoline, so the isomerization process is gaining importance in the present refining context as an excellent safe alternative to increase the octane number of gasoline. The main aim of the naphtha isomerization unit is to modify the molecular structure of light naphtha to transform it into a more valuable gasoline blend stock, and simultaneously the benzene content is reduced by saturation of the benzene fraction. In this work, Aspen HYSYS version 12.1 is used to simulate the hydrogen once-through isomerization unit of an Egyptian refinery plant, located in Alexandria, in order to determine the properties, composition, and octane number of the isomerate product. Many potential changes are investigated in order to find the best design that efficiently raises octane number with the least amount of expense. Firstly, the plant is modified by adding one fractionator either before or after the reactor, then by adding two fractionators before and after the reactor; then the configuration which gives the highest product octane number with the highest Return on Investment (ROI) is chosen as the recommended optimum configuration. The results show that using two fractionators before and after the reactor is the best configuration. Optimization of this best configuration resulted in an increase in octane number by 7% and a decrease in the total cost by 13%.

Keywords: isomerization; recycling naphtha; octane improver; optimization; de-isopentanizer

Citation: Osman, W.S.; Fadel, A.E.; Salem, S.M.; Shoaib, A.M.; Gadallah, A.G.; Bhran, A.A. Optimum Design of Naphtha Recycle Isomerization Unit with Modification by Adding De-Isopentanizer. *Processes* **2023**, *11*, 3406. https://doi.org/10.3390/pr11123406

Academic Editors: Dicho Stratiev, Dobromir Yordanov and Aijun Guo

Received: 19 October 2023
Revised: 2 December 2023
Accepted: 5 December 2023
Published: 11 December 2023

Copyright: © 2023 by the authors. Licensee MDPI, Basel, Switzerland. This article is an open access article distributed under the terms and conditions of the Creative Commons Attribution (CC BY) license (https:// creativecommons.org/licenses/by/ 4.0/).

1. Introduction

Isomerization is a process that has become one of the most promising techniques for upgrading gasoline quality; this is due to the process's ability to produce high-octane gasoline by converting straight-chain paraffins to the branched forms of iso-paraffins, while simultaneously reducing the number of pollutants released into the environment. There are different types of isomerization; one of the most common types is geometric isomerization. Geometric isomerization results in the same molecular formula, but the atoms are arranged differently in space due to the presence of double bonds. Another type of isomerization is positional isomerization; positional isomers have the same molecular formula but differ in the location of the functional group in the carbon chain [1].

Catalytic reforming and isomerization are the two main processes used to improve octane number by hydrocarbon molecule rearrangement [2,3]. However, catalytic reforming also involves breaking down large hydrocarbons into smaller more valuable molecules [4]. The two processes differ in feedstock, operating conditions, and quality of the product;

catalytic reforming has a limited ability to process naphtha with a high content of normal paraffin. The reformate, produced from the reforming process, has a much higher content of benzene than permissible by the current environmental regulations in many countries.

Isomerization is considered as a more refined and economical way of increasing the octane rating. The quality of isomerate depends on several factors such as temperature, naphthene content, and liquid hourly space velocity (LHSV); increasing temperature positively affects the reaction rates. In addition, as the naphthene content of the feed increases, the amount of hydrogen required to open the naphthene ring increases. However, a severe reduction in LHSV will result in channeling [5].

Many studies have been done to improve the performance of the isomerization process [6,7]. Naqvi et al. reviewed the isomerization catalyst used, main reactions, reaction mechanisms, and classification of the isomerization processes [8]. Nikitav Checantsev and Gyngazova introduced a mathematical model for light naphtha isomerization units with different compositions of raw materials, which gives isomerate composition agreement with experimental data obtained from the industrial isomerization units of Russian refineries. Their proposed isomerization mathematical model enables the user to compare the efficiency of different isomerization units and select the more suitable variant of process optimization for a given raw material. The calculations are carried out on an isomerization process scheme with recycling n-pentane [9].

Hamadi and Kadhim introduced a material balance and kinetic model for penex isomerization, in which material balance calculations have been performed for the prediction of kinetics, which is the rate constant for conversion of n-paraffin to olefin "K_1", rate constant for conversion of olefin to i-paraffins "K_2", and activation energy. Their study showed that increasing temperature results in an increase in K_1 and a decrease in K_2 [10]. The optimization of process variables was introduced by Shahata et al. in 2018; in their work, the variables affecting isomerization product octane numbers such as feed composition, temperature, hydrogen-to-feed ratio, and LHSV have been analyzed and optimized using response surface methodology (RSM) [11]. Chuzlov et al. developed a mathematical model for a light naphtha catalytic isomerization unit, where the plant operation with catalytic isomerization and separation columns has been optimized. They aimed to select the optimal modes of separation columns to achieve the desired separation between the units [12]. Jarullah et al. introduced a new naphtha isomerization process, called AJAM, where the isomerization reactor model was validated using data from Baiji North Refinery (BNR). In their study, it is found that adding a de-isopentanizer "DIP" has a positive effect on the research octane number (RON), isomerate properties, and operation cost. Their study concluded that the proposed AJAM isomerization process gives the maximum RON, isomerate yield, and minimum cost compared to molecular sieve technologies [13]. Nagabhatla Viswanadham et al. converted naphtha feedstock into high-octane gasoline blending stock, which is rich in iso-paraffin and suitable for fuel applications. They used three catalyst systems, which exhibit different acidities. Nano crystalline ZSM-5, containing inter-crystalline voids, is also studied in their research to investigate the effect of micro porosity on the product selectivity; then, the quality of isomerate in terms of total iso-paraffins is analyzed. Studies were also conducted on two single-component feeds, n-heptane, and n-octane, to understand the effect of hydrocarbon chain length on the reactivity and product selectivity in the process [14]. Yu. N. Lebedevincrease et al. showed that fitting isomerization units with a de-isohexanizer "DIH" tower increases the RON of isomerate by a minimum of 4–5 points; the product from the stabilizer is fed to this tower to separate low-octane n-hexane and methyl pentanes, which are taken back with the side stream into the reactor for repeated conversion [15].

The availability of low-value naphtha and other such feedstocks calls for the development of efficient methods for adding value to the feedstocks through octane number enhancement. The feedstock has a low octane number most times (<60), which is not reliable for fuel applications, in which high-octane gasoline is required. Therefore, the isomerization of n-paraffins attracted much attention for the refinery processes. In addition, Euro-4 and Euro-5 standards did not only restrict the content of benzene to less than 1 vol.%, but also put restrictions on the total aromatics content; it must be less than 35 vol.%. To meet these environmental restrictions, reformate is usually diluted with isomerate in the ratio of 1:1. So, isomerization became the largest tonnage process after reforming. Saad Zafer showed that UOP offers several schemes, in which low-octane components are separated and recycled back to the reactors. These recycling modes of operation can lead to the production of a product with a higher octane number. He also confirmed that the addition of a de-isopentanizer (DIP) and a super de-isohexanizer (DIH) would achieve the highest octane from a fractionation hydrocarbon recycle flow scheme. Moreover, the scheme with de-isopentanizer (DIP) before the reactor section allows the production of isomerate with high octane number, increases the conversion level of n-pentanes, and at the same time reduces the reactor duty [16].

In this research, a new modification is developed by adding two fractionators before and after the reactor, where more economic savings to the refinery could be achieved. The improvement in process economics is not only related to obtaining high-quality product, but also comes from operating cost savings due to optimizing process conditions. This improvement was illustrated by applying the proposed modifications to the investigated case study.

The study shows how octane number is affected by separating i-pentane from feed before entering the reactor and recycling n-hexane to the reactor. The optimum conditions to produce the highest octane with minimum cost are also found in this study, using Aspen HYSYS V.12.1. Soave Redlich Kwong (SRK) fluid package is used to provide an estimation for the isomerate composition and the properties of all process streams. The Peng–Robinson Equation of State (EOS) is generally the recommended property package, as it predicts properties of mixtures ranging from well-defined light hydrocarbon systems to complex oil mixtures and provides optimized state equations for the rigorous handling of hydrocarbon systems. However, it is approved that the SRK fluid package is more suitable for isomerization reaction calculations [17].

2. Methodology

The method used in this work can be summarized in the following steps:

1. Hydrogen once through the isomerization unit with de-hexanizer (DH) after the reactor section in the Base Case (BC) is simulated with Aspen HYSYS V12.1., and then the model is validated.
2. Three alternative modifications to the existing case study have been applied and the effect of each modification on the naphtha octane number is monitored; the proposed modifications are as follows:
   - Removing de-hexanizer from the isomerization unit [Proposed Case 1 (PC1)].
   - Replacing the existing de-hexanizer tower with de-iso-pentanizer ahead of the reactor section [Proposed Case 2 (PC2)].
   - Installing de-iso-pentanizer and de-hexanizer at the same time [Proposed Case 3 (PC3)].
3. The configuration, which gives the highest octane number and ROI, is chosen as the best modification.
4. The best process modification is optimized using the original multi-variable optimizer in Aspen HYSYS V. 12.1 and the optimum conditions for the highest octane number and lower cost are determined.

2.1. Process Description

2.1.1. Base Case

The process presented in this research work is an isomerization unit of an Egyptian plant located in Alexandria, in which the octane number is upgraded from 66 to 82 in a penex process using a chlorinated alumina-based catalyst. In that process, low-octane components such as n-hexane and methyl pentane are recycled to the reactor, as shown in

Figure 1, to increase octane number (isomerization with de-hexanizer) [18]. Naphtha feed comes from an atmospheric distillation unit, and from cracking units as hydrocracker and coker units. In this isomerization unit, naphtha and make-up hydrogen are first passed through driers to remove any traces of water to avoid poisoning of the Penex catalyst. After that, naphtha and hydrogen are mixed and then heated by exchanging heat with the first and second reactor effluents. Chlorine is injected into the reactor charge to provide acid sites on the catalyst's surface that are necessary for the isomerization reaction. The feed reached the reaction temperature by a fired heater. The effluent of the first reactor is then cooled using exchangers before entering the second reactor to remove the generated heat from exothermic reactions in the first reactor bed. The reactor's effluent is then fed to a stabilizer to separate light gases (C_4^- and hydrogen) from the product. The overhead gases are neutralized, and LPG is produced. The stabilized isomerate undergoes fractionation to maximize its octane number using a de-hexanizer, in which unconverted hexanes and low-octane products are separated from products. They are recycled to be mixed with fresh feed to improve product octane number. This Base Case has the lowest cost of the recycle flow schemes and supplies a high octane isomerate product; this scheme allows increasing hexane conversion but does not raise the content of isopentanes in the product. So, higher octane could be achieved by adding other fractionators [16].

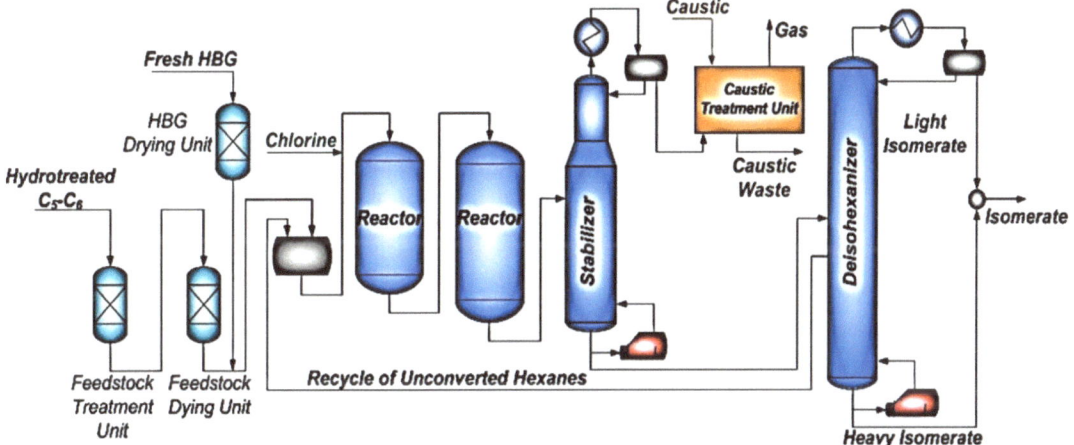

Figure 1. Flow diagram of base case [18].

2.1.2. Proposed Case 1

Once-through isomerization process is the most widely used isomerization process for producing moderate octane upgrades of light naphtha, in this process is similar to base case except that de-isohexanizer is removed as shown in Figure 2; this process is highly common, less expensive, and the simplest isomerization process unit but its main disadvantage is limited octane boost, so for higher octane another configuration with naphtha recycling is used [8,16].

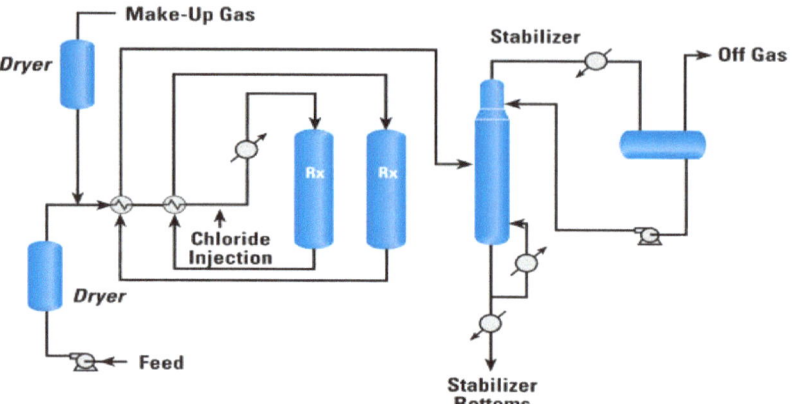

Figure 2. Flow diagram of first proposed case1 "once through isomerization" [19].

2.1.3. Proposed Case 2

In this process, the feed stream enters a de-isopentanizer, in which i-C_5 is separated overhead and sent to the gasoline blending pool. I-C_5 is already an isomer, so its removal would only lower the unit's capacity. The bottoms of the de-isopentanizer containing n-C_5 and C_6's are dried and hydrogenated and passed through the reactor to isomerize the hydrocarbons. After separating hydrogen reactor effluent, it enters a stabilizer where the propane and lighter hydrocarbons are removed to be used as fuel gases. The bottom product is sent to the blending pool, as shown in Figure 3. This process has many advantages such as reducing throughput and increasing the driving force for isomerization. It produces isomerate with a high-octane number as it increases the conversion level of n-pentanes, while lowering reactor duty and space velocity. It is reasonable when the isopentane's content in the feed is more than 13% [8,16].

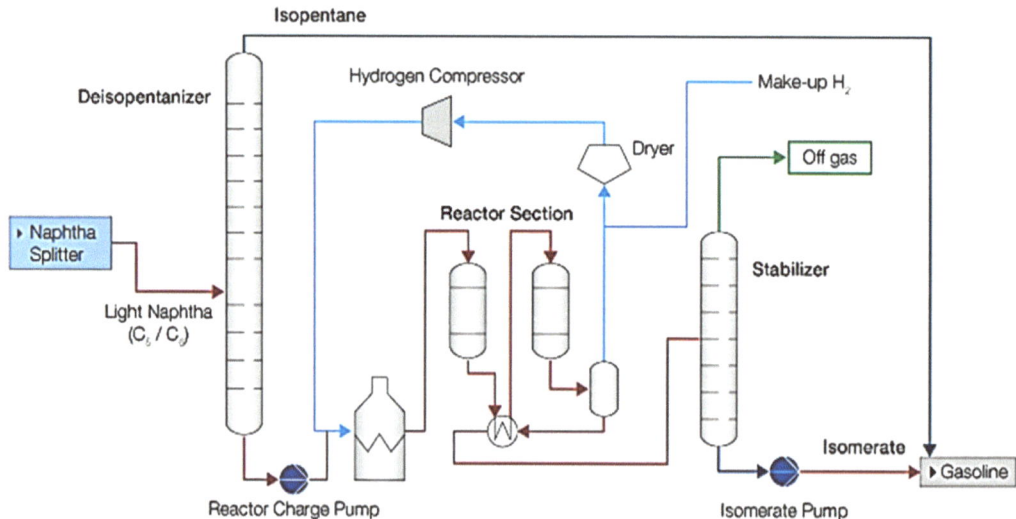

Figure 3. Flow diagram of second proposed case 2 [20].

2.1.4. Proposed Case 3

In this proposed case, both fractionators (de-isopentanizer and a de-hexanizer) are introduced to the base case study. The flow diagram of the process was not found in the literature survey, but the configuration of the process will be illustrated in Figure 4, which shows the simulated proposed configuration. The feed stream enters a de-isopentanizer, in which i-C_5 is separated overhead and sent to the gasoline blending pool to lower the unit's capacity. The bottoms of the de-isopentanizer, containing n-C_5 and C_6's, are dried for maximum catalyst activity. The bottoms are then hydrogenated and passed through the reactor to isomerize the hydrocarbons. After separating hydrogen reactor effluent, it enters a stabilizer to boost conversion levels. The stabilized isomerate undergoes fractionation to maximize the octane number of the isomerate using de-hexanizer in which unconverted hexanes and low-octane products are separated from products. They are then recycled to be mixed with reactor feed to improve product octane number. This method is applied to feed containing significant amounts of isopentane. Less normal pentane would isomerize because of the equilibrium reaction, as overall concentration would be constrained by the iso-pentane in the feed. The equilibrium is pushed forward and more of the normal pentanes can isomerize when isopentane is removed from the feed. In this unit, the de-hexanizer is employed, and normal C_5 and C_6 are recycled to the reactor, resulting in greater octane of the produced fuel [8,16].

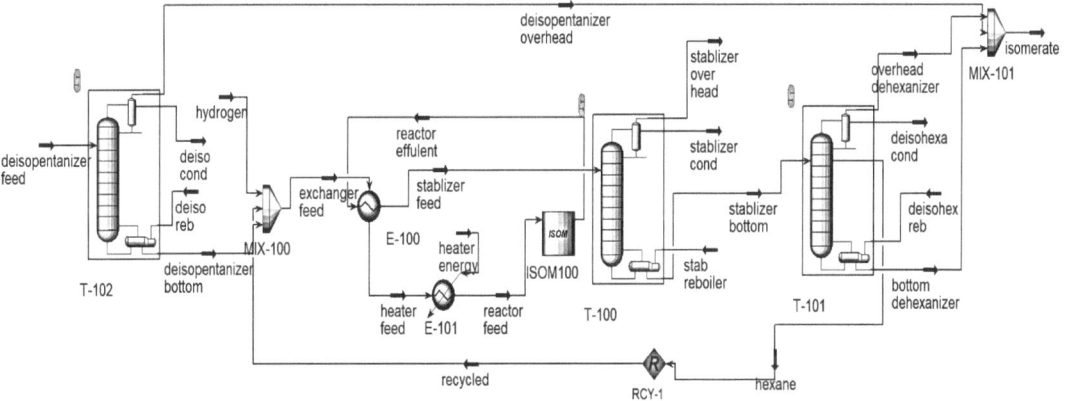

Figure 4. Simulation for third proposed case.

2.1.5. Feed Properties and Its Requirement

Feed of the four isomerization units has temperature, pressure, and molar flow as 72 °C, 10.3 barg, and 582 kmole/h, respectively. The feed is hydrotreated using cobalt, molybdenum, and nickel oxide as catalysts. Light naphtha composition and properties are listed in Tables 1 and 2. Makeup hydrogen is produced from the platforming unit in the same company; the liquid volume flow of makeup gas is 7.94 m³/h and detailed makeup gas composition is tabulated in Table 2. This process does not require costly feed pre-fractionation for the removal of C_6 cyclic or C_7^+ hydrocarbons, as it could process feeds with high levels of C_6 cyclic and C_7^+ components. In addition, feeds with noticeable levels of benzene can be processed without the need to separate the saturated section, which allows the removal of benzene in the light naphtha, while an octane upgrade takes place. To maintain catalyst activity, feed should be treated; it is allowed for feed, which contains up to 15 percent C_7^+ with low effect on design requirements. The feed should not contain benzene higher than 5%. Sulfur is undesirable in the process; it must be removed in the hydrotreater, as it reduces the rate of reaction and octane number of products. Water, nitrogen, and oxygen-containing compounds will poison the catalyst and lower its lifetime, so feed and hydrogen should be dried to remove water to eliminate forming acids [21,22].

Table 1. Naphtha feed and hydrogen conditions [23].

Properties	Naphtha Feed	Hydrogen
Vapor fraction	0.0	1.0
Temperature, °C	72.0	38.0
Pressure, barg	10.3	44.6
Molar flowrate, kgmole/h	582.0	241.0
Mass flowrate, kg/h	47,807.5	1246.5
Liquid volume flowrate, m^3/h	70.7	7.9

Table 2. Naphtha feed and hydrogen composition [23].

Component, Mole Fraction	Naphtha Feed	Hydrogen
H_2	0.0000	0.9014
Methane	0.0000	0.0318
Ethane	0.0000	0.0282
Propane	0.0000	0.0233
I-butane	0.0000	0.0055
n-butane	0.0011	0.0000
I-pentane	0.1169	0.0013
n-pentane	0.133	0.0063
Cyclopentane	0.0195	0.0000
2,2-Dimethyl butane	0.0049	0.0001
2,3-Dimethyl butane	0.0166	0.0002
2-Methyl pentane	0.104	0.0004
3-Methyl pentane	0.0937	0.0001
Hexane	0.3072	0.0001
Cyclohexane	0.0869	0.0000
Benzene	0.0318	0.0000
Cycloheptane	0.0584	0.0000
n-heptane	0.0260	0.0000
H_2O	0.0000	0.0012

2.1.6. Catalyst

Catalyst composed of chlorinated alumina impregnated with 0.25 wt. percentage of platinum is loaded in fixed-bed reactors. No oxygen is allowed to contact the catalyst during loading, as the chloride alumina bond is highly sensitive to oxygen compounds, so oxygen compounds are removed using a molecular sieve. Catalyst loading is dense, so the amount of catalyst in the reactor is increased and continuous addition of perchloro ethylene is necessary to maintain acidity.

2.2. Simulation

Aspen HYSYS is used in this work to simulate the base case study and the three proposed cases. In order to determine the composition and attributes of each stream as well as the product octane number, each case includes a unique simulation model based on the same feed composition and flow rate. Isomerization unit operation in Hysys is a detailed kinetic model of the isomerization unit. It models isomerization, hydrocracking, ring opening, saturation, and heavy reactions. The isomerization reactor is manually tuned since the isomerization unit models one reactor. The isomerization reactor is modeled using the Aspen EORXR model. Isomerization and hydrogenation reactions are reversible, while the other reaction classes are irreversible. Each reaction class is first order with respect to the primary reactant. The reactor has a diameter of 2.7 m and a 7.9 m length; catalyst-specific density is 0.8367 with a void Fraction of 0.25 [24].

2.2.1. Simulation of Base Case

In this process, a de-hexanizer is used after the stabilizer for recycling low-octane components such as straight-chain normal hexane and methyl pentane to the reactor for improving the octane of the produced gasoline as shown in Figure 5. The results of the simulation are presented in Table 3.

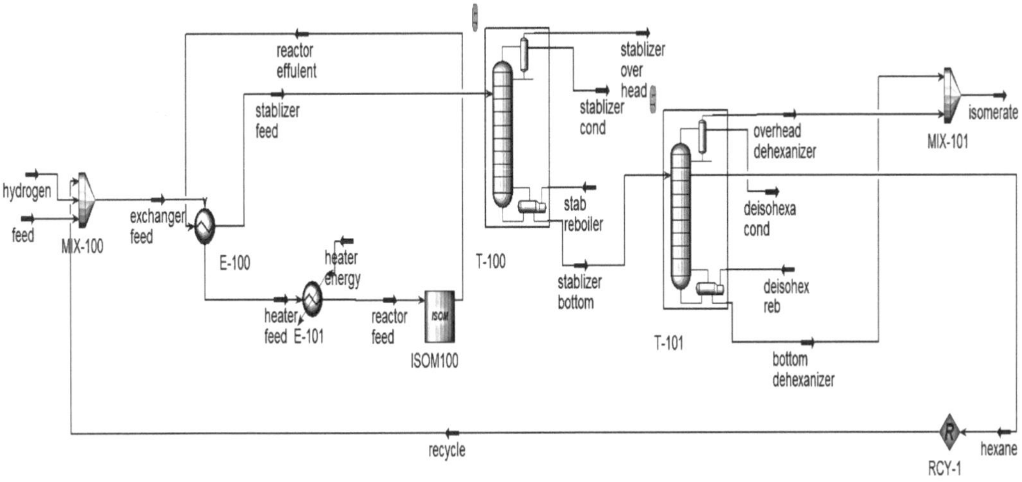

Figure 5. Simulation of the base case.

Table 3. Different streams conditions and composition for base case.

Item	Reactor Effluent	Stabilizer Feed	Reactor Feed	Stabilizer over Head	Stabilizer Bottom	Overhead of De-Humanizer	Bottom of De-Hexanizer	Hexane	Isomerate
Temperature, °C	179.89	138.00	145.00	36.00	177.26	72.78	124.28	105.88	80.33
Pressure, barg	32.99	15.38	33.00	13.93	15.10	1.03	2.00	1.89	1.03
Molar flowrate, kmole/h	977.48	977.48	1063.32	176.05	801.43	467.70	92.39	241.33	560.1
Mass flowrate, kg/h	69,793	69,793	69,746	2928	66,865	37,863	8304	20,698	46,167
H_2	0.122	0.122	0.204	0.678	0.000	0.000	0.000	0.000	0.000
Methane	0.009	0.009	0.007	0.048	0.000	0.000	0.000	0.000	0.000
Ethane	0.008	0.008	0.006	0.044	0.000	0.000	0.000	0.000	0.000
Propane	0.014	0.014	0.005	0.078	0.000	0.000	0.000	0.000	0.000
i-butane	0.010	0.010	0.001	0.056	0.000	0.000	0.000	0.000	0.000
n-butane	0.006	0.006	0.001	0.033	0.000	0.000	0.000	0.000	0.000
i-pentane	0.127	0.127	0.064	0.062	0.141	0.242	0.000	0.000	0.202
n-pentane	0.050	0.050	0.074	0.002	0.060	0.103	0.000	0.000	0.086
Cyclopentane	0.012	0.012	0.011	0.000	0.014	0.024	0.000	0.000	0.020
2,2-DMC_4	0.115	0.115	0.003	0.000	0.140	0.239	0.000	0.000	0.200
2,3-DMC_4	0.039	0.039	0.011	0.000	0.048	0.077	0.000	0.009	0.064
2-MC_5	0.150	0.150	0.081	0.000	0.183	0.258	0.003	0.105	0.216
3-MC_5	0.096	0.096	0.113	0.000	0.118	0.057	0.019	0.273	0.050
n-hexane	0.062	0.062	0.220	0.000	0.076	0.000	0.065	0.228	0.011
Cyclohexane	0.086	0.086	0.109	0.000	0.105	0.000	0.201	0.272	0.033
Benzene	0.000	0.000	0.017	0.000	0.000	0.000	0.000	0.000	0.000
Cycloheptane	0.053	0.053	0.052	0.000	0.065	0.000	0.335	0.087	0.055
2,3-DMC_5	0.000	0.000	0.000	0.000	0.000	0.000	0.000	0.000	0.000
n-heptane	0.014	0.014	0.016	0.000	0.017	0.000	0.128	0.009	0.021
H_2O	0.000	0.000	0.000	0.000	0.000	0.000	0.000	0.000	0.000

2.2.2. Simulation of Proposed Case 1

A once-through isomerization process is more affordable since there is no longer a need for a recycling gas compressor in the isomerization process. This process requires adding chloride continuously to maintain the catalyst's activity, necessitating the use of a caustic scrubber to neutralize the acidity of the off-gases and prevent corrosion. Additionally, a make-up gas drier is required to remove moisture and extend the catalyst's lifespan.

Figure 6 shows the simulation of the once-through isomerization process. The simulation results are tabulated in Table 4. This once-through operation produces research octane number (RON) improvement depending on the distribution of isomers in the feed stream. Lower octane components should be isolated and recycled back into the reactors to increase the octane number. As shown in Table 4, the concentration of straight chain components as well as the aromatics are decreased, while the branched-chain components are increased in the stabilized gasoline product. This confirms the upgrading of the produced gasoline octane number.

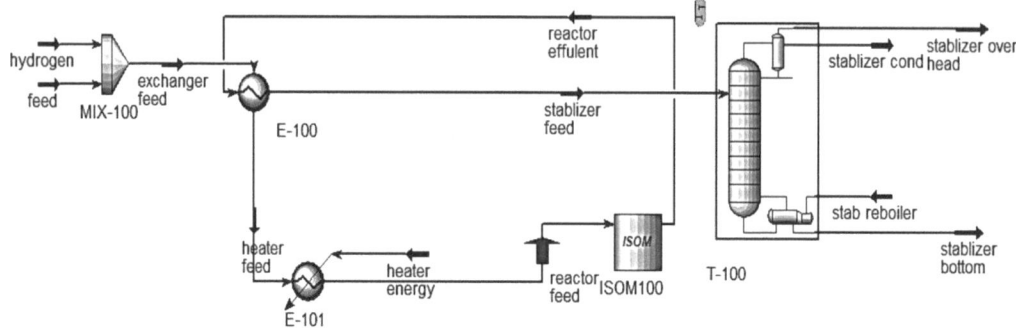

Figure 6. Simulation for first proposed case.

Table 4. Different stream conditions and composition for first proposed case.

Properties	Feed	Hydrogen	Exchanger Feed	Heat Feed	Reactor Effluent	Stabilizer Feed	Reactor Feed	Stabilizer over Head	Stabilizer Bottom
Pressure, barg	10.3	44.6	10.3	33.9	33.1	15.4	33.9	13.9	15.1
Temperature, °C	72.0	38.0							
Molar flowrate, kmole/h	582.0	241.0	823.0	823.0	757.2	757.2	823.0	196.3	560.9
Mass flowrate, kg/h	47,808	1,247	49,054	49,054	49,193	49,193	49,054	2,907	46,286
H_2	0.000	0.901	0.264	0.264	0.189	0.189	0.264	0.728	0.000
methane	0.000	0.032	0.009	0.009	0.011	0.011	0.009	0.042	0.000
Ethane	0.000	0.028	0.008	0.008	0.010	0.010	0.008	0.038	0.000
Propane	0.000	0.023	0.007	0.007	0.015	0.015	0.007	0.056	0.000
I-butane	0.000	0.006	0.002	0.002	0.009	0.009	0.002	0.033	0.000
n-butane	0.001	0.000	0.001	0.001	0.005	0.005	0.001	0.019	0.000
I-pentane	0.117	0.001	0.083	0.083	0.153	0.153	0.083	0.081	0.178
n-pentane	0.133	0.006	0.096	0.096	0.056	0.056	0.096	0.002	0.075
Cyclopentane	0.020	0.000	0.014	0.014	0.015	0.015	0.014	0.000	0.020
2,2-DMC_4	0.005	0.000	0.004	0.004	0.107	0.107	0.004	0.000	0.145
2,3-DMC_4	0.017	0.000	0.012	0.012	0.035	0.035	0.012	0.000	0.047
2-MC_5	0.104	0.000	0.074	0.074	0.129	0.129	0.074	0.000	0.174
3-MC_5	0.094	0.000	0.066	0.066	0.082	0.082	0.066	0.000	0.110
n-pentane	0.307	0.000	0.217	0.217	0.051	0.051	0.217	0.000	0.069
cyclohexane	0.087	0.000	0.062	0.062	0.063	0.063	0.062	0.000	0.085
benzene	0.032	0.000	0.023	0.023	0.000	0.000	0.023	0.000	0.000
cycloheptane	0.058	0.000	0.041	0.041	0.044	0.044	0.041	0.000	0.060
n-heptane	0.026	0.000	0.018	0.018	0.015	0.015	0.018	0.000	0.021
H_2O	0.000	0.001	0.000	0.000	0.000	0.000	0.000	0.000	0.000

2.2.3. Simulation of Second Proposed Case

In this case, de-isopentanizer is used ahead of the reactor to separate isopentane from the input stream, as illustrated in Figure 7; the simulation results of the considered process are listed in Table 5.

Table 5. Different stream conditions and composition for second proposed case.

Properties	Heater Feed	Reactor Effluent	Stabilizer Feed	Reactor Feed	Stabilizer over Head	Stabilizr Bottom	Isomerate	Deiso-Pentanizr Bottom	I-Pentane
Temperature, °C	124.04	172.83	127.00	133.00	37.00	173.00	80.45	82.99	49.40
Pressure, barg	33.85	33.85	15.38	33.85	13.93	15.10	1.00	1.00	1.00
Molar flowrate, kmole/h	764.07	696.19	696.19	764.07	180.49	515.70	574.63	523.07	58.93
Mass flowrate, kg/h	44,811	44,961	44,961	44,811	2215	42,746	46,989	43,565	4243
H_2	0.284	0.202	0.202	0.284	0.780	0.000	0.000	0.000	0.000

Table 5. Cont.

Properties	Heater Feed	Reactor Effluent	Stabilizer Feed	Reactor Feed	Stabilizer over Head	Stabilizr Bottom	Isomerate	Deiso-Pentanizr Bottom	I-Pentane
methane	0.010	0.012	0.012	0.010	0.045	0.000	0.000	0.000	0.000
ethane	0.009	0.011	0.011	0.009	0.032	0.003	0.003	0.000	0.000
propane	0.007	0.016	0.016	0.007	0.037	0.009	0.008	0.000	0.000
i-butane	0.002	0.009	0.009	0.002	0.015	0.007	0.006	0.000	0.000
n-butane	0.000	0.005	0.005	0.000	0.007	0.004	0.005	0.000	0.011
i-pentane	0.015	0.106	0.106	0.015	0.068	0.120	0.207	0.021	0.965
n-pentane	0.101	0.040	0.040	0.101	0.015	0.049	0.046	0.145	0.024
Cyclopentane	0.015	0.016	0.016	0.015	0.001	0.022	0.019	0.022	0.000
2,2-DMC$_4$	0.004	0.114	0.114	0.004	0.001	0.154	0.138	0.006	0.000
2,3-DMC$_4$	0.013	0.037	0.037	0.013	0.000	0.051	0.045	0.019	0.000
2-MC$_5$	0.079	0.141	0.141	0.079	0.000	0.190	0.171	0.116	0.000
3-MC$_5$	0.071	0.090	0.090	0.071	0.000	0.121	0.109	0.104	0.000
n-hexane	0.234	0.057	0.057	0.234	0.000	0.076	0.069	0.342	0.000
Cyclohexane	0.066	0.066	0.066	0.066	0.000	0.090	0.080	0.097	0.000
benzene	0.024	0.000	0.000	0.024	0.000	0.000	0.000	0.035	0.000
Cycloheptane	0.045	0.045	0.045	0.045	0.000	0.060	0.054	0.065	0.000
n-heptane	0.020	0.017	0.017	0.020	0.000	0.023	0.020	0.029	0.000

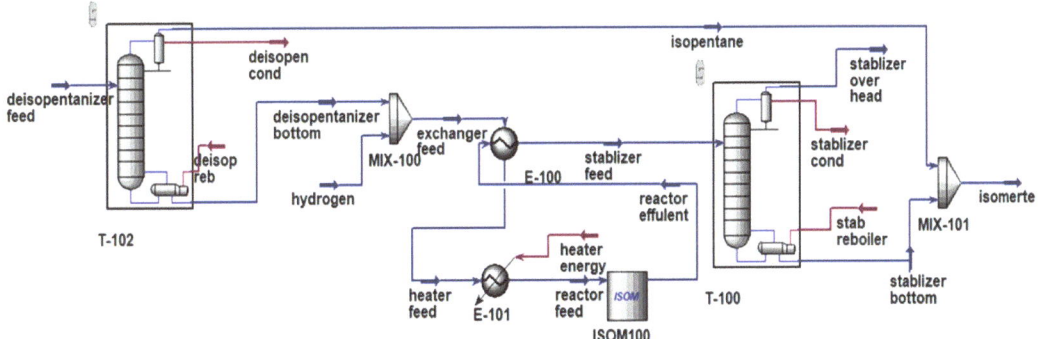

Figure 7. Simulation for second proposed case.

2.2.4. Simulation of Third Proposed Case

In this process, both fractionators (de-isopentanizer and a de-hexanizer) are introduced as described in Figure 4, resulting in greater octane of the produced fuel [14]; the simulation results are provided in Table 6.

Table 6. Different stream conditions and composition for third proposed case.

Properties	Reactor Effluent	Stabilizer Feed	Reactor Feed	Stabilizer over Head	Stabilizer Bottom	Overhead De-hexanizer	Bottom De-hexanizer	Isomerate	Deiso-Pentanizr Bottom	Recycle
Temperature, °C	160.78	150.00	138.00	36.00	183.19	71.32	122.52	77.26	83.00	99.74
Pressure, barg	36.48	31.30	36.50	13.93	15.10	1.03	2.00	1.00	1.00	1.72
Molar flowrate, kmole/h	1649	1649	1714	195	1455	395	108	562	523	951
Mass flowrate, kg/h	126,468	126,468	126,466	2591	123,877	32,755	9390	46,398	43,554	81,671
H$_2$	0.090	0.090	0.126	0.759	0.000	0.000	0.000	0.000	0.000	0.000
methane	0.005	0.005	0.005	0.041	0.000	0.000	0.000	0.000	0.000	0.000
ethane	0.004	0.004	0.004	0.037	0.000	0.000	0.000	0.000	0.000	0.000
propane	0.005	0.005	0.003	0.045	0.000	0.000	0.000	0.000	0.000	0.000
i-butane	0.003	0.003	0.001	0.025	0.000	0.000	0.000	0.000	0.000	0.000
n-butane	0.001	0.001	0.000	0.011	0.000	0.000	0.000	0.001	0.000	0.000
i-pentane	0.043	0.043	0.007	0.080	0.038	0.141	0.000	0.200	0.021	0.000
n-pentane	0.015	0.015	0.045	0.003	0.017	0.063	0.000	0.047	0.145	0.000
Cyclopentane	0.007	0.007	0.007	0.000	0.008	0.029	0.000	0.020	0.022	0.000
2,2-DMC$_4$	0.169	0.169	0.012	0.000	0.191	0.660	0.000	0.464	0.006	0.018
2,3-DMC$_4$	0.053	0.053	0.046	0.000	0.061	0.046	0.000	0.032	0.019	0.073
2-MC$_5$	0.200	0.200	0.215	0.000	0.227	0.058	0.000	0.041	0.116	0.323

Table 6. Cont.

Properties	Reactor Effluent	Stabilizer Feed	Reactor Feed	Stabilizer over Head	Stabilizer Bottom	Overhead De-hexanizer	Bottom De-hexanizer	Isomerate	Deiso-Pentanizr Bottom	Recycle
3-MC$_5$	0.126	0.126	0.152	0.000	0.143	0.004	0.000	0.003	0.104	0.216
n-hexane	0.077	0.077	0.178	0.000	0.087	0.000	0.004	0.001	0.342	0.133
cyclohexane	0.104	0.104	0.115	0.000	0.117	0.000	0.216	0.041	0.097	0.155
benzene	0.000	0.000	0.011	0.000	0.000	0.000	0.000	0.000	0.035	0.000
Cycloheptane	0.078	0.078	0.059	0.000	0.089	0.000	0.585	0.112	0.065	0.070
n-heptane	0.013	0.013	0.013	0.000	0.014	0.000	0.124	0.024	0.029	0.008
H$_2$O	0.000	0.000	0.000	0.000	0.000	0.000	0.000	0.000	0.000	0.000
H$_2$	0.090	0.090	0.126	0.759	0.000	0.000	0.000	0.000	0.000	0.000
methane	0.005	0.005	0.005	0.041	0.000	0.000	0.000	0.000	0.000	0.000

2.2.5. Validation of Base Case Simulation Result

The results of the simulated base case of isomerization unit were validated with the data extracted from an industrial case of isomerization unit at an Egyptian refinery plant located in Alexandria. A comparison between the real state of the base case and simulation results is shown in Figure 8; it confirms that there is a good agreement between the actual and simulated results. Therefore, the base case simulation model can be used to evaluate the performance of the proposed configurations. It is worth mentioning that a similar result was reported by Yu. N. Lebedev who proved that Kedr-89 Co. has revamped several existing isomerization units by adding a DIH tower and an increase in the RON of commercial isomerate has been achieved. The experience of Kedr-89 Co. showed also that fitting isomerization units with a DIH tower increases the RON of commercial isomerate by a minimum of 4–5 points, which nearly almost agrees with the base case result [15].

Figure 8. Comparison between real state of base case and simulation result.

2.2.6. Simulation Results Discussion

The light naphtha isomerization unit's simulation was carried out using the feed's real characteristics and composition. Several scenarios were simulated, and Table 7 displays the obtained process's octane number of the gasoline product. The employment of both fractionators, before and after the reactor, results in a superior grade of product. This is because the concentration of the normal paraffins at the reactor input increases due to the removal of i-pentane, which forces the reaction to undergo more isomerization. Additionally, the isomerization unit with both a de-hexanizer and a de-isopentanizer has a high-octane number for the produced isomerate compared to the unit with de-hexanizer alone, which is still higher than the unit applying a de-isopentanizer alone.

Table 7. Isomerate octane number for the four cases of isomerization unit modifications.

The Modified Isomerization Unit	Isomerate Reasearch Octane Number (RON)
PC1	77.06
PC2	78.15
BC	80.91
PC3	86.42

From (Aspen Hysys V12.1 Help) the Healy blend for RON and MON calculation uses the following formulas:

$$RON = RON_{sum} + 0.05411(\Delta RONMON_1 - RON_{sum} \times \Delta RONMON) + 0.00098\,(olf_{sum2} - olf^2_{sum}) - 0.00074(Arom_{sum2} - Arom^2_{sum})$$

$$MON = MON_{sum} + 0.03908(\Delta RONMON_2 - MON_{sum} \times \Delta RONMON) - 7.03 \times 10^{-7}(Arom_{sum2} - Arom^2_{sum})^2)$$

where

$RON_{sum} = \sum_i RON_i \times v_i$
$MON_{sum} = \sum_i MON_i \times v_i$
$olf_{sum} = \sum_i olf_i \times v_i$
$olf_{sum2} = \sum_i olf_i^2 \times v_i$
$Arom_{sum} = \sum_i Arom_i \times v_i$
$Arom_{sum2} = \sum_i Arom_i^2 \times v_i$
$\Delta RONMON = \sum_i (RON_i - MON_i) \times v_i$
$\Delta RONMON_1 = \sum_i RON_i(RON_i - MON_i) \times v_i$
$\Delta RONMON_2 = \sum_i MON_i(RON_i - MON_i) \times v_i$
v_i = volume fraction
for stream level blending:
$$Vol\ Frac = \frac{volume\ flow\ i}{volume\ flow\ of\ stream}$$
For component level blending
$$Vol\ Frac = \frac{volume\ flow\ of\ component\ i\ in\ stream}{total\ volume\ flow\ of\ component\ in\ all\ stream}$$

2.3. Economic Study of the Different Investigated Isomerization Processes

All chemical process elements, such as equipment, instruments, electricity, utilities, operating expenses, and feed and product prices are included in the economic assessment for each isomerization case, in order to select the optimal case. Based on the total fixed costs and profits, the payback period and returns on investments (ROI) are determined; a good investment will have a short payback period and a high ROI [25,26].

2.3.1. Capital Investment

Fixed and working capital investments are the two categories of capital investment [24]. Manufacturing fixed capital includes expenses such as those required for the full operation of the process, such as instruments, foundations, insulation, piping, and site separation. Working capital includes expenses required for operation. The sum of both is known as total capital investment.

Capital Costs Calculations

The costs for the current isomerization plant as well as the modified plants with the proposed changes must be calculated according to the current prices. Therefore, it is important for capital costs calculations to use the cost index, which relates the current price of equipment to its price in the past, as presented by the following equation [25–27]:

$$Present\ cost = Original\ cost \times \frac{index\ value\ at\ present\ time}{index\ value\ at\ time\ original\ cost\ was\ obtained}.$$

Based on applicable data for the built-in isomerization unit, capital costs were calculated. Figure 9 shows the total capital cost for the original as well as each modification scenario. It is noticed that the isomerization process with adding both a de-hexanizer and a de-isopentanizer has the highest capital cost. This can be attributed to the addition of two extra fractionators and the usage of expensive equipment for recycling unconverted hexanes. This increase in capital cost is a result of the use of additional reboilers, condensers, exchangers, and pumps, which are required with an increase in fractionators. De-hexanizer-based isomerization requires a greater initial investment than iso-pentanizer-based isomerization because a larger reaction section and higher recycling flow are required.

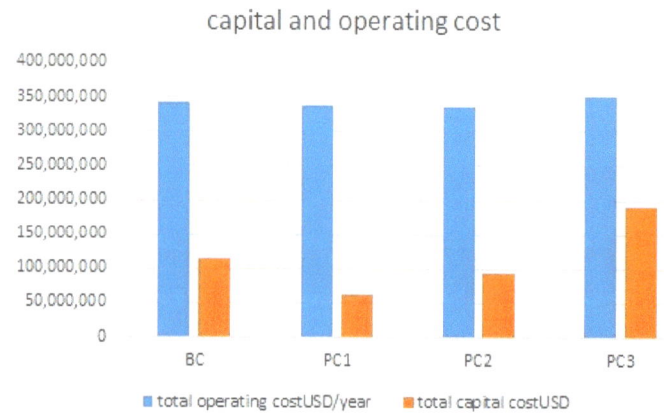

Figure 9. Capital and operating costs for the four investigated cases of isomerization.

2.3.2. Operating Costs

Raw material costs, operational labor costs, utilities, maintenance and repairs, operating supplies, laboratory charges, catalyst, solvent, depreciation, insurance, and municipal taxes are all included in operating costs. The operating cost also includes the costs of labor, catalysts, chemicals, make-up hydrogen, energy, steam, cooling water, and raw materials (naphtha).

Operating cost = raw material cost (naphtha cost) + electricity cost + steam cost + cooling water cost + labor cost + catalyst cost + chemicals cost + and make-up hydrogen cost [25,26].

Since the cost of feed and hydrogen for each unit is the same, all instances have the same raw material cost. According to the calculation of operating costs, the isomerization unit with both a de-isopentanizer and a de-hexanizer has the highest operating costs as addressed in Table 8.

Table 8. Operating costs of the four cases of isomerization processes [28].

Item	PC1	PC2	BC	PC3
Price of feed naphtha, USD/tone	918	918	918	918
Price of produced isomerate, USD/Gallon	2.71	2.72	2.9	3.2
Octane number of produced isomerate	77.06	78.15	80.91	86.42
Volume of produced isomerate, Gallon /hour	18,245	18,606	18,321.6	18,340
Hydrogen price, USD/MT	6746	6746	6746	6746
Total utilities cost, USD/year	5,221,710	2,029,990	8,965,580	16,845,500
Total raw materials cost, USD/year	307,268,000	307,268,000	307,267,000	307,268,000
Total operating cost, USD/year	338,357,000	335,180,000	342,897,000	351,879,000
Total product sales, USD/year	345,126,000	354,426,000	372,345,000	411,075,000

2.3.3. Profit, ROI, and Payback Period for Different Isomerization Scenarios

The main objective of every endeavor is to make money. Therefore, assessing profit not only determines the success of the project but also clarifies how we spend our money and provides funding for growing businesses. Profit is the refinery's net cash flow expressed in dollars per time unit. Profit is derived by subtraction of total operating costs from total expenses (total operating costs) as presented by Equation (2) [25]. It should be noted that the price of gasoline was calculated according to U.S. Energy Information Administration [25,27].

$$\text{Profit} = \text{Total income} - \text{Total expenses} \qquad (1)$$

$$\text{ROI} = (\text{average yearly profit}/\text{total capital cost}) \times 100 \qquad (2)$$

PC3 of the investigated isomerization processes has the best profit, since the product is of the highest quality; nevertheless, while having the highest operating and capital expenses, the high-grade gasoline generated allows income to exceed the necessary operating costs. Because the unconverted hexane could be recycled, the isomerization process by adding a de-hexanizer (PC3) is quite profitable. A once-through isomerization process (PC1) has the lowest profit because of the low-quality product that is generated after isomerization.

According to the results of the economic analysis, isomerization with adding both a de-hexanizer and a de-isopentanizer produces the greatest octane number and the shortest payback period, as shown in Table 9. As a result, isomerization using a de-hexanizer and a de-isopentanizer is optimized for minimum-cost modeling and is included in the simulation. The original steady state optimizer in Aspen HYSIS version 12.1 is used to minimize cost using two variables at the same time, temperature, and pressure of isomerization reactor feed.

Table 9. Profit, ROI, and payback period for different isomerization scenarios.

Item	BC	PC1	PC2	PC3
Profit, USD/year	6,769,000	19,246,000	29,448,000	59,196,000
ROI, %	10.69	20.25	17	30.99
Payback period, year	9.35	4.936	5.85	3.23

2.4. Process Optimization

The introduced four cases; simple once-through isomerization, isomerization with adding a de-isopentanizer, isomerization with adding a de-hexanizer, and isomerization with adding both of a de-hexanizer and a de-isopentanizer, are simulated to determine the best case with respect to octane number and ROI. The temperature and pressure of the isomerization reactor feed are selected as the optimization variables in this process as indicated in Table 10.

Table 10. Design variable range.

Variable	Minimum	Maximum
Temperature °C	120	160
Pressure barg	17.7	74

2.4.1. Design Variables

Design parameters include fixed parameters in all optimization runs such as feed conditions and are shown in Table 1. On the other hand, optimization variables include variables, which are allowed to change for the optimization calculation to achieve the optimum value [24]. Design variables used in the original optimizer to reach the lowest isomerization cost are the temperature and pressure of the isomerization reactor. Temperature is controlled by a thermodynamic equilibrium, which is favorable at low temperatures (<200 °C). Equilibrium limits maximum conversion at any given set of conditions. High temperatures increase the catalyst activity and the resulting research octane number. However, at very high temperatures, the concentration of iso-paraffins in the product will decrease since a crack in hydrocarbons to light gases has occurred as a side reaction; this consequently reduces the yield. The increase in pressure does not affect the yield of isomerate but increases the operating cost. On the other hand, decreasing the pressure below a certain value will result in a decrease in the activity of the catalyst, as heavy compounds such as cyclic C_6 compounds will block the active sites of the catalyst and decrease its activity. The purpose of the range is to scale the gradients of the cost function and constraints and give similar gradient magnitude for each variable. The gradients of the objective function and constraints vary inversely with the variable ranges [24].

The objective of the optimization is to minimize the total cost, taking into consideration the raw material cost, stabilizer reboiler heating cost, stabilizer condenser cooling cost, heater cost, fractionators reboiler heating cost, and fractionators condenser cooling cost. The original steady state optimizer in Aspen HYSYS version 12.1 is used for cost calculations, which aims to minimize cost, where the temperature and pressure of the feed to the isomerization reactor are the two main affecting variables.

Isomerization unit target is to upgrade the octane number of light naphtha, which is related to anti-knocking quality of gasoline; this is achieved by modifying the structure of straight chain components to be branched chain components.

Optimization of an isomerization process includes two targets: minimum cost and high-octane number of the isomerate product. The operating cost includes the costs of raw material, utility, labor, catalyst, chemicals, and makeup hydrogen. Labor, catalyst, and chemicals costs are fixed in all optimizations runs, and this consequently leads to include only raw material and utility costs in the objective function. The price value is used to calculate the objective function value. Equation (3) is used for determining the objective function value [24]:

$$\text{Objective Function: Value} = \text{Price} \times \text{Current Value} \quad (3)$$

Objective function = de-isopentanizer Cond utility heat flow(KJ/h) × 7.89 ×10^{-6} ($/kJ) × 7000 (h/year) + de-isopentanizer reboiler utility heat flow (KJ/h) × 7.5 × 10^{-5} × 7000 (h/year) + heater utility heat flow(KJ/h) × 5.7 × 10^{-4} ($/KJ) × 7000 (h/year) + stabilizer Cond utility heat flow(KJ/h) × 7.89 × 10^{-6} ($/KJ) × 7000 +stabilizer reboiler utility heat flow (KJ/h) × 8.62 × 10^{-4} ($/KJ) × 7000 (h/year) + deisohexanizer Cond (KJ/h) × 7.89 × 10^{-6} ($/KJ) × 7000 (h/year) + deisohexanizer reboiler utility heat flow (KJ/h) × 5.7 × 10^{-4} × ($/KJ) × 7000 (h/year) + feed mass flow rate (kg/h) × 0.918 ($/Kg) × 7000 (h/year) + hydrogen mass flow rate (kg/h) × 6.74 × 10^{-3} ($/KG) × 7000 (h/year) [28].

Constrain equation: octane number $\geq$ 86.

2.4.2. Energy Analysis

The utility costs include de-isopentanizer reboiler heat flow, de-isopentanizer condenser heat flow, heater utility heat flow, de-hexanizer reboiler heat flow, de-hexanizer condenser heat flow, stabilizer condenser heat flow, and stabilizer reboiler heat flow costs.

This objective function is minimized to find the optimum conditions. The optimization results reveal that the optimum temperature and pressure of the reactor feed are 155 °C and 45.4 barg, respectively.

It is noticed that the optimized temperature and pressure are greater than operational ones; however, when compared as shown in Table 11, it is discovered that the heat flow of the heater, stabilizer reboiler and condenser, and de-hexanizer reboiler and condenser are lower as the reactor feed temperature is higher, resulting in minimizing cost. This process resulted in an increase in octane numbers by 7% and a decrease in the total cost by 13%.

Table 11. Heat flows of different types of utilities for the optimized and non-optimized isomerization process with adding of a de-hexanizer and a de-isopentanizers.

Utility Type	Heat Flow of Non-Optimized Process, kJ/h	Heat Flow of the Optimized Process, kJ/h
De-isopentanizer condenser	19,035,232.2	19,035,232
De-isopentanizer reboiler	21,340,938.3	21,340,938
De-hexanizer condenser	104,831,445.3	63,822,765
De-hexanizer reboiler	138,039,323.6	49,638,262
Stabilizer reboiler	70,816,415.7	55,973,348
Stabilizer condenser	59,885,821.4	44,419,607
Heater energy	12,891,639.9	11,214,280

3. Conclusions

The aim of the current research work is directed to studying, improving, and optimizing an isomerization plant located in Alexandria, Egypt. Three types of changes in the main structure of the isomerization process are introduced. The changes consider the addition of one or two fractionation columns before or after the reactor. The purpose of these fractionators is separating the unreacted normal (unbranched) paraffins to be recycled to the reactor for increasing the octane number of the isomerate product. The simulation and optimization tool used in this paper is Aspen HYSYS version 12.1.

The simulation results showed that the octane number and ROI of the isomerization process using two fractionators (a de-hexanizer and a de-isopentanizer) before and after the reactor increased to 86.5 and 29.9%, respectively. For the process of adding a de-isopentanizer before the reactor, the octane number and ROI reached 78.15 and 20%, respectively. Regarding the isomerization process with adding a de-hexanizer after the reactor, the octane number of 81 and ROI of 17% are obtained. Therefore, adding two fractionators to the original isomerization plant is more profitable with the highest product octane number compared with the other investigated configurations.

This work also studies the optimization of this selected best process to be more profitable. The optimization of this process seeks to find the optimum conditions for the reactor feed. The optimization results showed that the optimum temperature and pressure of the reactor feed are 155 °C and 45.4 bar_g, respectively. It is noticed that the obtained optimum conditions of the reactor feed stream led to the maximum product's octane number and minimum heat flow of the de-hexanizer and stabilizer, which resulted in a significant decrease in utility costs. The optimization results reveal an increase in octane numbers by 7% and a decrease in the total cost by 13%. These results prove the economic effectiveness of the proposed modification and optimization on the existent isomerization process, which can be applied to similar processes to increase their profitability.

Author Contributions: Conceptualization, W.S.O., S.M.S. and A.A.B.; methodology, W.S.O., A.M.S. and S.M.S.; software, A.M.S. and A.E.F.; validation, A.E.F., W.S.O. and A.A.B.; formal analysis, A.E.F. and S.M.S.; investigation, A.E.F., A.M.S. and A.G.G.; resources, W.S.O. and A.A.B.; data curation, A.E.F., A.M.S. and A.G.G.; writing—original draft preparation, A.E.F. and W.S.O.; writing—review and editing, A.M.S., A.G.G. and A.A.B.; visualization, A.M.S., S.M.S. and A.G.G.; supervision, W.S.O., S.M.S. and A.A.B.; funding acquisition, A.G.G. and A.A.B. All authors have read and agreed to the published version of the manuscript.

Funding: This work was supported and funded by the Deanship of Scientific Research at Imam Mohammad Ibn Saud Islamic University (IMSIU) (grant number IMSIU-RG23064).

Data Availability Statement: Data are available upon request through the corresponding author.

Conflicts of Interest: The authors declare no conflict of interest.

References

1. Hasini, A. Pediaa. Available online: https://pediaa.com/HasiniA/what-is-the-difference-between-isomerization-and-reforming/ (accessed on 20 July 2023).
2. Oyekan, S. *Catalytic Naphtha Reforming Process*; Taylor & Francis Group, LLC: Boca Raton, FL, USA, 2019.
3. Valavarasu, G.; Sairam, B. Light Naphtha Isomerization Process: A Review. *Pet. Sci. Technol.* **2013**, *31*, 580–595. [CrossRef]
4. Petrov, I.; Stratiev, D.; Shishkova, I.; Yordanov, D. A hybrid reformer performance analysis reveals the reason for reformate octane deterioration. *Oil Gas Eur. Mag.* **2021**, *47*, 14–20.
5. Tamizhdurai, P.; Ramesh, A.; Krishnan, P.; Narayanan, S.; Shanthi, K.; Sivasanker, S. Effect of acidity and porosity changes of dealuminated mordenite on n-pentane, n-hexane and light naphtha isomerization. *Microporous Mesoporous Mater.* **2019**, *287*, 192–202. [CrossRef]
6. Shakor, Z.M.; Ramos, M.J.; AbdulRazak, A.A. A detailed reaction kinetic model of light naphtha isomerization on Pt/zeolite catalyst. *J. King Saud Univ.-Eng. Sci.* **2022**, *34*, 303–308. [CrossRef]
7. Hamied, R.S.; Shakor, Z.M.; Sadeiq, A.H.; Razak, A.A.A.; Khadim, A.T. Kinetic Modeling of Light Naphtha Hydroisomerization in an Industrial Universal Oil Products Penex™ Unit. *Energy Eng.* **2023**, *120*, 1371–1386. [CrossRef]
8. Naqvi, S.R.; Bibi, A.; Naqvi, M.; Noor, T.; Nizami, A.S.; Rehan, M.; Ayoub, M. New trends in improving gasoline quality and octane through naphtha isomerization: A short review. *Appl. Petrochem. Res.* **2018**, *8*, 131–139. [CrossRef]
9. Chekantsev, N.V.; Gyngazova, M.S. Mathematical modeling of light naphtha (C5, C6) isomerization process. *J. Chem. Eng.* **2014**, *238*, 120–128. [CrossRef]
10. Hamadi, A.S.; Kadhim, R.A. Material Balance and Reaction Kinetics Modeling for Penex Isomerization Process in Daura Refinery. *MATEC Web Conf.* **2017**, *111*, 02012. [CrossRef]
11. Shahata, W.M.; Mohamed, M.F.; Gad, F.K. Monitoring and modelling of variables affecting isomerate octane number produced from an industrial isomerization process. *J. Pet.* **2018**, *27*, 945–953. [CrossRef]
12. Chuzlov, V.A.; Chekantsev, N.V.; Ivanchina, E.D. Development of Complex Mathematical Model of Light Naphtha Isomerization and Rectification Processes. *Procedia Chem.* **2014**, *10*, 236–243. [CrossRef]
13. Jarullah, A.T.; Abed, F.M.; Ahmed, A.M.; Mujtaba, I.M. Optimization of Several Industrial and Recently Developed AJAM Naphtha Isomerization Processes Using Model Based Techniques. *Computers* **2019**, *126*, 403–420.
14. Viswanadham, N.; Saxena, S.K.; Garg, M. Octane number enhancement studies of naphtha over noble metal loaded zeolite catalysts. *J. Ind. Eng. Chem.* **2013**, *19*, 950–955. [CrossRef]
15. Lebedev, Y.N.; Ratovskii, Y.Y.; Karmanov, E.V.; Zaitseva, T.M.; Pod'yablonskaya, T.V. Revamping of isomerization units. *Chem. Technol. Fuels Oils* **2010**, *46*, 244–247. [CrossRef]
16. Zafar, S. Academia. Penex Process. Available online: https://www.academia.edu/9687674/Penex_Process (accessed on 13 November 2023).
17. Abd Hamid, M. *HYSYS: An Introduction to Chemical Engineering Simulation for UTM Degree++ Program*; Universiti Teknologi Malaysia: Skudai, Malaysia, 2007.
18. Chuzlov, V.A.; Molotov, K.V. Semantic Scholor. Available online: https://www.semanticscholar.org/paper/Analysis-of-Optimal-Process-Flow-Diagrams-of-Light-Chuzlov-Molotov/c19bc5029bd217c5cd3c12e44df7d16d5b1aaca6/ (accessed on 6 December 2023).
19. Hassan, E. Hassanelbanhawi. Available online: http://hassanelbanhawi.com/processes/isomerization-process/ (accessed on 13 November 2023).
20. Sluzer Technology. Available online: https://www.eia.gov/dnav/pet/PET_PRI_GND_DCUS_NUS_M.htm (accessed on 13 November 2023).
21. Surinder, P. *Refining Processes Handbook*, 1st ed.; Gulf Professional Publishing, Ed.; Elsevier: Houston, TX, USA, 2003.
22. Meyer, R.A. *Handbook of Petroleum Refining Processes*, 3rd ed.; McGraw-Hill Education LLC: New York, NY, USA, 2004.
23. General Operating Manual of Isomerization Unit of an Egyptian Petroleum Refinery Plant, UOP Manuals. 1997. Available online: https://pdfcoffee.com/nht-isom-pdf-free.html (accessed on 20 August 2023).
24. AspenTech. *Aspen HYSYS Petroleum Refining Unit Operations & Reactor Models*; Aspen Technology: Bedford, MA, USA, 2016.
25. Peters, M.S. *Plant Design and Economics for Chemical Engineers*, 5th ed.; McGraw Hill Education LLC: New York, NY, USA, 2003.
26. Gary, J.H.; Handwerk, G.E.; Kaiser, M.J. *Petroleum Refining: Technology and Economics*, 5th ed.; CRC Press: Boca Raton, FL, USA, 2007.
27. Plant Cost Index, Chemical Engineering. Available online: https://personalpages.manchester.ac.uk/staff/tom.rodgers/Interactive_graphs/CEPCI.html?reactors/CEPCI/index.html (accessed on 15 August 2023).
28. US Energy Information Administration. Retail Motor Gasoline and On-Highway Diesel Fuel Prices, Monthly Energy Review. 2022. Available online: https://www.eia.gov/petroleum/gasdiesel/ (accessed on 20 August 2023).

Disclaimer/Publisher's Note: The statements, opinions and data contained in all publications are solely those of the individual author(s) and contributor(s) and not of MDPI and/or the editor(s). MDPI and/or the editor(s) disclaim responsibility for any injury to people or property resulting from any ideas, methods, instructions or products referred to in the content.

Article

Preparation and Application of New Polyhydroxy Ammonium Shale Hydration Inhibitor

Xiaofeng Chang [1], Quande Wang [2,3], Jiale Hu [2], Yan Sun [1], Shijun Chen [2], Xuefan Gu [3] and Gang Chen [2,3,*]

[1] CNPC Chuanqing Drilling Engineering Company Ltd., Xi'an 710018, China
[2] Engineering Research Center of Oil and Gas Field Chemistry, Universities of Shaanxi Provence, Xi'an Shiyou University, Xi'an 710065, China; 20212070871@stumail.xsyu.edu.cn (Q.W.)
[3] Shaanxi Province Key Laboratory of Environmental Pollution Control and Reservoir Protection Technology of Oilfields, Xi'an Shiyou University, Xi'an 710065, China
* Correspondence: gangchen@xsyu.edu.cn

Abstract: Wellbore instability caused by the hydration of shale formations during drilling is a major problem in drilling engineering. In this paper, the shale inhibition performance of polyhydroxy-alkanolamine was evaluated using an anti-swelling test, linear swelling test, wash-durable test and montmorillonite hydration and dispersion experiment. Additionally, the shale inhibition mechanism of polyhydroxy-alkanolamine was studied via Fourier transform infrared spectroscopy (FTIR), particle size, zeta potential, thermogravimetric analysis (TGA) and scanning electron microscopy (SEM). The results show that the use of polyhydroxy-alkanolamine (EGP-2) could result in a relatively lower linear swelling rate of montmorillonite, and the linear swelling rate of 0.3% EGP-2 is 26.98%, which is stronger than that of 4% KCl. The anti-swelling rate of 0.3% EGP-2 is 43.54%, and the shrinkage–swelling rate of 0.3% EGP-2 is 34.62%. The study on the inhibition mechanism revealed that EGP-2 can permeate and adsorb on the surface of montmorillonite. The rolling recovery rate of easily hydrated shale was as high as 79.36%, which greatly reduces the dispersion ability of water to easily hydrated shale. The results of this study can be used to maintain the stability of a wellbore, which is conducive to related research.

Keywords: hydration; infiltration; adsorption; wellbore stability

1. Introduction

Shale oil has been one of the outstanding technologies in the world in recent years [1]. In the process of oil field drilling, due to the hydration swelling of water-sensitive shale, drilling instability problems such as drilling scouring, pipe jamming, rock debris disintegration and bit ball often occur in shale formation [2,3]. According to the chemical characteristics of shale and drilling fluid, when water-sensitive shale (with a high montmorillonite content) is immersed in water-based drilling fluid, the shale may swell and disperse rapidly [4–6]. Therefore, many shale inhibitors have been widely used in water-based drilling fluids. Unfortunately, because of the environmental requirements, the use of most of shale inhibitors is limited. [7–9]. High-performance water-based drilling fluid adopts the basic idea of strengthening inhibition overall, relying on multiple treatment agents for synergistic suppression, and basically achieves the strong inhibitory effect of oil-based drilling fluid. In recent years, polyhydroxy-ammonium has received the extensive attention of researchers because of its more significant application effects in terms of inhibition, lubricity and stable rheology [10]. In addition, our research team has also conducted research in the field of drilling fluid treatment agents [11–13]. Therefore, we have proposed environmentally friendly alcohol amine inhibitors with multi-hydroxyl. Polyhydroxy-alkanolamine inhibitors can provide multiple adsorption sites on a montmorillonite surface and enhance the adsorption of inhibitors on the montmorillonite surface [14,15]. The binding of montmorillonite is mainly realized through hydrogen bonding, anchoring, electrostatic adsorption and hydrophobic action, which effectively inhibits the hydration, swelling and dispersion of montmorillonite [16–18]. At present, polyhydroxy-alkanolamines have excellent compatibility with traditional additives and can meet the requirements of environmental protection. They have been applied in many water-based-drilling fluids, and have very broad application prospects.

In this study, polyhydroxy-alkanolamine was used to permeate and adsorb on the surface of shale, thereby reducing the hydration of the montmorillonite minerals in shale formation and stabilizing the wellbore. In this paper, the shale inhibition performance of polyhydroxy-alkanolamine was evaluated via experimental methods, and its shale inhibition mechanism was comprehensively analyzed.

2. Experimental Materials and Methods

2.1. Materials and Reagents

Epoxy propanol and ethylenediamine were purchased from Xi'an Chemical Reagent Factory. Ethanol and acetone were purchased from the Shanghai Xinghuo chemical plant. Potassium chloride and sodium carbonate were purchased from the Tianjin Zhiyuan chemical reagent factory. Calcium-based montmorillonite and sodium-based montmorillonite were purchased from Xi'an Fengyun Chemical Co., Ltd. (Xi'an Fengyun Chemical Co., Ltd., Xi'an, China) Polyvinyl alcohol (PVA), guar gum (GG), CMC and modified starch (MS) were purchased from Yangzhou Runda Oilfield Chemical Co., Ltd. (Yangzhou Runda Oilfield Chemical Co., Ltd., Yangzhou, China)

2.2. Synthesis

A certain amount of ethylenediamine, epoxy propanol and solvents was placed in a round-bottom flask equipped with a reflux condenser and refluxed with magnetic stirring for 4 h. After cooling to room temperature, the solvent in the solution was evaporated to obtain the product. The reaction mechanism is shown in Figure 1. The names of synthetic inhibitors are shown in Table 1.

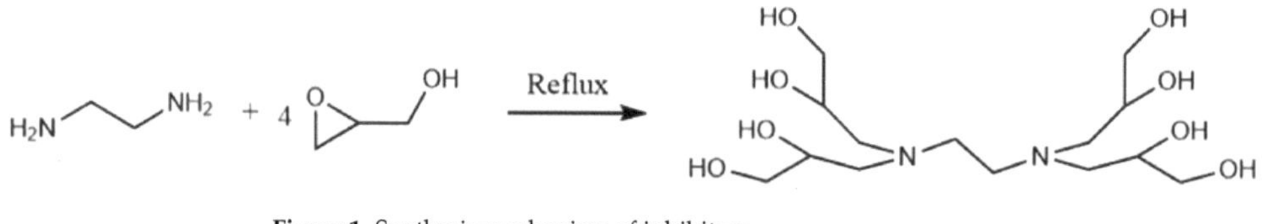

Figure 1. Synthesis mechanism of inhibitors.

Table 1. Nomenclature of inhibitors.

Reagent	Reagent	Solvent	Proportion	Nomenclature
Ethylenediamine	Epoxy propanol	Distilled water	1:1	EGD-1
			1:2	EGD-2
			1:3	EGD-3
		Ethanol	1:1	EGA-1
			1:2	EGA-2
			1:3	EGA-3
		Acetone	1:1	EGP-1
			1:2	EGP-2
			1:3	EGP-3

2.3. Optimization of Synthesis Conditions

The inhibition performance of synthetic products on montmorillonite is affected by the material ratio, concentration and medium of synthetic reaction. Therefore, the synthetic products with the best inhibition performance were preliminarily selected through inhibition performance parameters such as anti-swelling rate and linear swelling rate. In addition, the shale inhibition performance of polyhydroxy-alkanolamine was evaluated in water-based drilling fluid and its mechanism was studied. The relationship between the influencing factors can be better analyzed. Therefore, the L9 (3^3) orthogonal experiment table was designed, and the linear swelling rate of montmorillonite after adding the inhibitor for 2 h was taken as the index of the hydration inhibition effect. The results are shown in Tables 2 and 3.

Table 2. Orthogonal experimental factors.

Factors	Solvent (A)	Ratio of Amine to Alcohol (B)	Concentration (C)
1	Distilled water	1:1	0.1%
2	Acetone	1:2	0.3%
3	Ethanol	1:3	1.0%

Table 3. Analysis of orthogonal experiment results.

Number	A	B	C
1	1	1	1
2	1	2	2
3	1	3	3
4	2	1	2
5	2	2	3
6	2	3	1
7	3	1	3
8	3	2	1
9	3	3	2

2.4. Anti-Swelling and Shrinkage–Swelling Evaluation

The industry-standard evaluation method for montmorillonite stabilizers of drilling fluid, SY/T 5971-2016 [19], was referred to for evaluating the influence of the inhibitor on the anti-swelling rate of montmorillonite. Inhibitor solutions of different concentrations were prepared. Montmorillonite (0.5× g) was weighed and put into a 10 mL centrifuge tube. A certain amount of the inhibitor solution was added into the centrifuge tube, and then fully stirred and shaken. After left to stand for 2 h, with a centrifuge at the speed of 1500 r/min for 15 min, the volume, V_a, was recorded. The inhibitor solution was replaced by water and kerosene, and the swelling volume of montmorillonite in water and kerosene was recorded as V_b and V_0, respectively. The calculation formula of the anti-swelling rate of montmorillonite is shown in (1):

$$B_1 = \frac{V_b - V_a}{V_b - V_0} \times 100\% \tag{1}$$

where B_1 is the anti-swelling rate of montmorillonite; V_a is the swelling volume of montmorillonite in the inhibitor solution, in mL; V_b is the swelling volume of montmorillonite in water, in mL; V_0 is the swelling volume of montmorillonite in kerosene, in mL.

Montmorillonite (2× g) was added to the centrifuge tube. Kerosene (7 mL) was added to centrifuge tube No. 1, and distilled water was added to other centrifuge tubes. After being fully stirred and left to stand for 4 h, it was centrifuged for 15 min at the speed of 3000 r/min, and then the montmorillonite volume was recorded after centrifugation. The volume of montmorillonite in kerosene is V_0, and the volume of distilled water is recorded as V_W. After that, the supernatant in the centrifuge tube was poured out, and 7 mL inhibitor solutions of different concentrations were added, fully shaken, stirred and left to stand for 4 h before centrifugation. The montmorillonite volume was recorded as V_S. The calculation formula of the shrinkage–swelling rate of montmorillonite is shown in (2):

$$B_2 = \frac{V_w - V_s}{V_w - V_0} \times 100\% \tag{2}$$

where B_2 is the shrinkage–swelling rate of montmorillonite; V_S is the swelling volume of montmorillonite in the inhibitor solution, in mL; V_w is the swelling volume of montmorillonite in water, in mL; V_0 is the swelling volume of montmorillonite in kerosene, in mL.

2.5. Wash-Durable Test

The evaluation of the water washing resistance of the montmorillonite inhibitor was based on the enterprise standard Q/SH 0053-2010 of China Petroleum and Chemical Corporation on technical requirements for montmorillonite stabilizers [20].

2.6. Montmorillonite Hydration and Dispersion Experiment

Inhibitor solutions of different concentrations were prepared at room temperature. Sodium-based montmorillonite (5 g) was added to the above solutions, shaken well and left to stand for 24 h. The swelling volume of montmorillonite in different solutions was recorded and the inhibition performance of the inhibitor was evaluated.

2.7. Linear Swelling

The industry-standard shale inhibitor evaluation method, SY/T 6335-1997 [21], for drilling fluid was referred to for evaluating the influence of the inhibitor on the linear swelling rate of montmorillonite. The calculation formula for the linear swelling rate of montmorillonite is shown in (3):

$$\text{Sr} = \frac{Ro}{\Delta L} \times 100\% \tag{3}$$

where Sr is the linear swelling rate of montmorillonite; Ro represents the swelling of montmorillonite, in mm; ΔL is the core thickness, in mm.

2.8. Performance in Drilling Fluid

Briefly, the preparation of 4% calcium montmorillonite drilling fluid was as follows. Calcium montmorillonite (14 g) and sodium carbonate (0.7 g) were added to tap water (350 mL), stirred at a high speed for 2 h and aged at 298 K for 24 h for use [22]. The preparation of treatment mud went as follows. The drilling fluid and treatment agent were aged for 6 h, stirred at a high speed for 10 min and tested for their performance [23]. The rheological properties, filtration properties and lubrication properties of the drilling fluid, such as AV (apparent viscosity), PV (plastic viscosity), YP (yield point), FL (API filtration) and tg (friction coefficient), were determined. A viscometer (ZNN-D6S, Hetongda Co., Ltd. Qingdao, China), medium pressure filtration instrument (GJSS-B12K, Haitongda Co., Ltd. Qingdao, China) and viscosity coefficient instrument (Qingdao Hetongda Co., Ltd. Qingdao, China) were adopted in accordance with the formulas in Chinese National Standard GB/T 16783.1-2006 [24].

2.9. Shale Rolling Recovery Experiment

The shale was crushed, and 6–10 mesh shale pieces were screened out for use in the experiments. Before the experiments, the shale pieces were dried at $100 \pm 2\ °C$ for 2 h. An amount of 50 g of shale pieces (6–10 mesh) was weighted and added to 350 mL of the inhibition solution, transferred into a stainless-steel aging cell and aged at 120 °C for 16 h. After aging, a 40-mesh standard sieve was used to filter the shale pieces, and the material left on the sieve was dried at 105 °C and weighed (M_1). Equation (4) was used to calculate the shale recovery rate.

$$\text{Shale recovery} = \frac{M_1}{50} \times 100\% \tag{4}$$

where M_1 is the mass of the recovered shale pieces after drying (g).

2.10. FT-IR Analysis

The dried inhibitor samples were ground. During the test, the ground samples were mixed with KBr at a ratio of 1:100, put into the tablet press and pressed into transparent flakes. Additionally, the soil samples were scanned and analyzed using an infrared spectrometer [25].

2.11. Particle Distribution Measurement

The dried inhibitor samples were used to measure particle sizes using a laser particle size experiment, so as to obtain the median particle size and average particle size of the montmorillonite particles in mud treated with the treatment agent. The change in montmorillonite particle size was analyzed according to these data [26].

2.12. Zeta Potential Measurement

The zeta potential of the supernatant of the solution was measured via the omni multiangle particle size and using a high-sensitivity zeta potential analyzer. The changes in the zeta potential of graphite with different dosages of adsorbent were analyzed [27].

2.13. SEM and TGA

The montmorillonite samples were dispersed in the inhibitor solution and hydrated for 24 h, and then the water was separated from it and dried at 105 °C for TGA and SEM. The TGA experiment was conducted on a TGA/DSC thermal analysis instrument (1/1600, METTLER TOLEDO, Inc., Columbus, OH, USA) at a ramp of 20 °C/min from room temperature to 825 °C under a nitrogen flow. The surface morphology of the montmorillonite samples was evaluated using a digital microscope imaging scanning electron microscope (model SU6000, serial NO. HI-2102-0003) at a 40.0 kV accelerating voltage on the basis of the reported method [28,29].

3. Results and Discussion

3.1. Screening of Synthesis Conditions

The orthogonal test results of the influence of the inhibitors synthesized by using ethylenediamine and epoxy propanol in different solvents on montmorillonite swelling are shown in Table 4, the experiment results of range analysis are shown in Table 5 and the main effect diagram of the mean value from the orthogonal experiment is shown in Figure 2.

Table 4. Orthogonal test results.

Number	Swelling Rate/%	Number	Swelling Rate/%
1	48.41	6	46.61
2	35.25	7	50.61
3	48.93	8	42.13
4	35.70	9	47.08
5	29.75		

Table 5. Analysis of experimental results obtained via range method.

Project	A	B	C
K1	44.20	44.91	40.10
K2	37.35	41.33	39.34
K3	46.61	41.92	48.72
Range	9.25	3.58	9.37
Patch	2	3	1

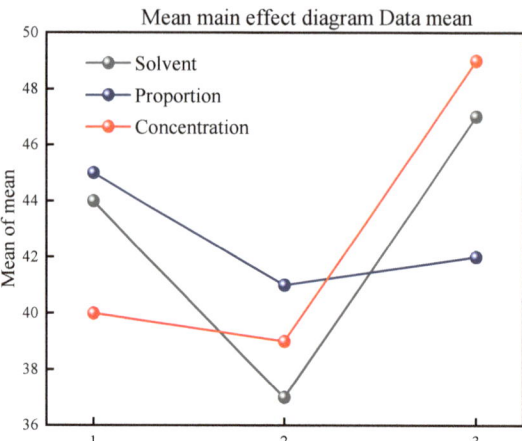

Figure 2. Main effect diagram of mean value from orthogonal experiment.

It can be seen from Tables 4 and 5 and Figure 2 that the inhibitor synthesized via ethylenediamine and epoxy propanol has the most significant inhibition effect on montmorillonite; ethylenediamine and epoxy propanol react in a molar ratio of alcohol to amine functional groups of 1:2, the solvent is acetone, and the inhibitor dosage is 1.0%. As a consequence, the amount of inhibitor is the main factor affecting the linear swelling rate of montmorillonite, followed by the reaction medium, and the molar ratio of ethylenediamine to epoxy propanol, which has the least effect.

3.2. Anti-Swelling and Shrinkage–Swelling

The effects of inhibitors on the anti-swelling rate and shrinkage–swelling rate of montmorillonite were evaluated. The results are shown in Tables 6 and 7 and Figure 3. It can be seen from Table 6 that when the synthetic molar ratio is 1:2 and the concentration is 0.3%, the synthetic products in different solvents have different effects on the anti-swelling rate and shrinkage–swelling rate of montmorillonite. The anti-swelling rate of 0.3% EGP-2 is 43.54%, and the shrinkage–swelling rate is 34.62%. The anti-swelling rate of 0.3% EGA-2 is 24.56%, and the shrinkage–swelling rate is 18.50%. This shows that the same concentration and the same molar ratio also have a certain impact on the inhibition performance of the corresponding products when changing the solvent. When the solvent is acetone, the anti-swelling rate and shrinkage–swelling rate of the product are relatively high, and the inhibition performance of clay is the most significant.

Table 6. Anti-swelling rate and shrinkage–swelling rate of montmorillonite synthesized via different solvents in the same proportion and concentration.

Inhibitors	Anti-Swelling Rate/%	Shrinkage–Swelling Rate/%
0.3% EGD-2	36.78	34.62
0.3% EGA-2	24.56	18.50
0.3% EGP-2	43.54	34.62

Table 7. Anti-swelling rate and shrinkage–swelling rate of montmorillonite synthesized in different proportions in the same solvents and concentrations.

0.3% EGP	Anti-Swelling Rate/%	Shrinkage–Swelling Rate/%
EGP-1	26.32	11.54
EGP-2	43.54	34.62
EGP-3	28.78	16.78

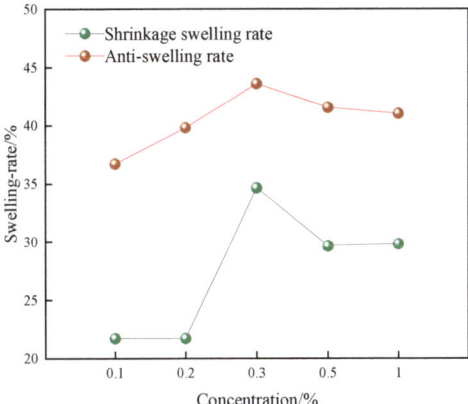

Figure 3. Effect of EGP-2 concentration on anti-swelling rate and shrinkage–swelling rate of montmorillonite.

The effects of EGP synthesized in acetone solvent with different molar ratios on the anti-swelling rate and shrinkage–swelling rate of montmorillonite are shown in Table 7. It can be seen from Table 7 that EGP-2 has the greatest impact on the anti-swelling rate and shrinkage–swelling rate of montmorillonite when the concentration is the same and the synthetic molar ratio is 1:2. The anti-swelling rate of EGP-2 is 43.54%, which is 39.55% of that of EGP-1. The shrinkage–swelling rate of EGP-2 is 34.62%, which is 66.67% of that of EGP-1. The results show that when the concentration and solvent are the same and the ratio is 1:2, the inhibitor has the most significant inhibition effect on montmorillonite.

The influence of the EGP-2 concentration on the montmorillonite anti-swelling rate and shrinkage–swelling rate is evaluated as shown in Figure 3. It can be seen from Figure 3 that with the increase in concentration, the anti-swelling rate and shrinkage–swelling rate increase first and then decrease. When the concentration of EGP-2 is 0.3%, the anti-swelling rate and shrinkage–swelling rate are the highest, at 43.54% and 34.62%, respectively. After that, the concentration continues to rise, and the anti-swelling rate and shrinkage–swelling rate begins to decrease slowly. The reason may be that the concentration of EGP-2 is too high, which causes flocculation with montmorillonite and affects its inhibition performance.

3.3. Wash-Durable Test

EGP inhibition performance can be evaluated through the wash-durable rate experiment. The volume change of montmorillonite immersed in different solutions can be measured quantitatively and regularly via centrifugation, as shown in Table 8. It can be seen from Table 8 that after the montmorillonite was added to the EGP aqueous solution, the swelling volume decreased significantly. The wash-durable rate of the 0.3% EGP-2 aqueous solution is 79.55%, which is 20.53% of that of 4.0%KCl and 10.42% of that of 0.1% EGP-2. The results show that EGP-2 can be more firmly adsorbed on the surface of montmorillonite. Therefore, the inhibition performance of EGP-2 was further evaluated.

Table 8. Results of wash-durable rate experiment (25 °C).

Solution	Swelling Volume/mL	Swelling Volume after Water Washing/mL	Wash-Durable/%
Distilled water	8.5	\	\
4.0% KCl	5.5	8.7	63.22
0.1% EGP-2	6.2	8.7	71.26
0.3% EGP-2	7.0	8.8	79.55
1.0% EGP-2	6.5	8.5	76.47

3.4. Montmorillonite Hydration and Dispersion

Through the montmorillonite hydration experiment, the inhibition performance of EGP-2 on montmorillonite was evaluated. Sodium-based montmorillonite (5 g) was added to EGP-2 solutions of different concentrations, shaken and left to stand for 24 h. It was then then observed and the findings recorded. Figure 4 shows the experimental results after it was left to stand for 24 h, with clean water as the comparison. It can be seen from Figure 4 that the swelling volume of montmorillonite with EGP-2 added is significantly lower than that of montmorillonite in clean water. Additionally, the swelling volume of montmorillonite decreases with the increase in concentration. This shows that the higher the concentration is, the stronger the inhibition of EGP-2 on montmorillonite is, which effectively inhibits the hydration and dispersion of montmorillonite. However, the inhibitor needs to act in the drilling working fluid together with other treatment agents. It is easy for an excessive concentration to cause flocculation and affect other properties of the working fluid. Therefore, we will continue to evaluate the compatibility of the inhibitor and drilling fluid in a later stage.

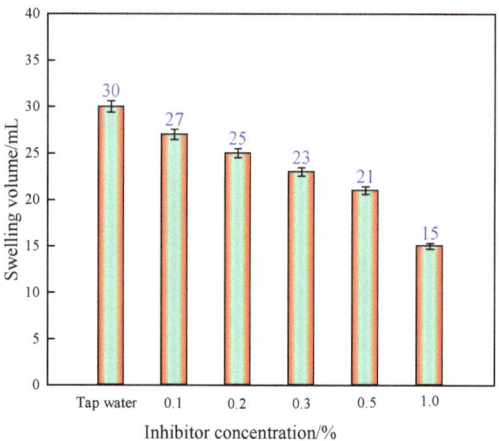

Figure 4. Experimental results of montmorillonite hydration and dispersion.

3.5. Linear Swelling

During the drilling process, wellbore collapse and instability have a very bad irreversible impact on the exploitation of the oilfield [30]. The linear swelling rate measured in laboratory experiments can reflect the instability degree of shaft wall collapse to a certain extent. Therefore, the effect of EGP-2 on the linear swelling of montmorillonite was evaluated via the montmorillonite tablet pressing method. The results are shown in Figure 5. It can be seen from Figure 5 that montmorillonite is rapidly hydrated and expanded within 20 min, and the linear swelling rate increases rapidly. After 40 min, the growth rate tends to slow down. After 120 min, the growth rate reaches a relatively stable state. At this time, the linear swelling rates of 0.2% and 0.3% EGP-2 are low, at 35.71% and 26.98%, which are 42.69% and 56.70% of those with clean water. Additionally, these values are 22.10% and 41.14% of the swelling rate of 4.0% KCl, and lead to strong inhibition performance. The reason for this phenomenon may be that EGP-2 has a large adsorption energy, which can replace the water molecules adsorbed on the surface of montmorillonite and destroy the orderly arranged water molecule structure layer between the surface and layers of the soil sample. Thus, it plays a crucial role in inhibiting the hydration and dispersion of montmorillonite. Furthermore, in the actual operation process, it is beneficial to stabilize the borehole wall. At the same time, the bit mud pack phenomenon is reduced and oil recovery is improved.

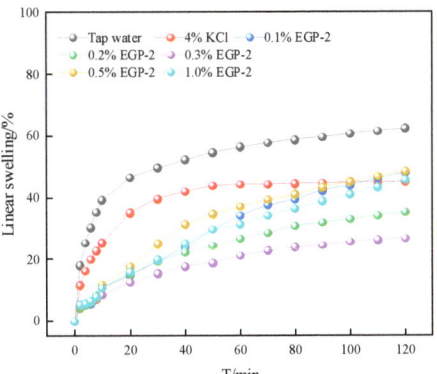

Figure 5. Effect of EGP-2 concentration on linear swelling of montmorillonite.

3.6. Performance in Drilling Fluid

At room temperature, 0.1%, 0.3% and 1.0% EGP-2 were added to the drilling fluid. The effect of different concentrations of EGP-2 on the performance of water-based drilling fluid was evaluated. It can be seen from Table 9 that the apparent viscosity (AV), dynamic shear force (YP), plastic viscosity (PV) and sliding block resistance coefficient (tg) of the drilling fluid increased to a certain extent after the inhibitors at different concentrations were added. When the concentration was 0.3%, the filtration loss (FL) was the lowest, at 13.0 mL. It is compared with that of the drilling fluid, in which the AV is increased by 2.0 times, the YP is increased by 2.1 times and the PV is increased by 1.7 times. However, the filtration rate was reduced to a certain extent, to 18.2%, which shows that the filtration rate was effectively controlled. In addition, when the EGP-2 concentration was 0.1%, the FL increased to 13.21% of that of the drilling fluid. When the concentration was 1.0%, the filtration rate0 increased to 6.29% of that of the drilling fluid. The results show that there was no filtration reduction, the filtration rate was too high, the mud cake was too thick and the solid content in the drilling fluid was reduced, which affected the drilling speed.

Table 9. Effect of EGP-2 concentration on drilling fluid performance.

Additive	AV/(mPa·s)	PV/(mPa·s)	YP/Pa	YP/PV Pa/(mPa·s)	FL/mL	tg
Mud	2.00	1.4	0.60	0.43	15.9	0.0437
Mud + 0.1% EGP-2	3.75	1.5	2.25	1.50	18.0	0.1051
Mud + 0.3% EGP-2	4.00	3.0	1.00	0.33	13.0	0.1139
Mud + 1.0% EGP-2	3.75	1.5	2.25	1.50	16.9	0.1317

At room temperature, 0.3% EGP-2 was added to CMC-, PVA-, MS- and GG-treated mud. It can be seen from Table 10 that the performance parameters of drilling fluid increased after the treatment agents were added. After 0.3% EGP-2 was added to the CMC treated mud, the AV increased by 45.95%, the YP increased by 21.74%, the PV increased by seven times, and the FL and the tg were also increased to a certain extent. Then, the flowability parameters of the PVA-treated mud changed greatly after the inhibitor was added to the PVA treated mud. The AV, PV and YP all increased. The AV increased, which strengthened the suspension capacity. However, the tg showed no change and had no effect on the lubricity of the drilling fluid. In addition, the MS treatment agent could effectively control the filtration of the drilling fluid and adjust the rheology of the drilling fluid, with a significant anti-sloughing effect. Therefore, after 0.3% EGP-2 was added to the MS-treated mud, the FL was further effectively controlled and reduced from 10.8 mL to 5.8 mL. The AV, YP and YP/PV were 1.01, 2.78 and 3.73 times those of MS, respectively. At the same time, GG had increased viscosity in the water-based drilling fluid and a certain filtration reduction property. Therefore, after 0.3% EGP-2 was added to GG-treated mud, the AV and PV were 1.09 and 1.22 times those of of GG-treated mud, respectively. However, the filtration rate and the tg were basically unchanged. In other words, a certain amount of EGP-2 being added to CMC-, PVA-, MS- and GG-treated mud can effectively improve the rheological properties of various drilling fluids. Briefly, 0.3% EGP-2 has good compatibility with CMC, PVA, MS and GG, but it has the best compatibility with MS.

Table 10. Effect of 0.3% EGP-2 on performance of different drilling fluids.

Additive	AV /(mPa·s)	PV /(mPa·s)	YP /Pa	YP/PV Pa/(mPa·s)	FL/mL	tg
Mud	2.00	1.4	0.60	0.43	15.9	0.0437
0.5% CMC	10.00	9.0	1.00	0.11	4.8	0.0875
0.5% CMC + 0.3% EGP-2	18.50	11.5	7.00	0.61	5.9	0.1763
1.0% PVA	7.00	7.00	0.00	0.00	4.6	0.1944
1.0% PVA + 0.3% EGP-2	11.75	9.0	2.75	0.23	7.4	0.1944
1.0% MS	6.90	6.0	0.90	0.15	10.8	0.1405
1.0% MS + 0.3% EGP-2	7.00	4.5	2.50	0.56	5.8	0.1853
0.3% GG	16.00	9.0	7.00	0.44	16.0	0.0437
0.3% GG + 0.3% EGP-2	17.50	11.0	6.50	0.37	14.0	0.0524

3.7. Shale Rolling Recovery

Organic amine inhibitors are relatively expensive, and the amount added to the drilling fluid during the drilling process generally does not exceed 1%. Taking into account the actual addition of various shale inhibitors to the drilling fluid, shale recovery tests were conducted to evaluate the inhibitory performances of tap water, 7% KCl, 0.3% NW-1 (a low molecular weight quaternary ammonium salt shale inhibitor) and 0.3% EGP-2 on easily hydrated shale. The experiment results are shown in Figure 6. It can be seen from Figure 6 that the shale recovery rate of tap water is 9.52%, indicating that shale samples are very easy to hydrate, and that hydration dispersion is serious. KCl is a common inorganic salt shale inhibitor. The recovery rate of shale is 18.56%, indicating that 7% KCl solution can basically not inhibit the hydration and dispersion of shale formation. However, low-molecular quaternary ammonium salt is a new shale inhibitor. Because of its excellent inhibition properties, it has been used more and more in drilling fluids. The low-molecular quaternary ammonium salt shale inhibitor NW-1 was used in this paper. The shale recovery rate of 0.3% NW-1 is 61.23%, indicating that the quaternary ammonium salt shale inhibitor has a certain effect on shale. The shale recovery rate of 0.3% EGP-2 is 79.36%, which is higher than that of NW-1 with the same concentration. EGP-2 contains a large number of adsorbed hydroxyl functional groups which can be firmly adsorbed on the shale surface through hydrogen bonding and electrostatic interaction. The shale diffusion electric double layer was compressed, so as to replace the water between shale layers.

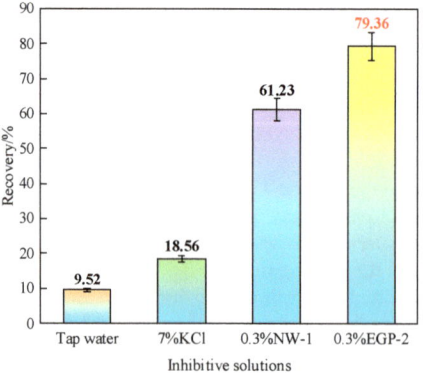

Figure 6. Shale recovery rates from tap water, 7% KCl, 0.3% NW-1 and 0.3% EGP-2.

3.8. FTIR Analysis

The montmorillonite particle samples were analyzed by pressing infrared spectrum, as shown in Figure 7. It can be seen from Figure 7 that the montmorillonite treated with 0.3% EGP-2 has vibration peaks at 3620 cm^{-1} and 3422 cm^{-1}, which can be attributed to the characteristic peak of -OH. And the characteristic peak near 1034 cm^{-1} and 798 cm^{-1} are the anti-stretching vibration of Si-O-Si. However, it is compared with the montmorillonite, the FTIR spectra of the treated montmorillonite shows no obvious change. The reason may be that some -OH and Si-O-Si on the montmorillonite are masked by EGP-2, which has no obvious effect on the lattice structure of the montmorillonite.

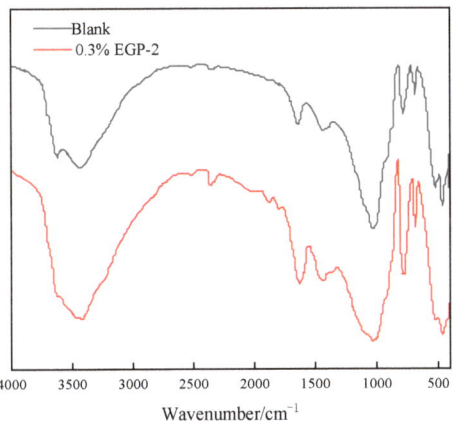

Figure 7. Infrared spectra of montmorillonite before and after 0.3% EGP-2 treatment.

3.9. Particle Distribution

The inhibitor has a certain microscopic effect on the particle size of montmorillonite. The influence of synthetic products on the particle size of montmorillonite particles was analyzed by laser particle size analysis of un-treated montmorillonite particles and montmorillonite particles treated with different solutions [31]. It can be seen from Table 11 and Figure 8 that the average particle size and median particle size of un-hydrated montmorillonite are 14.270 μm and 11.020 μm, respectively. The average particle size and median particle size of fully hydrated montmorillonite in clean water are 7.903 μm and 4.660 μm, respectively. In addition, after 0.3% EGP-2 was added, the average un-hydrated particle size was reduced to 43.01% of the original particle size, and the median particle size was reduced to 35.59% of the original median particle size. The average particle size and median particle size were increased after hydration, and were 1.62 times and 2.31 times those of the original hydration group, respectively.

Table 11. Average particle size and median particle size of sodium-based montmorillonite in 0.3% EGP-2 solution.

Treatment of Montmorillonite	The Average Particle Size/μm	Median Particle Size/μm
Un-treated	14.270	11.020
Water treated	7.903	4.660
0.3% EGP-2 un-treated	8.132	7.098
0.3% EGP-2 treated	12.832	10.779

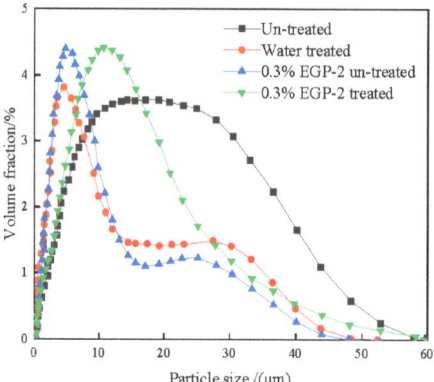

Figure 8. Effect of 0.3% EGP-2 on particle size distribution of sodium-based montmorillonite before and after hydration.

3.10. Zeta Potential

The hydration swelling and dispersion of montmorillonite are caused by many factors. These factors depend not only on the composition and structure of montmorillonite, but also on the composition of exchangeable cations and the properties of the dispersion medium. The value of the zeta potential of the dispersing medium solution is closely related to that of the dispersing state of montmorillonite. The smaller the montmorillonite particle size is, the greater the absolute value of zeta potential is, and the montmorillonite particles in the system are more dispersed and stable. That is, the dispersion force is greater than the cohesion [32,33]. On the contrary, the smaller the absolute value of the zeta potential is, the more it tends to agglomerate and shrink. That is, the attraction is strong to disperse the force, which makes it easy for particles to agglomerate and gather together. The relationship between zeta potential on the surface of montmorillonite particles and EGP-2 solution concentration is shown in Figure 8. Due to the lattice substitution phenomenon, an excess negative charge is generated in the crystal structure of montmorillonite minerals, so montmorillonite particles show a negative charge. It can be seen from Figure 9, the zeta potential on the surface of montmorillonite particles in clean water is −21.41 mv. This shows that montmorillonite particles have significant dispersibility in clean water. In Figure 9, with the increase in the EGP concentration in clean water, the zeta potential of the solution decreased, and the system reached a new stable equilibrium state of agglomeration dispersion. This shows that EGP can effectively inhibit the hydration and dispersion of montmorillonite.

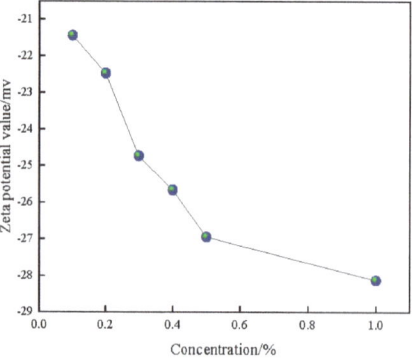

Figure 9. Effect of EGP−2 concentration on zeta potential of electric double layer adsorbed on montmorillonite surface.

3.11. SEM

SEM was used to analyze the micromorphology of montmorillonite particles treated and dried with 0.3% EGP-2 and clean water to evaluate the effect of EGP-2 on the microstructure of montmorillonite. The results are shown in Figure 10. Figure 10a shows the SEM microstructure of un-hydrated montmorillonite. (b) and (c) are the SEM microstructures of montmorillonite after hydration treatment in clean water and in 0.3% EGP-2 solution for 24 h and after drying. It can be seen from Figure 9 that montmorillonite was strongly dispersed in clean water, and the fine particles of montmorillonite were significantly reduced after 0.3% EGP-2 was added. This indicates that after 0.3% EGP-2 was added, the inhibitor entered the montmorillonite interlayer. The montmorillonite layers are combined via electrostatic adsorption and hydrogen bonding to effectively inhibit the hydration swelling and dispersion of montmorillonite. This phenomenon shows that it has a significant inhibitory effect on montmorillonite [34].

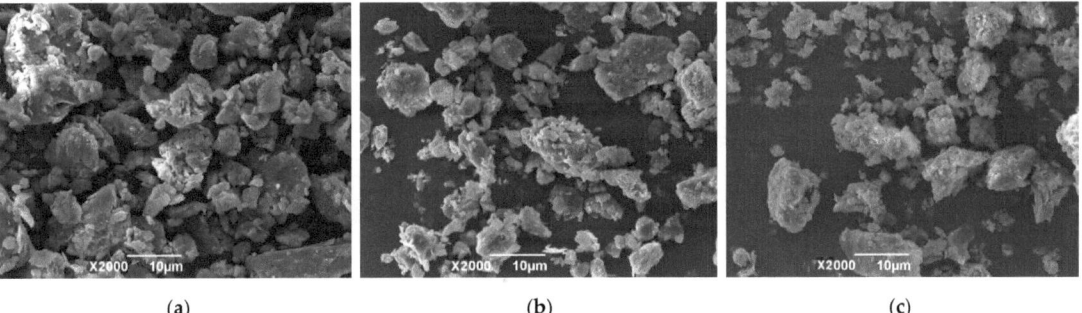

(a)   (b)   (c)

Figure 10. SEM images of montmorillonite in different solvents. (**a**) Un-hydrated montmorillonite; (**b**) hydrated montmorillonite; (**c**) 0.3% EGP-2.

3.12. TGA

Montmorillonite contains a lot of water. With an increase in temperature, the adsorbed water, interlayer water and hydroxyl water in montmorillonite are removed in turn [35,36]. Therefore, TGA can be used to determine the weight loss rate of montmorillonite treated with different inhibitors, so as to evaluate the effect of inhibitors on the water absorption, hydration swelling and dispersion of montmorillonite. After the montmorillonite was soaked in clean water and 0.3% EGP-2 solution for 24 h, it was dried at 105 °C for TGA. It can be seen from Figure 11 that as the temperature gradually increases, the water between montmorillonite layers begins to evaporate and the weight of montmorillonite particles begins to decrease. Apparently, when the temperature rises from 50 °C to 350 °C, the weight loss rate of montmorillonite treated in clean water is 4.10%, and that of montmorillonite treated in EGP-2 solution is 1.46%. The weight loss rate of the sample soaked in EGP-2 solution was significantly lower than that of the sample soaked in clean water. This indicates that EGP-2 can obviously prevent the penetration of water molecules into shale, and has a certain inhibitory effect on the hydration swelling and dispersion of montmorillonite. The characteristics of macroscopic performance are that the weight loss rate of montmorillonite decreases and the water absorption is small.

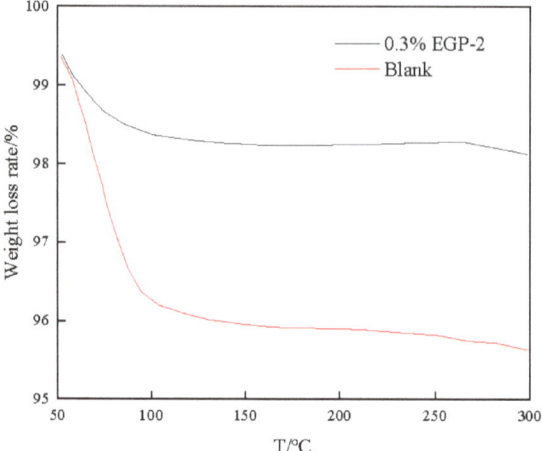

Figure 11. TG curve of montmorillonite after soaked in 0.3% EGP-2 solution for 24 h and dried.

3.13. Mechanism

The mechanism of inhibiting hydration and of the swelling of polyhydroxy-alkanolamine inhibitors in montmorillonite was systematically discussed, based on diffusion double layer theory. It is generally believed that the core purpose of inhibitors is to reduce the repulsion between montmorillonite crystal layers and prevent contact between water and montmorillonite particles [37–39]. As shown in Figure 12, EGP-2 has a polyhydroxy structure, which can provide multiple adsorption points on the surface of montmorillonite, and can be well embedded between montmorillonite layers. Additionally, the closely bound montmorillonite layers can reduce the trend of water molecules entering the montmorillonite layers. The inhibitor is adsorbed on the montmorillonite surface to neutralize the negative charge of montmorillonite, or attached to the crystalline layer of the montmorillonite to reduce the charge between the crystalline layer and the surface [40–42]. At the same time, it can combine montmorillonite through electrostatic adsorption, hydrogen bonding, anchoring and hydrophobic interaction, and effectively inhibit the hydration, swelling and dispersion of montmorillonite. Secondly, the adsorption between the dissociated primary amine group of EGP-2 and the crystalline layer of active montmorillonite pulls together the upper and lower crystalline layers of montmorillonite [43,44] to prevent the swelling of the crystalline layer caused by hydration, so as to obtain strong shale inhibition performance.

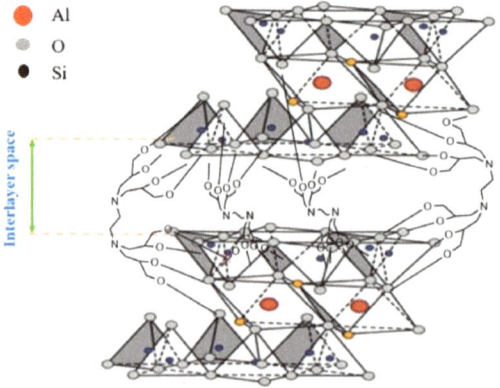

Figure 12. Inhibiting mechanism of EGP-2 against shale hydration.

4. Conclusions

In this study, a polyhydroxy-alkanolamine inhibitor was synthesized from ethylenediamine and epoxy propanol. The inhibition performance of 0.3% EGP-2 was studied in detail. The results show that 0.3% EGP-2 has obvious hydration inhibition performance. Firstly, the linear swelling rate of 0.3% EGP-2 is only 26.98%, which is 56.70% and 41.14% lower than that of tap water and 4% KCl, respectively. The inhibition mechanism was also studied via FTIR, particle size analysis, SEM and TGA. The synthesized inhibitor has a polyhydroxy structure, which can provide multiple adsorption sites on the montmorillonite surface, and enhance the adsorption of the inhibitor to montmorillonite. In addition, the inhibitor is adsorbed on the montmorillonite surface and the montmorillonite is negatively charged or attached to the montmorillonite crystal layer to reduce the charge between the crystal layer and the surface. At the same time, the binding of montmorillonite is realized through electrostatic adsorption, hydrogen bonding, anchoring and hydrophobic action, which can effectively inhibit the hydration, swelling and dispersion of montmorillonite and reduce wellbore instability caused by shale hydration. Therefore, the polyhydroxy-alkanolamine inhibitor has obvious an inhibition property in montmorillonite.

Author Contributions: Conceptualization, G.C.; Methodology, J.H. and Y.S.; Formal analysis, X.C. and S.C.; Investigation, Q.W. and S.C.; Resources, J.H.; Data curation, J.H. and Y.S.; Writing—original draft, Q.W.; Writing—review & editing, X.G. and G.C.; Visualization, X.G.; Supervision, G.C.; Project administration, X.C. All authors have read and agreed to the published version of the manuscript.

Funding: The work was supported financially by the Key Scientific Research Program of Shaanxi Provincial Department of Education (22JY052) and Youth Innovation Team of Shaanxi University.

Institutional Review Board Statement: Not applicable.

Informed Consent Statement: Not applicable.

Data Availability Statement: Not applicable.

Acknowledgments: The authors are grateful for the work carried out by Modern Analysis and Testing Center of Xi'an Shiyou University.

Conflicts of Interest: The authors declare no conflict of interest.

References

1. Wilson, M.J.; Wilson, L. Clay mineralogy and shale instability: An alternative conceptual analysis. *Sci. Lett.* **2014**, *49*, 127–145. [CrossRef]
2. Chen, G.; Yan, J.; Li, L.; Zhang, J.; Gu, X.F.; Song, H. Preparation and performance of amine-tartaric salt as potential clay swelling inhibitor. *Appl. Clay Sci.* **2017**, *138*, 12–16. [CrossRef]
3. Wang, J.; Yan, J.; Ding, T. Progresses in the researches on high performance water base muds. *Drill. Fluid. Complet. Fluid.* **2007**, *24*, 71–75. [CrossRef]
4. Bai, X.; Wang, H.; Luo, Y.; Zheng, X.; Zhang, X.; Zhou, S.; Pu, X. The structure and application of amine-terminated hyperbranched polymer shale inhibitor for water-based drilling fluid. *Appl. Polym. Sci.* **2017**, *134*, 45466. [CrossRef]
5. Faridi, S.; Mobinikhaledi, A.; Moghanian, H.; Shabanian, M. Synthesis of novel modified acrylamide copolymers for montmorillonite flocculants in water-based drilling fluid. *BMC Chem.* **2023**, *17*, 125. [CrossRef]
6. Ehsan, S.H.; Iman, N.; Khalil, S.; Mosayyeb, K.; Amir, M.H.; Abbas, M. An investigation into shale swelling inhibition properties of dodecyltrimethylammonium chloride (DTAC) for water-based drilling fluids. *Energy Sci. Eng.* **2023**, *223*, 211465. [CrossRef]
7. Muhammad, S.K.; Abdullah, S.S.; Usamah, A.A.; Ibnelwaleed, A. Review on polymer flooding: Rheology, adsorption, stability, and field applications of various polymer systems. *Polym. Rev.* **2015**, *55*, 491–530. [CrossRef]
8. Gu, X.; Zhang, J.; Zhang, J.; Chen, G.; Ma, C.; Zhang, Z. Stabilization of montmorillonite by ammoniated lignosulfonates and its use in water-based drilling fluid. *Sci. Adv. Mater.* **2017**, *9*, 928–933. [CrossRef]
9. Al-Hameedi, T.T.A.; Alkinani, H.H.; Dunn-Norman, S.; Al-Alwani, M.A.; Alshammari, A.F.; Alkhamis, M.M.; Mutar, R.A.; Al-Bazzaz, W.H. Experimental investigation of environmentally friendly drilling fluid additives (mandarin peels powder) to substitute the conventional chemicals used in water-based drilling fluid. *J. Pet. Explor. Prod. Technol.* **2020**, *10*, 407–417. [CrossRef]
10. Zhao, L.; Zhu, H.; Tian, G.; An, Y. A novel hyperbranched polyethyleneimine-graphene composite as shale inhibitor for drilling fluid. *RSC Adv.* **2023**, *13*, 2611–2619. [CrossRef]
11. Ahmed, H.; Kamal, M.; Al-Harthi, M. Polymeric and low molecular weight shale inhibitors: A review. *Fuel* **2019**, *251*, 187–217. [CrossRef]

12. Song, Z.; Zhang, L.; Huang, L.; Liu, X.; Zhang, J.; Du, W.; Chen, G. Preparation and application of a novel polyammonium as potent shale hydration inhibitor. *J. Macromol. Sci. Phys. Part A* **2020**, *57*, 326–331. [CrossRef]
13. Zhang, W.; Liu, X.; Liang, L.; Xiong, J. Experimental Study on the Adaptability of Plugging Drilling Fluids to Wellbore Stability in Hard Brittle Shale Formations. *ACS Omega* **2022**, *7*, 48034–48046. [CrossRef] [PubMed]
14. Wu, J.; Xu, H.; Xie, Y.; Zhou, X. A research and application of strong inhibition drilling fluid. *Appl. Mech. Mater.* **2014**, *675*, 1481–1484. [CrossRef]
15. Han, Y.; Song, Z.; Huang, W.; Cao, J. Shale inhibitive properties of polyether diamine in water-based drilling fluid. *Pet. Sci. Technol.* **2011**, *78*, 510–515. [CrossRef]
16. Qu, Y.; Lai, X.; Zou, L.; Su, Y. Polyoxyalkyleneamine as shale inhibitor in water-based drilling fluids. *Appl. Clay Sci.* **2009**, *44*, 264–265. [CrossRef]
17. Rana, A.; Arfaj, M.K.; Saleh, T.A. Graphene grafted with glucopyranose as a shale swelling inhibitor in water-based drilling mud. *Appl. Clay Sci.* **2020**, *199*, 105806. [CrossRef]
18. Movahedi, H.; Jamshidi, S.; Hajipour., M. Hydrodynamic Analysis and Cake Erosion Properties of a Modified Water-Based Drilling Fluid by a Polyacrylamide/Silica Nanocomposite during Rotating-Disk Dynamic Filtration. *ACS Omega* **2022**, *7*, 44223–44240. [CrossRef]
19. *SY/T 5971-2016*; Performance Evaluation Method of Clay Stabilizer for Fracturing and Acidification and Water Injection in Oil and Gas Fields. China National Energy Administration: Beijing, China, 2016.
20. *Q/SH 0053-2010*; Technical Requirements for Montmorillonite Stabilizers. China Petroleum and Chemical Corporation: Beijing, China, 2010.
21. *SY/T 6335-1997*; Evaluation Procedure of Drilling Fluids Shale Inhibitor. China National Petroleum Corporation: Beijing, China, 1997.
22. Zhang, Y.; Luo, H.; Xiao, N.; Shi, L. Design and application of green drilling fluid of strong inhibition. *EES* **2019**, *227*, 042020. [CrossRef]
23. Jing, Y.; Zhang, J.; Du, W.; Hu, W.; Xie, J.; Qu, C.; Chen, G. Preparation and evaluation of ammonium-succinic salts as shale swelling inhibitor and its application in water-based drilling fluid. *Russ. J. Phys. Chem. B* **2021**, *15*, 102–108. [CrossRef]
24. *GB/T 16783.1-2006*; Petroleum and Natural Gas Industries—Field Testing of Drilling Fluids—Part 1: Water-Based Fluids (English Version). Chinese National Standard: Beijing, China, 2006.
25. Moslemizadeh, A.; Aghdam, K.; Shahbazi, K.; Zendehboudi, S. A triterpenoid saponin as an environmental friendly and biodegradable clay swelling inhibitor. *J. Mol. Liq.* **2017**, *247*, 269–280. [CrossRef]
26. Aggrey, W.N.; Asiedu, N.Y.; Adenutsi, C.; Anumah, P. A novel non-ionic surfactant extract derived from *Chromolaena odorata* as shale inhibitor in water based drilling mud. *Heliyon* **2019**, *5*, 01697. [CrossRef]
27. Shi, Q.; Wang, W.; Zhang, H.; Bai, H.; Liu, K.; Zhang, J.; Li, Z.; Zhu, W. Porous biochar derived from walnut shell as an efficient adsorbent for tetracycline removal. *Bioresour. Technol.* **2023**, *383*, 129213. [CrossRef]
28. Huang, D.; Xie, G.; Luo, P.; Deng, M.; Wang, J. Synthesis and mechanism research of a new low molecular weight shale inhibitor on swelling of sodium montmorillonite. *Energy Sci. Eng.* **2020**, *8*, 1501–1509. [CrossRef]
29. Du, W.; Wang, X.; Chen, G.; Zhang, J.; Slaný, M. Synthesis, property and mechanism analysis of a novel polyhydroxy organic amine shale hydration inhibitor. *Minerals* **2020**, *10*, 128. [CrossRef]
30. Xie, C.; Jia, N.; He, L. Study on the instability mechanism and grouting reinforcement repair of large-scale underground stopes. *Adv. Civ. Eng.* **2020**, *1*, 8832012. [CrossRef]
31. Zhang, B.; Wang, Q.; Wei, Y.; Wei, W.; Du, W.; Zhang, J.; Chen, G.; Michal, S. Preparation and swelling inhibition of mixed metal hydroxide to montmorillonite clay. *Minerals* **2022**, *12*, 459. [CrossRef]
32. Wang, Q.; Michal, S.; Gu, X.; Miao, Z.; Du, W.; Zhang, J.; Chen, G. Lubricity and rheological properties of highly dispersed graphite in clay-water-based drilling fluids. *Materials* **2022**, *15*, 1083. [CrossRef]
33. Rahman, M.T.; Negash, B.M.; Idris, A.; Miah, M.I.; Biswas, K. Experimental and COSMO-RS Simulation Studies on the Effects of Polyatomic Anions on Clay Swelling. *ACS Omega* **2021**, *6*, 26519–26532. [CrossRef]
34. Rana, A.; Saleh, T.A.; Arfaj, M.K. Nanosilica modified with moringa extracts to get an efficient and cost-effective shale inhibitor in water-based drilling muds. Chemical Engineering and Processing—Process Intensification. *Chem. Eng. Process.-Process. Intensif.* **2021**, *168*, 108589. [CrossRef]
35. Zhang, Y.; Xu, P.; Xu, M.; Pu, L.; Wang, X. Properties of Bentonite Slurry Drilling Fluid in Shallow Formations of Deepwater Wells and the Optimization of Its Wellbore Strengthening Ability While Drilling. *ACS Omega* **2022**, *7*, 39860–39874. [CrossRef]
36. Ahmed, K.; Murtaza, M.; Abdulraheem, A.; Kamal, M.S.; Mahmoud, M. Imidazolium-Based Ionic Liquids as Clay Swelling Inhibitors: Mechanism, Performance Evaluation, and Effect of Different Anions. *ACS Omega* **2020**, *5*, 26682–26696. [CrossRef]
37. Du, W.; Pu, X.; Sun, J.; Luo, X.; Zhang, Y.; Li, L. Synthesis and evaluation of a novel monomeric amine as sodium montmorillonite swelling inhibitor. *Adsorp. Sci. Technol.* **2018**, *36*, 655–668. [CrossRef]
38. Murtaza, M.; Gbadamosi, A.; Ahmad, H.; Hussain, S.M.S.; Kamal, M.S.; Mahmoud, M.; Patil, S. A Magnetic Surfactant Having One Degree of Unsaturation in the Hydrophobic Tail as a Shale Swelling Inhibitor. *Molecules* **2023**, *28*, 1878. [CrossRef]
39. Jiang, G.; Li, X.; Zhu, H.; Yang, L.; Li, Y.; Wang, T.; Wu, X. Improved shale hydration inhibition with combination of gelatin and KCl or EPTAC, an environmentally friendly inhibitor for water-based drilling fluids. *J. Appl. Polym. Sci.* **2019**, *136*, 47585. [CrossRef]

40. Murtaza, M.; Kamal, M.S.; Mahmoud, M. Application of a Novel and Sustainable Silicate Solution as an Alternative to Sodium Silicate for Clay Swelling Inhibition. *ACS Omega* **2020**, *5*, 17405–17415. [CrossRef] [PubMed]
41. Vryzas, Z.; Kelessidis, V. Nano-based drilling fluids: A review. *Energies* **2017**, *10*, 540. [CrossRef]
42. Xie, G.; Xiao, Y.; Deng, M.; Luo, Y.; Luo, P. Low Molecular Weight Branched Polyamine as a Clay Swelling Inhibitor and Its Inhibition Mechanism: Experiment and Density Functional Theory Simulation. *Energy Fuels* **2020**, *34*, 2169–2177. [CrossRef]
43. Xuan, Y.; Jiang, G.; Li, Y.; Wang, J.; Genget, H. Inhibiting effect of dopamine adsorption and polymerization on hydrated swelling of montmorillonite. *Colloids Surf. A Physicochem. Eng. Asp.* **2013**, *422*, 50–60. [CrossRef]
44. Mei, T.; Lan, J.; Dong, Y.; Zhang, S.; Tao, H.; Hou, H. A novel expansive soil hardener: Performance and mechanism of immersion stability. *RSC Adv.* **2022**, *12*, 30817–30828. [CrossRef] [PubMed]

Disclaimer/Publisher's Note: The statements, opinions and data contained in all publications are solely those of the individual author(s) and contributor(s) and not of MDPI and/or the editor(s). MDPI and/or the editor(s) disclaim responsibility for any injury to people or property resulting from any ideas, methods, instructions or products referred to in the content.

Article

Research on the Damage Model of Cold Recycled Mixtures with Asphalt Emulsion under Freeze-Thaw Cycles

Ye Yang [1,2], Zongguang Sun [1], Yanhai Yang [2,*], Chonghua Wang [2] and Lin Qi [3,*]

1. College of Transportation Engineering, Dalian Maritime University, Dalian 116026, China; yangye@sjzu.edu.cn (Y.Y.); sun@dlmu.edu.cn (Z.S.)
2. School of Transportation and Geomatics Engineering, Shenyang Jianzhu University, Shenyang 110168, China; chonghw@126.com
3. School of Civil Engineering, Shenyang Urban Construction University, Shenyang 110167, China
* Correspondence: yhyang@sjzu.edu.cn (Y.Y.); qilin6126@126.com (L.Q.)

Abstract: Cold recycled mixtures with asphalt emulsion (CRME) suffer the majority of damage from freezing and thawing cycles in seasonal freezing regions. However, an effective model for describing the internal damage evolution behavior of the CRME is still lacking. The objective of this study is to explore the performance of the destroy and damage model of the CRME subjected to freezing and thawing cycles with various water contents. The damage degree of performance at 60 °C and −10 °C, as well as the mechanical properties, were first analyzed in the laboratory. Then, the damage evolution models were established based on macroscopic properties, reliability, and damage theory. The results showed that the performance of the CRME decreased obviously as the number of freezing and thawing cycles increased; after 20 freezing and thawing cycles, the damage degree of 60 °C shear strength and 15 °C and −10 °C indirect tensile strength were 21.5%, 20.6%, and 19.8% at dry condition, but they were 34.9%, 31.8%, and 44.8% at half water saturation condition and 51.5%, 49.1%, and 56.1% at complete water saturation condition; the existence of water and the phase transition of water changed the failure characteristics of the CRME; the correlation coefficient of the damage model parameters was more than 0.98, so the damage evolution model could reveal the internal damage evolution law. Clearly, the freezing and thawing cycles accelerated the damage caused by CRME.

Keywords: asphalt emulsion; cold recycled mixtures; damage model; freezing and thawing cycles; property destroy

Citation: Yang, Y.; Sun, Z.; Yang, Y.; Wang, C.; Qi, L. Research on the Damage Model of Cold Recycled Mixtures with Asphalt Emulsion under Freeze-Thaw Cycles. *Processes* **2023**, *11*, 3031. https://doi.org/10.3390/pr11103031

Academic Editors: Dicho Stratiev, Dobromir Yordanov, Aijun Guo and Amir Tabakovic

Received: 31 August 2023
Revised: 13 October 2023
Accepted: 19 October 2023
Published: 21 October 2023

Copyright: © 2023 by the authors. Licensee MDPI, Basel, Switzerland. This article is an open access article distributed under the terms and conditions of the Creative Commons Attribution (CC BY) license (https://creativecommons.org/licenses/by/4.0/).

1. Introduction

With increasing of the road service life, an increasing number of early-built roads require annual maintenance, causing a dramatic enhancement in the amount of old asphalt material [1]. The disposal of old asphalt materials demands a large amount of land and pollutes the environment [2]. The topic of resource conservation and environmental friendliness has gradually risen to prominence in road construction. Asphalt pavement recycling has become an excellent technique in road construction and maintenance [3,4]. Due to the depression of aggregate, cost, and carbon emissions, cold recycling technology has been widely accepted globally and adopted in many countries [5–7].

Zhang J et al. [8] studied the influences of compaction and water contents on the properties of the CRME, and a design approach for CRME using single compaction was presented. Han Z et al. [9] demonstrated that the vertical vibration testing method showed more excellent mechanical and fatigue performances than Marshall compaction and Superpave Gyratory Compactor on cold recycled mixtures. And the number and diameter of voids and fractal dimension of the vertical vibration testing method samples were similar to actual core samples in the vertical direction. Chen T et al. [10] proposed that cement and asphalt emulsion need to be completely mixed before the mixing between aggregate and mortar to achieve the more excellent property of the cold recycled mixture; moreover, aggregate stirred with asphalt emulsion firstly may be an excellent design. Gao L et al. [11] showed that the cold in-place recycling mixtures tend to have larger size and a lower amount of air voids. Kim Y et al. [12] stated that emulsion form and residual asphalt stiffness of reclaimed asphalt pavement (RAP) materials had impacted on the dynamic modulus, flow number, and flow time. Jiang J et al. [13] obtained that the polymer modifiers could enhance the high-temperature property obviously, and adding chloroprene rubber latex seemed to be a more excellent idea to enhance the high-temperature stability of asphalt emulsion. Zhang J et al. [14] found that a recycling agent had an impact on the fracture energy indicator of more than 60%. Yan J et al. [15] proposed cement had active influences on early-age strength and long-term property of cold recycled mixtures. Yang Y et al. [16] showed cold recycled mixtures had more excellent low-temperature property when adding cement was between 1% and 2%. Dong S et al. [17] concluded the rejuvenation agent, styrene–butadiene rubber latex, and Buton rock asphalt could enhance the comprehensive property of the modified CRME. Moreover, the rejuvenation agent had the largest influence. Du S [18] found polyester fiber, polypropylene fiber, polyacrylonitrile fiber, lignin fiber, and basalt fiber could improve the performance of the emulsion recycled mixture. Polyester fiber had better advancement on fatigue life than others. Xu S et al. [19] found the new cold-mix SBS modified emulsified asphalt had better mechanical performance, rutting performance, and water stability than the normal hot and warm mix asphalt mixtures. In comparison with deicing agents containing calcium chloride, the deicing agents containing calcium magnesium acetate obviously could reduce the disruptive influences of freeze–thaw cycles on the mechanical performance of cold recycled mixtures using polymer-modified bitumen emulsion [20]. Yang Y et al. [21] discovered the numerical value and quantity of the tensile force chain in DEM raised markedly; as the stress ratio increased, the fatigue performance decreased significantly. Lin J et al. [22] presented the viscoelastic of the CRME was worse than HMA. The fatigue life of the CRME was 10%−20% normal asphalt mixture at high strain. Xia Y et al. [6] proposed the initial cracking point appeared at approximately 60% of the fatigue life based on the SCB fatigue test through image analysis. The value of the destroyed variable was 0.06–0.17 at the initial cracking point according to the cracking model.

However, the road performance of the CRME decayed obviously, and diseases such as crushing and loosening appeared in the seasonal frozen region [23]. Water was the key factor for the destruction. Due to temperature variation, the water would freeze and thaw with the changing seasons, causing significant damage to the CRME [24]. Lachance-Tremblay et al. [25] demonstrated the linear viscoelastic properties containing glass aggregates were significantly altered during freezing and thawing cycles. The addition of hydrated lime containing glass aggregates obviously decreased the linear viscoelastic property. Freezing and thawing cycles enhanced the interior destruction of the asphalt mixture, resulting in air voids increasing and adhesion decreasing [26]. Fan Z et al. [27] observed that the fatigue life of asphalt mixtures reduced with saturation and freezing–thawing cycles increasing. Fu L. et al. [28] showed that freezing and thawing cycles changed the failure type of asphalt mixtures, made it harder for microcracks to form early on, sped up the growth of macrocracks, and made it easier for asphalt and aggregates to separate. Wang T. et al. [29] found the tensile modulus of steel slag, basalt, and recycled aggregate permeable asphalt concrete decreased by 80–90% after 20 freezing–thawing cycles. Ud Din et al. [30] found freezing and thawing could obviously impact the compressive strength, air voids, fatigue cracking, and the rutting of the asphalt pavement. Fatigue and rutting were more sensitive to climatic conditions. Xu H et al. [31] presented the interior void evolution law: expansion of original voids; connection of independent voids; occurrence of new voids, demonstrating the nonnegligible impact of pore structure on dynamic flow law subjected to freezing and thawing cycles [32]. Wang J et al. [33] put forward the damage mechanism of the biobased cold-mix epoxy asphalt subjected to freezing and thawing cycles: post-curing and damage of the cross-linking network; agglomeration and aging of asphalt; diffusion and reaction of water. Jin D et al. [34] found asphalt emulsion chip seal showed a decrease in interlayer shear strength and interlayer tensile strength under repeated loading, freezing, and thawing cycles. The weak bond between asphalt emulsion and aggregate could be due to repeated loading and freezing and thawing behaviors. Zhao H et al. [35] found the indirect tensile strength, the modulus, and the fracture properties of cold recycled mixtures using foamed asphalt significantly decreased subjected to freezing and thawing cycles. Lövqvist L et al. [36] presented a new thermodynamics-based multi-scale model of freezing and thawing destruction in asphalt mixtures, which also calculated the destruction from water and traffic. Chen Y et al. [37] presented the freeze–thaw cycles made the nonlinear characteristics of the stress–strain relationship of the asphalt mixture remarkable. Yang Y. et al. [38] concluded the void ratio of CRME went up by 1.06%, the ultrasonic wave velocity and high and low temperature performance all went down, and the splitting strength went down by 26.3% after 20 unsatisfied freezing–thawing cycles. Under freezing and thawing cycles, the voids of vacuum-saturated samples were primarily characterized by the formation of new voids, void expansion, and void bonding [39].

In summary, researchers have conducted a large number of studies on mix design, air void characteristics, performance evaluation, early strength, additives, and fatigue performance to improve the CRME. Although extensive research has been conducted on normal asphalt mixtures during freezing and thawing cycles, a few studies have been conducted on the CRME, despite the fact that its application in a seasonally frozen area is crucial. CRME has greater air voids (8–13%) than normal asphalt mixture. The water could easily permeate the CRME and weaken the bond among asphalt, old asphalt, new aggregate, and old aggregate. The adhesion has an immediate impact on the performance of the CRME. Therefore, the aim of this research is to explore the performance degradation and damage model of the CRME under freezing and thawing cycles with various water contents. The uniaxial penetration test and indirect tensile test are carried out to evaluate the high–low temperature performance and mechanical properties. The damage degree of the 60 °C shear strength and 15 °C and −10 °C indirect tensile strength are calculated and analyzed. Finally, the damage model of CRME is developed to reveal the internal law of damage evolution based on macroscopic properties, reliability, and damage theory.

2. Materials and Methods

2.1. Materials

Table 1 illustrates the characteristics of asphalt emulsion referencing JTG T5521-2019 [40]. The RAP was milled from a first-class highway in Shenyang, China and divided into 0 mm, 0.075 mm, 0.15 mm, 0.3 mm, 0.6 mm, 1.18 mm, 2.36 mm, 4.75 mm, 9.5 mm, 13.2 mm, 16 mm, and finally 19 mm. Referring to JTG T5521-2019 [40], the sand equivalent value of RAP was 65%, which met the specification requirements that is not less than 50%. The characteristics of the new aggregate satisfied the requirement of the JTG F40-2004 [41], which was divided into the single size. The biggest size of RAP could not satisfy the gradation composition of CRME referencing to JTG T5521-2019 in China [40]. A total of 19–26.5 mm of new aggregate was added. Drinking water and 32.5# of regular Portland cement were added in the meantime.

Table 1. Characteristics of asphalt emulsion [24].

Characteristic	Requirements	Results
Demulsification speed	Slow-cracking	Slow-cracking
Particle charge	Cation (+)	Cation (+)
Remained content on 1.18 mm/wt%	≤0.1	0.021
Solid content/wt%	>60	63.6
Penetration (25 °C, 100 g, 5 s)/0.1 mm	50~130	69.5
Softening point/°C	—	45.6
Ductility (15 °C)/cm	≥40	76.5
Solubility in trichloroethylene/wt%	≥97.5	99.1

Table 1. Cont.

Characteristic	Requirements	Results
Storage stability at 1 d/wt%	≤1	0.4
Storage stability at 5 d/wt%	≤5	2.6

2.2. Mixture Design and Preparation of the Samples

2.2.1. Mixture Design

The selected gradation and composition of RAP and new aggregate are displayed in Table 2 [16]. The cement dosage was adopted by the early result, which was 1.5 wt% [16]. The selected gradation of the CRME is shown in Figure 1. The optimum water content of CRME was determined referencing JTG E40-2007 [42], which was 3.0 wt%. The optimum asphalt emulsion content of CRME was determined referencing to JTG T5521-2019 [40], which was 3.5 wt%.

Table 2. Selected gradation of RAP and new aggregates.

	Size/mm	26.5	19	16	13.2	9.5	4.75	2.36	1.18	0.6	0.3	0.15	0.075
Passing rate/%	RAP (68.95%)	100	100	88.8	78.7	63.5	38.1	22.8	13.7	7.6	4.1	2.0	1.0
	New Aggregate (29.55%)	100	93.9	88.8	78.7	63.5	38.1	22.8	13.7	7.6	4.1	2.0	1.0

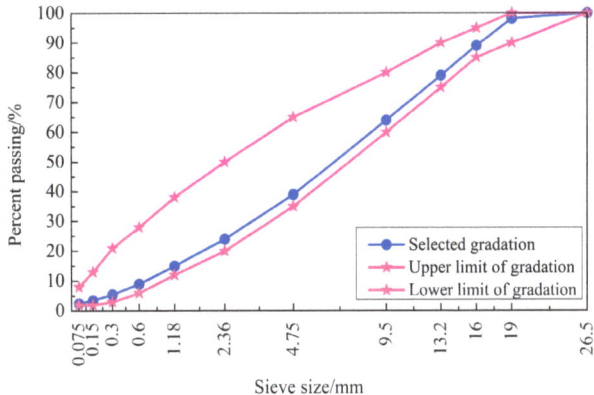

Figure 1. Selected gradation of CRME.

2.2.2. Preparation of the Samples

The Superpave gyratory compactor (AFG2C) was applied to form the samples. The 1.25° rotation compaction angle, 600 kPa vertical compressive stress, and 30 rpm were set in a Superpave gyratory compactor. The diameter of the sample was 100 ± 0.5 mm. The CRME samples were molded under the optimum mixture composition. Firstly, the mixture was placed into the mold and compacted up to 63.5 mm in height. Then, all the samples were cured in a 60 °C environmental oven for more than 40 h. Finally, the samples were put in an indoor temperature environment for longer than 12 h [40].

2.3. Experimental Methods

2.3.1. Freezing and Thawing Test

The cured sample was subjected to a freezing and thawing test with various water content. The dry condition, half water saturation condition, and complete water saturation condition were adopted. The parallel four samples were carried out for every test under a saturated condition and different freezing and thawing cycles.

(1) Dry condition, namely 0% water saturation condition. The cured samples were directly covered with plastic preservative film.
(2) Complete water saturation condition, namely 100% water saturation condition. Firstly, the cured samples were vacuumed for 15 min in water. The vacuum pressure was 98.3~98.7 kPa. Secondly, the vacuumed samples were kept in normal pressure water for longer than 2 h until absorbing water completely. Thirdly, the surface of vacuum saturated samples was dried through the wet cloth and covered with plastic preservative film.
(3) Half water-saturation condition, namely 50% water saturation condition. The cured samples were weighed. The weighted samples were vacuum saturated according to (2). The weight of the vacuum-saturated sample was measured. The environmental furnace then reduced the weight of water absorption by half. Finally, the surface of the half water-saturated specimens was covered with plastic preservative film and placed in an indoor environment for more than 12 h.

The samples with different water contents were frozen and thawed. The sample was stored at −20 °C and 20 °C for 6 h, respectively, completing one freeze-thaw cycle. The whole samples were frozen-thawed zero, five, ten, fifteen, and twenty times, respectively [27,43]. The frozen-thawed samples were used to evaluate the characteristics of CRME after drying. The partial samples are shown in Figure 2.

Figure 2. The partial samples before experiment.

2.3.2. Uniaxial Penetration Test

The uniaxial penetration test was used to evaluate the high-temperature performance of CRME at 60 ± 1 °C. The 1 mm per minute was used as the loading rate referencing JTG D50-2017 [44]. The electromechanical universal tester (70-S18B2) (Controls S.R.L., Milan, Italy) was used for the test to obtain the maximum load. The shear strength was obtained by Equation (1).

$$R_S = f \times P/A \tag{1}$$

where R_S, f, P, and A represent the shear strength (MPa), the sample dimension correction coefficient $f = 0.34$, the maximum loading (N), and the cross-sectional area (mm^2), respectively.

2.3.3. Indirect Tensile Test

The indirect tensile test was performed at 15 ± 0.5 °C based on the loading rate of 50 mm per minute to evaluate the mechanical property referencing JTG E20-2011 [45].

However, the indirect tensile test was performed at $-10 \pm 0.5\,°C$ based on the loading rate of 1 mm per minute to reveal the low-temperature cracking resistance referencing JTG E20-2011 [45]. The electromechanical universal tester (70-S18B2) (Controls S.R.L., Milan, Italy) was used for the indirect tensile test to obtain the limit load. The indirect tensile strength was obtained by Equation (2).

$$R_T = 0.006287 F/h \tag{2}$$

where R_T, F, and h represent the indirect tensile strength (MPa), the limit loading (N), and the height of the sample (mm), respectively.

2.4. Modeling Method

2.4.1. Basic Model Assumptions

If the CRME could satisfy the basic assumptions of the general model of reliability and damage theory, the damage evolution law of CRME could be analyzed under freezing–thawing cycles [46,47]. The modelling of each surface of the cube subjected to the same damage was adopted to investigate the damage situation of CRME under freezing and thawing cycles with various water contents.

Situation 1: The interior of CRME was considered continuous and homogeneous. RAP, new aggregate, cement, and asphalt emulsion conform to the random distribution and were proportionally smaller than the sample. Consequently, the sample could be considered as homogenous material.

Situation 2: The boundary of the CRME was in the same freezing and thawing conditions. The damage was developed from outside to inside gradually under freeze–thaw cycles with various water content. Therefore, all microscopic unit points with the shortest distance between the interior and boundary of CRME satisfied the damage evolution law. Each surface of the cube subjected to the same damage was drawn in Figure 3.

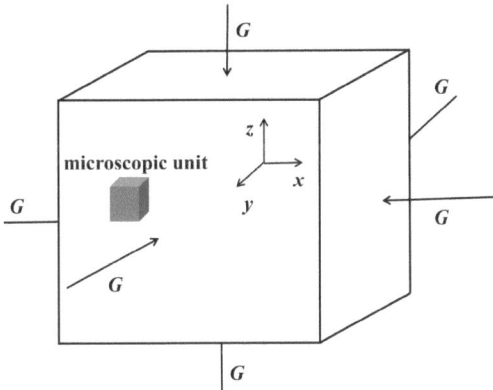

Figure 3. Each surface of the cube suffers the same amount of damage.

Situation 3: The destroyed occurrence of CRME was from the gradually accumulated interior damage as freezing and thawing cycles increased. The failure possibility of every component increased over time in CRME exposed to freezing and thawing cycles with various water contents. Therefore, it was considered that the destruction of CRME accorded to the Weibull damage distribution under freezing and thawing cycles, as represented by Equation (3).

$$F(t) = 1 - \exp\left[-(\lambda t)^\alpha\right] \tag{3}$$

where t, λ, and α represent the number of freezing and thawing cycles (time), the scale factor (dimensionless), and the shape factor (dimensionless), respectively.

Situation 4: Each point was subjected to the same amount of damage. Based on the characteristics of the Weibull distribution, the failure curve shape of each point was the same approximately. Consequently, it was possible to conclude that the shape factor α was the same. If the microscopic unit point had any coordinate (x, y, z), then Equation (4) could be used to determine the shape factor α.

$$\lambda(x, y, z) = \lambda(|x|, |y|, |z|) \tag{4}$$

2.4.2. Model Derivation

The microscopic unit (x, y, z) was selected randomly in CRME. The probability density function of the internal point from the microscopic unit was $f(x, y, z; t)$ at t time. Therefore, the number of damaged microscopic units was $V(x, y, z; t)$ at time t. The random variable satisfied the spatial Poisson distribution requirement. Therefore, Equation (5) represents the probability P of internal point failure.

$$P = f(x, y, z; t)\, d\varsigma d\eta d\sigma \tag{5}$$

According to the mathematical expectation of the Poisson distribution, the mathematical expectation of $V(x, y, z; t)$ could be derived as shown in Equation (6).

$$E(V) = nP = dx\, dy\, dz\, d\varsigma^{-1}\, d\eta^{-1}\, d\sigma^{-1} f(x, y, z; t)\, d\varsigma d\eta d\sigma = f(x, y, z; t)\, dx\, dy\, dz \tag{6}$$

where the n represents the quantity of sample points in the space area.

The failure volume of the whole section was shown in Equation (7).

$$V = \iint_{V_0} E(V) \tag{7}$$

According to the previous studies [47], the study defined the degree of damage using Equation (8).

$$D = V/V_0 \tag{8}$$

where D, V, V_0 represent the degree of damage (%), the volume of the damaged unit (dimensionless), and the volume of the original unit (dimensionless), respectively.

According to Equations (3)–(8), the damage degree equation could be obtained as shown in Equation (9).

$$D = V_0^{-1} \iint_{V_0} f(x, y, z; t) dx dy dz = V_0^{-1} \iint_{V_0} \alpha (\lambda t)^{\alpha-1} \exp\left[-(\lambda t)^\alpha\right] dx dy dz \tag{9}$$

2.4.3. Numerical Algorithm of Damage Evolution

Equation (9) could be altered through discretization of the calculated spatial region. In the calculated spatial region, each boundary was divided into N parts on average, and N was a dual number. Based on situation 2, the i-layer unit number distribution was identical. According to Equation (10), the units with the shortest distance from the model boundary were determined.

$$N_i = 6N^2 - 24iN + 24i^2 - 12N + 24i + 8 \tag{10}$$

where $i = 0, 1, 2 \cdots\cdots (n = N/2 - 1)$, respectively.

At t time, the distribution function of i-layer unit damage was $Fi(t)$. When the number of sample points of the Poisson distribution was large, the Poisson distribution could be transformed into the Bernoulli distribution based on the relationship between the Poisson distribution and the Bernoulli distribution, namely N_i damage in the unit of the i layer. The mathematical expectation of the event Φ_i was shown in Equation (11).

$$E(\Phi_i) = N_i F_i(t) \tag{11}$$

Based on situation 3, Equation (12) could be obtained.

$$F_i(t) = 1 - \exp[-(\lambda t)^\alpha] \quad (12)$$

The scale factor λ_i was simulated with the linear formula, and the mesh was sufficiently divided. The influence of micro-unit size could be neglected. The scale factor λ_i could be shown in Equation (13).

$$\lambda_i = \lambda_0 - 2iv/(N-2) \quad (13)$$

where λ and v represent the scale factor (dimensionless) and the gradient factor (dimensionless), $i = 0, 1, 2 \cdots (n = N/2 - 1)$, respectively.

The microscopic unit was in the outer layer at $i = 0$, and $\lambda_i = \lambda_0$. The microscopic unit was in the inner layer at $i = N/2 - 1$, and $\lambda_i = \lambda_0 - v$. The average scale factor of the outer and inner layers of the CRME could be substituted into the calculation. The mathematic expectation of the unit damage event ω at time t could be obtained as shown in Equation (14).

$$E(\omega) = \sum_{i=0}^{N/2-1} E(\phi_i) = \sum_{i=0}^{N/2-1} N_i F_i(t) \quad (14)$$

According to the Equation (14), the expected value of regional damage degree could be calculated. As shown in Equation (15).

$$E(D) = E(\omega)/V_0 = N^{-3} \sum_{i=0}^{N/2-1} \left(6N^2 - 24iN + 24i + 8\right) \times \left\{1 - exp\left[-\left(\lambda_0 t - \frac{ivt}{N/2-1}\right)^\alpha\right]\right\} \quad (15)$$

$E(D) = 0$ at $t = 0$, which showed that the damage degree of CRME was 0 without freezing and thawing cycles. $E(D) = 1$ at $t \to \infty$, which showed that the damage degree of CRME was 1 after infinite freezing and thawing cycles. Based on the application of the equal strain assumption in macroscopic phenomenological damage mechanics, the damage degree of the CRME after freezing and thawing cycles could be calculated according to Equation (16).

$$D_n = (E_0 - E_n)/E_0 \quad (16)$$

where D_n, E_0, and E_n represent the degree of damage of CRME after n freezing and thawing cycles, the performance of the CRME without freezing and thawing cycles, and the performance of CRME after n freezing and thawing cycles, respectively.

3. Results and Discussions

3.1. Experimental Results

The results of the 60 °C uniaxial penetration test and 15 °C, and −10 °C indirect tensile strength test under freezing and thawing cycles with various water contents are shown in Table 3.

3.2. Damage Models

The damage models of the high–low temperature performance and mechanical property of the CRME were used to investigate the damage situation. The damage degree of CRME was calculated based on the Equation (16). The damage degree results of CRME are displayed in Table 4. Figure 4 illustrates the damage degree change trend of CRME under freezing and thawing cycles with various water content.

Table 3. Test results of CRME under freezing and thawing cycles with various water contents.

Freeze-Thaw Cycles/Times	60 °C Shear Strength/MPa			15 °C Indirect Tensile Strength/MPa			−10 °C Indirect Tensile Strength/MPa		
	Dry Condition	Half Water Saturation Condition	Complete Water Saturation Condition	Dry Condition	Half Water Saturation Condition	Complete Water Saturation Condition	Dry Condition	Half Water Saturation Condition	Complete Water Saturation Condition
0	0.573 (0.041)	0.548 (0.040)	0.556 (0.039)	0.65 (0.023)	0.63 (0.015)	0.66 (0.003)	1.11 (0.008)	1.05 (0.012)	1.07 (0.019)
5	0.542 (0.024)	0.483 (0.033)	0.459 (0.057)	0.60 (0.016)	0.56 (0.011)	0.55 (0.003)	1.03 (0.023)	0.90 (0.018)	0.86 (0.010)
10	0.491 (0.015)	0.431 (0.018)	0.374 (0.020)	0.57 (0.011)	0.49 (0.007)	0.46 (0.008)	0.96 (0.031)	0.77 (0.026)	0.70 (0.009)
15	0.468 (0.029)	0.396 (0.022)	0.317 (0.012)	0.54 (0.005)	0.44 (0.012)	0.38 (0.007)	0.92 (0.014)	0.65 (0.009)	0.55 (0.011)
20	0.455 (0.038)	0.374 (0.031)	0.283 (0.019)	0.51 (0.017)	0.41 (0.006)	0.32 (0.008)	0.86 (0.014)	0.58 (0.006)	0.47 (0.007)

The data of () are the standard deviation.

Table 4. The damage degree results of CRME under freezing and thawing cycles with various water content.

Freeze-Thaw Cycles/Times	Damage Degree of 60 °C Shear Strength/%			Damage Degree of 15 °C Indirect Tensile Strength/%			Damage Degree of −10 °C Indirect Tensile Strength/%		
	Dry Condition	Half Water Saturation Condition	Complete Water Saturation Condition	Dry Condition	Half Water Saturation Condition	Complete Water Saturation Condition	Dry Condition	Half Water Saturation Condition	Complete Water Saturation Condition
0	0	0	0	0	0	0	0	0	0
5	7.7	11.1	16.7	5.4	11.9	17.4	7.2	14.3	19.6
10	12.3	22.2	30.3	14.3	21.4	32.7	13.5	26.7	34.6
15	16.9	30.2	42.4	18.3	27.7	43.0	17.1	38.1	48.6
20	21.5	34.9	51.5	20.6	31.8	49.1	19.8	44.8	56.1

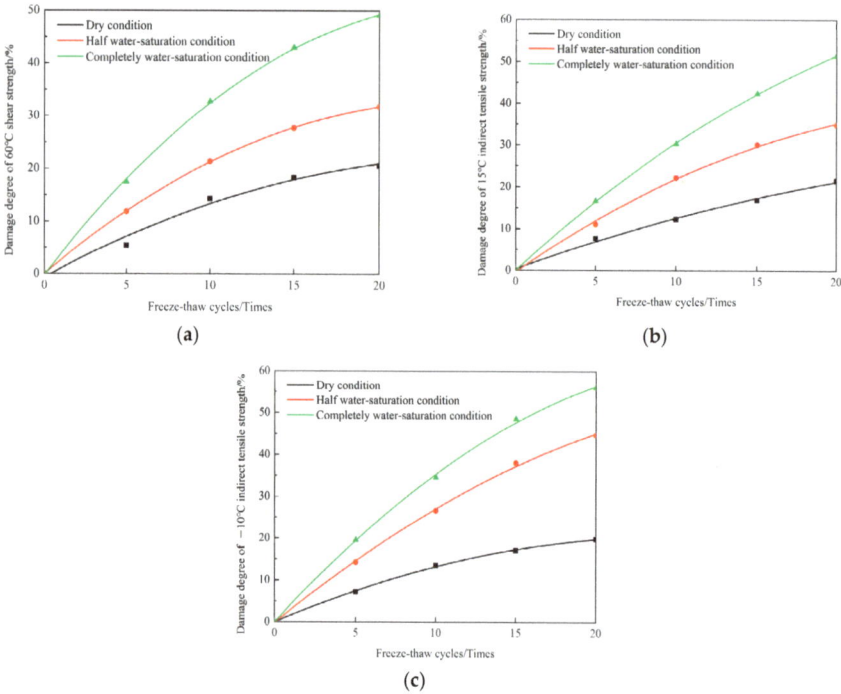

Figure 4. Damage degree change trend under freezing–thawing cycles with various water contents: (a) 60 °C shear strength; (b) 15 °C indirect tensile strength; (c) −10 °C indirect tensile strength.

As shown in Table 4 and Figure 4, with the number of freezing and thawing cycles increasing, the damage degree of the high–low temperature performance and mechanical property of CRME increased. As the saturation rate rises, the performance changes under freezing–thawing cycles become more pronounced. It indicated that the temperature cycle would damage the CRME and that the water would exacerbate the damage of the CRME during the temperature cycle.

Three parameters (α, λ_0, v) of the damage evolution model could be achieved by the nonlinear fitting of Equation (15) according to the damage degree of CRME from Table 4. Therefore, the damage evolution model could be established. The calculation results of the parameters would be affected by the number of grids N. The fitting results would become more accurate as the number of grids N increased. The parameters of the damage evolution model would also be more accurate. However, the iteration times of the damage evolution model would become higher as the number of grids N increased, which would affect the computational efficiency. Therefore, it was necessary to determine an appropriate N value. The MATLAB (2018A) software was used to nonlinearly fit the parameters of the damage evolution model. The initial value of N was set to 4, and $N = N + 2$ was used for the cyclic calculation until the parameters were stable. The degree of damage of high–low temperature performance and mechanical property of the CRME and the number of freezing and thawing cycles were fitted with different water contents. The predicted data became stable, and the calculation result was accurate when $N = 48$. In order to obtain a stable model and accurate results, $N = 100$ was adopted for calculation during the study.

3.3. Parameter Analysis of Damage Model

The damage evolution models were established based on the damage degree data calculated by different properties under 20 freezing and thawing cycles. The calculated performance parameters are shown in Table 5. The damage degree evolution diagrams of 60 °C shear strength and 15 °C and −10 °C indirect tensile strength are shown in Figures 5–7.

Table 5. Parameters results of damage model.

Performance	Water-Saturated Condition	Correlation Coefficient	Parameters of Damage Model		
			The Shape Factor α	The Scale Factor λ	The Gradient Factor v
15 °C indirect tensile strength	Dry condition	0.995	0.7873	0.0208	0.0197
	Half water saturation condition	0.997	1.0427	0.0455	0.0451
	Complete water saturation condition	0.996	1.3223	0.0838	0.0831
60 °C shear strength	Dry condition	0.985	0.7821	0.0252	0.0218
	Half water saturation condition	0.998	0.9898	0.0488	0.0466
	Complete water saturation condition	0.999	1.2009	0.0875	0.0871
−10 °C indirect tensile strength	Dry condition	0.994	0.9115	0.0265	0.0234
	Half water saturation condition	0.999	1.2011	0.0675	0.0668
	Complete water saturation condition	0.988	1.4273	0.1046	0.0988

Table 5 showed that the damage evolution model of CRME fit well and that the correlation coefficients were greater than 0.98 when freezing and thawing cycles happened. The shape factor, scale factor, and gradient factor showed different characteristics of the CRME under freezing and thawing cycles with different water contents. Figures 5–7 showed that the model fitting effect was good and the error was small.

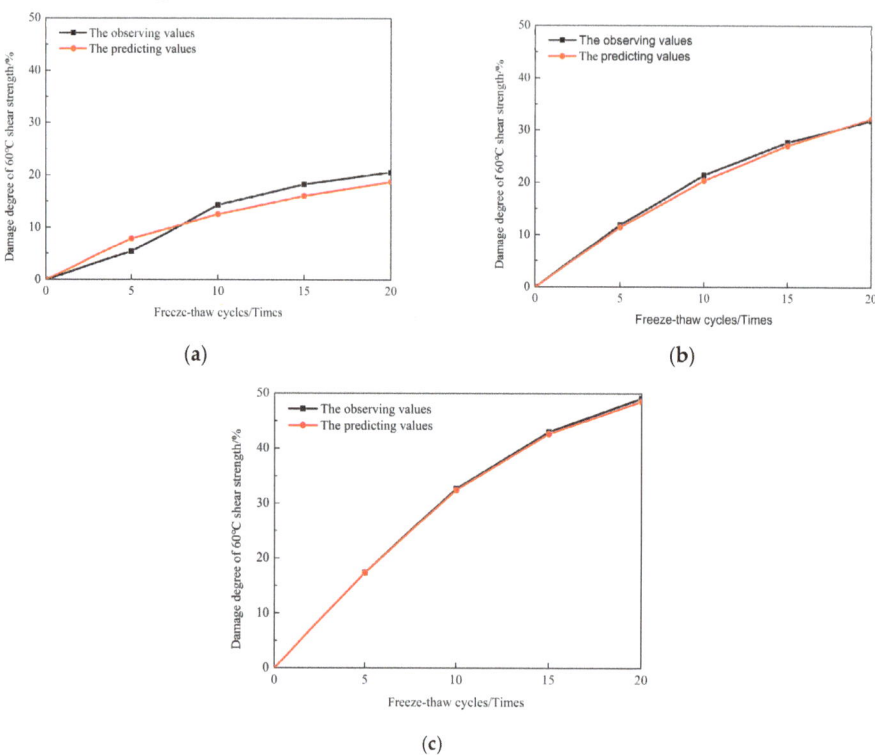

Figure 5. Damage degree evolution diagram of 60 °C shear strength: (**a**) dry condition; (**b**) half water saturation condition; (**c**) complete water saturation condition.

The shape factor revealed the failure characteristics of the inner points of the CRME under freezing and thawing cycles with different water contents [47]. Table 5 showed that the shape factors of 60 °C shear strength and 15 °C and −10 °C indirect tensile strength increased from 0.7873 to 1.3223, 0.7821 to 1.2009, 0.9115 to 1.4273, respectively. The shape factors of the CRME were similar to hot asphalt mixtures [46,47]. It indicated the inner points failure of the CRME gradually accumulated with the increasing of water contents. The presence of water and the phase transition of water changed the internal failure characteristics of the CRME [24,39]. The shape factors of 60 °C shear strength and 15 °C and −10 °C indirect tensile strength were different at various water contents, which showed that water contents had different influences on the same performance of CRME.

The scale factor indicated the resistance ability of the internal points of the CRME under freezing and thawing cycles with various water contents. The scale factor was mainly determined by air voids, gradation, additives, and so on [47]. The greater the value of the scale factor, the weaker the ability to resist freezing and thawing damage [46]. As shown schematically in Table 5, the scale factors of 60 °C shear strength and 15 °C and −10 °C indirect tensile strength increased from 0.0208 to 0.0838, 0.0252 to 0.0875, 0.0265 to 0.1046, respectively. The scale factors of the CRME were similar to hot asphalt mixtures [46,47]. It indicated that the resistance ability of CRME decreased with the increasing of water contents. Moreover, the −10 °C indirect tensile strength was influenced by water contents obviously. The frost heaving force from the phase transition of water accelerated the formation of new voids and the connection of voids, which resulted in a significant decrease in performance under freezing and thawing cycles with different water contents [39].

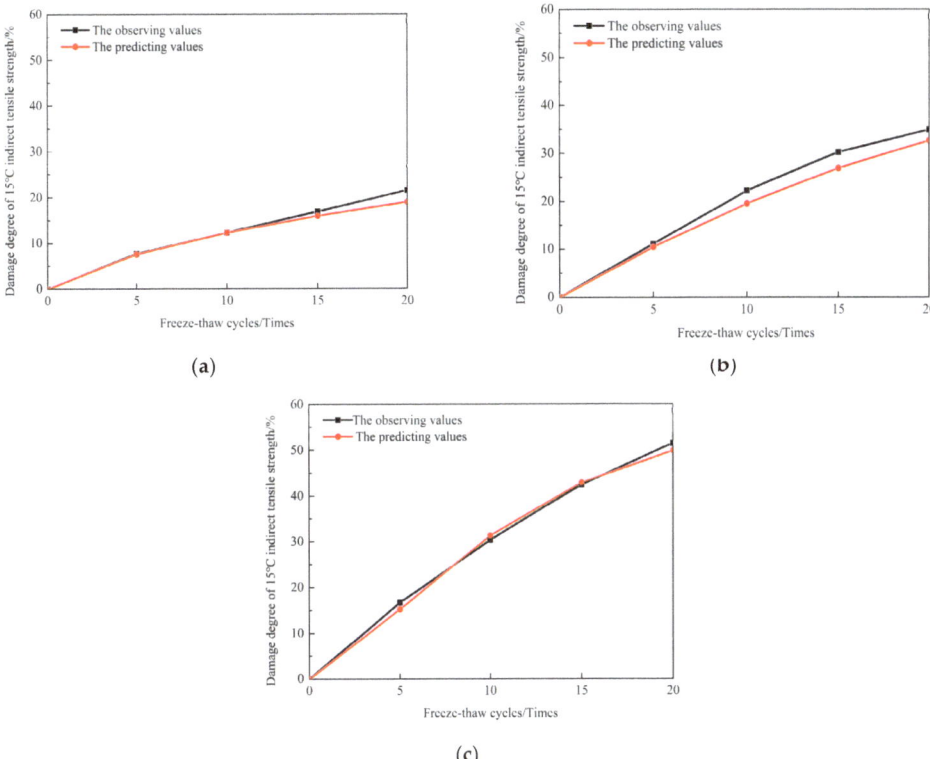

Figure 6. Damage degree evolution diagram of 15 °C indirect tensile strength: (**a**) dry condition; (**b**) half water saturation condition; (**c**) complete water saturation condition.

The gradient factor showed the difference in destruction development of the interior points of the CRME under freezing and thawing cycles with different water contents [47]. The absolute value of the gradient factor represented the difference. When the absolute value of the gradient factor was small, the damage to the internal points occurred at the same time, indicating that the material was homogeneous. The gradient factor was positive, which indicated that the damage developed from the surface to the interior. The gradient factor was negative, which indicated that the damage developed from the interior to the surface [46]. The gradient factors of 60 °C shear strength and 15 °C and −10 °C indirect tensile strength increased from 0.0197 to 0.0831, 0.0218 to 0.0871, 0.0234 to 0.0988, respectively. The gradient factor of the CRME was positive, which indicated that the damage developed from the surface to the interior in CRME under freezing and thawing cycles. However, the absolute value of the gradient factor for hot asphalt mixtures was less 10^{-7} [46,47]. It shows that the homogeneity of the CRME was worse than hot mix asphalt. Moreover, the gradient factors of 60 °C shear strength and 15 °C and −10 °C indirect tensile strength increased gradually with the water contents. It indicated the damage of the CRME gradually accumulated with the increasing of water contents.

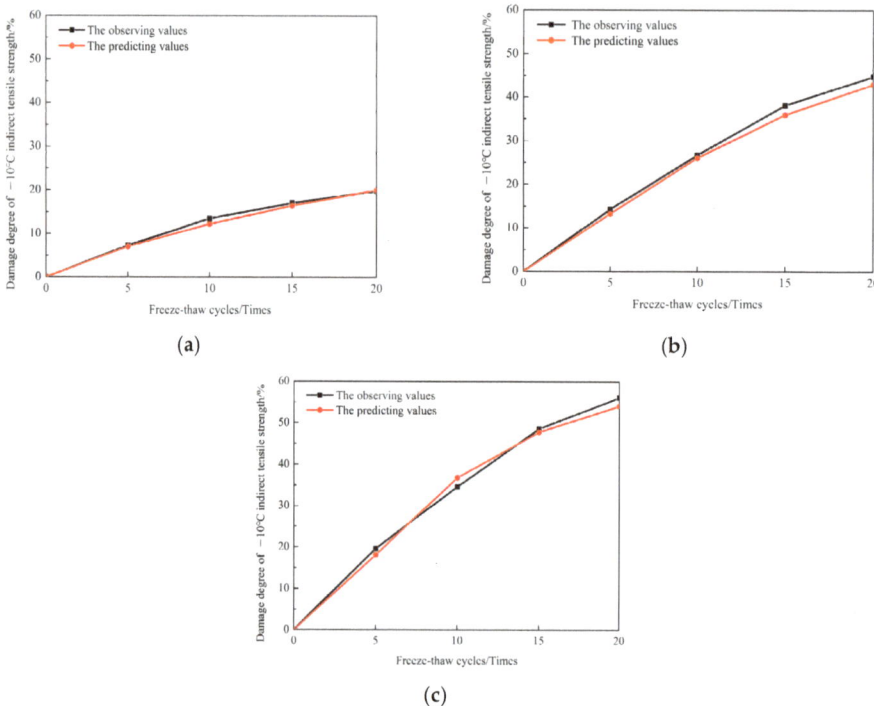

Figure 7. Damage degree evolution diagram of −10 °C indirect tensile strength: (**a**) dry condition; (**b**) half water saturation condition; (**c**) completely water saturation condition.

4. Conclusions

In this paper, the damage model investigated the damage characteristics of CRME under freezing–thawing cycles with various water contents. The following conclusions were drawn:

1. The damage degree of 60 °C shear strength and −10 °C and 15 °C indirect tensile strength of the CRME increases with the freezing and thawing cycles increasing. As the water content increases, the damage degree of performance increases significantly under freezing and thawing cycles.
2. The fitting accuracy of the damage evolution model of CRME was good under freezing and thawing cycles, and the correlation coefficients were greater than 0.98.
3. The shape factor and gradient factor of 60 °C shear strength and −10 °C and 15 °C indirect tensile strength gradually increased with the increasing degree of saturation. On the contrary, the scale factors gradually decreased with the increase in saturation degree.
4. With the water content increasing, the generation of new voids and the interconnection of voids occurred. The homogeneity of the CRME became worse, resulting in a significant decrease in performance under freezing and thawing cycles with different water contents.
5. Based on the results of the present study and other studies on the CRME subjected to freezing–thawing cycles with various water contents, it is recommended that future studies examine the fatigue performance, dynamic characteristic, and cracking behaviors and establish a multi-scale model to reflect damage mechanisms.

Author Contributions: Conceptualization, Y.Y. (Ye Yang) and Z.S.; methodology, Y.Y. (Ye Yang) and L.Q.; software, Y.Y. (Ye Yang) and C.W.; validation, Y.Y. (Ye Yang); formal analysis, Y.Y. (Ye Yang) and L.Q.; investigation, Y.Y. (Yanhai Yang); resources, Y.Y. (Yanhai Yang); data curation, Y.Y. (Ye Yang) and L.Q.; writing—review and editing, Y.Y. (Ye Yang), Z.S., and C.W.; supervision, Y.Y. (Yanhai Yang). All authors have read and agreed to the published version of the manuscript.

Funding: This study was supported by the National Natural Science Foundation of China (grant numbers 52278454) and Traffic Science and Technology Project of Liaoning Province, China [grant numbers 202216].

Data Availability Statement: Not applicable.

Acknowledgments: This research was performed at Dalian Maritime University and Shenyang Jianzhu University.

Conflicts of Interest: The authors declare no conflict of interest.

References

1. Huang, W.; Cao, M.; Xiao, L.; Li, J.; Zhu, M. Experimental study on the fatigue performance of emulsified asphalt cold recycled mixtures. *Constr. Build. Mater.* **2023**, *369*, 130607. [CrossRef]
2. Ji, J.; Li, J.; Wang, J.; Suo, Z.; Li, H.; Yao, H. Early strength of cold recycled emulsified asphalt mixtures. *J. Mater. Civ. Eng.* **2023**, *35*, 04023088. [CrossRef]
3. Hu, G.; Yang, Q.; Qiu, X.; Zhang, D.; Zhang, W.; Xiao, S.; Xu, J. Use of DIC and AE for investigating fracture behaviors of cold recycled asphalt emulsion mixtures with 100% RAP. *Constr. Build. Mater.* **2022**, *344*, 128278. [CrossRef]
4. Han, D.; Liu, G.; Xi, Y.; Zhao, Y. Research on long-term strength formation and performance evolution with curing in cold recycled asphalt mixture. *Case Stud. Constr. Mater.* **2023**, *18*, e01757. [CrossRef]
5. Zhao, Z.; Ni, F.; Zheng, J.; Cheng, Z.; Xie, S. Evaluation of curing effects on bitumen emulsion-based cold in-place recycling mixture considering field-water evaporation and heat-transfer conditions. *Coatings* **2023**, *13*, 1204. [CrossRef]
6. Xia, Y.; Lin, J.; Chen, Z.; Cai, J.; Hong, J.; Zhu, X. Fatigue cracking evolution and model of cold recycled asphalt mixtures during different curing times. *Materials* **2022**, *15*, 4476. [CrossRef]
7. Xiao, F.; Yao, S.; Wang, J.; Li, X.; Amirkhanian, S. A literature review on cold recycling technology of asphalt pavement. *Constr. Build. Mater.* **2018**, *180*, 579–604. [CrossRef]
8. Zhang, J.; Zheng, M.; Xing, X.; Pei, J.; Zhang, J.; Li, H.; Xu, P.; Wang, D. Investigation on the designing method of asphalt emulsion cold recycled mixture based on one-time compaction. *J. Clean. Prod.* **2021**, *286*, 124958. [CrossRef]
9. Han, Z.; Liu, Z.; Jiang, Y.; Wu, P.; Li, S.; Sun, G.; Zhang, L. Engineering properties and air void characteristics of cold recycled mixtures with different compaction methods. *J. Build. Eng.* **2023**, *77*, 107430. [CrossRef]
10. Chen, T.; Luan, Y.; Ma, T.; Zhu, J.; Ma, S. Mechanical and microstructural characteristics of different interfaces in cold recycled mixture containing cement and asphalt emulsion. *J. Clean. Prod.* **2020**, *258*, 120674. [CrossRef]
11. Gao, L.; Ni, F.; Luo, H.; Charmot, S. Characterization of air voids in cold in-place recycling mixtures using X-ray computed tomography. *Constr. Build. Mater.* **2015**, *84*, 429–436. [CrossRef]
12. Kim, Y.; Lee, H.D. Performance evaluation of Cold In-Place Recycling mixtures using emulsified asphalt based on dynamic modulus, flow number, flow time, and raveling loss. *KSCE J. Civ. Eng.* **2012**, *16*, 586–593. [CrossRef]
13. Jiang, J.; Ni, F.; Zheng, J.; Han, Y.; Zhao, X. Improving the high-temperature performance of cold recycled mixtures by polymer-modified asphalt emulsion. *J. Pavement Eng.* **2018**, *21*, 41–48. [CrossRef]
14. Zhang, J.; Zheng, M.; Pei, J.; Zhang, J.; Li, R. Research on low temperature performance of emulsified asphalt cold recycled mixture and improvement measures based on fracture energy. *Materials* **2020**, *13*, 3176. [CrossRef] [PubMed]
15. Yan, J.; Leng, Z.; Li, F.; Zhu, H.; Bao, S. Early-age strength and long-term performance of asphalt emulsion cold recycled mixes with various cement contents. *Constr. Build. Mater.* **2017**, *137*, 153–159. [CrossRef]
16. Yang, Y.; Yang, Y.; Qian, B. Performance and microstructure of cold recycled mixes using asphalt emulsion with different contents of cement. *Materials* **2019**, *12*, 2548. [CrossRef] [PubMed]
17. Dong, S.; Wang, D.; Hao, P.; Zhang, Q.; Bi, J.; Chen, W. Quantitative assessment and mechanism analysis of modification approaches for cold recycled mixtures with asphalt emulsion. *J. Clean. Prod.* **2021**, *323*, 129163. [CrossRef]
18. Du, S. Effect of different fibres on the performance properties of cold recycled mixture with asphalt emulsion. *J. Pavement Eng.* **2021**, *23*, 1–10. [CrossRef]
19. Xu, S.; Ruan, P.; Lu, Z.; Liang, L.; Han, B.; Hong, B. Effects of the high temperature and heavy load on the rutting resistance of cold-mix emulsified asphalt mixture. *Constr. Build. Mater.* **2021**, *298*, 123831. [CrossRef]
20. Azadgoleh, M.A.; Modarres, A.; Ayar, P. Effect of polymer modified bitumen emulsion production method on the durability of recycled asphalt mixture in the presence of deicing agents. *Constr. Build. Mater.* **2021**, *307*, 124958. [CrossRef]
21. Yang, Y.; Yue, L.; Cui, H.; Yang, Y. Simulation and evaluation of fatigue damage of cold recycled mixtures with bitumen emulsion. *Constr. Build. Mater.* **2023**, *364*, 129976. [CrossRef]

22. Lin, J.; Hong, J.; Xiao, Y. Dynamic characteristics of 100% cold recycled asphalt mixture using asphalt emulsion and cement. *J. Clean. Prod.* **2017**, *156*, 337–344. [CrossRef]
23. Guo, W.; Guo, X.; Chen, W.; Li, Y.; Sun, M.; Dai, M. Laboratory assessment of deteriorating performance of nano hydrophobic silane silica modified asphalt in spring-thaw season. *Appl. Sci.* **2019**, *9*, 2305. [CrossRef]
24. Yang, Y.; Sun, Z.; Yang, Y.; Yue, L.; Chen, G. Effects of freeze–thaw cycles on performance and microstructure of cold recycled mixtures with asphalt emulsion. *Coatings* **2022**, *12*, 802. [CrossRef]
25. Lachance-Tremblay, E.; Perraton, D.; Vaillancourt, M.; Benedetto, H. Effect of hydrated lime on linear viscoelastic properties of asphalt mixtures with glass aggregates subjected to freeze-thaw cycles. *Constr. Build. Mater.* **2018**, *184*, 58–67. [CrossRef]
26. You, L.; You, Z.; Dai, Q.; Guo, S.; Wang, J.; Schultz, M. Characteristics of water-foamed asphalt mixture under multiple freeze-thaw cycles, Laboratory evaluation. *J. Mater. Civ. Eng.* **2018**, *30*, 04018270. [CrossRef]
27. Fan, Z.; Xu, H.; Xiao, J.; Tan, Y. Effects of freeze-thaw cycles on fatigue performance of asphalt mixture and development of fatigue-freeze-thaw (FFT) uniform equation. *Constr. Build. Mater.* **2020**, *242*, 118043. [CrossRef]
28. Fu, L.; Zhou, H.; Yuan, P.; An, W.; Chen, X. Damage fracture characterization of asphalt mixtures considering freeze-thaw cycling and aging effects based on acoustic emission monitoring. *Materials* **2021**, *14*, 5930. [CrossRef]
29. Wang, T.; Chen, Y.; Zhu, C.; Liu, H.; Ma, C.; Wang, X.; Qu, T. High- and low-temperature fracture behavior of pervious asphalt mixtures under different freeze–thaw cycles based on acoustic emission technique. *Arab. J. Geosci.* **2022**, *15*, 1542. [CrossRef]
30. Ud Din, I.M.; Mir, M.S.; Farooq, M.A. Effect of freeze-thaw cycles on the properties of asphalt pavements in cold regions: A Review. *Transp. Res. Procedia* **2020**, *48*, 3634–3641. [CrossRef]
31. Xu, H.; Guo, W.; Tan, Y. Internal structure evolution of asphalt mixtures during freeze-thaw cycles. *Mater. Des.* **2015**, *86*, 436–446. [CrossRef]
32. Xu, H.; Shi, H.; Zhang, H.; Li, H.; Leng, Z.; Tan, Y. Evolution of dynamic flow behavior in asphalt mixtures exposed to freeze-thaw cycles. *Constr. Build. Mater.* **2020**, *255*, 119320. [CrossRef]
33. Wang, J.; Yu, X.; Ding, G.; Si, J.; Xing, M.; Xie, R. Strength and toughness attenuation mechanism of biobased cold-mixed epoxy asphalt under freeze–thaw cycles. *Int. J. Pavement Eng.* **2022**, 1–9. [CrossRef]
34. Jin, D.; Yin, L.; Xin, K.; You, Z. Comparison of asphalt emulsion-based chip seal and hot rubber asphalt-based chip seal. *Case Stud. Constr. Mater.* **2023**, *18*, e02175. [CrossRef]
35. Zhao, H.; Ren, J.; Chen, Z.; Luan, H.; Yi, J. Freeze and thaw field investigation of foamed asphalt cold recycling mixture in cold region. *Case Stud. Constr. Mater.* **2021**, *15*, e00710. [CrossRef]
36. Lövqvist, L.; Balieu, R.; Kringos, N. Multiscale model for predicting freeze-thaw damage in asphalt mixtures. *Int. J. Pavement Eng.* **2022**, *23*, 5048–5065. [CrossRef]
37. Cheng, Y.; Yu, D.; Tan, G.; Zhu, C. Low-temperature performance and damage constitutive model of eco-friendly basalt fiber–diatomite-modified asphalt mixture under freeze–thaw cycles. *Materials* **2018**, *11*, 2148. [CrossRef]
38. Yang, Y.; Cui, H.; Yang, Y.; Zhang, H.; Liu, H. Effect of freeze-thaw cycle on performance of unsaturated emulsified asphalt cold recycled mixture. *J. Jilin Univ. Eng. Technol. Ed.* **2022**, *52*, 2352–2359. [CrossRef]
39. Yang, Y.; Wang, H.; Yang, Y. Characterization of air voids in cold recycled mixtures with emulsified asphalt under freeze-thaw cycles. *Mater. Rev.* **2022**, *36*, 69–75.
40. *JTG T5521-2019*; Technical Specifications for Highway Asphalt Pavement Recycling. China Communications Press: Beijing, China, 2019.
41. *JTG F40-2004*; Technical Specifications for Construction of Highway Asphalt Pavements. China Communications Press: Beijing, China, 2004.
42. *JTG E40-2007*; Test Methods of Soils for Highway Engineering. China Communications Press: Beijing, China, 2007.
43. Duojie, C.; Si, W.; Ma, B.; Hu, Y.; Xue, L.; Wang, X. Assessment of freeze-thaw cycles impact on flexural tensile characteristics of asphalt mixture in cold regions. *Math. Probl. Eng.* **2021**, *2021*, 6697693. [CrossRef]
44. *JTG D50-2017*; Specifications for Design of Highway Asphalt Pavement. China Communications Press: Beijing, China, 2017.
45. *JTG E20-2011*; Standard Test Methods of Bitumen and Bituminous Mixtures for Highway Engineering. China Communications Press: Beijing, China, 2011.
46. Tan, Y.; Zhao, L.; Lan, B.; Liang, M. Research on freeze-thaw damage model and life prediction of asphalt mixture. *J. Highw. Transp. Res. Dev.* **2011**, *28*, 1–7.
47. Chen, Y.; Yu, D.; Tan, G.; Wang, W.; Zhang, P. Evolution on freeze-thaw damage of basalt fiber asphalt mixture. *J. Harbin Eng. Univ.* **2019**, *40*, 518–524.

Disclaimer/Publisher's Note: The statements, opinions and data contained in all publications are solely those of the individual author(s) and contributor(s) and not of MDPI and/or the editor(s). MDPI and/or the editor(s) disclaim responsibility for any injury to people or property resulting from any ideas, methods, instructions or products referred to in the content.

Article

Research and Evaluation of Foam-Drainage Corrosion-Inhibition Hydrate Anti-Aggregation Integrated Agent

Weijun Ni [1], Guohao Yang [1], Jie Dong [2,3,*], Yansong Pan [2], Gang Chen [2] and Xuefan Gu [4,*]

[1] College of Petroleum Engineering, Xi'an Shiyou University, Xi'an 710065, China; wjni@xsyu.edu.cn (W.N.); 21211010004@stumail.xsyu.edu.cn (G.Y.)
[2] Shaanxi University Engineering Research Center of Oil and Gas Field Chemistry, Xi'an Shiyou University, Xi'an 710065, China; 22212071107@stumail.xsyu.edu.cn (Y.P.); gangchen@xsyu.edu.cn (G.C.)
[3] Sinopec Shanghai Gaoqiao Petrochemical Co., Ltd., Shanghai 200129, China
[4] Shaanxi Province Key Laboratory of Environmental Pollution Control and Reservoir Protection Technology of Oilfields, Xi'an Shiyou University, Xi'an 710065, China
* Correspondence: 20212070841@stumail.xsyu.edu.cn (J.D.); xuefangu@xsyu.edu.cn (X.G.)

Abstract: In natural gas exploitation, foam drainage, corrosion inhibition and hydrate inhibition of wellbore fluid are conventional operations. However, there is often a problem where multiple chemical agents cannot be effectively used together and can only be used separately, resulting in complex production processes. In this study, the final integrated formulation was determined: 0.1% sodium alpha-olefin sulfonate (AOST) + 0.3% dodecyl dimethyl betaine (BS-12) + 0.3% sodium lignosulfonate + 0.5% hydrazine hydrate. The minimum tension of the integrated agent could be reduced to 23.5 mN/m. The initial foaming height of the integrated agent was 21.5 cm at 65 °C, the liquid-carrying capacity was 143 mL, and the liquid-carrying rate reached 71.5%. The maximum corrosion depth also decreased from 11.52 μm without the addition of hydrazine hydrate, gradually decreasing to 5.24 μm as the concentration of hydrazine hydrate increased. After adding an integrated agent, the growth rate of hydrates was slow and aggregation did not easily occur, and the formation temperature was also more demanding. Therefore, the integrated agent has a inhibitory effect on the formation of hydrates and has a good anti-aggregation effect. From the observation of the microstructure, the emulsion is an oil-in-water type, and the integrated agent adsorbs at the oil–water interface, preventing the dispersed water droplets in the oil phase from coalescing in one place. The oil-in-water type emulsion is more likely to improve the performance of the natural gas hydrate anti-aggregation agent.

Keywords: foaming agent; foaming stability; surface tension; microstructure; salt resistance

1. Introduction

As an effective method to solve bottom-hole fluid accumulation, foam-drainage agents have become an economically efficient and commonly used auxiliary recovery method, and most studies have verified their economic and effective characteristics. In order to develop a high-performance foam-dispersant system, different types of surfactants were compounded [1–9]. In the process of natural gas development, there is not only the problem of liquid accumulation, but also the problem of hydrate and pipeline corrosion in an environment of low temperature and high pressure. For research into an integrated agent that has the simultaneous functions of foam drainage, corrosion inhibition and hydrate anti-polymerization, the combination of any two commonly used agents may produce antagonism [10–17]. For example, methanol is often added for the purpose of hydrate anti-polymerization to alleviate the accumulation of hydrate, and methanol has an obvious effect as an anti-polymerization agent, However, methanol plays a defoaming role in foam dispersants, while commonly used corrosion inhibitors lack the performance of hydrate anti-aggregation.

Cage hydrates are ice-like compounds composed of small gas molecules encapsulated in water molecules. The formation of natural gas hydrates in oil and gas pipelines may lead to the failure of natural gas flow and serious safety and environmental issues. The use of anti-condensates is a promising method to reduce the risks of natural gas hydrates in actual production [18]. Therefore, effectively suppressing the generation and blockage of hydrates is a very important and urgent problem for all oil and gas production. One of the most effective methods to improve natural gas extraction is to suppress the generation of natural gas hydrates. Due to the fact that the use of anti-polymerization agents is not limited by temperature (supercooling) conditions and the concentration of use is below 3%, the price of anti-polymerization agents is relatively high [19]. Considering the economic benefits, in practical production applications, different types of inhibitors are often mixed and reused to reduce costs. This can significantly improve both economic composition and the inhibition effect. At present, this method is the most widely used in the development and application of natural gas in domestic and foreign gas fields to suppress hydrate generation and accumulation [20,21].

To address the issues of high water content in gas wells, hydrate formation under low temperature and high pressure, and wellbore-corrosion susceptibility, a foam-drainage hydrate anti-aggregation corrosion-inhibitor system has been developed. By utilizing experimental and theoretical research, we evaluated the foaming and stabilizing properties of the foam-drainage hydrate anti-aggregation corrosion-inhibitor system, and revealed the relationship between the structure of the foaming agent and the foaming performance [22–26]. We tested the phase-change point of hydrate formation caused by the system, and explored the corrosion-inhibition performance of the system for injection and production systems such as wellbore [27–30]. Therefore, based on these three points, a foam-agent system with the multiple performances of foaming, polymerization prevention and corrosion inhibition has been developed.

2. Experimental

2.1. Materials

AOST was purchased from Lusen Chemical Co., Ltd. (Linyi, China). BS-12 was purchased from Huajun New Materials Co., Ltd. (Huainan, China). Methanol and petroleum ether were purchased from Fuyu Fine Chemical Co., Ltd. (Tianjin, China). All products were used as received without further purification.

2.2. Surface-Tension Measurement

The surface tension of each solution was measured by the hanging-ring method at room temperature. Before the measurements, the tensiometer (Kruss K 100, Hamburg, Germany) was used to test the surface tension of a distilled water sample to confirm the accuracy of the instrument; the surface tension of distilled water measured in this manner was 72.65 mN/m. Each measurement was repeated at least three times and results reported as the average.

2.3. Foaming-Capacity Evaluation

A high-speed agitation method was used to generate foams using a high-speed mixer (GJ-3S, Qingdao Haitongda Special Instrument Co., Ltd., Qingdao, China). In each test, 100 mL surfactant solution was agitated at 7000 r/min for 3 min at ambient conditions. After the foam preparation, the foam was transferred into a graduated cylinder immediately. The volume and half-life time (the time that 50 mL of free-water phase accumulated at the bottom of the cylinder) of the foam were recorded. Each test was repeated in triplicate. All measurements were performed at 25 °C and atmospheric pressure.

2.4. Salt-Resistance Evaluation

Generally, the salinity of formation water has a strong adverse effect on the generation of foam. To study the effect of concentration and species of inorganic ions on the foaming ability and related foaming stability of the surfactants, surfactant solutions with different salt concentrations (NaCl, KCl, $MgCl_2$, $CaCl_2$) were prepared.

2.5. Temperature Resistance

The temperature in a well has a significant effect on the performance of foaming agents. Therefore, the Ross–Miles method was used to measure the foaming capacity and stability of the formula at temperatures ranging from 30 to 70 °C. Each test was repeated three times.

2.6. Methanol Effect Evaluation

During gas production, methanol was usually used to prevent the formation of gas hydrate. However, the presence of methanol may also retard the performance of foaming agents. Therefore, it was necessary to check the methanol's influence on the foaming ability of the optimized foaming agents. In this section, the foaming performance of optimized surfactant solutions with 0, 5, 10 and 15% methanol was tested in a temperature range of 40 to 70 °C using the Ross–Miles method.

2.7. Liquid-Carrying-Capacity Test

According to the performance requirements for the foam-discharge agent in the Changqing Gas Field, the liquid-carrying performance of the integrated agent required evaluation. After aging 200 mL of the integrated agent at 65 °C for 30 min, 3.0 L/min of N_2 was introduced into the dedicated foam tube. After 15 min, the volume vs. of the remaining liquid in the foam tube was recorded. The formula for calculating the liquid-carrying rate is:

$$W = \frac{200 - V_s}{200} \times 100\%$$

where W is liquid-carrying rate (%), Vs is the remaining liquid in the foam tube.

2.8. Adsorption Experiment

By scanning the wavelength of a UV spectrophotometer, the adsorption capacity of different concentrations of 4DF-4 as a whole agent on iron powder was tested, and the adsorption relationship between 4DF-4 as a foaming agent and metals was evaluated using a standard curve.

2.9. Surface Micromorphology of Steel Sheet

A DSX-500 (OLYMPUS, Tokyo, Japen) fully automatic three-dimensional imaging microscope was used to scan steel sheets in bright field (BF) mode, the scanning area of the Q235 sample was 277 μm × 277 μm, in order to obtain 2D and 3D images as well as height maps.

2.10. Micro-Morphology of Hydrates

The assembled hydrate-growth observation instrument, consisting of temperature control system, low-temperature reaction system, and image processing system, was used to observe the micro-morphology of hydrate growth of 20% tetrahydrofuran aqueous solution and 20% tetrahydrofuran integrated agent solution at different times.

2.11. Contact-Angle Experiment

The contact angle of water and oil droplets on the surface of glass treated with reagents was measured using a contact-angle measuring instrument.

2.12. Thermodynamic Analysis of Hydrates

The phase-transition point of hydrate with 20% tetrahydrofuran aqueous solution and 20% tetrahydrofuran surfactant solution was measured by DSC.

2.13. Emulsification Experiment and Microstructure Analysis after Emulsification

Samples of 10 mL of different concentration multiples (times 0.5, 1, 1.5, 2) were taken of the integrated agent and condensate oil in a 1:1 ratio and placed in a centrifuge tube. They were placed in a 45 °C water bath at a constant temperature for 10 min and then taken out. They were shaken in the left and right hands 50 times each to form an emulsion, then placed in a water bath and the time and amount of water released was recorded. The precipitation rate was calculated:

$$V_w = \frac{V_T}{V_0} 100\%$$

where V_w is precipitation rate (%), V_T is the volume of water that separates water (mL), V_0 is the total volume of water (mL).

Samples of 100 mL of different concentration multiples (times 0.5, 1, 1.5, 2) were taken of the integrated agent and crude oil in a 1:1 ratio and placed in a high stirring cup. After stirring according to the high-stirring evaluation method, the emulsion was placed under a polarizing microscope to observe the micro-morphology of the emulsion of the integrated agent and oil at different concentrations.

3. Results and Discussion

3.1. Measurement of Surface Tension

From Tables 1 and 2, it can be seen that the interfacial tension value gradually decreased with the increase in the concentration of the integrated agent, and the tension changed more rapidly in the low-concentration range. This is mainly because the surface molecules of the solution are oriented and continuously form a single molecular layer of the integrated agent. The hydrophobic end arrangement increased, and the surface tension decreased until the critical micelle concentration was reached. At this point, the surface tension appeared to have a turning point, and the surface tension value was 23.5 mN/m, Due to the lack of interfacial activity in the micelles inside the solution, the interfacial tension tends to stabilize. As the concentration increased, there was a slight increase in surface tension, which may be due to the diversification of the integrated agent and the formation of complex micelles, thereby affecting the molecular concentration on the surface and causing changes in surface and interfacial tension [31,32]. The same applies to the variation of interfacial tension, with a minimum value of 2.3×10^{-2} mN/m.

Table 1. Surface tension values of the integrated agent at different concentrations.

Concentration/%	0.00001	0.0001	0.001	0.005	0.01	0.05	0.1	0.5	0.8	1.2
Tension value/mN/m	32.6	31.3	30.1	26.1	25.4	23.5	23.9	24.7	24.3	24.8

Table 2. The interfacial tension value of the one-piece agent at different concentrations (60 °C).

Concentration/%	0.024	0.06	0.12	0.24	0.6	1.2
Tension value/mN/m	2.12	1.244	7.1×10^{-1}	2.3×10^{-2}	1.2×10^{-1}	1.5×10^{-1}

3.2. Mineral-Content Impact Test

From Table 3, it was found that after the addition of salt, the four types of salts had an adverse effect on the foaming ability of the integrated agent. The negative effect of salt on the foaming ability of the integrated agent may be attributed to the obstruction of electrostatic repulsion between charged bubble surfaces, thereby reducing the foaming ability. However, relatively speaking, the salt resistance of the all-in-one agent was ranked as follows: KCl > NaCl > $MgCl_2$ > $CaCl_2$.

Table 3. Foaming performance of the integrated agent under different salt concentrations.

Concentration of NaCl/%	Initial Height of the Foam/cm	Concentration of KCl/%	Initial Height of the Foam/cm	Concentration of CaCl$_2$/%	Initial Height of the Foam/cm	Concentration of MgCl$_2$/%	Initial Height of the Foam/cm
0	21.3	0	21.3	0	21.3	0	21.3
2.5	16.7	2.5	17.8	2.5	8.3	2.5	14.8
5	15.6	5	18.0	5	5.9	5	10.1
10	12.3	10	17.5	10	4.2	10	6.6
20	3.9	20	8.7	20	2.5	20	3.2

3.3. Temperature-Resistance Evaluation

It can be seen from Table 4 that the initial foam height increased with the increasing temperature, but the higher the temperature, the faster the defoaming speed of the foam, and the stability decreased. When the temperature was raised, the activity of the integrated agent molecules was enhanced, and foam was more likely to be generated. When the test temperature was low (30, 40 °C), the height of the foam almost did not change with the extension of time. This is because when the temperature is low, the water loss rate of the liquid film is slow, and the gas movement is slow, resulting in the low diffusion ability of the gas in the small bubbles to the large bubbles, so that the foam has better stability. The higher temperature (50~70 °C) will make the water molecules more likely to evaporate, the loss rate of liquid on the liquid film will be accelerated, and the thickness of the liquid film will continue to decrease due to the loss of liquid, so the foam is more likely to break, leading to the decrease in the height of the foam. In addition, high temperature will also accelerate the diffusion of gas in the foam and accelerate the diffusion of gas in small bubbles to large bubbles, thus shortening the life of the foam.

Table 4. Foaming properties of the one-piece agent at different temperatures.

Temperature/°C	0 min/cm	5 min/cm	10 min/cm	15 min/cm	20 min/cm
30	21.3	21.7	21.7	21.3	21.0
40	21.5	22.0	21.9	20.5	20.3
50	21.9	22.3	20.0	13.8	7.9
60	22.3	22.9	12.5	7.8	5.4
70	22.6	23.6	7.3	3.9	3.0

3.4. Methanol-Resistance Test

Different concentrations of methanol were added to verify the impact of methanol on the integrated agent, ensuring that the existing methanol in the formation interfered with the foam removal performance of the integrated agent when used as an anti-aggregation agent. It can be seen from Table 5 that the initial height of the foam decreased from 18.5 to 14.0 cm when the concentration of methanol continued to increase. With the extension of time, the height of the foam changed little, and the height of the foam decreased slightly. This is because methanol molecules are easily spread on the surface of liquid film, and they do not have amphiphilic properties. They grab the arrangement position of the integral agent molecules on the surface of the liquid film, leading to the inability of the ordered and directional arrangement of the monolayers in the interface. It has a defoaming effect. The experiment shows that methanol does have an impact on the foaming performance of the integrated agent, but the impact is not significant.

Table 5. Foaming performance of the one-piece agent under different methanol concentrations.

Concentration/%	0 min/cm	5 min/cm	10 min/cm	15 min/cm	20 min/cm
5	18.5	18.5	18.0	18.0	17.9
10	17.0	17.0	16.9	16.9	16.7
20	14.0	13.9	13.8	13.5	13.3
30	14.0	13.5	13.3	13.2	12.9

3.5. Analysis of Foam Microstructure

It can be seen from Figure 1 that the microstructure of foam with different concentrations of integrated agent is similar under the polarizing microscope, but over the same time, with the increase in concentration, the numbers of small foam increased significantly, the liquid film thickness was thicker, and the liquid loss rate slowed down. At a certain concentration, with the increase in time, the liquid on the foam liquid film was gradually lost and the gas wrapped by the foam continuously diffused, the volume of foam gradually increased, the thickness of the liquid film decreased, and small bubbles continued to bubble into the atmosphere until the foam burst. It can be seen from the figure that at 20 min, no matter whether the concentration of the integrated agent was 0.5, 1, 1.5 times or twice the standard concentration, the foam morphology had no obvious polygon structure, which means that the integrated agent molecules were arranged in an orderly fashion on the liquid film to maintain the water content of the liquid film, reduce its flow loss and gas diffusion, and finally maintain the stability of the foam. In addition, the foam took a long time to be broken, which can also prevent it from falling back in the process of carrying liquid accumulation upward, so the microscopic view of foam can well demonstrate the performance of the foam discharge capacity of the integrated agent.

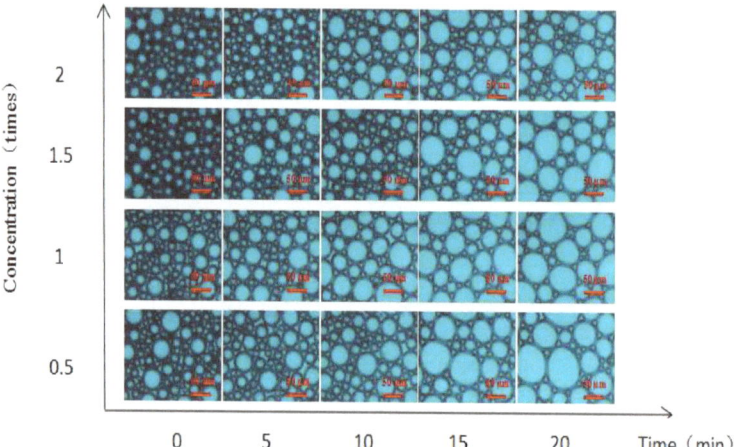

Figure 1. The microstructure of the integrated agent at different times.

3.6. Liquid-Carrying Capacity

In practical applications, the foam removal agent needs to carry the accumulated liquid from the bottom of the well out of the formation, so it was necessary to simulate the actual operation with the assistance of a certain airflow to achieve the corresponding liquid-carrying capacity. The magnitude of the liquid-carrying rate also represents the strength of the foam-removal capacity. Moreover, in actual production, the foam-removal agent also needs to overcome the influence of temperature. Therefore, the experimental temperature was set at 65 °C, and a certain flow rate of N_2 was introduced to record the liquid-carrying capacity, which was compared with the representative company's liquid-carrying-capacity standard, The experimental results are shown in the following table. It can be seen from Table 6 that the initial foaming height of the integrated agent measured at 65 °C was 215 mL, and the foaming height after 5 min was 245 mL, because high temperature will enhance the activity of surfactant molecules, so the foam height will increase in a short time. The liquid-carrying capacity of the integrated agent was 143 mL, with a liquid-carrying rate of 71.5%, which is much higher than the requirements of the Changqing Gas Field for the liquid-carrying capacity of the foam-discharge agent. Therefore, this integrated agent has certain on-site application value.

Table 6. Foaming ability and liquid-carrying ability of one-piece agent (65 °C).

Content	Changqing Gas Field (Yulin)/mL	Changqing Gas Field (Shenmu)/mL	One-Piece Agent/mL
Foam height (0 min)	120	110	215
Foam height (5 min)	70	60	245
Liquid-carrying capacity (0~15 min)	120	110	143

3.7. Viscoelasticity of Foam

As shown in Figure 2, within a certain concentration range of $1 \times 10^{-7} \sim 1 \times 10^{-5}$ g/mL, the intermolecular force increased and the interfacial activity increased, resulting in an increase in the interfacial expansion modulus and viscoelasticity. As the concentration of the integrated agent ($1 \times 10^{-4} \sim 1 \times 10^{-2}$ g/mL) continued to increase, the interfacial expansion modulus and viscoelasticity decreased. The high concentration of the integrated agent will lead to an accelerated diffusion exchange between the interface and the bulk phase, resulting in the reduction in the interfacial expansion modulus [33], and the foam tends to be stable. Not only the concentration increased; there were maximum values for the expansion modulus, elastic and viscous modulus, and phase angle, which were 32.32 mN/m, 29.86 mN/m, 483.33 mN/m, and 31.96°, respectively.

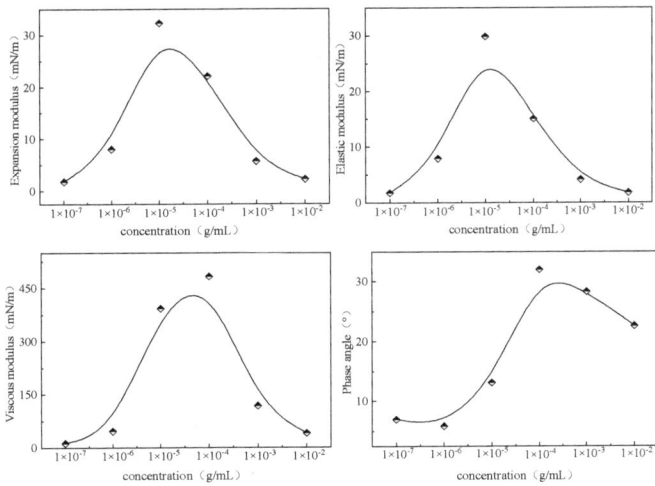

Figure 2. Interfacial viscoelasticity measurements at different concentrations.

3.8. Adsorption Experiment

Figure 3 of the adsorption experiment shows the UV spectra of the integrated agent with different concentration multiples. The absorption peak generated at 362 nm showed a significant red shift with the increase in concentration and Fe powder, and the absorption peaks were all enhanced. This may be due to the integrated agent adsorbing on the surface of Fe atoms and coordinating with metal ions. This indicates that the integrated agent molecules adsorb on the surface of carbon steel, forming a tight and stable adsorption film that can effectively prevent the occurrence of steel plate corrosion.

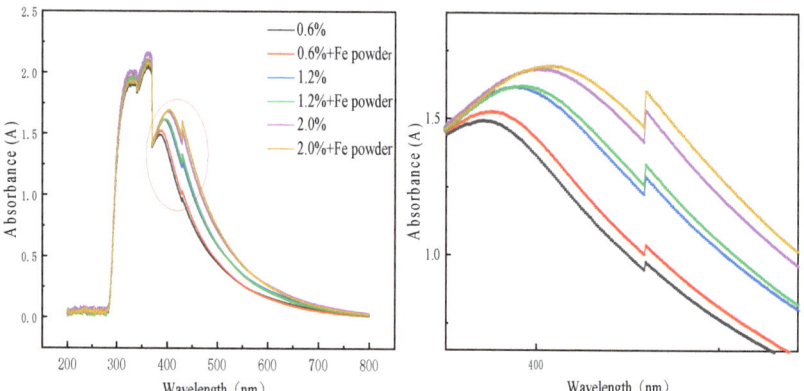

Figure 3. Wavelength scanning of the one-piece agent at different concentrations.

3.9. Surface Micromorphology of Metal

A model of the steel sheet surface and pitting pits shown on the right of Figure 4 was established, and the morphology of the steel sheet was indirectly observed. From the 2D images in Figure 4, it can be observed that the surface of the steel sheet was smooth, and the 4DF system had a significant promoting effect on the corrosion inhibition of the steel sheet. As the concentration of hydrazine hydrate increased, the surface roughness decreased and the corrosion degree of the steel sheet significantly decreased. Compared with the blank group (without any additives), the 4DF system showed a significant reduction in pitting pits. The more purple in the 3D and height maps, the deeper the pitting pits. Figure 4 showed that the purple area significantly decreased and the pitting range significantly decreased, following the increase in hydrazine hydrate concentration. The maximum corrosion depth decreased to 5.24 μm, proving that the 4DF system can effectively suppress the corrosion of steel sheets and play a good corrosion-inhibition role.

3.10. Microscopic Morphology of Hydrate Growth

Due to the difficulty in forming hydrates in normal environments, the formation of tetrahydrofuran hydrates using self-built instruments was studied and discussed. Figure 5 shows the growth morphology of the hydrates as time increased at 2 °C. It can be seen that from 0 s onwards, hydrates continued to form at the edge of the liquid surface and attracted each other towards the middle of the droplets. This is because there is a cohesive force between the formed hydrate and the forming hydrate, which forces them to attract and aggregate with each other. Moreover, there is a certain repulsive effect at the interface between the formed hydrate and the formed hydrate, causing the formed hydrate to continuously aggregate towards the middle.

As shown in Figure 6, At −1 °C, the structure of the THF hydrate was more loose and the hydrate formation rate slowed down compared to the THF hydrate added as a whole agent. At 30 s, the 20% THF hydrate was basically completely formed and mostly generated giant crystals, while the hydrate containing an organic agent was only generated on a large scale at 60 s. At 0 °C for 60 s, the hydrate crystal structure formed by 20% THF was significantly more compact. At 1 °C, the risk of hydrate formation was significantly reduced after the addition of an integrated agent, which grew slowly and was looser compared to the hydrates formed without an integrated agent. It did not aggregate into large-scale crystals due to the arrangement and adsorption of integrated agent molecules on the surface of the hydrates. The charge of hydrophilic groups in the integrated agent can repel each other, thereby preventing the aggregation of hydrates [28]. In summary, the integrated agent has an inhibitory effect on the formation of THF hydrates and has a good anti-aggregation effect.

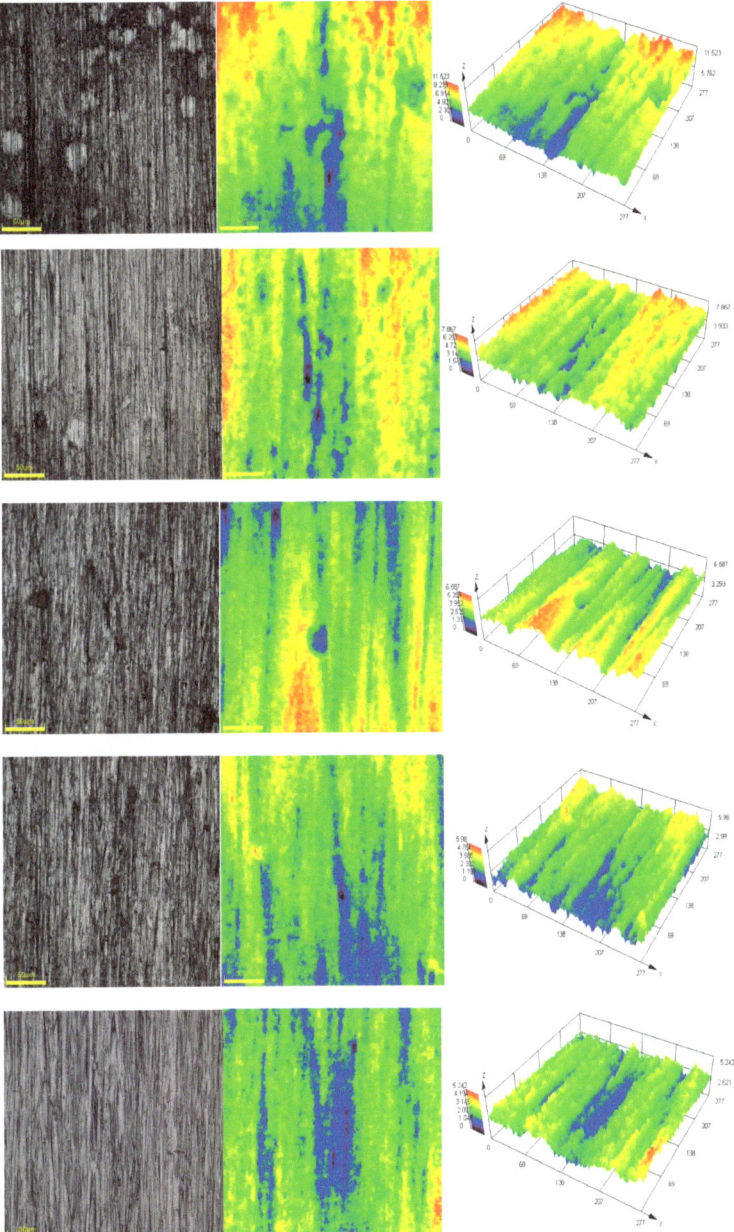

Figure 4. Two-dimensional view, height map and three dimensional view (1000 magnification) of the steel sheet under different concentrations of hydrazine hydrate in the all-in-one agent.

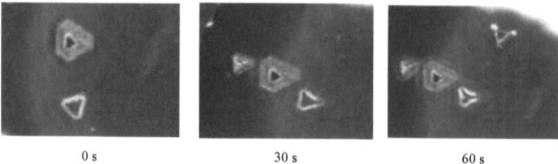

Figure 5. Growth morphology of hydrate at 2 °C (100 magnification).

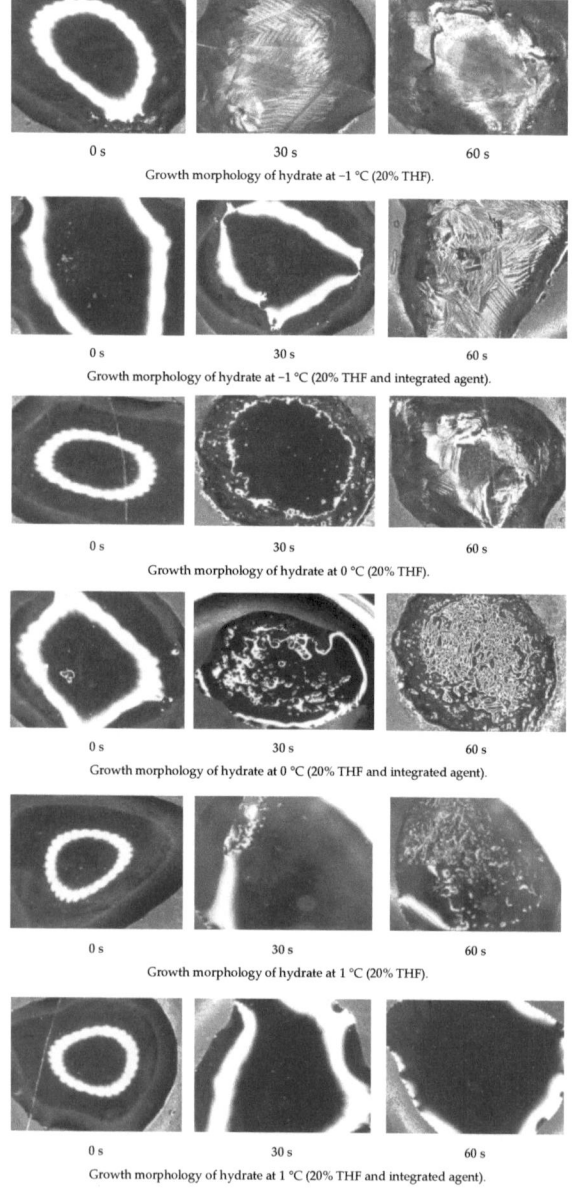

Growth morphology of hydrate at −1 °C (20% THF).

Growth morphology of hydrate at −1 °C (20% THF and integrated agent).

Growth morphology of hydrate at 0 °C (20% THF).

Growth morphology of hydrate at 0 °C (20% THF and integrated agent).

Growth morphology of hydrate at 1 °C (20% THF).

Growth morphology of hydrate at 1 °C (20% THF and integrated agent).

Figure 6. Microscopic view of hydrate formation of bulk agent at different temperatures.

3.11. Contact-Angle Experiment

As shown in Figure 7, compared to the cleaned-glass surface after treatment, the glass surface soaked with the integrated agent was significantly more hydrophilic and oil friendly. Through measurement, it was found that the integrated agent had better hydrophilicity, which is consistent with the anti-aggregation mechanism. On the one hand, the hydrophilic groups of the integrated agent were adsorbed on the surface of the hydrate, while the surfaces of adjacent hydrates were prevented from approaching each other due to the hydrophobic and hydrophilic groups' charge properties; On the other hand, the addition of an all-in-one agent disrupted the activity of the water molecules by hydrophilic groups, resulting in a decrease in the amount of hydrate formation. The anti-aggregation mechanism of the hydrates is shown in Figure 8.

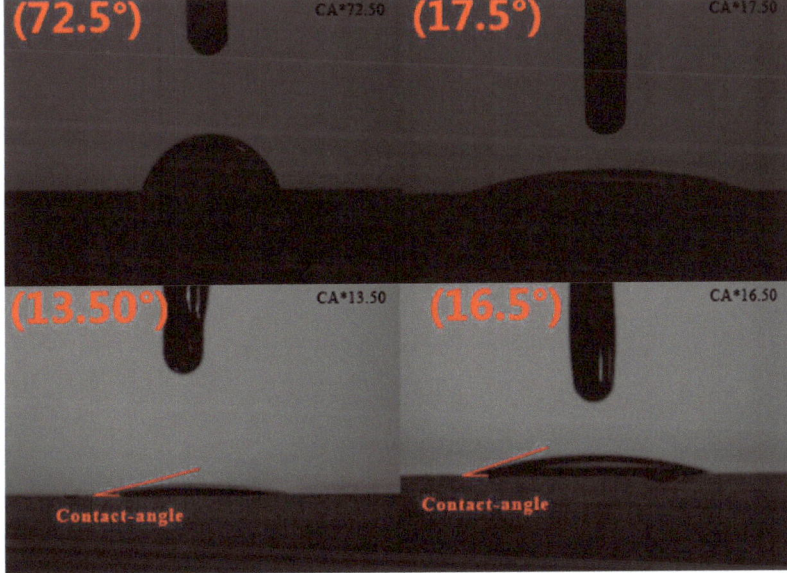

Figure 7. Contact-angle measurement of the one-piece agent (water at the top, oil at the bottom).

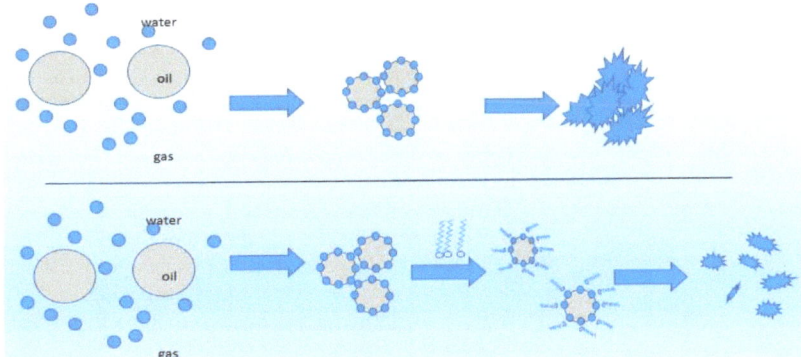

Figure 8. Anti-aggregation mechanism diagram.

3.12. Thermodynamic Analysis of Hydrates

As shown in Figure 9, with the operation of the cooling program, the solution gradually transformed from liquid to solid, and the formation of hydrates released heat, resulting in a change in calorific value. As a result, an upward heat release peak appeared in the image. At this time, the initial point of heat change was the phase transition point of the hydrates. As shown on the left of Figure 9, the phase transition point of 20% THF hydrate was 4.32 °C, indicating that THF hydrate begins to grow at this temperature. The right side of Figure 9 shows the phase transition point of the hydrate after the addition of an integrated agent. Compared with the 20% THF hydrate, the phase transition point decreased by 1.92 °C, significantly reducing the risk of hydrate formation. This is because the molecules of the integrated agent not only hinder the hydrogen bonding of water molecules to form a cage-like structure of hydrates, but also interfere with the activity of the water molecules, effectively reducing the aggregation of water and matter.

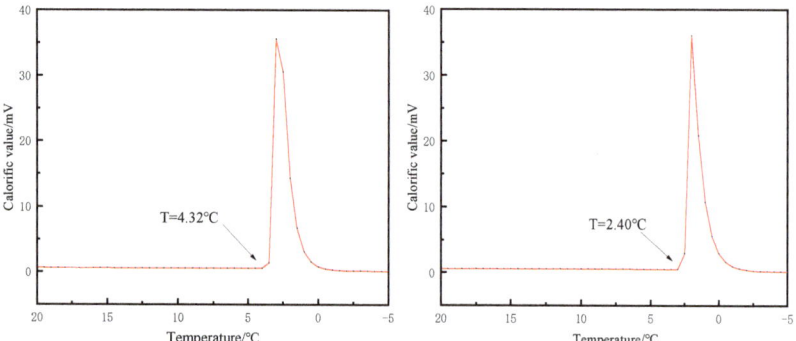

Figure 9. DSC curve of 20% THF solution with and without the integrated agent ((**left**) is without integrated agent; (**right**) is with integrated agent).

3.13. Emulsification Experiment and Microstructure Analysis after Emulsification

As shown in Figure 10, with the increase in the concentration of the integrated agent, the stability of the emulsion after uniform emulsification increased, and the amount of water released at the same time decreased. When standing at 45 °C for 1 min, the water evolution rates of different concentrations were 18, 12, 0, and 0%, respectively, indicating that the emulsion has good stability in a short period of time and can ensure good emulsification performance. After standing at 45 °C for 10 min, the water separation rate of the solution was 100, 74, 0 and 0%, respectively, which indicates that there is no difficult demulsification of lotion at 10 min, which is conducive to subsequent recovery. As shown in Figure 11, the amount and rate of water evolution at different concentrations increased with time and eventually stabilized. The emulsification performance of the integrated agent represents both the ability to foam and the ability to prevent hydrate aggregation. The better emulsification stability of the integrated agent is of great significance for the production of natural gas.

It can be seen from Figure 12 that at 0 min, the sizes of the lotions formed by mixing different concentrations of integrated agent and crude oil in a ratio of 1:1 were different. As the concentration of the integrated agent increased, the diameter of the emulsion became smaller, and the more small emulsions there were, the better the emulsifying ability and stability. In the figure, it can be seen that, as time went on, after emulsification with 1 and 1.5 times the emulsion, the emulsion continued to coalesce and its stability gradually deteriorated, providing the conditions for the demulsification of the emulsion. As the emulsion is an oil-in-water type, the integrated agent adsorbs at the oil–water interface, preventing the dispersed water droplets in the oil phase from coalescing in one place.

The oil-in-water type emulsion is more likely to improve the performance of the anti-aggregation agent.

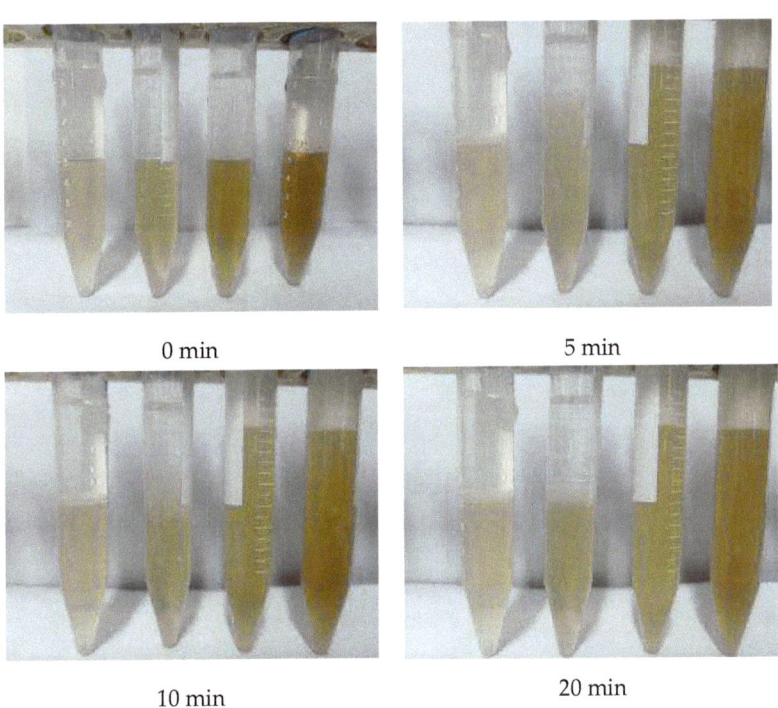

Figure 10. Emulsification experiments of different concentrations of the all-in-one agent (from left to right, 0.5, 1, 1.5, and double concentrations of the one-body solution).

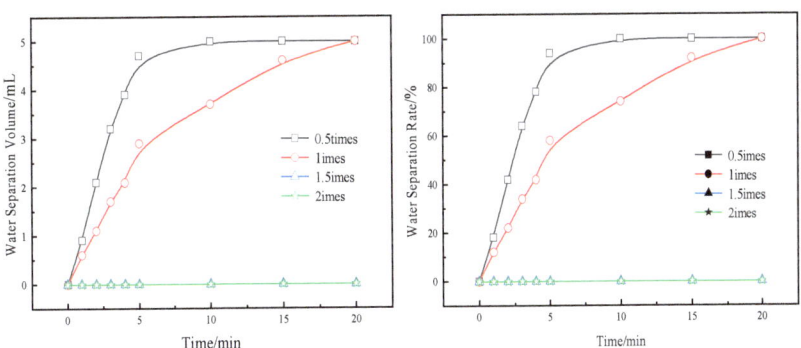

Figure 11. The water separation rate of the all-in-one emulsion at different times.

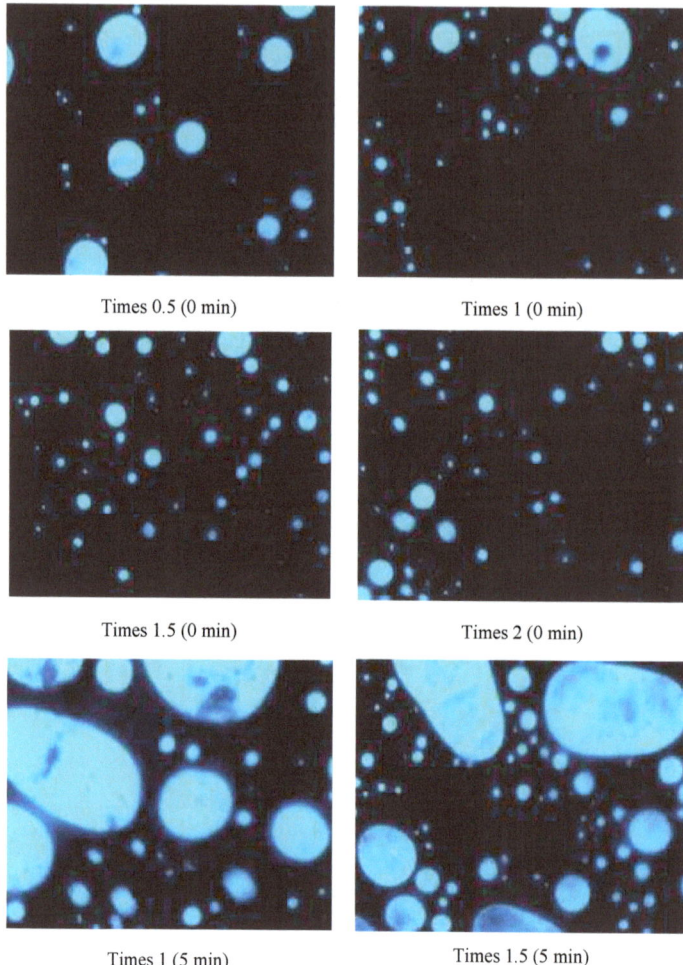

Figure 12. Microemulsion at different concentrations.

4. Conclusions

In this study, the final integrated formulation was determined: 0.1% sodium alpha-olefin sulfonate (AOST) + 0.3% dodecyl dimethyl betaine (BS-12) + 0.3% sodium lignosulfonate + 0.5% hydrazine hydrate. With this formulation, the performances of foaming, polymerization prevention and corrosion inhibition were improved. After adding this integrated agent, the growth rate of hydrates was slow and the maximum corrosion depth decreased to 5.24 μm. The good performance of this anti-aggregation agent is largely because of its oil-in-water type emulsion, preventing the dispersed water droplets in the oil phase from coalescing in one place. These excellent abilities to produce foam and inhibit corrosion indicate that they can be used in the oil and petrochemical industry for foam drainage and to inhibit corrosion, which have a certain practical uses.

Author Contributions: W.N.: data curation, investigation and writing—original draft; G.Y.: validation, conceptualization, supervision; J.D.: data curation, investigation, formal analysis; Y.P.: investigation, methodology, data curation; X.G.: project administration, funding acquisition; G.C.: writing—review and editing, validation, and supervision. All authors have read and agreed to the published version of the manuscript.

Funding: This work is funded by Scientific Research Program Funded by Shaanxi Provincial Education Department (Program No. 22JY052).

Data Availability Statement: The data that support the findings of this study are available from the corresponding author upon reasonable request.

Acknowledgments: The authors also thank the support of The Youth Innovation Team of Shaanxi University and the work of the Modern Analysis and Testing Center of Xi'an Shiyou University.

Conflicts of Interest: The authors declare no conflict of interest.

References

1. Zhang, T.; Wang, S.Z.; Dong, C.H. Experimental study on the emergency disposal agent for methanol leakage. *Adv. Mat. Res.* **2017**, *1142*, 306–313. [CrossRef]
2. Gu, X.F.; Gao, L.; Li, Y.F.; Dong, K.; Zhang, J.; Du, W.C.; Qu, C.T.; Chen, G. Performance and mechanism of span surfactants as clean flow improvers for crude oil. *Pet. Chem.* **2020**, *60*, 140–145. [CrossRef]
3. Behera, M.R.; Varade, S.R.; Ghosh, P.; Paul, P.; Negi, A.S. Foaming in micellar solutions: Effects of surfactant, salt, and oil concentrations. *Ind. Eng. Chem. Res.* **2014**, *53*, 18497–18507. [CrossRef]
4. Qu, C.; Wang, J.; Yin, H.; Lu, G.; Li, Z.; Feng, Y. Condensate oil-tolerant foams stabilized by an anionic–sulfobetaine surfactant mixture. *ACS Omega* **2019**, *4*, 1738–1747. [CrossRef]
5. Negm, N.A.; El Farargy, A.F.; Mohammed, D.E.; Mohamad, H.N. Environmentally friendly nonionic surfactants derived from tannic acid: Synthesis, characterization and surface activity. *J. Surfactants Det.* **2012**, *15*, 433–443. [CrossRef]
6. Lee, J.J.; Nikolov, A.; Wasan, D. Surfactant micelles containing solubilized oil decrease foam film thickness stability. *J Colloid Interface Sci.* **2014**, *415*, 18–25. [CrossRef] [PubMed]
7. Yoshimura, T.; Ichinokawa, T.; Kaji, M.; Esumi, K. Synthesis and surface-active properties of sulfobetaine-type zwitterionic gemini surfactants. *Colloids Surf. A* **2006**, *273*, 208–212. [CrossRef]
8. Li, Y.; Bai, Q.; Li, Q.; Huang, H.; Ni, W.; Wang, Q.; Xin, X.; Zhao, B.; Chen, G. Preparation of Multifunctional Surfactants Derived from Sodium Dodecylbenzene Sulfonate and Their Use in Oil-Field Chemistry. *Molecules* **2023**, *28*, 3640. [CrossRef] [PubMed]
9. Chen, G.; Cheng, C.; Zhang, J.; Sun, Y.; Hu, Q.; Qu, C.T.; Dong, S.B. Synergistic effect of surfactant and alkali on the treatment of oil sludge. *J. Petrol. Sci. Eng.* **2019**, *183*, 106420. [CrossRef]
10. Koczo, K.; Tselnik, O.; Falk, B. Silicon-based foamants for foam assisted lift of aqueous-hydrocarbon mixtures. In Proceedings of the SPE International Symposium on Oilfield Chemistry, The Woodlands, TX, USA, 11–13 April 2011; OnePetro: Richardson, TX, USA, 2011. [CrossRef]
11. Chen, G.; Lin, J.; Liu, Q.N.; Zhang, J.; Wu, Y.; Li, H.; Ma, Y.; Qu, C.T.; Song, W.Q. Corrosion inhibition and the structure-efficiency relationship study of two cationic surfactants. *Anti-Corros. Methods Mater.* **2019**, *66*, 388–393. [CrossRef]
12. Pavelyev, R.S.; Zaripova, Y.F.; Yarkovoi, V.V.; Vinogradova, S.S.; Razhabov, S.; Khayarov, K.R.; Nazarychev, S.A.; Stoporev, A.S.; Mendgaziev, R.I.; Semenov, A.P.; et al. Performance of Waterborne Polyurethanes in Inhibition of Gas Hydrate Formation and Corrosion: Influence of Hydrophobic Fragments. *Molecules* **2020**, *25*, 5664. [CrossRef]
13. Elhenawy, S.; Khraisheh, M.; Almomani, F.; Al-Ghouti, M.A.; Hassan, M.K.; Al-Muhtaseb, A. Towards Gas Hydrate-Free Pipelines: A Comprehensive Review of Gas Hydrate Inhibition Techniques. *Energies* **2022**, *15*, 8551. [CrossRef]
14. Mandal, S.; Bej, S.; Banerjee, P. Insights into the uses of two azine decorated d10-MOFs for corrosion inhibition application on mild steel surface in saline medium: Experimental as well as theoretical investigation. *J. Mol. Liq.* **2023**, *381*, 109846. [CrossRef]
15. Raviprabha, K.; Bhat, R.S. Corrosion inhibition of mild steel in 0.5 M HCL by substituted 1,3,4-oxadiazole. *Egypt. J. Pet.* **2023**, *32*, 1–10. [CrossRef]
16. Pesha, T.; Mulaudzi, V.L.; Cele, M.L.; Mothapo, M.P.; Ratshisindi, F. Evaluation of corrosion inhibition effect of glycerol stearate on aluminium metal by electrochemical techniques. *Arab. J. Chem.* **2023**, *16*, 104798. [CrossRef]
17. Zhang, H.; Pang, X.; Gao, K. Localized CO_2 corrosion of carbon steel with different microstructures in brine solutions with an imidazoline-based inhibitor. *Appl. Surf. Sci.* **2018**, *442*, 446–460. [CrossRef]
18. Christogonus, A.O.; Arinze, C.M. Experimental and DFT evaluation of adsorption and inhibitive properties of Moringa oliefera extract on mild steel corrosion in acidic media. *Arab. J. Chem.* **2020**, *13*, 9270–9282. [CrossRef]
19. Bai, Y.; Zhang, J.; Dong, S.; Li, J.; Zhang, R.; Pu, C.; Chen, G. Effect of anion on the corrosion inhibition of cationic surfactants and a mechanism study. *Desalination Water Treat.* **2020**, *188*, 130–139. [CrossRef]
20. Enabulele, D.O.; Bamigboye, G.O.; Solomon, M.M.; Durodola, B. Exploration of the Corrosion Inhibition Potential of Cashew Nutshell on Thermo-Mechanically Treated Steel in Seawater. *Arab. J. Sci. Eng.* **2022**, *48*, 223–237. [CrossRef]
21. Hussain, H.H.; Husin, H. Review on Application of Quaternary Ammonium Salts for Gas Hydrate Inhibition. *Appl. Sci.* **2020**, *10*, 1011. [CrossRef]
22. Paz, P.; Netto, T.A. On the Rheological Properties of Thermodynamic Hydrate Inhibitors Used in Offshore Oil and Gas Production. *J. Mar. Sci. Eng.* **2020**, *8*, 878. [CrossRef]
23. Habib, S.; Nawaz, M.; Kahraman, R.; Ahmed, E.M.; Shakoor, R.A. Effect of the modified hybrid particle on the corrosion inhibition performance of polyolefin based coatings for carbon steel. *J. Sci. Adv. Mater. Devices* **2022**, *7*, 100466. [CrossRef]

24. Xu, X.; Wei, H.Y.; Liu, M.G.; Zhou, L.S.; Shen, G.Z.; Li, Q.; Hussain, G.; Yang, F.; Fathi, R.; Chen, H.G.; et al. Nitrogen-doped carbon quantum dots for effective corrosion inhibition of Q235 steel in concentrated sulphuric acid solution. *Mater. Today Commun.* **2021**, *29*, 102872. [CrossRef]
25. Ulhaq, M.I.; Saleem, Q.; Ajwad, H.; Aleisa, R.M.; Alanazi, N.M.; Leoni, M.; Zahrani, I.; Makogon, T. Corrosion inhibition of carbon steel in a sour (H_2S) environment by an acryloyl-based polymer. *ACS Omega* **2023**, *8*, 18047–18057. [CrossRef]
26. Obot, I.B.; Obi-Egbedi, N.O. Adsorption properties and inhibition of mild steel corrosion in sulphuric acid solution by ketoconazole: Experimental and theoretical investigation. *Corros. Sci.* **2009**, *52*, 198–204. [CrossRef]
27. Jiang, L.L.; Xu, N.; Liu, Q.B.; Cheng, Z.C.; Liu, Y.; Zhao, J.F. Review of Morphology Studies on Gas Hydrate Formation for Hydrate-Based Technology. *Cryst. Growth Des.* **2020**, *20*, 8148–8161. [CrossRef]
28. Zandi, M.S.; Hasanzadeh, M. The self-healing evaluation of microcapsule-based epoxy coatings applied on AA6061 Al alloy in 3.5% NaCl solution. *Anti-Corros. Methods Mater.* **2017**, *64*, 225–232. [CrossRef]
29. Sliem, M.H.; El Basiony, N.M.; Zaki, E.G.; Sharaf, M.A.; Abdullah, A.M. Corrosion Inhibition of Mild Steel in Sulfuric Acid by a Newly Synthesized Schiff Base: An Electrochemical, DFT, and Monte Carlo Simulation Study. *Electroanalysis* **2020**, *32*, 3145–3158. [CrossRef]
30. El-Hajjaji, F.; Ech-Chihbi, E.; Rezki, N.; Benhiba, F.; Taleb, M.; Chauhan, D.S.; Quraishi, M. Electrochemical and theoretical insights on the adsorption and corrosion inhibition of novel pyridinium-derived ionic liquids for mild steel in 1 M HCl. *J. Mol. Liq.* **2020**, *314*, 113737. [CrossRef]
31. Navidfar, A.; Bulut, O.; Baytak, T.; Iskender, H.; Trabzon, L. Boosted viscoelastic and dynamic mechanical behavior of binary nanocarbon based polyurethane hybrid nanocomposite foams. *J. Compos. Mater.* **2022**, *56*, 2907–2920. [CrossRef]
32. Alaboalirat, M.; Qi, L.; Arrington, K.J.; Qian, S.; Keum, J.K.; Mei, H.; Littrell, K.C.; Sumpter, B.G.; Carrillo, J.M.; Verduzco, R.; et al. Amphiphilic Bottlebrush Block Copolymers: Analysis of Aqueous Self-Assembly by Small-Angle Neutron Scattering and Surface Tension Measurements. *Macromolecules* **2019**, *52*, 465–476. [CrossRef]
33. Dong, S.B.; Liu, C.W.; Han, W.W.; Li, M.Z.; Zhang, J.; Chen, G. The Effect of the Hydrate Antiagglomerant on Hydrate Crystallization at the Oil-Water Interface. *ACS Omega* **2020**, *5*, 3315–3321. [CrossRef]

Disclaimer/Publisher's Note: The statements, opinions and data contained in all publications are solely those of the individual author(s) and contributor(s) and not of MDPI and/or the editor(s). MDPI and/or the editor(s) disclaim responsibility for any injury to people or property resulting from any ideas, methods, instructions or products referred to in the content.

Article

Synergistic Catalysis of Reservoir Minerals and Exogenous Catalysts on Aquathermolysis of Heavy Oil

Yunlei Zang [1,2], Huaizhu Liu [3], Dong Chen [3], Shu Zhang [1], Shanjian Li [1] and Gang Chen [1,2,*]

1. Shaanxi Province Key Laboratory of Environmental Pollution Control and Reservoir Protection Technology of Oilfields, Xi'an Shiyou University, Xi'an 710065, China; 21211070913@stumail.xsyu.edu.cn (Y.Z.); 20212070889@stumail.xsyu.edu.cn (S.Z.)
2. Shaanxi University Engineering Research Center of Oil and Gas Field Chemistry, Xi'an Shiyou University, Xi'an 710065, China
3. Tangshan Jiyou Ruifeng Chemical Co., Ltd., Tangshan 063200, China; jxzx_chd@petrochina.com.cn (D.C.)
* Correspondence: gangchen@xsyu.edu.cn

Abstract: In this study, based on existing heavy oil extraction technology, combined with the mineral composition in a reservoir, the synergistic catalytic effect of reservoir minerals and exogenous catalysts under the reaction system of a hydrogen-rich environment not only reduces the viscosity of thick oil but also reduces the extraction cost and further improves the recovery rate of heavy oil. In this study, the impacts of different reservoir minerals and exogenous catalysts on the aquathermolysis of heavy oil were investigated. The research results showed that the sodium montmorillonite within the reservoir minerals exhibited an optimal catalytic effect, and the synergistic catalytic effect of sodium montmorillonite and catalyst C-Fe (catechol iron) resulted in a viscosity reduction rate of 60.47%. Furthermore, the efficiency of different alcohols as hydrogen donors was screened, among which ethanol had the best catalytic effect. Under the optimal reaction conditions, the viscosity reduction rate after the addition of ethanol was 75.25%. Infrared spectroscopy, elemental analysis, thermogravimetry, and differential scanning calorimetry were used to study the changes in heavy oil before and after hydrothermal cracking. Element analysis showed that the synergistic catalytic effect of sodium-based montmorillonite and catalyst C-Fe increased the hydrocarbon ratio from 0.116 to 0.117, and the content of S and N elements decreased. This fully confirms the catalytic effect of sodium-based montmorillonite and C-Fe catalyst for he hydrogenation reaction of the unsaturated carbon in heavy oil.

Keywords: reservoir minerals; heavy oil; catalytic aquathermolysis; synergistic

Citation: Zang, Y.; Liu, H.; Chen, D.; Zhang, S.; Li, S.; Chen, G. Synergistic Catalysis of Reservoir Minerals and Exogenous Catalysts on Aquathermolysis of Heavy Oil. *Processes* **2023**, *11*, 2635. https://doi.org/10.3390/pr11092635

Academic Editors: Albert Ratner, Dicho Stratiev and Dobromir Yordanov

Received: 26 July 2023
Revised: 21 August 2023
Accepted: 31 August 2023
Published: 4 September 2023

Copyright: © 2023 by the authors. Licensee MDPI, Basel, Switzerland. This article is an open access article distributed under the terms and conditions of the Creative Commons Attribution (CC BY) license (https://creativecommons.org/licenses/by/4.0/).

1. Introduction

The global demand for oil will rise by more than 40% by 2025. About 70% of the world's total oil reserves are made up of heavy oil, extra heavy oil, and bituminous heavy oil, all of which have geological reserves that are significantly bigger than those of regular crude oil [1]. China has reserves of more than 4 billion tons in more than 70 heavy oil fields. The majority of these heavy oil reservoirs are located in the Liaohe, Huanxiling, Xinjiang Karamay, and Shengli Oilfields. Conventional heavy oil is rich in compounds with high boiling points and viscosities, resulting in the poor fluidity of heavy oil, which poses great difficulties for heavy oil exploitation [2]. Common heavy oil viscosity reduction methods include thermal viscosity reduction, chemical viscosity reduction, microbial viscosity reduction, and dilute viscosity reduction. Among the various thermal viscosity reduction methods, steam stimulation (CSS), steam flooding (SF), steam-assisted gravity drainage (SAGD), and steam-injection-based combustion of oil layers are the primary techniques [3], but these technologies lead to high energy consumption and have a high environmental impact. Chemical viscosity reduction mainly includes emulsion dispersion viscosity reduction, oil-soluble viscosity reducer viscosity reduction, etc. [4,5], which are highly selective but costly and complicated to operate. Microbial viscosity reduction technology is environmentally friendly and low cost, but the treatment time is long; dilution viscosity reduction technology is simple and the effect is immediate, but it is energy-dependent and may lead to the degradation in oil quality.

Catalytic modification and viscosity reduction is a typical combination of thermal viscosity reduction and chemical viscosity reduction, a heavy oil modification and viscosity reduction technology. By injecting the catalyst into a heavy oil reservoir, the combined effect of high temperature and the catalyst removes the impurities in the heavy oil and cracks the heavy constituents into light constituents, which reduces the apparent viscosity of the heavy oil [6,7]. In addition, the structure of gums and asphaltenes contains many functional groups that can form hydrogen bonds, and the hydrothermal cracking reaction causes a hydrogenation reaction, cracking reaction, and ring-opening reaction [8,9]. When the catalyst and hydrogen donor ethanol are added, the metal ions fully act on the S atoms to catalyze the acid polymerization and hydrogas shift reactions, resulting in the formation of free radicals by breaking the C-S bonds. In order to improve the recovery rate of heavy oil, the majority of research efforts have been directed towards developing crude oil fluidity improvers [10–13] and heavy oil aquathermolysis catalysts [14,15]. Currently, transition metal catalysts are mainly categorized into water-soluble catalysts and oil-soluble catalysts [16]. Water-soluble catalysts are some of the commonly used chemicals in the petroleum industry. Maity et al. [17] used the metals Ru and Fe as catalysts in asphaltene reforming experiments with desulfurization effects of 21% and 18%, respectively. The results showed that the first-row transition metals and AL^{3+} ions have high catalytic activity for thiophene and tetrahydrothiophene, and these metals convert large molecules into small molecules by breaking the C-S bond. Zhong et al. [18] studied the changes in viscosity and average molecular weight of heavy oil in the presence of eight metal ions, such as Fe^{2+}, Co^{2+}, Ni^{2+}, and so on, and the results showed that the metal ions all have certain viscosity-reducing effects on heavy oil. Clark et al. [19,20] investigated the application of several catalysts in hydrothermal cracking reactions, pointing out that transition metal salts can break C-S bonds in heavy oil components, accelerate the removal of organic sulfur in heavy oil, and generate light hydrocarbons, CO_2, H_2, and H_2S, resulting in an irreversible decrease in the viscosity of heavy oil. Subsequently, a large number of applied studies have been carried out at home and abroad [21,22]. Among them, Chen et al. synthesized a series of catalysts with transition metal ions as the center, and these catalysts had a good catalytic viscosity reduction effect. Oil-soluble catalysts can more fully contact with the oil phase, but the implementation conditions of this technology are harsh, and the extraction cost is high. Zhao et al. [23] succeeded in reducing the viscosity of Liaohe thick oil by more than 90% using nickel- and cobalt-based catalysts as well as petroleum sulfonates as emulsifiers at a lower temperature of 180 °C. Muneer et al. [24] used oil-soluble transition-metal catalysts (Fe, Co, Ni) to catalyze hydrothermal decomposition of heavy oil during steam injection. The catalytic performance of these catalysts is good at 300 °C, and they can be used to improve the quality of thick oil and reduce the viscosity of thick oil, among which Ni has the best catalytic performance.

As shown in the oil production profile in Figure 1, heavy oil has the most contact with minerals in the reservoir [25,26]. Minerals have great potential to participate in chemical reactions during the injection of high-temperature steam into the reservoir. So far, there has been no research on the aquathermolysis reaction that is catalyzed by foreign catalysts and in situ minerals. In this work, we explored the possibility of heavy oil aquathermolysis synergistically catalyzed through the application of exogenous catalysts in conjunction with in situ minerals. The synergistic catalytic effect of different reservoir minerals and exogenous catalysts and the effect of the addition of ethanol on aquathermolysis were studied under optimum reaction conditions. The compositional changes in the heavy oil before and after the reaction were characterized using elemental analysis, DSC, and TGA.

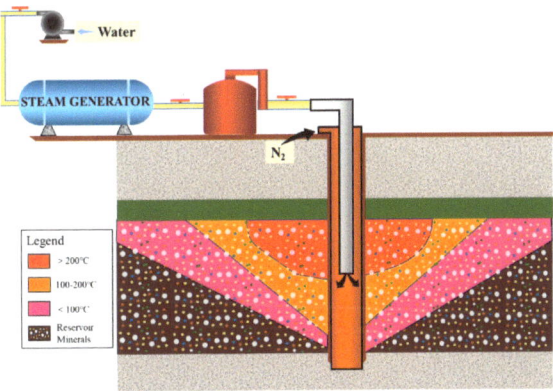

Figure 1. Schematic diagram of oil field recovery.

2. Materials and Methods

2.1. Materials

Commercially available chemical reagents of analytical grade were utilized in this experiment without undergoing additional purification processes prior to their usage. The reservoir minerals used in the experiment were all uniformly pulverized powders, which could be used directly. The crude oil samples utilized in this study were sourced from the Nanyang Oilfield in Henan, China. Oil sample properties are shown in Table 1.

Table 1. The physical parameters of heavy oil.

Pour Point/°C	Asphaltene, %	Saturated HC, %	Aromatic HC, %	Resin, %
20.0	23.44	31.16	28.73	16.67

2.2. Synthesis of the Catalyst

A certain mass of catechol was dissolved in ethanol, and an iron chloride aqueous solution was prepared according to the molar ratio of iron chloride to catechol of 1:2. The iron chloride aqueous solution was slowly dropped into catechol ethanol solution, mixed evenly, stirred at 70 °C for 4 h, and dried to obtain a catechol iron (C−Fe) catalyst. The preparation of C−Fe is shown in Figure 2.

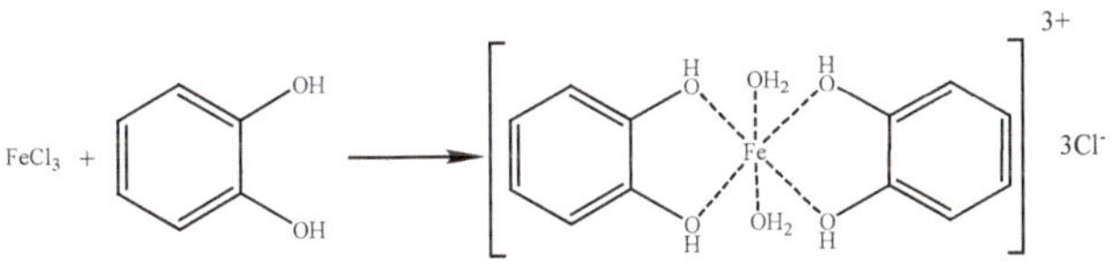

Figure 2. Catalyst synthesis and structures.

2.3. Characterization of the Complex

A Fourier transform infrared spectrometer, was used with the pressed-disk technique, and the spectral range of the measurement process was 400−4000 cm^{-1}.

2.4. Aquathermolysis of Heavy Oil

In a high-temperature and high–pressure reactor, the oil sample was combined with certain amounts of water, reservoir minerals, exogenous catalysts, and hydrogen donor. The reaction took place at 200 °C for 4 h, and the working pressure was 0.2−0.3 mpa.

2.5. Product Evaluation

The viscosity of heavy oils was measured in accordance with ASTM D97-96. The viscosity reduction rate, denoted as $\Delta\eta\%$, was determined using the formula $((\eta_0 - \eta)/\eta_0) \times 100$, where η_0 and η (mPa·s) represent the viscosities of the oil prior to and subsequent to the reaction [27,28]. Furthermore, the analysis of heavy oil components was carried out in accordance with the China Petroleum Industry Standard SY/T 5119-2016. An elementar vario EL cube was used to determine the elemental compositions (C, H, N, and S) of the original oil and the improved oil. The distribution of carbon in crude oil at various temperatures was assessed via thermogravimetric analysis. Under a nitrogenous environment, the oil samples were heated at a rate of 10 °C/min from 30 °C to 550 °C. According to SY/T 0545−2012, the wax precipitation point of the heavy oil was tested. Using Mettler−Toledo DSC822e DSC (Mettler Toledo Limited, Shanghai, China) equipment, the different scanning calorimetry (DSC) analyses of heavy oil were all performed within a temperature range of −25 to 50 °C, a flow rate of 50 mL/min, and a nitrogen environment.

3. Results and Discussion

3.1. Characterization of the Catalyst

Figure 3 displays the infrared spectra of the catalyst and ligand. The absorption peaks of the ligand at 1616 cm^{-1}, 1517 cm^{-1}, and 1469 cm^{-1} are the absorption peaks of the benzene ring. The corresponding absorption peaks at 1616 cm^{-1}, 1483 cm^{-1}, and 1430 cm^{-1} in the catalyst are also the absorption peaks of the benzene ring. The stretching vibration peak of −OH in the ligand catechol is around 3457 cm^{-1}, and the peak is strong and sharp. After the association with the iron ion is completed, where the stretching vibration peak position of the hydroxyl group is at 3222 cm^{-1}, and the peak width is strong, the infrared absorption position shifts. It shows that the −OH of the ligand coordinated with metal ions, and the ligand formed a stable complex.

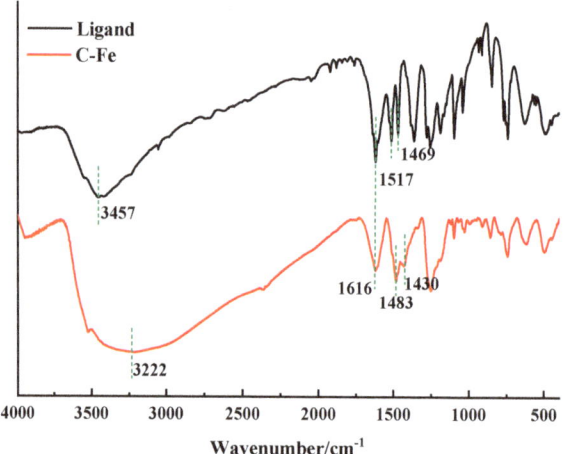

Figure 3. Infrared spectra of the ligand catechol and the C−Fe complex.

3.2. Effect of Reaction Temperature on Aquathermolysis

We aimed to investigate the viscosity–temperature properties of the oil samples after a hydrothermal cracking reaction at different reaction temperatures. As shown in Figure 4, the oil samples already had a good viscosity reduction effect at low temperature, and the higher the temperature, the better the viscosity reduction effect. The viscosity reduction rate of the oil samples reached its maximum at 200 °C. Due to the increase in temperature, the energy given to the system became larger, which caused the chemical bonds of the recombinant components in the oil samples to break, resulting in a viscosity decrease.

When the temperature was too high, the hydrothermal cracking reaction polymerization reaction dominated, and coking occurred at the bottom of the reactor. Therefore, 200 °C was selected as the optimum reaction temperature.

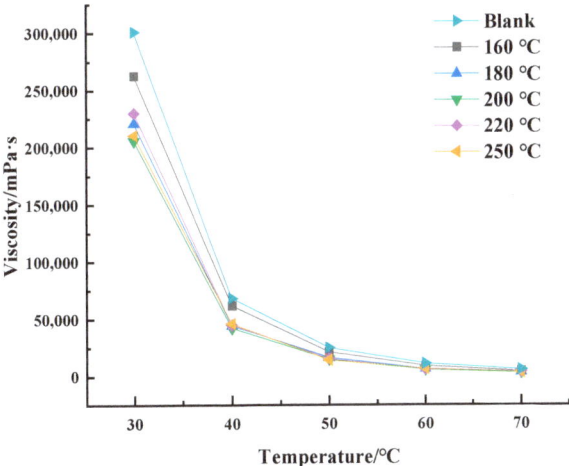

Figure 4. Effect of different reaction temperatures on the viscosity of oil samples.

3.3. Effect of Reaction Time on Aquathermolysis

After determining the reaction temperature at which the oil samples were subjected to a hydrothermal cracking reaction, we continued to examine the effect of different reaction times on the viscosity–temperature properties of the oil samples after hydrothermal cracking. As shown in Figure 5, the viscosity of the oil samples decreased with increasing reaction time, and the hydrothermal cracking reaction had the best viscosity-reducing effect on the oil samples when it reached 4 h. The viscosity of the oil samples gradually recovered as the reaction time increased, which indicated that the hydrothermal cracking reaction was essentially completed at 4 h. Therefore, the reaction duration was determined to be 4 h.

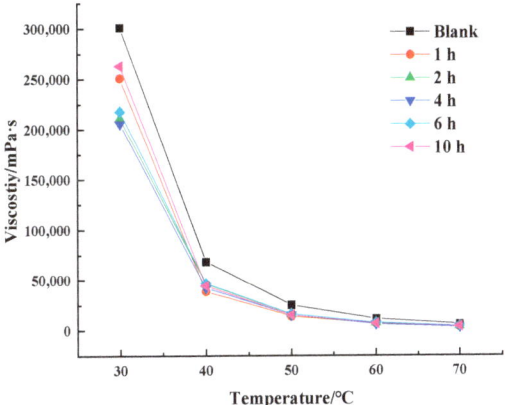

Figure 5. Effect of different reaction times on the viscosity of oil samples.

3.4. Effect of Water

Figure 6 clearly illustrates the substantial impact of the water-to-oil mass ratio on viscosity. The viscosity of heavy oil falls dramatically with an increase in the water to oil mass ratio when the water-to-oil ratio is between 0 and 0.3. For water-to-oil ratios between

0.3 and 0.5, the viscosity of heavy oil shows a positive correlation with the corresponding water-to-oil mass ratio. This phenomenon can be attributed to the occurrence of the reaction of a water–gas shift (WGSR) [29] between the heavy oil and water. This is due to the fact that in the hydrothermal cracking reaction, the main role of water is to give the active hydrogen needed for the reaction system, and as the amount of water is increased, the amount of active hydrogen that can be provided by water increases, resulting in the hydrothermal cracking reaction being carried out more thoroughly and inhibiting the polymerization of free radicals. When the amount of water is too large, it plays a certain role in diluting the free radicals produced in the reaction process, resulting in an increase in the viscosity of the oil samples. Simultaneously, considering the dilution of catalyst in subsequent catalytic reactions due to the increase in the water amount [30], the subsequent experiments adopted a water-to-oil mass ratio of 0.3 as the reaction condition.

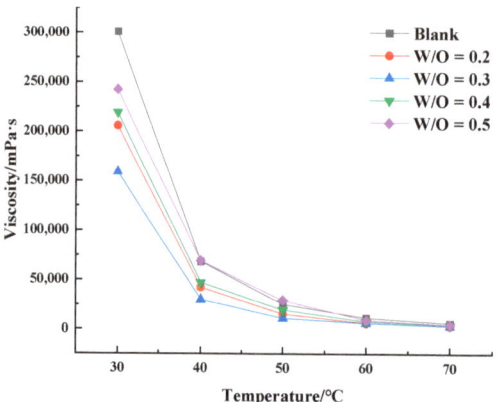

Figure 6. Effects of different water additions on aquathermolysis.

3.5. Effect of Reservoir Minerals on Aquathermolysis

Six minerals were selected to carry out the aquathermolysis reaction under the reaction conditions determined above. As evidenced by the analysis in Figure 7, clay minerals typically have a distinct catalytic reduction effect. Strong adsorption, cation exchange capacity (CEC), and strong acid centers of the clay may be responsible for this phenomenon. The viscosity comparison performed at 30 °C demonstrated that sodium montmorillonite exhibited the most significant reduction in viscosity, reaching up to 41.53%. This was followed by kaolin, showing a viscosity reduction rate of 40.10%, and ferrous sulfide, with a viscosity reduction rate of 40.00%. The findings indicate that minerals exhibit a notable influence on aquathermolysis.

3.6. The Effect of Hydrogen Donors on the Aquathermolysis of Heavy Oil

The type of alcohol has a non-negligible effect on the hydrothermal cracking of heavy oil. Different types of hydrogen donors all contributed to viscosity reduction, as shown in the analysis in Figure 8. Among them, isopropanol had the best hydrocracking impact in heavy oil, but its viscosity reduction effect under the dilution effect was less than ideal. Currently, isopropanol is commercially available at USD 1030 per ton and ethanol at USD 895 per ton, which is significantly costlier than ethanol. Therefore, in subsequent experiments, ethanol was selected as the hydrogen donor to reduce the viscosity. As the ethanol-to-oil ratio increased, Figure 9 shows that the viscosity of heavy oil significantly decreased. The subsequent studies used an ethanol-to-oil mass ratio of 0.3 as the reaction condition due to the dilution impact of the catalyst in the subsequent catalytic reaction caused by the rise in ethanol concentration.

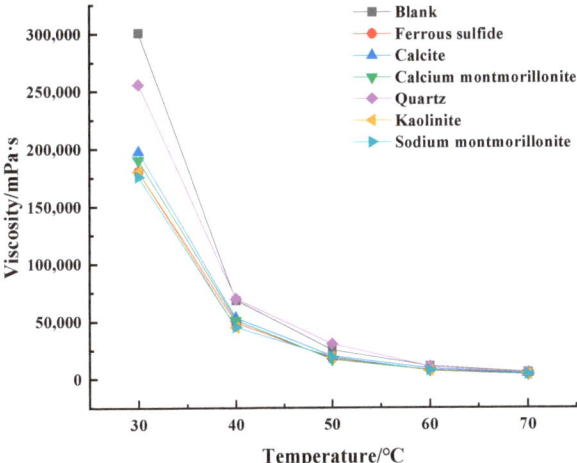

Figure 7. Influence of aquathermolysis of heavy oil with different minerals.

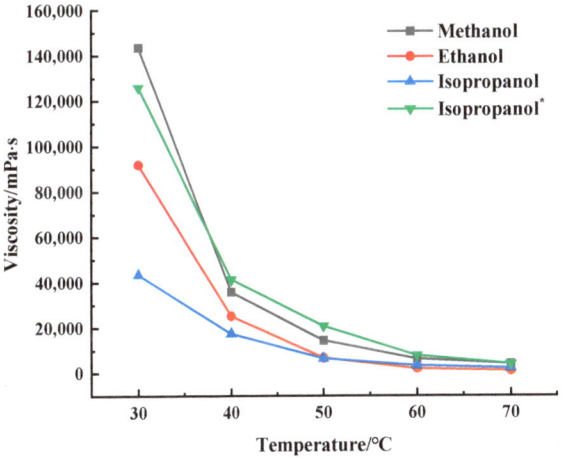

Figure 8. Influence of hydrogen donor on aquathermolysis reaction of heavy oil (isopropanol-hydrogen donor; isopropanol *—A diluent solvent at room temperature).

3.7. Analysis of the Viscosity of Heavy Oil Catalyzed by Various Catalysts

Figure 10 indicates that in the synergistic catalysis of minerals and C-Fe, the synergistic viscosity reduction effect of C-Fe and sodium montmorillonite was the best. The viscosity was reduced by 60.47% at 30 °C in comparison with the blank oil sample. Compared with the viscosity after aquathermolysis, the viscosity decreased by 42.23%. Therefore, the reaction system of sodium montmorillonite and C-Fe was selected for the subsequent experiment.

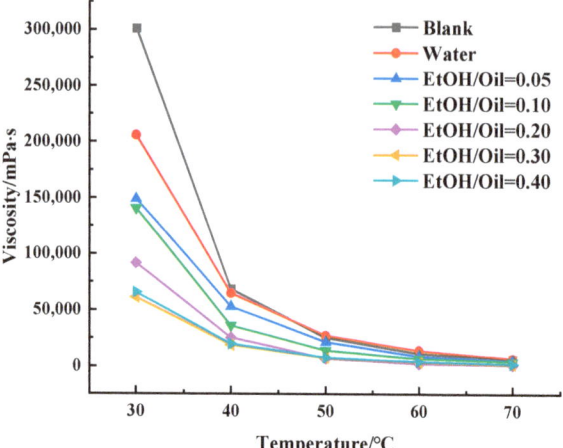

Figure 9. Effect of ethanol dosage on the aquathermolysis.

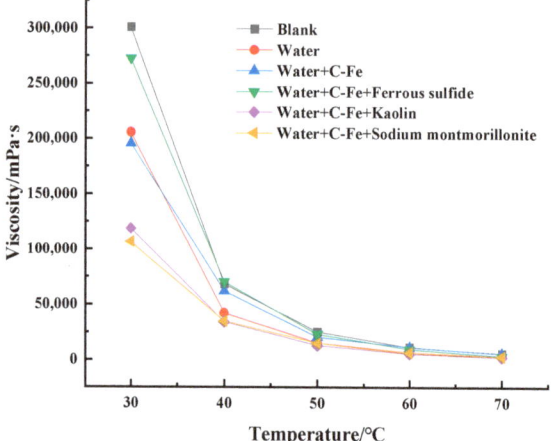

Figure 10. Influence of synergistic catalysis between reservoir minerals and catalyst on heavy oil viscosity.

Figure 11 shows that the catalytic aquathermolysis reaction between heavy oil and water exhibited a certain viscosity reduction rate of up to 31.56%. Compared with the oil–water reaction, the addition of water and C-Fe to the heavy oil resulted in an increase of 3.32% in the viscosity reduction rate. After adding water and sodium montmorillonite to the oil, the viscosity reduction rate was increased by 9.97% compared with that of the oil–water reaction. Although the catalytic impact of the two together was not immediately apparent, it had a certain viscosity reduction catalytic effect on the aquathermolysis of the heavy oil. After adding water, C-Fe, and sodium montmorillonite to the heavy oil, the viscosity reduction rate was 18.94% higher than that of the oil–water sodium montmorillonite, indicating that the exogenous catalyst and clay have a synergistic catalytic effect on the aquathermolysis of heavy oil. The viscosity reduction rate of the heavy oil after the addition of water, C-Fe, sodium montmorillonite, and ethanol was 14.78% greater than that after the addition of oil–water, C-Fe, and sodium montmorillonite, demonstrating that ethanol has a superior hydrogen supply impact during the catalytic aquathermolysis of heavy oil.

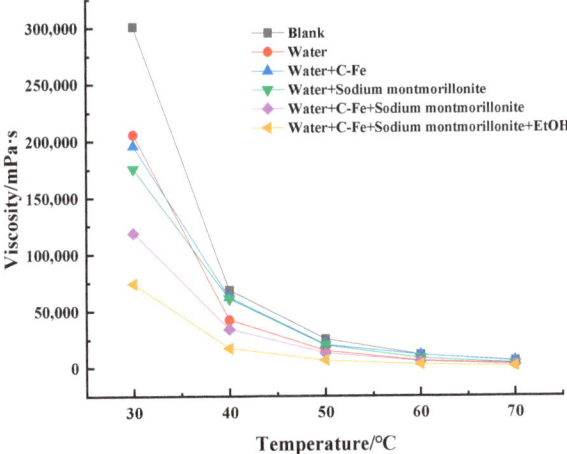

Figure 11. Performance of oil samples in reducing viscosity under various reaction circumstances.

3.8. Determination of SARA before and after Reaction

The results in Table 2 show that when the hydrothermal cracking reaction was completed, the saturated and aromatic hydrocarbon fractions contained in the oil samples increased, and the asphaltene and colloidal fractions decreased, which also indicates that most of the large molecules in the recombined fractions of the oil samples underwent ring-opening and hydrogenation reactions. The addition of the composite catalyst promoted the conversion of the recombined components in the oil samples, consumed more free radicals, reduced the occurrence of copolymerization reactions, and increased the content of light components, thus improving the viscosity reduction efficiency.

Table 2. Oil sample SARA analysis before and after the reaction.

Oil Sample	Saturates, %	Aromatics, %	Asphaltenes, %	Resins, %
Blank	23.44	31.16	28.73	16.67
After reaction with C-Fe and sodium montmorillonite	30.28	36.20	25.98	7.54
After reaction with C-Fe and sodium montmorillonite and EtOH	33.15	37.74	23.19	5.92

3.9. Elemental Analysis (EA)

An analysis was conducted on the variation in the element content in the heavy oil before and after the aquathermolysis reaction. Table 3 presents the results of this study. The findings demonstrate that the concentrations of carbon, nitrogen, and sulfur reduced during pure aquathermolysis, while the amounts of hydrogen marginally rose. This suggests that water contributes hydrogen to the heavy oil aquathermolysis process, increasing the saturation of macromolecules in heavy oil. The synergistic effect of sodium montmorillonite and the catalyst leads to the increase in hydrogen content, the decrease in sulfur content, and the increase in H/C ratio. The data obtained affirms the synergistic effect of sodium clay and the catalyst on the hydrogenation process of unsaturated carbon in heavy oil. After the addition of ethanol, the elemental analysis revealed a higher hydrogen content and increased nitrogen, sulfur, and H/C ratio. It showed that ethanol has a stronger ability to provide protons for the reaction, promoting the generation of small molecules and the breaking of C-N, C-S, and other bonds in the oil samples to produce more heteroatomic compounds. More importantly, it can also promote the conversion of more asphaltenes, gums, and other recombinant components into light components, thus improving the oil quality.

Table 3. Oil sample elemental content before and after the reaction.

Oil Sample	Elemental Content/%				C/H
	C	H	N	S	
Blank	86.20	10.02	1.88	0.65	0.116
After the aquathermolysis	85.90	10.04	1.41	0.56	0.116
After reaction with C-Fe and sodium montmorillonite	86.19	10.10	1.58	0.44	0.117
After reaction with C-Fe and sodium montmorillonite and EtOH	83.99	10.29	1.30	0.44	0.122

3.10. Thermogravimetric Analysis (TGA)

Figure 12 shows the TGA curves, while Table 4 presents the corresponding mass loss of the heavy oil before and after the reaction. After aquathermolysis catalyzed by sodium clay and a catalyst, it was observed that the weight loss rate of the oil with a boiling point less than 150 °C and more than 450 °C decreased, while the weight loss rate of the oil with a boiling point between 350 and 450 °C increased. The weight loss rate of light oil with a boiling point less than 150 °C increased after the aquathermolysis was catalyzed by sodium montmorillonite, catalyst, and an ethanol promoter. In addition, at a temperature above 350 °C, a significant reduction in mass loss was observed [31,32], which confirms that the addition of a composite catalyst promotes the conversion of asphaltenes, resins, and other heavy components to light components during the reaction process, leading to the increase in the light component content of oil samples, and then the viscosity of oil samples decreases.

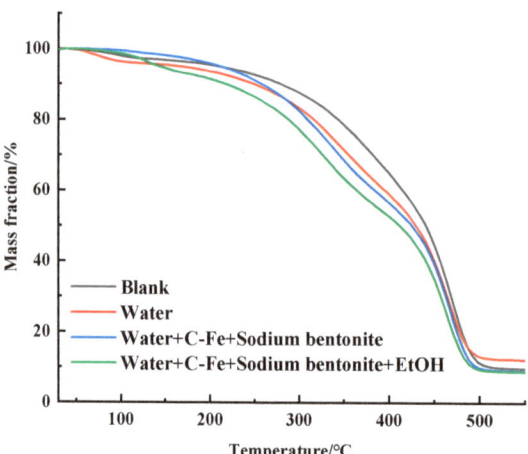

Figure 12. The TGA curves of the heavy oil before and after aquathermolysis.

Table 4. Weight loss rate of oil samples after different reaction systems.

Reaction System	Weight Loss Ratio/%			
	0–150 °C	150–350 °C	350–450 °C	>450 °C
Blank	3.10	18.36	34.82	43.72
Water	4.42	24.05	31.90	39.63
Water + C-Fe + sodium montmorillonite	1.83	29.35	29.77	39.05
Water + C-Fe + sodium montmorillonite + EtOH	5.33	30.82	28.94	34.91

3.11. Differential Scanning Calorimetry Analysis (DSC)

Figure 13 illustrates the findings from a DSC study of the wax formation process of crude oil under various reaction conditions. Compared with the blank oil sample, the wax precipitation point after aquathermolysis increased from 43.00 °C to 43.07 °C. After the synergistic catalytic cracking of C-Fe and sodium montmorillonite, the wax precipitation point of the oil sample increased from 43.00 °C to 43.71 °C, and the wax precipitation point increased to 45.07 °C after the addition of ethanol. The aforementioned study shows that resins in the heavy oil are broken down and transformed into asphaltenes, which serve as the primary nucleus of the wax precipitation and hasten the formation of wax crystals, raising the wax precipitation point.

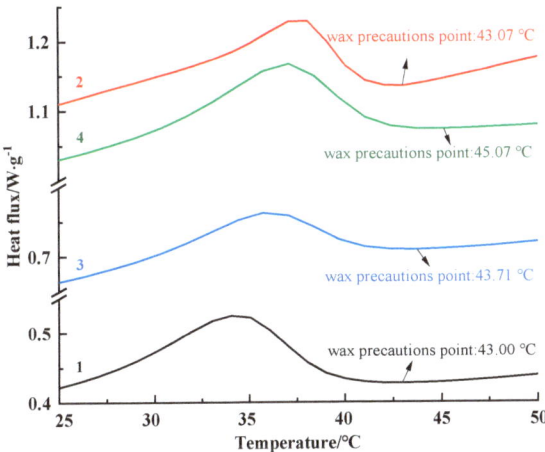

Figure 13. The DSC curves of the heavy oil before and after aquathermolysis. (1—blank; 2—water; 3—water + C-Fe + sodium montmorillonite; 4—water + C-Fe + sodium montmorillonite + ethanol).

3.12. Mechanism

Due to the layered structure of clay, there are numerous cations in its octahedral voids and numerous broken bonds on the surface of clay minerals, which have strong adsorption effects on organic macromolecules. The synergistic dual catalytic mechanism of exogenous catalysts and clay minerals is shown in Figures 14 and 15, which can be mainly described in the following stages: (1) The exogenous catalyst acts on the heteroatoms in the heavy components, destroying the hydrogen bonds between the molecules of some high-carbon hydrocarbon compounds, which results in the rupture of C-S, C=O, C-N bonds, etc. (2) The transition metal in the exogenous catalyst is easily exchanged with the sodium ion in the sodium montmorillonite, thus becoming the active center in the reaction. The presence of abundant vacant orbitals enables transition metals to readily engage with the electron-rich species present in heavy oil, thereby significantly enhancing the catalytic efficiency of the aquathermolysis decomposition in heavy oil [33,34]. (3) Due to the existence of Lewis acid on the surface of montmorillonite, high-carbon hydrocarbon compounds provide it with an electron, and simultaneously generate free radicals. The free radicals rearrange to promote the cleavage of C-C bonds and the formation of short-chain alkanes [35]. Clay minerals act as Brønsted acids to provide protons (H^+) for the organic matter adsorbed by it. Protons (H^+) are generated through the dissociation of the adsorbed water and interlayer water molecules that are bound to exchangeable cations. The primary reaction pathway for these protons involves the formation of transition-state carbocations [36,37]. (4) Upon the adsorption of water molecules onto the surface of clay minerals, the Lewis acid exhibits a high electron affinity, facilitating the sharing of an electron pair with the hydroxyl group in water. Consequently, the hydroxyl group becomes firmly adsorbed onto the surface of the Lewis acid, while the remaining H⁺ is readily released. This converts the Lewis acid into a Bronsted acid. When clay minerals are dehydrated, Bronsted acid sites are gradually converted into Lewis acids due to the lack of protons [38]. In this reaction system, montmorillonite activates the reactant water/steam, reduces the reaction activation energy, accelerates the breaking speed of some hydrogen bonds between the molecules of high-carbon hydrocarbon compounds, and improves the effectiveness of reducing the viscosity of heavy oil.

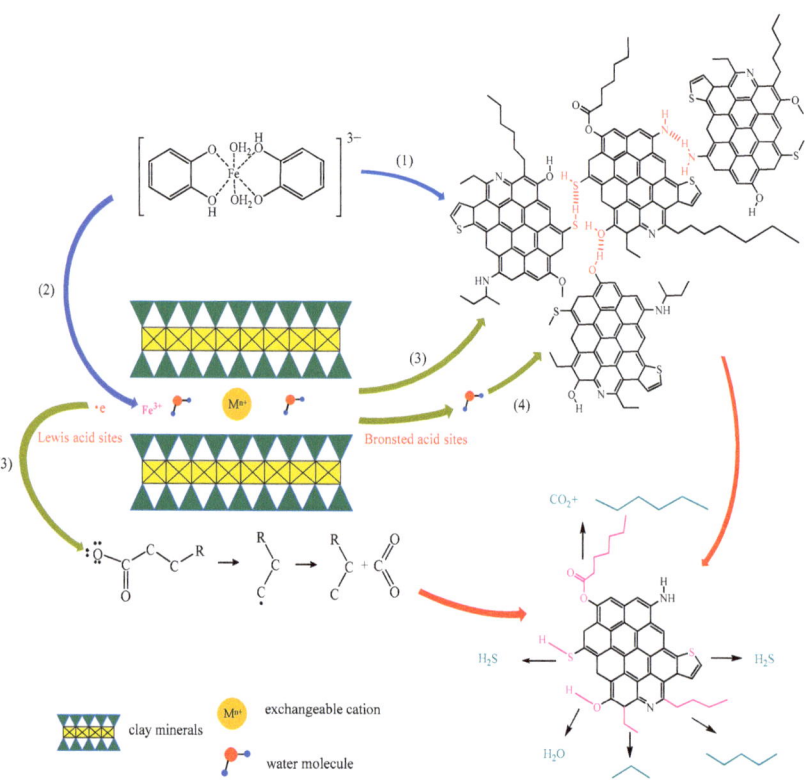

Figure 14. Synergistic catalysis mechanism of exogenous catalysts and clay minerals.

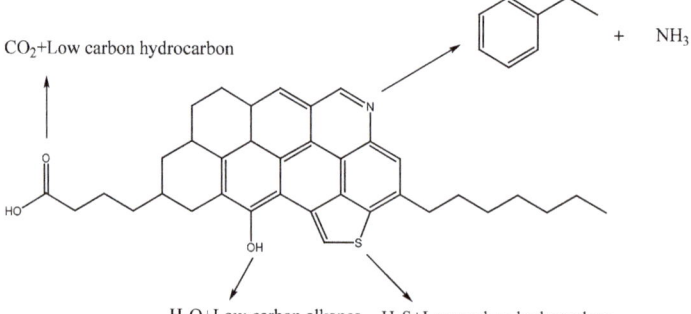

Figure 15. Chemical changes occurring in the hydrothermal cracking of heavy oil.

4. Summary and Conclusions

In conclusion, reaction time, oil-to-water ratio, and mineral type all affect the viscosity reduction effect of heavy oil–water thermal cracking. In addition, the addition of external catalysts and hydrogen donors can enhance the catalytic effect in reducing viscosity. Under optimized conditions, the viscosity reduction rates of oil–water, oil–water+ sodium montmorillonite, oil–water+ sodium montmorillonite +C-Fe, and oil–water+ sodium montmorillonite + C-Fe + ethanol oil samples reached 31.56%, 41.53%, 60.47%, and 75.25%, indicating that exogenous catalysts and in situ clay have a synergistic catalytic effect on the aquathermolysis of heavy oil. After the catalytic aquathermolysis of heavy oil, the thermogravimetric analysis showed that the light components increased, and the oil–water + sodium montmorillonite + C-Fe oil samples changed significantly. DSC showed that with the wax precipitation point of crude oil, the wax peaks all shifted to the right, and the wax content increased. Under the synergistic catalytic aquathermolysis of heavy oil with exogenous catalyst and minerals, it is helpful to break the C-C, C-N, and C-S bonds. The addition of a hydrogen donor further improves the viscosity reduction effect. This work will benefit related research on oilfield exploration.

Author Contributions: Y.Z.: data curation, investigation, and writing—original draft; H.L.: validation, conceptualization, supervision; D.C.: data curation, investigation, formal analysis; S.Z.: investigation, methodology, data curation; S.L.: project administration, funding acquisition; G.C.: writing—review and editing, validation, and supervision. All authors have read and agreed to the published version of the manuscript.

Funding: This research was funded by National Science Foundation of China (program No. 50874092) and Scientific Research Program Funded by Shaanxi Povincial Education Department (program No. 22JY052).

Data Availability Statement: Not applicable.

Acknowledgments: The authors also thank the support of The Youth Innovation Team of Shaanxi University and the work of Modern Analysis and Testing Center of Xi'an Shiyou University.

Conflicts of Interest: The authors declare no conflict of interest.

References

1. Shaban, S.; Dessouky, S.; Badawi, A.E.F.; El Sabagh, A.; Zahran, A.; Mousa, M. Upgrading and viscosity reduction of Heavy oil by catalyst ionic liquid. *Energy Fuel* **2014**, *28*, 6545–6553. [CrossRef]
2. Li, Y.; Li, Q.; Wang, X.; Yu, L.; Yang, J. Aquathermolysis of heavy crude oil with ferric oleate catalyst. *Pet. Sci.* **2018**, *15*, 613–624. [CrossRef]
3. Pang, Z.; Wang, Q.; Tian, C.; Chen, J. Study on Hydrothermal Cracking of Heavy Oil under the Coexisting Conditions of Supercritical Water and Non-condensate Gas. *ACS Omega* **2023**, *8*, 18029–18040. [CrossRef]
4. Guo, K.; Li, H.; Yu, Z. In-situ heavy and extra-heavy oil recovery: A review. *Fuel* **2016**, *185*, 886–902. [CrossRef]
5. Muraza, O.; Galadima, A. Aquathermolysis of heavy oil: A review and perspective on catalyst development. *Fuel* **2015**, *157*, 219–231. [CrossRef]
6. Vakhin, A.V.; Khelkhal, M.A.; Mukhamatdinov, I.I.; Mukhamatdinova, R.E.; Tajik, A.; Slavkina, O.V.; Malaniy, S.Y.; Gafurov, M.R.; Nasybullin, A.R.; Morozov, O.G. Changes in Heavy Oil Saturates and Aromatics in the Presence of Microwave Radiation and Iron-Based Nanoparticles. *Catalysts* **2022**, *12*, 514. [CrossRef]
7. Huang, S.; Cao, M.; Huang, Q.; Liu, B.; Jiang, J. Study on reaction equations of heavy oil aquathermolysis with superheated steam. *Int. J. Environ. Sci. Technol.* **2019**, *16*, 5023–5032. [CrossRef]
8. Ushakova, A.; Zatsepin, V.; Khelkhal, M.; Sitnov, S.; Vakhin, A. In Situ Combustion of Heavy, Medium, and Light Crude Oils: Low-Temperature Oxidation in Terms of a Chain Reaction Approach. *Energy Fuels* **2022**, *36*, 7710–7721. [CrossRef]
9. Demirbas, A.; Bafail, A.; Nizami, A.S. Heavy oil upgrading: Unlocking the future fuel supply. *Pet. Sci. Technol.* **2016**, *34*, 303–308. [CrossRef]
10. Hou, J.; Li, C.; Gao, H.; Chen, M.; Huang, W.; Chen, Y.; Zhou, C. Recyclable oleic acid modified magnetic $NiFe_2O_4$ nanoparticles for catalytic aquathermolysis of Liaohe heavy oil. *Fuel* **2017**, *200*, 193–198. [CrossRef]
11. Chang, J.; Fujimoto, K.; Tsubaki, N. Effect of Initiative Additives on Hydro-Thermal Cracking of Heavy Oils and Model Compound. *Energy Fuels* **2003**, *17*, 457–461. [CrossRef]
12. Chen, G.; Yuan, W.; Yan, J.; Meng, M.; Guo, Z.; Gu, X.; Zhang, J.; Qu, C.; Song, H.; Jeje, A. Zn(II) Complex Catalyzed Coupling Aquathermolysis of Water-Heavy Oil-Methanol at Low Temperature. *Pet. Chem.* **2018**, *58*, 197–202. [CrossRef]

13. Chen, G.; Yan, J.; Bai, Y.; Gu, X.; Zhang, J.; Li, Y.; Jeje, A. Clean aquathermolysis of heavy oil catalyzed by Fe(III) complex at relatively low temperature. *Pet. Sci. Technol.* **2017**, *35*, 113–119. [CrossRef]
14. Mukhamed'yarova, A.N.; Gareev, B.I.; Nurgaliev, D.K.; Aliev, F.A.; Vakhin, A.V. A Review on the Role of Amorphous Aluminum Compounds in Catalysis: Avenues of Investigation and Potential Application in Petrochemistry and Oil Refining. *Processes* **2021**, *9*, 1811. [CrossRef]
15. Clark, P.; Dowling, N.; Hyne, J.; Lesage, K. The chemistry of organosulphur compound types occurring in heavy oils: 4. the high-temperature reaction of thiophene and tetrahydrothiophene with aqueous solutions of aluminium and first-row transition-metal cations. *Fuel* **1987**, *66*, 1353–1357. [CrossRef]
16. Ma, L.; Zhang, S.; Zhang, X.; Dong, S.; Yu, T.; Slaný, M.; Chen, G. Enhanced aquathermolysis of Heavy oil catalysed by bentonite supported Fe (III) complex in the present of ethanol. *J. Chem. Technol. Biotechnol.* **2022**, *97*, 1128–1137. [CrossRef]
17. Maity, S.K.; Ancheyta, J.; Marroquín, G. Catalytic Aquathermolysis Used for Viscosity Reduction of Heavy Crude Oils: A Review. *Energy Fuels* **2010**, *24*, 2809–2816. [CrossRef]
18. Zhong, L.; Liu, Y.; Fan, H.; Jiang, S.J. Liaohe Extra-Heavy Crude Oil Underground Aquathermolytic Treatments Using Catalyst and Hydrogen Donors under Steam Injection Conditions. In Proceedings of the SPE International Improved Oil Recovery Conference in Asia Pacific, Kuala Lumpur, Malaysia, 8–9 October 2003. [CrossRef]
19. Clark, P.; Hyne, J. Chemistry of organosulphur compound types occurring in heavy oil sands: 3. Reaction of thiophene and tetrahydrothiophene with vanadyl and nickel salts. *Fuel* **1984**, *63*, 1649–1654. [CrossRef]
20. Chen, G.; Yuan, W.; Wu, Y.; Zhang, J.; Song, H.; Jeje, A.; Song, S.; Qu, C. Catalytic aquathermolysis of heavy oil by coordination complex at relatively low temperature. *Pet. Chem.* **2017**, *57*, 881–884. [CrossRef]
21. Zhao, F.; Liu, Y.; Lu, N.; Xu, T.; Zhu, G.; Wang, K. A review on upgrading and viscosity reduction of heavy oil and bitumen by underground catalytic cracking. *Energy Rep.* **2021**, *7*, 4249–4272. [CrossRef]
22. Al-Muntaser, A.A.; Varfolomeev, M.A.; Suwaid, M.A.; Saleh, M.M.; Djimasbe, R.; Yuan, C.; Zairov, R.R.; Ancheyta, J. Effect of decalin as hydrogen-donor for in-situ upgrading of Heavy crude oil in presence of nickel-based catalyst. *Fuel* **2022**, *313*, 122652. [CrossRef]
23. Zhao, F.; Liu, Y.; Fu, Z.; Zhao, X. Using hydrogen donor with oil-soluble catalysts for upgrading Heavy oil. *Russ. J. Appl. Chem.* **2014**, *87*, 1498–1506. [CrossRef]
24. Muneer, A.S.; Varfolomeev, M.A.; Al-muntaser, A.A.; Yuan, C.; Valentina, L.S.; Almaz, Z.; Farit, G.V.; Ilfat, Z.R.; Dmitrii, A.; Artem, E.C. In-situ catalytic upgrading of heavy oil using oil-soluble transition metal-based catalysts. *Fuel* **2020**, *282*, 118753. [CrossRef]
25. Zhao, F.; Wang, X.; Wang, Y.; Shi, Y. Study of catalytic aquathermolysis of heavy oil in the presence of a hydrogen donor. *J. Chem. Pharm. Res.* **2012**, *48*, 273–282. [CrossRef]
26. Zhou, Z.; Slaný, M.; Kuzielová, E.; Zhang, W.; Ma, L.; Dong, S.; Zhang, J.; Chen, G. Influence of reservoir minerals and ethanol on catalytic aquathermolysis of Heavy oil. *Fuel* **2022**, *307*, 121871. [CrossRef]
27. Kuzmić, A.E.; Radošević, M.; Bogdanić, G.; Srića, V.; Vuković, R. Studies on the influence of long chain acrylic esters polymers with polar monomers as crude oil flow improver additives. *Fuel* **2008**, *87*, 2943–2950. [CrossRef]
28. Hu, J.; Gan, J.; Li, J.; Luo, Y.; Wang, G.; Wu, L.; Gong, Y. Extraction of crude oil from petrochemical sludge: Characterization of products using thermogravimetric analysis. *Fuel* **2017**, *188*, 166–172. [CrossRef]
29. Ovalles, C.; Filgueiras, E.; Morales, A.; Scott, C.E.; Gonzalez-Gimenez, F.; Embaid, B.P. Use of a dispersed iron catalyst for upgrading extra-heavy crude oil using methane as source of hydrogen. *Fuel* **2003**, *82*, 887–892. [CrossRef]
30. Aliev, F.A.; Mukhamatdinov, I.I.; Sitnov, S.A.; Ziganshina, M.R.; Onishchenko, Y.V.; Sharifullin, A.V.; Vakhin, A.V. In-situ Heavy oil aquathermolysis in the presence of nanodispersed catalysts based on transition metals. *Processes* **2021**, *9*, 127. [CrossRef]
31. Cornejo, J.; Celis, R.; Pavlovic, I.; Ulibarri, M.A. Interactions of pesticides with clays and layered double hydroxides: A review. *Clay Miner.* **2008**, *43*, 155–175. [CrossRef]
32. Boulet, P.; Greenwell, H.C.; Stackhouse, S.; Coveney, P.V. Recent advances in understanding the structure and reactivity of clays using electronic structure calculations. *Theochem* **2005**, *762*, 33–48. [CrossRef]
33. Wu, L.M.; Zhou, C.H.; Keeling, J.; Tong, D.S.; Yu, W.H. Towards an understanding of the role of clay minerals in crude oil formation, migration and accumulation. *Earth. Sci. Rev.* **2012**, *115*, 373–386. [CrossRef]
34. Johns, W.D. Clay mineral catalysis and petroleum generation. *Annu. Rev. Earth. Planet. Sci.* **1979**, *7*, 183–198. [CrossRef]
35. Brown, D.R.; Rhodes, C.N. Bronsted and Lewis acid catalysis with ion-exchanged clays. *Catal. Lett.* **1997**, *45*, 35–40. [CrossRef]
36. Bruce, C.H. Smectite dehydration-its relation to structural development and hydrocarbon accumulation in Northern Gulf of Mexico Basin. *AAPG Bull.* **1984**, *68*, 673–683. [CrossRef]
37. Reddy, C.R.; Bhat, Y.S.; Nagendrappa, G.; Prakash, B.J. Bronsted and Lewis acidity of modified montmorillonite clay catalysts determined by FT-IR spectroscopy. *Catal. Today.* **2009**, *141*, 157–160. [CrossRef]
38. Yan, L.; Stucki, J.W. Effects of structural Fe oxidation state on the coupling of interlayer water and structural Si-O stretching vibrations in montmorillonite. *Langmuir* **1999**, *15*, 4648–4657. [CrossRef]

Disclaimer/Publisher's Note: The statements, opinions and data contained in all publications are solely those of the individual author(s) and contributor(s) and not of MDPI and/or the editor(s). MDPI and/or the editor(s) disclaim responsibility for any injury to people or property resulting from any ideas, methods, instructions or products referred to in the content.

Article

A Volume Fracturing Percolation Model for Tight Reservoir Vertical Wells

Dianfa Du [1,*], Peng Liu [1,2,*], Lichuan Ren [1,3], Yuan Li [1], Yujie Tang [1] and Fanghui Hao [1]

[1] National Key Laboratory of Deep Oil and Gas, School of Petroleum Engineering, China University of Petroleum (East China), Qingdao 266580, China; 13386424053@163.com (L.R.); liyuan9877@126.com (Y.L.); tyjxiaoshuaige@163.com (Y.T.); haocomet@163.com (F.H.)
[2] Oil Production Engineering Institute of Daqing Oilfield Limited Company, Daqing 163000, China
[3] Engineering and Technology Branch of CNOOC Energy Development Co., Tianjin 300452, China
* Correspondence: dudf@upc.edu.cn (D.D.); lpxiaoshuaige@163.com (P.L.)

Abstract: Based on the non-linear seepage characteristics of tight reservoirs and the reconstruction mode of vertical wells with actual volume fracturing, a seven-area percolation model for volume fracturing vertical wells in tight reservoirs is established. Laplace transform and Pedrosa transform are applied to obtain analytical solutions of bottom hole pressure and vertical well production under a constant production regime. After verifying the correctness of the model, the influence of the fracture network parameters on the pressure and production is studied. The research results indicate that as the permeability modulus increases, the production of volume fracturing vertical wells decreases. The penetration ratio of the main crack and the half-length of the main crack have a small impact on production, while the diversion capacity of the main crack has a significant impact on the initial production, but it is ultimately limited by the effective volume of the transformation. Under constant pressure conditions, the greater the width and permeability of the ESRV region, the higher the vertical well production rate is. The smaller the aspect ratio of the ESRV region, the higher the mid-term yield and the faster the yield decrease. The research results show guiding significance for the design of vertical well volume fracturing in tight reservoirs.

Keywords: volume fracturing vertical well; nonlinear seepage; Laplace transform; productivity

Citation: Du, D.; Liu, P.; Ren, L.; Li, Y.; Tang, Y.; Hao, F. A Volume Fracturing Percolation Model for Tight Reservoir Vertical Wells. *Processes* **2023**, *11*, 2575. https://doi.org/10.3390/pr11092575

Academic Editors: Dicho Stratiev, Dobromir Yordanov and Aijun Guo

Received: 3 August 2023
Revised: 16 August 2023
Accepted: 17 August 2023
Published: 28 August 2023

Copyright: © 2023 by the authors. Licensee MDPI, Basel, Switzerland. This article is an open access article distributed under the terms and conditions of the Creative Commons Attribution (CC BY) license (https://creativecommons.org/licenses/by/4.0/).

1. Introduction

The development potential of tight oil reservoirs is enormous. According to incomplete statistics, the geological reserves of tight oil resources in China are 7.4–8 billion tons, which is of great significance to the Chinese petroleum industry. Due to the low permeability and strong heterogeneity of tight reservoirs, the production of tight oil is relatively low [1–5]. Volume fracturing is the main technical means for the transformation and development of tight oil reservoirs [6–9]. Unlike conventional fracturing techniques, volume fracturing can crush the reservoir, creating a secondary fracture network near the main fracture that has been fractured, increasing the volume of the transformation, shortening the fluid migration distance in the area, reducing seepage resistance, and improving oil recovery [10–14].

At present, the research on analytical models for volume fracturing of horizontal wells in tight reservoirs is relatively in-depth, and the types of models are diverse [15–18]. Brown et al. [19] established a three-area composite model for fracturing horizontal wells, with reservoirs divided into three areas: main fracture area, reformed area (SRV), and unreformed area, and through analytical solutions, the pressure and productivity dynamics of conventional oil reservoir fracturing wells were studied. Brohi et al. [20] established a three-area composite model for unconventional gas reservoirs based on the Brown model by characterizing the modified area with dual pore media and the unmodified area with single pore media. In addition, Stalgorova et al. [21] established a five-area composite model for horizontal wells to describe the situation where the main fractures of volume fracturing were not fully modified, and analyzed the problems in the theoretical derivation and practical application of linear flow models. On the basis of previous research, Zeng et al. [22] established a seven-area composite model for volume fracturing of horizontal wells in tight oil reservoirs. This model considers the heterogeneity of geological parameters in different main fracture areas and the situation where longitudinal fractures do not penetrate the reservoir. At the same time, the wellbore pressure drop loss between different fracture sections was calculated, making the model closer to the actual situation of the mine. Unlike volume fracturing horizontal wells, the analytical model for volume fracturing vertical wells is mainly based on the "composite radial flow" model. Zhu et al. [23] established a three-area composite model for volume fracturing vertical wells in tight oil reservoirs, which is divided into three regions: the main fracture area, the elliptical modified area, and the unreformed area. The transformed area adopts a fractal medium model to characterize the fracture network, while the unreformed area takes into account the starting pressure gradient of the matrix. The model applies the equivalent seepage resistance method to obtain a steady-state production capacity solution. Zhu et al. [24] found that the reconstruction area of vertical wells with volume fracturing is closer to a rectangle according to the microseismic cloud map, applied the linear flow model of horizontal wells with volume fracturing to vertical wells, and established a five-area model of vertical wells with volume fracturing that considers the reservoir stress sensitivity and has a rectangular reconstruction volume. The regional division is consistent with the five-area model of horizontal wells with volume fracturing. Although scholars have conducted extensive research on the seepage law of volume fracturing, there is relatively little research on multi-stage volume fracturing in vertical wells [25–28]. Currently, most of the seepage models for tight oil reservoirs with volume fracturing in vertical wells are radial composite models, and the assumption that the reconstruction area is a cylinder does not match the results of on-site microseismic monitoring [29–32]. Therefore, the establishment of a seven-area seepage model for volume fracturing of tight oil reservoirs is of great significance.

Tight reservoirs have dense lithology, porosity less than 10%, permeability less than 0.1×10^{-3} μm^2, and pore throat diameter at the micro-nanometer level, with obvious microscale effect, which leads to tight reservoirs presenting nonlinear seepage characteristics. This article divides the renovation area into seven seepage areas based on the nonlinear seepage characteristics of tight oil reservoirs and the renovation mode of actual volume fracturing vertical wells. An analytical modeling approach was used to establish a seepage model for seven areas of volume-fractured straight wells in tight reservoirs after reasonable simplification of the fracture by certain physical assumptions, and the pressure and production solutions under a constant production regime were obtained through Laplace transformation. The flow stages were divided and the influence of fracture network parameters on the seepage law was studied. In the actual exploration and development process, it is generally multi-stage combined production after segmented volume fracturing. For multi-stage combined production, the dynamic splitting method of multi-stage combined production and the Blasingame curve algorithm fitting technology can be used to invert the ESRV and other fracture network parameters. Due to the limitation of space, this paper does not cover the issue of multi-stage combined production, which will be discussed separately in the future.

2. Physical Model

Vertical well volume fracturing technology can "break" the reservoir, forming a transformation area composed of primary and secondary fracture networks. The complex fracture network generated increases the effective transformation volume (ESRV) and increases the fracture conductivity. The complex fracture network in the ESRV area of volume fracturing wells in tight oil reservoirs results in different seepage characteristics from porous media, requiring regional analysis. The author adopts a hypothetical method, assuming that the vertical well is located at the center of a rectangular sealed reservoir and that there is a finite conductivity fracture on the vertical well section. The model is divided into the following areas: the unreformed areas (areas 3, 4, 5, and 6) are single medium; the effective renovation area (area 1), is characterized by a dual medium model; the main crack area F. According to symmetry, one-eighth of the seepage area is taken for research and calculation, as shown in Figure 1.

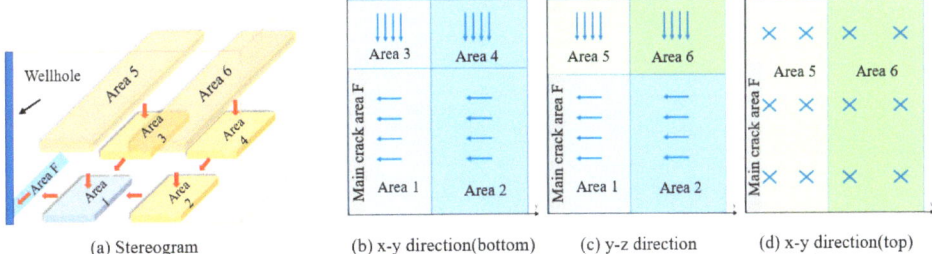

Figure 1. Schematic diagram of physical model.

Based on the volume fracturing characteristics of tight oil reservoirs, the following assumptions are made: ① The influence of starting pressure gradient is considered in the unreformed area, and the influence of permeability stress sensitivity of cracks is considered in the transformed area, and the main fracture area. ② Sealing of the outer boundary of the oil reservoir. ③ The main crack is a vertical crack with symmetrical wings, considering that the crack network does not fully penetrate the reservoir vertically. ④ The liquid is single-phase and slightly compressible. ⑤ The seepage process is isothermal seepage. ⑥ Neglecting the influence of gravity and capillary force. ⑦ The fluid flow direction, boundary, and coupling conditions in each region of the oil reservoir are:

Unreformed area: The outer boundary of area 6, which is not penetrated by the main crack and not compressed longitudinally, is closed, the inner boundary pressure is continuous, and the fluid flows to areas 4 and 2. The boundary conditions of area 5 and area 6 are the same, with fluid flowing towards areas 3 and 1. The outer boundary of area 4 is closed, and the inner boundary pressure is continuous, which is supplemented by the fluid in area 6 and flows towards area 2. The boundary conditions of area 3 are the same as those of area 4, supplemented by fluid from area 5 and flowing toward area 1. The outer boundary of area 2 is closed, and the inner boundary pressure is continuous, supplemented by fluids from areas 6 and 4 and flows towards area 1.

Effective transformation area: The flow rate at the outer boundary of area 1 is continuous, the pressure at the inner boundary is continuous, and the fracture system is supplemented by the matrix system and fluids from areas 5, 3, and 2, flowing towards the main fracture.

Main fracture area F: The fluid in the main fracture flows into the wellbore, with the outer boundary closed, and the inner boundary conditions determined by the production system.

3. Mathematical Model

3.1. Definition of Dimensionless Quantity

Dimensionless pressure (under fixed production conditions):

$$p_{jD} = \frac{K_{\text{ref}} h (p_i - p_j)}{1.842 \times 10^{-3} q_F \mu B} \tag{1}$$

where K_{ref} is the reference permeability, μm^2, the subscript ref represents the reference value; h is the thickness of the formation, m; p_j is the pressure, MPa, the subscript j represents different partitions; q_F is the main fracture yield, $m^3 \cdot d^{-1}$; and B is the volume coefficient of crude oil, dimensionless.

Dimensionless production:

$$q_{FD} = \frac{q_F \mu B}{2\pi K_{ref} h_{ref}(p_i - p_{wf})} \quad (2)$$

where p_{wf} is the bottom hole flow pressure, MPa; h_{ref} is the reference thickness, m.

Dimensionless conductivity coefficient:

$$\eta_{iD} = \frac{\eta_i}{\eta_{ref}} \quad (3)$$

$$\eta_{ref} = \frac{K_{ref}}{u_{ref}(\phi C_t)_{ref}} \quad (4)$$

where μ_{ref} is the reference viscosity, mPa·s; ϕ is porosity, dimensionless; C_t is the comprehensive compression coefficient, MPa^{-1}.

Dimensionless time:

$$t_D = \frac{3.6\eta_{ref} t}{L_{ref}^2} \quad (5)$$

where L_{ref} is the reference length, m; t is time, s.

Dimensionless starting pressure gradient:

$$G_D = \frac{K_{ref} L_{ref} h \lambda_m}{1.842 \times 10^{-3} q_F \mu B} \quad (6)$$

where λ_m is the starting pressure gradient, MPa·m^{-1}.

Dimensionless distance:

$$\begin{aligned} x_{FD} &= x_f/L_{ref} \\ x_{eD} &= x_e/L_{ref} \\ y_{1D} &= y_1/L_{ref} \\ y_{eD} &= y_e/L_{ref} \\ z_{1D} &= z_1/L_{ref} = h_F/(2L_{ref}) \\ z_{2D} &= z_2/L_{ref} = h/(2L_{ref}) \\ w_D &= w_F/L_{ref} \end{aligned} \quad (7)$$

where x_f is the half-length of the main crack, m; x_e is the distance from the well in the x-direction to the reservoir boundary, m; y_1 is the half-width of the effective renovation area, m; y_e is the distance from the well in the y-direction to the reservoir boundary, m; z_1 is the half-height of the main crack, m; h_F is the main crack height, m, the subscript F represents the main crack; z_2 is the half-height of the reservoir, m; and w_F is the half-height of the reservoir, m.

Dimensionless fracture conductivity:

$$F_{CD} = \frac{K_{Fi} w_F}{K_{ref} L_{ref}} \quad (8)$$

Crossflow coefficient:

$$\lambda = \alpha \frac{K_{1m}}{K_{1fi}} L_{ref}^2 \quad (9)$$

where K_{1m} is the matrix permeability of area 1, μm^2; α is the form factor, dimensionless; K_{1fi} is the initial permeability of the secondary crack in the area 1, μm^2.

Elastic storage capacity ratio:

$$\omega = \frac{(\phi C_t)_{1f}}{(\phi C_t)_{1f} + (\phi C_t)_{1m}} \quad (10)$$

Dimensionless starting pressure gradient:

$$\lambda_D = C_L \lambda_m L_{ref} \tag{11}$$

where C_L is the compressibility coefficient of the liquid volume, MPa^{-1}.

3.2. Mathematical Model Establishment and Solution

3.2.1. Area 6

This area is characterized by fractures that do not penetrate the reservoir, assuming a one-dimensional flow in the z-direction with a starting pressure gradient.

According to the principle of material balance, the continuity equation is obtained as follows:

$$\frac{\partial(\rho_6 v_6)}{\partial z} = -\frac{\partial(\rho_6 \phi_6)}{\partial t} \tag{12}$$

where ρ is the fluid density, kg·m^{-3}; v is the seepage rate m·h^{-1}.

The motion equation considering the starting pressure gradient is:

$$v_6 = -\frac{K_6}{\mu}\left(\frac{\partial \rho_6}{\partial z} - \lambda_m\right) \tag{13}$$

The equation of state for rocks and fluids is:

$$\rho_6 = \rho_0[1 + C_L(p_6 - p_0)] \tag{14}$$

$$\phi_6 = \phi_0 + C_f(p_6 - p_0) \tag{15}$$

By substituting the motion equation and rock fluid state equation into the continuity equation, the seepage control equation for this area can be obtained as follows:

$$\frac{\partial^2 p_6}{\partial z^2} - \lambda_m C_L \frac{\partial p_6}{\partial z} = \frac{\phi \mu C_{t6}}{K_6} \frac{\partial p_6}{\partial t} \tag{16}$$

The outer boundary conditions of a finite enclosed oil reservoir are:

$$\left.\frac{\partial p_6}{\partial z}\right|_{z_D = z_{2D}} = 0 \tag{17}$$

The pressure at the interface between area 6 and areas 2 and 4 is continuous, and the internal boundary conditions are:

$$p_6|_{z_D=z_{1D}} = p_2|_{z_D=z_{1D}} = p_4|_{z_D=z_{1D}} \tag{18}$$

According to the definition of dimensionless variables, the equation is dimensionless and subjected to a Laplace transformation based on dimensionless time t_D, resulting in:

$$\frac{\partial^2 \overline{p}_{6D}}{\partial z_D^2} - \lambda_D \frac{\partial \overline{p}_{6D}}{\partial z_D} = \frac{s}{\eta_{6D}} \overline{p}_{6D} \tag{19}$$

$$\left.\frac{\partial \overline{p}_{6D}}{\partial z_D}\right|_{z_D = z_{2D}} = 0 \tag{20}$$

$$\overline{p}_{6D}|_{z_D=z_{1D}} = \overline{p}_{2D}|_{z_D=z_{1D}} = \overline{p}_{4D}|_{z_D=z_{1D}} \tag{21}$$

where s is the Laplace space variable.

The solution of the seepage differential equation can be obtained by combining the above equation:

$$\overline{p}_{6D} = c_6 \overline{p}_{2D}|_{z_D=z_{1D}} = c_6 \overline{p}_{4D}|_{z_D=z_{1D}} \tag{22}$$

Among them:

$$c_6 = \frac{\left(-\frac{r_{62}}{r_{61}}\right)e^{r_{61}(z_D-z_{2D})} + e^{r_{62}(z_D-z_{2D})}}{\left(-\frac{r_{62}}{r_{61}}\right)e^{r_{61}(z_{1D}-z_{2D})} + e^{r_{62}(z_{1D}-z_{2D})}}$$

$$r_{61} = \frac{\lambda_D + \sqrt{\lambda_D^2 + \frac{4s}{\eta_{6D}}}}{2}, r_{62} = \frac{\lambda_D - \sqrt{\lambda_D^2 + \frac{4s}{\eta_{6D}}}}{2}$$

Taking the partial derivative of $\overline{p}_{6D}$ at $z_D = z_{1D}$ yields:

$$\left.\frac{\partial \overline{p}_{6D}}{\partial z_D}\right|_{z_D=z_{1D}} = -\beta_6 \overline{p}_{2D}|_{z_D=z_{1D}} = -\beta_6 \overline{p}_{4D}|_{z_D=z_{1D}} \tag{23}$$

Among them:

$$\beta_6 = -\frac{-r_{62}e^{r_{61}(z_{1D}-z_{2D})} + r_{62}e^{r_{62}(z_{1D}-z_{2D})}}{\left(-\frac{r_{62}}{r_{61}}\right)e^{r_{61}(z_{1D}-z_{2D})} + e^{r_{62}(z_{1D}-z_{2DD})}}$$

3.2.2. Area 5

The seepage control equation for region 5 is:

$$\frac{\partial^2 \overline{p}_{5D}}{\partial z_D^2} - \lambda_D \frac{\partial \overline{p}_{5D}}{\partial z_D} = \frac{s}{\eta_{5D}} \overline{p}_{5D} \tag{24}$$

$$\left.\frac{\partial \overline{p}_{5D}}{\partial z_D}\right|_{z_D=z_{2D}} = 0 \tag{25}$$

$$\overline{p}_{5D}|_{z_D=z_{1D}} = \overline{p}_{1fD}|_{z_D=z_{1D}} = \overline{p}_{3D}|_{z_D=z_{1D}} \tag{26}$$

The solution of the seepage differential equation is:

$$\overline{p}_{5D} = c_5 \overline{p}_{1fD}|_{z_D=z_{1D}} = c_5 \overline{p}_{3D}|_{z_D=z_{1D}} \tag{27}$$

Among them:

$$c_5 = \frac{\left(-\frac{r_{52}}{r_{51}}\right)e^{r_{51}(z_D-z_{2D})} + e^{r_{52}(z_D-z_{2D})}}{\left(-\frac{r_{52}}{r_{51}}\right)e^{r_{51}(z_{1D}-z_{2D})} + e^{r_{52}(z_{1D}-z_{2D})}}$$

$$r_{51} = \frac{\lambda_D + \sqrt{\lambda_D^2 + \frac{4s}{\eta_{5D}}}}{2}, r_{52} = \frac{\lambda_D - \sqrt{\lambda_D^2 + \frac{4s}{\eta_{5D}}}}{2}$$

Taking the partial derivative of $\overline{p}_{5D}$ at $z_D = z_{1D}$ yields:

$$\left.\frac{\partial \overline{p}_{5D}}{\partial z_D}\right|_{z_D=z_{1D}} = -\beta_5 \overline{p}_{1D}|_{z_D=z_{1D}} = -\beta_5 \overline{p}_{3D}|_{z_D=z_{1D}} \tag{28}$$

Among them:

$$\beta_5 = -\frac{-r_{52}e^{r_{51}(z_{1D}-z_{2D})} + r_{52}e^{r_{52}(z_{1D}-z_{2D})}}{\left(-\frac{r_{52}}{r_{51}}\right)e^{r_{51}(z_{1D}-z_{2D})} + e^{r_{52}(z_{1D}-z_{2D})}}$$

3.2.3. Area 4

The fluid in area 4 flows towards area 2 in the x-direction and is supplemented by fluid from area 6 in the z-direction. The seepage control equation is:

$$\frac{\partial^2 \bar{p}_{4D}}{\partial x_D^2} - \lambda_D \frac{\partial \bar{p}_{4D}}{\partial x_D} + \frac{K_6}{K_4 z_{1D}} \frac{\partial \bar{p}_{6D}}{\partial z_D}\bigg|_{z_D=z_{1D}} = \frac{s}{\eta_{4D}} \bar{p}_{4D} \tag{29}$$

order $\alpha_4 = \frac{K_6 \beta_6}{K_4 z_{1D}} + \frac{s}{\eta_{4D}}$, and by simplifying it into the above equation, we can obtain:

$$\frac{\partial^2 \bar{p}_{4D}}{\partial x_D^2} - \lambda_D \frac{\partial \bar{p}_{4D}}{\partial x_D} = \alpha_4 \bar{p}_{4D} \tag{30}$$

Closed oil reservoir, with external boundary conditions as follows:

$$\frac{\partial \bar{p}_{4D}}{\partial x_D}\bigg|_{x_D=x_{eD}} = 0 \tag{31}$$

The pressure at the interface between area 4 and area 2 is continuous, and the internal boundary conditions are:

$$\bar{p}_{4D}|_{x_D=x_{FD}} = \bar{p}_{2D}|_{x_D=x_{FD}} \tag{32}$$

By combining the internal and external boundary conditions and the seepage control equation, it is obtained that:

$$\bar{p}_{4D} = c_4 \bar{p}_{2D}|_{x_D=x_{FD}} \tag{33}$$

Among them:

$$c_4 = \frac{\left(-\frac{r_{42}}{r_{41}}\right) e^{r_{41}(x_D - x_{eD})} + e^{r_{42}(x_D - x_{eD})}}{\left(-\frac{r_{42}}{r_{41}}\right) e^{r_{41}(x_{FD} - x_{eD})} + e^{r_{42}(x_{FD} - x_{eD})}}$$

$$r_{41} = \frac{\lambda_D + \sqrt{\lambda_D^2 + 4\alpha_4}}{2}, r_{42} = \frac{\lambda_D - \sqrt{\lambda_D^2 + 4\alpha_4}}{2}$$

Taking the partial derivative of $\bar{p}_{4D}$ at $x_D = x_{FD}$ yields:

$$\frac{\partial \bar{p}_{4D}}{\partial x_D}\bigg|_{x_D=x_{FD}} = -\beta_4 \bar{p}_{2D}|_{x_D=x_{FD}} \tag{34}$$

Among them:

$$\beta_4 = -\frac{-r_{42} e^{r_{41}(x_{FD} - x_{eD})} + r_{42} e^{r_{42}(x_{FD} - x_{eD})}}{\left(-\frac{r_{42}}{r_{41}}\right) e^{r_{41}(x_{FD} - x_{eD})} + e^{r_{42}(x_{FD} - x_{eD})}}$$

3.2.4. Area 3

The fluid flows in the x-direction towards area 1 and is supplemented by fluid from area 5 in the z-direction. The seepage control equation is:

$$\frac{\partial^2 \bar{p}_{3D}}{\partial x_D^2} - \lambda_D \frac{\partial \bar{p}_{3D}}{\partial x_D} + \frac{K_5}{K_3 z_{1D}} \frac{\partial \bar{p}_{5D}}{\partial z_D}\bigg|_{z_D=z_{1D}} = \frac{s}{\eta_{3D}} \bar{p}_{3D} \tag{35}$$

Order $\alpha_3 = \frac{K_5 \beta_5}{K_3 z_{1D}} + \frac{s}{\eta_{3D}}$, and by simplifying it into the above equation, we can obtain:

$$\frac{\partial^2 \bar{p}_{3D}}{\partial x_D^2} - \lambda_D \frac{\partial \bar{p}_{3D}}{\partial x_D} = \alpha_3 \bar{p}_{3D} \tag{36}$$

Closed oil reservoir, with external boundary conditions as follows:

$$\left.\frac{\partial \overline{p}_{3D}}{\partial x_D}\right|_{x_D=x_{eD}} = 0 \quad (37)$$

The pressure at the interface between area 3 and area 1 is continuous, and the internal boundary conditions are:

$$\overline{p}_{3D}|_{x_D=x_{FD}} = \overline{p}_{1fD}|_{x_D=x_{FD}} \quad (38)$$

By combining the internal and external boundary conditions and the seepage control equation, it is obtained that:

$$\overline{p}_{3D} = c_3 \overline{p}_{1fD}|_{x_D=x_{FD}} \quad (39)$$

Among them:

$$c_3 = \frac{\left(-\frac{r_{32}}{r_{31}}\right)e^{r_{31}(x_D-x_{eD})} + e^{r_{32}(x_D-x_{eD})}}{\left(-\frac{r_{32}}{r_{31}}\right)e^{r_{31}(x_{FD}-x_{eD})} + e^{r_{32}(x_{FD}-x_{eD})}}$$

$$r_{31} = \frac{\lambda_D + \sqrt{\lambda_D^2 + 4\alpha_3}}{2}, r_{32} = \frac{\lambda_D - \sqrt{\lambda_D^2 + 4\alpha_3}}{2}$$

Taking the partial derivative of $\overline{p}_{3D}$ at $x_D = x_{FD}$ yields:

$$\left.\frac{\partial \overline{p}_{3D}}{\partial x_D}\right|_{x_D=x_{FD}} = -\beta_3 \overline{p}_{1fD}|_{x_D=x_{FD}} \quad (40)$$

Among them:

$$\beta_3 = -\frac{-r_{32}e^{r_{31}(x_{FD}-x_{eD})} + r_{32}e^{r_{32}(x_{FD}-x_{eD})}}{\left(-\frac{r_{32}}{r_{31}}\right)e^{r_{31}(x_{FD}-x_{eD})} + e^{r_{32}(x_{FD}-x_{eD})}}$$

3.2.5. Area 2

The fluid flows in the y-direction towards area 1 and is supplemented by fluid from area 6 in the z-direction, and area 4 in the x-direction. The seepage control equation is:

$$\frac{\partial^2 \overline{p}_{2D}}{\partial y_D^2} - \lambda_D \frac{\partial \overline{p}_{2D}}{\partial y_D} + \frac{K_6}{K_2 z_{1D}} \left.\frac{\partial \overline{p}_{6D}}{\partial z_D}\right|_{z_D=z_{1D}} + \frac{K_4}{K_2 x_{FD}} \left.\frac{\partial \overline{p}_{4D}}{\partial x_D}\right|_{x_D=x_{FD}} = \frac{s}{\eta_{2D}} \overline{p}_{2D} \quad (41)$$

Order $\alpha_2 = \frac{K_6 \beta_6}{K_2 z_{1D}} + \frac{K_4 \beta_4}{K_2 x_{FD}} + \frac{s}{\eta_{2D}}$, and by simplifying it into the above equation, we can obtain:

$$\frac{\partial^2 \overline{p}_{2D}}{\partial y_D^2} - \lambda_D \frac{\partial \overline{p}_{2D}}{\partial y_D} = \alpha_2 \overline{p}_{2D} \quad (42)$$

Closed oil reservoir, with external boundary conditions as follows:

$$\left.\frac{\partial \overline{p}_{2D}}{\partial y_D}\right|_{y_D=y_{eD}} = 0 \quad (43)$$

The pressure at the interface between area 2 and area 1 is continuous, and the internal boundary conditions are:

$$\overline{p}_{2D}|_{y_D=y_{1D}} = \overline{p}_{1fD}|_{y_D=y_{1D}} \quad (44)$$

By combining the internal and external boundary conditions and the seepage control equation, it is obtained that:

$$\overline{p}_{2D} = c_2 \overline{p}_{1fD}|_{y_D=y_{1D}} \quad (45)$$

Among them:

$$c_2 = \frac{\left(-\frac{r_{22}}{r_{21}}\right)e^{r_{21}(y_D-y_{eD})} + e^{r_{22}(y_D-y_{eD})}}{\left(-\frac{r_{22}}{r_{21}}\right)e^{r_{21}(y_{1D}-y_{eD})} + e^{r_{22}(y_{1D}-y_{eD})}}$$

$$r_{21} = \frac{\lambda_D + \sqrt{\lambda_D^2 + 4\alpha_2}}{2}, r_{22} = \frac{\lambda_D - \sqrt{\lambda_D^2 + 4\alpha_2}}{2}$$

Taking the partial derivative of $\bar{p}_{2D}$ at $y_D = y_{1D}$ yields:

$$\left.\frac{\partial \bar{p}_{2D}}{\partial y_D}\right|_{y_D=y_{1D}} = -\beta_2 \bar{p}_{1fD}\big|_{y_D=y_{1D}} \tag{46}$$

Among them:

$$\beta_2 = -\frac{-r_{22}e^{r_{21}(y_{1D}-y_{eD})} + r_{22}e^{r_{32}(y_{1D}-y_{eD})}}{\left(-\frac{r_{22}}{r_{21}}\right)e^{r_{21}(y_{1D}-y_{eD})} + e^{r_{32}(y_{1D}-y_{eD})}}$$

3.2.6. Area 1

This area is effectively modified with a developed secondary fracture network, where we assume a dual medium and use the W R quasi steady state model. The fluid in the fracture system of area 1 flows in the y-direction towards the main fracture area F, while being supplemented by fluids from area 5, area 3, area 2, and the matrix system. The fracture system is sensitive to permeability.

The continuity equation of the crack system in this area is:

$$-\frac{\partial(\rho_1 v_{1f})}{\partial y} + \rho_1 q_{21} + \rho_1 q_{31} + \rho_1 q_{51} + \rho_1 q_{1mf} = \frac{\partial(\rho_1 \phi_{1f})}{\partial t} \tag{47}$$

The motion equation considering permeability sensitivity is:

$$v_{1f} = -\frac{K_{1fi} e^{\gamma(p_{1f}-p_0)}}{\mu} \frac{\partial p_{1f}}{\partial y} \tag{48}$$

where γ is the permeability modulus, MPa^{-1}.

The equation of state for rocks and fluids is:

$$\rho_1 = \rho_0[1 + C_L(p_{1f} - p_0)] \tag{49}$$

$$\phi_{1f} = \phi_0 + C_f(p_{1f} - p_0) \tag{50}$$

The supplementary items of source and exchange:

$$q_{21} = \frac{K_2}{\mu y_{1D}} \left.\frac{\partial p_2}{\partial y}\right|_{y=y_{1D}} \tag{51}$$

$$q_{31} = \frac{K_3}{\mu x_{FD}} \left.\frac{\partial p_3}{\partial x}\right|_{x=x_{FD}} \tag{52}$$

$$q_{51} = \frac{K_5}{\mu z_{1D}} \left.\frac{\partial p_5}{\partial z}\right|_{z=z_{1D}} \tag{53}$$

$$q_{1mf} = \alpha \frac{K_{1m}}{\mu}(p_{1m} - p_{1f}) \tag{54}$$

The continuity equation of the matrix system is:

$$q_{1mf} = -\phi_{1m} C_{t1m} \frac{\partial p_{1m}}{\partial t} \tag{55}$$

The motion, state equation and supplementary equation are introduced into the continuity equation and dimensionless to obtain the seepage control equation:

Matrix system:
$$\lambda(p_{1fD} - p_{1mD}) = \frac{1-\omega}{\eta_{1D}} \frac{\partial p_{1mD}}{\partial t_D} \tag{56}$$

Crack system:
$$e^{-\gamma_D p_{1fD}}\left[\frac{\partial^2 p_{1fD}}{\partial y_D^2} - \gamma_D\left(\frac{\partial p_{1fD}}{\partial y_D}\right)^2\right] + \frac{K_2}{K_{fi}y_{1D}}\frac{\partial p_{2D}}{\partial y_D}\bigg|_{y_D=y_{1D}} + \frac{K_3}{K_{1fi}x_{FD}}\frac{\partial p_{3D}}{\partial x_D}\bigg|_{x_D=x_{FD}} + \frac{K_5}{K_{1fi}z_{1D}}\frac{\partial p_{5D}}{\partial z_D}\bigg|_{z_D=z_{1D}} - \lambda(p_{1fD} - p_{1mD}) = \frac{\omega}{\eta_{1D}}\frac{\partial p_{1fD}}{\partial t_D} \tag{57}$$

The flow at the interface between area 1 and area 2 is continuous, and the outer boundary conditions are:

$$e^{\gamma_D p_{1fD}}\frac{\partial p_{1fD}}{\partial y_D}\bigg|_{y_D=y_{1D}} = \frac{K_2}{K_{1fi}}\frac{\partial p_{2D}}{\partial y_D}\bigg|_{y_D=y_{1D}} \tag{58}$$

The pressure at the interface between area 1 and the main crack area F is continuous, and the internal boundary conditions are:

$$p_{1fD}\big|_{y_D=\frac{w_D}{2}} = p_{FD}\big|_{y_D=\frac{w_D}{2}} \tag{59}$$

Due to the presence of crack stress sensitivity, the equation is nonlinear and difficult to solve directly. By applying the Pedrosa transformation, it can be transformed into a linear equation.

Transforming pressure p_{1fD} into functions of perturbation τ_{1fD}:

$$p_{1fD} = -\frac{1}{\gamma_D}\ln(1 - \gamma_D \tau_{1fD}) \tag{60}$$

When τ_{1fD} is expanded to n-th order, there are:

$$\frac{1}{1-\gamma_D \tau_{1fD}} = 1 + \gamma_D \tau_{1fD} + \gamma_D^2 \tau_{1fD}^2 + \cdots \gamma_D^n \tau_{1fD}^n \tag{61}$$

$$-\frac{1}{\gamma_D}\ln(1-\gamma_D \tau_{1fD}) = \tau_{1fD} + \frac{1}{2}\gamma_D \tau_{1fD}^2 + \frac{1}{3}\gamma_D \tau_{1fD}^3 + \cdots \frac{1}{n}\gamma_D \tau_{1fD}^n \tag{62}$$

Considering that γ_D is generally a small value, only the zero-order expansion to obtain τ_{1fD0} can satisfy the accuracy requirement.

After performing zero-order Pedrosa transformation on p_{1fD} and Laplace transformation on t_D, the seepage control equation is obtained as follows:

$$\lambda(\overline{\tau}_{1fD0} - \overline{p}_{1mD}) = \frac{(1-\omega)s}{\eta_{1D}}\overline{p}_{1mD} \tag{63}$$

$$\frac{\partial^2 \overline{\tau}_{1fD0}}{\partial y_D^2} + \frac{K_2}{K_{1fi}y_{1D}}\frac{\partial \overline{p}_{2D}}{\partial y_D}\bigg|_{y_D=y_{1D}} + \frac{K_3}{K_{1fi}x_{FD}}\frac{\partial \overline{p}_{3D}}{\partial x_D}\bigg|_{x_D=x_{FD}} + \frac{K_5}{K_{1fi}z_{1D}}\frac{\partial \overline{p}_{5D}}{\partial z_D}\bigg|_{z_D=z_{1D}} - \lambda(\overline{\tau}_{1fD0} - \overline{p}_{1mD}) = \frac{\omega s}{\eta_{1D}}\overline{\tau}_{1fD0} \tag{64}$$

$$\frac{\partial \overline{\tau}_{1fD0}}{\partial y_D}\bigg|_{y_D=y_{1D}} = \frac{K_2}{K_{1fi}}\frac{\partial \overline{p}_{2D}}{\partial y_D}\bigg|_{y_D=y_{1D}} \tag{65}$$

$$\overline{\tau}_{1fD0}\big|_{y_D=\frac{w_D}{2}} = \overline{\tau}_{FD0}\big|_{y_D=\frac{w_D}{2}} \tag{66}$$

Order $\alpha_1 = \frac{K_2\beta_2}{K_{1fi}y_{1D}} + \frac{K_3\beta_3}{K_{1fi}x_{FD}} + \frac{K_5\beta_5}{K_{1fi}z_{1D}} + \frac{\omega s}{\eta_{1D}} + \frac{\lambda(1-\omega)s}{\lambda\eta_{1D}+(1-\omega)s}$, the above equation can be simplified as:

$$\frac{\partial^2 \overline{\tau}_{1fD0}}{\partial y_D^2} = \alpha_1 \overline{\tau}_{1fD0} \tag{67}$$

The solution for area 1 is obtained by combining the internal and external boundary conditions as follows:

$$\overline{\tau}_{1D0} = A_1 \cosh[(y_D - y_{1D})\sqrt{\alpha_1}] + B_1 \sinh[(y_D - y_{1D})\sqrt{\alpha_1}] \tag{68}$$

Among them:

$$A_1 = \frac{\overline{\tau}_{FD0}|_{y_D=\frac{w_D}{2}}}{\cosh[(\frac{w_D}{2} - y_{1D})\sqrt{\alpha_1}] + b\sinh[(\frac{w_D}{2} - y_{1D})\sqrt{\alpha_1}]}$$

$$B_1 = bA_1, b = -\frac{K_2\beta_2}{K_{1fi}\sqrt{\alpha_1}}$$

Taking the partial derivative of $\overline{\tau}_{1D0}$ at $y_D = \frac{w_D}{2}$ yields:

$$\left.\frac{\partial \overline{\tau}_{1D0}}{\partial y_D}\right|_{y_D=\frac{w_D}{2}} = e_1 \sqrt{\alpha_1} \overline{\tau}_{FD0}|_{y_D=\frac{w_D}{2}} \tag{69}$$

Among them:

$$e_1 = \frac{b\cosh[(\frac{w_D}{2} - y_{1D})\sqrt{\alpha_1}] + \sinh[(\frac{w_D}{2} - y_{1D})\sqrt{\alpha_1}]}{\cosh[(\frac{w_D}{2} - y_{1D})\sqrt{\alpha_1}] + b\sinh[(\frac{w_D}{2} - y_{1D})\sqrt{\alpha_1}]}$$

3.2.7. Area F

The main fracture area, where fluid flows towards the wellbore in the x-direction and is supplemented by fluid from area 1 in the y-direction, has permeability sensitivity. The seepage control equation in this area is:

$$e^{-\gamma_D p_{FD}}\left[\frac{\partial^2 p_{FD}}{\partial x_D^2} - \gamma_D(\frac{\partial p_{FD}}{\partial x_D})^2\right] + \frac{2K_{1fi}e^{-\gamma_D p_{1fD}}}{K_{Fi}w_D}\left.\frac{\partial p_{1fD}}{\partial y_D}\right|_{y_D=\frac{w_D}{2}} = \frac{1}{\eta_{FD}}\frac{\partial p_{FD}}{\partial t_D} \tag{70}$$

Assuming the crack tip is closed, the outer boundary condition is:

$$\left.e^{\gamma_D p_{FD}}\frac{\partial p_{FD}}{\partial x_D}\right|_{x_D=x_{FD}} = 0 \tag{71}$$

The oil well is produced at a fixed production rate, and the internal boundary condition is:

$$\left.e^{-\gamma_D p_{FD}}\frac{\partial p_{FD}}{\partial x_D}\right|_{x_D=0} = -\frac{\pi}{F_{CD}} \tag{72}$$

where F_{CD} is the dimensionless conductivity of the main crack.

The internal boundary condition for constant pressure production in oil wells is:

$$p_{FD}|_{x_D=0} = 1, \left.e^{-\gamma_D p_{FD}}\frac{\partial p_{FD}}{\partial x_D}\right|_{x_D=0} = -\frac{\pi q_{wfD}}{F_{CD}} \tag{73}$$

Similarly, the zero-order Pedrosa transformation is introduced to transform it into a linear equation and Laplace transformation is performed, resulting in:

$$\frac{\partial^2 \overline{\tau}_{FD0}}{\partial x_D^2} + \frac{2K_{fii}}{K_{Fi}w_D}\left.\frac{\partial \overline{\tau}_{1fD0}}{\partial y_D}\right|_{y_D=\frac{w_D}{2}} = \frac{s}{\eta_{FD}}\overline{\tau}_{FD0} \tag{74}$$

$$\left.\frac{\partial \overline{\tau}_{\text{FD0}}}{\partial x_{\text{D}}}\right|_{x_{\text{D}}=x_{\text{FD}}} = 0 \tag{75}$$

Fixed production system:

$$\left.\frac{\partial \overline{\tau}_{\text{1fD0}}}{\partial x_{\text{D}}}\right|_{x_{\text{D}}=0} = -\frac{\pi}{F_{\text{CD}}s} \tag{76}$$

Fixed pressure production system:

$$\left.\overline{\tau}_{\text{FD0}}\right|_{x_{\text{D}}=0} = \frac{1-e^{-\gamma_{\text{D}}}}{s\gamma_{\text{D}}}, \left.\frac{\partial \overline{\tau}_{\text{FD0}}}{\partial x_{\text{D}}}\right|_{x_{\text{D}}=0} = -\frac{\pi \overline{q}_{\text{wfD}}}{F_{\text{CD}}} \tag{77}$$

Order $\alpha_{\text{F}} = \frac{s}{\eta_{\text{FD}}} - \frac{2e_1 K_{1\text{fi}}\sqrt{\alpha_1}}{K_{\text{Fi}}w_{\text{D}}}$, the above equation can be simplified as:

$$\frac{\partial^2 \overline{\tau}_{\text{FD0}}}{\partial x_{\text{D}}^2} = \alpha_{\text{F}} \overline{\tau}_{\text{FD0}} \tag{78}$$

The boundary conditions for simultaneous production can be solved as follows:

$$\overline{\tau}_{\text{FD0}} = \frac{\pi \cosh[(x_{\text{D}}-x_{\text{FD}})\sqrt{\alpha_{\text{F}}}]}{F_{\text{CD}}s\sqrt{\alpha_{\text{F}}}\sinh(x_{\text{FD}}\sqrt{\alpha_{\text{F}}})} \tag{79}$$

When $x_{\text{D}} = 0$, the dimensionless bottom hole pressure solution in the Lagrangian space for constant production rate is obtained as:

$$\overline{\tau}_{\text{wfD}} = \frac{\pi}{F_{\text{CD}}s\sqrt{\alpha_{\text{F}}}\tanh(x_{\text{FD}}\sqrt{\alpha_{\text{F}}})} \tag{80}$$

By combining the boundary conditions of constant pressure, the dimensionless bottom hole production in the Lagrangian space can be solved as:

$$\overline{q}_{\text{wfD}} = \frac{(1-e^{-\gamma_{\text{D}}})F_{\text{CD}}\sqrt{\alpha_{\text{F}}}}{\gamma_{\text{D}}\pi s}\tanh(x_{\text{FD}}\sqrt{\alpha_{\text{F}}}) \tag{81}$$

Perform Stehfest numerical inversion on the pressure solution in Laplace space to obtain the dimensionless perturbation pressure solution in real space:

$$\tau_{\text{wfD}}(t_{\text{D}}) = \frac{\ln 2}{t_{\text{D}}}\sum_{i=1}^{N} V_i \overline{\tau}_{\text{wfD}}\left(\frac{\ln 2}{t_{\text{D}}}i\right) \tag{82}$$

Among them:

$$V_i = (-1)^{\frac{N}{2}+1}\sum_{K=[\frac{i+1}{2}]}^{\min(i,\frac{N}{2})} \frac{K^{\frac{N}{2}}(2K)!}{(\frac{N}{2}-K)!K!(K-1)!(i-K)!(2K-i)!}$$

In engineering applications, N is an even number between 4 and 12, and is generally selected based on actual debugging.

Finally, the perturbed pressure solution is subjected to inverse Pedrosa transformation to obtain a dimensionless pressure solution under constant production conditions:

$$p_{\text{wfD}}(t_{\text{D}}) = -\frac{\ln\{1-\gamma_{\text{D}}\tau_{\text{wfD}}(t_{\text{D}})\}}{\gamma_{\text{D}}} \tag{83}$$

Similarly, the dimensionless production solution under constant pressure conditions can be obtained:

$$q_{\text{wfD}}(t_{\text{D}}) = \frac{\ln 2}{t_{\text{D}}} \sum_{i=1}^{N} V_i \bar{q}_{\text{wfD}}(\frac{\ln 2}{t_{\text{D}}} i) \tag{84}$$

4. Model Validation

The established volume fracturing seven-area composite flow model was validated using analytical and numerical simulation methods.

4.1. Comparative Validation of Analytical Models

When the fractures in the volume fracturing seven-area composite flow model completely penetrate the reservoir, and the permeability sensitivity of main fractures and the secondary fracture network in the effectively modified area are not considered, neither is the starting pressure gradient of the unmodified area, and the model degenerates into the dual medium five-area linear flow model proposed by Stalgorova et al. Here, we compare the degraded seven-area composite flow model with the five-area linear flow model.

As shown in Figure 2, the pressure and pressure derivative results for both coincide exactly, proving the correctness of the pressure solution of the model.

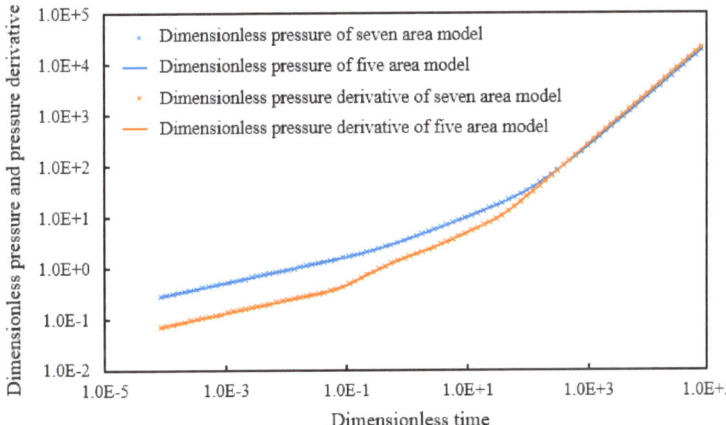

Figure 2. Comparison of analytical model pressure.

4.2. Numerical Simulation Comparison Verification

Compare the seven-area model with numerical simulation software using numerical simulation methods. A numerical model was established using CMG, which can reflect the characteristics of seepage in actual volume fractured vertical wells. The numerical simulation model is shown in Figure 3. The effective renovation area adopts a dual medium model, while the unmodified area adopts a single pore medium to simulate. By using the zoning function, the stress sensitivity effect of cracks is set in the effective renovation area and the main crack area, and the starting pressure gradient is set in the original unmodified area. The other model data are shown in Table 1, and Figure 4 shows the comparison between the theoretical calculation and numerical simulation yield results of the volume fracturing seven-area composite flow model (without considering skin factors). It can be seen that the yield curve is basically consistent, further verifying the correctness of the model yield solution.

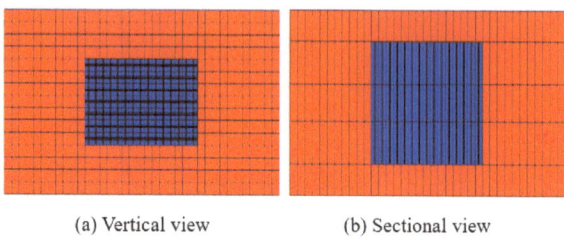

(a) Vertical view (b) Sectional view

Figure 3. Numerical model diagram.

Table 1. Table of basic parameters of numerical model.

Parameter	Numerical Value	Parameter	Numerical Value
Reservoir length/m	370	Initial permeability of ESRV fracture system/μm^2	5×10^{-3}
Reservoir width/m	150	Fracture porosity	0.2
Reservoir thickness/m	30	Initial permeability of main fracture/μm^2	1
Main crack seam height/m	20	Half-length of main crack/m	75
Matrix porosity	0.1	Main crack width/m	0.01
Matrix permeability/μm^2	1×10^{-3}	ESRV half-width/m	35
Comprehensive compressibility coefficient of matrix	0.0001	Original formation pressure/MPa	20
Comprehensive compression coefficient of cracks/MPa^{-1}	0.001	Bottom hole flowing pressure/MPa	15
Oil volume factor	1.1	Starting pressure gradient/(MPa·m^{-1})	0.02
Crude oil viscosity/(mPa·s)	5	Permeability modulus/MPa^{-1}	0.01

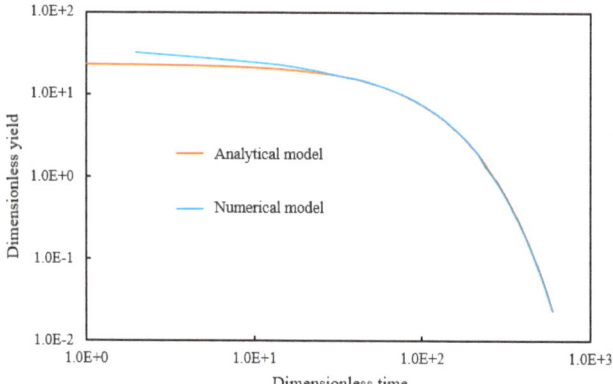

Figure 4. Numerical model validation solution.

4.3. Division of Flow Stages

The dimensionless bottom hole pressure and pressure derivative curve is drawn under the fixed production system of volume fracturing vertical wells in double logarithmic coordinates, as shown in Figure 5. It can be divided into six flow stages: ① In the linear flow stage of the main fracture and ESRV regional fracture network, the slope of the dimensionless pressure and pressure derivative curves is 0.25. ② Matrix fracture scouring phase in the ESRV area, where the pressure and pressure derivative curves begin to be non-parallel at the beginning of the phase and the pressure derivative becomes depressed. ③ In the linear flow stage of the ESRV area, the pressure and pressure derivatives are once again parallel to each other, with slopes of 0.5. ④ During the boundary flow stage of the ESRV area, the flow continues to extend along the crack network of the renovation area and reaches the boundary of the ESRV area. ⑤ Linear flow in unmodified areas, liquid supply to ESRV area in unmodified areas. ⑥ During the stage of reservoir boundary influence, the slope is related to the type of reservoir boundary, and the slope of a closed reservoir is 1.

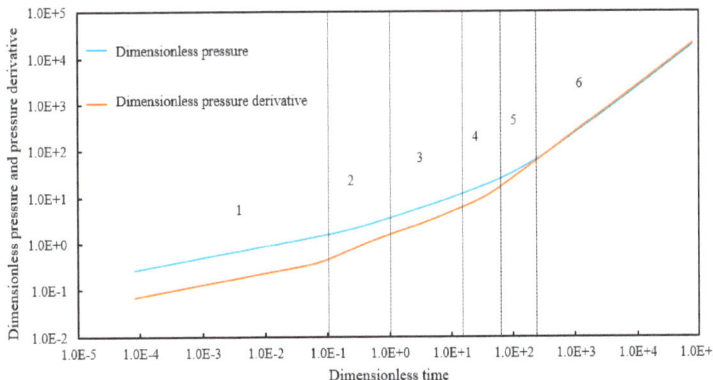

Figure 5. Dynamic curve of vertical well pressure during volume fracturing in tight oil reservoirs.

5. The Influence of Mesh Parameters on Flow Patterns

We use Matlab to program and calculate the analytical solution of the model, analyzing the impact of different parameters on pressure and production. In the pressure curve graph, the relevant parameters with the symbol in the legend represent the pressure derivative curve.

5.1. Starting Pressure Gradient

From Figure 6, it can be seen that the starting pressure gradient has a significant impact on production capacity from the boundary flow stage of the ESRV region in the middle to late stages. In the early stage, the fracture network of the effective modification area reduced the seepage resistance and weakened the impact of the starting pressure gradient on dimensionless pressure, pressure reciprocal, and dimensionless production. As the starting pressure gradient increases in the middle and later stages, the pressure consumption in the unmodified area increases to maintain production under fixed production conditions. As a result, the dimensionless pressure rises faster, and the pressure derivative also increases accordingly. Under constant pressure conditions, a larger starting pressure gradient leads to greater seepage resistance of fluid flowing into the effective modified area in the unmodified area, and the dimensionless production is lower.

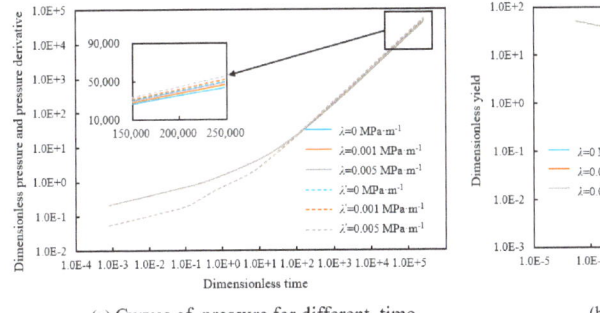
(a) Curves of pressure for different time

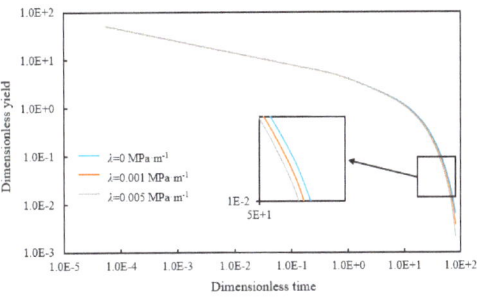
(b) Curves of yield for different time

Figure 6. The influence of starting pressure gradient on pressure and production.

5.2. Permeability Modulus

From Figure 7, it can be seen that the permeability modulus measures the sensitivity of fractures to pressure changes. The stress sensitivity effect causes the permeability of primary and secondary fractures to decrease with the decrease in formation pressure during the production process. From the production curve, it can be seen that the stress sensitivity effect affects the entire reservoir development stage. As the permeability modulus increases, the degree of fracture closure increases, the permeability decreases, the production decreases, and the pressure derivative curve rises faster under constant pressure conditions.

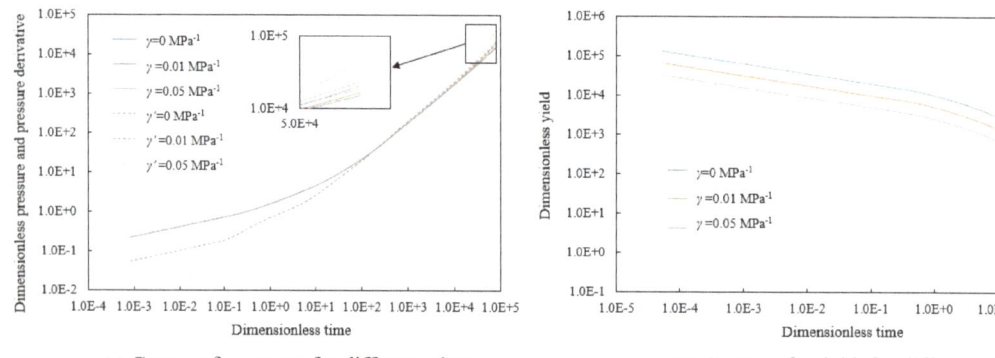

(a) Curves of pressure for different time   (b) Curves of yield for different time

Figure 7. The influence of permeability modulus on pressure and production.

5.3. Main Crack Penetration Ratio

From Figure 8, it can be seen that the fracture penetration ratio affects the pressure and productivity of volume fracturing wells starting from the boundary flow stage of the effective transformation area. When the length of the main crack and the width of the renovation area are fixed, the crack penetration ratio increases and the effective renovation volume increases. In the renovation area, the crack network develops, and the pressure conductivity is stronger than in the unreformed area. Therefore, under fixed production conditions, as the crack penetration ratio increases, the rise of dimensionless pressure and pressure derivative curves slows down, and the start time of upward warping becomes later. For constant pressure conditions, as the fracture penetration ratio increases, the degree of transformation increases in the reservoir, and there are more flow channels in the fracture network, resulting in higher oil well production.

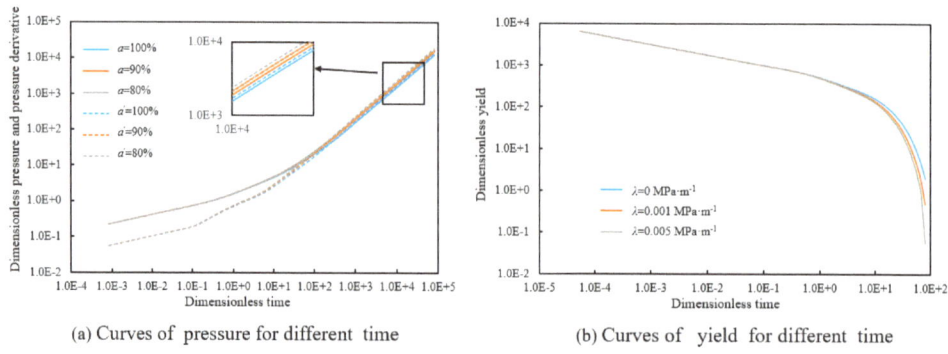

(a) Curves of pressure for different time   (b) Curves of yield for different time

Figure 8. The influence of main crack penetration ratio on pressure and production.

5.4. Half-Length of Main Crack

From Figure 9, it can be seen that the half-length of the main fracture is similar to the penetration ratio of the main fracture, which directly determines the size of the effective reconstruction area. Starting from the linear flow stage of the reconstruction area, it affects the pressure and productivity of the volume fracturing well. When the height of the main crack and the width of the renovation area are constant, the half-length of the main crack increases, the rise of the dimensionless pressure and pressure derivative curve is slower for fixed production conditions, and the start time of upward warping is later. For constant pressure conditions, as the half-length of the main fracture increases, the oil drainage area becomes larger, and the production of the oil well increases. Unlike the limitation of reservoir thickness on fracture height, the variation range of fracture length is relatively large, and its impact on dimensionless pressure and production curve is more significant.

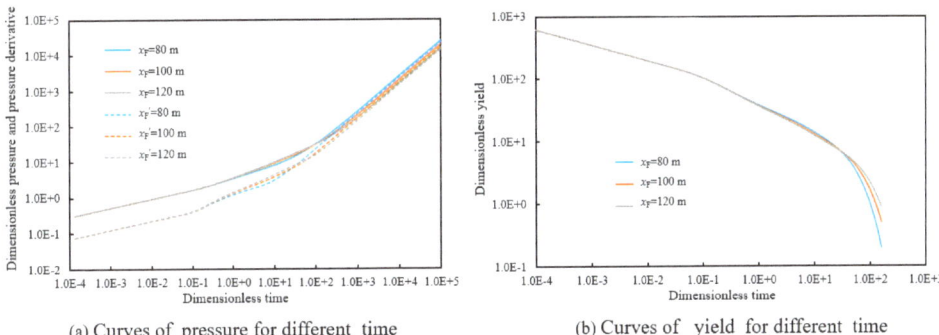

(a) Curves of pressure for different time

(b) Curves of yield for different time

Figure 9. The influence of half-length of main fractures on pressure and production.

5.5. ESRV Area Width

From Figure 10, it can be seen that the width of the ESRV area has an impact starting from the matrix crack flow stage of the effective transformation area. As the width of the ESRV region increases, the dimensionless pressure and pressure derivative decrease under constant production conditions, while the dimensionless production increases under constant pressure conditions. From the production curve, it can be seen that the width of the secondary fracture network has a significant impact on production. When the ESRV width is 0, it is conventional fracturing. From the production curve, it can be seen that volume fracturing is significantly better than conventional fracturing, which can significantly improve the production capacity of tight oil reservoirs.

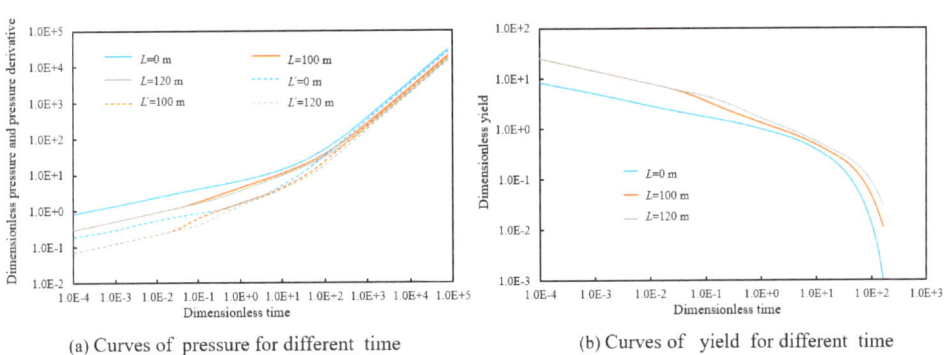

(a) Curves of pressure for different time

(b) Curves of yield for different time

Figure 10. The effect of ESRV area width on pressure and production.

5.6. Main Fracture Conductivity

From Figure 11, it can be seen that the conductivity of the main fracture mainly affects the early and middle flow stages covered by the main fracture and the effective renovation area. As the fracture conductivity increases, the dimensionless pressure curve is lower in the early and middle stages and corresponds to higher production in the early and middle stages. From the production curve, it can be seen that the high conductivity of the main fracture can quickly increase the production capacity of the effective transformation area, and shorten the development cycle of tight oil reservoirs, but it is ultimately limited by the size of the effective transformation volume and the permeability of the formation matrix, indicating that the matching relationship between the three should be optimized during the development process.

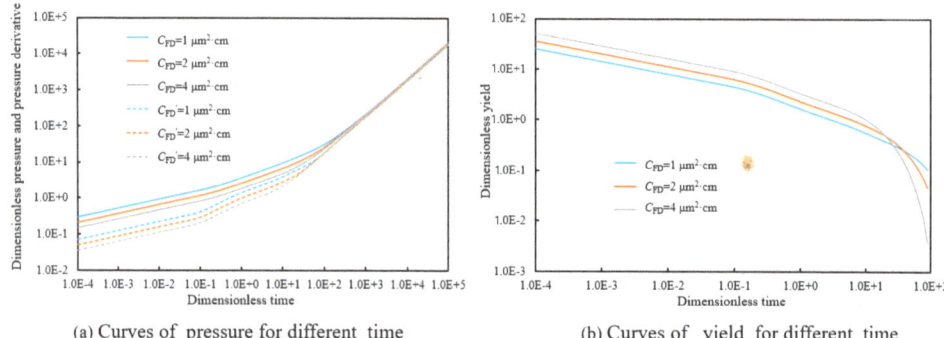

Figure 11. The influence of main fracture conductivity on pressure and production.

5.7. ESRV Regional Permeability

From Figure 12, it can be seen that the permeability of the fracture network in the ESRV region has a significant impact on the linear flow and matrix flow of cracks in the effectively modified area characterized by dual media. The permeability of the fracture network represents the degree of transformation in the volume fracturing ESRV area. As the permeability of the fracture network increases, the liquid supply capacity of the ESRV area becomes stronger, the dimensionless pressure and pressure derivative become smaller, the dimensionless production becomes larger, and entering the boundary flow stage of the reformed area happens earlier, which is ultimately limited by the effective modification volume and formation matrix permeability.

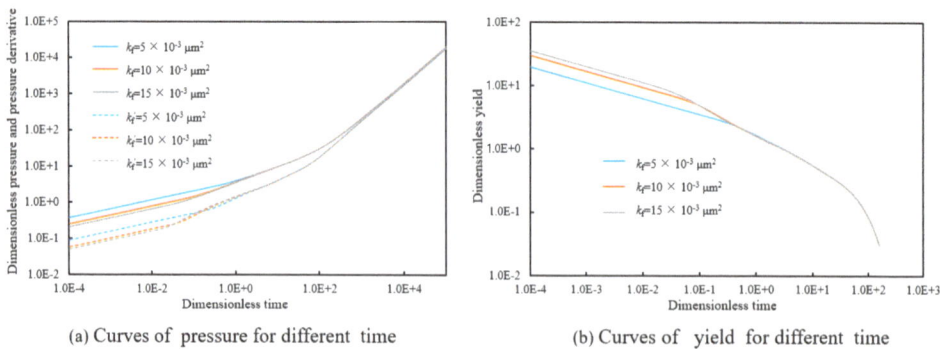

Figure 12. The influence of permeability in ESRV region on pressure and production.

5.8. ESRV Area Aspect Ratio

From Figure 13, it can be seen that under the same effective renovation volume, the aspect ratio of the ESRV area determines the starting time of the linear flow stage in the renovation area. The aspect ratio of the ESRV area is the ratio of the length of the main crack to the renovation bandwidth. With the increase in the aspect ratio, the effective renovation area is narrower and longer, the bandwidth is smaller, the pressure wave propagates to the ESRV bandwidth boundary earlier, contacts the unmodified area earlier, and enters the flow phase at the boundary of the modified area, which is reflected in the mid-term dimensionless pressure and pressure derivative curves start to rise earlier. From the production curve, it can be seen that as the aspect ratio of the ESRV region increases, the mid-term production becomes higher and the production declines faster. This is because the aspect ratio of the ESRV region is smaller (when the aspect ratio is maintained to be larger than 1), the area of direct communication between the ESRV region and the matrix of the unmodified region, i.e., the oil drainage area is larger, and the production capacity is released more quickly.

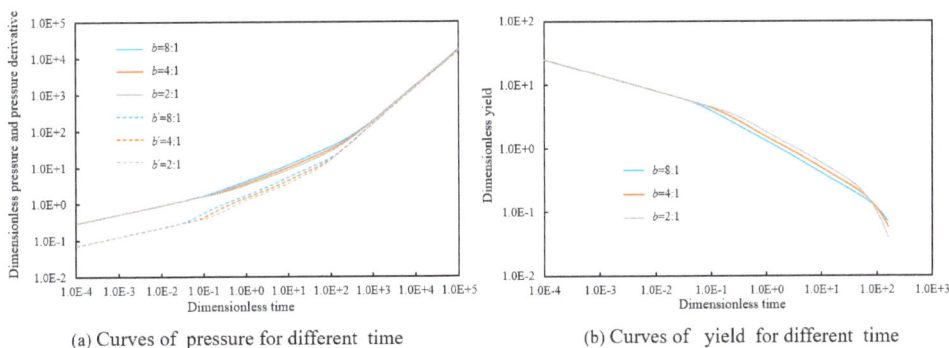

Figure 13. The influence of ESRV area aspect ratio on pressure and production.

6. Conclusions

1. Based on the reservoir transformation characteristics of actual volume fracturing vertical wells, the volume fracturing transformation area was finely divided, and a seven-area seepage mathematical model for volume fracturing vertical wells in tight oil reservoirs was established. The pressure solution under constant production conditions and production solution under constant pressure conditions were solved using methods such as Laplace transform and Pedrosa transform. The accuracy of the model was verified using analytical and numerical simulation methods, respectively.

2. Based on the dimensionless pressure and pressure derivative curve, the flow of vertical well volume fracturing wells in tight oil reservoirs is divided into six stages: main fractures, linear network flow in the ESRV region, matrix fracture channeling flow in the ESRV region, linear flow in the ESRV region, boundary flow in the ESRV region, linear flow in the unmodified region, and reservoir boundary influence.

3. The production of volume fracturing vertical wells is influenced by permeability modulus, main fracture conductivity, ESRV area width, and ESRV area permeability. The production decreases with the increase in permeability modulus. The high conductivity of the main fracture can quickly release the production capacity of the effectively transformed area, and shorten the development cycle of tight oil reservoirs, but it is ultimately limited by the size of the effectively transformed volume. Under constant pressure conditions, the yield increases with increasing ESRV area width and ESRV area permeability.

4. By using well testing parameters, the seven-area seepage model for volume fracturing in tight reservoirs can be used to reverse calculate fracture parameters, providing guidance for reservoir development design.

Author Contributions: Methodology, D.D. and L.R.; writing—review and editing, P.L.; formal analysis, D.D. and Y.L.; writing—original draft, D.D. and L.R.; supervision, Y.T. and F.H. All authors have read and agreed to the published version of the manuscript.

Funding: This research received no external funding.

Data Availability Statement: Data available on request.

Conflicts of Interest: The authors declare no conflict of interest.

References

1. Fisher, M.K.; Wright, C.A.; Davidson, B.M.; Steinsberger, N.P.; Buckler, W.S.; Goodwin, A.; Fielder, E.O. Integrating Fracture Mapping Technologies To Improve Stimulations in the Barnett Shale. *SPE Prod. Facil.* **2005**, *20*, 85–93. [CrossRef]
2. Dongyan, F.; Jun, Y.; Hai, S.; Hui, Z.; Wei, W. A Composite Model of Hydraulic Fractured Horizontal Well with Stimulated Reservoir Volume in Tight Oil & Gas Reservoir. *J. Nat. Gas Sci. Eng.* **2015**, *24*, 115–123.
3. Maxwell, S.C.; Urbancic, T.I.; Steinsberger, N.; Energy, D.; Zinno, R. Microseismic Imaging of Hydraulic Fracture Complexity in the Barnett Shale. Presented at the SPE Annual Technical Conference and Exhibition, San Antonio, TX, USA, 29 September–2 October 2002; OnePetro: Richardson, TX, USA, 2002.
4. Mayerhofer, M.J.; Lolon, E.P. Integration of Microseismic Fracture Mapping Results With Numerical Fracture Network Production Modeling in the Barnett Shale. Presented at the SPE Annual Technical Conference and Exhibition, San Antonio, TX, USA, 24–27 September 2006; OnePetro: Richardson, TX, USA, 2006.
5. Guo, T.; Zhang, S.; Qu, Z.; Zhou, T.; Xiao, Y.; Gao, J. Experimental Study of Hydraulic Fracturing for Shale by Stimulated Reservoir Volume. *Fuel* **2014**, *128*, 373–380. [CrossRef]
6. Cui, G.; Tan, Y.; Chen, T.; Feng, X.-T.; Elsworth, D.; Pan, Z.; Wang, C. Multidomain Two-Phase Flow Model to Study the Impacts of Hydraulic Fracturing on Shale Gas Production. *Energy Fuels* **2020**, *34*, 4273–4288. [CrossRef]
7. Cipolla, C.L.; Warpinski, N.R.; Mayerhofer, M.J.; Lolon, E.P. The Relationship Between Fracture Complexity, Reservoir Properties, and Fracture-Treatment Design. *SPE Prod. Oper.* **2010**, *25*, 438–452. [CrossRef]
8. Brehonnet, P.; Tanguy, N.; Vilbe, P.; Calvez, L.C. An Alternative Method for Numerical Inversion of Laplace Transforms. *IEEE Trans. Circuits Syst. II-Express Briefs* **2006**, *53*, 434–437. [CrossRef]
9. Ali, A.J.; Siddiqui, S.; Dehghanpour, H. Analyzing the Production Data of Fractured Horizontal Wells by a Linear Triple Porosity Model: Development of Analysis Equations. *J. Pet. Sci. Eng.* **2013**, *112*, 117–128. [CrossRef]
10. Huang, X.; Zhang, R.; Chen, M.; Zhao, Y.; Xiao, H.; Zhang, L. Simulation of the Production Performance of Fractured Horizontal Wells in Shale Gas Reservoirs Considering the Complex Fracture Shape. *Energy Fuels* **2022**, *36*, 1358–1373. [CrossRef]
11. Chu, H.; Liao, X.; Chen, Z.; Zhao, X.; Liu, W.; Dong, P. Transient Pressure Analysis of a Horizontal Well with Multiple, Arbitrarily Shaped Horizontal Fractures. *J. Pet. Sci. Eng.* **2019**, *180*, 631–642. [CrossRef]
12. Sheng, G.; Su, Y.; Wang, W.; Javadpour, F.; Tang, M. Application of Fractal Geometry in Evaluation of Effective Stimulated Reservoir Volume in Shale Gas Reservoirs. *Fractals-Complex. Geom. Patterns Scaling Nat. Soc.* **2017**, *25*, 1740007. [CrossRef]
13. Cao, L.; Li, X.; Zhang, J.; Luo, C.; Tan, X. Dual-Porosity Model of Rate Transient Analysis for Horizontal Well in Tight Gas Reservoirs with Consideration of Threshold Pressure Gradient. *J. Hydrodyn.* **2018**, *30*, 872–881. [CrossRef]
14. Sonnenberg, S.A.; Pramudito, A. Petroleum Geology of the Giant Elm Coulee Field, Williston Basin. *AAPG Bull.* **2009**, *93*, 1127–1153. [CrossRef]
15. Wang, Y.; Liu, X. Stress-Dependent Unstable Dynamic Propagation of Three-Dimensional Multiple Hydraulic Fractures with Improved Fracturing Sequences in Heterogeneous Reservoirs: Numerical Cases Study via Poroelastic Effective Medium Model. *Energy Fuels* **2021**, *35*, 18543–18562. [CrossRef]
16. Qi, W.; Yun, X.; Xiaoquan, W.; Tengfei, W.; Shouliang, Z. Volume Fracturing Technology of Unconventional Reservoirs: Connotation, Design Optimization and Implementation. *Pet. Explor. Dev.* **2012**, *39*, 377–384.
17. He, Y.; Cheng, S.; Rui, Z.; Qin, J.; Fu, L.; Shi, J.; Wang, Y.; Li, D.; Patil, S.; Yu, H.; et al. An Improved Rate-Transient Analysis Model of Multi-Fractured Horizontal Wells with Non-Uniform Hydraulic Fracture Properties. *Energies* **2018**, *11*, 393. [CrossRef]
18. Zeng, B.; Cheng, L.; Li, C. Low Velocity Non-Linear Flow in Ultra-Low Permeability Reservoir. *J. Pet. Sci. Eng.* **2011**, *80*, 1–6. [CrossRef]
19. Brown, M.; Ozkan, E.; Raghavan, R.; Kazemi, H. Practical Solutions for Pressure-Transient Responses of Fractured Horizontal Wells in Unconventional Shale Reservoirs. *SPE Reserv. Eval. Eng.* **2011**, *14*, 663–676. [CrossRef]
20. Brohi, I.; Pooladi-Darvish, M.; Aguilera, R. Modeling Fractured Horizontal Wells As Dual Porosity Composite Reservoirs—Application to Tight Gas, Shale Gas and Tight Oil Cases. Presented at the SPE Western North American Region Meeting, Anchorage, AL, USA, 7–11 May 2011; OnePetro: Richardson, TX, USA, 2011.

21. Stalgorova, E.; Mattar, L. Analytical Model for Unconventional Multifractured Composite Systems. *SPE Reserv. Eval. Eng.* **2013**, *16*, 246–256. [CrossRef]
22. Zeng, J.; Wang, X.; Guo, J.; Zeng, F. Analytical Model for Multi-Fractured Horizontal Wells in Tight Sand Reservoir with Threshold Pressure Gradient. Presented at the SPE Asia Pacific Hydraulic Fracturing Conference, Beijing, China, 24–26 August 2016; OnePetro: Richardson, TX, USA, 2016.
23. Zhu, Y.; Yue, M.; Gao, Y. Nonlinear percolation model and productivity analysis for volume fracturing of tight oil layers. *J. China Univ. Min. Technol.* **2014**, *43*, 248–254.
24. Zhu, L.; Liao, X.; Chen, Z. Pressure Transient Analysis of Vertically Fractured Well in Tight Oil Reservoirs with Rectangle Stimulated Reservoir Volume. Presented at the SPE Kingdom of Saudi Arabia Annual Technical Symposium and Exhibition, Dammam, Saudi Arabia, 24–27 April 2017; OnePetro: Richardson, TX, USA, 2017.
25. Li, Q.; Zhao, D.; Yin, J.; Zhou, X.; Li, Y.; Chi, P.; Han, Y.; Ansari, U.; Cheng, Y. Sediment Instability Caused by Gas Production from Hydrate-bearing Sediment in Northern South China Sea by Horizontal Wellbore: Evolution and Mechanism. *Nat. Resour. Res.* **2023**, *32*, 1595–1620. [CrossRef]
26. Li, Q.; Zhao, C.; Yang, Y.; Ansari, U.; Han, Y.; Li, X.; Cheng, Y. Preliminary experimental investigation on long-term fracture conductivity for evaluating the feasibility and efficiency of fracturing operation in offshore hydrate-bearing sediments. *Ocean. Eng.* **2023**, *281*, 114949. [CrossRef]
27. Wang, F.; Liu, X.; Jiang, B.; Zhou, H.; Chen, W.; Chen, Y.; Li, X. Low-loading Pt nanoparticles combined with the atomically dispersed FeN4 sites supported by FeSA-N-C for improved activity and stability towards oxygen reduction reaction/hydrogen evolution reaction in acid and alkaline media. *J. Colloid. Interface Sci.* **2023**, *635*, 514–523. [CrossRef] [PubMed]
28. Li, M.; Zhou, Z.; Chen, M.; Wu, J. Topological Representative Element Volume of Fractured Rock Mass. *Appl. Sci.* **2022**, *12*, 2844. [CrossRef]
29. Wang, J.; Xiong, Y.; Lu, Z.; Shi, J.; Wu, J. Influence of Volume Fracturing on Casing Stress in Horizontal Wells. *Energies* **2021**, *14*, 2057. [CrossRef]
30. Chen, Z.; Xu, G.; Zhou, J.; Liu, J. Fracture Network Volume Fracturing Technology in High-temperature Hard Formation of Hot Dry Rock. *Acta Geol. Sin.-Engl. Ed.* **2021**, *95*, 1828–1834. [CrossRef]
31. Li, Z.; Yan, X.; Wen, M.; Bi, G.; Ma, N.; Ren, Z. Transient Pressure Behavior of Volume Fracturing Horizontal Wells in Fractured Stress-Sensitive Tight Oil Reservoirs. *Processes* **2022**, *10*, 953. [CrossRef]
32. Qu, H.; Zhang, J.; Zhou, F.; Peng, Y.; Pan, Z.; Wu, X. Evaluation of hydraulic fracturing of horizontal wells in tight reservoirs based on the deep neural network with physical constraints. *Pet. Sci.* **2023**, *20*, 1129–1141. [CrossRef]

Disclaimer/Publisher's Note: The statements, opinions and data contained in all publications are solely those of the individual author(s) and contributor(s) and not of MDPI and/or the editor(s). MDPI and/or the editor(s) disclaim responsibility for any injury to people or property resulting from any ideas, methods, instructions or products referred to in the content.

Article

Persistent Free Radicals in Petroleum

Lina M. Yañez Jaramillo [1], Joy H. Tannous [2] and Arno de Klerk [1,*]

[1] Department of Chemical and Materials Engineering, University of Alberta, 9211-116th Street, Edmonton, AB T6G 1H9, Canada; yanezjar@ualberta.ca
[2] Department of Chemical and Petroleum Engineering, United Arab Emirates University, Al Ain P.O. Box 15551, United Arab Emirates; j.tannous@uaeu.ac.ae
* Correspondence: deklerk@ualberta.ca; Tel.: +1-780-248-1903; Fax: +1-780-492-2881

Abstract: The persistent free radical content in petroleum is of the order 10^{18} spins/g (1 µmol/g), with higher and lower values found depending on origin and in different distillation fractions. The field of persistent free radicals in petroleum was reviewed with the aim of addressing and explaining apparent inconsistencies between free radical persistence and reactivity. The macroscopic average free radical concentration in petroleum is persistent over geological time, but individual free radical species in petroleum are short-lived and reactive. The persistent free radical concentration in petroleum can be explained in terms of a dynamic reaction equilibrium of free radical dissociation and association that causes a finite number of species at any given time to be present as free radicals. Evidence to support this description are observed changes in free radical concentration related to change in Gibbs free energy when the bulk liquid properties are changed and responsiveness of free radical concentration to dynamic changes in temperature. Cage effects, solvent effects, steric protection, and radical stabilization affect free radical reaction rate but do not explain the persistent free radical concentration in petroleum. The difference between persistent free radicals in straight-run petroleum and converted petroleum is that straight-run petroleum is an equilibrated mixture, but converted petroleum is not at equilibrium and the free radical concentration can change over time. Based on the limited data available, free radicals in straight-run petroleum appear to be part of the compositional continuum proposed by Altgelt and Boduszynski. Persistent free radical species are partitioned during solvent classification of whole oil, with the asphaltenes (*n*-alkane insoluble) fraction having a higher concentration of persistent free radicals than maltenes (*n*-alkane soluble) fraction. Attempts to relate persistent free radical concentration to petroleum composition were inconclusive.

Keywords: persistent free radicals; petroleum; compositional continuum

Citation: Yañez Jaramillo, L.M.; Tannous, J.H.; de Klerk, A. Persistent Free Radicals in Petroleum. *Processes* **2023**, *11*, 2067. https://doi.org/10.3390/pr11072067

Academic Editors: Dicho Stratiev, Dobromir Yordanov and Aijun Guo

Received: 31 May 2023
Revised: 26 June 2023
Accepted: 6 July 2023
Published: 11 July 2023

Copyright: © 2023 by the authors. Licensee MDPI, Basel, Switzerland. This article is an open access article distributed under the terms and conditions of the Creative Commons Attribution (CC BY) license (https://creativecommons.org/licenses/by/4.0/).

1. Introduction

Persistent free radicals are present in high-molecular-mass natural raw materials like petroleum and coal. The concentration of these free radical species can be quantified using electron spin resonance (ESR) or electron paramagnetic resonance (EPR) spectrometry. This technique exploits the magnetic moment of the unpaired electron, which makes substances with an unpaired electron paramagnetic.

The concentration and electronic environment of unpaired electrons in a substance can be detected by subjecting the material to a magnetic field. When subjected to an external magnetic field, those unpaired electrons that are aligned with the magnetic field will have a lower energy than those unpaired electrons aligned against the magnetic field. When sufficient energy ($h.\nu$) is provided for the unpaired electrons to change their spin state under the influence of a magnetic field (B_0), the amount of energy absorbed, as well as the frequency of the electromagnetic radiation, provides information about the concentration and nature of the unpaired electron. Specifically, this relationship is defined as the Landé *g*-factor (Equation (1)).

$$g = \frac{h.\nu}{\mu_B.B_0} \qquad (1)$$

In this equation, h is the Planck's constant = 6.626×10^{-34} J/s, ν is the microwave frequency of the ESR in Hz, μ_B is the Bohr magneton = 9.273×10^{-28} J/Gauss, and B_0 is the magnetic field in Gauss. Organic free radicals can easily be distinguished from other paramagnetic species present in petroleum, such as the vanadyl ion (VO^{2+}), based on the difference in g-factor. The unpaired electrons in organic free radicals have g-factors close to that of a free electron, $g = 2.0023$.

This study is limited to persistent organic free radicals.

Reported concentrations of the organic free radicals in heavy petroleum and coal are typically of the order 10^{18} spins/g. This is equivalent to about 1 µmol/g. Higher and lower values can be found depending on the origin and distillation range of the material (Table 1) [1,2]. If one then considers the high average molecular mass of heavy petroleum fractions and coal, the concentration of persistent free radical species in molar concentration is around 0.1 mol%.

Table 1. Persistent free radical content in petroleum and coal [1,2].

Material	Free Radical Content		Reference
	(spins/g)	(µmol/g)	
Athabasca bitumen	$0.9–1.1 \times 10^{18}$	1.5–1.8	[1]
Cold Lake bitumen	$0.9–1.1 \times 10^{18}$	1.5–1.8	[1]
Coal (low rank) [a]	$2.5–5.3 \times 10^{18}$	4.2–8.8	[2]
Coal (high rank) [b]	$7.2–25 \times 10^{18}$	12–42	[2]

[a] Carbon content range 77–85%; [b] Carbon content range 89–97%.

The persistence of free radicals in petroleum and coal is intriguing because these free radical species appear to have been present over geological time. Free radical persistence over geological time is incongruent with the description of free radicals as reactive species.

Herein lies a conundrum for those interested in petroleum conversion processes that proceed by free radical chemistry, such as visbreaking and coking. The reactions taking place in thermal conversion processes are usually described in terms of free radical initiation, propagation, and termination reactions [3]. The notion is that sufficient temperature is required for homolytic bond dissociation to produce free radicals, i.e., initiation, so that thermal conversion can take place. Yet, as was pointed out, the amount of persistent free radicals present in heavy petroleum fractions is already of the order 0.1 mol%. The implication is that thermal conversion can proceed at a lower temperature than required for initiation by homolytic bond dissociation.

The purpose of this work is to review the field of persistent free radicals in petroleum. It is a specific aim to address and explain the apparent inconsistencies between free radical persistence and reactivity. It is a further aim to explore the relationship between the nature of the free radical species and how it is affected by and related to bulk properties. To do so and to guide the narrative, several questions will be posed and answered to the extent possible. To illustrate specific concepts, the focus will be on petroleum and thermal conversion processes applied to petroleum, although the work can be equally applied to other materials.

2. What Is Meant by Persistent Free Radicals?

The term *persistent free radical* was defined by Griller and Ingold [4] as "... a radical that has a lifetime significantly greater than methyl under the same conditions...". They were also at pains to point out that there is a difference between "persistent", "stable", and "stabilized" free radicals.

The term *stable free radical* was reserved for [4]: "... a radical so persistent and so unreactive... under ambient conditions that the pure radical can be handled and stored in the lab with no more precautions than would be used for the majority of commercially available organic chemicals". A commonly encountered example is molecular oxygen (O_2), which is a stable diradical species.

Most persistent free radical species can therefore not be classified as stable free radicals according to the preceding definition. Their persistence depends on their chemical environment and physical state [5]. It is therefore possible that under appropriate circumstances, free radical species that would not normally be persistent appear to be persistent.

The triphenylmethyl radical is a prototypical example of a persistent free radical species, which is stabilized by delocalization of the unpaired electron that is delocalized into the adjacent systems of π-bonds of the phenyl groups [4]. This makes it a *stabilized free radical*, but it is not a stable free radical that can be isolated and stored for an extended period of time. In fact, the extent of stabilization of the triphenylmethyl radical is about the same as for a benzylic radical because the three phenyl rings are not in the same plane but at an angle to each other, like a propeller. Both electron delocalization and steric hinderance contribute to the persistence, with a half-life of the triphenylmethyl radical in dilute solution that is of the order of milliseconds [6].

The conundrum that arose due to observed free radical persistence in petroleum and the apparent lack of reactivity was an artifact of semantics. In the petroleum community the meaning of the term "persistent free radical" morphed into a description that implied that the radicals were both long-lived and unreactive. This was a false impression. It was demonstrated that the persistent free radical species in petroleum were reactive [7], and evidence of hydrogen transfer at 60–100 °C was presented [8,9]. A change in free radical concentration was also reported after keeping petroleum samples at 60 °C for 2 h [10]. It therefore appears unlikely that one would be able to isolate and store the pure radical species found in petroleum as unreactive materials, which are requirements for classification as stable free radicals according to the terminology of Griller and Ingold [4].

In petroleum, the macroscopically measured concentration of organic free radical species remains constant at constant ambient conditions. The apparent longevity of the free radical species in petroleum meets the criterion of description as persistent free radicals but does not imply anything about the nature of the radicals, radical reactivity, or reason for the radical persistence.

3. What Makes Free Radicals in Petroleum Persistent?

3.1. Cage Effect

When radicals are formed from non-radical precursors, two radicals are formed in close proximity to each other and the reaction yield in the liquid phase is usually less than in the gas phase for the exact same reaction and conditions. To explain this difference, reference is made to the concept of a cage effect [11,12].

The cage effect can be explained in terms of the effect of the solvent molecules surrounding free radicals, which effectively forms a solvent cage around the newly formed radicals (Figure 1). Multiple collisions may have to take place before the radicals can diffuse past those solvent molecules surrounding them to escape the solvent cage. This could increase the probability of recombination, since the newly formed radical species are neighbors in solution. Considering that all species in solution are surrounded by other molecules, Lorand [11] elected to reserve the term *cage* only for the solvent molecules surrounding a pair of newly generated radicals that were generated by the same event, so-called geminate radicals. The cage effect is therefore the consequence of the lower diffusion rate in the liquid phase compared to the gas phase. The extent to which the cage effect will affect a specific reaction is dependent on the properties of the liquid phase that affects the diffusion rate.

For solvents that are mixtures, bulk liquid viscosity is not necessarily a good predictor of the cage effect. It was shown that cage recombination rate was poorly related to bulk viscosity (η, Pa.s) but was instead related to the inverse diffusion coefficient ($1/D$, s/m^2) they called "microviscosity" [13–15], which has the same units as inverse kinematic viscosity ($1/\nu$, s/m^2).

Figure 1. Schematic representation of solvent molecules surrounding a newly formed radical pair that is referred to as the solvent cage.

The cage effect is a purely physical phenomenon. The solvent can of course also affect the rate of radical recombination reactions by affecting the stability of the free radicals. These chemical interactions are solvent-effects [16] and are discussed in Section 3.3. Changes in recombination rate due to chemical interaction with the solvent molecules within the cage are not considered a cage effect.

One of the explanations that was put forward in the petroleum literature for the presence of persistent free radicals in petroleum was that of the cage effect [17]. Caging by aggregation was offered as the explanation for persistence over time and to explain how some radicals could survive under strong reducing conditions [18]. As envisioned, the interaction was more than just a physical caging effect because the interaction was not just decreasing the diffusion rate to slow mass transport; it was an interaction that effectively prevented reaction with the free radicals species. Along similar lines, it was postulated that free radicals played a role in the aggregation of asphaltenes [19], although in that work, aggregation was not used as an explanation for free radical persistence; it was instead a consequence of persistent free radicals in petroleum.

Aggregation is caused by chemical interaction or reaction between species that leads to an increase in the molecular weight of the aggregate when compared to the species involved in aggregation. Aggregation may then appear to physically keep the free radical persistent because aggregates can also de-aggregate, which is the reverse reaction. Thus, despite evidence for the relationship between aggregation and the free radical nature of the species involved in aggregation, this is not a cage effect but a reaction that appears to be causing a physical effect.

At the same time, aggregates when present in petroleum can cause a cage effect, as noted by Gray et al. [20]: "Free radical species that form within nanoaggregates due to thermal reactions would be restricted in their ability to react with the bulk liquid phase". The newly formed radicals are still within the aggregate and the aggregate presents a more formidable diffusion barrier than monomeric species in solution. The physical restriction imposed by the aggregate structure is a cage effect because it is a physical obstacle that reduces the diffusion rate of the newly formed radical species. No claims were made in that work [20] that the radicals formed within aggregates would persist indefinitely, only that the radical species would have more restricted access to the bulk liquid phase.

For the sake of argument, the concept of a cage effect can be applied to persistent free radical species in petroleum. The cage effect can explain how solvent molecules surrounding a persistent free radical species can shield it from radical–radical termination reactions, but it cannot explain how radical–radical termination reactions can be prevented. Even if the petroleum viscosity is very high, the diffusion coefficient in the liquid phase is not zero, which means that the rate of radical–radical termination reactions can only be slowed down. Analogously, if the free radical species are trapped within an aggregate structure, the radical termination is prevented only if the aggregate persists indefinitely. Since it was shown that persistent free radicals are reactive, this is not the case. In conclusion, the persistence of free radicals in petroleum cannot be explained by a cage effect.

3.2. Steric Protection

One of the causes of free radical persistence is steric protection [4], which affects the reaction rate of the free radical. Pendant groups surrounding the free radical center may physically hinder the approach of a reagent to the radical center, thereby reducing the probability of reaction during an interaction. The longevity of the free radical is increased, and meeting the criterion for being described as a persistent free radical (see Section 2) is easily met.

The size and nature of the pendant groups surrounding the free radical center may also affect the stability of the free radical. For example, Rüchardt [21] showed the relative impact of different pendant groups on the bond dissociation energy (BDE), which was related to the hybridization of the atom where the free radical is located, and more specifically to the bond angles of the pendant groups. Bulkier groups can also cause higher strain in the molecule, resulting in a greater relief when going from a tetrahedral (sp^3) to trigonal planar (sp^2) hybridization [6]. Thus, in addition to the steric protection offered by the pendant groups, the pendant groups also affect the thermodynamic stability of the free radical, which should be considered when assessing the impact of steric protection on reaction rate. This will be discussed in Section 3.3.

In the case of straight-run petroleum, its free radical concentration remains invariant. If this is due to steric protection, the steric protection must be absolute. Acevedo et al. [18] demonstrated that it was possible to reduce the free radical concentration of a petroleum asphaltenes fraction by boiling it in tetrahydrofuran (boiling point 66 °C). Since treatment at such mild conditions is unlikely to cause skeletal rearrangement to change the extent of steric protection of the persistent free radicals, steric protection cannot be used as explanation for free radical persistence over geological time.

Alili et al. [7] purposefully investigated the impact of steric effects on free radical reactivity of petroleum asphaltenes. Compounds with different pendant groups surrounding C=C were used as probe reagents to evaluate the relative reactivity of persistent free radicals in the asphaltenes fraction. The probe reagents themselves imposed steric restrictions on reaction. As expected, the reaction rate of reagents with sterically crowded C=C was slower, but with the exception of tetraphenyl ethylene, all other probe reagents resulted in measurable conversion during reaction with persistent free radicals in asphaltenes within 1 h at 250 °C (Figure 2) [7].

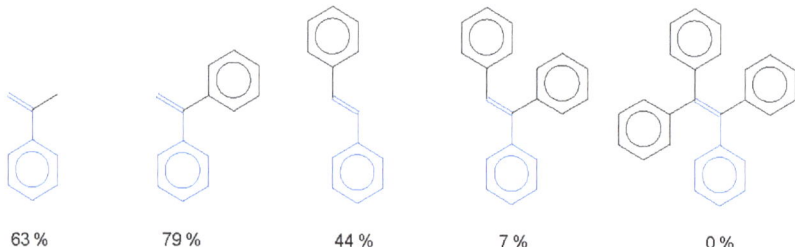

Figure 2. Conversion of different probe reagents at 250 °C for 1 h with industrially produced n-pentane insoluble asphaltenes from Athabasca bitumen with a persistent free radical content of 2.1×10^{18} spins/g [7].

In conclusion, although the impact of steric protection of free radical species in petroleum cannot be disregarded, it does not offer an explanation for free radical persistence over geological time.

3.3. Radical Stabilization Effects

The stabilization of free radicals can be viewed in terms of the rate of their formation and disappearance. Radical stabilization has been described in terms of (i) thermodynamic stabilization, which is related to the bond dissociation energy (BDE) of the bond leading to radical formation, with contributing factors such as hyperconjugation, resonance, and captodative effects; and (ii) kinetic stabilization, which is controlled by the steric hindrance at a radical center and solvent stabilization effects.

While hyperconjugation makes reference to a "donation" of electrons from a σ-bond to a p-orbital which is electron deficient, resonance finds similarity with hyperconjugation with the difference that the electron is delocalized in order to stabilize the radical and lower BDE [21]. Another factor contributing to the thermodynamic stability is the captodative effect. The captodative effect refers to the presence and combined action of electron donating and electron withdrawing groups on a radical center. The stability results from the combination of having an electron donor and an electron acceptor substituent on the radical center that enables additional resonance structures that involve a separation of charge [22,23].

It should be pointed out that thermodynamic stabilization generally does not lead to the formation of persistent free radicals and that the lifetime of free radicals are determined mainly by kinetic stabilization effects [4].

Kinetic stabilization due to steric protection was discussed in Section 3.2, and it was already concluded that this type of stabilization is insufficient to explain free radical persistence over a geological time period as is observed in petroleum. A second type of kinetic stabilization is that provided by the properties of the bulk liquid or solvent.

One type of solvent effect that plays a role relates to the formation of solvent–radical complexes, causing a redistribution of the π-electron density [24,25]. For example, Isenberg and Baird [26] reported on the efficiency of polar solvents in which neutral molecules dissociate due to the solvent's polarity lowering the energy by a specific interaction between the solvent and the radical.

Another type of solvent effect is related to the Gibbs free energy (ΔG) of the reagents and products from free radical decomposition in solution [5,16]. The ΔG of the free radical species in solution is not necessarily the same as that of the material from which the free radical species is formed, or the products from free radical termination. If the free radical species have lower ΔG in solution than that of the termination products, there is an added energy barrier to overcome. This will affect the equilibrium composition but may also lead to a kinetic effect.

The kinetic stabilization effects can lead to free radical persistence in the sense that the free radical lifetime is greater than that of a methyl radical under the same conditions but do not explain how free radicals can remain persistent over geological time.

3.4. Dynamic Reaction Equilibrium

Persistent free radicals in petroleum may be stabilized by several factors, none of which could explain the longevity of the free radicals over such a long time period. Furthermore, it was shown that the free radicals in petroleum are reactive. When the straight-run petroleum is perturbed through a change in temperature or composition, there is an impact. It is necessary to explain both the long-term free radical persistence and reactivity of the persistent free radicals.

The existence, persistence, and reactivity of persistent free radicals in petroleum can be described by a dynamic equilibrium between associated radical pairs and their dissociated forms [5,7]. This is illustrated by Figure 3. Such a description does not require the longevity of any individual radical species and it describes the persistence in terms of the relative rates of dissociation and association reactions.

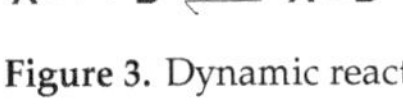

A• - •B ⇌ A—B

Figure 3. Dynamic reaction equilibrium of free radical pairs as explanation of both longevity and reactivity of persistent free radicals in petroleum.

The description of persistent free radicals in petroleum can be viewed in an analogous way to the description of persistent ions in water. There is a dynamic equilibrium in water between associated ion pairs (H_2O) and their dissociated forms ($H^+ + OH^-$). No individual ionic species remains persistent, but due to the dynamic nature of the equilibrium, at constant conditions, the concentration of dissociated ion pairs in the water remains invariant over time.

What makes the description of the dynamic equilibrium associated with persistent free radicals in petroleum more difficult is that it is not a simple binary combination. The free radical species A• and B• in Figure 3 are not only engaged in a simple equilibrium with A–B but also all of the other free radical species—C•, D•, E•, and so forth—and the different potential binary combinations thereof. The macroscopically observed persistent free radical concentration is then the result of the multicomponent equilibrium of all radical species and combinations of radical species.

What evidence exists for this description of persistent free radicals in petroleum, and can this description provide a viable explanation for the observations reported in literature?

3.4.1. Impact of Bulk Liquid Composition

One aspect of the impact of the solvent on free radicals that was noted in Section 3.3 was the influence of the solvent on the ΔG of the free radical species in solution. If the persistent free radical species in petroleum is engaged in dynamic reaction equilibrium, then a change in the bulk liquid properties should have an impact on the free radical concentration. This was indeed what was reported.

It was found that the concentration of solvent affected the measured concentration of free radicals in petroleum (Table 2) [1]. To be clear, the concentration of the free radical species is expressed on the basis of the amount of analyte, the petroleum, which takes the dilution into account (i.e., number of spins/g of analyte). The data were taken from a single study because the quantification of free radical content has several pitfalls [27] which may introduce discrepancies in the absolute numbers reported between studies.

Table 2. Change in free radical concentration in heavy gas oil (HGO) when ESR measurements were performed at different concentrations of heavy gas oil in toluene [1].

HGO Concentration (wt%)	Free Radical Concentration	
	(spins/g HGO)	(µmol/g HGO)
4.6	8.7×10^{17}	1.4
11	4.0×10^{17}	0.67
20	2.3×10^{17}	0.38
22	2.0×10^{17}	0.34
37	1.4×10^{17}	0.23
49	1.1×10^{17}	0.18

The change in the free radical concentration of the petroleum shown in Table 2 is a consequence of the change in bulk liquid composition. In straight-run heavy gas oil, the free radical concentration at ambient conditions was of the order 1×10^{17} spins/g but increased to 8×10^{17} spins/g when diluted to 5 wt% in toluene.

In the example shown in Table 2, the impact of changing the bulk liquid composition on the equilibrium free radical concentration was considerable. When this is interpreted in terms of ΔG, toluene stabilized dissociated free radicals in solution better than the petroleum fraction. The observation is consistent with the increased stabilization of chlorine radicals by aromatic solvents reported before [28], and presumably for a similar reason.

The bulk liquid composition can also be changed in different ways by making use of different solvents at the same concentration.

The effect of different solvents on the persistent free radical concentration in bitumen has been previously evaluated. Khulbe et al. [29] evaluated different solvents in the quantification of free radicals and noted that the number of free radicals in the bitumen–solvent or asphaltenes–solvent solution was dependent on the nature of the solvent. In their work, it was observed that the persistent free radical concentration of the analyte decreased exponentially with an increase in the dipole moment of the solvent.

In a study by Tannous et al. [30], it was also found that at the same level of petroleum dilution the type of solvent affected the free radical concentration. However, this study did not find a relationship between the free radical concentration in the solution with the dipole moment of the solvent. Additionally, bulk properties of the solvent such as molecular weight, refractive index, density, and viscosity were not correlated to the free radical concentration of the analyte. Table 3 [30] illustrates the effect of the type of solvent on the persistent free radical concentration. The measurements were all performed at the same concentration of bitumen.

Table 3. Change in free radical concentration in bitumen when ESR measurements were performed at the same concentration of bitumen, but different solvents [30].

Solvent	Free Radical Concentration	
	(spins/g Bitumen)	(μmol/g Bitumen)
Carbon disulfide	1.44×10^{18}	2.4
2,3-Benzofuran	0.99×10^{18}	1.6
Cumene	0.92×10^{18}	1.5
Toluene	0.76×10^{18}	1.3
Tetrahydrothiophene	0.76×10^{18}	1.3
Diphenyl sulfide	0.63×10^{18}	1.0

Here, it is important to point out that some solvents are "lossy", and this can affect the quality factor (Q-factor) of an ESR, which will affect the signal intensity in relation to the amount of free radicals present [27,31]. In practical terms, the Q-factor is a relationship between the amount of energy stored in the ESR per unit time and the amount of energy lost per unit time. As long as this ratio remains constant, the ESR spectrometer can be calibrated to quantify the free radical concentration of unknown samples against the concentration of free radicals in a known standard. When all samples are measured using the same type of ESR hardware, ESR probes, and bulk solvent, the Q-factor remains the same. However, when the bulk solvent is changed, there is a risk that the Q-factor may change.

The study by Tannous et al. [30] did not explicitly determine whether there was a change in Q-factor, but this was evaluated in the study by Elofson et al. [32]. They compared measurements of the free radical concentration of petroleum asphaltenes samples sealed in a capillary tube placed in different solvents and the same petroleum asphaltenes dissolved in those same solvents. It was reported that there was no change in Q-factor for benzene, toluene, pyridine, quinoline, and tetralin, with a constant free radical concentration measured for the asphaltenes sealed in the capillary tube. They noted that the free radical concentration changed when the asphaltenes were dissolved in the solvents, which means that the change was not due to a change in Q-factor, but due to the interaction of the solvent with the asphaltenes. The only solvent that was tested for which the Q-factor changed was nitrobenzene.

It can be concluded that variation in the nature and concentration of solvent species at constant temperature caused a change in the measured persistent free radical content of petroleum. This is consistent with a description of persistent free radicals in terms of dynamic reaction equilibrium that will be affected by changes in ΔG caused by the bulk liquid properties.

3.4.2. Impact of Temperature

Reaction equilibrium is usually a function of temperature. If the persistent free radical concentration is a consequence of dynamic reaction equilibrium, it is expected that the measured concentration of free radicals should change with temperature. It is further expected that the free radical concentration should increase with temperature, because the dissociation is endothermic. This is unlikely to be a monotonic trend over a wide temperature range because the free radicals are reactive, and over time, at elevated temperature, it is expected that the measured free radical concentration will also be affected by non-equilibrium reactions.

The temperature dependence of free radical concentration is somewhat masked by the effect of Curie's law. The Curie law states that the mass magnetic susceptibility (χ) of a paramagnetic substance is proportional to the inverse temperature ($1/T$, K^{-1}). Whether the Curie law applies to all petroleum fractions is unclear. The work of Elofson et al. [32] showed little or no evidence that the Curie law was obeyed over the temperature range -196 to $+23\,°C$ for five different asphaltenes samples, although some temperature dependent changes were observed. Conversely, Hernández et al. [33] claimed that the Curie law was obeyed over the temperature range -183 to $+237\,°C$ for three different asphaltenes samples, although the data indicated that the fit was only approximate. Malhotra and Graham [34] also reported that bitumen and n-heptane solubility fractions obeyed the Curie law over the temperature range -263 to $+27\,°C$.

A further challenge to such temperature dependent measurements is the reactivity of the material. As mentioned before, there were measurable changes in composition observed at 60 and $100\,°C$ within 1–2 h [8–10]. Differently put, given sufficient time at elevated temperature, the free radicals will participate in some reactions that are not equilibrium reactions.

There is nevertheless evidence that the persistent free radical content in petroleum samples dynamically increase, as the temperature is dynamically increased from ambient conditions to about $150\,°C$ [35,36].

Since the species in petroleum that are responsible for its persistent free radical nature are the products of transformations that took place over geological time, the near instantaneous responsiveness to changes in temperature and bulk properties (Section 3.4.1) points to a dynamic reaction equilibrium.

4. Are Persistent Free Radicals in Straight-Run and Converted Petroleum Different?

It would be convenient if the description of persistent free radicals for straight-run and converted petroleum is the same. The evidence that was presented to show that the apparent persistence of free radicals in petroleum is due to dynamic reaction equilibrium (Section 3.4) relied mostly on measurements made using straight-run petroleum and petroleum fractions.

It stands to reason that when persistent free radicals are found in converted petroleum products, the same arguments could be applied to explain the longevity of free radicals in terms of dynamic reaction equilibrium. However, there are some important differences in equilibration and the reaction pathways available to persistent free radicals in straight-run and converted petroleum:

(i) The species that give rise to the observed persistent free radicals in straight-run petroleum are species that over geological time, exhausted their reactive pathways to more stable products within the mixture. The straight-run material is an equilibrated mixture. When the petroleum is subjected to conversion, the material is no longer equilibrated.

(ii) Both hydrogen transfer and methyl transfer reactions can take place at meaningful rates at temperatures below the onset of thermal cracking [8,9,37–39]. There is evidence that petroleum processing at milder conditions than normally associated with thermal conversion leads to changes in the composition and properties of the petroleum. For example, changes in physical properties and spectroscopy of bitumen were clearly visible over a period of 8 h exposure to temperature of $150\,°C$ under inert gas atmosphere [40]. After heating bitumen to $70\,°C$ over a period of 5.5 h, gas evolution was measurably increased over the baseline emissions at $25\,°C$ [41]. These are just two examples to illustrate that the temperature threshold for reactive change is in petroleum with a high persistent free radical content is quite low.

(iii) Conversion of petroleum changes the bulk liquid composition. It has already been shown that a change in bulk liquid composition will affect the concentration of free radicals. Depending on the severity of the change, the converted petroleum may also contain additional hydrogen acceptor species, such as olefins. Under inert ambient storage, the converted petroleum will continue to change, with changes in the persistent free radical content and properties of the material being apparent over a period of weeks (Table 4) [42].

Table 4. Changes in converted petroleum during storage at ambient conditions under inert atmosphere [42].

Storage Time (Weeks)	Free Radical Concentration		Refractive Index at 20 °C	Density at 20 °C (kg/m^3)
	(spins/g)	(µmol/g)		
0	1.9×10^{18}	3.1	1.5749	986.6
8	1.6×10^{18}	2.7	1.5774	997.1
20	1.3×10^{18}	2.1	1.5809	1001.1

To avoid the complication of dealing with non-equilibrated materials, subsequent questions about persistent free radicals in petroleum will be limited to straight-run materials. At the same time, some of the observations may equally apply to converted petroleum products, although no specific support for extending the conclusions to converted products is presented in this study.

Finally, it should be noted that exposure of straight-run petroleum to air and light can, over time, affect the free radical concentration. For example, the bond dissociation energy for free radical formation to initiate new free radical reactions can be provided by light of a sufficiently short wavelength (typically ultraviolet light) [43].

5. Is Persistent Free Radical Concentration Part of the Compositional Continuum?

One of the most powerful concepts in the characterization of petroleum is the concept of the compositional continuum. To quote from Altgelt and Boduszynski [44], "... compositional trends in fractions of increasing boiling point are continuous and that this continuity extends even to nondistillable residues". This continuity was demonstrated for many properties, but the work did not include quantification of the free radical content. Nevertheless, there was an expectation that the compositional features giving rise to the persistent free radical nature of petroleum would also follow the compositional continuum.

There is a common trend that can be observed in the characterization of straight-run petroleum in terms of its distillation fractions. As the atmospheric equivalent boiling point of the distillation fraction increases, the persistent free radical content also increases. Atmospheric distillate does not have a detectable amount of persistent free radicals. As the boiling point of the petroleum fractions further increases, it is found that for light vacuum gas oil (LVGO), heavy vacuum gas oil (HVGO), and vacuum residue (VR), the increase in boiling point range corresponds to an increase in the persistent free radical concentration of those fractions (Table 5) [1].

Table 5. Persistent free radical concentration in straight-run distillation fractions of Athabasca bitumen [1].

Distillation Fraction	Free Radical Concentration	
	(spins/g)	(µmol/g)
Light vacuum gas oil	7.8×10^{17}	1.3
Heavy vacuum gas oil	8.7×10^{17}	1.4
Vacuum residue	1.4×10^{18}	2.3

The atmospheric equivalent boiling point temperature of petroleum is correlated with the average molecular weight of the material [44]. The compositional continuum can be rationalized by viewing the composition in terms of the probability of finding a specific structural element for species with a specific molecular weight. For example, there is a threshold molecular weight below which it is not possible to find trinuclear aromatic species, but beyond this threshold molecular weight, it is possible to find species that contain a trinuclear aromatic substructure.

This reasoning can be applied to species that form persistent free radicals. It is postulated that there are specific structural requirements that must be met by species to participate in the dynamic reaction equilibrium involved in maintaining a persistent free radical concentration. For example, we can see how specific structural groupings with condensed hydrocarbon rings that have an odd number of carbons (Figure 4) would naturally give rise to species that have a free radical nature. The likelihood of finding such structural elements increases with increasing molecular weight.

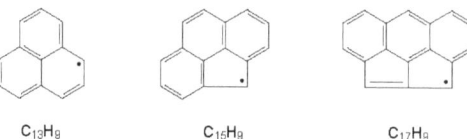

$C_{13}H_9$ $C_{15}H_9$ $C_{17}H_9$

Figure 4. Examples of condensed aromatic structures with an odd number of carbons that could potentially exist as a free radical (as shown) in dynamic reaction equilibrium with another free radical to give rise to a finite persistent free radical concentration in petroleum.

The simplest condensed aromatic structure with an odd number of carbons that is prone to free radical formation is indene, which forms the indenyl radical (•C_9H_7). Although indene is in the atmospheric distillate, with an atmospheric equivalent boiling point temperature of 182 °C, upon heating, it self-reacts to form a product with measurable persistent free radical content [45].

The aforementioned observations about the potential link between persistent free radical nature and structural elements in species explains why there is the expectation that persistent free radical content is a property that can be described in terms of the compositional continuum. Unfortunately, the only study that the authors are aware of that reported on the measured relationship between molecular weight and persistent free radical content is that by Rudnick and Tueting (Figure 5) [46].

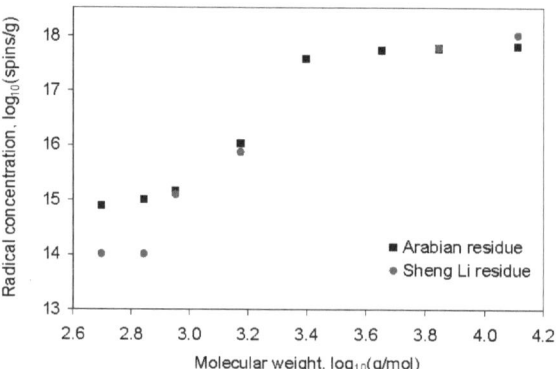

Figure 5. Relationship between persistent free radical concentration and average molecular weight of two straight-run oils, redrawn using the data from Rudnick and Tueting [46].

In the study by Rudnick and Tueting [46], two straight-run oils were separated using preparative size exclusion chromatography and characterized using ESR to determine the persistent free radical content. The free radical concentration was determined based on a calibration with 1,1-diphenyl-2-picryl-hydrazyl (DPPH), and measurement reproducibility was reported to be within ±15% relative [46]. Based on current understanding, the molecular weights are likely over-estimated [47], but this does not detract from the value of this study, which employed a single consistent measure of molecular weight.

According to the data in Figure 5, the persistent free radical content has a regular relationship with molecular weight, which, in turn, is related to the atmospheric equivalent boiling point of the petroleum. Thus, both Table 5 and Figure 5 presented data showing an increase in persistent free radical content with an increase in atmospheric equivalent boiling point temperature. Based on the limited evidence presented, it appears that persistent free radical content in straight-run petroleum is a property that is part of the compositional continuum.

6. How Is Persistent Free Radical Concentration Related to Petroleum Composition?

Continuing from the tentative conclusion that the persistent free radical concentration is part of the compositional continuum of petroleum (see Section 5), it would be useful to know how the persistent free radical concentration is related to petroleum composition. Properties of petroleum that are part of the compositional continuum may also be correlated to the free radical concentration since both are correlated to atmospheric equivalent boiling point temperature. The challenge is therefore to differentiate between properties that are just correlated because they are both part of the compositional continuum and those that are not only correlated but also causally related to the origin of the persistent free radicals.

It is unlikely that a clear answer to the question can be provided with the current state of knowledge about persistent free radicals in petroleum. Some possible relationships can nevertheless be explored.

6.1. Aromatic Carbon Content in Relation to Free Radical Concentration

The example presented in Figure 4 suggested that there might be a causal relationship between the abundance of specific aromatic species and the persistent free radical concentration. Although that specific example was meant to be illustrative, it nevertheless presented a plausible relationship between aromatic carbon content and free radical concentration.

The persistent free radical concentration of different materials was reported along with their aromatic fraction [2,48], which indicated a relationship between these properties. The relationship spanned many different materials, which included converted materials from petroleum and coal.

However, the observation should be interpreted with caution. The apparent relationship between the aromatic fraction and the free radical concentration is not restricted to the aromatic carbon content, nor does it imply that the reported relationship involved carbon-centered radicals. In fact, further evidence was provided that extended the relationship to the heteroatom content of the materials, which is discussed next (Section 6.2).

6.2. Heteroatom Content in Relation to Free Radical Concentration

Generally speaking, carbon-centered radicals have g-factors closer to that of a "free electron" compared to heteroatom-centered radicals that have slightly higher values [27].

For pure compounds, the g-factor and hyperfine splitting of the ESR signal can provide detailed information about the nature of the radical center. Hyperfine splitting, or hyperfine coupling, is when the unpaired electron is coupled with a nearby nucleus with non-integer spin number, such as ^1H, ^{13}C, and ^{14}N. The coupling affects the energy needed for the change in spin orientation. Hyperfine splitting in ESR is analogous to the effect of spin-spin coupling of nuclei in nuclear magnetic resonance (NMR) spectrometry.

However, the ESR spectrum of the organic radicals in petroleum consists only of a single absorption. In complex mixtures, the overlapping signals of many different radical species obscure the hyperfine splitting, and the observed g-factor (Equation (1)) becomes the weighted average of the mixture.

Yen and Sprang [49,50] pointed out that the heteroatom content in free radical species caused a systematic change in the g-factor of the organic radical peak. Specifically, it was claimed that there was a linear relationship between the g-factor and the sum of the N, O, and S elemental content in petroleum and coal. Retcofsky et al. [51] showed similar trends between the g-factor and O and S content in coals, and Elofson et al. [32] also presented data that suggested that there was a relationship between the g-value and heteroatom content. On the other hand, Malhotra and Buckmaster [52] found that the relationship, although observed, was not always statistically significant at 99% level of confidence.

The relationship between g-factor and free radical concentration is of interest because both are macroscopic averages that contain information about the nature of the free radicals. An increase in g-factor implies that, on average, there is a larger contribution of heteroatom-centered free radicals or an increase in carbon-centered radicals in proximity to heteroatoms and other radical centers that may cause a shift in the g-factor.

6.3. Watson K-Factor in Relation to Free Radical Concentration

The persistent free radical concentration in petroleum was expected to be the result of both the composition of the petroleum and the change in composition with boiling point, as is the case with other properties that follow the compositional continuum. It was therefore of interest to see whether the Watson K-factor (K_W) was a property relationship that allowed the normalization of the impact of the compositional properties and distillation profile in relation to free radical concentration.

The K_W is an empirical measure in petroleum refining that combines the mean atmospheric equivalent boiling point temperature (T_{50}, °R) and density expressed as specific gravity (SG) to give an indication of composition (Equation (2)) [53].

$$K_W = \frac{\sqrt[3]{T_{50}}}{SG} \quad (2)$$

The values for K_W practically range from around 10.5 for very aromatic and naphthenic oils to around 13.0 for very paraffinic oils.

It was found that for oil sands bitumen from different locations that had similar values of K_W, the persistent free radical concentrations varied more than could be explained by experimental uncertainty (Table 6) [1,54,55]. The mean boiling points for these materials were close, and it is known that the distillation profiles for Athabasca and Cold Lake bitumens are quite similar [56]. Although the values in Table 6 were not from the same study, the studies were from the same laboratory using the same analytical protocol. It is therefore tentatively concluded that the K_W does not adequately capture the properties that determine the persistent free radical concentration.

Table 6. Comparison of different straight-run oil sands bitumen samples in terms of Watson K-factor (K_W), mean boiling temperature (T_{50}), and persistent free radical concentration [1,54,55].

Sample	K_W	T_{50}		Free Radical Concentration		Reference
		(°R)	(°C)	(spins/g)	(µmol/g)	
Cold Lake bitumen	11.2	1530	577	9.5×10^{17}	1.6	[1,54]
Athabasca bitumen	11.2	1489	554	1.6×10^{18}	2.7	[55]

7. Are Persistent Free Radicals in Petroleum Found Only in the Asphaltenes Fraction?

A solubility class of petroleum that is often encountered as a topic of study is asphaltenes [57]. Asphaltenes are defined as a material that is insoluble in an n-alkane solvent but soluble in an aromatic solvent. There are several standard test methods for the separation of asphaltenes from petroleum—for example ASTM D2007 [58], ASTM D4124 [59], and ASTM D6560 [60]—and asphaltenes are also encountered as an industrial product obtained from solvent deasphalting as process [53,56,57].

Persistent free radicals in the petroleum partition between the n-alkane soluble (maltenes) fraction and n-alkane insoluble (asphaltenes) fraction. The free radical concentration is not necessarily an additive property. Asphaltenes separated from petroleum have a higher persistent free radical content than the whole petroleum, and the maltenes separated from petroleum have a lower persistent free radical content (Table 7) [55]. The persistent free radicals in petroleum are therefore not limited to only the asphaltenes. In fact, the persistent free radical concentrations of several crude oils that were measured and reported, had little or no measurable *n*-pentane insoluble asphaltenes fraction [32].

Table 7. Partitioning of persistent free radicals in Athabasca bitumen from Nexen Long Lake between the maltenes (*n*-heptane soluble) and asphaltenes (*n*-heptane insoluble) fractions [55].

Sample	Free Radical Concentration	
	(spins/g)	(µmol/g)
Whole petroleum	1.6×10^{18}	2.7
Maltenes fraction	1.1×10^{18}	1.8
Asphaltenes fraction	3.4×10^{18}	5.6

As one would expect, the persistent free radicals in asphaltenes have features in common with persistent free radicals in whole petroleum, namely, the responsiveness of the free radical concentration to changes in solvent environment and dynamic changes in temperature (see Section 3.4) [29,61].

In the study by Adams et al. [62], the *n*-pentane insoluble asphaltenes fractions from different crude oils were further separated by size exclusion chromatography into different molecular weight fractions, and the free radical concentration of each fraction was determined by ESR spectrometry. The relationship between free radical concentration and molecular weight found is shown in Figure 6 [62].

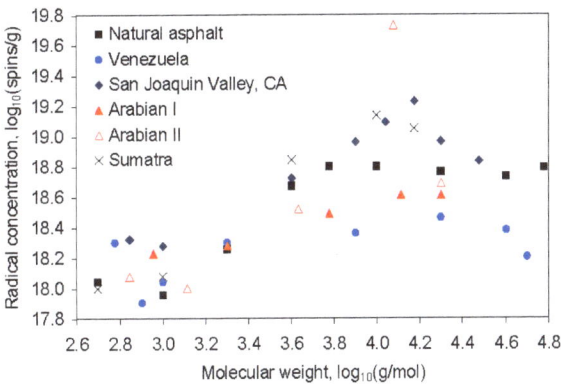

Figure 6. Relationship between persistent free radical concentration and average molecular weight of different asphaltenes, redrawn using the data from Adams et al. [62].

The increase in persistent free radical concentration with the increase in molecular weight observed for whole petroleum (Figure 5) is also, to some extent, seen in the asphaltenes (Figure 6). The trend, broadly speaking, is one where the free radical concentration increases with molecular weight, but it is not a monotonic increase, and for several of the asphaltenes, the free radical concentration passed through a maximum with an increase in molecular weight.

The molecular weights were determined in a consistent way [62], but (as mentioned before) the values are too high based on current understanding [47]. The higher-molecular-weight fractions from size exclusion chromatography likely represent a higher extent of molecular-level aggregation [63], with a correspondingly larger difference between the monomeric molecular weight and reported value.

Other studies that report both free radical concentration and molecular weight [18,64] also found that the free radical concentration increased somewhat with an increase in molecular weight, but when sufficient data was available to see a trend, the trend was not monotonous.

8. Conclusions

The stated purpose of this work was to review the field of persistent free radicals in petroleum and to explain the apparent inconsistencies between free radical persistence and reactivity. The main conclusions were as follows:

(a) There is a difference between the longevity of an individual free radical species and the macroscopic average of free radical longevity in petroleum. Individual species in petroleum may be termed persistent free radicals because their longevity exceeds that of the methyl radical, but the individual free radical species in petroleum are short-lived and reactive. It is the macroscopic average free radical concentration in petroleum that persisted over geological time, not that of individual free radical species.

(b) The persistent free radical concentration in petroleum can be explained in terms of a dynamic reaction equilibrium of free radical dissociation and association that causes a finite number of species at any given time to be present as free radicals. Evidence to support this description are the change in free radical concentration related to changes in the Gibbs free energy of the system when the bulk liquid properties are changed, as well as the responsiveness of free radical concentration to dynamic change in temperature.

(c) Cage effects, solvent effects, steric protection, and radical stabilization affect the reaction rate of free radicals in petroleum, but these phenomena are not responsible for the macroscopically observed persistent free radical concentration in petroleum.

(d) The main difference between persistent free radicals in straight-run petroleum and those in converted petroleum is that the former system has been equilibrated over geologic time, whereas the latter is not equilibrated. The free radical concentration in straight-run petroleum at constant conditions is time invariant, whereas the free radical concentration in converted petroleum can change over time, even at ambient conditions.

(e) The persistent free radical concentration in petroleum distillation fractions increases with an increase in atmospheric equivalent boiling point of the distillation fraction. Based on the limited evidence presented, it appears that persistent free radical content in straight-run petroleum is a property that is part of the compositional continuum postulated by Altgelt and Boduszynski.

(f) Separation of petroleum into solubility fractions causes a partitioning of the free radical species. The asphaltenes (*n*-alkane insoluble material) fraction of whole petroleum has a higher concentration of persistent free radicals, and the maltenes (*n*-alkane soluble material) fraction has a lower concentration of persistent free radicals than whole petroleum. As expected, the free radicals in the solubility fractions have the properties of the free radicals in the whole petroleum, which includes responsiveness to changes in solvent environment and dynamic changes in temperature.

(g) Attempts to relate persistent free radical concentration to petroleum composition were inconclusive.

Author Contributions: The authors contributed equally to this work. All authors have read and agreed to the published version of the manuscript.

Funding: This research received no external funding.

Institutional Review Board Statement: Not applicable.

Informed Consent Statement: Not applicable.

Data Availability Statement: This research made use only of previously published data and the origin and experimental details can be found in the cited literature noted in this study.

Acknowledgments: We would like to acknowledge people that unwittingly served as inspiration for the research presented here. Gareth and Sandra Eaton, for their work on quantitative electron spin resonance spectrometry, and Dicho Stratiev, for sharing a wealth of industrial data and insights on thermal conversion processes with the research community.

Conflicts of Interest: The authors declare no conflict of interest.

References

1. Tannous, J.H.; De Klerk, A. Quantification of the free radical content of oilsands bitumen fractions. *Energy Fuels* **2019**, *33*, 7083–7093. [CrossRef]
2. Chang, H.-L.; Wong, G.K.; Lin, J.-R.; Yen, T.F. Electron spin resonance study of bituminous substances and asphaltenes. In *Asphaltenes and Asphalts*; Yen, T.F., Chilingarian, G.V., Eds.; Developments in Petroleum Science Volume 40 B; Elsevier: Amsterdam, The Netherlands, 2000; Volume 2, pp. 229–280.
3. Raseev, S. *Thermal and Catalytic Processes in Petroleum Refining*; Marcel Dekker: New York, NY, USA, 2003.
4. Griller, D.; Ingold, K.U. Persistent carbon-centered radicals. *Acc. Chem. Res.* **1976**, *9*, 13–19. [CrossRef]
5. Forrester, A.R.; Hay, J.M.; Thomson, R.H. *Organic Chemistry of Stable Free Radicals*; Academic Press: London, UK, 1968.
6. Parsons, A.F. *An Introduction to Free Radical Chemistry*; Blackwell Science: Oxford, UK, 2000.
7. Alili, A.S.; Siddiquee, M.N.; De Klerk, A. Origin of free radical persistence in asphaltenes: Cage effect and steric protection. *Energy Fuels* **2020**, *34*, 348–359. [CrossRef]
8. Styles, Y.; De Klerk, A. Sodium conversion of oilsands bitumen-derived asphaltenes. *Energy Fuels* **2016**, *30*, 5214–5222. [CrossRef]
9. Naghizada, N.; Prado, G.H.C.; De Klerk, A. Uncatalyzed hydrogen transfer during 100–250 °C conversion of asphaltenes. *Energy Fuels* **2017**, *31*, 6800–6811. [CrossRef]
10. Petrakis, L.; Grandy, D.W. An electron spin resonance spectrometric investigation of natural, extracted and thermally altered kerogenous materials. *Geochim. Cosmochim. Acta* **1980**, *44*, 763–768. [CrossRef]
11. Lorand, J.P. The cage effect. In *Inorganic Reaction Mechanisms, Part II*; Progress in Inorganic Chemistry; Edwards, J.O., Ed.; Wiley and Sons, Inc.: New York, NY, USA, 1972; Volume 17, pp. 207–325.
12. Koenig, T.; Fischer, H. "Cage" effects. In *Free Radicals*; Kochi, J.K., Ed.; Wiley and Sons, Inc.: New York, NY, USA, 1973; Volume 1, pp. 157–189.
13. Barry, J.T.; Berg, D.J.; Tyler, D.R. Radical cage effects: Comparison of solvent bulk viscosity and microviscosity in predicting the recombination efficiencies of radical cage pairs. *J. Am. Chem. Soc.* **2016**, *138*, 9389–9392. [CrossRef]
14. Barry, J.T.; Berg, D.J.; Tyler, D.R. Radical cage effects: The prediction of radical cage pair recombination efficiencies using microviscosity across a range of solvent types. *J. Am. Chem. Soc.* **2017**, *139*, 14399–14405. [CrossRef]
15. Li, X.; Ogihara, T.; Abe, M.; Nakamura, Y.; Yamago, S. The effect of viscosity on the diffusion and termination reaction of organic radical pairs. *Chem.-Eur. J.* **2019**, *25*, 9846–9850. [CrossRef]
16. Reichardt, C. *Solvents and Solvent Effects in Organic Chemistry*, 3rd ed.; Wiley-VCH: Weinheim, Germany, 2003.
17. Mujica, V.; Nieto, P.; Puerta, L.; Acevedo, S. Caging of molecules by asphaltenes. A model for free radical preservation in crude oils. *Energy Fuels* **2000**, *14*, 632–639. [CrossRef]
18. Acevedo, S.; Escobar, G.; Ranaudo, M.A.; Piñate, J.; Amorín, A. Observations about the structure and dispersion of petroleum asphaltenes aggregates obtained from dialysis fractionation and characterization. *Energy Fuels* **1997**, *11*, 774–778. [CrossRef]
19. Zhang, Y.; Siskin, M.; Gray, M.R.; Walters, C.C.; Rodgers, R.P. Mechanisms of asphaltene aggregation: Puzzles and a new hypothesis. *Energy Fuels* **2020**, *34*, 9094–9107. [CrossRef]
20. Gray, M.R.; Yarranton, H.W.; Chacón-Patiño, M.L.; Rodgers, R.P.; Bouyssiere, B.; Giusti, P. Distributed properties of asphaltene nanoaggregates in crude oils: A review. *Energy Fuels* **2021**, *35*, 18078–18103. [CrossRef]
21. Rüchardt, C. Relations between structure and reactivity in free-radical chemistry. *Angew. Chem. Int. Ed. Engl.* **1970**, *9*, 830–843. [CrossRef]
22. Stella, L.; Janousek, Z.; Merényi, R.; Viehe, H.G. Stabilization of radicals by "capto-dative" substitution –C–C addition to radicophilic olefins. *Angew. Chem. Int. Ed. Engl.* **1978**, *17*, 691–692. [CrossRef]
23. Viehe, H.G.; Janousek, Z.; Merényi, R.; Stella, L. The captodative effect. *Acc. Chem. Res.* **1985**, *18*, 148–154. [CrossRef]
24. Huyser, E.S. Solvent effects in free-radical reactions. In *Advances in Free Radical Chemistry*; Williams, G.H., Ed.; Academic Press: London, UK, 1965; Volume 1, pp. 77–153.
25. Gendell, J.; Freed, J.H.; Fraenkel, G.K. Solvent effects in electron spin resonance. *Chem. Phys.* **1962**, *37*, 2832–2841. [CrossRef]
26. Isenberg, I.; Baird, S.L., Jr. Solvent effects in radical ion formation. *J. Am. Chem. Soc.* **1962**, *84*, 3803–3805. [CrossRef]
27. Eaton, G.R.; Eaton, S.S.; Barr, D.P.; Weber, R.T. *Quantitative EPR*; Springer: New York, NY, USA, 2010.
28. Russell, G.A. Solvent effects in the reactions of free radicals and atoms. *J. Am. Chem. Soc.* **1957**, *79*, 2977–2978. [CrossRef]
29. Khulbe, K.C.; Mann, R.S.; Lu, B.C.-Y.; Lamarche, G.; Lamarche, A.-M. Effects of solvents on free radicals of bitumen and asphaltenes. *Fuel Process. Technol.* **1992**, *32*, 133–141. [CrossRef]
30. Tannous, J.H.; Tulegenova, A.; De Klerk, A. Effect of solvents on persistent free radical content in the absence of reactions. *Energy Fuels* **2022**, *36*, 5253–5266. [CrossRef]
31. Dalal, D.P.; Eaton, S.S.; Eaton, G.R. The effects of lossy solvents on quantitative EPR studies. *J. Magn. Reson.* **1981**, *44*, 415–428. [CrossRef]
32. Elofson, R.M.; Schulz, K.F.; Hitchon, B. Geochemical significance of chemical composition and ESR properties of asphaltenes in crude oils from Alberta, Canada. *Geochim. Cosmochim. Acta* **1977**, *41*, 567–580. [CrossRef]

33. Hernández, M.S.; Coll, D.S.; Silva, P.J. Temperature dependence of the electron paramagnetic resonance spectrum of asphaltenes from Venezuelan crude oils and their vacuum residues. *Energy Fuels* **2019**, *33*, 990–997. [CrossRef]
34. Malhotra, V.M.; Graham, W.R.M. Characterization of P.R. Spring (Utah) tar sand bitumen by the EPR technique: Free radicals. *Fuel* **1983**, *62*, 1255–1264. [CrossRef]
35. Yokono, T.; Obara, T.; Sanada, Y.; Shimomura, S.; Imamura, T. Characterization of Carbonization Reaction of Petroleum Residues by Means of High-Temperature ESR and Transferable Hydrogen. *Carbon* **1986**, *24*, 29–32. [CrossRef]
36. Dappe, V.; Ben Tayeb, K.; Vezin, H.; Mariette, S.; Serve, O.; Livadaris, V. Effect of Thermal Treatment of Different Petroleum Fractions: Characterization by in situ EPR Spectroscopy. *Energy Fuels* **2020**, *34*, 12026–12032. [CrossRef]
37. Rüchardt, C.; Gerst, M.; Ebenhoch, J. Uncatalyzed transfer hydrogenation and transfer hydrogenolysis: Two novel types of hydrogen-transfer reactions. *Angew. Chem. Int. Ed.* **1997**, *36*, 1406–1430. [CrossRef]
38. Tannous, J.H.; De Klerk, A. Methyl and hydrogen transfer in free radical reactions. *Energy Fuels* **2020**, *34*, 1698–1709. [CrossRef]
39. Payan, F.; De Klerk, A. Hydrogen transfer in asphaltenes and bitumen at 250 °C. *Energy Fuels* **2018**, *32*, 9340–9348. [CrossRef]
40. Yañez Jaramillo, L.M.; de Klerk, A. Partial upgrading of bitumen by thermal conversion at 150–300 °C. *Energy Fuels* **2018**, *32*, 3299–3311. [CrossRef]
41. Jha, K.N.; Montgomery, D.S.; Strausz, O.P. Chemical composition of gases in Alberta bitumens and in low-temperature thermolysis of oil sand asphaltenes and maltenes. In *Oil Sand and Oil Shale Chemistry*; Strausz, O.P., Lown, E.M., Eds.; Verlag Chemie: New York, NY, USA, 1978; pp. 33–54.
42. Yan, Y.; Prado, G.H.C.; De Klerk, A. Storage stability of products from visbreaking of oilsands bitumen. *Energy Fuels* **2020**, *34*, 9585–9598. [CrossRef]
43. Ellis, C.; Wells, A.A.; Heyroth, F.F. *The Chemical Action of Ultraviolet Rays*; Reinhold: New York, NY, USA, 1941.
44. Altgelt, K.H.; Boduszynski, M.M. *Composition and Analysis of Heavy Petroleum Fractions*; Marcel Dekker: New York, NY, USA, 1994.
45. Tannous, J.H.; De Klerk, A. Asphaltenes formation during thermal conversion of deasphalted oil. *Fuel* **2019**, *255*, 115786. [CrossRef]
46. Rudnick, L.R.; Tueting, D.R. Variation of free radical concentration with molecular weight in petroleum feedstocks. *Fuel Sci. Technol. Int.* **1989**, *7*, 57–68. [CrossRef]
47. Podgorski, D.C.; Corilo, Y.E.; Nyadong, L.; Lobodin, V.V.; Bythell, B.J.; Robbins, W.K.; McKenna, A.M.; Marshall, A.G.; Rodgers, R.P. Heavy petroleum composition. 5. Compositional and structural continuum of petroleum revealed. *Energy Fuels* **2013**, *27*, 1268–1276. [CrossRef]
48. Yen, T.F.; Erdman, J.G.; Saraceno, A.J. Investigation of the nature of free radicals in petroleum asphaltenes and related substances by Electron Spin Resonance. *Anal. Chem.* **1962**, *34*, 694–700. [CrossRef]
49. Yen, T.F.; Sprang, S.R. ESR g-values of bituminous materials. *Prepr. Pap.-Am. Chem. Soc. Div. Petrol. Chem.* **1970**, *15*, A65–A76.
50. Yen, T.F.; Sprang, S.R. Contribution of E.S.R. analysis toward diagenic mechanisms in bituminous deposits. *Geochim. Cosmochim. Acta* **1977**, *41*, 1007–1018. [CrossRef]
51. Retcofsky, H.L.; Hough, M.R.; Maguire, M.M.; Clarkson, R.B. Nature of the free radicals in coals, pyrolyzed coals, solvent-refined coal, and coal liquefaction products. In *Coal Structure*; Gorbaty, M.L., Ouchi, K., Eds.; Advances in Chemistry; American Chemical Society: Washington, DC, USA, 1981; Volume 192, pp. 37–58.
52. Malhotra, V.M.; Buckmaster, H.A. 9 and 34 GHz EPR Study of the free radicals in various asphaltenes: Statistical correlation of the g-values with heteroatom content. *Org. Geochem.* **1985**, *8*, 235–239. [CrossRef]
53. Kaiser, M.J.; De Klerk, A.; Gary, J.H.; Handwerk, G.E. *Petroleum Refining. Technology, Economics, and Markets*, 6th ed.; CRC Press: Boca Raton, FL, USA, 2020.
54. Wang, L.; Zachariah, A.; Yang, S.; Prasad, V.; De Klerk, A. Visbreaking oilsands-derived bitumen in the temperature range of 340–400 °C. *Energy Fuels* **2014**, *28*, 5014–5022. [CrossRef]
55. Yañez Jaramillo, L.M.; De Klerk, A. Is solubility classification a meaningful measure in thermal conversion? *Energy Fuels* **2022**, *36*, 8649–8662. [CrossRef]
56. Gray, M.R. *Upgrading Oilsands Bitumen and Heavy Oil*; University of Alberta Press: Edmonton, AB, Canada, 2015.
57. Ramirez-Corredores, M.M. *The Science and Technology of Unconventional Oils*; Academic Press: London, UK, 2017; pp. 41–222.
58. *ASTM D2007*; Standard Test Method for Characteristic Groups in Rubber Extender and Processing Oils and Other Petroleum-derived Oils by the Clay-Gel Absorption Chromatographic Method. ASTM International: West Conshohocken, PA, USA, 2020.
59. *ASTM D4124*; Standard Test Method for Separation of Asphalt into Four Fractions. ASTM International: West Conshohocken, PA, USA, 2018.
60. *ASTM D6560*; Standard Test Method for Determination of Asphaltenes (Heptane Insolubles) in Crude Petroleum and Petroleum Products. ASTM International: West Conshohocken, PA, USA, 2022.
61. Niizuma, S.; Steele, C.T.; Gunning, H.E.; Strausz, O.P. Electron spin resonance study of free radicals in Athabasca asphaltene. *Fuel* **1977**, *56*, 249–256. [CrossRef]
62. Adams, J.Q.; Altgelt, K.H.; LeTourneau, R.L.; Lindeman, L.P. Free radical concentrations in gel permeation fractions of asphaltenes from different crude oils. *Prepr. Pap.-Am. Chem. Soc. Div. Petrol. Chem.* **1966**, *12*, B140–B144.

63. Andersen, S.I. Effect of precipitation temperature on the composition of n-heptane asphaltenes. *Fuel Sci. Technol. Int.* **1994**, *12*, 51–74. [CrossRef]
64. Schultz, K.F.; Selucky, M.L. ESR measurements on asphaltene and resin fractions from various separation methods. *Fuel* **1981**, *60*, 951–956. [CrossRef]

Disclaimer/Publisher's Note: The statements, opinions and data contained in all publications are solely those of the individual author(s) and contributor(s) and not of MDPI and/or the editor(s). MDPI and/or the editor(s) disclaim responsibility for any injury to people or property resulting from any ideas, methods, instructions or products referred to in the content.

Review

Biodiesel Production from Waste Cooking Oil: A Perspective on Catalytic Processes

Montserrat Cerón Ferrusca [1], Rubi Romero [1,*], Sandra Luz Martínez [2], Armando Ramírez-Serrano [2] and Reyna Natividad [1,*]

[1] Chemical Engineering Laboratory, Centro Conjunto de Investigación en Química Sustentable, UAEM-UNAM, Universidad Autónoma del Estado de México, Km 14.5 Toluca-Atlacomulco Road, Toluca 50200, Mexico; mcerfer96@gmail.com

[2] Faculty of Chemistry, Universidad Autónoma del Estado de México, Toluca 50120, Mexico; slmartinezv@uaemex.mx (S.L.M.); aramirezs75@hotmail.com (A.R.-S.)

* Correspondence: rromeror@uaemex.mx (R.R.); rnatividadr@uaemex.mx (R.N.)

Abstract: Presently, the use of fossil fuels is not ecologically sustainable, which results in the need for new alternative energies such as biodiesel. This work presents a review of the classification of the lipidic feedstocks and the catalysts for biodiesel production. It also presents the pros and cons of the different processes and feedstocks through which biodiesel is obtained. In this context, cooking oil (WCO) has emerged as an alternative with a high potential for making the process sustainable. A detected limitation to achieving this is the high content of free fatty acids (FFA) and existing problems related to homogeneous and heterogeneous catalysts. To overcome this, the use of bifunctional catalysts is being evaluated by the scientific community. Thus, this work also explores the advances in the study of bifunctional catalysts, which are capable of simultaneously carrying out the esterification of free fatty acids (FFA) and the triglycerides present in the WCO. For the sake of an improved understanding of biodiesel production, flow diagrams and the mechanisms implied by each type of process (enzymatic, homogenous, and heterogeneous) are provided. This article also highlights some of the challenges in catalyst development for sustainable biodiesel production from low-grade raw materials.

Keywords: biodiesel; waste cooking oil; bifunctional catalysts; transesterification

Citation: Cerón Ferrusca, M.; Romero, R.; Martínez, S.L.; Ramírez-Serrano, A.; Natividad, R. Biodiesel Production from Waste Cooking Oil: A Perspective on Catalytic Processes. *Processes* **2023**, *11*, 1952. https://doi.org/10.3390/pr11071952

Academic Editors: Dicho Stratiev, Dobromir Yordanov and Aijun Guo

Received: 15 May 2023
Revised: 17 June 2023
Accepted: 21 June 2023
Published: 28 June 2023

Copyright: © 2023 by the authors. Licensee MDPI, Basel, Switzerland. This article is an open access article distributed under the terms and conditions of the Creative Commons Attribution (CC BY) license (https://creativecommons.org/licenses/by/4.0/).

1. Introduction

1.1. Biodiesel Global Scenario

The energy model that currently prevails is highly dependent on the usage of fossil fuels and supports various sectors such as transportation, industry, and agriculture, among others [1]. However, this model has become less and less viable due to the reduction in the non-renewable energy source, its increasing price, and the fact that this type of fuel favors an elevation in greenhouse gas emissions, some of which have been shown to have an impact on people's health as they are related to various types of cancer [2–4]. As stated by the United Nations' Sustainable Development Goals (SDG), regarding sustainable energy access (SDG7) and climate change (SDG13), several countries have started to take actions to reduce carbon emissions by at least 43% by 2030 and to not reach an increase in global temperature of 1.5 °C between 2030 and 2050 (IPCC, 2018) [5].

The aforementioned problems have motivated the development of other cleaner energy options. An example is biodiesel, because of its capability to be produced from vegetable and/or animal fats while also being able to be used in diesel engines without major changes because it poses physicochemical characteristics similar to those of high-performance diesel [6–8]. This biofuel improves engine performance in addition to having cleaner combustion because it has an oxygenated molecule that allows it to reduce CO_2 emissions by up to 80% [6,9].

In the last decade, there has been an increase in biodiesel production of approximately 4–14%, which is an economic advantage due to its growing demand [10]. Figure 1 shows the distribution of biodiesel production per geographical area in 2021 (42.7 billion liters) [11]. It can be observed in this figure that Europe produces the highest percentage of biodiesel (34%) around the globe. Biodiesel production from 2023 to 2027 is expected to grow from 50 to 52.5 billion liters, respectively [12].

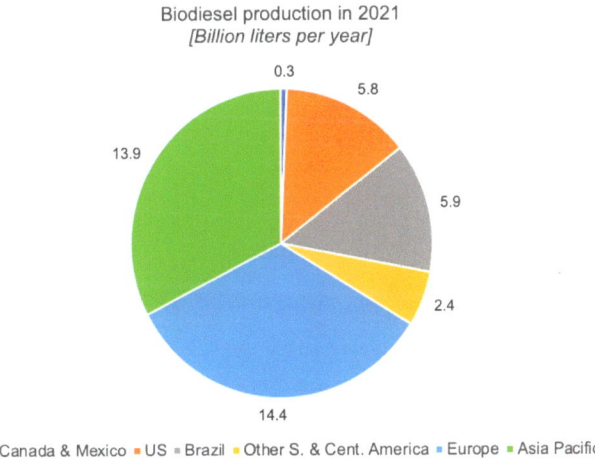

Figure 1. Global distribution of biodiesel production in 2021 with data from [11].

However, the production of this biofuel still cannot match its demand in multiple countries, mainly due to its production cost, which is derived from 60–80% of the cost of the lipid raw material [4,9]. Figure 2 shows biodiesel consumption in 2021 (45.6 billion liters) [11]. It is not surprising that the highest consumption percentage also lies in Europe (35%), and Canada and Mexico are some of the lowest consumers (1.4%).

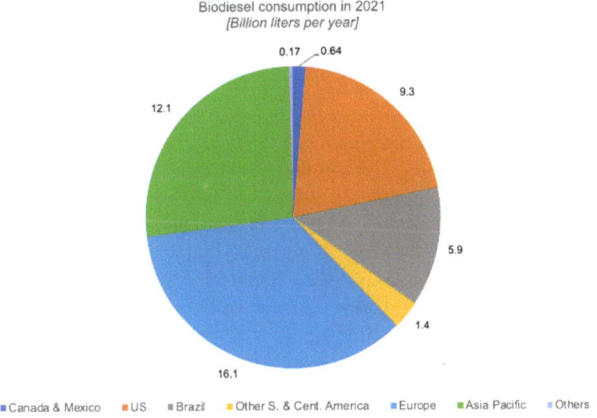

Figure 2. Global distribution of biodiesel consumption in 2021 with data from [11].

In addition, there are several countries where the legislation to promote the production of biodiesel is nonexistent and there are no established regulations about the composition of biodiesel with petroleum diesel mixtures, as has been the case in other countries in Europe and America.

In recent years, many biodiesel-producing companies have used feedstock that is more competitive and accessible than edible seed oils, such as waste oils. Furthermore, since the beginning of the Ukraine–Russia conflict, the price of biofuels has increased due to the shortage or increase in price of raw materials [13], and several European countries have been forced to use cheaper oils or waste cooking oil (WCO) to obtain biodiesel.

1.2. Biodiesel Feedstock

Figure 3 shows the feedstocks from which this biofuel can be produced. Furthermore, the context of their use will be discussed.

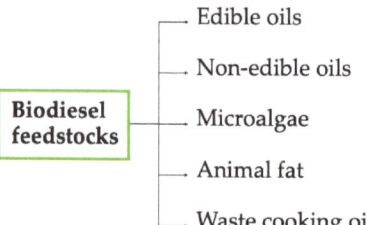

Figure 3. Feedstocks for biodiesel production.

- *Edible Oils (EO):* This raw material has been used and studied for several decades mainly because, of its purity [14]. Nevertheless, its use is currently in great controversy, mainly due to the ethical dilemma derived from its nutritional value in the market [6]. In addition, the use of this type of raw material increases the cost of biodiesel production [14]. Some of the most commonly used refined oils are soybean, peanut, corn, and sunflower [6].
- *Non-edible Oils (NEO):* The need to discover low-cost raw materials that do not compete with the food market has led to various investigations for biodiesel production from non-edible oils and reusable oils [6,14]. NEO has shown a reduction in biodiesel production costs and is highly available in several parts of the world [6]. Around the world, in different areas (mainly Africa and Asia), various species of plants are known to have an oil content of ≥20% within their seeds, which makes them potential sources of edible oils [14]. However, the main disadvantage of using NEO as a raw material comes from their high free fatty acid (FFA) content since they would saponify when in contact with a basic catalyst [6]. To obtain a high-quality biodiesel from this feedstock, it is necessary to conduct esterification prior to the transesterification reaction [15]. However, carrying out two processes considerably increases the final cost of biodiesel production. Among the non-edible oils used to obtain biodiesel are: *Jatropha curcas, Croton megalocarpus, Ricinus communis, Cerbera odollam, Celastrus paniculatus, Lepidium perfoliatum Linn, Ailanthus altissima (Mill.), Capparis spinosa L., Calophyllum inophyllum, Carthamus lanatus L.*, neem, jojoba, date seed, palm kernel oil, medlar seeds, karanja, and mahua [4,6,16–21]. Different from these oils, there are others such as that from the *Raphnus raphanistrum* L. seed, which is easy to grow and whose oil FFA content is very low, which allows the transesterification reaction to be carried out in a single step, which would solve the aforementioned drawbacks [17].
- *Microalgae:* This group of unicellular organisms can be cultivated in multiple climatic conditions and can be a great source of biomass with a high fat content (between 40–60%) [22,23]. This raw material has some considerable advantages, such as its rapid growth, its ability to grow in wastewater bodies, and its high lipid content. However, some of their main disadvantages are the need for large amounts of nutrients such as nitrogen and phosphorus, and some species of microalgae produce harmful toxins [22,24] and the need for large areas of land for their cultivation [25]. Some examples of microalgae that produce biodiesel are *Chlamydomonas, Chlorella vulgaris,*

Chlorophyceae, Chrysophyceae, Crypthecodinium cohnii, Cylindrothec, Dinophyceae, Isochrysis, Monallanthus salina, Nannochliropsis, Rhodophyceae, and *Xanthophyceae* [14,26–30].

- *Animal Fat (AF):* This feedstock is available in large quantities and generally is taken from waste generated by slaughterhouses or food processing industries [31]. This residue is considered an economically viable raw material, being used mainly in Europe, the United States, and Brazil, where it is considered the 2nd most used raw material for biodiesel production [31–33]. As with reusable oils and non-edible oils, AF has high fatty acid contents (5–40%) [34,35]. Therefore, it is necessary to use a catalyst capable of handling the high fatty acid contents or a process of two steps (esterification and transesterification) to obtain commercial-quality biodiesel [22,32]. Among the most commonly used animal fats are chicken fat, lard, tallow (sheep or beef), and mixtures of all of the above [22].
- *Waste Cooking Oil (WCO) or Used Cooking Oil (UCO):* The usage of this feedstock allows for a reduction in the production cost of biodiesel by 70–80%, in addition to being a raw material with high availability [2,36,37]. This lipid raw material can be considered a viable option, mainly because it is a waste without nutritional value generated by restaurants, households, and food processing industries [38]. WCO can be classified as a combination of triglycerides and free fatty acids that have undergone physicochemical changes, which occur when the oils are subjected to high temperatures and humidity for food preparation [37].
- The use of WCO to obtain biodiesel has a double benefit: economically, it allows a decrease in the cost of its production, and environmentally, it allows a reduction in environmental contamination in water bodies and soils derived from its incorrect disposal [39]. To obtain biodiesel from WCO, it is necessary to carry out three stages: pretreatment, transesterification reaction, and biodiesel purification.

When EO or microalgae oils are used as lipid feedstocks, it is possible to obtain high-quality biodiesel through the use of a conventional basic catalyst in the transesterification reaction. The above is attributed to the low content of free fatty acids (FFA) in the raw material. Nonetheless, when unrefined or waste raw materials are used, it is not possible to omit a pre-treatment of the raw material. The objective of the pre-treatment is to eliminate solid particles and contaminants from the cooking process. Depending on the catalyst to be used, it may be imperative to perform acid esterification to reduce the amount of FFA present in the lipid raw material, followed by basic transesterification. However, this two-step process implies major energy consumption and higher production costs [14].

Recently, other unconventional feedstocks to produce biodiesel have begun to gain relevance, such as those obtained from instant coffee production (spent coffee grounds, SCG) or fat derived from insect biomass (black soldier fly larvae, *H. illucens*, BSF) [40–44]. Worldwide, it is estimated that 60 million tons of spent coffee grounds (SCG) are generated [45]. The coffee residue contains a high amount of fat (10–20%), and from this percentage, 80–90% are glycerides, becoming a potential raw material to produce biodiesel [46]. With SCG oil, biodiesel yields of 97.11–97.18% have been achieved [40,44]. Insects have a high fat content (34–58%) compared to vegetable oils, which range from 15–46% [43]. For this reason, fats derived from insects are attracting more interest in the production of biodiesel. Some of the insects that have been studied are mealworm beetles, blowflies, meat flies, houseflies, black soldier flies, and superworms [43,47–50]. Recently, the larva of the black soldier fly H. illucens (BSFL) is the one that has generated the most expectations because it has a high amount of fat (50%) [51,52], which can vary depending on the diet of the BSFL; reporting important percentages of fatty acids: lauric acid (47.47%) [53], oleic acid (41.90%), and palmitic acid (39.83%) [54]. Various methods have been used to obtain biodiesel from BSF: acid-catalyzed esterification followed by alkali-catalyzed transesterification [55–60]; enzymatic catalysis (Novozym 435) [61], direct transesterification (the lipid extraction and transesterification are carried out in one step) [62,63], and non-catalytic transesterification (without lipid extraction, direct conversion of biodiesel from dry BSFL) [59]. Depending on the process for obtaining biodiesel and the diet that the BSFL have had, the biodiesel yield ranges from 90–98%.

Waste Cooking Oil as a Feedstock for Biodiesel Production

Since 2014, the main exporting countries of WCO to the EU have been increasing, being mainly China, Indonesia, Malaysia, Russia, the United States, and Saudi Arabia [64]. In 2019, WCO represented the second-most important feedstock, which translates to 21% of the total feedstock for biodiesel production. In the European Union, the greatest biodiesel producers were Germany, the Netherlands, Portugal, the United Kingdom, Spain, and Austria, representing 90% of the use of WCO. However, in 2020, WCO collection decreased during the COVID-19 pandemic as many countries in the EU closed or restricted restaurant services [65].

According to Claeys et al. [66], almost one fifth of all European biofuels are made from WCO, which has also seen the highest growth compared to any other biomass-based diesel raw materials in Europe and North America in recent years. Globally, 6.6 million tons of WCO biofuel were consumed in 2021, representing 5% of the total biofuels market [66]. The size of the global WCO market was $6.1 billion in 2022 and is projected to attain $8.9 billion by 2028, registering a 6.3% compound annual growth rate (CAGR) from 2023 to 2028 [67].

Due to the aforementioned, used cooking oil represents a viable alternative to satisfy the demand for biodiesel, in addition to contributing to the proper handling and disposal of this residue. This process contributes to the global politics of establishing a circular economy; furthermore, because of the use of residue as a raw material, the environmental impact categories are positively affected.

However, it is imperative to take into consideration the quality of the WCO since the quality of the biodiesel obtained depends on it. During the frying process, oils are heated to temperatures above 100 °C and can be used repeatedly, which leads to a degradation of the quality of the oil because, during this process, thermal, hydrolytic, oxidative reactions, polymerization and cracking [68,69], chemically modify the original oil. These changes alter the properties of the WCO, presenting a higher content of free fatty acids (FFA), which may affect the transesterification reaction, favoring the formation of soaps (saponification) when basic catalysts are used. Other properties that are affected by the frying process are viscosity, change in surface tension, flash point, color, and moisture content [69,70]. For this reason, it is compulsory to conduct an adequate characterization of the residual cooking oil to guarantee that the biodiesel produced meets quality standards and contributes to the achievement of the sustainable development goals. Tables 1 and 2 show the fatty acid composition and the properties of several WCO samples, respectively. As can be observed, the composition and properties hinge on the type of oil and the handling it has had.

Table 1. Fatty acid composition of WCO.

Type of Fatty Acid	% [71][a]	% [72][b]	% [72][c]	% [73][d]	% [74][e]	% [75][f]	% [76][g]	% [77][h]
lauric (C12:0)	0.03	-	-	-	-	-	-	-
myristic (C14:0)	0.16	-	-	0.77	-	1.00	-	-
palmitic (C16:0)	12.03	0.36	5.98	31.88	11.00	39.00	8.48	18.14
palmitoleic (C16:1)	0.17	-	-	-	-	-	-	-
margaric (C17:0)	0.12	-	-	-	-	-	-	-
stearic (C18:0)	4.40	-	-	6.45	4.00	4.50	2.73	4.73
oleic (C18:1)	23.58	0.8	2.74	41.04	24.00	44.60	66.79	38.86
linoleic (C18:2)	52.48	0.10	33.89	17.98	54.00	10.90	20.14	36.45
arachidic (C20:0)	0.33	-	-	-	-	-	1.86	-
linolenic (C18:3)	6.65	-	-	0.43	7.00	-	-	1.82

Table 1. Cont.

Type of Fatty Acid	% [71] [a]	% [72] [b]	% [72] [c]	% [73] [d]	% [74] [e]	% [75] [f]	% [76] [g]	% [77] [h]
erucid (C22:1)	-	0.26	-	-	-	-	-	-
caprylic(C8:0)	-	-	-	-	-	-	-	-
undecylic (C11:0)	-	-	0.52	-	-	-	-	-
Others	-	0.20	-	-	-	-	-	-

[a] Waste oil from local food industry in Toluca, Mexico. [b] Waste sunflower oil from restaurants (fish and chips) in Durban, South Africa. [c] Waste sunfoil from restaurants (chips) in Durban, South Africa. [d] Waste oil from local restaurants in Bushehr, Iran. [e] Waste oil from canteen of Malaviya National Institute of Technology, Jaipur India. [f] Waste oil from local source-UTP Cafeteria in Seri Iskandar, Perak. [g] Waste oil from local restaurant in Mérida, Yucatán. México. [h] Waste oil from a restaurant in Malaysia.

Table 2. Properties of waste cooking oil samples.

WCO Properties	[68] [a]	[72] [b]	[72] [c]	[74] [d]	[75] [e]	[76] [f]	[78] [g]	[79] [h]
Acid value (mg KOH/g)	0.31	2.29	1.44	1.2	2.04	7.06	2.8	2.7
Viscosity at 40 °C (mm^2/s)	49.40	31.38	35.23	54.00	51.04	42.98	13.45	-
Water content (wt%)	0.14	0.36	5.98	-	0.12	0.04	0.09	0.3

[a] Waste oil from a restaurant in Toluca, Mexico. [b] Waste sunflower oil from restaurants (fish and chips) from Durban, South Africa. [c] Waste sunfoil from restaurants (chips) from Durban, South Africa. [d] Waste oil from canteen of Malaviya National Institute of Technology, Jaipur India. [e] Waste oil from local source-UTP Cafeteria, Seri Iskandar, Perak. [f] Waste oil from local restaurant in Mérida, Yucatán. México. [g] Waste oil from home activities, Suez, Egypt. [h] Waste oil from fast food.

As previously mentioned, during the frying process, the properties of the oils are modified. Saturated fatty acids like stearic acid, palmitic acid, and monounsaturated fatty acids like oleic acid increase in relation to polyunsaturated fatty acids like linoleic acid [72,80]. This is important because biodiesel obtained from feedstocks with a high content of saturated or monounsaturated fatty acids has superior resistance to oxidation. The oxidation rates for fatty acids (C18) are: linolenic > linoleic > oleic. A high oxidation rate can cause damage to fuel pumps and injectors [81].

This work will discuss biodiesel synthesis methods, emphasizing esterification and transesterification; the different types of catalysts that can be used in biofuel synthesis will also be discussed, as well as some of their advantages and disadvantages. The present work seeks to highlight the advances in the study of the development of bifunctional catalysts and the challenges for sustainable biodiesel production from waste cooking oil (WCO), although some results with other raw materials like refined oil and oil from microalgae are presented to highlight the relevance of those results obtained with WCO.

2. Biodiesel Preparation Methods and Strategies

2.1. Pyrolysis

Pyrolysis, otherwise called thermal cracking, is a process that consists of decomposing organic matter by heating it at high temperatures in an atmosphere devoid of air or oxygen [82]. The resulting properties of the fuel obtained by this method are very similar to those of petroleum diesel; however, the equipment used for thermal cracking is expensive and releases gases into the environment, eliminating the environmental advantage of biodiesel [83].

2.2. Esterification

This reaction is generally used as the pretreatment of lipid feedstocks with high FFA contents, such as WCO. As you can see in Scheme 1, the esterification reaction involves the production of fatty acid monoalkyl esters (FAMEs) from the reaction of FFAs with alcohol and the use of a catalyst [4].

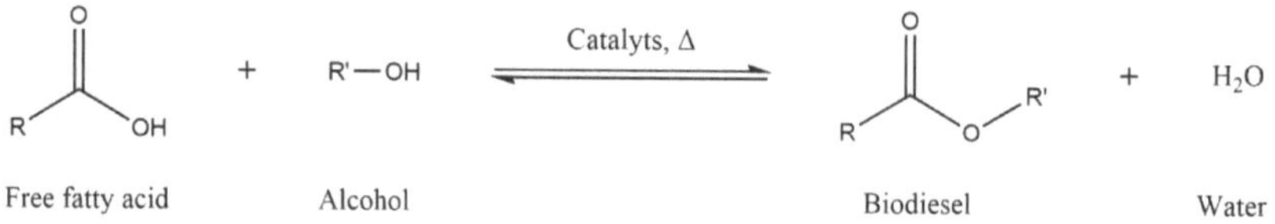

Scheme 1. Esterification reaction of free fatty acid from WCO.

Commonly, this reaction is favored by acid catalysis, with sulfuric acid (H_2SO_4) being the most widely used catalyst [4].

2.3. Transesterification

This is the process that has been used the most for biodiesel production on an industrial scale because only three raw materials are required to produce it: oil, alcohol, and a catalyst [32,84]. Scheme 2 shows this reaction, which consists of the transformation of the triglycerides contained in oils, an alcohol, and a catalyst to obtain fatty acid monoalkyl esters (FAMEs) [4]. This procedure has proven to be capable of producing good-quality biodiesel, depending on the lipid feedstock used. The transesterification reaction requires the use of triglycerides, which results in the need for a lipid raw material with a high degree of purity, mainly due to the high sensitivity of most catalysts to the presence of FFA in percentages greater than 2% [32,84]. The transesterification reaction consists of three steps: the conversion of triglycerides (TG) into diglycerides (DG), these into monoglycerides (MG), and finally obtaining glycerol (G).

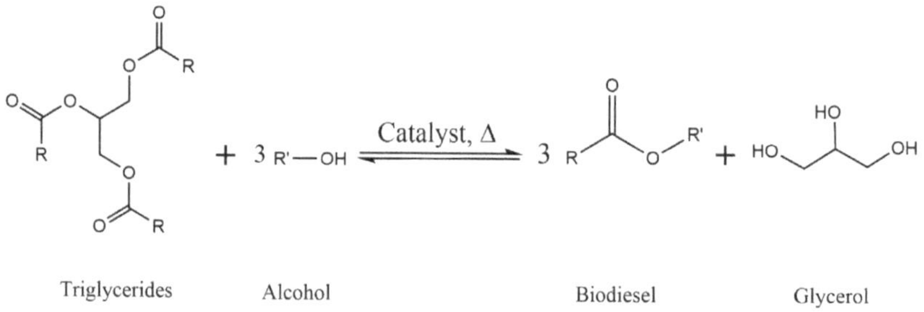

Scheme 2. Transesterification reaction of triglycerides.

To obtain quality biodiesel from a lipid raw material with a high free fatty acid content (>2% by weight), it is suggested to carry out a pretreatment process, such as esterification, thus ensuring the quality of the final product [85]. However, this double process implies a meaningful increase in the production cost of biodiesel.

Direct Transesterification

The direct (or in situ) transesterification reaction occurs when the extraction and transesterification of lipids from the biomass are carried out in the same step. This reaction is further enhanced when a co-solvent is used [62,86–88]. The co-solvent increases the solubility of alcohol in lipids. Originally, in direct transesterification, methanol was used as a reagent and solvent at the same time, which implied an excess of methanol that caused the activity of the catalyst in the reaction to decrease as well as its effect as a disruptor agent of the cell wall, so the yield of biodiesel also decreased [44,89]. Generally, organic solvents such as chloroform, h-hexane, n-pentane, acetone, diethyl ether, isopropanol, and petroleum ether have been used in direct transesterification [46,62,89], with the aim of reducing the amounts of methanol and avoiding the aforementioned problems. However these types of chemical reagents are toxic and can cause serious environmental problems [44,90]. For this reason, several studies have reported the use of more environmentally friendly co-solvents such as 2-methyltetrahydrofuran (2-MeTHF), cyclopentyl methyl ether (CPME), and 1,8-Diazabicyclo [5.4.0]undec-7-ene (DBU) solvents [91–93].

2.4. Electrolysis

The electrolysis method allows the use of feedstocks with a high content of FFA and water [94–96]. Some of the advantages of electrolysis are that no pretreatment is required to decrease free fatty acids and lipid moisture [97]. In addition, methoxide ions keep forming rapidly in the electrolysis cell [94]. At the cathode, hydroxide ions are obtained from the electrolysis of water molecules (Equation (1)), which then react with the methanol molecules to produce methoxide ions (Equation (2)). OH− ions are formed at the cathode, while H+ ions form at the anode (Equation (3)) [96,98], which ensures that esterification and transesterification can be carried out in the same electrolytic cell [99]. By adding NaCl to the mixture (Equation (4)) [96], the reaction rate rises due to the increase in conductivity [100]. The transesterification reaction requires the presence of methoxide ions that attack the carbon of the carbonyl group to obtain methyl esters [101,102].

Cathodic Reaction:
$$2H_2O + 2e^- \rightarrow H_2 + 2OH^- \quad (1)$$

Proton Transfer Reaction:
$$CH_3OH + OH^- \rightarrow CH_3O^- + H_2 \quad (2)$$

Anodic Reaction:
$$2H_2O \rightarrow O_2 + 4H^+ + 4e^- \quad (3)$$
$$2Cl^- \rightarrow Cl_2 + 2e^- \quad (4)$$

The biodiesel produced by any of the aforesaid methods, depending on purity, can be used directly in the engines or in blends. Blending or dilution consists of mixing biodiesel or vegetable oil with diesel. This strategy aims to reduce the utilization of fossil fuels in addition to the decrease in the viscosity of the mixture, which improves the efficiency of compression engines [82,103]. Fossil fuel dilutions are made with some additives (biodiesel, animal fat, vegetable oil, bioethanol, etc.). Some of the most common blends are B10 (90% additive and 10% diesel) and B20 (80% additive and 20% diesel) [82]. In this context, biodiesel is known as a bioadditive. This process, however, presents important disadvantages, such as the generation of gums when oils with high FFA content are used and the generation of carbon deposits inside the tanks and engines. In addition, for a diesel engine to be able to use vegetable oils, significant changes in the materials of the pipes and injectors need to be made [82]. To avoid these problems, some authors suggest mixing the oils before carrying out the transesterification reaction, which would not only solve the problem of insufficient raw materials but also improve the quality of the biofuel [104].

3. Catalysis in the Production of Biodiesel

It is well known that the transesterification reaction occurs at slow reaction rates, and for biodiesel production to become sustainable, it is necessary to reduce reaction times and reaction temperatures, for which the use of catalysts is required [105,106]. The reduction of these two variables implies lower energy consumption and therefore lower environmental impacts [107] and costs.

The catalysis studied in biodiesel production has three main categories: (1) homogeneous catalysis, (2) enzymatic catalysis, and (3) heterogeneous catalysis. Next, each of the categories and their subdivisions will be discussed.

3.1. Homogeneous Catalysis

In homogeneous catalysis, reactants and the catalyst are in the same phase, which is generally liquid. These catalysts are frequently used in industrial-scale processes because they present higher reaction rates than heterogeneous catalysis.

However, they have some disadvantages, for example, the impossibility of recovering the catalyst when the reaction is finished, in addition to the need for a purification process where large amounts of residual water are generated [108]. Figure 4 presents the biodiesel production process using homogeneous catalysts.

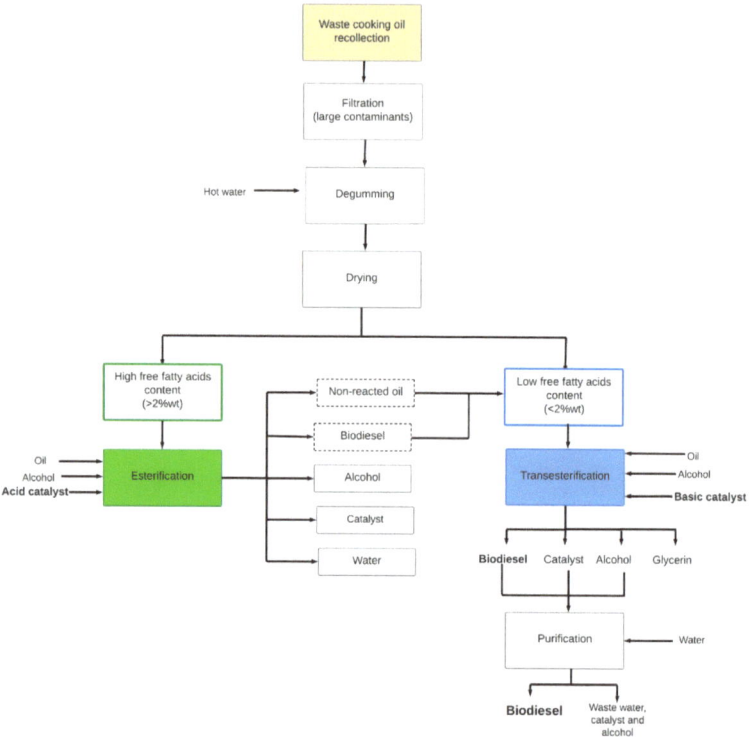

Figure 4. Schematic of biodiesel production process using homogeneous catalysts.

Next, the subdivisions of this type of catalysis are discussed: (1) Homogeneous acid catalysis and (2) Homogeneous basic catalysis.

3.1.1. Homogeneous Acid Catalysis

This type of catalyst admits the use of unrefined lipid raw materials because they present a high tolerance to FFA. Though this process is slower than basic catalysis.

Next, Table 3 shows some examples of homogeneous acid catalysts, in addition to the type of feedstock used for the production of biodiesel, the reaction conditions used, and the %FAMEs obtained. It can be seen in Table 3 that the preferred acids to be used as catalysts are hydrochloric, sulfuric, and phosphoric acids.

Despite the fact that this kind of catalyst has a high tolerance to the FFA content within the lipid raw material, its use has not been extended at an industrial level, mainly because of its corrosion hazards, so its use poses environmental and safety risks [22]. In addition, to remove this type of catalyst from the final biodiesel, it is necessary to carry out multiple washes with water, which implies a considerable environmental impact.

The reaction temperatures required in this type of catalysis can range from 60 °C to 200 °C, depending on the process used for biodiesel production. Conventional batch processes generally require higher temperatures and longer reaction times. However, some research papers suggest the use of microwave-assisted reaction systems or ultrasound to reduce these disadvantages [122].

Table 3. Examples of homogeneous acid catalysts used in biodiesel production.

Catalyst	Oil	Reaction Conditions	Methyl Esters Content (%FAMEs)	References
HCl	Microalgae	T = 76.67 °C; 0.54 M; M:o = 7.92:1; t = 1.73 h	98.19	[109]
H_2SO_4	Chrysophyllum albidum	T = 65 °C; CC% 2%wt; M:o = 12:1; t = 0.33 h	98.15	[2]
Orthophosphoric acid H_3PO_4	Calophyllum inophyllum L.	T = 60 °C; CC% 0.8%wt; M:o = 9:1; t = 1.25 h	97.14	[110]
H_2SO_4	S. obliquus lipids	T = 60 °C; CC% 10%wt; M:o = 30:1; t = 4 h	96.68	[111]
H_2SO_4	Microalgae	T = 80 °C; CC% 3%wt; M:o = 9:1; t = 8 h	96.5	[112]
H_2SO_4	WCOEsterification	T = 60 °C; CC% 5%wt; M:o = 12:1; t = 3 h	95.4	[113]
Superphosphoric acid $H_{(n+2)}P_{(n)}O_{(3n+1)}$	Palm oil	T = 70 °C; CC% 9%wt; M:o = 12:1	95	[114]
H_2SO_4	Jatropha oil	T = 60 °C; CC% 4%wt; M:o = 7:1; t = 1 h	92.4	[115]
H_2SO_4	Corn oil	T = 200 °C; CC% 0.2%wt; E:o = 18:1; t = 0.5 h	92	[116]
H_2SO_4	Palm oil	T = 60 °C; CC% 5%wt; M:o = 9:1; t = 4.5 h	91.1	[117]
H_2SO_4	Soybean oil	T = 60 °C; CC% 3.5%wt; M:o = 9:1; t = 1 h	90.6	[118]
H_2SO_4	Oleic acid	T = 60 °C; CC% 5%wt; M:o = 3:1; t = 2 h	89.3	[119]
H_2SO_4	WCO	T = 80 °C; CC% 1.5–3.5 %mol; M:o = 50:1; t = 4 h; 170–180 kPa pressure	97.0	[120]
HCl	Waste Coconut Oil Esterification	T = 80 °C; CC% 3%wt; M:o = 10:1; t = 1 h	90.45	[121]

T—Reaction temperature, CC—Catalyst weight, M:o—Methanol:oil molar ratio, E:o—ethanol:oil molar ratio, t—Reaction time.

In addition, as can be observed in Table 3, the percentage contents of FAMEs obtained are very close to the one required by the European Union Quality Standard (UNE-EN 1403), which requires a minimum of 96.5% FAMEs. It is also important to emphasize that the lipid raw materials used in this research are mainly refined oils. However, we must not forget the environmental and safety disadvantages that arise during the use and storage of these catalysts.

Generally, this type of catalysis is used in conjunction with basic catalysis, being used as a pretreatment for unrefined lipid raw materials or with a free fatty acid content greater than 1%. First, an acid esterification is performed to decrease the FFA content (<1%), and later, a basic transesterification is carried out.

The mechanism of this process is shown in Scheme 3. It begins with the protonation of the carboxylic group of the ester (this step is the most important in the catalyst-reactive relationship), followed by the action of the acid catalyst (H^+), followed by the nucleophilic attack of the alcohol, producing a tetrahedral intermediate. This intermediate breaks down to form a diacylglyceride ion and the ester alkyl of the fatty acid; these steps continue until three fatty acid esters are formed and, subsequently, the glycerol is released.

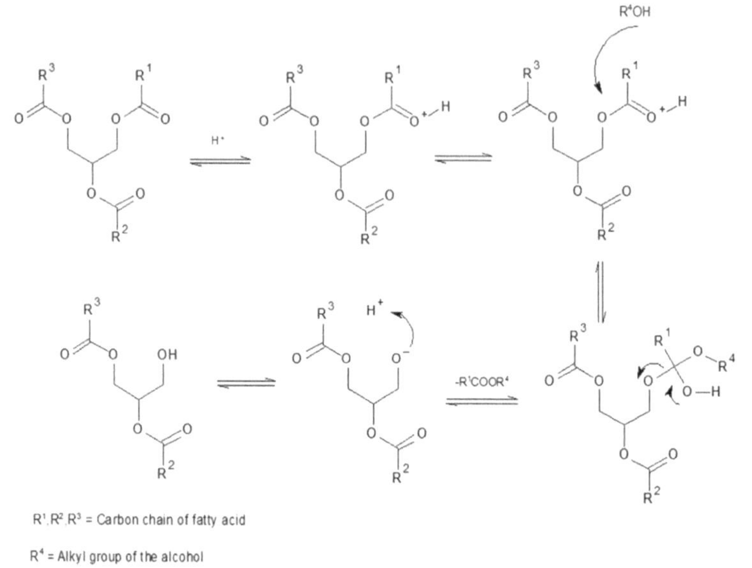

R^1, R^2, R^3 = Carbon chain of fatty acid

R^4 = Alkyl group of the alcohol

Scheme 3. Homogeneous acid transesterification mechanism [71].

3.1.2. Homogeneous Basic Catalysis

This type of catalysis is the most extensively utilized at the industrial level, as homogeneous basic catalysts are low-cost and easy to access [106]. It is also due to their high reaction rates, which implies shorter reaction times, lower methanol:oil molar ratios than acid catalysis, and mild reaction temperatures. Furthermore, the use of this catalysis allows the elimination of corrosion problems related to the use of acid catalysts. The transesterification reaction employing basic catalysts is faster than with homogeneous acid catalysts [123,124]. The most commonly used basic catalysts are KOH, NaOH, and CH_3ONa. Some examples of these catalysts can be seen in Table 4.

Table 4. Examples of basic homogeneous catalysts used in biodiesel production.

Catalyst	Oil	Reaction Conditions	Methyl Esters Content (%FAMEs)	References
NaOH	WCO	T = 62.4 °C; CC% 1.16%wt; M:o = 9.4:1; t = 0.017 h Esterification (1.56%wt FFA) Transesterification (0.35%wt FFA)	99.7	[125]
CH_3ONa	Refined palm oil	T = 55 °C; CC% 0.32%wt; M:o = 5.48:1; t = 0.67 h	98	[126]
KOH	Black mustard oil	T = 57.1 °C; CC% 0.4%wt; M:o = 20.39%wt; t = 0.9 h; 0.8%wt FFA	97.3	[127]
KOH	Jatropha curcas-WCO	T = 50 °C; CC% 1%wt; M:o = 6:1; t = 2 h; 1%wt FFA	97.1	[128]
CH_3ONa	WCO	T = 65 °C; CC% 0.75%wt; M:o = 9:1; t = 0.13 h; 2.4%wt FFA	97.1	[129]
NaOH	Black mustard oil	T = 59.5 °C; CC% 0.5%wt; M:o = 21.5%wt; t = 1 h; 0.8%wt FFA	96.9	[127]
KOH	Waste Cotton oil	T = 50 °C; CC% 0.65%wt; M:o = 7:1; t = 0.16 h	96.44 (Microwave)	[130]

Table 4. *Cont.*

Catalyst	Oil	Reaction Conditions	Methyl Esters Content (%FAMEs)	References
KOH	WCO	T = 65 °C; CC% 1.2%wt; M:o = 6:1; t = 1 h; 1.25%wt FFA	93.2	[131]
NaOH	Mango oil	T = 60 °C; CC% 1%wt; M:o = 6:1; t = 3 h; 0.06% FFA	92.7	[132]
KOH	WCO	T = 60 °C; CC% 1.2%wt; M:o = 5:1; t = 2 h; 0.41%wt FFA	92	[133]
CH_3ONa	WCO	T = 25 °C; CC% 0.75%wt; M:o = 6:1; t = 0.05 h; <2%wt FFA	87.0	[134]
NaOH	WCO	T = 56.5 °C; CC% 0.75%wt; M:o = 12:1; t = 3.25 h; 0.92%wt FFA	82	[135]
KOH	WCO	T = 60 °C; CC% 1%wt; M:o = 6:1; t = 0.5 h; 0.93%wt FFA	94.01	[136]
CH_3OK	WCO	T = 60 °C; CC% 1%wt; M:o = 6:1; t = 0.5 h; 0.93%wt FFA	99	[136]
KOH	WCO	T = 60 °C; CC% 1%wt; M:o = 8:1; t = 2 h	92.5	[137]
NaOH	WCO	T = 65 °C; CC% 0.8%wt; M:o = 12:1; t = 0.033 h	98.2 (Microwave)	[138]
KOH	Soybean WCO	T = 60 °C; CC% 0.5%wt; t = 2 h	93.2	[139]

T—Reaction temperature, CC—Catalyst weight, M:o—Methanol:oil molar ratio, t—Reaction time.

By contrasting Tables 3 and 4, it can be concluded that both acid and basic catalysis allow the production of biodiesel at mild temperatures (~60 °C). The obtained yields with basic catalysis tend to be higher with lower reaction times. The methanol:oil ratio (M:o) is also observed to be lower under basic catalysis. This does not represent an improvement only in the process cost but also in energy consumption and therefore in environmental impacts like global warming potential (carbon footprint), which is expected to decrease [107].

Some of the disadvantages of homogeneous basic catalysts include the need to perform washes to remove the catalyst at the end of the reaction, as well as not being able to recover the catalyst [9,140]. The most important disadvantage of this type of catalyst, however, lies in its high sensitivity to the presence of water or FFA within the lipid raw material, since this type of catalyst needs to use refined feedstocks (<1%wt) or with a content of FFA <2% weight [141–143].

Generally, to reach high-quality biodiesel from WCO, it is necessary to perform a previous acid esterification (Scheme 1). In esterification, FFA present in oils is transformed into biodiesel, which leads to a reduction of the percentage content of FFA in the lipid raw material, making it possible to carry out a basic transesterification without saponification.

Nevertheless, recent research has shown that the use of systems assisted by ultrasound allows for high-quality biodiesel production using WCO with elevated FFA content and basic catalysts. This is due to the fact that ultrasound waves influence heating at the molecular level, allowing internal heating to be distributed evenly [130].

Table 4 shows that percentage contents of FAMEs higher than the minimum required by the UNE-EN 1403 standard (96.5% FAMEs minimum) can be obtained. However, in most cases, the acidity values reported for the used cooking oils were low (<2%wt), which is considered the limit for obtaining high-quality biodiesel. It can also be observed that in the case of feedstocks with a FFA with a higher content than refined oils (>1%wt), it is necessary to conduct a prior esterification to obtain biodiesel with a standard quality. The above-mentioned agrees with that reported by Hsiao and Mohadesi, who required carrying out prior esterification to obtain high-quality biodiesel.

The mechanism using basic catalysts (Scheme 4) can be accomplished by the attack of the alkoxide ion on the electrophilic carbon of the triglyceride, forming an alkyl ester (tetrahedral intermediate). Subsequently, the catalyst is deprotonated, and the proton is joined to the diglyceride anion until esters and glycerol are formed.

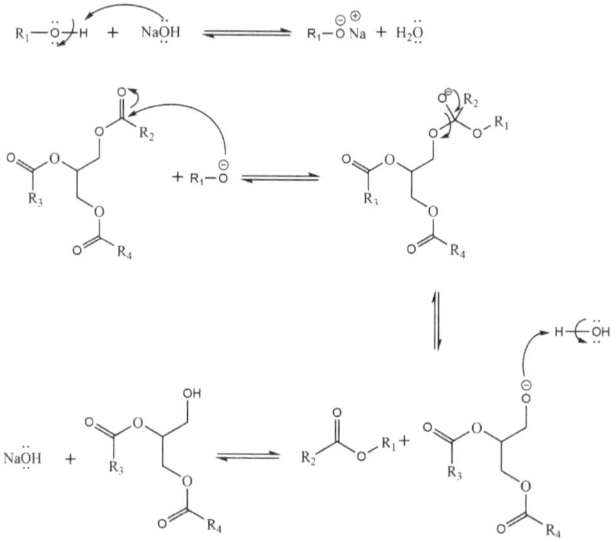

R_1: Alkyl group of the alcohol
R_2, R_3 y R_4: Carbon chain of fatty acid

Scheme 4. Homogeneous basic transesterification. Adapted with permission from [101]. Copyright 2010 Elsevier.

As mentioned above, the transesterification reaction using homogeneous catalysts involves 3 stages: the triglyceride (TG) reacts with alcohol to obtain diglycerides (DG) $TG + ROH \leftrightarrow DG + R'CO_2R$, this reacts with alcohol to form monoglycerides (MG) $DG + ROH \leftrightarrow MG + RCO_2R$ and finally, it reacts with alcohol to produce methyl esters and glycerol (GL) $MG + ROH \leftrightarrow GL + RCO_2R$.

For the determination of the kinetics of transesterification, DG and MG can be omitted since methyl esters are the final product of this reaction, allowing us to use a simple mathematical model that expresses total conversion as a single step. With respect to the reversible reactions, they can also be depreciated due to the excess of methanol in the product. Furthermore, in this reaction, there are no mass transfer problems, the kinetic process is chemically controlled [144], and the kinetics of transesterification can be considered irreversible pseudo-first order [145].

3.2. Enzymatic Catalysis

Recently, this type of biocatalyst has gathered the attention of researchers due to its potential to produce quality biodiesel from high FFA content feedstocks with yields close to 100% and a reduction of impurities in the final product. In addition, the formation of soap is eliminated, the enzymes have a high tolerance to water content, have minor energy consumption since the reaction is conducted at low temperatures, can be recycled when immobilized, and are easily separated and purified from the products at the end of the reaction [146]. However, it still presents limitations on an industrial scale as a result of the high cost, deactivation of the enzyme, and low reaction rate [147]. Furthermore, as can be seen in Table 5, the yields achieved are not as high as those achieved by basic catalysis (see Table 4).

Enzymatic catalysts are mainly divided into three types: extracellular lipases, intracellular lipases, and free enzymes (see Table 5) [148,149].

Table 5. Examples of enzymatic catalysts used in the biodiesel production.

Catalyst	Oil	Reaction Conditions	Methyl Esters Content (%FAMEs)	References
Callera TM Trans Lipase	Soybean	T = 35 °C; CC% 1.45%wt; M:o = 4.5:1; t = 24 h	96.9	[150]
Lipozyme (Thermomyces lanuginosus)	Wasted fenix oil	T = 31 °C; CC% 9.7%wt; M:o = 4.3:1; t = 6.9 h	93.8	[151]
Pseudonomas cepacia	Jatropha	T = 8 °C; CC% 5%wt; M:o = 4:1; t = 50 h	98.0	[152]
Rice bran lipase	Rice bran oil	T = 40 °C; CC%; M:o = 6:1; t = 288 h	83.4	[153]
Novozym 435	Waste Fish oil	T = 35 °C; CC% 50%wt; E:o = 35.45:1; t = 8 h	82.91	[154]
Novozym® 435	WCO	T = 50 °C; CC% 40%wt; M:o = 6:1; t = 14 h	72.0	[155]
Chromobactrium viscosum	Jatropha curcas	T = 30 °C; CC% 10%wt; M:o = 4:1; t = 4 h	51–65	[156]
B. stearothermophilus and S. aureus lipases (Inmobilized)	WCO	T = 55 °C; CC% 1%wt (50% of each lipase); M:o = 6:1; t = 24 h	97.66	[157]
Oreochromis niloticus lipase	WCO	T = 45 °C; CC% 30 kUnit; M:o = 4:1; t = 28 h	96.5	[158]
Candida rugosa and Rhizomucor miehei lipases (Inmovilized)	WCO	T = 45 °C; CC% 1%wt (50% of each lipase); M:o = 6:1; t = 24 h	96.5	[159]
Burkholderia cepacia lipase (Immobilized)	WCO	T = 35 °C; CC% 25%wt; M:o = 6:1; t = 25 h	85.2	[160]
Candida sp. lipase	WCO	T = 40 °C; CC% 1%wt; t = 12 h	80	[161]
Lipase from porcine pancreas	WCO	T = 40 °C; CC% 7.5%wt; M:o = 9:1; t = 10 h	92.33	[162]

T—Reaction temperature, CC—Catalyst weight, M:o—Methanol:oil molar ratio, E:o—ethanol:oil molar ratio, t—Reaction time.

In the case of extracellular lipases, they offer great selectivity, preventing the generation of by-products such as soaps and baits. However, they are expensive to produce due to their complicated synthesis process, they can be easily deactivated by the wrong alcohol selection, their reaction times are higher than basic catalysis (3–288 h), and enzimatic catalysts have a high affinity for glycerin, which implies a drawback in their separation [22]. Intracellular lipases can be used directly as catalysts, which makes them cheaper since expensive processes such as extraction and purification are omitted [22]. In 2021, Acherki et al. [163] reported the use of the Eversa® Transform 2.0 liquid enzyme with jatropha oil and butanol, obtaining 83% biodiesel conversion (T = 42 °C, 9.79%wt catalyst). One of the advantages of this enzyme is its low cost, the handling of oils with high FFA contents, and the fact that no purification steps are required. A Finally, it is known that free enzymes or liquid enzymes offer better miscibility and mass transfer, although they cannot be reutilized.

Figure 5 represents a process scheme using enzymes. When using WCO, it is necessary to carry out a filtration to separate the solid particles. Later, it is recommended to dry the oil in order to eliminate excess water since the presence of a lot of water may be undesirable, without forgetting that water is necessary to maintain the catalytic activity of enzymes [101].

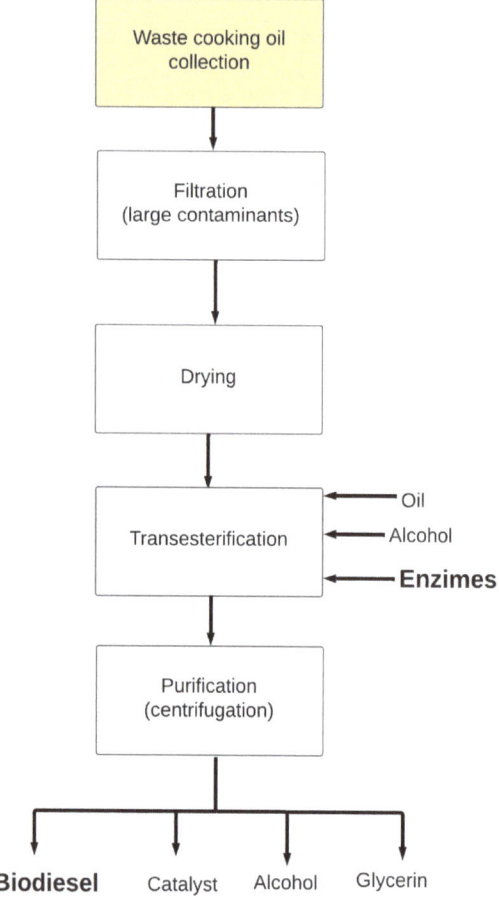

Figure 5. Schematic of biodiesel production process using enzimatic catalysts.

The transesterification mechanism using an enzymatic catalyst involves two steps: 1. Hydrolysis of the esters to produce FFA; 2. Esterification to obtain esters (FAME). Furthermore, it is assumed that the transesterification reactions with alcohol (methanol) are simultaneous with the hydrolysis reactions [164–166]. Scheme 5 shows the mechanism proposed by Andrade et al. [165] for enzymatic transesterification of castor oil, where: TG = triglycerides, DG = diglycerides, MG = monoglycerides, FAME = fatty acid methyl esters, FFA = free fatty acids, MeOH = methanol, W = water, GLY = glycerol, and E = enzyme.

3.3. Heterogeneous Catalysis

This kind of catalysis occurs when the reagents and the catalyst are in different phases, the most common being that the catalyst is in solid form. Heterogeneous catalysis arose from the need to reduce production costs implied by homogeneous catalysts.

These catalysts caught the attention of researchers because they can be separated and reused many times before losing their catalytic activity, which allows cost reduction in biodiesel production by reducing post-treatment complexity [167]. This is the reason heterogeneous catalysis is considered the most effective way to produce biodiesel from lipid raw materials with high FFA content [167].

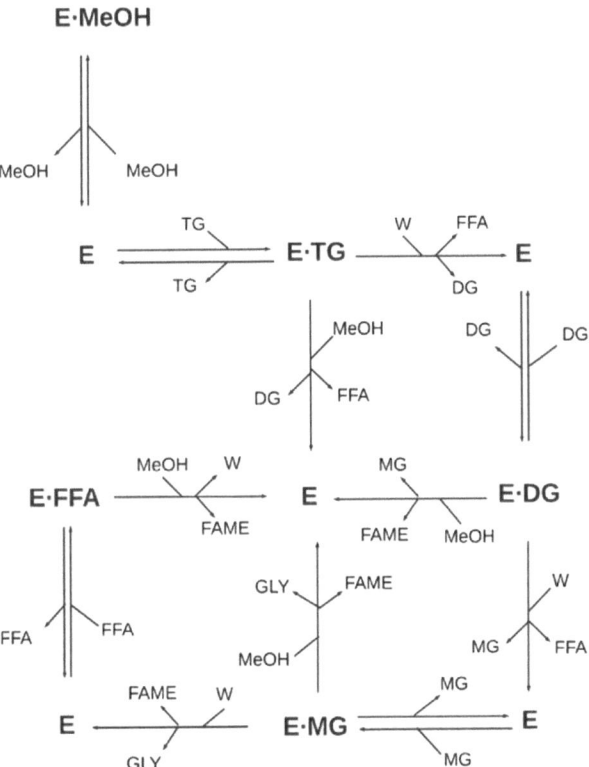

Scheme 5. Mechanism for the enzymatic transesterification of castor oil. Adapted with permission [165]. Copyright 2017 American Chemical Society.

However, the main objection to the use of these catalysts lies in the contamination of the final product derived from the leaching of the active sites and in the mass transfer problems derived from the solid-liquid biphasic reaction [22]. Figure 6 shows the processes of heterogeneoeus catalysis.

Next, the subdivisions of this type of catalysis are discussed: (1) Heterogeneous acid catalysis and (2) Heterogeneous basic catalysis.

3.3.1. Heterogeneous Acid Catalysis

This type of catalyst is effective for biodiesel production from lipids with high FFA content [167]. This type of catalyst can simultaneously perform the esterification of the FFA and the transesterification of the triglycerides present in the lipid raw materials since these catalysts have Brönsted acid sites and Lewis acid sites capable of promoting esterification reactions and ester exchange reactions [168,169]. Although transesterification can also be conducted on acid sites, this proceeds at a very low rate [170].

The most commonly used acid heterogeneous catalysts are mixed metal oxides, heteropoly acid derivates, ion exchange resins, sulfonated carbon-based catalysts, and sulfated catalysts [170,171]. Table 6 below shows some examples of heterogeneous acid catalysts, as well as the raw material from which biodiesel was produced, the reaction conditions used, and the %FAMEs obtained.

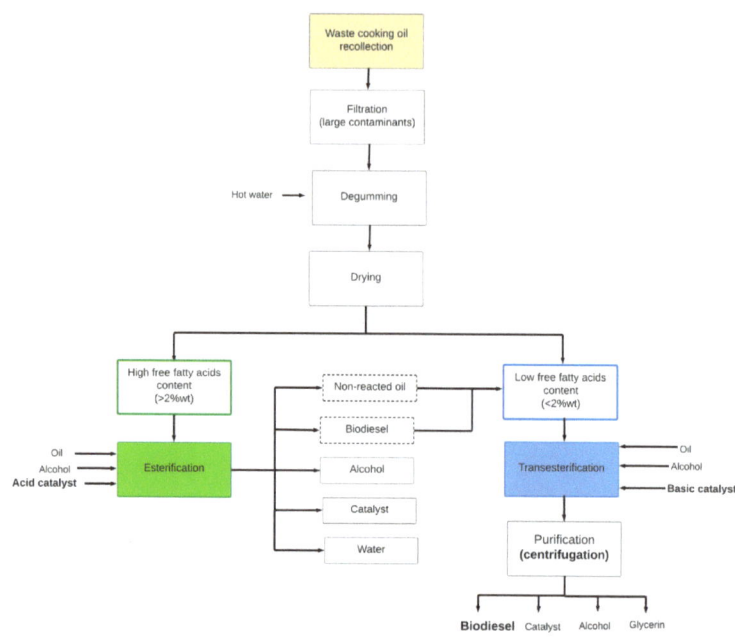

Figure 6. Schematic of biodiesel production process employing heterogeneous catalysts.

Table 6. Examples of heterogeneous acid catalysts used for biodiesel production.

Catalyst	Oil	Reaction Conditions	Methyl Esters Content (%FAMEs)	References
4-BDS	Palm oil	T = 110 °C; CC% 20%wt; M:o = 30:1; t = 7 h	98.1	[172]
(ZS/Si) Zinc stearate	WCO	T = 200 °C; CC% = 3%wt; M:o = 18:1; t = 10 h; 15%wt FFA	98	[173]
Sulfonated hypercrosslinked exchange resin	WCO	T = 60 °C; CC% 5%wt; M:o = 12:1; t = 2 h	97	[174]
C-SO$_3$H	Oleic acid	T = 80 °C; CC% 8%wt; M:o = 21:1; t = 1 h	96.77	[175]
TPA/Bentonite	WCO	T = 100 °C; CC% 0.7 g; M:o = 10:1; t = 4.5 h, 11.2%wt FFA	96	[37]
SO$_4$/Fe-Al-TiO$_2$	WCO	T = 90 °C; CC% = 3%wt; M:o = 10:1; t = 2.5 h; 2%wt FFA	96	[176]
S-TiO$_2$/SBA-15	WCO	T = 200 °C; CC% = 1%wt; M:o = 15:1; t = 0.5 h; 2.92%wt FFA	94.96	[177]
WO$_3$/ZrO$_2$	S. obliquus lipids	T = 100 °C; CC% = 15%wt; M:o = 12:1; t = 3 h	94.58	[111]
Carbon acid catalyst	WCO Prior esterification	T = 100 °C; CC% 5%wt; M:o = 22:1; t = 3 h	92.3	[178]
H$_2$SO$_4$/Bamboo ashes	Oleic acid	T = 65 °C; CC% 0.3 g; Metanol: 2.7 g; t = 8 h	92.1	[84]
Carbon acid catalyst	Chicken fat	T = 200 °C; CC% 3%wt; M:o = 9:1; t = 6 h; 50%wt FFA	90.8	[178]
RS-SO$_3$H	WCO	T = 70 °C; CC% 5%wt; M:o = 18:1; t = 1 h	90.38	[78]

Table 6. Cont.

Catalyst	Oil	Reaction Conditions	Methyl Esters Content (%FAMEs)	References
Bi_2SiO_5	Oleic acid	T = 70 °C; CC% 10%wt; M:o = 20:1; t = 6 h; 2.8%wt FFA	90.0	[179]
Xylose derived sulfonated carbon catalyst	WCO	T = 80 °C; CC% 0.3 g; M:o = 120:1; t = 2 h	89.6	[180]
SO_4^{-2}/ZrO_2	WCO	T = 150 °C; CC% 10%wt; M:o = 10:1; t = 4 h; 2.7%wt FFA	86	[181]
$MgF_x(OH)_{2-x}$	WCO	T = 150 °C; CC% 5%wt; M:o = 30:1; t = 5 h; 13%wt FFA	75.29	[182]

T—Reaction temperature, CC—Catalyst weight, M:o—Methanol:oil molar ratio, t—Reaction time.

As can be seen in Table 6, these catalysts are capable of producing biodiesel with a high amount of FAMEs from lipid raw materials whose FFA content is higher than refined oils (such as animal fats and WCO). For conventional batch systems, this type of catalyst requires longer reaction times as well as higher reaction temperatures (60–220 °C) [101,183]. Some of their main advantages are found in their ease of recovery, their ability to be reused, the reduction of their corrosive nature (compared with homogeneous), and the possibility of esterification and transesterification taking place simultaneously.

The works cited in Table 6 show that most of the WCOs used have an FFA content greater than 2%wt, which means those lipidic raw materials are considered low-quality oils. Despite the above, most of the catalysts manage to obtain >90% FAMEs at the end of the reaction; nonetheless, relatively long reaction times (2–7 h) were required to reach these percentages. In addition, many of these catalysts require MeOH:oil molar ratios greater than 10:1. This leads to mass transfer problems (catalyst separation problems), increased production costs [68,105] and a negative effect on environmental impact categories such as global warming potential and photochemical oxidation [107].

The foregoing has motivated the search for catalysts that are capable of reducing such reaction conditions, in addition to seeking to reduce the environmental impact derived from the corrosive nature of this type of catalyst.

The mechanism of the esterification reaction (Scheme 6) by acid catalysts, begins with the donation of an H^+ to the carboxylic acid, later it undergoes the nucleophilic attack by the hydroxyl group of the methanol to continue with the reaction until the water is eliminated [184].

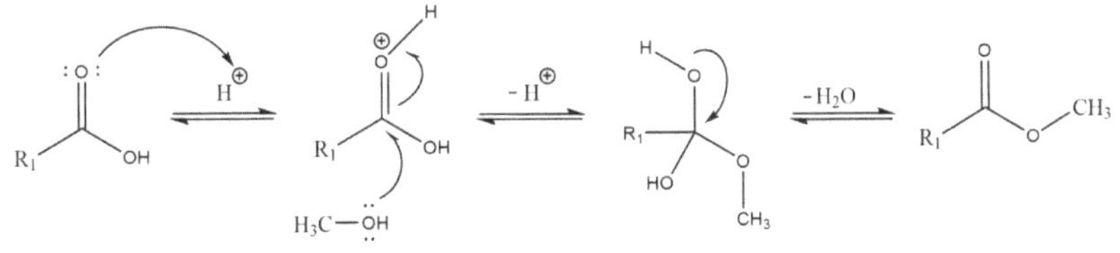

Scheme 6. Mechanism of acid catalyzed esterification of FFA [71].

According to several experimental studies using heterogeneous acid catalysts with high FFA content oils, the experimental data approximates a pseudohomogeneous irreversible reaction [168,185]; first order for both FFA content and methanol concentration. The above agrees with Zeng et al. [184], who found that when heterogeneous acid catalysts are used, the esterification reaction follows a second-order mechanism.

3.3.2. Heterogeneous Basic Catalysis

This type of catalyst has been extensively investigated as it shows attractive catalytic activities under mild reaction conditions as well as easy recovery and the ability to be reused [106,186].

Nonetheless, using these catalysts during the transesterification reaction of oils with a high FFA content might result in a reduction in the quality of the biodiesel obtained because the saponification reaction is favored [167]. This not only lowers the biodiesel yield but also implies two main consequences: it makes it harder to separate glycerol from biodiesel in addition to consuming the added catalyst [187]. Furthermore, this type of catalyst is highly sensitive to poisoning when exposed to air (absorbing CO_2 and humidity) [186].

The most frequently used basic heterogeneous catalysts are zeolites, transition metal oxides, hydrotalcite-based catalysts, mixed metal oxides, and alkaline earth metal oxides [170]. These catalysts have good reaction kinetics and adsorption capacities and are widely available in nature, which makes them low-cost [187].

Table 7 shows some examples of basic heterogeneous catalysts, as well as the sort of raw material from which biodiesel was produced, the reaction conditions used, and the %FAMEs obtained at the end of the reaction.

Table 7. Examples of basic heterogeneous catalysts used in biodiesel production.

Catalyst	Type of Oil Used	Reaction Conditions	Yield (%FAMEs)	References
K_2CO_3/Sepiolite	Turnip oil	T = 70 °C; CC% 2%wt; E:o = 12:1; t = 4 h	99.9	[188]
Na_2ZrO_3	*Jatropha curcas* L. oil	T = 65 °C; CC% 5%wt; M:o = 65:1; t = 8 h	99.9	[189]
CaO	WCO	T = 80 °C; CC% 2%wt; M:o = 9:1; t = 0.17 h	98.7	[190]
CaO	WCO	T = 55 °C; CC% 6%wt; M:o = 8.3:1; t = 0.67 h	98.62	[191]
CaO	(Mixture of blended oil)	T = 61.61 °C; CC% 4.5%wt; M:o = 8:1; t = 1.08 h	98.0	[192]
KOH/limestone	WCO	T = 65 °C; CC% 5.36%wt; M:o = 12.26:1; t = 0.97 h	97.15	[193]
MgO-NaOH	WCO	T = 50 °C; CC% 3%wt; M:o = 6:1; t = 6 h	97	[194]
CH_3ONa/Bentonita	Sunflower oil	T = 55 °C; CC% 2%wt; M:o = 12:1; t = 1.17 h	94.33	[195]
MgO	WCO	T = 65 °C; CC% 2%wt; M:o = 24:1; t = 1 h	93.3	[196]
SrO	WCO	T = 65 °C; CC% 3%wt; M:o = 9:1; t = 0.07 h	93	[197]
CaO	Waste Cotton Oil	T = 50 °C; CC% 1.3%wt; M:o = 9.6:1; t = 0.16 h	89.94	[130]
α-Fe_2O_3-Al_2O_3	WCO	T = 65 °C; CC% 1%wt; M:o = 15:1; t = 3 h	87.78	[198]
KOH/Diatomita	Palm oil	T = 75 °C; CC% 5%wt; M:o = 9:1; t = 2 h	84.56	[199]

T—Reaction temperature, CC—Catalyst weight, M:o—Methanol:oil molar ratio, t—Reaction time.

Nevertheless, a major disadvantage of these catalysts involves the decrease of their catalytic activity derived from the adhesion of reaction by-products, which results in the deactivation of the catalytic materials [200].

The results observed in Table 7 indicate that when there is a raw material with a greater FFA content than a refined oil (such as non-edible oils and WCO), they require higher temperatures of reaction (to increase the collisions among molecules and to improve the reaction rate), higher methanol:oil molar ratios, and a higher catalyst loading to obtain biodiesel with a higher FAME content.

The aforementioned reaction conditions are linked to the basicity of the material used and possible mass transfer problems. As an example of the above, it is well known that using alcohol in excess will result in mass transfer problems [201].

Most of the works cited in Table 6 use WCO with FFA contents lower than 2%wt, which allows this type of catalyst to obtain 85–99.9% FAMEs after the transesterification reaction. Though we must remember that international standards require a 96.5% FAMEs content to consider that the biodiesel has quality enough for its usage in engines.

On the other hand, it is essential to remember that basic catalysts have a high sensitivity to the FFA content, which is why, in the case of a low-quality raw material (>2%wt FFA), it is necessary to reduce said content of FFA, for which an acid esterification reaction is usually used as a pretreatment.

In addition, it is necessary to carry out process optimization. Some investigations have suggested the use of microwave-assisted or ultrasonic systems to overcome the mass transfer problems that occur in conventionally stirred processes, thus reducing reaction times [170].

The mechanism of transesterification using a basic heterogeneous catalyst (Scheme 7) begins with the formation of the methoxide anion, followed by the attack of the carbon of the carbonyl group by the methoxide anion, forming an intermediate, to obtain the ester and a diglyceride anion, which are compounds more stable. Subsequently, the attack of the cation by the diglyceride anion occurs, forming the diglyceride regenerating the catalyst (CaO). The mechanism is repeated until the methyl esters (biodiesel) and glycerol are formed.

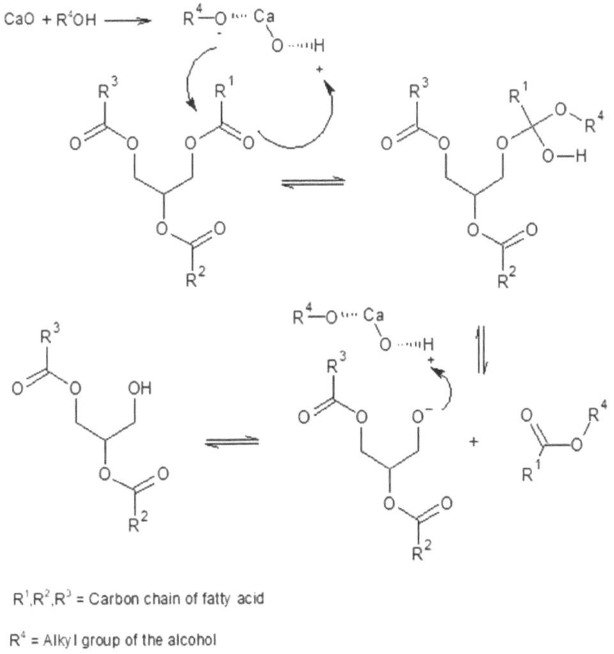

R^1, R^2, R^3 = Carbon chain of fatty acid

R^4 = Alkyl group of the alcohol

Scheme 7. Heterogeneous base-catalyzed mechanism for the transesterification of triglycerides [71].

Nain et al. [202] analyzed two kinetic models based on Langmuir-Hinshelwood-Hougen-Watson (LHHW) and Eley-Rideal (ER) mechanisms of the transesterfication reaction of canola oil and quicklime (CaO) as a heterogeneous catalyst. They concluded that the best model, according to their experimental data, is the Eley-Rideal mechanism and that the controlling step is the surface reaction [202]. This is consistent with the ER model, especially when a highly basic catalyst is used, like CaO, BaO, or SrO [203]. Likewise, they observed that there was no adsorption of triglycerides on the surface of the catalyst, this being caused by the rapid adsorption of methanol [202].

3.3.3. Bifunctional Catalysis

As previously mentioned, biodiesel's final quality is clearly related to the content of FFA in the feedstock. In feedstocks with a low content of FFA (<2%wt), a transesterification reaction is good enough to obtain a high-quality product. Furthermore, the high sensitivity of the transesterification reaction to the FFA content results in its saponification or in obtaining low-quality biodiesel. To avoid the above drawbacks and ensure the quality of the final product, it is necessary to carry out a process consisting of two steps, which consist of a prior esterification reaction (to transform the FFA into FAMEs) and later a transesterification of the triglycerides (see Figure 7).

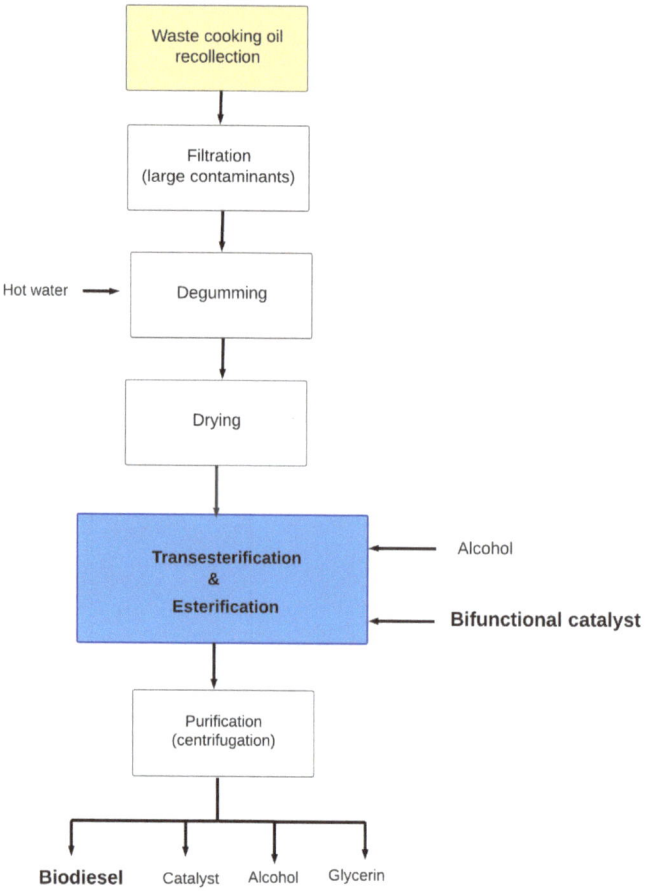

Figure 7. Schematic of biodiesel production process using bifunctional catalysts.

In the related literature, there is a broad variety of bifunctional catalysts used for biodiesel synthesis. These catalysts generally consist of mixtures of some support and metal oxides. Nevertheless, it is also possible to find bio-based catalysts [204,205]. Additionally, it is precisely these catalysts based on biomass that have gained more attention in recent years due to their economic origin and because they are friendly to the environment [206].

The obstacles mentioned above for catalysts in transesterification reactions have allowed the development of research focused on obtaining sustainable technology for biodiesel production. Within these investigations, the attention of researchers has been centered on the use of bifunctional catalysts, also known as acid-base catalysts. These catalysts involve the conjugation between a metal and metal oxides, which gives them both acid and basic sites [207,208].

Below, Table 8 shows some examples of bifunctional catalysts, as well as the sort of lipidic raw material employed, the reaction conditions used, and the %FAMEs obtained at the end of the reaction.

Table 8. Examples of bifunctional catalysts used in biodiesel production.

Catalyst	Oil Used	Reaction Conditions	Methyl Esters Content (%FAMEs)	References
Fly ash	WCO	T = 59 °C; CC = 11.2%wt; M:o = 3.1:1; t = 6 h	100	[209]
CaO(10%)-Fe$_2$O$_3$(10%)	WCO	T = 65 °C; CC = 3%wt; M:o = 18:1; t = 3 h	98.3	[210]
TiO$_2$/PrSO$_3$H	WCO	T = 60 °C; CC = 4.5%wt; M:o = 15:1; t = 9 h	98.3	[211]
RHC/K$_2$O-20%/Ni-5%	WCO	T = 65 °C; CC = 4%wt; M:o = 12:1; t = 2 h	98.2	[212]
CaO/Al$_2$O$_3$	WCO	T = 60 °C; CC = 2.5%wt; M:o = 12:1; t = 3 h	98.23	[213]
MgO/MgSO$_4$	WCO	T = 50 °C; CC = 6.4%wt; M:o = 10.8:1; t = 0.8 h	98.8	[214]
LiNbO$_3$	WCO	T = 65 °C; CC = 2%wt; M:o = 24:1; t = 6 h	98.08	[140]
CaO/Al$_2$O$_3$	WCO	T = 65 °C; CC = 1%wt; M:o = 11:1; t = 4 h	98	[215]
KOH/AC	WCO	T = 45 °C; CC = 1%wt; M:o = 18:1; t = 1 h	97.8	[216]
SrTi$_{0.85}$Fe$_{0.15}$O$_3$	Palm oil	T = 170 °C; CC = 5%wt; M:o = 18:1; t = 3 h	97.52	[217]
Sn-CaO	WCO	T = 85.15 °C; CC = 2.2%wt; M:o = 16.1:1; t = 3.42 h	97.39	[218]
SrO-ZnO/Al$_2$O$_3$	WCO	T = 75 °C; CC = 15%wt; M:o = 10:1; t = 5 h	95.7	[219]
10W/BV	WCO	T = 65 °C; CC = 8%wt; M:o = 6:1; t = 7 h	96	[220]
Sulfonated RHC	WCO	T = 50 °C; CC = 3.5%wt; M:o = 13:1; t = 0.84 h	96	[221]
2.6SrO-ZnO/Al$_2$O$_3$ (2.6SZA)	WCO	T = 75 °C; CC = 15%wt; E:o = 10:1; t = 5 h	95.7	[219]
PKSAC-K$_2$CO$_3$(30%)CuO(5%)	WCO	T = 75 °C; CC = 15%wt; M:o = 10:1; t = 5 h	95	[222]
WO$_3$-Zr$_2$O$_3$ (7WZ)	WCO	T = 80 °C; CC = 2%wt; M:o = 15:1; t = 1 h	94.4	[167]
SrTiO$_3$	Palm oil	T = 170 °C; CC = 6%wt; M:o = 15:1; t = 3 h	93.14	[223]
BBFC	Neen seed oil	T = 61.9 °C; CC = 2.58%wt; M:o = 14.76:1; t = 1.21 h	92.89	[224]
CaO-CeO$_2$	WCO	T = 70 °C; CC = 4%wt; M:o = 9:1; t = 1.2 h	90.14	[225]
CaO-Ca$_2$Fe$_2$O$_5$-CaFeO$_3$	WCO	T = 60 °C; CC = 5%wt; M:o = 12:1; t = 2 h	90	[71]
Cu/Zn/γ-Al$_2$O$_3$	Low grade	T = 65 °C; CC = 10%wt; M:o = 20:1; t = 2 h	88.82	[226]
MgO-SnO$_2$	WCO	T = 60 °C; CC = 2%wt; M:o = 18:1; t = 2 h	88	[227]
7% SR/ZrO$_2$	WCO	T = 70 °C; CC = 1%wt; M:o = 15:1; t = 0.34 h	85	[228]

T—Reaction temperature, CC—Catalyst weight, M:o—Methanol:oil molar ratio, E:o—Ethanol:oil molar ratio, t—Reaction time.

In Table 8, it can be seen there is a wide variety of materials that can be used to synthesize bifunctional catalysts. To dope the support, metals such as tungsten [167], lanthanum [229,230], strontium [219], iron [71,229], and zirconium [231,232]. It is also important to note that each metal will have its own catalyst characteristics, such as the crystalline phases present and acid strength. The catalytic features will depend on oxidation states, the synthesis method used, and the catalyst precursor [71].

The combination of Lewis and Brönsted acid sites within the bifunctional catalyst gives them a greater tolerance to FFA content in the lipid feedstock than basic catalysts, in addition to eliminating the low catalytic activity of acid catalysts [140]. They are also easily recoverable, which simplifies the end of the end of the need for takeout washings [140]. The above leads to a reduction in the process's total cost.

Two of the main advantages of bifunctional catalysts are: (1) they are able to concurrently carry out the esterification as well as the transesterification [140]; and (2) these catalysts can be designed for specific needs, which allows them to have high selectivity [183]. In the case of biodiesel production, this permits the use of low-purity oils without complex production and purification processes [9].

The supports used in the synthesis of these catalysts are also very important since they can be obtained from various metal oxides such as Li_2CO_3 [140], CaO [213,225], ZrO_4H_4 [167], and Al_2O_3 [219], among others. These supports will provide different densities of basic sites, pore sizes, and surface areas, which will affect the final properties of the catalyst and directly influence the percentage content of FAMEs obtained at the end of the reaction.

In the search for cheap raw materials, multiple materials were discovered that are sources of metal oxides; some of them are considered waste, which makes them low-cost raw materials as CaO sources such as eggshell [233] and recycled waste oyster shells [234]. As a result of the high tolerance to the FFA content of the bifunctional catalysts, we can see that most of those listed in Table 8 managed to obtain a high FAME content (>90%) at the end of the reaction.

Despite having reaction times ranging from 20 min to 9 h, it is possible to obtain high-quality biodiesel from a low-quality raw material in a single-step process considering that FFA esterification and triglycerides transesterification are carried out concurrently, which allows the reduction of production costs and the environmental impact of energy consumption.

In addition, the works presented in Table 8 show that with this type of catalyst, in most cases, it is possible to work with mild reaction temperatures. Depending on the catalyst used, using higher reaction temperatures allows the catalyst to use feedstocks with higher water contents (8%wt) without affecting the %FAMEs obtained, as reported by Li [235].

As can also be observed in Table 9, the use of nanocatalysts/magnetic catalysts. Several investigations of nanocatalysts, most of them bifunctional, have been reported in recent years. Nanocatalysts' advantages are their high efficiency, minimal generation of chemical residues, safety, reduced global warming, economic efficiency, and energy efficiency [236]. However, one of the most important disadvantages of this type of catalyst is the difficulty of separating it from the reaction mixture. Therefore, they have been synthesized using magnetic metals to facilitate their separation and using biomass materials in several of them. A nano-magnetic catalyst ($K/ZrO_2/g\text{-}Fe_2O_3$) was synthesized by Liu et al. [237] for the transesterification of soybean oil, obtaining promising results with 5% by weight of catalyst, a methanol-oil molar ratio of 10:1, a temperature of reaction of 65 °C, and 3 h of reaction. A yield of 93.6% of biodiesel was obtained, presenting good magnetic characteristics that allowed the adequate separation of the reaction products. Liu et al. [237] synthesized a bifunctional magnetic catalyst based on bamboo charcoal, potassium, and iron ($K/BC\text{-}Fe_2O_3$) to obtain biodiesel using soybean oil. This catalyst presented excellent catalytic activity and good recoverability, reaching 98% yield with 2.5% catalyst, a methanol:oil 8:1 molar ratio, a reaction time of 1 h, and a temperature of 60 °C.

In Scheme 8, the mechanism of the transesterification reaction using bifunctional catalysts can be observed. It is carried out in three steps: (a) adsorption of the FFA from the WCO on the acid sites and adsorption of methanol on the basic sites of the catalyst; (b) reaction on the catalyst surface; and (c) desorption of methyl esters, glycerol, and water. In this scheme, Enguilo et al., using a Fe/CaO bifunctional catalyst, postulate that iron (the proton donor) provides the sites for both FFA esterification and triglyceride transeserification.

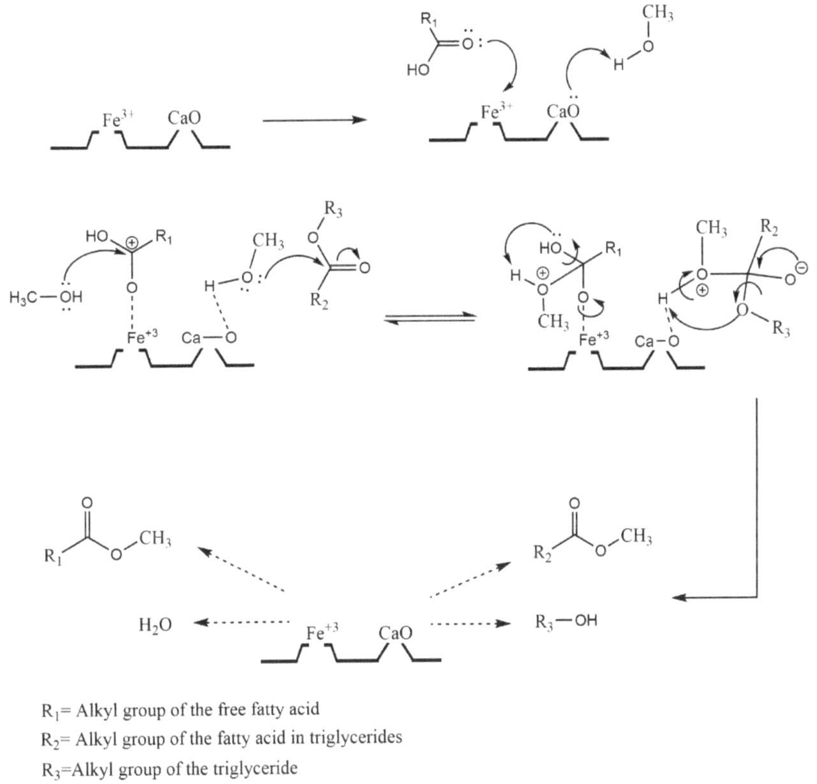

R_1= Alkyl group of the free fatty acid
R_2= Alkyl group of the fatty acid in triglycerides
R_3=Alkyl group of the triglyceride

Scheme 8. Bifunctional transesterification mechanism of used cooking oil [71].

An area of opportunity to further our knowledge regarding the use of bifunctional catalysts to produce biodiesel is being able to establish the catalyst composition related to a specific FFA content. In addition, it is crucial for the sustainability of the process to conduct life cycle assessments, not only of the processes but also of the catalyst making, since several authors have reported this to be one of the most important stages contributing to the environmental impact [107,238].

In addition, it is crucial for the sustainability of the process to conduct life cycle assessments, not only of the processes but also of the catalyst making, since several authors have reported this to be one of the most important stages contributing to the environmental impact.

Table 9 shows the advantages, disadvantages, and economic feasibility of catalysts used for biodiesel production.

Table 9. Pros, cons and economic feasibility of catalyst type used for biodiesel production.

Catalyst	Pros	Cons	Economic Feasibility	References
Homogeneous acid	- High tolerance to the presence of water and FFA - Ability to use low-cost raw materials	- Environmentally harmful - Safety risky - Corrosive nature - Needs higher methanol:oil molar ratios - Higher reaction temperatures - Slower reaction rates - Longer reaction times - Generation of large amounts of wastewater	The high quality of the raw material significantly affects the production cost of biodiesel. The corrosive nature of these catalysts results in an economically unfeasible process.	[22,122,140,239]
Homogeneous basic	- Lower cost. - High availability - Lower methanol:oil ratios - Mild reaction temperatures - No corrosive problems - Relatively short reaction times	- High sensitivity to the presence of water and FFA - Need of refined raw materials - The need of a previous esterification to manage raw materials with elevated FFA content - High reaction rate - Generation of large amounts of wastewater	The high quality of the raw material significantly affects the production cost of biodiesel. It can be considered as an economically viable option to produce biodiesel from high-quality oils.	[9,106,123,124, 140–143,239]
Enzymatic	- No catalyst leaching is generated - Easy recovery. - Mild reaction conditions - High tolerance to the presence of FFA - Lower reaction temperatures - Ability to be recycled - Easy recovery - Great selectivity	- High cost of most enzymes - Easily disactivated by wrong alcohol selection - Slower reaction rates - Enzyme deactivation	The high quality of the raw material significantly affects the production cost of biodiesel. These catalysts are good examples to produce biodiesel from low-quality feedstocks in one step.	[23,239–241]
Heterogeneous acid	- High tolerance to the presence of FFA - Reduction of corrosive nature - Ability to carry out esterification and transesterification simultaneously - Ability to use cheaper raw materials - Ability to be easily separated and recycled - Reduce purification costs	- Active sites leaching - Mass transfer problems - Slow reaction rate for transesterification reaction - Needs higher methanol:oil molar ratios - Higher reaction temperatures - Longer reaction times	High profit at minimal investment. The high quality of the raw material significantly affects the production cost of biodiesel.	[101,170,183, 206,239]
Heterogeneous basic	- Ability to be easily separated and recycled - Reduce purification costs - Mild reaction conditions - Lower cost - High availability - Lower methanol:oil rates - Shorter reaction times	- Active sites leaching - Mass transfer problems - High sensitivity to the presence of FFA - Sensitive to poisoning by absorbing humidity and CO_2 - Deactivation derived from adherence of reaction by-products	High profit at minimal investment. The high quality of the raw material significantly affects the production cost of biodiesel. It can be considered as an economically viable option to produce biodiesel from high-quality oils.	[106,167,186, 206,239]
Bifunctional and Nanocatalysts/magnetic	- High tolerance to the presence of FFA - Ability to use cheaper raw materials - Ability to be easily separated and recycled - Ability to carry out esterification and transesterification simultaneously - Reduce purification costs - Mild reaction conditions - Acid-base conjugation eliminates low activity of acid catalysts - High selectivity - They can be designed with specific characteristics	- Active sites leaching - Mass transfer problems - Higher synthesis cost depending on the used metal - Complicated synthesis	The high quality of the raw material significantly affects the production cost of biodiesel. These catalysts are good examples to produce biodiesel from low-quality feedstocks in one step.	[9,140,183,237, 239]

4. Reactors for Biodiesel Production

In recent years, biodiesel production has focused on trying to reduce production costs by using various feedstocks that make them decrease, since the raw material represents 60–80% of the production cost. Therefore, the development of catalysts as well as the types of reactors have been essential to optimizing and developing new sustainable technologies. In the previous section, different types and characteristics of the catalysts used to obtain biodiesel were shown. As for the reactors, they have an important role in the yield of biodiesel since they must be optimized to achieve greater sustainability, technical advantages, and economic viability. In the process of obtaining biodiesel, vegetable edible and non-edible oils are mainly used, although oil-containing materials such as seeds, rice bran, spent coffee grounds, fat derived from insect biomass, animal fat, waste cooking oil, and products from edible oil have also been employed as feedstocks [6,19,26,38,43,47]. In some studies, pure acids such as oleic, caprylic, and capric acids, as well as pure triolein, have been utilized [242]. The reactors that are typically used for biodiesel production are shown in Figure 8.

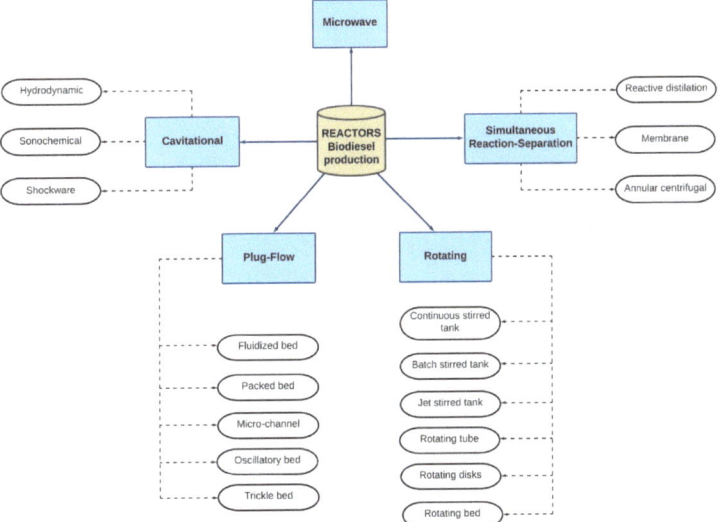

Figure 8. Types of reactors for biodiesel production. Adapted with permission [243] Copyright 2019 Elsevier.

In plug–flow reactors, products have consistent quality. They use liquids with diverse viscous ranges and have low maintenance and capital costs.

Rotating reactors have tubes, discs, and impellers that require different energy and rotational power, directly affecting the biodiesel quality. These reactors are expensive due to the large amount of energy needed [22].

The most widely used plug flow reactor is the tubular, or PFR, where the reagents are fed, at a constant speed, through one end of the reactor with an adequate residence time to allow the reagents to mix while they flow towards the outlet. When handling viscous liquids, PFRs present laminar flows, so it is necessary to use injection devices (a T mixer) or mechanical mixers. Some of the advantages of PFRs are that they do not require constant maintenance, are built in small spaces, and have low capital costs [243,244].

The cavitation reactors usually used to obtain biodiesel are hydrodynamic and sonochemical. Cavitation reactors are multiphase reactors that intensify the process using acoustic or flow energy, causing a cavitation phenomenon and, therefore, an increase in turbulence, thereby improving mass transfer. This cavitation phenomenon achieves high values of temperature and pressure [243–245].

Simultaneous reaction-separation reactors perform the chemical reaction, extraction, and separation of the products in a single stage. This type of reactor achieves better quality and a higher biodiesel yield because there is an optimal mixture. Of these reactors, the membrane ones are the most used in the production of biofuels since they do not require additional units in the process. Reactive distillation has also been used for the simultaneous reaction-separation process, which presents advantages over other reactors, such as short reaction times and improved yields because the products are extracted immediately after production. Costs decrease since additional operating units are not required [243,244].

Table 10 shows some research regarding the use of chemical reactors to obtain biodiesel from waste cooking oil. To intensify the production of this biofuel, techniques such as supercritical conditions [31], microwaves [170,246,247], ultrasonic [248], hydrodynamic cavitation [245], and spinning disk [249] have been used to eliminate resistance to mass transfer between alcohol and oil and have short periods and low energy consumption compared to industrial processes that are currently used [245].

Table 10. Examples of bifunctional catalysts used in biodiesel production.

Type of Reactor	Oil	Catalyst	Catalyst Load (%)	Alcohol:Oil Ratio	Reaction Temperature (°C)	Yield (%FAMEs)	References
Continuous Flow-Microwave	WCO	SrO/SiO_2	41	12:1	65	99.2	[247]
Hydrodynamic cavitation	WCO	KOH	1	6:1	60	98.1	[245]
Ultrasonic	WCO	KOH	1	7.4:1	60	96.5	[250]
Microreactor	WCO	KOH	2	12:1	50	>95.00	[251]
Rotating flask oscillatory flow	Coconut CWO	KOH	1	6:1	60	93.72	[252]
Reactive distillation	WCO	CaO	Bed height of 150 mm	4:1	65	93.48	[253]
Microtubes (prior esterification)	WCO	H_2SO_4	1	9:1	65	91.76	[254]
Microwave Irradiation	WCO	KOH	0.5	5:1	-	91.63	[246]
Batch stirred tank	WCO	Fe/CaO	7	12:1	60	90.0	[71]

As seen in Table 10, moderate reaction temperatures (60 °C) and several homogeneous and heterogeneous catalysts are used in different types of chemical reactors, obtaining yields of at least 90% in all of them with WCO.

Tangy et al. [247] reported the highest yield using WCO (99.2%) in a continuous flow reactor for microwave-assisted transesterification and heterogeneous catalysts (SrO/SiO_2). However, it is necessary to improve the process and see other catalyst synthesis options to prevent SrO leaching and make the FFA content fed to the reactor more efficient.

On the other hand, microreactors, whose advantages include small diffusion distances, increased specific surface area, high heat and mass transfer rates, and greater safety, have driven the study of capillary reactors for biodiesel production [251,254]. Tanawannapong et al. [254] reported biodiesel production from waste cooking oil using a microtube reactor with a 1.2 cm length and an internal diameter of 0.508 mm along with a T mixer at the inlet of the reactor; a methyl ester content of 91.7% was obtained in a 5 s reaction time; this study verifies that the transesterification reaction takes a shorter time as compared to the batch reactor. Although satisfactory initial results are observed, the technology still requires advancements in certain areas. Further research is needed to develop operating procedures that include the usage of feedstock, possessing increased levels of free fatty acids, and exploiting heterogeneous catalysts, in addition to high costs and complexities in the fabrication of glass and silicon microdevices [255].

In summary, the cost-effectiveness of the transesterification reaction to produce biodiesel rests heavily on many process parameters, namely the oil type and composition, type and amount of the catalyst, type and quantity of alcohol, residence time and temperature, and process intensification method. Actually, the last parameters depend upon catalyst type, and therefore its cost and activity greatly affect not only the overall cost of the process [107,206,256] but also the environmental impacts [107]. Actually, it has been demonstrated by Alanis et al. that the metal precursor used to prepare the catalyst has a significant impact on the production cost and energy consumption because the catalyst activity is modified. Therefore, in order to minimize environmental impacts and the overall cost of the catalyst preparation and the biodiesel production process, an optimization of the catalyst synthesis must be conducted.

The batch operation remains the most common process for the production of biodiesel. However, continuous production has advantages, such as small spaces for their installation, reduced operating costs, low investment, and ensuring a product of consistent quality. This approach is ideal when a fast response is required and offers higher heat transfer and selectivity than the batch method. As a result of all of this, the biodiesel industry now has its eyes on the continuous process model, hoping to solve batch production problems.

5. A Perspective on Biodiesel Production in Different Countries and Biodiesel Commercialization Improvement Strategies

In the last decade, the production and consumption of biodiesel in different countries in the world have been increasing due to the increase in energy demand derived from the growth of the human population [257]. This has allowed these countries to embrace policies related to biodiesel production.

- In the US, biodiesel is commonly used by the transportation sector through blends with fossil fuels, such as B10 or B20. Demand for biodiesel in the US is expected to increase as fossil fuels are replaced. As an example, biodiesel production in 2023 is expected to be 37% higher than in 2022 due to the implementation of economic incentives by the government [258].
- The Canadian government has improved biodiesel production through subsidies to decrease the cost of biofuel production and comply with the agreements established in the 2030 Agenda. As an example, biodiesel production in 2026 is expected to be 313 M liters, compared to the 147 M liters awaited this year [258].
- In Latin America, the biodiesel production expected in 2023 is 635 M liters. In Brazil, the variety of climates and the large expanse of soil allow it to cultivate various oilseeds. Aside that, this country has policies that promote this biofuel usage [258].
- In Europe and the UK the biodiesel production expected in 2013 is 37% higer than in 2022 [258]. Due to the implementation of different policies in the EU, biodiesel will be more accessible in order to reduce the use of fossil fuels.

Despite the abundance of available studies about biodiesel production from waste cooking oil, there are still various strategies that could improve its commercialization. These are presented below.

(a) Implementing efficient collection systems according to local regulations for the correct disposal of lipid waste of animal or vegetable origin. Then the need for these regulations arises because large quantities of this residue are produced worldwide, which increases proportionally to the human population's increase. To promote the recollection and correct disposition of WCO, several countries have implemented different incentives. For instance, China's government offers several subsidies, such as training, a collecting system focused on the market, and professional disposal. In Japan, the subsidies offered to biofuel producers allow for greater economic competitiveness by reducing production costs. In Spain, there is a WCO recollection program where collection bins are set up in some neighborhoods of Barcelona and Valladolid [259].

(b) Designing industrial-scale processes based on a circular economy perspective: In recent years, this concept has been introduced with the idea of reducing waste to

a minimum, which implies the employment of renewable energy sources to use energy more efficiently and reuse process water [260,261].
(c) Life Cycle Sustainability Assessment (LCSA) of existing processes. This is mandatory to estimate the environmental impacts of biodiesel production through different processes, which ultimately will aid the government and industry in making decisions about the less harmful process [259,262,263].

This tool has been applied to evaluate different biodiesel production processes, such as the one conducted by Talens Peiró et al. [264] which found that the transesterification process contributed 68% to the total impact. Lombardi et al. [265] reported a comparison against several methods of biodiesel production, and it shows that NaOH-catalyzed transesterification of WCO can lead to decreased environmental impacts [265]. Alanís et al. [107] compared the environmental impacts of biodiesel production from WCO catalyzed by a heterogeneous bifunctional catalyst synthesized with two different iron salt precursors [107].

6. Conclusions

Biodiesel can be obtained by the esterification and transesterification of waste cooking oil (WCO) as a raw material by homogeneous or heterogeneous catalysis. The type of biodiesel production process impacts the quality of biodiesel. In this context, transesterification is highly preferred. The feedstock and catalysis type used to produce biodiesel determine the stages of the process. The homogenously catalyzed process implies two more steps than the latter, and those are esterification under acid conditions (usually adding H_2SO_4) and elimination of the transesterification catalyst (usually a base like NaOH or KOH) by washing with water. Enzymatic catalysis to conduct the process is not a viable option due to the long reaction times and cost of the enzyme. Bifunctional catalysts are solids that contain both acid and basic sites and are able to reduce the number of process stages by simultaneously conducting esterification of free fatty acids and triglyceride transesterification. This eliminates the need to add an acid and the high consumption of water to clean the biodiesel.

The challenges to overcome in biodiesel production using WCO and bifunctional catalysts are reducing costs and energy consumption, using catalysts whose synthesis does not demand high loads of energy, and conducting life cycle assessments in order to establish the environmental impacts of each process and provide a relevant criterion to make the decision of electing or not electing a specific production process.

From the assessed processes to conduct the transesterification of WCO, the ones including microwaves, microreactors, and reactive distillation seem to be the most promising ones in terms of yield, reaction time, and number of involved stages.

Biodiesel from WCO usually does not meet all the standards, mainly that of methyl esters content and viscosity. In order to use biodiesel from WCO, it is suggested to use it in blends, to use co-solvents or to improve the pre-treatment of the raw material.

Author Contributions: Conceptualization, R.R. and R.N.; analysis, R.R., R.N. and M.C.F.; investigation, M.C.F., S.L.M. and A.R.-S.; resources, R.R. and R.N.; data curation, S.L.M. and A.R.-S.; writing—original draft preparation, M.C.F.; writing—review and editing, R.R. and R.N.; visualization, M.C.F. and A.R.-S.; supervision, R.R. and R.N.; project administration, R.R.; funding acquisition, R.R. All authors have read and agreed to the published version of the manuscript.

Funding: This research was funded by COMECYT-Mexico (FICDTEM-2023-32) and the Universidad Autonoma del Estado de Mexico through research project 6871/2022CIB.

Data Availability Statement: Not applicable.

Acknowledgments: M.C.F. thanks CONAHCYT for the postgraduate studies scholarship (Number 1000624). The authors are grateful to CCIQS (UAEM-UNAM) for providing support. The technical support of María Citlalit Martínez Soto is also acknowledged.

Conflicts of Interest: The authors declare no conflict of interest.

References

1. Ogunkunle, O.; Ahmed, N.A. A Review of Global Current Scenario of Biodiesel Adoption and Combustion in Vehicular Diesel Engines. *Energy Rep.* **2019**, *5*, 1560–1579. [CrossRef]
2. Kasirajan, R. Biodiesel Production by Two Step Process from an Energy Source of Chrysophyllum Albidum Oil Using Homogeneous Catalyst. *S. Afr. J. Chem. Eng.* **2021**, *37*, 161–166. [CrossRef]
3. Hafeez, S.; Al-Salem, S.M.; Manos, G.; Constantinou, A. Fuel Production Using Membrane Reactors: A Review. *Environ. Chem. Lett.* **2020**, *18*, 1477–1490. [CrossRef]
4. Al-Muhtaseb, A.H.; Osman, A.I.; Murphin Kumar, P.S.; Jamil, F.; Al-Haj, L.; Al Nabhani, A.; Kyaw, H.H.; Myint, M.T.Z.; Mehta, N.; Rooney, D.W. Circular Economy Approach of Enhanced Bifunctional Catalytic System of CaO/CeO$_2$ for Biodiesel Production from Waste Loquat Seed Oil with Life Cycle Assessment Study. *Energy Convers. Manag.* **2021**, *236*, 114040. [CrossRef]
5. Rogelj, J.; Shindell, D.; Jiang, K.; Fifita, S.; Forster, P.; Ginzburg, V.; Handa, C.; Kheshgi, H.; Kobayashi, S.; Kriegler, E.; et al. Mitigation Pathways Compatible with 1.5 °C in the Context of Sustainable Development. Available online: https://www.ipcc.ch/site/assets/uploads/sites/2/2022/06/SR15_Chapter_2_LR.pdf (accessed on 6 April 2023).
6. Adenuga, A.A.; Oyekunle, J.A.O.; Idowu, O.O. Pathway to Reduce Free Fatty Acid Formation in *Calophyllum inophyllum* Kernel Oil: A Renewable Feedstock for Biodiesel Production. *J. Clean. Prod.* **2021**, *316*, 128222. [CrossRef]
7. Borah, M.J.; Das, A.; Das, V.; Bhuyan, N.; Deka, D. Transesterification of Waste Cooking Oil for Biodiesel Production Catalyzed by Zn Substituted Waste Egg Shell Derived CaO Nanocatalyst. *Fuel* **2019**, *242*, 345–354. [CrossRef]
8. Lv, E.; Dou, T.; Ding, S.; Lu, J.; Li, Z.; Yi, W.; Li, J.; Ding, J. Membrane Dehydration-Enhanced Esterification for Biodiesel Production from a Potential Feedstock of *Firmiana platanifolia* L.f. Seed Oil. *Chem. Eng. Res. Des.* **2020**, *153*, 1–7. [CrossRef]
9. Zhang, H.; Li, H.; Hu, Y.; Venkateswara Rao, K.T.; Xu, C.C.; Yang, S. Advances in Production of Bio-Based Ester Fuels with Heterogeneous Bifunctional Catalysts. *Renew. Sustain. Energy Rev.* **2019**, *114*, 109296. [CrossRef]
10. Teo, S.H.; Islam, A.; Chan, E.S.; Thomas Choong, S.Y.; Alharthi, N.H.; Taufiq-Yap, Y.H.; Awual, M.R. Efficient Biodiesel Production from Jatropha Curcus Using CaSO$_4$/Fe$_2$O$_3$-SiO$_2$ Core-Shell Magnetic Nanoparticles. *J. Clean. Prod.* **2019**, *208*, 816–826. [CrossRef]
11. BP International. *Statistical Review of World Energy 2022*; BP International: London, UK, 2022.
12. Transport Biofuels—Renewables 2022—Analysis—IEA. Available online: https://www.iea.org/reports/renewables-2022/transport-biofuels#forecast-summary (accessed on 6 April 2023).
13. Esfandabadi, Z.S.; Ranjbari, M.; Scagnelli, S.D. The Imbalance of Food and Biofuel Markets amid Ukraine-Russia Crisis: A Systems Thinking Perspective. *Biofuel Res. J.* **2022**, *9*, 1640–1647. [CrossRef]
14. Athar, M.; Zaidi, S. A Review of the Feedstocks, Catalysts, and Intensification Techniques for Sustainable Biodiesel Production. *J. Environ. Chem. Eng.* **2020**, *8*, 104523. [CrossRef]
15. Paiz, S.; Costa, J.M., Jr.; Pontes, P.C.; Juliana, J.D.; de Moraes, D.B.; de Souza, C.G.; Naveira-Cotta, C.P. Experimental Parametric Analysis of Biodiesel Synthesis in Microreactors Using Waste Cooking Oil (WCO) in Ethilic Route. *J. Braz. Soc. Mech. Sci. Eng.* **2022**, *44*, 179. [CrossRef]
16. Munir, M.; Saeed, M.; Ahmad, M.; Waseem, A.; Sultana, S.; Zafar, M.; Srinivasan, G.R. Optimization of Novel *Lepidium perfoliatum* Linn. Biodiesel Using Zirconium-Modified Montmorillonite Clay Catalyst. *Energy Sources Part A Recovery Util. Environ. Eff.* **2019**, *44*, 6632–6647. [CrossRef]
17. Munir, M.; Ahmad, M.; Rehan, M.; Saeed, M.; Lam, S.S.; Nizami, A.S.; Waseem, A.; Sultana, S.; Zafar, M. Production of High Quality Biodiesel from Novel Non-Edible *Raphnus raphanistrum* L. Seed Oil Using Copper Modified Montmorillonite Clay Catalyst. *Environ. Res.* **2021**, *193*, 110398. [CrossRef]
18. Munir, M.; Ahmad, M.; Mubashir, M.; Asif, S.; Waseem, A.; Mukhtar, A.; Saqib, S.; Siti Halimatul Munawaroh, H.; Lam, M.K.; Shiong Khoo, K.; et al. A Practical Approach for Synthesis of Biodiesel via Non-Edible Seeds Oils Using Trimetallic Based Montmorillonite Nano-Catalyst. *Bioresour. Technol.* **2021**, *328*, 124859. [CrossRef]
19. Munir, M.; Ahmad, M.; Saeed, M.; Waseem, A.; Nizami, A.S.; Sultana, S.; Zafar, M.; Rehan, M.; Srinivasan, G.R.; Ali, A.M.; et al. Biodiesel Production from Novel Non-Edible Caper (*Capparis spinosa* L.) Seeds Oil Employing Cu–Ni Doped ZrO$_2$ Catalyst. *Renew. Sustain. Energy Rev.* **2021**, *138*, 110558. [CrossRef]
20. Jabeen, M.; Munir, M.; Abbas, M.M.; Ahmad, M.; Waseem, A.; Saeed, M.; Kalam, M.A.; Zafar, M.; Sultana, S.; Mohamed, A.; et al. Sustainable Production of Biodiesel from Novel and Non-Edible *Ailanthus altissima* (Mill.) Seed Oil from Green and Recyclable Potassium Hydroxide Activated *Ailanthus cake* and Cadmium Sulfide Catalyst. *Sustainability* **2022**, *14*, 10962. [CrossRef]
21. Munir, M.; Saeed, M.; Ahmad, M.; Waseem, A.; Alsaady, M.; Asif, S.; Ahmed, A.; Shariq Khan, M.; Bokhari, A.; Mubashir, M.; et al. Cleaner Production of Biodiesel from Novel Non-Edible Seed Oil (*Carthamus lanatus* L.) via Highly Reactive and Recyclable Green Nano CoWO$_3$@rGO Composite in Context of Green Energy Adaptation. *Fuel* **2023**, *332*, 126265. [CrossRef]
22. Mohiddin, M.N.B.; Tan, Y.H.; Seow, Y.X.; Kansedo, J.; Mubarak, N.M.; Abdullah, M.O.; Chan, Y.S.; Khalid, M. Evaluation on Feedstock, Technologies, Catalyst and Reactor for Sustainable Biodiesel Production: A Review. *J. Ind. Eng. Chem.* **2021**, *98*, 60–81. [CrossRef]
23. Jalilian, N.; Najafpour, G.D.; Khajouei, M. Macro and Micro Algae in Pollution Control and Biofuel Production—A Review. *ChemBioEng Rev.* **2020**, *7*, 18–33. [CrossRef]
24. Pikula, K.; Zakharenko, A.; Stratidakis, A.; Razgonova, M.; Nosyrev, A.; Mezhuev, Y.; Tsatsakis, A.; Golokhvast, K. The Advances and Limitations in Biodiesel Production: Feedstocks, Oil Extraction Methods, Production, and Environmental Life Cycle Assessment. *Green Chem. Lett. Rev.* **2020**, *13*, 11–30. [CrossRef]

25. Yaashikaa, P.R.; Keerthana Devi, M.; Senthil Kumar, P. Algal Biofuels: Technological Perspective on Cultivation, Fuel Extraction and Engineering Genetic Pathway for Enhancing Productivity. *Fuel* **2022**, *320*, 123814. [CrossRef]
26. Sanju, S.; Thakur, A.; Misra, P.; Shukla, P.K. Algal Biomass and Biofuel Production. In *Bioprospecting of Microorganism-Based Industrial Molecules*; John Wiley & Sons: Hoboken, NJ, USA, 2021; pp. 357–376. [CrossRef]
27. Clifford, M.; Prakash, R.; Rai, M.P. Latest Advances and Status Analysis of Nanomaterials for Microalgae Photosystem, Lipids and Biodiesel: A State of Art. *J. Environ. Chem. Eng.* **2023**, *11*, 109111. [CrossRef]
28. Manzoor, M.; Hussain, A.; Ahmad, Q.A.; Chaudhary, A.; Schenk, P.M.; Deepanraj, B.; Loke Show, P. Biodiesel Quality Assessment of Microalgae Cultivated Mixotrophically on Sugarcane Bagasse. *Sustain. Energy Technol. Assess.* **2022**, *53*, 102359. [CrossRef]
29. Yang, G.; Yu, J. Advancements in Basic Zeolites for Biodiesel Production via Transesterification. *Chemistry* **2023**, *5*, 438–451. [CrossRef]
30. Yaashikaa, P.R.; Kumar, P.S.; Karishma, S. Bio-Derived Catalysts for Production of Biodiesel: A Review on Feedstock, Oil Extraction Methodologies, Reactors and Lifecycle Assessment of Biodiesel. *Fuel* **2022**, *316*, 123379. [CrossRef]
31. Andreo-Martínez, P.; Ortiz-Martínez, V.M.; Salar-García, M.J.; Veiga-del-Baño, J.M.; Chica, A.; Quesada-Medina, J. Waste Animal Fats as Feedstock for Biodiesel Production Using Non-Catalytic Supercritical Alcohol Transesterification: A Perspective by the PRISMA Methodology. *Energy Sustain. Dev.* **2022**, *69*, 150–163. [CrossRef]
32. Rezania, S.; Oryani, B.; Park, J.; Hashemi, B.; Yadav, K.K.; Kwon, E.E.; Hur, J.; Cho, J. Review on Transesterification of Non-Edible Sources for Biodiesel Production with a Focus on Economic Aspects, Fuel Properties and by-Product Applications. *Energy Convers. Manag.* **2019**, *201*, 112155. [CrossRef]
33. Adepoju, T.F.; Akens, H.A.; Ekeinde, E.B. Synthesis of Biodiesel from Blend of Seeds Oil-Animal Fat Employing Agricultural Wastes as Base Catalyst. *Case Stud. Chem. Environ. Eng.* **2022**, *5*, 100202. [CrossRef]
34. Encinar, J.M.; Nogales-Delgado, S.; Sánchez, N. Pre-Esterification of High Acidity Animal Fats to Produce Biodiesel: A Kinetic Study. *Arab. J. Chem.* **2021**, *14*, 103048. [CrossRef]
35. Srinivasan, G.R.; Jambulingam, R. Comprehensive Study on Biodiesel Produced from Waste Animal Fats—A Review. *J. Environ. Sci. Technol.* **2018**, *11*, 157–166. [CrossRef]
36. Chen, H.X.; Xia, W.; Wang, S. Biodiesel Production from Waste Cooking Oil Using a Waste Diaper Derived Heterogeneous Magnetic Catalyst. *Braz. J. Chem. Eng.* **2022**, 1–10. [CrossRef]
37. Khan, H.M.; Iqbal, T.; Ali, C.H.; Yasin, S.; Jamil, F. Waste Quail Beaks as Renewable Source for Synthesizing Novel Catalysts for Biodiesel Production. *Renew. Energy* **2020**, *154*, 1035–1043. [CrossRef]
38. Soji-Adekunle, A.R.; Asere, A.A.; Ishola, N.B.; Oloko-Oba, I.M.; Betiku, E. Modelling of Synthesis of Waste Cooking Oil Methyl Esters by Artificial Neural Network and Response Surface Methodology. *Int. J. Ambient Energy* **2019**, *40*, 716–725. [CrossRef]
39. Mahmood Khan, H.; Iqbal, T.; Haider Ali, C.; Javaid, A.; Iqbal Cheema, I. Sustainable Biodiesel Production from Waste Cooking Oil Utilizing Waste Ostrich (*Struthio camelus*) Bones Derived Heterogeneous Catalyst. *Fuel* **2020**, *277*, 118091. [CrossRef]
40. Goh, B.H.H.; Ong, H.C.; Chong, C.T.; Chen, W.H.; Leong, K.Y.; Tan, S.X.; Lee, X.J. Ultrasonic Assisted Oil Extraction and Biodiesel Synthesis of Spent Coffee Ground. *Fuel* **2020**, *261*, 116121. [CrossRef]
41. Nguyen, H.C.; Liang, S.H.; Chen, S.S.; Su, C.H.; Lin, J.H.; Chien, C.C. Enzymatic Production of Biodiesel from Insect Fat Using Methyl Acetate as an Acyl Acceptor: Optimization by Using Response Surface Methodology. *Energy Convers. Manag.* **2018**, *158*, 168–175. [CrossRef]
42. Nguyen, H.C.; Nguyen, N.T.; Su, C.-H.; Wang, F.-M.; Tran, T.N.; Liao, Y.-T.; Liang, S.-H. Biodiesel Production from Insects: From Organic Waste to Renewable Energy. *Curr. Org. Chem.* **2019**, *23*, 1499–1508. [CrossRef]
43. Mohan, K.; Sathishkumar, P.; Rajan, D.K.; Rajarajeswaran, J.; Ganesan, A.R. Black Soldier Fly (*Hermetia illucens*) Larvae as Potential Feedstock for the Biodiesel Production: Recent Advances and Challenges. *Sci. Total Environ.* **2023**, *859*, 160235. [CrossRef]
44. Nguyen, H.C.; Nguyen, M.L.; Wang, F.M.; Juan, H.Y.; Su, C.H. Biodiesel Production by Direct Transesterification of Wet Spent Coffee Grounds Using Switchable Solvent as a Catalyst and Solvent. *Bioresour. Technol.* **2020**, *296*, 122334. [CrossRef]
45. Forcina, A.; Petrillo, A.; Travaglioni, M.; di Chiara, S.; de Felice, F. A Comparative Life Cycle Assessment of Different Spent Coffee Ground Reuse Strategies and a Sensitivity Analysis for Verifying the Environmental Convenience Based on the Location of Sites. *J. Clean. Prod.* **2023**, *385*, 135727. [CrossRef]
46. Park, J.; Kim, B.; Lee, J.W. In-Situ Transesterification of Wet Spent Coffee Grounds for Sustainable Biodiesel Production. *Bioresour. Technol.* **2016**, *221*, 55–60. [CrossRef] [PubMed]
47. Li, Q.; Zheng, L.; Cai, H.; Garza, E.; Yu, Z.; Zhou, S. From Organic Waste to Biodiesel: Black Soldier Fly, *Hermetia illucens*, Makes It Feasible. *Fuel* **2011**, *90*, 1545–1548. [CrossRef]
48. Leung, D.; Yang, D.; Li, Z.; Zhao, Z.; Chen, J.; Zhu, L. Biodiesel from *Zophobas morio* Larva Oil: Process Optimization and FAME Characterization. *Ind. Eng. Chem. Res.* **2012**, *51*, 1036–1040. [CrossRef]
49. Zheng, L.; Hou, Y.; Li, W.; Yang, S.; Li, Q.; Yu, Z. Exploring the Potential of Grease from Yellow Mealworm Beetle (*Tenebrio molitor*) as a Novel Biodiesel Feedstock. *Appl. Energy* **2013**, *101*, 618–621. [CrossRef]
50. Yang, S.; Li, Q.; Gao, Y.; Zheng, L.; Liu, Z. Biodiesel Production from Swine Manure via Housefly Larvae (*Musca domestica* L.). *Renew. Energy* **2014**, *66*, 222–227. [CrossRef]
51. Ramos-Bueno, R.P.; González-Fernández, M.J.; Sánchez-Muros-Lozano, M.J.; García-Barroso, F.; Guil-Guerrero, J.L. Fatty Acid Profiles and Cholesterol Content of Seven Insect Species Assessed by Several Extraction Systems. *Eur. Food Res. Technol.* **2016**, *242*, 1471–1477. [CrossRef]

52. Pamintuan, K.R.S.; Cajayon, J.A.B.; Dableo, G.B. Growth Characteristics and Lipid Content of Black Soldier Fly (*Hermetia illucens*) Larva Reared in Milkfish Offal and Mixed Vegetable Wastes. In Proceedings of the ICBBE '19: 2019 6th International Conference on Biomedical and Bioinformatics Engineering, Shanghai, China, 13–15 November 2019; pp. 163–168. [CrossRef]
53. Wang, Y.S.; Shelomi, M. Review of Black Soldier Fly (*Hermetia illucens*) as Animal Feed and Human Food. *Foods* **2017**, *6*, 91. [CrossRef]
54. Sajjadi, B.; Raman, A.A.A.; Arandiyan, H. A Comprehensive Review on Properties of Edible and Non-Edible Vegetable Oil-Based Biodiesel: Composition, Specifications and Prediction Models. *Renew. Sustain. Energy Rev.* **2016**, *63*, 62–92. [CrossRef]
55. Elsayed, M.; Ran, Y.; Ai, P.; Azab, M.; Mansour, A.; Jin, K.; Zhang, Y.; Abomohra, A.E.F. Innovative Integrated Approach of Biofuel Production from Agricultural Wastes by Anaerobic Digestion and Black Soldier Fly Larvae. *J. Clean. Prod.* **2020**, *263*, 121495. [CrossRef]
56. Feng, W.; Wang, S.; Duan, X.; Wang, W.; Yang, F.; Xiong, J.; Wang, T.; Wang, C. A Novel Approach for Enhancing Lipid Recovery for Biodiesel Production from Wet Energy Biomass Using Surfactants-Assisted Extraction. *Renew. Energy* **2021**, *170*, 462–470. [CrossRef]
57. Leong, S.Y.; Kutty, S.R.M.; Bashir, M.J.K.; Li, Q. A Circular Economy Framework Based on Organic Wastes Upcycling for Biodiesel Production from *Hermetia illucens*. *Eng. J.* **2021**, *25*, 223–234. [CrossRef]
58. Wong, C.Y.; Kiatkittipong, K.; Kiatkittipong, W.; Lim, J.W.; Lam, M.K.; Wu, T.Y.; Show, P.L.; Daud, H.; Goh, P.S.; Sakuragi, M.; et al. *Rhizopus oligosporus*—Assisted Valorization of Coconut Endosperm Waste by Black Soldier Fly Larvae for Simultaneous Protein and Lipid to Biodiesel Production. *Processes* **2021**, *9*, 299. [CrossRef]
59. Jung, S.; Jung, J.M.; Tsang, Y.F.; Bhatnagar, A.; Chen, W.H.; Lin, K.Y.A.; Kwon, E.E. Biodiesel Production from Black Soldier Fly Larvae Derived from Food Waste by Non-Catalytic Transesterification. *Energy* **2022**, *238*, 121700. [CrossRef]
60. Park, J.Y.; Jung, S.; Na, Y.G.; Jeon, C.H.; Cheon, H.Y.; Yun, E.Y.; Lee, S.H.; Kwon, E.E.; Kim, J.K. Biodiesel Production from the Black Soldier Fly Larvae Grown on Food Waste and Its Fuel Property Characterization as a Potential Transportation Fuel. *Environ. Eng. Res.* **2022**, *27*, 200704. [CrossRef]
61. Nguyen, H.C.; Liang, S.H.; Doan, T.T.; Su, C.H.; Yang, P.C. Lipase-Catalyzed Synthesis of Biodiesel from Black Soldier Fly (*Hermetica illucens*): Optimization by Using Response Surface Methodology. *Energy Convers. Manag.* **2017**, *145*, 335–342. [CrossRef]
62. Nguyen, H.C.; Liang, S.H.; Li, S.Y.; Su, C.H.; Chien, C.C.; Chen, Y.J.; Huong, D.T.M. Direct Transesterification of Black Soldier Fly Larvae (*Hermetia illucens*) for Biodiesel Production. *J. Taiwan Inst. Chem. Eng.* **2018**, *85*, 165–169. [CrossRef]
63. Nguyen, H.C.; Nguyen, M.L.; Liang, S.H.; Su, C.H.; Wang, F.M. Switchable Solvent-Catalyzed Direct Transesterification of Insect Biomass for Biodiesel Production. *BioEnergy Res.* **2020**, *13*, 563–570. [CrossRef]
64. Van Grinsven, A.; van den Toorn, E.; van der Veen, R.; Kampman, B. *Used Cooking Oil (UCO) as Biofuel Feedstock in the EU*; CE Delft: Delft, The Netherlands, 2020; pp. 1–64.
65. EU Biodiesel. *Towards HVO*; Oils Fats Internationl: Redhill, UK, 2022.
66. Claeys, C. Used Cooking Oil (UCO) Feedstock Now Accounts for One-Fifth of All European Biofuels. In Proceedings of the ACI Oleofuels Conference, Marseille, France, 18–19 May 2022.
67. Global Information, Inc. (GII)—Premium Market Research Reports. Used Cooking Oil Market Size, Share, Price & Report 2023–2028. Available online: https://www.giiresearch.com/report/imarc1291431-used-cooking-oil-market-global-industry-trends.html. (accessed on 8 June 2023).
68. Muciño, G.G.; Romero, R.; Ramírez, A.; Martínez, S.L.; Baeza-Jiménez, R.; Natividad, R. Biodiesel Production from Used Cooking Oil and Sea Sand as Heterogeneous Catalyst. *Fuel* **2014**, *138*, 143–148. [CrossRef]
69. Suzihaque, M.U.H.; Alwi, H.; Kalthum Ibrahim, U.; Abdullah, S.; Haron, N. Biodiesel Production from Waste Cooking Oil: A Brief Review. *Mater. Today Proc.* **2022**, *63*, S490–S495. [CrossRef]
70. Azahar, W.N.A.W.; Bujang, M.; Jaya, R.P.; Hainin, M.R.; Mohamed, A.; Ngadi, N.; Jayanti, D.S. The Potential of Waste Cooking Oil as Bio-Asphalt for Alternative Binder—An Overview. *J. Teknol.* **2016**, *78*, 111–116. [CrossRef]
71. Enguilo Gonzaga, V.; Romero, R.; Gómez-Espinosa, R.M.; Romero, A.; Martínez, S.L.; Natividad, R. Biodiesel Production from Waste Cooking Oil Catalyzed by a Bifunctional Catalyst. *ACS Omega* **2021**, *6*, 24092–24105. [CrossRef] [PubMed]
72. Awogbemi, O.; Onuh, E.I.; Inambao, F.L. Comparative Study of Properties and Fatty Acid Composition of Some Neat Vegetable Oils and Waste Cooking Oils. *Int. J. Low-Carbon Technol.* **2019**, *14*, 417–425. [CrossRef]
73. Foroutan, R.; Esmaeili, H.; Mousavi, S.M.; Hashemi, S.A.; Yeganeh, G. The Physical Properties of Biodiesel-Diesel Fuel Produced via Transesterification Process from Different Oil Sources. *Phys. Chem. Res.* **2019**, *7*, 415–424. [CrossRef]
74. Bargole, S.S.; Singh, P.K.; George, S.; Saharan, V.K. Valorisation of Low Fatty Acid Content Waste Cooking Oil into Biodiesel through Transesterification Using a Basic Heterogeneous Calcium-Based Catalyst. *Biomass Bioenergy* **2021**, *146*, 105984. [CrossRef]
75. Chuah, L.F.; Yusup, S.; Aziz, A.R.A.; Klemeš, J.J.; Bokhari, A.; Abdullah, M.Z. Influence of Fatty Acids Content in Non-Edible Oil for Biodiesel Properties. *Clean Technol. Environ. Policy* **2016**, *18*, 473–482. [CrossRef]
76. Ben-Youssef, C.; Chávez-Yam, A.; Zepeda, A.; Rivera, J.M.; Rincón, S. Simultaneous Esterification/Transesterification of Waste Cooking Oil and *Jatropha Curcas* Oil with MOF-5 as a Heterogeneous Acid Catalyst. *Int. J. Environ. Sci. Technol.* **2021**, *18*, 3313–3326. [CrossRef]
77. Santya, G.; Maheswaran, T.; Yee, K.F. Optimization of Biodiesel Production from High Free Fatty Acid River Catfish Oil (*Pangasius Hypothalamus*) and Waste Cooking Oil Catalyzed by Waste Chicken Egg Shells Derived Catalyst. *SN Appl. Sci.* **2019**, *1*, 152. [CrossRef]

78. Mohamed, R.M.; Kadry, G.A.; Abdel-Samad, H.A.; Awad, M.E. High Operative Heterogeneous Catalyst in Biodiesel Production from Waste Cooking Oil. *Egypt. J. Pet.* **2020**, *29*, 59–65. [CrossRef]
79. Jume, B.H.; Gabris, M.A.; Rashidi Nodeh, H.; Rezania, S.; Cho, J. Biodiesel Production from Waste Cooking Oil Using a Novel Heterogeneous Catalyst Based on Graphene Oxide Doped Metal Oxide Nanoparticles. *Renew. Energy* **2020**, *162*, 2182–2189. [CrossRef]
80. Sharoba, A.M.; Ramadan, M.F. Impact of Frying on Fatty Acid Profile and Rheological Behaviour of Some Vegetable Oils. *J. Food Process. Technol.* **2017**, *3*, 161. [CrossRef]
81. McCormick, R.L.; Westbrook, S.R. Storage Stability of Biodiesel and Biodiesel Blends. *Energy Fuels* **2009**, *24*, 690–698. [CrossRef]
82. Maheshwari, P.; Haider, M.B.; Yusuf, M.; Klemeš, J.J.; Bokhari, A.; Beg, M.; Al-Othman, A.; Kumar, R.; Jaiswal, A.K. A Review on Latest Trends in Cleaner Biodiesel Production: Role of Feedstock, Production Methods, and Catalysts. *J. Clean. Prod.* **2022**, *355*, 131588. [CrossRef]
83. Abbaszaadeh, A.; Ghobadian, B.; Omidkhah, M.R.; Najafi, G. Current Biodiesel Production Technologies: A Comparative Review. *Energy Convers. Manag.* **2012**, *63*, 138–148. [CrossRef]
84. Munyentwali, A.; Li, H.; Yang, Q. Review of Advances in Bifunctional Solid Acid/Base Catalysts for Sustainable Biodiesel Production. *Appl. Catal. A Gen.* **2022**, *633*, 118525. [CrossRef]
85. Al-Muhtaseb, A.H.; Osman, A.I.; Jamil, F.; Mehta, N.; Al-Haj, L.; Coulon, F.; Al-Maawali, S.; Al Nabhani, A.; Kyaw, H.H.; Zar Myint, M.T.; et al. Integrating Life Cycle Assessment and Characterisation Techniques: A Case Study of Biodiesel Production Utilising Waste *Prunus Armeniaca* Seeds (PAS) and a Novel Catalyst. *J. Environ. Manag.* **2022**, *304*, 114319. [CrossRef]
86. Faried, M.; Samer, M.; Abdelsalam, E.; Yousef, R.S.; Attia, Y.A.; Ali, A.S. Biodiesel Production from Microalgae: Processes, Technologies and Recent Advancements. *Renew. Sustain. Energy Rev.* **2017**, *79*, 893–913. [CrossRef]
87. Katre, G.; Raskar, S.; Zinjarde, S.; Ravi Kumar, V.; Kulkarni, B.D.; RaviKumar, A. Optimization of the in Situ Transesterification Step for Biodiesel Production Using Biomass of *Yarrowia lipolytica* NCIM 3589 Grown on Waste Cooking Oil. *Energy* **2018**, *142*, 944–952. [CrossRef]
88. De Jesus, S.S.; Ferreira, G.F.; Moreira, L.S.; Filho, R.M. Biodiesel Production from Microalgae by Direct Transesterification Using Green Solvents. *Renew. Energy* **2020**, *160*, 1283–1294. [CrossRef]
89. Hidalgo, P.; Toro, C.; Ciudad, G.; Schober, S.; Mittelbach, M.; Navia, R. Evaluation of Different Operational Strategies for Biodiesel Production by Direct Transesterification of Microalgal Biomass. *Energy Fuels* **2014**, *28*, 3814–3820. [CrossRef]
90. Henderson, R.K.; Jiménez-González, C.; Constable, D.J.C.; Alston, S.R.; Inglis, G.G.A.; Fisher, G.; Sherwood, J.; Binks, S.P.; Curzons, A.D. Expanding GSK's Solvent Selection Guide—Embedding Sustainability into Solvent Selection Starting at Medicinal Chemistry. *Green Chem.* **2011**, *13*, 854–862. [CrossRef]
91. De Jesus, S.S.; Ferreira, G.F.; Wolf Maciel, M.R.; Maciel Filho, R. Biodiesel Purification by Column Chromatography and Liquid-Liquid Extraction Using Green Solvents. *Fuel* **2019**, *235*, 1123–1130. [CrossRef]
92. De Jesus, S.S.; Ferreira, G.F.; Fregolente, L.V.; Maciel Filho, R. Laboratory Extraction of Microalgal Lipids Using Sugarcane Bagasse Derived Green Solvents. *Algal Res.* **2018**, *35*, 292–300. [CrossRef]
93. Sicaire, A.G.; Vian, M.; Fine, F.; Joffre, F.; Carré, P.; Tostain, S.; Chemat, F. Alternative Bio-Based Solvents for Extraction of Fat and Oils: Solubility Prediction, Global Yield, Extraction Kinetics, Chemical Composition and Cost of Manufacturing. *Int. J. Mol. Sci.* **2015**, *16*, 8430–8453. [CrossRef]
94. Guan, G.; Kusakabe, K. Synthesis of Biodiesel Fuel Using an Electrolysis Method. *Chem. Eng. J.* **2009**, *153*, 159–163. [CrossRef]
95. Fereidooni, L.; Mehrpooya, M. Experimental Assessment of Electrolysis Method in Production of Biodiesel from Waste Cooking Oil Using Zeolite/Chitosan Catalyst with a Focus on Waste Biorefinery. *Energy Convers. Manag.* **2017**, *147*, 145–154. [CrossRef]
96. Moradi, P.; Saidi, M.; Najafabadi, A.T. Biodiesel Production via Esterification of Oleic Acid as a Representative of Free Fatty Acid Using Electrolysis Technique as a Novel Approach: Non-Catalytic and Catalytic Conversion. *Process Saf. Environ. Prot.* **2021**, *147*, 684–692. [CrossRef]
97. Fereidooni, L.; Tahvildari, K.; Mehrpooya, M. Trans-Esterification of Waste Cooking Oil with Methanol by Electrolysis Process Using KOH. *Renew. Energy* **2018**, *116*, 183–193. [CrossRef]
98. Abdollahi Asl, M.; Tahvildari, K.; Bigdeli, T. Eco-Friendly Synthesis of Biodiesel from WCO by Using Electrolysis Technique with Graphite Electrodes. *Fuel* **2020**, *270*, 117582. [CrossRef]
99. Syah Putra, R.; Hartono, P.; Julianto, S. ScienceDirect Conversion of Methyl Ester from Used Cooking Oil: The Combined Use of Electrolysis Process and Chitosan. *Energy Procedia* **2015**, *65*, 309–316. [CrossRef]
100. Rachman, S.A.; Komariah, L.N.; Andwikaputra, A.I.; Umbara, N.B. High Conversion and Yield of Biodiesel Using Electrolysis Method. *J. Phys. Conf. Ser.* **2018**, *1095*, 012040. [CrossRef]
101. Lam, M.K.; Lee, K.T.; Mohamed, A.R. Homogeneous, Heterogeneous and Enzymatic Catalysis for Transesterification of High Free Fatty Acid Oil (Waste Cooking Oil) to Biodiesel: A Review. *Biotechnol. Adv.* **2010**, *28*, 500–518. [CrossRef]
102. Huber, G.W.; Iborra, S.; Corma, A. Synthesis of Transportation Fuels from Biomass: Chemistry, Catalysts, and Engineering. *Chem. Rev.* **2006**, *106*, 4044–4098. [CrossRef]
103. Gandure, J.; Ketlogetswe, C.; Temu, A. Fuel Properties of Jatropha Methyl Ester and Its Blends with Petroleum Diesel. *ARPN J. Eng. Appl. Sci.* **2013**, *8*, 900–908.
104. Brahma, S.; Nath, B.; Basumatary, B.; Das, B.; Saikia, P.; Patir, K.; Basumatary, S. Biodiesel Production from Mixed Oils: A Sustainable Approach towards Industrial Biofuel Production. *Chem. Eng. J. Adv.* **2022**, *10*, 100284. [CrossRef]

105. Borges, M.E.; Díaz, L. Recent Developments on Heterogeneous Catalysts for Biodiesel Production by Oil Esterification and Transesterification Reactions: A Review. *Renew. Sustain. Energy Rev.* **2012**, *16*, 2839–2849. [CrossRef]
106. Shakorfow, A.M.; Mohamed, A.H. Homogenous Acidic and Basic Catalysts in Biodiesel Synthesis: A Review. *Acta Chem. Malays.* **2020**, *4*, 76–85. [CrossRef]
107. Alanis, C.; Ávila Córdoba, L.I.; Álvarez-Arteaga, G.; Romero, R.; Padilla-Rivera, A.; Natividad, R. Strategies to Improve the Sustainability of the Heterogeneous Catalysed Biodiesel Production from Waste Cooking Oil. *J. Clean. Prod.* **2022**, *380*, 134970. [CrossRef]
108. Gupta, A.R.; Rathod, V.K. Application of Catalysts in Biodiesel Production. In *Biodiesel Technology and Applications*; Scrivener Publishing: Beverly, MA, USA, 2023; pp. 85–136. [CrossRef]
109. Su, C.H. Recoverable and Reusable Hydrochloric Acid Used as a Homogeneous Catalyst for Biodiesel Production. *Appl. Energy* **2013**, *104*, 503–509. [CrossRef]
110. Kshirsagar, C.M.; Anand, R. Homogeneous Catalysed Biodiesel Synthesis from Alexandrian Laurel (*Calophyllum inophyllum* L.) Kernel Oil Using Ortho-Phosphoric Acid as a Pretreatment Catalyst. *Int. J. Green Energy* **2017**, *14*, 754–764. [CrossRef]
111. Guldhe, A.; Singh, P.; Ansari, F.A.; Singh, B.; Bux, F. Biodiesel Synthesis from Microalgal Lipids Using Tungstated Zirconia as a Heterogeneous Acid Catalyst and Its Comparison with Homogeneous Acid and Enzyme Catalysts. *Fuel* **2017**, *187*, 180–188. [CrossRef]
112. Loures, C.C.A.; Amaral, M.S.; Da Rós, P.C.M.; Zorn, S.M.F.E.; de Castro, H.F.; Silva, M.B. Simultaneous Esterification and Transesterification of Microbial Oil from *Chlorella minutissima* by Acid Catalysis Route: A Comparison between Homogeneous and Heterogeneous Catalysts. *Fuel* **2018**, *211*, 261–268. [CrossRef]
113. Dhawane, S.H.; Karmakar, B.; Ghosh, S.; Halder, G. Parametric Optimisation of Biodiesel Synthesis from Waste Cooking Oil via Taguchi Approach. *J. Environ. Chem. Eng.* **2018**, *6*, 3971–3980. [CrossRef]
114. Metre, A.V.; Nath, K. Super Phosphoric Acid Catalyzed Esterification of Palm Fatty Acid Distillate for Biodiesel Production: Physicochemical Parameters and Kinetics. *Pol. J. Chem. Technol.* **2015**, *17*, 88–96. [CrossRef]
115. Deng, X.; Fang, Z.; Liu, Y.H. Ultrasonic Transesterification of *Jatropha curcas* L. Oil to Biodiesel by a Two-Step Process. *Energy Convers. Manag.* **2010**, *51*, 2802–2807. [CrossRef]
116. Liu, J.; Nan, Y.; Tavlarides, L.L. Continuous Production of Ethanol-Based Biodiesel under Subcritical Conditions Employing Trace Amount of Homogeneous Catalysts. *Fuel* **2017**, *193*, 187–196. [CrossRef]
117. Deshmane, V.G.; Gogate, P.R.; Pandit, A.B. Ultrasound-Assisted Synthesis of Biodiesel from Palm Fatty Acid Distillate. *Ind. Eng. Chem. Res.* **2008**, *48*, 7923–7927. [CrossRef]
118. Santos, F.F.P.; Matos, L.J.B.L.; Rodrigues, S.; Fernandes, F.A.N. Optimization of the Production of Methyl Esters from Soybean Waste Oil Applying Ultrasound Technology. *Energy Fuels* **2009**, *23*, 4116–4120. [CrossRef]
119. Hanh, H.D.; Dong, N.T.; Okitsu, K.; Nishimura, R.; Maeda, Y. Biodiesel Production by Esterification of Oleic Acid with Short-Chain Alcohols under Ultrasonic Irradiation Condition. *Renew. Energy* **2009**, *34*, 780–783. [CrossRef]
120. Zhang, Y.; Dubé, M.A.; McLean, D.D.; Kates, M. Biodiesel Production from Waste Cooking Oil: 1. Process Design and Technological Assessment. *Bioresour. Technol.* **2003**, *89*, 1–16. [CrossRef]
121. Karnasuta, S.; Punsuvon, V.; Nokkaew, R. Biodiesel Production from Waste Coconut Oil in Coconut Milk Manufacturing. *Walailak J. Sci. Technol.* **2015**, *12*, 291–298.
122. Thanh, L.T.; Okitsu, K.; van Boi, L.; Maeda, Y. Catalytic Technologies for Biodiesel Fuel Production and Utilization of Glycerol: A Review. *Catalysts* **2012**, *2*, 191–222. [CrossRef]
123. Kulkarni, M.G.; Dalai, A.K. Waste Cooking Oil—An Economic Source for Biodiesel: A Review. *Ind. Eng. Chem. Res.* **2006**, *45*, 2901–2913. [CrossRef]
124. Carlucci, C. An Overview on the Production of Biodiesel Enabled by Continuous Flow Methodologies. *Catalysts* **2022**, *12*, 717. [CrossRef]
125. Mohadesi, M.; Aghel, B.; Maleki, M.; Ansari, A. Production of Biodiesel from Waste Cooking Oil Using a Homogeneous Catalyst: Study of Semi-Industrial Pilot of Microreactor. *Renew. Energy* **2019**, *136*, 677–682. [CrossRef]
126. Thoai, D.N.; Tongurai, C.; Prasertsit, K.; Kumar, A. A Novel Two-Step Transesterification Process Catalyzed by Homogeneous Base Catalyst in the First Step and Heterogeneous Acid Catalyst in the Second Step. *Fuel Process. Technol.* **2017**, *168*, 97–104. [CrossRef]
127. Aslan, V.; Eryilmaz, T. Polynomial Regression Method for Optimization of Biodiesel Production from Black Mustard (*Brassica nigra* L.) Seed Oil Using Methanol, Ethanol, NaOH, and KOH. *Energy* **2020**, *209*, 118386. [CrossRef]
128. Berchmans, H.J.; Morishita, K.; Takarada, T. Kinetic Study of Hydroxide-Catalyzed Methanolysis of *Jatropha curcas*—Waste Food Oil Mixture for Biodiesel Production. *Fuel* **2013**, *104*, 46–52. [CrossRef]
129. Hsiao, M.C.; Kuo, J.Y.; Hsieh, P.H.; Hou, S.S. Improving Biodiesel Conversions from Blends of High- and Low-Acid-Value Waste Cooking Oils Using Sodium Methoxide as a Catalyst Based on a High Speed Homogenizer. *Energies* **2018**, *11*, 2298. [CrossRef]
130. Sharma, A.; Kodgire, P.; Kachhwaha, S.S. Biodiesel Production from Waste Cotton-Seed Cooking Oil Using Microwave-Assisted Transesterification: Optimization and Kinetic Modeling. *Renew. Sustain. Energy Rev.* **2019**, *116*, 109394. [CrossRef]
131. Ouanji, F.; Kacimi, M.; Ziyad, M.; Puleo, F.; Liotta, L.F. Production of Biodiesel at Small-Scale (10 L) for Local Power Generation. *Int. J. Hydrogen Energy* **2017**, *42*, 8914–8921. [CrossRef]

132. Hiwot, T. Mango (*Magnifera indica*) Seed Oil Grown in Dilla Town as Potential Raw Material for Biodiesel Production Using NaOH-a Homogeneous Catalyst. *Chem. Int.* **2018**, *4*, 198–205.
133. Dias, J.M.; Alvim-Ferraz, M.C.M.; Almeida, M.F. Comparison of the Performance of Different Homogeneous Alkali Catalysts during Transesterification of Waste and Virgin Oils and Evaluation of Biodiesel Quality. *Fuel* **2008**, *87*, 3572–3578. [CrossRef]
134. Chen, K.S.; Lin, Y.C.; Hsu, K.H.; Wang, H.K. Improving Biodiesel Yields from Waste Cooking Oil by Using Sodium Methoxide and a Microwave Heating System. *Energy* **2012**, *38*, 151–156. [CrossRef]
135. Sivarethinamohan, S.; Hanumanthu, J.R.; Gaddam, K.; Ravindiran, G.; Alagumalai, A. Towards Sustainable Biodiesel Production by Solar Intensification of Waste Cooking Oil and Engine Parameter Assessment Studies. *Sci. Total Environ.* **2022**, *804*, 150236. [CrossRef]
136. Miyuranga, K.A.V.; Balasuriya, B.M.C.M.; Arachchige, U.S.P.R.; Jayasinghe, R.A.; Weerasekara, N.A. Comparison of Performance of Various Homogeneous Alkali Catalysts in Transesterification of Waste Cooking Oil. *Asian J. Chem.* **2022**, *34*, 3157–3161. [CrossRef]
137. Shende, K.; Sonage, S.; Dange, P.; Tandale, M. Optimization of Biodiesel Production Process from Waste Cooking Oil Using Homogeneous and Heterogeneous Catalysts through Transesterification Process. In *Proceedings of the 2nd International Conference on Advanced Technologies for Societal Applications—Volume 1*; Springer: Berlin, Germany, 2020; pp. 531–542. [CrossRef]
138. Hsiao, M.C.; Liao, P.H.; Lan, N.V.; Hou, S.S. Enhancement of Biodiesel Production from High-Acid-Value Waste Cooking Oil via a Microwave Reactor Using a Homogeneous Alkaline Catalyst. *Energies* **2021**, *14*, 437. [CrossRef]
139. Topare, N.S.; Patil, K.D.; Khedkar, S.V. Synthesis of Biodiesel from Waste Cooking Oil and Emission Characteristics of Its Blends. In Proceedings of the IOP Conference Series: Materials Science and Engineering, Tamil Nadu, India, 17–18 September 2020; p. 983. [CrossRef]
140. Dai, Y.M.; Li, Y.Y.; Chen, B.Y.; Chen, C.C. One-Pot Synthesis of Acid-Base Bifunctional Catalysts for Biodiesel Production. *J. Environ. Manag.* **2021**, *299*, 113592. [CrossRef]
141. Bhavani, A.G.; Sharma, V.K. Production of Biodiesel from Waste Cooking Oil: A Review. *J. Adv. Chem. Sci.* **2018**, *4*, 549–555. [CrossRef]
142. Elias, S.; Rabiu, A.M.; Okeleye, B.I.; Okudoh, V.; Oyekola, O. Bifunctional Heterogeneous Catalyst for Biodiesel Production from Waste Vegetable Oil. *Appl. Sci.* **2020**, *10*, 3153. [CrossRef]
143. Cao, Y.; Dhahad, H.A.; Esmaeili, H.; Razavi, M. MgO@CNT@K_2CO_3 as a Superior Catalyst for Biodiesel Production from Waste Edible Oil Using Two-Step Transesterification Process. *Process Saf. Environ. Prot.* **2022**, *161*, 136–146. [CrossRef]
144. Mueller, C.J.; Boehman, A.L.; Martin, G.C. An Experimental Investigation of the Origin of Increased NO_x Emissions When Fueling a Heavy-Duty Compression-Ignition Engine with Soy Biodiesel. *SAE Int. J. Fuels Lubr.* **2009**, *2*, 789–816. [CrossRef]
145. Pauline, J.M.N.; Sivaramakrishnan, R.; Pugazhendhi, A.; Anbarasan, T.; Achary, A. Transesterification Kinetics of Waste Cooking Oil and Its Diesel Engine Performance. *Fuel* **2021**, *285*, 119108. [CrossRef]
146. Mandari, V.; Devarai, S.K. Biodiesel Production Using Homogeneous, Heterogeneous, and Enzyme Catalysts via Transesterification and Esterification Reactions: A Critical Review. *BioEnergy Res.* **2021**, *15*, 935–961. [CrossRef]
147. Bajaj, A.; Lohan, P.; Jha, P.N.; Mehrotra, R. Biodiesel Production through Lipase Catalyzed Transesterification: An Overview. *J. Mol. Catal. B Enzym.* **2010**, *62*, 9–14. [CrossRef]
148. Avhad, M.R.; Marchetti, J.M. Uses of Enzymes for Biodiesel Production. In *Advanced Bioprocessing for Alternative Fuels, Biobased Chemicals, and Bioproducts*; Woodhead Publishing: Sawston, UK, 2019; pp. 135–152. [CrossRef]
149. Mohammed, A.R.; Bandari, C. Lab-Scale Catalytic Production of Biodiesel from Waste Cooking Oil—A Review. *Biofuels* **2020**, *11*, 409–419. [CrossRef]
150. Wancura, J.H.C.; Rosset, D.V.; Tres, M.V.; Oliveira, J.V.; Mazutti, M.A.; Jahn, S.L. Production of Biodiesel Catalyzed by Lipase from *Thermomyces lanuginosus* in Its Soluble Form. *Can. J. Chem. Eng.* **2018**, *96*, 2361–2368. [CrossRef]
151. Zhou, Y.; Li, K.; Sun, S. Simultaneous Esterification and Transesterification of Waste Phoenix Seed Oil with a High Free Fatty Acid Content Using a Free Lipase Catalyst to Prepare Biodiesel. *Biomass Bioenergy* **2021**, *144*, 105930. [CrossRef]
152. Shao, P.; Meng, X.; He, J.; Sun, P. Analysis of Immobilized Candida Rugosa Lipase Catalyzed Preparation of Biodiesel from Rapeseed Soapstock. *Food Bioprod. Process.* **2008**, *86*, 283–289. [CrossRef]
153. Choi, N.; No, D.S.; Kim, H.; Kim, B.H.; Kwak, J.; Lee, J.S.; Kim, I.H. In Situ Lipase-Catalyzed Transesterification in Rice Bran for Synthesis of Fatty Acid Methyl Ester. *Ind. Crops Prod.* **2018**, *120*, 140–146. [CrossRef]
154. Marín-Suárez, M.; Méndez-Mateos, D.; Guadix, A.; Guadix, E.M. Reuse of Immobilized Lipases in the Transesterification of Waste Fish Oil for the Production of Biodiesel. *Renew. Energy* **2019**, *140*, 1–8. [CrossRef]
155. Taher, H.; Nashef, E.; Anvar, N.; Al-Zuhair, S. Enzymatic Production of Biodiesel from Waste Oil in Ionic Liquid Medium. *Biofuels* **2017**, *10*, 463–472. [CrossRef]
156. Santos, S.; Puna, J.; Gomes, J. A Review on Bio-Based Catalysts (Immobilized Enzymes) Used for Biodiesel Production. *Energies* **2020**, *13*, 3013. [CrossRef]
157. Ben Bacha, A.; Alonazi, M.; Alharbi, M.G.; Horchani, H.; Ben Abdelmalek, I. Biodiesel Production by Single and Mixed Immobilized Lipases Using Waste Cooking Oil. *Molecules* **2022**, *27*, 8736. [CrossRef]
158. Patchimpet, J.; Simpson, B.K.; Sangkharak, K.; Klomklao, S. Optimization of Process Variables for the Production of Biodiesel by Transesterification of Used Cooking Oil Using Lipase from Nile *Tilapia viscera*. *Renew. Energy* **2020**, *153*, 861–869. [CrossRef]

159. Binhayeeding, N.; Klomklao, S.; Prasertsan, P.; Sangkharak, K. Improvement of Biodiesel Production Using Waste Cooking Oil and Applying Single and Mixed Immobilised Lipases on Polyhydroxyalkanoate. *Renew. Energy* **2020**, *162*, 1819–1827. [CrossRef]
160. Khoobbakht, G.; Kheiralipour, K.; Yuan, W.; Seifi, M.R.; Karimi, M. Desirability Function Approach for Optimization of Enzymatic Transesterification Catalyzed by Lipase Immobilized on Mesoporous Magnetic Nanoparticles. *Renew. Energy* **2020**, *158*, 253–262. [CrossRef]
161. Gong, H.; Gao, L.; Nie, K.; Wang, M.; Tan, T. A New Reactor for Enzymatic Synthesis of Biodiesel from Waste Cooking Oil: A Static-Mixed Reactor Pilot Study. *Renew. Energy* **2020**, *154*, 270–277. [CrossRef]
162. Khan, N.; Maseet, M.; Basir, S.F. Synthesis and Characterization of Biodiesel from Waste Cooking Oil by Lipase Immobilized on Genipin Cross-Linked Chitosan Beads: A Green Approach. *Int. J. Green Energy* **2019**, *17*, 84–93. [CrossRef]
163. Acherki, H.; Bouaid, A.; Marchetti, J.M. Optimization of the Enzymatic Butanolysis of Jatropha Oil for Biodiesel Production Using Eversa. *Biofuels Bioprod. Biorefining* **2022**, *16*, 219–227. [CrossRef]
164. Fjerbaek, L.; Christensen, K.V.; Norddahl, B. A Review of the Current State of Biodiesel Production Using Enzymatic Transesterification. *Biotechnol. Bioeng.* **2009**, *102*, 1298–1315. [CrossRef]
165. Andrade, T.A.; Errico, M.; Christensen, K.V. Evaluation of Reaction Mechanisms and Kinetic Parameters for the Transesterification of Castor Oil by Liquid Enzymes. *Ind. Eng. Chem. Res.* **2017**, *56*, 9478–9488. [CrossRef]
166. Cheirsilp, B.; Aran, H.; Limkatanyu, S. Impact of Transesterification Mechanisms on the Kinetic Modeling of Biodiesel Production by Immobilized Lipase. *Biochem. Eng. J.* **2008**, *42*, 261–269. [CrossRef]
167. Mansir, N.; Teo, S.H.; Mijan, N.A.; Taufiq-Yap, Y.H. Efficient Reaction for Biodiesel Manufacturing Using Bi-Functional Oxide Catalyst. *Catal. Commun.* **2021**, *149*, 106201. [CrossRef]
168. Gaurav, A.; Dumas, S.; Mai, C.T.Q.; Ng, F.T.T. A Kinetic Model for a Single Step Biodiesel Production from a High Free Fatty Acid (FFA) Biodiesel Feedstock over a Solid Heteropolyacid Catalyst. *Green Energy Environ.* **2019**, *4*, 328–341. [CrossRef]
169. Gupta, J.; Agarwal, M.; Dalai, A.K. An Overview on the Recent Advancements of Sustainable Heterogeneous Catalysts and Prominent Continuous Reactor for Biodiesel Production. *J. Ind. Eng. Chem.* **2020**, *88*, 58–77. [CrossRef]
170. Changmai, B.; Vanlalveni, C.; Ingle, A.P.; Bhagat, R.; Rokhum, L. Widely Used Catalysts in Biodiesel Production: A Review. *RSC Adv.* **2020**, *10*, 41625–41679. [CrossRef]
171. Rizwanul Fattah, I.M.; Ong, H.C.; Mahlia, T.M.I.; Mofijur, M.; Silitonga, A.S.; Ashrafur Rahman, S.M.; Ahmad, A. State of the Art of Catalysts for Biodiesel Production. *Front. Energy Res.* **2020**, *8*, 101. [CrossRef]
172. Lim, S.; Yap, C.Y.; Pang, Y.L.; Wong, K.H. Biodiesel Synthesis from Oil Palm Empty Fruit Bunch Biochar Derived Heterogeneous Solid Catalyst Using 4-Benzenediazonium Sulfonate. *J. Hazard. Mater.* **2020**, *390*, 121532. [CrossRef]
173. Jacobson, K.; Gopinath, R.; Meher, L.C.; Dalai, A.K. Solid Acid Catalyzed Biodiesel Production from Waste Cooking Oil. *Appl. Catal. B Environ.* **2008**, *85*, 86–91. [CrossRef]
174. Roslan, N.A.; Zainal Abidin, S.; Abdullah, N.; Osazuwa, O.U.; Abdul Rasid, R.; Yunus, N.M. Esterification Reaction of Free Fatty Acid in Used Cooking Oil Using Sulfonated Hypercrosslinked Exchange Resin as Catalyst. *Chem. Eng. Res. Des.* **2022**, *180*, 414–424. [CrossRef]
175. Saikia, K.; Ngaosuwan, K.; Assabumrungrat, S.; Singh, B.; Okoye, P.U.; Rashid, U.; Rokhum, S.L. Sulphonated Cellulose-Based Carbon as a Green Heterogeneous Catalyst for Biodiesel Production: Process Optimization and Kinetic Studies. *Biomass Bioenergy* **2023**, *173*, 106799. [CrossRef]
176. Gardy, J.; Osatiashtiani, A.; Céspedes, O.; Hassanpour, A.; Lai, X.; Lee, A.F.; Wilson, K.; Rehan, M. A Magnetically Separable SO_4/Fe-Al-TiO_2 Solid Acid Catalyst for Biodiesel Production from Waste Cooking Oil. *Appl. Catal. B Environ.* **2018**, *234*, 268–278. [CrossRef]
177. Hossain, M.N.; Bhuyan, M.S.U.S.; Alam, A.H.M.A.; Seo, Y.C. Optimization of Biodiesel Production from Waste Cooking Oil Using S–TiO_2/SBA-15 Heterogeneous Acid Catalyst. *Catalysts* **2019**, *9*, 67. [CrossRef]
178. Kumar, S.; Shamsuddin, M.R.; Farabi, M.A.; Saiman, M.I.; Zainal, Z.; Taufiq-Yap, Y.H. Production of Methyl Esters from Waste Cooking Oil and Chicken Fat Oil via Simultaneous Esterification and Transesterification Using Acid Catalyst. *Energy Convers. Manag.* **2020**, *226*, 113366. [CrossRef]
179. Mahmoud, H.R. Bismuth Silicate ($Bi_4Si_3O_{12}$ and Bi_2SiO_5) Prepared by Ultrasonic-Assisted Hydrothermal Method as Novel Catalysts for Biodiesel Production via Oleic Acid Esterification with Methanol. *Fuel* **2019**, *256*, 115979. [CrossRef]
180. Tran, T.T.V.; Kaiprommarat, S.; Kongparakul, S.; Reubroycharoen, P.; Guan, G.; Nguyen, M.H.; Samart, C. Green Biodiesel Production from Waste Cooking Oil Using an Environmentally Benign Acid Catalyst. *Waste Manag.* **2016**, *52*, 367–374. [CrossRef]
181. Rattanaphra, D.; Harvey, A.; Srinophakun, P. Simultaneous Conversion of Triglyceride/Free Fatty Acid Mixtures into Biodiesel Using Sulfated Zirconia. *Top. Catal.* **2010**, *53*, 773–782. [CrossRef]
182. Indrayanah, S.; Rosyidah, A.; Setyawati, H.; Murwani, I.K. Performance of Magnesium Hydroxide Fluorides as Heterogeneous Acid Catalyst for Biodiesel Production. *Rasayan J. Chem.* **2018**, *11*, 312–320. [CrossRef]
183. Faruque, M.O.; Razzak, S.A.; Hossain, M.M. Application of Heterogeneous Catalysts for Biodiesel Production from Microalgal Oil—A Review. *Catalysts* **2020**, *10*, 1025. [CrossRef]
184. Zeng, Z.; Cui, L.; Xue, W.; Chen, J.; Che, Y. Recent Developments on the Mechanism and Kinetics of Esterification Reaction Promoted by Various Catalysts. In *Chemical Kinetics*; IntechOpen: London, UK, 2012. [CrossRef]

185. Srilatha, K.; Ramesh Kumar, C.; Prabhavathi Devi, B.L.A.; Prasad, R.B.N.; Sai Prasad, P.S.; Lingaiah, N. Efficient Solid Acid Catalysts for Esterification of Free Fatty Acids with Methanol for the Production of Biodiesel. *Catal. Sci. Technol.* **2011**, *1*, 662–668. [CrossRef]
186. Said, N.H.; Ani, F.N.; Said, M.F.M. Review of the Production of Biodiesel from Waste Cooking Oil Using Solid Catalysts. *J. Mech. Eng. Sci.* **2015**, *8*, 1302–1311. [CrossRef]
187. Chanburanasiri, N.; Ribeiro, A.M.; Rodrigues, A.E.; Arpornwichanop, A.; Laosiripojana, N.; Praserthdam, P.; Assabumrungrat, S. Hydrogen Production via Sorption Enhanced Steam Methane Reforming Process Using Ni/CaO Multifunctional Catalyst. *Ind. Eng. Chem. Res.* **2011**, *50*, 13662–13671. [CrossRef]
188. Silveira, E.G.; Barcelos, L.F.T.; Perez, V.H.; Justo, O.R.; Ramirez, L.C.; Rêgo Filho, L.d.M.; de Castro, M.P.P. Biodiesel Production from Non-Edible Forage Turnip Oil by Extruded Catalyst. *Ind. Crops Prod.* **2019**, *139*, 111503. [CrossRef]
189. Martínez, A.; Mijangos, G.E.; Romero-Ibarra, I.C.; Hernández-Altamirano, R.; Mena-Cervantes, V.Y. In-Situ Transesterification of *Jatropha Curcas* L. Seeds Using Homogeneous and Heterogeneous Basic Catalysts. *Fuel* **2019**, *235*, 277–287. [CrossRef]
190. Aigbodion, V.S. Modified of CaO-Nanoparticle Synthesized from Waste Oyster Shells with Tin Tailings as a Renewable Catalyst for Biodiesel Production from Waste Cooking Oil as a Feedstock. *Chem. Afr.* **2022**, *6*, 1025–1035. [CrossRef]
191. Attari, A.; Abbaszadeh-Mayvan, A.; Taghizadeh-Alisaraie, A. Process Optimization of Ultrasonic-Assisted Biodiesel Production from Waste Cooking Oil Using Waste Chicken Eggshell-Derived CaO as a Green Heterogeneous Catalyst. *Biomass Bioenergy* **2022**, *158*, 106357. [CrossRef]
192. Adepoju, T.F.; Ibeh, M.A.; Babatunde, E.O.; Asuquo, A.J.; Abegunde, G.S. Appraisal of CaO Derived from Waste Fermented-Unfermented Kola Nut Pod for Fatty Acid Methylester (FAME) Synthesis from *Butyrospermum Parkii* (Shea Butter) Oil. *S. Afr. J. Chem. Eng.* **2022**, *33*, 160–171. [CrossRef]
193. Mohd Ali, M.A.; Gimbun, J.; Lau, K.L.; Cheng, C.K.; Vo, D.V.N.; Lam, S.S.; Yunus, R.M. Biodiesel Synthesized from Waste Cooking Oil in a Continuous Microwave Assisted Reactor Reduced PM and NOx Emissions. *Environ. Res.* **2020**, *185*, 109452. [CrossRef]
194. Rafati, A.; Tahvildari, K.; Nozari, M. Production of Biodiesel by Electrolysis Method from Waste Cooking Oil Using Heterogeneous MgO-NaOH Nano Catalyst. *Energy Sources Part A Recover. Util. Environ. Eff.* **2019**, *41*, 1062–1074. [CrossRef]
195. Naik, B.D.; Meivelu, U. Experimental Studies on Sodium Methoxide Supported Bentonite Catalyst for Biodiesel Preparation from Waste Sunflower Oil. *Environ. Prog. Sustain. Energy* **2020**, *39*, e13390. [CrossRef]
196. Ashok, A.; Kennedy, L.J.; Vijaya, J.J.; Aruldoss, U. Optimization of Biodiesel Production from Waste Cooking Oil by Magnesium Oxide Nanocatalyst Synthesized Using Coprecipitation Method. *Clean Technol. Environ. Policy* **2018**, *20*, 1219–1231. [CrossRef]
197. Lee, H.; der Liao, J.; Yang, J.W.; Hsu, W.D.; Liu, B.H.; Chen, T.C.; Sivashanmugan, K.; Gedanken, A. Continuous Waste Cooking Oil Transesterification with Microwave Heating and Strontium Oxide Catalyst. *Chem. Eng. Technol.* **2018**, *41*, 192–198. [CrossRef]
198. Widayat, W.; Putra, D.A.; Nursafitri, I. Preparation of α-Fe$_2$O$_3$-Al$_2$O$_3$ Catalysts and Catalytic Testing for Biodiesel Production. *Mater. Today Proc.* **2019**, *13*, 97–102. [CrossRef]
199. Kingkam, W.; Issarapanacheewin, S.; Nuchdang, S.; Pakawanit, P.; Puripunyavanich, V.; Rattanaphra, D. Experimental Investigation on Biodiesel Production through Simultaneous Esterification and Transesterification Using Mixed Rare Earth Catalysts. *Energy Rep.* **2022**, *8*, 857–870. [CrossRef]
200. Muciño, G.E.G.; Romero, R.; García-Orozco, I.; Serrano, A.R.; Jiménez, R.B.; Natividad, R. Deactivation Study of K$_2$O/NaX and Na$_2$O/NaX Catalysts for Biodiesel Production. *Catal. Today* **2016**, *271*, 220–226. [CrossRef]
201. Malani, R.S.; Shinde, V.; Ayachit, S.; Goyal, A.; Moholkar, V.S. Ultrasound–Assisted Biodiesel Production Using Heterogeneous Base Catalyst and Mixed Non–Edible Oils. *Ultrason. Sonochem.* **2019**, *52*, 232–243. [CrossRef]
202. Camacho, J.N.; Romero, R.; Galván Muciño, G.E.; Martínez-Vargas, S.L.; Pérez-Alonso, C.; Natividad, R. Kinetic Modeling of Canola Oil Transesterification Catalyzed by Quicklime. *J. Appl. Res. Technol.* **2018**, *16*, 446–454. [CrossRef]
203. Ilgen, O. Reaction Kinetics of Dolomite Catalyzed Transesterification of Canola Oil and Methanol. *Fuel Process. Technol.* **2012**, *95*, 62–66. [CrossRef]
204. Rashid, U.; Akinfalabi, S.-I.; Ibrahim, N.A.; Ngamcharussrivichai, C. Bio-Based Catalysts in Biodiesel Production. In *Nano and Biocatalysts for Biodiesel Production*; John Wiley & Sons: Hoboken, NJ, USA, 2021; pp. 201–248. [CrossRef]
205. Riadi, L.; Purwanto, E.; Kurniawan, H.; Oktaviana, R. Effect of Bio-Based Catalyst in Biodiesel Synthesis. *Procedia Chem.* **2014**, *9*, 172–181. [CrossRef]
206. Wang, B.; Wang, B.; Shukla, S.K.; Wang, R. Enabling Catalysts for Biodiesel Production via Transesterification. *Catalysts* **2023**, *13*, 740. [CrossRef]
207. Thangaraj, B.; Solomon, P.R.; Muniyandi, B.; Ranganathan, S.; Lin, L. Catalysis in Biodiesel Production—A Review. *Clean Energy* **2019**, *3*, 2–23. [CrossRef]
208. Naveenkumar, R.; Baskar, G. Optimization and Techno-Economic Analysis of Biodiesel Production from *Calophyllum inophyllum* Oil Using Heterogeneous Nanocatalyst. *Bioresour. Technol.* **2020**, *315*, 123852. [CrossRef]
209. Muñoz, R.; González, A.; Valdebenito, F.; Ciudad, G.; Navia, R.; Pecchi, G.; Azócar, L. Fly Ash as a New Versatile Acid-Base Catalyst for Biodiesel Production. *Renew. Energy* **2020**, *162*, 1931–1939. [CrossRef]
210. Ibrahim, N.A.; Rashid, U.; Hazmi, B.; Moser, B.R.; Alharthi, F.A.; Rokhum, S.L.; Ngamcharussrivichai, C. Biodiesel Production from Waste Cooking Oil Using Magnetic Bifunctional Calcium and Iron Oxide Nanocatalysts Derived from Empty Fruit Bunch. *Fuel* **2022**, *317*, 123525. [CrossRef]

211. Gardy, J.; Hassanpour, A.; Lai, X.; Ahmed, M.H.; Rehan, M. Biodiesel Production from Used Cooking Oil Using a Novel Surface Functionalised TiO_2 Nano-Catalyst. *Appl. Catal. B Environ.* **2017**, *207*, 297–310. [CrossRef]
212. Hazmi, B.; Rashid, U.; Ibrahim, M.L.; Nehdi, I.A.; Azam, M.; Al-Resayes, S.I. Synthesis and Characterization of Bifunctional Magnetic Nano-Catalyst from Rice Husk for Production of Biodiesel. *Environ. Technol. Innov.* **2021**, *21*, 101296. [CrossRef]
213. Simbi, I.; Aigbe, U.O.; Oyekola, O.; Osibote, O.A. Optimization of Biodiesel Produced from Waste Sunflower Cooking Oil over Bi-Functional Catalyst. *Results Eng.* **2022**, *13*, 100374. [CrossRef]
214. Bora, A.P.; Konda, L.D.; Pasupuleti, S.; Durbha, K.S. Synthesis of $MgO/MgSO_4$ Nanocatalyst by Thiourea–Nitrate Solution Combustion for Biodiesel Production from Waste Cooking Oil. *Renew. Energy* **2022**, *190*, 474–486. [CrossRef]
215. Kesserwan, F.; Ahmad, M.N.; Khalil, M.; El-Rassy, H. Hybrid CaO/Al_2O_3 Aerogel as Heterogeneous Catalyst for Biodiesel Production. *Chem. Eng. J.* **2020**, *385*, 123834. [CrossRef]
216. Naeem, M.M.; Al-Sakkari, E.G.; Boffito, D.C.; Gadalla, M.A.; Ashour, F.H. One-Pot Conversion of Highly Acidic Waste Cooking Oil into Biodiesel over a Novel Bio-Based Bi-Functional Catalyst. *Fuel* **2021**, *283*, 118914. [CrossRef]
217. Li, Y.; Niu, S.; Hao, Y.; Zhou, W.; Wang, J.; Liu, J. Role of Oxygen Vacancy on Activity of Fe-Doped $SrTiO_3$ Perovskite Bifunctional Catalysts for Biodiesel Production. *Renew. Energy* **2022**, *199*, 1258–1271. [CrossRef]
218. Bharti, R.; Singh, B.; Oraon, R. Synthesis of Sn-CaO as a Bifunctional Catalyst and Its Application for Biodiesel Production from Waste Cooking Oil. *Biofuels* **2023**, 1–11. [CrossRef]
219. Al-Saadi, A.; Mathan, B.; He, Y. Biodiesel Production via Simultaneous Transesterification and Esterification Reactions over $SrO-ZnO/Al_2O_3$ as a Bifunctional Catalyst Using High Acidic Waste Cooking Oil. *Chem. Eng. Res. Des.* **2020**, *162*, 238–248. [CrossRef]
220. Chaveanghong, S.; Smith, S.M.; Smith, C.B.; Luengnaruemitchai, A.; Boonyuen, S. Simultaneous Transesterification and Esterification of Acidic Oil Feedstocks Catalyzed by Heterogeneous Tungsten Loaded Bovine Bone under Mild Conditions. *Renew. Energy* **2018**, *126*, 156–162. [CrossRef]
221. Pratim, A.; Lutukurthi, B.; Paidinaidu, D.N.V.V.K.; Krishna, P.; Durbha, S. Valorization of Hazardous Waste Cooking Oil for the Production of Eco—Friendly Biodiesel Using a Low-Cost Bifunctional Catalyst. *Environ. Sci. Pollut. Res.* **2023**, *30*, 55596–55614. [CrossRef]
222. Abdullah, R.F.; Rashid, U.; Taufiq-Yap, Y.H.; Ibrahim, M.L.; Ngamcharussrivichai, C.; Azam, M. Synthesis of Bifunctional Nanocatalyst from Waste Palm Kernel Shell and Its Application for Biodiesel Production. *RSC Adv.* **2020**, *10*, 27183–27193. [CrossRef]
223. Li, Y.; Niu, S.; Wang, J.; Zhou, W.; Wang, Y.; Han, K.; Lu, C. Mesoporous $SrTiO_3$ Perovskite as a Heterogeneous Catalyst for Biodiesel Production: Experimental and DFT Studies. *Renew. Energy* **2022**, *184*, 164–175. [CrossRef]
224. Akhabue, C.E.; Osa-Benedict, E.O.; Oyedoh, E.A.; Otoikhian, S.K. Development of a Bio-Based Bifunctional Catalyst for Simultaneous Esterification and Transesterification of Neem Seed Oil: Modeling and Optimization Studies. *Renew. Energy* **2020**, *152*, 724–735. [CrossRef]
225. Suryajaya, S.K.; Mulyono, Y.R.; Santoso, S.P.; Yuliana, M.; Kurniawan, A.; Ayucitra, A.; Sun, Y.; Hartono, S.B.; Soetaredjo, F.E.; Ismadji, S. Iron (II) Impregnated Double-Shelled Hollow Mesoporous Silica as Acid-Base Bifunctional Catalyst for the Conversion of Low-Quality Oil to Methyl Esters. *Renew. Energy* **2021**, *169*, 1166–1174. [CrossRef]
226. Sulaiman, N.F.; Wan Abu Bakar, W.A.; Toemen, S.; Kamal, N.M.; Nadarajan, R. In Depth Investigation of Bi-Functional, $Cu/Zn/\Gamma$-Al_2O_3 Catalyst in Biodiesel Production from Low-Grade Cooking Oil: Optimization Using Response Surface Methodology. *Renew. Energy* **2019**, *135*, 408–416. [CrossRef]
227. Velmurugan, A.; Warrier, A.R. Production of Biodiesel from Waste Cooking Oil Using Mesoporous $MgO-SnO_2$ Nanocomposite. *J. Eng. Appl. Sci.* **2022**, *69*, 92. [CrossRef]
228. Javed, F.; Rizwan, M.; Asif, M.; Ali, S.; Aslam, R.; Akram, M.S.; Zimmerman, W.B.; Rehman, F. Intensification of Biodiesel Processing from Waste Cooking Oil, Exploiting Cooperative Microbubble and Bifunctional Metallic Heterogeneous Catalysis. *Bioengineering* **2022**, *9*, 533. [CrossRef]
229. Rezania, S.; Korrani, Z.S.; Gabris, M.A.; Cho, J.; Yadav, K.K.; Cabral-Pinto, M.M.S.; Alam, J.; Ahamed, M.; Nodeh, H.R. Lanthanum Phosphate Foam as Novel Heterogeneous Nanocatalyst for Biodiesel Production from Waste Cooking Oil. *Renew. Energy* **2021**, *176*, 228–236. [CrossRef]
230. Rattanaphra, D.; Temrak, A.; Nuchdang, S.; Kingkam, W.; Puripunyavanich, V.; Thanapimmetha, A.; Saisriyoot, M.; Srinophakun, P. Catalytic Behavior of La_2O_3-Promoted SO_4^{2-}/ZrO_2 in the Simultaneous Esterification and Transesterification of Palm Oil. *Energy Rep.* **2021**, *7*, 5374–5385. [CrossRef]
231. Mahmoud, H.R.; El-Molla, S.A.; Ibrahim, M.M. Biodiesel Production via Stearic Acid Esterification over Mesoporous ZrO_2/SiO_2 Catalysts Synthesized by Surfactant-Assisted Sol-Gel Auto-Combustion Route. *Renew. Energy* **2020**, *160*, 42–51. [CrossRef]
232. Vlasenko, N.V.; Kyriienko, P.I.; Yanushevska, O.I.; Valihura, K.V.; Soloviev, S.O.; Strizhak, P.E. The Effect of Ceria Content on the Acid–Base and Catalytic Characteristics of ZrO_2–CeO_2 Oxide Compositions in the Process of Ethanol to n-Butanol Condensation. *Catal. Lett.* **2020**, *150*, 234–242. [CrossRef]
233. Tshizanga, N.; Aransiola, E.F.; Oyekola, O. Optimisation of Biodiesel Production from Waste Vegetable Oil and Eggshell Ash. *S. Afr. J. Chem. Eng.* **2017**, *23*, 145–156. [CrossRef]

234. Amesho, K.T.T.; Lin, Y.C.; Chen, C.E.; Cheng, P.C.; Shangdiar, S. Kinetics Studies of Sustainable Biodiesel Synthesis from *Jatropha curcas* Oil by Exploiting Bio-Waste Derived CaO-Based Heterogeneous Catalyst via Microwave Heating System as a Green Chemistry Technique. *Fuel* **2022**, *323*, 12387. [CrossRef]
235. Liu, K.; Wang, R.; Yu, M. Biodiesel Production from Soybean Oils by a Novel Nano-Magnetic Solid Base Catalyst (K/ZrO$_2$/γ-Fe$_2$O$_3$). *RSC Adv.* **2017**, *7*, 51814–51821. [CrossRef]
236. Zhang, Y.; Duan, L.; Esmaeili, H. A Review on Biodiesel Production Using Various Heterogeneous Nanocatalysts: Operation Mechanisms and Performances. *Biomass Bioenergy* **2022**, *158*, 106356. [CrossRef]
237. Liu, K.; Wang, R.; Yu, M. An Efficient, Recoverable Solid Base Catalyst of Magnetic Bamboo Charcoal: Preparation, Characterization, and Performance in Biodiesel Production. *Renew. Energy* **2018**, *127*, 531–538. [CrossRef]
238. Foteinis, S.; Chatzisymeon, E.; Litinas, A.; Tsoutsos, T. Used-Cooking-Oil Biodiesel: Life Cycle Assessment and Comparison with First- and Third-Generation Biofuel. *Renew. Energy* **2020**, *153*, 588–600. [CrossRef]
239. Pasha, M.K.; Dai, L.; Liu, D.; Guo, M.; Du, W. An Overview to Process Design, Simulation and Sustainability Evaluation of Biodiesel Production. *Biotechnol. Biofuels* **2021**, *14*, 129. [CrossRef] [PubMed]
240. Watanabe, Y.; Shimada, Y.; Sugihara, A.; Tominaga, Y. Enzymatic Conversion of Waste Edible Oil to Biodiesel Fuel in a Fixed-Bed Bioreactor. *J. Am. Oil Chem. Soc.* **2001**, *78*, 703–707. [CrossRef]
241. Li, N.W.; Zong, M.H.; Wu, H. Highly Efficient Transformation of Waste Oil to Biodiesel by Immobilized Lipase from *Penicillium expansum*. *Process Biochem.* **2009**, *44*, 685–688. [CrossRef]
242. Hanh, H.D.; Dong, N.T.; Okitsu, K.; Maeda, Y.; Nishimura, R. Test Temperature Dependence of Transesterification of Triolein under Low-Frequency Ultrasonic Irradiation Condition. *Jpn. J. Appl. Phys.* **2007**, *46*, 4771–4774. [CrossRef]
243. Tabatabaei, M.; Aghbashlo, M.; Dehhaghi, M.; Panahi, H.K.S.; Mollahosseini, A.; Hosseini, M.; Soufiyan, M.M. Reactor Technologies for Biodiesel Production and Processing: A Review. *Prog. Energy Combust. Sci.* **2019**, *74*, 239–303. [CrossRef]
244. Rocha-Meneses, L.; Hari, A.; Inayat, A.; Yousef, L.A.; Alarab, S.; Abdallah, M.; Shanableh, A.; Ghenai, C.; Shanmugam, S.; Kikas, T. Recent Advances on Biodiesel Production from Waste Cooking Oil (WCO): A Review of Reactors, Catalysts, and Optimization Techniques Impacting the Production. *Fuel* **2023**, *348*, 128514. [CrossRef]
245. Chuah, L.F.; Yusup, S.; Abd Aziz, A.R.; Bokhari, A.; Klemeš, J.J.; Abdullah, M.Z. Intensification of Biodiesel Synthesis from Waste Cooking Oil (*Palm olein*) in a Hydrodynamic Cavitation Reactor: Effect of Operating Parameters on Methyl Ester Conversion. *Chem. Eng. Process. Process Intensif.* **2015**, *95*, 235–240. [CrossRef]
246. Ibrahim, R.I.; Reja, A.H.; Kadhim, A.J. Optimization Process for Biodiesel Production from Waste Cooking of Vegetable Oil by Microwave Irradiation. *Eng. Technol. J.* **2022**, *40*, 49–59. [CrossRef]
247. Tangy, A.; Pulidindi, I.N.; Perkas, N.; Gedanken, A. Continuous Flow through a Microwave Oven for the Large-Scale Production of Biodiesel from Waste Cooking Oil. *Bioresour. Technol.* **2017**, *224*, 333–341. [CrossRef]
248. Gaikwad, N.D.; Gogate, P.R. Synthesis and Application of Carbon Based Heterogeneous Catalysts for Ultrasound Assisted Biodiesel Production. *Green Process. Synth.* **2015**, *4*, 17–30. [CrossRef]
249. Chen, K.J.; Chen, Y.S. Intensified Production of Biodiesel Using a Spinning Disk Reactor. *Chem. Eng. Process. Process Intensif.* **2014**, *78*, 67–72. [CrossRef]
250. Aghbashlo, M.; Tabatabaei, M.; Hosseinpour, S. On the Exergoeconomic and Exergoenvironmental Evaluation and Optimization of Biodiesel Synthesis from Waste Cooking Oil (WCO) Using a Low Power, High Frequency Ultrasonic Reactor. *Energy Convers. Manag.* **2018**, *164*, 385–398. [CrossRef]
251. Tsaoulidis, D.; Farooqui, F.; Ortega, E.G.; Angeli, P. Scale-up Studies for Intensified Production of Biodiesel from Used Cooking Oil. *Bulg. Chem. Commun.* **2019**, *51*, 77–80. [CrossRef]
252. Muhammed Niyas, M.; Shaija, A. Biodiesel Production from Coconut Waste Cooking Oil Using Novel Solar Powered Rotating Flask Oscillatory Flow Reactor and Its Utilization in Diesel Engine. *Therm. Sci. Eng. Prog.* **2023**, *40*, 101794. [CrossRef]
253. Niju, S.; Begum, K.M.M.S.; Anantharaman, N. Continuous Flow Reactive Distillation Process for Biodiesel Production Using Waste Egg Shells as Heterogeneous Catalysts. *RSC Adv.* **2014**, *4*, 54109–54114. [CrossRef]
254. Tanawannapong, Y.; Kaewchada, A.; Jaree, A. Biodiesel Production from Waste Cooking Oil in a Microtube Reactor. *J. Ind. Eng. Chem.* **2013**, *19*, 37–41. [CrossRef]
255. Madhawan, A.; Arora, A.; Das, J.; Kuila, A.; Sharma, V. Microreactor Technology for Biodiesel Production: A Review. *Biomass Convers. Biorefin.* **2018**, *8*, 485–496. [CrossRef]
256. Lin, L.; Cunshan, Z.; Vittayapadung, S.; Xiangqian, S.; Mingdong, D. Opportunities and Challenges for Biodiesel Fuel. *Appl. Energy* **2011**, *88*, 1020–1031. [CrossRef]
257. Krishnan, S.G.; Pua, F.L.; Zhang, F. A Review of Magnetic Solid Catalyst Development for Sustainable Biodiesel Production. *Biomass Bioenergy* **2021**, *149*, 106099. [CrossRef]
258. International Energy Agency. *Renewables 2021*; IEA: Paris, France, 2021; p. 167.
259. Goh, B.H.H.; Chong, C.T.; Ge, Y.; Ong, H.C.; Ng, J.H.; Tian, B.; Ashokkumar, V.; Lim, S.; Seljak, T.; Józsa, V. Progress in Utilisation of Waste Cooking Oil for Sustainable Biodiesel and Biojet Fuel Production. *Energy Convers. Manag.* **2020**, *223*, 113296. [CrossRef]
260. Mena-Cervantes, V.Y.; Hernández-Altamirano, R.; García-Solares, S.M.; Arreola-Valerio, E. Biodiesel in Circular Economy. In *Biofuels in Circular Economy*; Springer Nature Singapore: Singapore, 2022; pp. 251–278.

261. Waudby, H.; Zein, S.H. A Circular Economy Approach for Industrial Scale Biodiesel Production from Palm Oil Mill Effluent Using Microwave Heating: Design, Simulation, Techno-Economic Analysis and Location Comparison. *Process. Saf. Environ. Prot.* **2021**, *148*, 1006–1018. [CrossRef]
262. Olivera, A.; Stella, C.; Saizar, C. Análisis de Ciclo de Vida Ambiental, Económico y Social. Una Herramienta Para La Evaluación de Impactos y Soporte Para La Toma de Decisiones. *INNOTEC Gestión* **2016**, *7*, 20–27.
263. Bey, N. Life Cycle Assessment: Theory and Practice. In *Life Cycle Assessment Theory and Practice*; Springer: Berlin/Heidelberg, Germany, 2017; pp. 519–544. [CrossRef]
264. Talens Peiró, L.; Lombardi, L.; Villalba Méndez, G.; Gabarrell i Durany, X. Life Cycle Assessment (LCA) and Exergetic Life Cycle Assessment (ELCA) of the Production of Biodiesel from Used Cooking Oil (UCO). *Energy* **2010**, *35*, 889–893. [CrossRef]
265. Lombardi, L.; Mendecka, B.; Carnevale, E. Comparative Life Cycle Assessment of Alternative Strategies for Energy Recovery from Used Cooking Oil. *J. Environ. Manag.* **2018**, *216*, 235–245. [CrossRef]

Disclaimer/Publisher's Note: The statements, opinions and data contained in all publications are solely those of the individual author(s) and contributor(s) and not of MDPI and/or the editor(s). MDPI and/or the editor(s) disclaim responsibility for any injury to people or property resulting from any ideas, methods, instructions or products referred to in the content.

Article

Ketones in Low-Temperature Oxidation Products of Crude Oil

Shuai Ma [1], Yunyun Li [1], Rigu Su [2], Jianxun Wu [1], Lingyuan Xie [1], Junshi Tang [3], Xusheng Wang [4], Jingjun Pan [2], Yuanfeng Wang [1], Quan Shi [1], Guangzhi Liao [5] and Chunming Xu [1,*]

[1] State Key Laboratory of Heavy Oil Processing, Petroleum Molecular Engineering Center (PMEC), China University of Petroleum, Beijing 102249, China; wyf_99@163.com (Y.W.)
[2] Engineering Technology Research Institute of PetroChina Xinjiang Oilfield Company, Karamay 834000, China
[3] PetroChina Research Institute of Petroleum Exploration and Development, Beijing 100120, China
[4] CAS Lanzhou Institute of Chemical Physics, Lanzhou 730000, China
[5] PetroChina Exploration & Production Company, Beijing 100007, China
* Correspondence: xcm@cup.edu.cn

Abstract: Ketone compounds are oxidation products of crude oil in the in-situ combustion (ISC) process. Revealing the molecular composition of ketones can provide theoretical guidance for understanding the oxidation process of crude oil and valuable clues for studying the combustion state of crude oil in the reservoir. In this study, low-temperature oxidation (LTO) processes were simulated in thermal oxidation experiments to obtain thermally oxidized oil at different temperatures (170 °C, 220 °C, 270 °C, and 320 °C). A combination of chemical derivatization and positive-ion electrospray (ESI) Fourier transform ion cyclotron resonance mass spectrometry (FT-ICR MS) was used to analyze the molecular composition of different kinds of ketones (fatty ketones, naphthenic ketones, and aromatic ketones) in the oxidized oils at different temperatures. The results showed that the concentration of aliphatic ketones and aliphatic cyclic ketones in the product oils decreased with the increase in temperature, while aromatic ketones increased with the increase in temperature. At the same oxidation temperature, the content of ketones follows this order: fatty ketones < cycloalkanes < aromatic ketones. The concentrations of ketones reached their maximum value at 170 °C and decreased at high temperatures due to over-oxidation. It was also found that nitrogen-containing compounds are more easily oxidized to ketone compounds than their hydrocarbon counterparts in the LTO process.

Keywords: in-situ combustion; low-temperature oxidization; ketone; crude oil; FT-ICR MS

1. Introduction

In-situ combustion (ISC) has great potential for the recovery of heavy oil with high viscosity and density. A large amount of heat is generated by the combustion of a small fraction of heavy oil, reducing the viscosity of heavy oil and enabling in-situ upgrading [1]. For nearly 100 years, the in-situ combustion (ISC) technique has been used in the U.S. in attempts to improve recovery from oil reservoirs. Despite its long history and the commercial success of some field projects, the process has not found widespread acceptance among operators due to failures in early field trials [2]. However, the majority of these failures occurred due to a poor understanding of the physical and chemical processes involved in ISC. Successful projects indicate that the process is applicable to a wide range of reservoirs, and the chances of failure can be minimized through a detailed characterization of crude oil from oil reservoirs and the adoption of mild engineering practices [3,4]. The reactions involved in the ISC process are generally categorized into three regimes: low-temperature oxidation (LTO), fuel deposition (FD), and high-temperature oxidation (HTO) [5]. Heavy oil undergoes a series of complex physical and chemical reactions in ISC, such as distillation, pyrolysis, and oxidation, to form coke, which serves as the fuel required for combustion [6]. The LTO products are the precursors of coke produced in the FD regime, which greatly affects the sustainability and advance of the combustion front [7]. A deeper understanding of the LTO reactions of heavy oil is helpful for improving the process conditions of field applications of ISC [8].

For many years, due to the complexity of crude oil, studies on the changes in the chemical composition of heavy oil that result from the LTO processes focused on the use of elementary and thermal analyses [9,10]. Extensive efforts have been made to analyze the characteristics of heavy oil LTO products, such as acid value and organic element content, which can provide more information on heavy oil oxidation [11,12]. To evaluate the oxidation characteristics of heavy oils, thermal analyses such as thermogravimetric analysis and differential scanning calorimetry (TG-DSC), pressure differential scanning calorimetry (PDSC), and thermogravimetric analysis coupled with a Fourier transform infrared spectrometer (TG-FTIR) have been applied [12,13]. However, thermal analyses cannot reveal the specific reactions that occurred during the LTO process. Zhao et al. [14] characterized oxidized oil using nuclear magnetic resonance (NMR) and electron paramagnetic resonance (EPR), indicating that the free radicals in oxidized oil are mainly located in aromatic hydrocarbons, aliphatic hydrocarbons, and oxygen atoms. It is found that some components of crude oil can be oxidized to oxygenated hydrocarbon compounds (e.g., aldehydes, ketones, and alcohols), which can be further oxidized to carbon oxides such as CO_2 [15]. The formation of these compounds further exacerbates the complexity of LTO products. Given their reactivity, ketones should be a class of compounds of interest. The additions across the C=O double bond are numerous in organic chemistry, including those with hydroperoxides [16]. Although ketones have been considered a key component in the LTO process, little is known about their presence, likely due, at least in part, to the lack of suitable analytical methods.

Gas chromatography–mass spectrometry (GC-MS), as an analytical method that can simultaneously separate and analyze complex organic substances, has been used to study the composition of crude oil during LTO [17,18]. Unfortunately, oxidized oils have higher boiling points and more complex compositions compared to crude oils, which exceed the upper limit of gas chromatography. Analytical developments have led to very powerful mass spectrometric (MS) methods for the study of fossil materials, but they have mainly been used for nitrogen, sulfur compounds, and acidic compounds, which are easily ionized when used with electrospray ionization (ESI) [19–21]. Non-polar oxygen-containing compounds, including furans and ketones, are not efficiently ionized in ESI [22,23]. In addition, MS is incapable of distinguishing compound isomers that have the same molecular formula. Therefore, in order to provide a comprehensive characterization of ketones in LTO products, the isolation of ketones from the rest of the LTO products is necessary. Ketones from fossil fuels have been traditionally separated by solid-phase extraction (SPE), liquid chromatography, and thin-layer chromatography [24–27]. However, these methods are insufficient to separate ketones from hydrocarbons, phenols, and other compounds with similar polarities to enable a definitive identification.

In recent years, a novel approach based on chemical derivatization followed by ESI high-resolution mass spectrometry has been used for the molecular characterization of ketones in fossil fuels [28–30]. The Girard-T reagent can be used to selectively create a positively charged quaternary ammonium moiety on carbonyls that can be accessed by ESI [31]. Although ketones can be ionized by positive-ion ESI [23], the derivatization largely improved the selectivity and sensitivity for the analysis of ketones in complex fossil fuels [32]. Alhassan and Andersson [28] compared two commercial derivatization reagents to selectively introduce a positive charge into the ketones for detection. It was found that the quaternary aminoxy compound was superior to Girard-T since better detectability and a larger number of ketones were found. Ketones in crude oil and coal tar were characterized by their molecular composition. Wang et al. [29] further validate that the Girard-T derivatization followed by positive-ion ESI MS analysis is suitable for the analysis of ketones in a trace amount, but it has discrimination on high double-bond equivalent (DBE) species (DBE $\geq$ 9).

In this study, heavy crude oil from the Xinjiang oilfield in China was oxidized at different temperatures using a batch reactor. The oxidized oils were separated from the residues, and their properties were assessed, including the contents of C, H, O, and N and SARA fractions (saturates, aromatics, resins, and asphaltenes). We applied chemical derivatization with Girard-T coupled with Fourier transform ion cyclotron resonance mass spectrometry (FT-ICR MS) to analyze ketones from the LTO products. This study will provide deep insights on the molecular composition of ketones in crude oil and their oxidation products at different reaction temperatures. The molecular composition of ketones will be helpful for the understanding of chemical reactions in the LTO's characteristics and mechanisms and will provide insights for ISC field applications.

2. Experimental Section

2.1. Samples and Regents

The heavy oil sample used in this study was collected from the Karamay Oilfield (Xinjiang, China), where in-situ combustion is being implemented. Crude oil from the same area was characterized in our previous study [33]. In general, crude oils in this oil field are biodegradable, having almost no light fraction and a boiling point lower than 200 °C.

Analytical-grade n-hexane, dichloromethane (DCM), chloroform, toluene, methanol, and ethanol were purchased from Beijing Chemical Reagents Company and purified by distillation with a 9600 spinning band distiller (B/R instrument, Easton Md, USA) before use. Analytical-grade Girard-T reagent and cation exchange resin (Amberlite IRC-50) were purchased from Aladdin Biochemical Technology Co., Ltd., Shanghai, China.

2.2. Oxidation Process

The oxidation experiments on the heavy oil were carried out in a batch reactor, as previously reported in [33]. A hot air flow was introduced into the reactor and bowed over the surface of the oil with a flow rate of 100 mL/min. The volatile components were flowed out of the reactor and cooled by a condenser. The reaction system was kept at a constant temperature for 2 h and then naturally cooled to room temperature. The reaction temperatures were controlled at 170, 220, 270, and 320 °C, which represented four different reaction degrees of the LTO process.

2.3. Bulk Property and Chemical Composition Analysis

The organic elemental composition of the heavy oil and its oxidation products was analyzed according to the Chinese standard method GB/T 19143-2017. The contents of carbon, hydrogen, and nitrogen were analyzed by a Vario EL Cube elemental analyzer (Elementar, Germany). The samples were decomposed by combustion at 950 °C, adsorbed and desorbed by a CO_2 and H_2O adsorption column, and detected by a thermal conductivity detector (TCD). The content of oxygen was analyzed by a Rapid OXY Cube elemental analyzer (Elementar, Germany). The samples were decomposed at 1450 °C, adsorbed and desorbed by a CO adsorption column, and detected by a TCD detector.

The saturates, aromatics, resins, and asphaltenes (SARA) composition of the heavy oil and its oxidation products was analyzed according to the Chinese industry standard method SY/T 5119-2016. Briefly, 30 mg sample was dissolved in 30 mL n-hexane, and the asphaltenes were separated by filtration after sufficient precipitation. A total of 3 g of silica gel and 2 g of alumina were added sequentially to the chromatographic column. The n-hexane solution was concentrated and added to the chromatographic column. The saturates, aromatics, and resins were sequentially eluted using 30 mL n-hexane, 20 mL DCM/n-hexane (2/1, v/v), 10 mL ethanol, and 10 mL chloroform as eluents. The solvent of each fraction was volatilized at low temperature and weighed until it reached a constant weight.

2.4. Derivatization and Separation of Ketones

To analyze the composition of ketones in the oils by using -ESI FT-ICR MS, the ketones were derived into strongly polar compounds. The derivation of the ketones in the heavy oil and its oxidation products was carried out by a chemical derivatization process with Girard-T reagent, which can introduce a charged quaternary ammonium moiety on carbonyl. The derivatization and separation procedures were based on previous work [31] with slight modifications, as shown in Figure 1. Briefly, 300 mg oil was dissolved in 2 mL DCM/methanol (1/1, v/v). The solution was stirred with 200 mg Girard-T reagent and 40 mg cation exchange resin at 40 °C for 14 h.

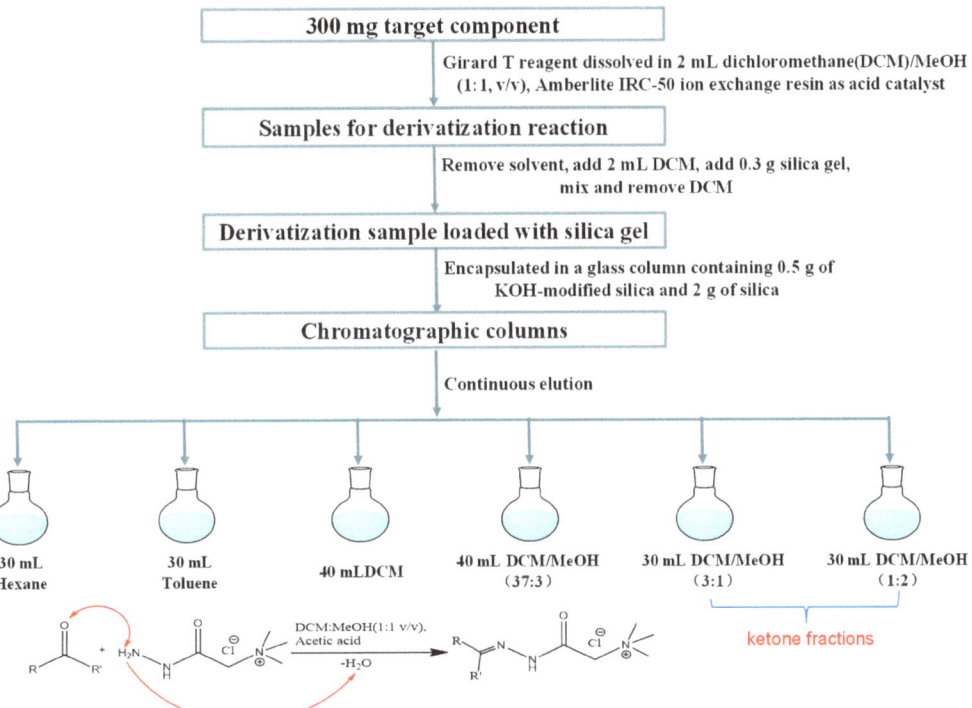

Figure 1. Sketch map of the separation of ketones and reaction schemes of ketones with Girard-T reagent.

After the reaction, the product was separated and purified by a chromatographic column composed of 2 g silica gel and 0.5 g KOH-modified silica gel. The unconverted oil matrixes were eluted with 30 mL n-hexane, 30 mL toluene, 40 mL DCM, and 40 mL DCM/methanol (37/3, v/v). The target derivatization products of the ketones were then eluted using 30 mL DCM/methanol (3/1, v/v) and 30 mL DCM/methanol (1/2, v/v) as eluents. The eluted solution was concentrated to 4 mL for analysis.

2.5. FT-ICR MS Analysis and Data Processing

The molecular composition of the ketones in the oils was obtained by analyzing the Girard-T reagent derivatives using an Apex-Ultra FT-ICR MS (Bruker, Germany) equipped with a 9.4 T magnet. The derivatives were diluted with toluene/methanol (1/1, v/v) to an appropriate concentration and directly pumped into the ESI source using a syringe pump at 180 μL/h. The ESI source was in positive-ion mode, and the key operating parameters were as follows: spray shielding voltage, −4500 V; front and terminal voltages of the capillary column, −4500 V and 320 V, respectively. The ions accumulated in the collision cell for 0.6 s and were transferred into the analysis cell for an ion injection time of 0.9 ms. The mass range was set to m/z 100–800. A total of 64 consecutive scans were accumulated for each analysis to improve the signal-to-noise ratio (S/N) of the mass spectrum.

The data processing has been described elsewhere [34]. Briefly, the data were calibrated using a known series, and the mass peak with S/N over 6 was exported by the Bruker DataAnalysis software (Version 3.4). A window of two nominal mass units chosen among the abundant peaks was randomly selected for manual assignment of the elemental composition of the peaks. For fast and reasonable calculation, the calculated molecular formula results were constrained by a range of double-bond equivalent (DBE) of less than 30. Once a peak was assigned to a molecular formula, it was used as a reference for assignment for other peaks with consecutive DBE values (with a mass interval of 2 Da) and/or carbon numbers (with a mass interval of 14 Da). The calculated results were further confirmed by the isotopic abundance. The Kendrick mass defect (KMD) plot of the uncalculated peaks was checked to make sure no classes were left out, which can be easily found as a row and/or consecutive rows [35].

3. Results and Discussion
3.1. Properties of Crude Oil

Table 1 lists the contents of C, H, O, and N and O/C and H/C in the crude oil and its oxidization products. The H/C ratio and the oxygen content imply that the crude oil dominates saturated moieties and has a high total acid number value [36]. It can be seen from the table that the contents of oxygen in the four oxidized oils are significantly higher than those of the crude oil. Therefore, it can be inferred that some oxygenates were generated during LTO. The O/C of crude oil is 0.012. Similarly, the O/C values of the oxidation products, from 0.012 to 0.018, are significantly higher compared to the crude oil, which was apparently caused by the introduction of oxygen atoms during the oxidation process. The H/C values are an important indicator of the degree of molecular condensation in fossil fuels. As the oxidation temperature increases, the H/C values of the oxidation products decrease gradually, indicating that the oxidation process promotes intramolecular condensation reactions such as cyclization and aromatization.

Table 1. Elemental contents of the crude oil and the oxidized oils.

Sample	C, wt%	H, wt%	O, wt%	N, wt%	O/C	H/C
Crude oil	85.91	12.38	1.42	0.28	0.012	1.73
170 °C	85.72	12.58	2.03	0.28	0.018	1.76
220 °C	86.42	12.18	1.87	0.28	0.016	1.69
270 °C	86.22	11.81	2.10	0.24	0.018	1.64
320 °C	86.68	11.45	2.12	0.21	0.018	1.58

The SARA composition of the crude oil and its oxidation products is listed in Table 2. Apparently, the content of saturates in the oxidation products gradually decreased with the increase in oxidation temperature, from an initial value of 53.21% to a final value of 30.18%. The content of aromatics showed a trend of first decreasing and then slightly increasing with the increase in oxidation temperature. The content of both resins and asphaltenes increased with the increase in oxidation temperature, with the asphaltic value showing the most significant increasing trend from 0.55% in the crude oil to 18.94% in the 320 °C product. It is well known that compounds in the saturates are dominated by chain and cyclic hydrocarbons; compounds in the aromatic fraction are mainly aromatic hydrocarbons and some weakly polar heteroatomic compounds (e.g., thiophenic compounds); and compounds in resins and asphaltenes are dominated by high condensation and/or strong polarity ones. The elemental compositions are consistent with the SARA compositions: on the one hand, the increase in O/C improves the polarity of the oxidation products, and on the other hand, the decrease in H/C increases the degree of condensation of the oxidation products. Both of these can lead to a decrease in the content of non-polar components (saturated and aromatic fractions) and an increase in the content of polar components (resins and asphaltenes) in the products.

Table 2. SARA composition of the crude oil and the oxidized oils.

Sample	Saturates (wt%)	Aromatics (wt%)	Resins (wt%)	Asphaltenes (wt%)	Yield (wt%)
Crude oil	53.21	22.20	12.81	0.55	88.78
170 °C	53.02	21.69	13.82	3.46	91.98
220 °C	45.68	17.26	15.87	13.08	91.90
270 °C	43.42	17.95	18.64	11.93	91.95
320 °C	40.18	18.07	20.61	18.94	97.80

The distribution of the elemental and SARA compositions shows the macroscopic properties of crude oil during the LTO process. Combined with high-resolution mass spectrometry, the molecular composition changes in crude oil during low-temperature oxidation can be discussed at the molecular level.

3.2. Molecular Composition of Ketones in the Oxidation Products

After Girard-T reagent derivatization, the molecular composition of ketones in petroleum can be characterized by high-resolution mass spectrometry equipped with an ESI source. The results of the high-resolution mass spectrometry analysis of ketones in crude oil and its products at different oxidation temperatures are shown in Figure 2. The two most abundant mass peaks in the left area are contaminants induced in the derivatization process. The inserts are mass spectra segments at around m/z 406, which illustrate the high mass resolution (about 500 K) of the mass spectra. High mass resolution and mass accuracy enable the unambiguous molecular assignments of these mass peaks. During the derivatization process, the mono-ketones of the O1 class (compounds with one oxygen atom in the molecules) are derivatized to produce N3O1 class species. It should be emphasized that previous studies have proven that only one carbonyl group of the diketone participates in the derivatization reaction, and the efficiency and conversion of both of its carbonyl groups participating in the reaction at the same time are very low [37]. The magnified plot of the mass point m/z 406 shows that significant N3O2, N3O3, and N3O4 classes appear in the oxidation products as the oxidation temperature increases. According to the present results, it can be confirmed that the oxygen atom in N3O1 is carbonyl oxygen; however, it is not sure that the oxygen atoms in the N3O2, N3O3, and N3O4 classes are all present in the form of carbonyl groups. In addition, the N3O1 class dominates the abundance distribution of both crude oil and oxidation product compound types. Therefore, the subsequent discussion in this study will mainly focus on the N3O1 class.

Figure 3 shows a histogram of the ion intensity of the N3O1 and N4O1 class species of the Girard-T derivatization products of the crude oil and its thermal oxidation products at different temperatures (170 °C, 220 °C, 270 °C, and 320 °C). The N4O1 class species should be nitrogen-containing ketones because compounds with four nitrogen atoms are rarely detected in crude oils without a separation for the enrichment of porphins and/or porphyrins [22]. As shown in Figure 3, the ketones of N3O1 in the oxidation products are more abundant than those in the crude oil. Meanwhile, the ketones of N4O1 reach their maximum intensity at 170 °C.

In order to quantitatively describe the composition changes in the ketones, an indicator of oxidation rate was defined according to Equation (1):

$$\text{Oxidation rate} = (I_{\text{product}} - I_{\text{crude oil}}) / I_{\text{crude oil}} \times 100\% \qquad (1)$$

where I_{product} and $I_{\text{crude oil}}$ are the total ion intensities of the product and the crude oil, respectively. The calculated oxidation rates are listed in Table 3. Apparently, the oxidation rate of the N3O1 class tended to increase with the increase in oxidation temperature, from 9.22% at 170 °C to 44.94% at 320 °C, almost doubling. In contrast, the oxidation rate of the N4O1 class showed a decreasing trend with the increase in oxidation temperature and even decreased to −63.98% at 320 °C. This may be caused by the increasing instability of the nitrogen-containing ketones at higher oxidation temperatures.

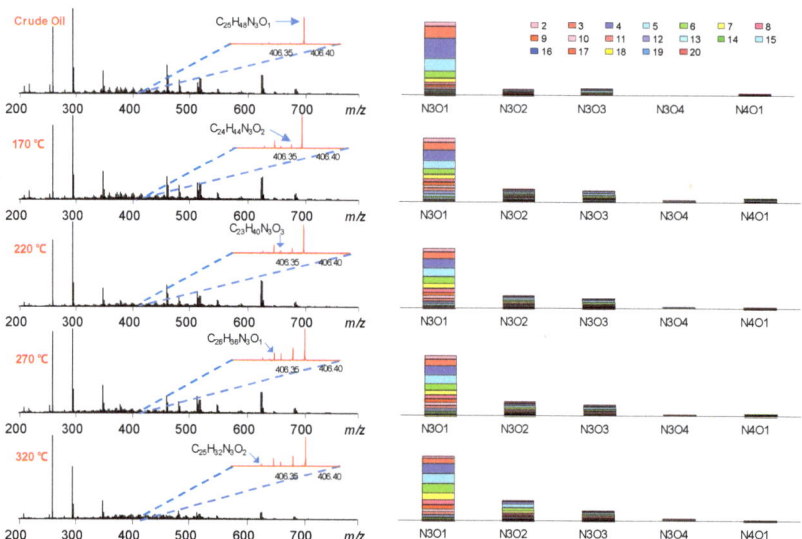

Figure 2. +ESI FT-ICR MS mass spectra (**left**) and compound-type abundance histograms (**right**) of the Gerard-T reagent derivatization products of crude oil and its oxidation products at 170 °C, 220 °C, 270 °C, and 320 °C. The legend in various colors corresponds to different DBE values, which are shown more clearly in Figure 4.

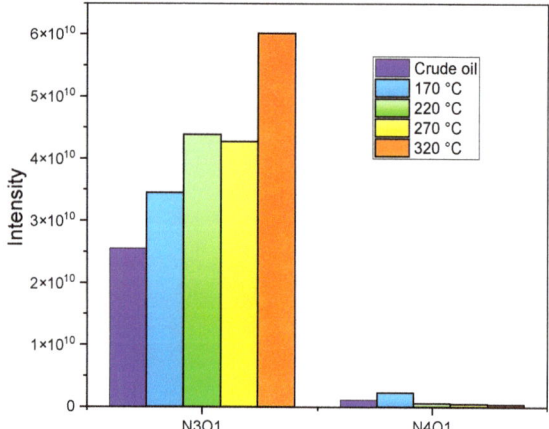

Figure 3. Ion intensities of N3O1 and N4O1 class species in the mass spectra. These compound classes correspond to ketones and nitrogen-containing ketones in oils.

Table 3. Oxidation rates of N3O1 and N4O1 classes at different oxidation temperatures.

Oxidation Temperature	ΔN3O1 (%)	ΔN4O1 (%)
170 °C	9.22	93.65
220 °C	28.69	−1.59
270 °C	24.03	−55.77
320 °C	44.94	−63.98

Figure 4 shows the ion relative abundance plots of DBE versus carbon number of the N3O1 and N4O1 class species assigned from the mass spectra of the Girard-T derivatives of crude oil and its thermal oxidation products. According to the derivatization mechanism, the N3O1 compounds correspond to ketones with five fewer carbon atoms and one fewer DBE. The distributions of the N3O1 class species shown in Figure 4 indicate that the ketones in the crude oil mainly have DBE values (one fewer than in the N3O1 class species) of 1, 2, 4, and 4, which correspond to acyclic, one-ring naphthenic, two-ring naphthenic, and three-ring naphthenic ketones, respectively. The carbon numbers of the ketones (five fewer than in the N3O1 class species) with high relative abundance in the crude oil are mainly in a range of about 15–30. With the increase in temperature, the relative abundance of ketones with DBE = 1 and 5–13 in the oxidized oils is significantly increased. It can be speculated that ketones (fatty ketones, alicyclic ketones, and aromatic ketones) were generated during LTO, and aromatic ketones are dominant. It can also be seen from Figure 3 that the compositional change is not continuous with the increase in temperature; this should be due to the continuous oxidation of the generated ketones, which converts ketones into acidic compounds or peroxides [38].

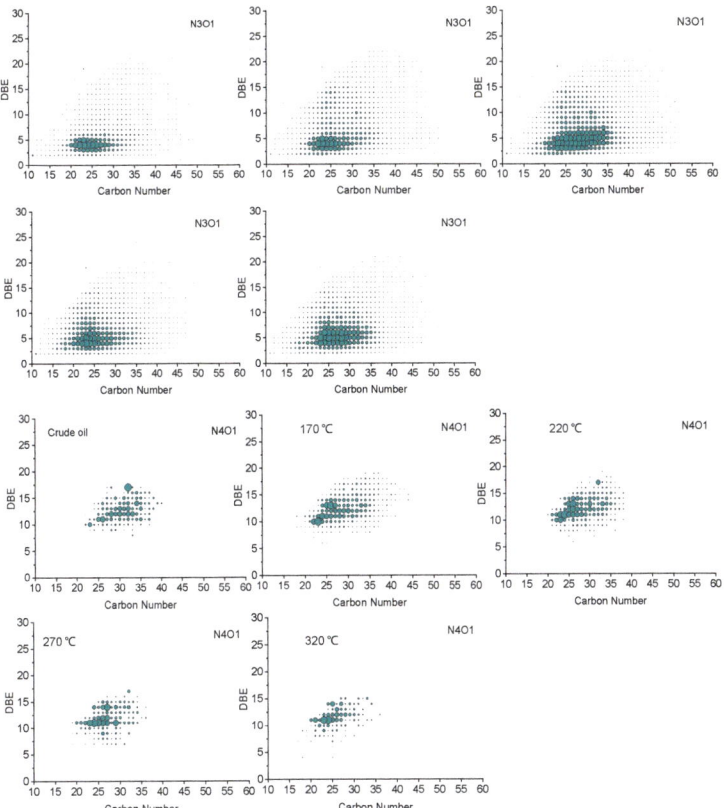

Figure 4. Ion relative abundance plots of DBE versus carbon number for N3O1 and N4O1 class species at different temperatures. Top: N3O1, corresponding to ketones; bottom: N4O1, corresponding to nitrogen-containing ketones.

Figure 4 and Table 3 show that nitrogen-containing compounds seem to be more easily oxidized to ketone compounds than hydrocarbons. This can be explained by the fact that the nitrogen atom in the hydrocarbon increases the molecular polarity, resulting in the formation of carbocation intermediates in the oxidation process. However, with increasing temperature, ketones are over-oxidized at temperatures higher than 170 °C, resulting in lower contents of ketones compared to crude oil [39].

The ketones detected in the oils can be classified into some groups according to their DBE values. Compounds with DBE values of 1, 2–4, and 5+ correspond to aliphatic ketones, alicyclic ketones, and aromatic ketones, respectively. Figure 5 shows the composition and classification of ketones in crude oil and its oxidation products. Aliphatic ketones and alicyclic ketones gradually decrease with an increase in temperature, while aromatic ketones gradually increase. This trend shows that aliphatic ketones, alicyclic ketones, and aromatic ketones have different transformation rules, indicating that aliphatic ketones and alicyclic ketones have a tendency to transform to aromatic ketones in the process of LTO. The decreasing trend of H/C with the increase in temperature in the preceding part of the text also confirms this conclusion. In addition, with the increase in oxidation temperature and the deepening of the oxidation degree, more aromatic ketones with a high condensation degree are generated, resulting in an O/C increase in oxidation products. High condensation and O/C can result in an increase in polar components (resins and asphaltenes), which corresponds well with the analysis results of the SARA composition. Crude oil is naphthenic in nature, so it is not surprising that cyclic ketones are the dominant ones in it. The increase in relative abundance of aromatic ketones could be caused by the oxidation of aromatic hydrocarbons or by the aromatization of cyclic ketones.

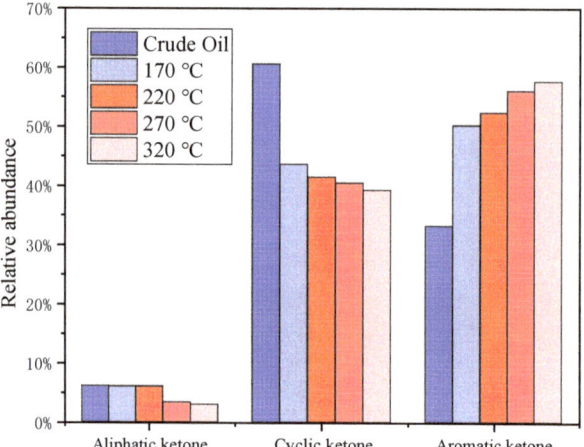

Figure 5. Relative abundance of different ketones. Aliphatic ketones, alicyclic ketones, and aromatic ketones are classified by DBE values of 1, 2–4, and 5+, respectively.

4. Conclusions

Low-temperature oxidation of crude oil was performed at four reaction temperatures. The chemical transformation of the crude oil during the oxidation process was revealed by the characterization of its bulk properties and molecular composition. With the increase in oxidation temperature, the O/C values of the products increased, the H/C values decreased gradually, and the content of polar components increased significantly. It was found that the oxidation rate of mono-ketones, which dominated the absolute abundance, tended to increase with the increase in oxidation temperature and was up to nearly 45% at 320 °C. In addition, both aliphatic and cyclic ketones tended to convert to aromatic ketones as the oxidation degree deepened. During oxidation, the oxygen content of the products increases with deeper oxidation, and mono-ketones are important carriers of these introduced oxygen elements. The conversion of aliphatic and cycloalkanones to aromatic ketones is an important reason for the decrease in H/C and the increase in condensation of the products. Ultimately, these intramolecular conversions containing the introduction of oxygen elements and the increase in condensation lead to an increase in polar components (resins and asphaltenes). Since the composition and abundance of ketones (especially mono-ketones) are closely related to the degree of oxidation, they have potential for applications in determining the different stages of the LTO process.

Author Contributions: Conceptualization, Y.L.; methodology, X.W. and Y.L.; formal analysis, S.M., Y.L., J.W. and L.X.; investigation, Y.W., S.M., Y.L. and R.S.; resources, R.S. and J.P.; writing—original draft preparation, S.M.; writing—review and editing, Y.L., J.W., L.X., Y.W. and Q.S.; supervision, C.X.; project administration, J.T. and G.L.; funding acquisition, J.P. and Q.S. All authors have read and agreed to the published version of the manuscript.

Funding: This work was supported by the National Key R&D Program of China (2018YFA0702400) and the PetroChina Exploration & Production Company (KS2020-01-05).

Data Availability Statement: Data will be made available on request from Authors.

Acknowledgments: This work was supported by the National Key R&D Program of China (2018YFA0702400) and the PetroChina Exploration & Production Company (KS2020-01-05).

Conflicts of Interest: The authors declare no conflict of interest.

References

1. Li, Y.; Wang, Z.; Hu, Z.; Xu, B.; Li, Y.; Pu, W.; Zhao, J. A review of in situ upgrading technology for heavy crude oil. *Pet* **2021**, *7*, 117–122. [CrossRef]
2. Horne, J.; Bousaid, I.; Dore, T.L.; Smith, L.B. Initiation of an in-situ combustion project in a thin oil column underlain by water. *J. Pet. Technol.* **1982**, *34*, 2233–2243. [CrossRef]
3. Ali, S.F. A current appraisal of in-situ combustion field tests. *J. Pet. Technol.* **1972**, *24*, 477–486. [CrossRef]
4. Howell, J.C.; Peterson, M.E. The Fry In Situ Combustion Project Performance And Economic Status. In Proceedings of the SPE Annual Technical Conference and Exhibition, Las Vegas, NV, USA, 23–26 September 1979. [CrossRef]
5. Turta, A. Chapter 18—In Situ Combustion. In *Enhanced Oil Recovery Field Case Studies*; Sheng, J.J., Ed.; Gulf Professional Publishing: Boston, MA, USA, 2013; pp. 447–541.
6. Hascakir, B.; Ross, C.M.; Castanier, L.M.; Kovscek, A.R. Fuel Formation and Conversion During In-Situ Combustion of Crude Oil. *Spe J.* **2013**, *18*, 1217–1228. [CrossRef]
7. Li, Y.-B.; Chen, Y.; Pu, W.-F.; Gao, H.; Bai, B. Experimental investigation into the oxidative characteristics of Tahe heavy crude oil. *Fuel* **2017**, *209*, 194–202. [CrossRef]
8. Zhao, S.; Pu, W.-F.; Su, L.; Shang, C.; Song, Y.; Li, W.; He, H.-Z.; Liu, Y.-G.; Liu, Z.-Z. Properties, combustion behavior, and kinetic triplets of coke produced by low-temperature oxidation and pyrolysis: Implications for heavy oil in-situ combustion. *Pet. Sci.* **2021**, *18*, 1483–1491. [CrossRef]
9. Huo, J.; Zhao, S.; Pan, J.; Pu, W.; Varfolomeev, M.A.; Emelianov, D.A. Evolution of mass losses and evolved gases of crude oil and its SARA components during low-temperature oxidation by isothermal TG-FTIR analyses. *J. Therm. Anal. Calorim.* **2021**, *147*, 4099–4112. [CrossRef]
10. Kok, M.V.; Varfolomeev, M.A.; Nurgaliev, D.K. Low-temperature oxidation reactions of crude oils using TGA-DSC techniques. *J. Therm. Anal. Calorim.* **2020**, *141*, 775–781. [CrossRef]
11. Zhao, S.; Pu, W.F.; Varfolomeev, M.A.; Yuan, C.D.; Zhang, J.Z.; Han, X.Q.; Yang, Y.; Peng, X.Q.; Wu, J.X. Comprehensive investigations into low temperature oxidation of heavy crude oil. *J. Pet. Sci. Eng.* **2018**, *171*, 835–842. [CrossRef]
12. Niu, B.; Ren, S.; Liu, Y.; Wang, D.; Tang, L.; Chen, B. Low-Temperature Oxidation of Oil Components in an Air Injection Process for Improved Oil Recovery. *Energy Fuels* **2011**, *25*, 4299–4304. [CrossRef]
13. Li, Y.-B.; Pu, W.-F.; Sun, L.; Jin, F.-Y.; Zhao, J.-Y.; Zhao, J.-Z.; Huang, T. Effect of formation factors on light crude oil oxidation via TG-FTIR. *J. Therm. Anal. Calorim.* **2014**, *118*, 1685–1695. [CrossRef]
14. Zhao, S.; Pu, W.; Varfolomeev, M.A.; Yuan, C.; Rodionov, A.A. Integrative Investigation of Low-Temperature Oxidation Characteristics and Mechanisms of Heavy Crude Oil. *Ind. Eng. Chem. Res.* **2019**, *58*, 14595–14602. [CrossRef]
15. Greaves, M.; Ren, S.; Rathbone, R. Air injection technique (LTO Process) for IOR from light oil reservoirs: Oxidation. In Proceedings of the SPE/DOE Improved Oil Recovery Symposium, Tulsa, OK, USA, 19–22 April 1998.
16. Petrov, L.V.; Solyanikov, V.M. Acid-catalyzed formation of free radicals in the reaction of hydroperoxides with ketones. *Russ. Chem. Bull.* **1996**, *45*, 340–345. [CrossRef]
17. Zhao, R.; Sun, J.; Fang, Q.; Wei, Y.; Song, G.; Xu, C.; Hsu, C.S.; Shi, Q. Evolution of Acidic Compounds in Crude Oil during In Situ Combustion. *Energy Fuels* **2017**, *31*, 5926–5932. [CrossRef]
18. Li, C.; Chen, Y.L.; Hou, J.J.; Zhou, C.G. A mechanism study on the viscosity evolution of heavy oil upon peroxide oxidation and pyrolysis. *Fuel* **2018**, *214*, 123–126. [CrossRef]

19. Smith, D.F.; Schaub, T.M.; Rahimi, P.; Teclemariam, A.; Rodgers, R.P.; Marshall, A.G. Self-association of organic acids in petroleum and Canadian bitumen characterized by low- and high-resolution mass spectrometry. *Energy Fuels* **2007**, *21*, 1309–1316. [CrossRef]
20. Fu, J.; Klein, G.C.; Smith, D.F.; Kim, S.; Rodgers, R.P.; Hendrickson, C.L.; Marshall, A.G. Comprehensive compositional analysis of hydrotreated and untreated nitrogen-concentrated fractions syncrude oil by electron ionization, field desorption ionization, and electrospray ionization ultrahigh-resolution FT-ICR mass spectrometry. *Energy Fuels* **2006**, *20*, 1235–1241. [CrossRef]
21. Purcell, J.M.; Juyal, P.; Kim, D.G.; Rodgers, R.P.; Hendrickson, C.L.; Marshall, A.G. Sulfur speciation in petroleum: Atmospheric pressure photoionization or chemical derivatization and electrospray ionization Fourier transform ion cyclotron resonance mass spectrometry. *Energy Fuels* **2007**, *21*, 2869–2874. [CrossRef]
22. Shi, Q.; Zhang, Y.; Chung, K.H.; Zhao, S.; Xu, C. Molecular Characterization of Fossil and Alternative Fuels Using Electrospray Ionization Fourier Transform Ion Cyclotron Resonance Mass Spectrometry: Recent Advances and Perspectives. *Energy Fuels* **2021**, *35*, 18019–18055. [CrossRef]
23. Ruddy, B.M.; Huettel, M.; Kostka, J.E.; Lobodin, V.V.; Bythell, B.J.; McKenna, A.M.; Aeppli, C.; Reddy, C.M.; Nelson, R.K.; Marshall, A.G.; et al. Targeted petroleomics: Analytical investigation of macondo well oil oxidation products from pensacola beach. *Energy Fuels* **2014**, *28*, 4043–4050. [CrossRef]
24. Long, H.; Shi, Q.; Pan, N.; Zhang, Y.; Cui, D.; Chung, K.H.; Zhao, S.; Xu, C. Characterization of Middle-Temperature Gasification Coal Tar. Part 2: Neutral Fraction by Extrography Followed by Gas Chromatography–Mass Spectrometry and Electrospray Ionization Coupled with Fourier Transform Ion Cyclotron Resonance Mass Spectrometry. *Energy Fuels* **2012**, *26*, 3424–3431. [CrossRef]
25. Neto, C.C.; Maçaira, A.; Pinto, R.; Nakayama, H.; Cardoso, J. New analytical approaches to organic geochemistry: Solid phase functional group extraction for bitumens and functional group markers for kerogens. *Phys. Chem. Earth* **1980**, *12*, 249–263. [CrossRef]
26. Strel'nikova, E.B.; Stakhina, L.D.; Petrenko, T.V. Preconcentration of petroleum organic acids and ketones by two-stage chromatography using a modified adsorbent. *J. Anal. Chem.* **2009**, *64*, 8–13. [CrossRef]
27. Harvey, T.G.; Matheson, T.W.; Pratt, K.C. Chemical class separation of organics in shale oil by thin-layer chromatography. *Anal. Chem.* **1984**, *56*, 1277–1281. [CrossRef]
28. Alhassan, A.; Andersson, J.T. Ketones in fossil materials—A mass spectrometric analysis of a crude oil and a coal tar. *Energy Fuels* **2013**, *27*, 5770–5778. [CrossRef]
29. Wang, P.; Zhang, Y.; Xu, C.; Zhang, W.; Zhu, G.; Li, Z.; Ji, H.; Shi, Q. Molecular Characterization of Ketones in a Petroleum Source Rock. *Energy Fuels* **2018**, *32*, 11136–11142. [CrossRef]
30. Wang, Z.; Chen, X.; Liang, Y.; Shi, Q. Molecular characterization of carbonyl compounds in atmospheric fine particulate matters (PM2.5) in Beijing by derivatization with Girard's reagent T combined with positive-ion ESI Orbitrap MS. *Atmos. Res.* **2022**, *273*. [CrossRef]
31. Chen, X.; Xu, C.; Zhang, W.; Ma, C.; Liu, X.; Zhao, S.; Shi, Q. Separation and Molecular Characterization of Ketones in a Low-Temperature Coal Tar. *Energy Fuels* **2018**, *32*, 4662–4670. [CrossRef]
32. Wang, Z.; Ge, Y.; Bi, S.; Liang, Y.; Shi, Q. Molecular characterization of organic aerosol in winter from Beijing using UHPLC-Orbitrap MS. *Sci. Total Environ.* **2022**, *812*. [CrossRef]
33. Li, Y.; Liao, G.; Wang, Z.; Su, R.; Ma, S.; Zhang, H.; Wang, L.; Wang, X.; Pan, J.; Shi, Q. Molecular composition of low-temperature oxidation products in a simulated crude oil In-situ combustion. *Fuel* **2022**, *316*. [CrossRef]
34. Shi, Q.; Pan, N.; Long, H.; Cui, D.; Guo, X.; Long, Y.; Chung, K.H.; Zhao, S.; Xu, C.; Hsu, C.S. Characterization of Middle-Temperature Gasification Coal Tar. Part 3: Molecular Composition of Acidic Compounds. *Energy Fuels* **2013**, *27*, 108–117. [CrossRef]
35. Hsu, C.S.; Qian, K.; Chen, Y.C. An innovative approach to data analysis in hydrocarbon characterization by on-line liquid chromatography-mass spectrometry. *Anal. Chim. Acta* **1992**, *264*, 79–89. [CrossRef]
36. Zhang, S.; Huo, J.; Sun, X.; Yang, F.; Wang, P.; Wu, J.; Zhang, Y.; Shi, Q. Molecular Composition Reveals Unique Rheological Property of Karamay Heavy Crude Oil. *Energy Fuels* **2021**, *35*, 473–478. [CrossRef]
37. Chen, X. *Analysis on Separation and Molecular Composition of Ketone Compounds from Low-Temperature Tar*; China University of Petroleum: Beijing, China, 2017.
38. Khansari, Z.; Kapadia, P.; Mahinpey, N.; Gates, I.D. A new reaction model for low temperature oxidation of heavy oil: Experiments and numerical modeling. *Energy* **2014**, *64*, 419–428. [CrossRef]
39. Zhou, Y.; Lin, S. Influence of nitrogen compounds on oxidation property of saturated hydrocarbon. *J. Pet. Univ. Nat. Sci. Ed.* **2001**, *25*, 33–35.

Disclaimer/Publisher's Note: The statements, opinions and data contained in all publications are solely those of the individual author(s) and contributor(s) and not of MDPI and/or the editor(s). MDPI and/or the editor(s) disclaim responsibility for any injury to people or property resulting from any ideas, methods, instructions or products referred to in the content.

Article

A New Approach for Synthesizing Fatty Acid Esters from Linoleic-Type Vegetable Oil

Sofia M. Kosolapova, Makar S. Smal, Viacheslav A. Rudko * and Igor N. Pyagay

Scientific Center "Issues of Processing Mineral and Technogenic Resources", Saint Petersburg Mining University, 199106 Saint Petersburg, Russia; sofy.k.97@mail.ru (S.M.K.); smal.makar@icloud.com (M.S.S.); igor-pya@yandex.ru (I.N.P.)
* Correspondence: rva1993@mail.ru

Abstract: Countries around the world recognize the numerous social, economic and environmental advantages of promoting liquid biofuels. They invest in its development and introduce tax incentives for its manufacture and tariffs of production regulation. In most studies, the process of synthesizing fatty acid esters takes a long time from 1 to 8 h. In this work, the synthesis of fatty acid esters was carried out in the range of volumetric ratios of ethanol to linoleic type oil in order to increase the kinetics of the process. The main parameters of the synthesis were studied by use of magnetic stirred tank reactors in a parallel reactor system, H.E.L. The synthesis was carried out in the presence of a homogeneous alkaline catalyst. The volumetric ratio of ethanol to oil was maintained at 1:1, 2:1, 3:1, 4:1 and 5:1. The amount of catalyst added to the reaction mixture ranged from 0.25 to 2.5% by the weight of the reaction alcohol. The dryness of ethanol varied from 91 to 99%. Effective process conditions have been established to reduce the reaction time from 2.5 h to 5 min while maintaining a high degree of conversion. The results obtained during the study suggest the possibility of using a continuous reactor to produce fatty acid esters from linoleic raw materials containing up to 16% of free fatty acids. This also means the possibility of using second generation biofuel feedstock.

Keywords: biofuels; rapeseed oil; ethanol; homogeneous catalysis; transesterification; fatty acid esters

1. Introduction

Due to the reduction in crude oil reserves and the harmful effects of the toxic emissions of conventional diesel fuel on the environment, biodiesel has become important over the past few years as an environmentally friendly, sustainable and renewable energy source [1–3]. According to the Energy Outlook Review forecast, it is expected that by the year 2030, a mixture of 30% biodiesel with petrodiesel (B30) will be promoted as an alternative to petrodiesel [4,5]. According to the estimates of the world community, biodiesel accounts for 70% of the transport fuel that will be in demand by 2040 [6,7].

Since biodiesel is made from natural ingredients, vegetable oil, animal fat or waste oil, it is biodegradable and renewable. Despite the fact that biodiesel has various advantages over conventional diesel fuel, it is still necessary to solve numerous technical and economic problems [8–11]. Among them are the lower cost of diesel fuel derived from oil, the choice of suitable catalysts and the development of technology for the economical and efficient synthesis of biodiesel.

Since 60–80% of the cost of biodiesel is due to its raw materials, the most difficult task is to choose inexpensive raw materials from a wide range of available sources [4,12,13]. Conditionally, three generations of biodiesel raw materials are distinguished. The raw materials of the first generation are oilseed crops. Initially, this raw material was seen as a promising option to reduce the extraction and use of traditional fuels. However, worries have arisen about the use of food crops as raw materials and their impact on arable land, biodiversity and global food needs [14–17].

Biofuels of the second generation are produced from non-food lignocellulose or wood biomass as well as agricultural waste. This raw material is grown on infertile lands or on arable lands, but is a by-product of the main crop and is not used directly in the production of food [18]. For example, straw, pulp, perennial herbs, yellow grease and solid household waste can act as raw materials for the second generation. The advantage of second-generation raw materials is an increase in waste-free production and the use of resources unclaimed in industry. Nevertheless, there are still some limitations related to economic efficiency since there are problems with expanding production to a commercial level [14].

The raw material of the third-generation biofuels is the biomass of micro- and macroalgae cultivated in ponds or reservoirs on land or in the sea. The advantages of this type of feedstock are high yields with minimal impacts on freshwater resources and the possibility of production in seawater or wastewater. On the other hand, their production requires a large amount of energy and fertilizers. Moreover, the resulting fuel has a shorter shelf life than other types of biofuels and is inferior in low-temperature properties [14].

Based on the advantages and disadvantages presented, the most practical application in the world is still found in first-generation raw materials. Among the EU countries and North and South America, soybeans and rapeseed have become the most popular oilseed crops. In Southeast Asia, it is the fruits and seeds of the oil palm. The main source of biodiesel production in the world is rapeseed oil (53% of all raw materials for biodiesel production) [19].

In the Russian Federation, rapeseed is one of the most promising oilseed crops for biodiesel production. According to the NeoAnalytics research of 2021, rapeseed oil production in Russia amounted to 701.4 thousand tons and increased by 11.8% over the year. At the same time, the volume of the domestic consumption of rapeseed oil in Russia remains small and accounts for only 1.34% of the total market (sunflower oil occupies more than 50%). Most of the rapeseed oil produced in Russia (more than 85%) is exported.

Based on this information, it can be concluded that the use of rapeseed oil as a raw material for biodiesel is more reasonable for the Russian market.

Depending on the choice of feedstock containing an excess of free fatty acids or their triglycerides, one of two reactions will be most effective for obtaining FAE—acid esterification for FFA and basic transesterification for triglycerides (Figures 1 and 2). The choice of reaction will determine the catalyst. Bronsted acid catalysts, such as H_2SO_4, are more active in the esterification reaction due to their availability and high catalytic activity; the basic homogeneous catalysts in the transesterification reaction are potassium and sodium hydroxides [20–22].

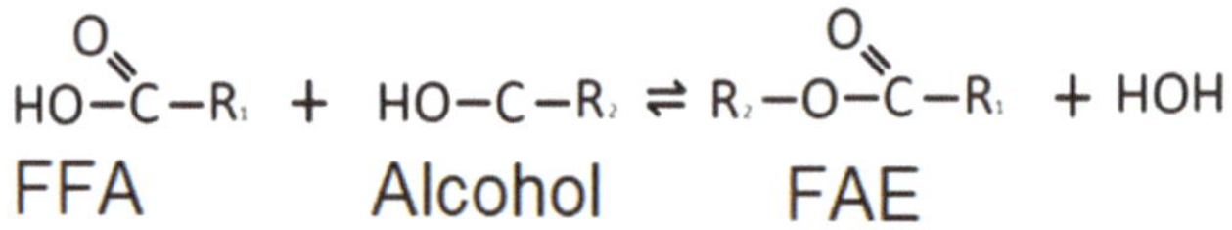

$$HO-\overset{O}{\underset{}{C}}-R_1 + HO-C-R_2 \rightleftharpoons R_2-O-\overset{O}{\underset{}{C}}-R_1 + HOH$$

FFA   Alcohol   FAE

Figure 1. Free fatty acid esterification reaction.

$$\begin{array}{c} CH_2-O-\overset{O}{C}-R_1 \\ CH-O-\overset{O}{C}-R_2 \\ CH_2-O-\overset{O}{C}-R_3 \end{array} + 3HO-C-R_4 \rightleftharpoons \begin{array}{c} CH_2-OH \\ CH-OH \\ CH_2-OH \end{array} + \begin{array}{c} R_4-O-\overset{O}{C}-R_1 \\ R_4-O-\overset{O}{C}-R_2 \\ R_4-O-\overset{O}{C}-R_3 \end{array}$$

Triglyceride   Alcohol   Glycerol   FAE

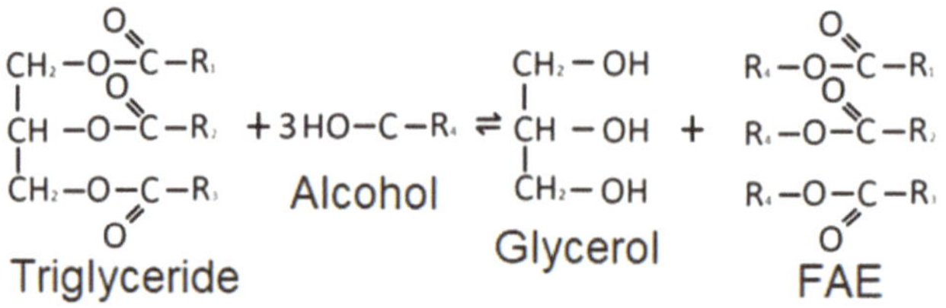

Figure 2. Transesterification reaction of vegetable oil.

Both reactions are reversible. Therefore, the addition of an excess of reaction alcohol is necessary in order to shift the equilibrium of the reaction towards the formation of products. In the esterification reaction, it is also required to remove a by–product—water—from the reaction system. In the case of vegetable oils, represented mainly by triglycerides, the transesterification reaction will be preferable.

The quality of the feedstock—the content of free fatty acids and impurities—affects the properties of the biodiesel. If the amount of free fatty acids in the raw material exceeds 1%, then the side saponification reaction reduces the yield and the rate of formation of FAE, which creates difficulties for the following technological processes [23,24]. For the same reason, water is an undesirable impurity in the feedstock since, in the presence of water, the FFAs quickly react with the catalyst, deactivating and reducing its concentration in the reaction mixtures.

The fatty acid composition of the starting oil affects some key properties of biodiesel, such as cetane number, pour point, flash point, oxidation resistance, etc. [4,25]. To improve the quality of the resulting biofuels, the refining of the raw materials (vegetable oils) is often carried out. However, this process requires complex technological operations, such as hydration, distillation refining and the use of solid activated adsorbents [26], which affects the increase in the cost of raw materials.

Existing studies and technologies for the production of biofuels by the method of alkaline transesterification make a bias towards the use of methanol as an alkylating component due to its high reactivity [27,28]. However, methanol has a high toxicity. Its maximum permissible concentration (MPC) in the air of the working area is 5 mg/m^3 (Table 1).

Table 1. Monohydric alcohols MPC.

Alcohol	Molecular Formula	MPC of the Working Area, mg/m^3
Methanol	CH_3OH	5
Ethanol	C_2H_5OH	1000–2000
Propanol	C_3H_7OH	10
Butanol	C_4H_9OH	10

A complete or partial alternative to methanol in the synthesis of fatty acid esters can be its homologues—ethyl, propyl, butyl alcohols, etc. [29–31]. Studies show that the use of alcohols with a longer and branched carbon chain increases the calorific value of esters obtained from them and improves the value of the pour point [32]. However, it is worth considering the influence of the spatial volume of the molecule—the steric effect. Thus, an increase in the carbon chain of an alcohol atom can slow down the reaction transesterification or make it impossible; therefore, methyl or ethyl alcohols are most often used.

In this list, ethyl alcohol has a number of advantages that determine the choice of this monatomic alcohol in the synthesis of liquid biofuels. Firstly, ethyl alcohol occupies the position closest to methanol in the homologous series of monatomic alcohols. Therefore, its reactivity will be greater than that of other similar alkylating agents—isopropanol and isobutanol. Secondly, the MPC of ethyl alcohol is many times higher than the MPC of other alcohols (Table 1). Thirdly, unlike others homologues obtained during the processing of petroleum products, there is a technology for obtaining bioethanol from vegetable raw materials [33–35].

The disadvantage of ethanol is the formation of an azeotropic mixture with water (4–6%) with a boiling point of 78.5 °C. Therefore, the use of ethanol in the process of transesterification requires a deeper drying of the alcohol, which increases the complexity of the technological scheme. Nevertheless, due to the advantages of ethyl alcohol as an alternative to methanol, research is currently underway in parallel with the study of the triglyceride methanolysis transesterification of vegetable oils in the presence of ethanol [36–39].

Most studies devoted to the basic transesterification of vegetable oils recognize the work in the optimal range of the initial components' molar ratios. This is 6–10 moles of alcohol per 1 mole of oil. However, the use of such a molar ratio has an impact on the kinetics of the reaction, since during the entire process the reaction mixture will remain in a heterogeneous state. Initially, there will be oil and alcohol phases, and at the exit from the process—an essential and a glycerin. In turn, this will affect the productivity and cost of commercial products.

For example, in research papers, the basic synthesis of FAE in the range of the molar ratios of ethanol:oil, equal to 6 ÷ 14:1, is taken from 1 to 6 h [36,37,40].

Reducing the reaction time can be achieved by reducing the volume of the reaction mixture. In this option, the FAE synthesis can be implemented in plug-flow microreactors (PRE) [39,41]. However, the use of reactors with small cross sections reduces the plant productivity.

On the other hand, the issue can be solved by homogenizing the reaction mixture during synthesis. As is known, the ethyl esters of fatty acids contribute to the homogenization of the reaction mixture [42]. However, in this case, part of the desired reaction product will be involved in the recycling of the technological scheme.

In this article, we suggest combining the above decisions and increasing the ratio of components towards a volumetric excess of ethanol. Therefore, the reaction mixture will be homogenized during the process. As a consequence, it will increase the rate of the transesterification reaction and make it possible to use a bigger cross section for the plug-flow reactor.

2. Experimental Section

2.1. Materials and Reagents

As objects of the study, two types of vegetable oil were used—refined sunflower (RSO) and unrefined rapeseed (URO). The acid number and acidity of the oils were determined according to ISO 660-83 "Animal and vegetable fats and oils. Determination of acid value and acidity" by the titrimetric method.

The fatty acid composition of vegetable oil was determined according to GOST 30418-96 "Vegetable oils. Method for determination of fatty acid content".

Moisture content in oils was determined according to ISO 662-2019 "Animal and vegetable fats and oils. Determination of moisture and volatile matter content".

The results of the analysis of RSO and URO oils are presented below. (Table 2, Figure 3).

Table 2. Acidity and acid value of feedstock.

Oil Type	Acid Value, mg KOH/g Oil	% Acid	Moisture, %Mass
Refined Sunflower Oil	3.49	1.76	0.076
Unrefined Rapeseed Oil	32.36	16.27	0.063

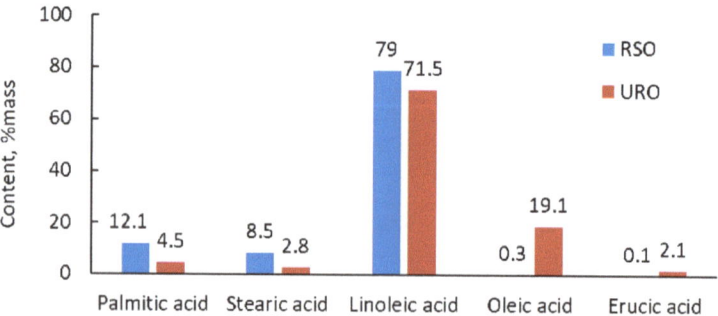

Figure 3. Fatty acid composition of sunflower (RSO) and rapeseed (URO) oil.

To prepare biodiesel by basic catalyzed transesterification, potassium and sodium hydroxides were used. Technical ethyl alcohol containing 5% water was used as the reaction alcohol.

2.2. Alcohol Drying

Absolute ethanol was obtained using GOST 30418-96 "Vegetable oils. Method for determination of fatty acid content". The principle method consists of boiling ethanol in the presence of CaO for 6–8 h, followed by distillation of absolute alcohol from the mixture (Figure 4). The required amount of calcium oxide was calculated from the lime slaking reaction:

$$CaO + H_2O = Ca(OH)_2 + Q$$

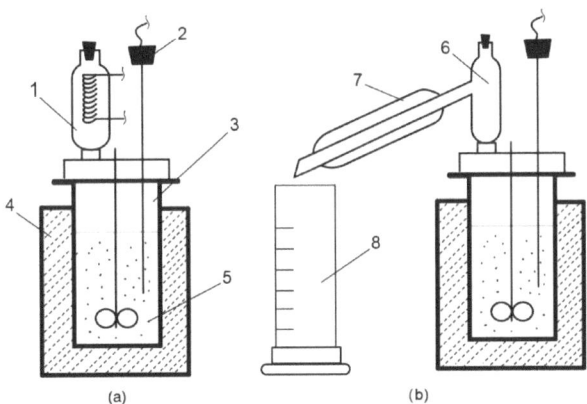

Figure 4. Schematic illustration of a laboratory unit for drying alcohol: (**a**) suspension mixing step; (**b**) absolute alcohol distillation step; 1—reflux condenser; 2—temperature probe; 3—glass reactor with magnetic bar stirrer; 4—mantle heater; 5—ethanol-CaO suspension; 6—Wurtz's nozzle; 7—condenser; 8—distillation receiver.

For example, for 100 mL of 95% ethanol, the following mass of calcium oxide will be required:

$$m_{CaO} = 0.28 \text{ mol} * 56 \text{ g/mol} = 15.7 \text{ g}$$

It is understood that increased water content in alcohol leads to the need to add a large amount of CaO to the alcohol; consequently, a suspension would be generated. The suspension can be overheated during the alcohol dehydration, which makes the reaction system unstable and results in the loss of absolute ethanol. Therefore, in order to optimize the drying process, the temperature in the reactor was lowered to 65–75 °C (depending on the density of the suspension). Uniform mix was achieved with magnetic bar stirrer.

The purity of the alcohol was checked with a refractometer using the graphic dependence of the optical density on the composition of the ethanol–water mixture (Figure 5). Reactive alcohol with water content in the range of 2–9% was obtained by mixing absolute ethanol with distilled water in a certain ratio.

2.3. Synthesis of Fatty Acid Esters (FAEs)

The synthesis of fatty acid ethyl esters was carried out at ethanol excess in a stirred tank reactor in Auto-MATE system H.E.L (Figure 6) with a reflux condenser and a magnetic stirrer [43–45]. The volumetric ratio of ethanol to oil was maintained at 1:1, 2:1, 3:1, 4:1 and 5:1. The amount of catalyst added to the reaction mixture ranged from 0.25 to 2.5% by weight of the reaction alcohol. The dryness of ethanol varied from 91 to 99%.

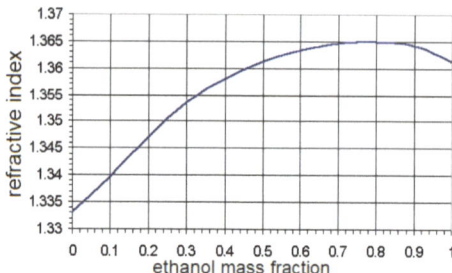

Figure 5. The refractive index dependence of the solution on the mass fraction of ethanol in water at 20 °C.

Figure 6. The ideal mixing reactor used for synthesis (Auto-MATE Reactor System H.E.L).

The transesterifications were carried out at 70 °C and 200–250 rpm for 2–4 h. Upon completion of the synthesis, the upper ether phase was separated from the glycerol phase by using a separation funnel.

In cases where a homogeneous phase was formed as a result of transesterification, it was filtered. The ethereal phase was purified from excess alcohol by distillation, then the glycerol phase was separated using a separating funnel.

The pilot study was divided into two blocks. Based on the theory of the transesterification reaction, it can be said that refined oil is a higher quality type of upstream material. That is why, in the first block basic process, conditions were determined by the example of refined sunflower oil. Then—in the second block of the study—unrefined rapeseed oil was used as a feedstock. In this block, the influence of unrefined oil on the parameters of the transesterification process was investigated.

Moreover, in another series of experiments, the synthesis of FAEs from sunflower and rapeseed oils was carried out using mixtures of absolute ethyl alcohol with water in the range of 91–99%.

2.3.1. Refined Sunflower Oil (RSO) Transesterification—Classical Method

An amount of 10 mL of refined sunflower oil and KOH catalyst in an amount of 0.5 to 2.5% by ethanol weight were placed in a 250 mL steel reactor. Then, 10 to 40 mL of ethanol was added to the reaction mixture and the stirring process was started. Ethyl alcohol was not subjected to pretreatment. The water content in it was 4–5%.

The reaction mixture was heated to 70 °C with constant stirring at 200–250 rpm. The mixing time was 2.5 h (Table 3). The process was stopped after the specified time. The reactor was unloaded after complete cooling. The ether phase was analyzed for the content of fatty acid esters by chromato-mass spectrometry.

Table 3. FAE-RSO synthesis conditions.

No. Test Series	1		2		3	4
Temperature, °C	70		70		70	70
Stirring speed, rpm	200 ÷ 250		200 ÷ 250		200 ÷ 250	200 ÷ 250
Catalyst	KOH	NaOH	KOH	NaOH	KOH	KOH
Catalyst quantity, mass% (by weight of alcohol)	1		1		0.5 ÷ 2.5	1
Ethanol drying degree, %vol.	95		95		95	91 ÷ 99
Synthesis time, hour	2.5		0 ÷ 2.5		2.5	2.5
V_{al}/V_{oil}	1 ÷ 5		3		3	3

2.3.2. Crude Rapeseed Oil (URO) Transesterification—Improved Method

In the first series of tests, the FAEs of unrefined rapeseed oil were obtained by the same method as the FAEs of refined sunflower oil. However, after observations about the kinetics of the process, the synthesis method was subject to change in order to measure the degree of conversion of raw materials for small periods of time.

An amount of 10 mL of unrefined rapeseed oil and KOH catalyst in an amount of 0.25 to 2.0% by ethanol weight were placed in a 250 mL steel reactor. The feedstock with the catalyst was heated in the reactor to 80 °C with constant stirring at 200–250 rpm. Then, without stopping the process, 10 to 50 mL of ethanol was added to the reaction mixture (Table 3). The temperature of 70 °C was reached in the reactor in 30 s by reducing the mantle heating.

The reaction mixture was stirred at constant temperature for 0.25–95 min. Then, the synthesis process was stopped by rapid cooling of the reactor. The ether phase was analyzed for the content of fatty acid esters by chromato-mass spectrometry.

The choice of starting point in the study of transesterification of rapeseed oil was based on a priori knowledge about the effect of FFA in the composition of vegetable oils on the process of alkaline transesterification. This is why a zero experiment was carried out with rapeseed oil (Tables 3 and 4).

Table 4. FAE-URO synthesis conditions.

No. Test Series	0	1	2		3		4
Temperature, °C	70	70	70		70		70
Stirring speed, rpm	200 ÷ 250	200 ÷ 250	200 ÷ 250		200 ÷ 250		200 ÷ 250
Catalyst	KOH	KOH	KOH		KOH		KOH
Catalyst quantity, mass% (by weight of alcohol)	1	1	0.25 ÷ 2		0.5	1	0.5
Ethanol drying degree, % vol.	93	91 ÷ 99	95	99	99		99
Synthesis time, hour	2.5	2.5	2.5		2.5		0 ÷ 2.5
V_{al}/V_{oil}	3	3	3		1 ÷ 5		3

2.4. Analysis of FAEs Composition

Fatty acid ethyl esters (FAEs) were determined using gas chromato-mass spectrometry equipped with an RTX HP-5MS (30 m × 0.25 mm) column equipped with flame ionization detector (FID). Helium was the carrier gas. The sample was injected at a flow rate of 0.5 mL/min. The injector temperature was 280 °C, and the detector temperature was 260 °C. The initial temperature of the oven was 120 °C for 2 min, increased at 5 °C/min to 250 °C, held for 10 min [46,47].

The internal standard method was used to determine the yield of the target product. A 10 μL sample of the ether fraction was introduced into 1 mL of a solvent containing a known amount of an internal standard. Dodecane was used as an internal standard ($C_{12}H_{26}$). The concentration of the target product was calculated by the (1):

$$C_{FAE} = \frac{S_{FAE}}{S_{st}} \cdot C_{st} \qquad (1)$$

where C_{FAE} and C_{st}—the ether and internal standard concentrations; $\frac{S_{FAE}}{S_{st}}$—the ratio of ether peak area to internal standard peak area.

The FAEs yield was calculated as the ratio of the number of synthesized product moles to the theoretical amount of product received at full product conversion:

$$\gamma_{FAE} = \frac{\vartheta_{exp}}{\vartheta_{teor}} \cdot 100\% \qquad (2)$$

where γ_{FAE}—the product yield; ϑ_{exp}—the number of synthesized product moles; ϑ_{teor}—the product moles received at full product conversion.

The ϑ_{teor} was calculated from the amount of raw material:

$$\vartheta_{teor} = \frac{\vartheta_{oil}}{3} \qquad (3)$$

2.5. FTIR Analysis of FAEs

The Fourier Transform Infrared (FTIR) spectra of FAEs were determined by using the FTIR spectrophotometer Nicolet 6700 (Thermo Scientific, USA). The ZnSe cell was used for this purpose. The FTIR spectrum was measured within a range of 400–4000 cm^{-1} with 4 cm^{-1} resolution.

3. Results and Discussions

3.1. Influence of the Water Content

As a result of the synthesis of rapeseed oil esters under zero experiment conditions, the yield of the product was lower than in the transesterification of sunflower oil. The FAE-URO yield did not exceed 24%.

The change in the yield of fatty acid esters (FAEs) could be affected by two factors: the acidity of the vegetable oil and the drying degree of the ethanol. The use of the refined oil with a low FFA content made it possible to eliminate the side reaction of saponification and use ethyl alcohol with a drying degree of 95–97%, while in the zero experiment with unrefined raw materials the ethanol of lower quality was used (93%). This conclusion confirms the dependence of the FAE yield on the drying degree of the ethanol (Figure 7).

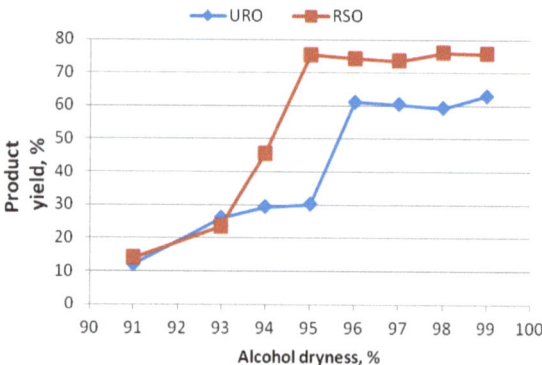

Figure 7. The FAEs' yield dependence of alcohol drying degree.

The yield of the target product remains low at concentration of water in alcohol >4%. At a water concentration of <4%, a jump in values is observed in the graph and a "plateau" is reached. The maximum yield of FAEs is achieved by using absolute ethanol (99%). When refined sunflower oil is used as a raw material, the jump in the yield of the target product shifts to the left. A high yield of the target product is achieved with a content of up to 5% water in ethanol for this type of raw material.

3.2. Influence of the Oil: Alcohol Ratio

Figure 8 shows the results of the first and third test series with refined sunflower oil and unrefined rapeseed oil, respectively.

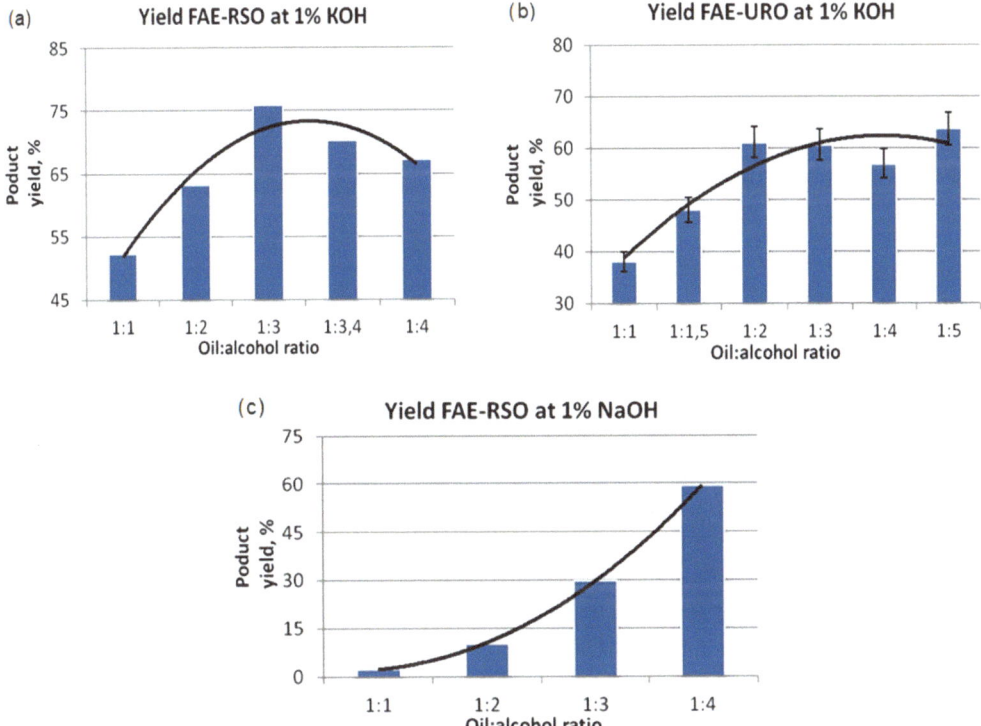

Figure 8. Effect of the proportions of oil:ethanol components on the yield of FAE-RSO and FAE-URO catalyzed by 1% KOH (**a**,**b**) and 1% NaOH (**c**).

We observe a linear increase in the concentration of the target product with an increase in the oil–alcohol ratio in the reaction catalyzed by potassium hydroxide (Figure 7). This corresponds to increases in the oil conversion degree and the yield of the target product, respectively.

The maximum conversion of the oil is achieved with an oil:ethanol ratio of 1:3. A further increase in proportions leads to a decrease in this value. On the one hand, this negative effect can be attributed to a decrease in the oil concentration in the system. On the other hand, increasing the volume of the reaction mixture requires more energy and time to completely heat and blend the components. Another reason can be an increase in water concentration in the system, leading to the deactivation of the catalyst.

An exponential increase in the yield of FAEs is observed in the transesterification reaction catalyzed by 1% wt. sodium hydroxide (Figure 8b). However, the maximum oil conversion is beyond the selected ratio range. In this case, to achieve maximum efficiency, more reactive alcohol is required and, consequently, the volume of the reaction mixture in the reactor increases.

This can be explained by the lower activity of Na compared with K. Since K is in the fourth rad of the alkali metal group of the periodic table it has one more energy level than Na in the third row.

Thus, it can be concluded that potassium hydroxide is more effective as a catalyst in comparison with sodium hydroxide in the example of the transesterification of refined sunflower oil.

In the case of unrefined rapeseed oil, it can be seen that the maximum FAE yield is achieved at a ratio of 1:2. After this point, the indicators level off (Figure 8b). In the synthesis of FAE-URO, 99% ethanol has been used. This explains why the concentration of the target product was not reduced by an increase in the oil–ethanol ratio, as was observed in the synthesis of FAE-RSO. Therefore, it can be concluded that the moisture content of ethanol has a predominant effect on the result obtained in the FAE-RSO synthesis (Figure 8a).

3.3. Influence Catalyst Concentration

We can see that the concentration of potassium hydroxide below 1% is not sufficient to initiate the transesterification process of refined sunflower oil (Figure 9). The FAE yield at a KOH catalyst concentration of 0.5% did not exceed 50%. There is an extreme concentration of the target product in the reaction mixture after the synthesis of FAE-RSO in the presence of 1% wt. KOH. A further increase in concentration results in a gradual decrease in the FAEs' yield. This decrease is correlated with a power function (Figure 8). This effect can be explained by the fact that an increase in catalyst content in the system above 1% leads to the esters' hydrolysis in the presence of water. Potassium salts of fatty acids are the products of this hydrolysis. The formation of potassium salts as a product of hydrolysis has been proven to make the reaction mixture more viscous, and therefore reduce the conversion rate [48–50].

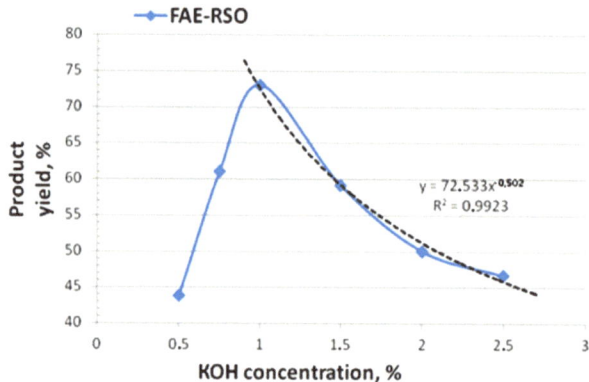

Figure 9. FAE-RSO yield dependence on different KOH catalyst content.

In the case of an increase in the content of FFA in the oil, the quality of alcohol has more influence on the transesterification process. Therefore, the optimal concentration of the potassium hydroxide would change (Figure 10). For instance, the peak of the FAEs' yield on the graph had shifted towards a decrease in the catalyst content due to the use of absolute ethanol. For this reason, a 0.25% KOH point was added to bring the optimum point into the limits of the curve's extreme values (Figure 10a). In the previous section, we determined the effect of the oil–alcohol ratio on the FAE yield at 1% KOH catalyst. To confirm the optimal catalyst concentration, we have built an additional curve at 0.5% KOH

(Figure 10b). It can be seen that, for a concentration of KOH at 0.5%, the optimal ratio is 1:3. For a concentration of 1% KOH, it is 1:2.

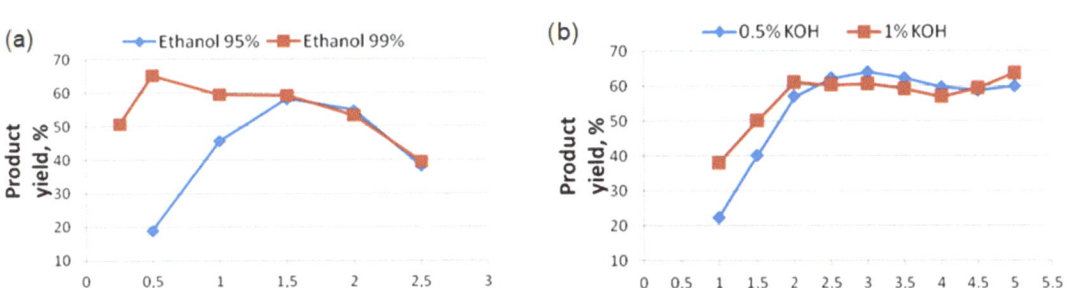

Figure 10. FAE-URO yield dependence on: (**a**) catalyst content; (**b**) oil-ethanol ratio.

It took more catalyst to use ethanol without pre-drying. Moreover, the optimum point is located below (Figure 10a). These results also confirm the negative effect of the water content not only on the reaction balance, but on the catalyst efficiency due to its deactivation by side saponification processes [23,24]. Therefore, less quality ethanol will require more KOH. Increasing the KOH content beyond the optimum point leads to the yield decrease the same way as in the sunflower oil experiment.

3.4. Process Kinetics

Since the FAEs synthesis takes place in the system of excess ethanol, this reaction can be attributed to the pseudo-first order reaction [51]. Graphs (Figure 11a,b) show the kinetic curves constructed for the first and second order reactions. The correlation coefficient of the first order curve is greater than the correlation coefficient of the second order curve. Therefore, it can be concluded about the first order of the transesterification reaction.

The KOH kinetic curve passes above the NaOH kinetic curve (Figure 11). This confirms the fact that potassium hydroxide is a more efficient catalyst than sodium hydroxide.

The results of the FAE-URO synthesis, according to the method applied to refined oil, are presented in Figure 12. The kinetic curve of rapeseed oil transesterification with absolute ethanol is shown below in Figure 13.

It can be seen from the graph that the presence of water in the system strongly affects the rate of the reaction. Thus, in the process of studying the kinetics of the zero experiment, the FAE-URO yield remained low (Figure 12).

At the same time, the use of absolute alcohol (99%) made it possible to reach a plateau of oscillations relative to the equilibrium line. This indicates that the concentration of the target product has already reached its maximum in less than 15 min (Figure 13a,b).

Figure 13 shows the results of the synthesis of FAE-URO in excess of absolute ethanol according to the optimized method. The maximum degree of the FAE-URO conversion is already reached in the second minute of the process. Then, a plateau of values takes place. These values fluctuate relative to the conditional equilibrium line (Figure 13a).

This result can be justified by the homogenization of the reaction mixture during synthesis in a volumetric excess of ethanol and by the small total volume of the mixture in the reactor (<50 mL). The improved synthesis method together with the optimal process conditions allows us to make an assumption about the possibility of a transition from the ideal mixing reactor model of the ideal displacement reactor.

Thus, in the paper [52], the authors compare two reactor models—oscillatory flow reactor (OFR) and stirred tank reactor (STR). The synthesis time of the stirred tank reactor in their work was 60 min. It is worth noting that, in paper [52], the synthesis in the stirred tank reactor was carried out at a molar ratio of waste cooking oil to methanol of 1:6. Furthermore, there was a large volume of reactor loading (5 L).

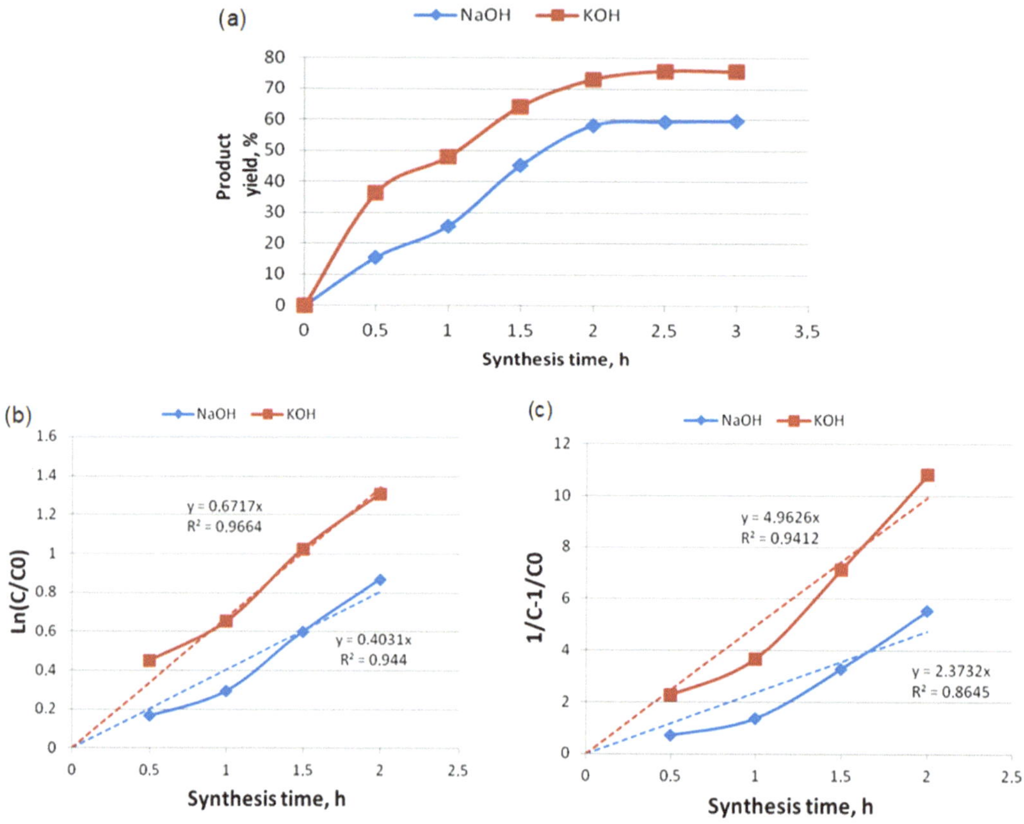

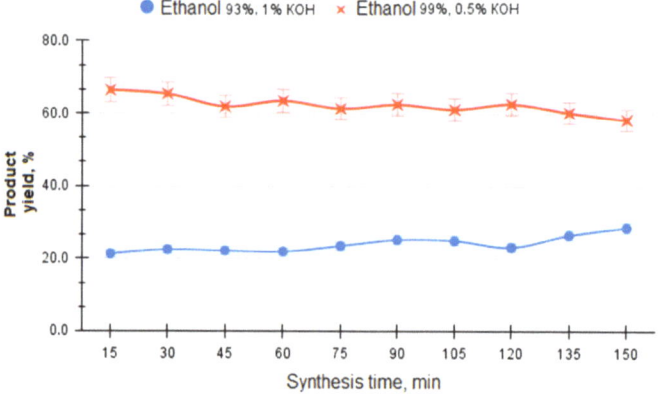

Figure 11. FAE-RSO synthesis kinetics: (**a**) the product yield change with time; (**b**) first order reaction kinetic curve; (**c**) second order reaction kinetic curve.

Figure 12. The FAE-URO synthesis kinetics in the period from 15 min to 2.5 h.

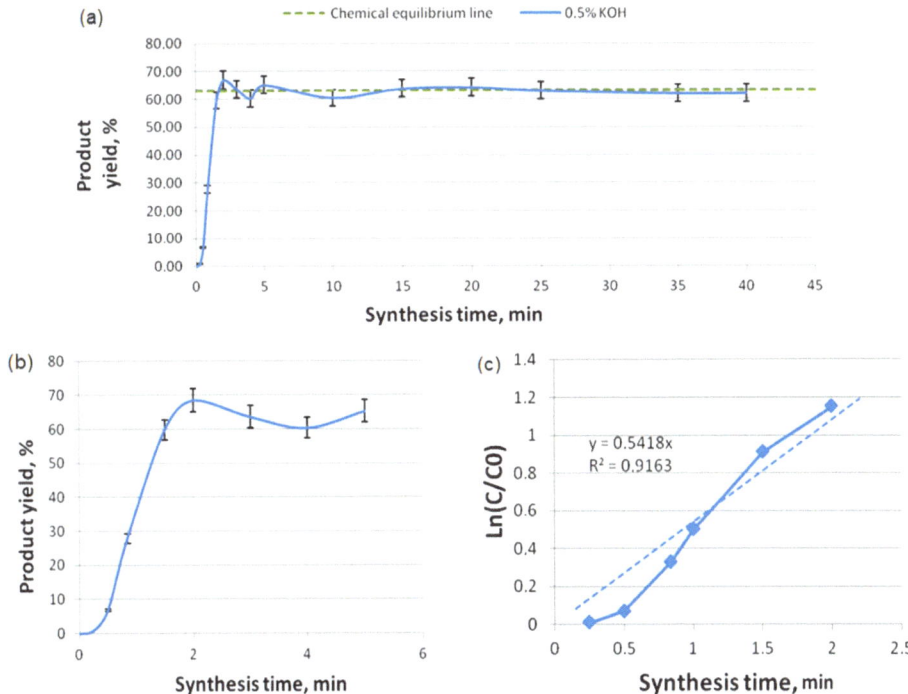

Figure 13. The FAE-URO synthesis kinetics: (**a**) whole period up to 2.5 h; (**b**) in the period less than 15 min; (**c**) kinetic curve of the first order reaction.

3.5. FAEs' Composition

The IR spectra show characteristic peaks confirming the qualitative composition similarity of the product with a mixture of fatty acid esters (Figure 14a,b). First of all, this is a peak of stretching vibrations of the carbonyl group C=O bond, the shift of which coincides with a narrow range for the esters of long chain fatty acids (1736–1744 cm^{-1}) [53]. For sunflower and rapeseed oil, this peak has a wave number of 1743 cm^{-1}, which corresponds to the fluctuation range characteristic of triglycerides (1744–1748 cm^{-1}).

Moreover, characteristic of FAEs is a pair of peaks of the stretching vibrations of the C-O bond. This most intense peak is around 1170 cm^{-1} (1178 cm^{-1} on the graph) with a less strong band around 1245 cm^{-1} (1243 cm^{-1} peak on the graph). In contrast to the FAEs' IR spectrum, the characteristic peaks of the stretching vibrations of the C-O bond in triglycerides are shifted and are located at about 1236, 1164 (more intense) and 1100 cm^{-1}. For sunflower oil, these peaks are 1236, 1159 and 1098 cm^{-1}. For rapeseed oil, these peaks are 1237, 1160 and 1096 cm^{-1} (Figure 14a).

In the FAEs' IR spectrum, there is a small wide band of –O-H bond vibrations corresponding to the carboxylic acid group (3500–2500 cm^{-1}). There is also a small peak around 1560 cm^{-1}. This peak is characteristic of vibrations of the carbonyl group in the structures of the potassium and sodium salts of fatty acids [54]. This can indicate the presence of water, catalyst, and soap residues in the FAEs. These impurities can be removed from the product by washing with weak solutions of sulfuric or phosphoric acid and water [55].

GC-MS analysis made it possible to determine the qualitative composition of the resulting FAEs mixture (Figure 15a,b). Since the initial raw material was linoleic type oil, the ethyl ester of linoleic acid predominates in the composition (Figure 15c). FAE-RSO contains no ethyl esters of oleic and erucic fatty acids because of the sunflower oil composition.

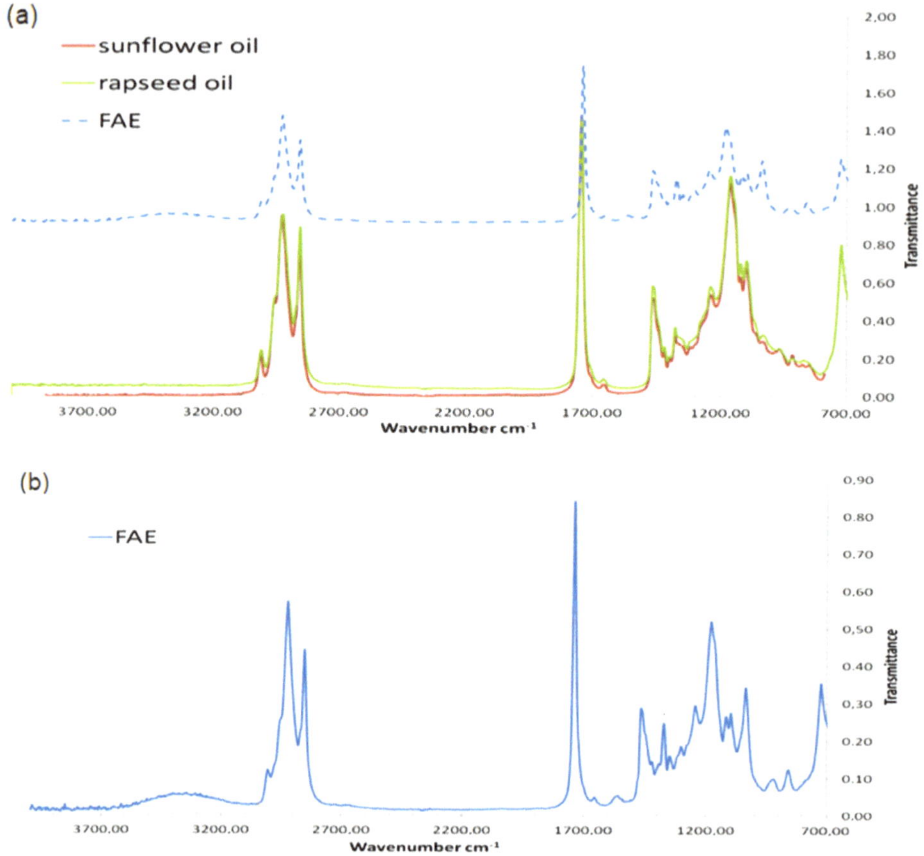

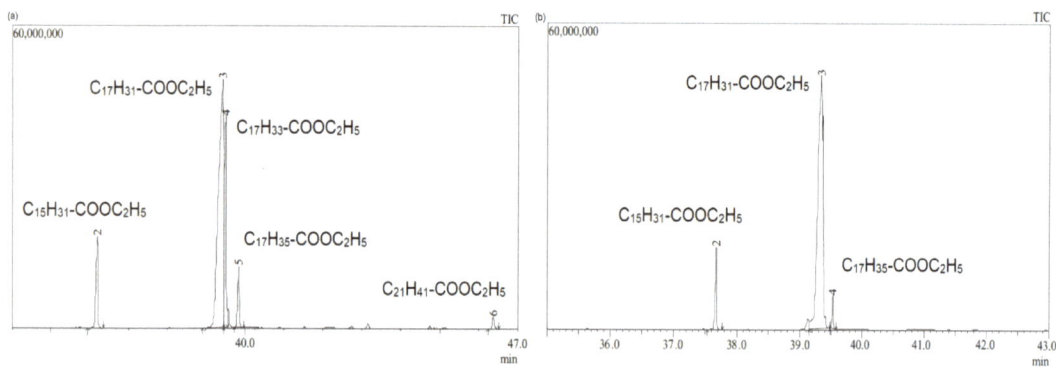

Figure 14. IR spectra of the FAEs and feedstock.

Figure 15. *Cont.*

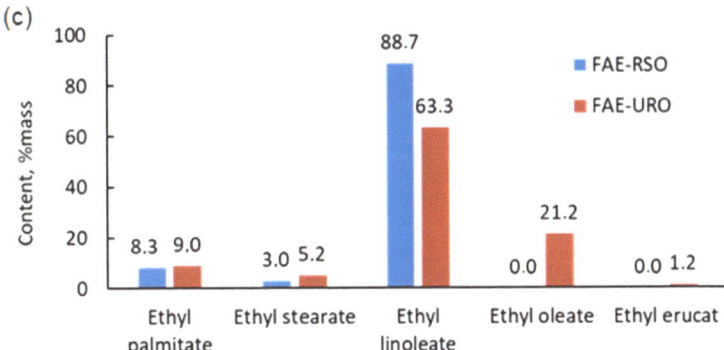

Figure 15. FAE Total Ion Chromatogram: (**a**) FAE-URO; (**b**) FAE-RSO; (**c**) FAE's composition.

4. Conclusions

The production of ethyl ester from refined sunflower and unrefined rapeseed linoleic type oil through the classical and optimized method of alkali-catalyzed transesterification in volumetric excess of ethanol was investigated. In both methods, the ideal mixing reactor model was used.

The results most significant for this study were obtained by changing the oil:ethanol ratio. The use of volumetric ratios and absolute ethanol made it possible to reduce the reaction time from 2.5 h to 5 min while maintaining a high degree of conversion. This allowed us to consider the technological scheme with the use of a linear flow reactor or perfect displacement reactor. The improved synthesis method also made it possible to fix the conversion rate at different points of the kinetic curve by inhibiting the reaction by abruptly cooling the reactor. With this method, it becomes possible to plot the kinetic curve of processes occurring over short time intervals.

The materials presented serve to augment the study of the vegetable oils transesterification process. In the case of refined oil, despite the water content of the reaction alcohol in the amount of 5% and the replacement of methanol with ethyl alcohol, alkaline catalysis made it possible to achieve a high yield of the target product—75%. The optimal synthesis conditions for refined sunflower oil were a KOH catalyst in a content equal to a 1% mass of the ethanol, a volume ratio oil:alcohol equal to 1:3, a stirring time of 2.5 h, and a temperature of 70 °C.

In homogeneous alkaline catalysis, the quality of the raw materials and the reaction alcohol has a strong influence on the balance of the reaction and, as a consequence, on the yield of the target product. For instance, the change in the acid value of the oil due to the change to the unrefined raw material led to a decrease in the target product yield and higher requirements for the quality of the reactive alcohol. This conclusion was confirmed by experimental evidence. Thus, while the sunflower oil esters yield was 75.8% for 95% ethanol, it was only 30.1% for unrefined rapeseed oil under the same synthesis conditions.

It is optimal to use absolute ethanol for unrefined rapeseed oil. However, due to the complexity of obtaining this alcohol drying degree, a range of concentrations of 96–99% can be considered. In this case, more time will be needed for the synthesis process.

The use of watered alcohol also affects the amount of catalyst used in the process. The optimum point on the graphical yield curve is shifted towards an increase in the KOH content. These values were 0.5 and 1.5%, respectively, for the absolute and 95% ethanol.

The analysis of the component ratio effect on the target product yield confirmed the earlier conclusion about the optimal value. The largest yield of the FAEs was obtained at 0.5% of KOH and the oil:ethanol ratio of 1:3. Therefore, the optimal synthesis conditions for unrefined rapeseed oil were: the use of absolute ethanol (99%), oil:ethanol volume ratio of 1:3 and the KOH catalyst content equal to 0.5% mass of ethanol.

Further research on this topic will be devoted to the implementation of a displacement reactor model for the optimal conditions for the synthesis of the fatty acid esters defined in this work.

It should be noted that the question of the further purification of fatty acid esters from excess ethanol, the glycerin phase, and the homogeneous catalyst remains relevant in this study. It will be considered in the following works.

Author Contributions: Investigation, writing—original draft preparation, methodology, visualization, S.M.K.; investigation, writing—original draft preparation, M.S.S.; conceptualization, writing—review and editing, project administration, V.A.R.; formal analysis, supervision, I.N.P. All authors have read and agreed to the published version of the manuscript.

Funding: This research received no external funding.

Data Availability Statement: Not applicable.

Conflicts of Interest: The authors declare no conflict of interest.

Abbreviations

TFA	Triglycerides of Fatty Acids
FFA	Free Fatty Acids
FAE/FAEs	Fatty Acid Esters
RSO	Refined Sunflower Oil
URO	Unrefined Rapeseed Oil
FAE-RSO	Fatty Acid Esters of Refined Sunflower Oil
FAE-URO	Fatty Acid Esters of Unrefined Rapeseed Oil

References

1. Litvinenko, V.; Tsvetkov, P.; Dvoynikov, M.; Buslaev, G. Barriers to implementation of hydrogen initiatives in the context of global energy sustainable development. *J. Min. Inst.* **2020**, *244*, 421. [CrossRef]
2. Pashkevich, M.; Bech, J.; Matveeva, V.; Alekseenko, A. Biogeochemical assessment of soils and plants in industrial, residential and recreational areas of Saint Petersburg. *J. Min. Inst.* **2020**, *241*, 125. [CrossRef]
3. Litvinenko, V.; Bowbrick, I.; Naumov, I.; Zaitseva, Z. Global guidelines and requirements for professional competencies of natural resource extraction engineers: Implications for ESG principles and sustainable development goals. *J. Clean. Prod.* **2022**, *338*, 130530. [CrossRef]
4. Athar, M.; Zaidi, S. A review of the feedstocks, catalysts, and intensification techniques for sustainable biodiesel production. *J. Environ. Chem. Eng.* **2020**, *8*, 104523. [CrossRef]
5. Shishkova, I.; Stratiev, D.; Kolev, I.V.; Nenov, S.; Nedanovski, D.; Atanassov, K.; Ivanov, V.; Ribagin, S. Challenges in Petroleum Characterization—A Review. *Energies* **2022**, *15*, 7565. [CrossRef]
6. Ershov, M.A.; Savelenko, V.D.; Makhova, U.A.; Makhmudova, A.E.; Zuikov, A.V.; Kapustin, V.M.; Abdellatief, T.M.M.; Burov, N.O.; Geng, T.; Abdelkareem, M.A.; et al. Current Challenge and Innovative Progress for Producing HVO and FAME Biodiesel Fuels and Their Applications. *Waste Biomass Valorization* **2022**, *14*, 505–521. [CrossRef]
7. Ershov, M.A.; Savelenko, V.D.; Shvedova, N.S.; Kapustin, V.M.; Abdellatief, T.M.M.; Karpov, N.V.; Dutlov, E.V.; Borisanov, D.V. An evolving research agenda of merit function calculations for new gasoline compositions. *Fuel* **2022**, *322*, 124209. [CrossRef]
8. Tcvetkov, P. Climate Policy Imbalance in the Energy Sector: Time to Focus on the Value of CO_2 Utilization. *Energies* **2021**, *14*, 411. [CrossRef]
9. Sultanbekov, R.; Islamov, S.; Mardashov, D.; Beloglazov, I.; Hemmingsen, T. Research of the Influence of Marine Residual Fuel Composition on Sedimentation Due to Incompatibility. *J. Mar. Sci. Eng.* **2021**, *9*, 1067. [CrossRef]
10. Litvinenko, V.; Petrov, E.; Vasilevskaya, D.; Yakovenko, A.; Naumov, I.; Ratnikov, M. Assessment of the role of the state in the management of mineral resources. *J. Min. Inst.* **2023**, *259*, 95–111. [CrossRef]
11. Ershov, M.; Potanin, D.; Gueseva, A.; Abdellatief, T.M.M.; Kapustin, V. Novel strategy to develop the technology of high-octane alternative fuel based on low-octane gasoline Fischer-Tropsch process. *Fuel* **2020**, *261*, 116330. [CrossRef]
12. Kuznetsova, T.; Politaeva, N.; Smyatskaya, Y.; Ivanova, A. Lemna Minor Cultivation for Biofuel Production. *IOP Conf. Ser. Earth Environ. Sci.* **2019**, *272*, 022058. [CrossRef]
13. Sverguzova, S.; Sapronova, Z.; Zubkova, O.; Svyatchenko, A.; Shaikhieva, K.; Voronina, Y. Electric steelmaking dust as a raw material for coagulant production. *J. Min. Inst.* **2023**, *260*, 279–288. [CrossRef]
14. Alalwan, H.A.; Alminshid, A.H.; Aljaafari, H.A.S. Promising evolution of biofuel generations. Subject review. *Renew. Energy Focus* **2019**, *28*, 127–139. [CrossRef]

15. Kononchuk, O.; Alekseev, A.; Zubkova, O.; Udovitsky, V. Scientific Background for Processing of Aluminum Waste. *E3S Web Conf.* **2017**, *21*, 02003. [CrossRef]
16. Stratiev, D.; Shishkova, I.; Ivanov, M.; Dinkov, R.; Argirov, G.; Vasilev, S.; Yordanov, D. Validation of Diesel Fraction Content in Heavy Oils Measured by High Temperature Simulated Distillation and Physical Vacuum Distillation by Performance of Commercial Distillation Test and Process Simulation. *Appl. Sci.* **2022**, *12*, 11824. [CrossRef]
17. Ershov, M.A.; Grigorieva, E.V.; Abdellatief, T.M.M.; Chernysheva, E.A.; Makhin, D.Y.; Kapustin, V.M. A new approach for producing mid-ethanol fuels E30 based on low-octane hydrocarbon surrogate blends. *Fuel Process. Technol.* **2021**, *213*, 106688. [CrossRef]
18. Boutesteijn, C.; Drabik, D.; Venus, T.J. The interaction between EU biofuel policy and first- and second-generation biodiesel production. *Ind. Crops Prod.* **2017**, *106*, 124–129. [CrossRef]
19. Janda, K.; Stankus, E. *Munich Personal RePEc Archive Biofuels Markets and Policies in Russia*; University Library of Munich: Munich, Germany, 2017.
20. Balajii, M.; Niju, S. Biochar-derived heterogeneous catalysts for biodiesel production. *Environ. Chem. Lett.* **2019**, *17*, 1447–1469. [CrossRef]
21. Pashkevich, M.A.; Kharko, P.A. The use of a composite mix to remove metals from acidic drainage waters at tailings facilities. *Obogashchenie Rud* **2022**, *4*, 40–47. [CrossRef]
22. Cheremisina, E.; Cheremisina, O.; Ponomareva, M.; Bolotov, V.; Fedorov, A. Kinetic features of the hydrogen sulfide sorption on the ferro-manganese material. *Metals* **2021**, *11*, 90. [CrossRef]
23. Murad, P.C.; Hamerski, F.; Corazza, M.L.; Luz, L.F.L.; Voll, F.A.P. Acid-catalyzed esterification of free fatty acids with ethanol: An assessment of acid oil pretreatment, kinetic modeling and simulation. *React. Kinet. Mech. Catal.* **2018**, *123*, 505–515. [CrossRef]
24. Lucena, I.L.; Saboya, R.M.A.; Oliveira, J.F.G.; Rodrigues, M.L.; Torres, A.E.B.; Cavalcante, C.L.; Parente, E.J.S.; Silva, G.F.; Fernandes, F.A.N. Oleic acid esterification with ethanol under continuous water removal conditions. *Fuel* **2011**, *90*, 902–904. [CrossRef]
25. Stratiev, D.; Shishkova, I.; Dinkov, R.; Nenov, S.; Sotirov, S.; Sotirova, E.; Kolev, I.; Ivanov, V.; Ribagin, S.; Atanassov, K.; et al. Prediction of petroleum viscosity from molecular weight and density. *Fuel* **2023**, *331*, 125679. [CrossRef]
26. Chew, S.C.; Ali, M.A. Recent advances in ultrasound technology applications of vegetable oil refining. *Trends Food Sci. Technol.* **2021**, *116*, 468–479. [CrossRef]
27. Gea, S.; Irvan, I.; Wijaya, K.; Nadia, A.; Pulungan, A.N.; Sihombing, J.L.; Rahayu, R. Bio-oil hydrodeoxygenation over acid activated-zeolite with different Si/Al ratio. *Biofuel Res. J.* **2022**, *9*, 1630–1639. [CrossRef]
28. Silitonga, A.S.; Masjuki, H.H.; Mahlia, T.M.I.; Ong, H.C.; Atabani, A.E.; Chong, W.T. A global comparative review of biodiesel production from jatropha curcas using different homogeneous acid and alkaline catalysts: Study of physical and chemical properties. *Renew. Sustain. Energy Rev.* **2013**, *24*, 514–533. [CrossRef]
29. Raita, M.; Champreda, V.; Laosiripojana, N. Biocatalytic ethanolysis of palm oil for biodiesel production using microcrystalline lipase in tert-butanol system. *Process Biochem.* **2010**, *45*, 829–834. [CrossRef]
30. Salisbury, C.; O'Cathain, A.; Edwards, L.; Thomas, C.; Gaunt, D.; Hollinghurst, S.; Nicholl, J.; Large, S.; Yardley, L.; Lewis, G.; et al. Effectiveness of an integrated telehealth service for patients with depression: A pragmatic randomised controlled trial of a complex intervention. *Lancet Psychiatry* **2016**, *3*, 515–525. [CrossRef]
31. Eremeeva, A.M.; Kondrasheva, N.K.; Khasanov, A.F.; Oleynik, I.L. Environmentally Friendly Diesel Fuel Obtained from Vegetable Raw Materials and Hydrocarbon Crude. *Energies* **2023**, *16*, 2121. [CrossRef]
32. de Oliveira, V.F.; Parente, E.J.S.; Manrique-Rueda, E.D.; Cavalcante, C.L.; Luna, F.M.T. Fatty acid alkyl esters obtained from babassu oil using C1–C8 alcohols and process integration into a typical biodiesel plant. *Chem. Eng. Res. Des.* **2020**, *160*, 224–232. [CrossRef]
33. Oloyede, C.T.; Jekayinfa, S.O.; Alade, A.O.; Ogunkunle, O.; Laseinde, O.T.; Adebayo, A.O.; Abdulkareem, A.I.; Smaisim, G.F.; Fattah, I.M.R. Synthesis of Biobased Composite Heterogeneous Catalyst for Biodiesel Production Using Simplex Lattice Design Mixture: Optimization Process by Taguchi Method. *Energies* **2023**, *16*, 2197. [CrossRef]
34. Kondrasheva, N.; Eremeeva, A. Production of biodiesel fuel from vegetable raw materials. *J. Min. Inst.* **2023**, *260*, 248–256. [CrossRef]
35. Lugani, Y.; Rai, R.; Prabhu, A.A.; Maan, P.; Hans, M.; Kumar, V.; Kumar, S.; Chandel, A.K.; Sengar, R.S. Recent advances in bioethanol production from lignocelluloses: A comprehensive review with a focus on enzyme engineering and designer biocatalysts. *Biofuel Res. J.* **2020**, *7*, 1267–1295. [CrossRef]
36. Belozertseva, N.E.; Bogdanov, I.A.; Altynov, A.A.; Balzhanova, A.T.; Belinskaya, N.S.; Kirgina, M.V. Selection of the most beneficial raw materials for the synthesis of biodiesel from a standpoint of its yield and physicochemical properties. *Proc. Univ. Appl. Chem. Biotechnol.* **2020**, *10*, 114–123. [CrossRef]
37. Fadhil, A.B.; Abdulahad, W.S. Transesterification of mustard (Brassica nigra) seed oil with ethanol: Purification of the crude ethyl ester with activated carbon produced from de-oiled cake. *Energy Convers. Manag.* **2014**, *77*, 495–503. [CrossRef]
38. Pinnarat, T.; Savage, P.E. Noncatalytic esterification of oleic acid in ethanol. *J. Supercrit. Fluids* **2010**, *53*, 53–59. [CrossRef]
39. Santana, H.S.; Tortola, D.S.; Reis, É.M.; Silva, J.L.; Taranto, O.P. Transesterification reaction of sunflower oil and ethanol for biodiesel synthesis in microchannel reactor: Experimental and simulation studies. *Chem. Eng. J.* **2016**, *302*, 752–762. [CrossRef]

40. Veljković, V.B.; Biberdžić, M.O.; Banković-Ilić, I.B.; Djalović, I.G.; Tasić, M.B.; Nježić, Z.B.; Stamenković, O.S. Biodiesel production from corn oil: A review. *Renew. Sustain. Energy Rev.* **2018**, *91*, 531–548. [CrossRef]
41. Natarajan, Y.; Nabera, A.; Salike, S.; Dhanalakshmi Tamilkkuricil, V.; Pandian, S.; Karuppan, M.; Appusamy, A. An overview on the process intensification of microchannel reactors for biodiesel production. *Chem. Eng. Process.-Process Intensif.* **2019**, *136*, 163–176. [CrossRef]
42. Permyakova, I.A.; Vol'khin, V.V.; Kazakov, D.A.; Kaczmarski, K.; Kudryashova, O.S.; Sukhoplecheva, E.A. Phase Equilibria in Triacylglycerols–Ethanol–Oleic Acid–Athyl Oleate Quasi-Quaternary System. *Eurasian Chem. J.* **2014**, *16*, 257–264. [CrossRef]
43. Golubev, V.; Litvinova, T. Dynamic simulation of industrial-scale gibbsite crystallization circuit. *J. Min. Inst.* **2021**, *247*, 88–101. [CrossRef]
44. Raupov, I.; Burkhanov, R.; Lutfullin, A.; Maksyutin, A.; Lebedev, A.; Safiullina, E. Experience in the Application of Hydrocarbon Optical Studies in Oil Field Development. *Energies* **2022**, *15*, 3626. [CrossRef]
45. Cheremisina, O.; Litvinova, T.; Sergeev, V.; Ponomareva, M.; Mashukova, J. Application of the Organic Waste-Based Sorbent for the Purification of Aqueous Solutions. *Water* **2021**, *13*, 3101. [CrossRef]
46. Povarov, V.; Efimov, I. Use of the UNIFAC model in the calculation of physicochemical properties of ecotoxicants for technological and ecoanalytical purposes. *J. Min. Inst.* **2023**, *260*, 238–247. [CrossRef]
47. Gerasimov, A.; Ustinov, I.; Zyryanova, O. Use of clay-containing waste as pozzolanic additives. *J. Min. Inst.* **2023**, *260*, 313–320. [CrossRef]
48. Alhassan, F.H.; Uemura, Y. Isopropanolysis of Cottonseed Oil to Biodiesel via Potassium Hydroxide Catalyst. *Procedia Eng.* **2016**, *148*, 473–478. [CrossRef]
49. Encinar, J.M.; González, J.F.; Rodríguez, J.J.; Tejedor, A. Biodiesel fuels from vegetable oils: Transesterification of Cynara cardunculus L. Oils with ethanol. *Energy Fuels* **2002**, *16*, 443–450. [CrossRef]
50. Vicente, G.; Martínez, M.; Aracil, J. Optimization of Brassica carinata oil methanolysis for biodiesel production. *J. Am. Oil Chem. Soc.* **2005**, *82*, 899–904. [CrossRef]
51. Crapiste, G.H.; Brevedan, M.I.V.; Carelli, A.A. Oxidation of sunflower oil during storage. *J. Am. Oil Chem. Soc.* **1999**, *76*, 1437–1443. [CrossRef]
52. García-Martín, J.F.; Barrios, C.C.; Alés-Álvarez, F.J.; Dominguez-Sáez, A.; Alvarez-Mateos, P. Biodiesel production from waste cooking oil in an oscillatory flow reactor. Performance as a fuel on a TDI diesel engine. *Renew. Energy* **2018**, *125*, 546–556. [CrossRef]
53. Knerelman, E.I.; Yarullin, R.S.; Davydova, G.I.; Startseva, G.P.; Churkina, V.Y.; Matkovsky, P.E.; Aldoshin, S.M. Comparative features of the infrared spectra C18-carboxic acids, their methyl esters (biodiesel) and triglycerides (vegetable oils). *Vestn. Kazan. Tekhnol. Univ.* **2008**, *6*, 68–78.
54. Sultanova, G.I.; Sayfetdinova, G.A.; Rakhmatullina, A.P.; Akhmedyanova, R.A.; Liakumovich, A.G. Effect of potassium salts of stearic and oleic acids on the emulsion copolymerization of styrene and alpha-methylstyrene. *Bull. Kazan Technol. Univ.* **2006**, *2*, 67–71.
55. Gomes, M.G.; Santos, D.Q.; De Morais, L.C.; Pasquini, D. Purification of biodiesel by dry washing, employing starch and cellulose as natural adsorbents. *Fuel* **2015**, *155*, 1–6. [CrossRef]

Disclaimer/Publisher's Note: The statements, opinions and data contained in all publications are solely those of the individual author(s) and contributor(s) and not of MDPI and/or the editor(s). MDPI and/or the editor(s) disclaim responsibility for any injury to people or property resulting from any ideas, methods, instructions or products referred to in the content.

Article

SAR-AD Method to Characterize Eight SARA Fractions in Various Vacuum Residues and Follow Their Transformations Occurring during Hydrocracking and Pyrolysis

Jeramie J. Adams [1,*], Joseph F. Rovani [1], Jean-Pascal Planche [1], Jenny Loveridge [1], Alex Literati [1], Ivelina Shishkova [2], Georgi Palichev [3], Iliyan Kolev [2,3], Krassimir Atanassov [3,4], Svetoslav Nenov [5], Simeon Ribagin [3], Danail Stratiev [3], Dobromir Yordanov [4] and Jianqiang Huo [6]

1. Western Research Institute, Laramie, WY 82072, USA
2. LUKOIL Neftohim Burgas, 8104 Burgas, Bulgaria
3. Institute of Biophysics and Biomedical Engineering, Bulgarian Academy of Sciences, Academic Georgi Bonchev 105, 1113 Sofia, Bulgaria
4. Department of Industrial Technologies and Management, University Prof. Dr. Assen Zlatarov, Professor Yakimov 1, 8010 Burgas, Bulgaria
5. Department of Mathematics, University of Chemical Technology and Metallurgy, Kliment Ohridski 8, 1756 Sofia, Bulgaria
6. Department of Chemical Engineering, University of Wyoming, 1000 E University Avenue, Laramie, WY 82071, USA
* Correspondence: jadams32@uwyo.edu

Citation: Adams, J.J.; Rovani, J.F.; Planche, J.-P.; Loveridge, J.; Literati, A.; Shishkova, I.; Palichev, G.; Kolev, I.; Atanassov, K.; Nenov, S.; et al. SAR-AD Method to Characterize Eight SARA Fractions in Various Vacuum Residues and Follow Their Transformations Occurring during Hydrocracking and Pyrolysis. *Processes* **2023**, *11*, 1220. https://doi.org/10.3390/pr11041220

Academic Editor: Miguel Ladero Galán

Received: 6 March 2023
Revised: 24 March 2023
Accepted: 6 April 2023
Published: 15 April 2023

Copyright: © 2023 by the authors. Licensee MDPI, Basel, Switzerland. This article is an open access article distributed under the terms and conditions of the Creative Commons Attribution (CC BY) license (https://creativecommons.org/licenses/by/4.0/).

Abstract: Model compounds were used to provide some chemical boundaries for the eight-fraction SAR-AD[TM] characterization method for heavy oils. It was found that the Saturates fraction consists of linear and highly cyclic alkanes; the Aro-1 fraction consists of molecules with a single aromatic ring; the Aro-2 fraction consists of mostly 2 and 3-ring fused aromatic molecules, the pericondensed 4-ring molecule pyrene, and molecules with 3–5 rings that are not fused; and the Aro-3 fraction consists of 4-membered linear and catacondensed aromatics, larger pericondensed aromatics, and large polycyclic aromatic hydrocarbons. The Resins fraction consists of mostly fused aromatic ring systems containing polar functional groups and metallated polar vanadium oxide porphyrin compounds, and the Asphaltene fraction consists of both island- and archipelago-type structures with a broad range of molecular weight variation, aromaticity, and heteroatom contents. The behavior of the eight SAR-AD[TM] fractions during hydrocracking and pyrolysis was investigated, and quantitative relations were established. Intercriteria analysis and evaluation of SAR-AD[TM] data of hydrocracked vacuum residue and sediment formation rate in commercial ebullated bed vacuum residue hydrocracking were performed. It showed that total asphaltene content, toluene-soluble asphaltenes, and colloidal instability index contribute to sediment formation, while Resins and Cyclohexane-soluble asphaltenes had no statistically meaningful relation to sediment formation for the studied range of operation conditions.

Keywords: vacuum residue; hydrocracking; SARA composition; SAR-AD; asphaltene solubility profile; intercriteria analysis

1. Introduction

Feedstock selection is the critical primary factor influencing most profitable petroleum refining processes. Vacuum residue feedstock characterization is of pivotal importance for bottom of the barrel hydrocracking upgrading processes [1–5]. The characterization of the vacuum residues is not trivial due to their low volatility, high melting point, and extremely complex composition. More than 95% of the molecules have never been isolated or identified from vacuum residues and thus remain unknown [6]. The typical characterization of the petroleum distillates (that includes boiling point distribution and density, allowing prediction of some important structure parameters) is not feasible for the vacuum residual oils due to their low volatility [7]. This has motivated researchers to devise methods to quantify similar classes of compounds using the saturates, aromatics, resins, and asphaltenes (SARA) composition analysis [8]. These analyses have provided an effective method to understand some aspects of bottom of the barrel upgrading processes [3,9–25].

Throughout the years, different methodologies have been developed to perform SARA analysis [26–48]. In general, the SARA analysis methodologies applied by different researchers can be divided into three main groups of chromatographic platforms: liquid chromatography, thin layer chromatography/flame ionization detection (TLC/FID), and high-performance liquid chromatography (HPLC) [42]. However, differences in the chromatographic platforms, sample preparation used for various methods can vary significantly, and methodologies can vary by utilizing different sorbent and solvent phases. With respect to sample preparation, some methods perform the asphaltene separation prior to chromatographing the maltenes (SAR fractions). This is generally favored since a significant portion of asphaltenes become irreversibly adsorbed to the sorbent phase, which can change the sorbent's activity. As an added layer of complexity, there are various solvents that can be used to precipitate asphaltenes, which will affect the quantity of resins and asphaltenes. In general, smaller alkyl chain solvents precipitate more asphaltenes than longer alkyl chain solvents, e.g., pentane vs. heptane, and branched lower solubility parameter solvents like isooctane can precipitate more asphaltenes relative to more linear alkane isomers. Other methods allow for in situ analysis for quantification of the SAR fractions and asphaltenes for the whole residue. Aside from sample preparation, the other dominant factor that affects the SAR separation is the sorbent and solvent systems used to perform the chromatography. Different sorbent and solvent combinations affect the cut points and overlap in molecular species during chromatography. As a result, data obtained from the same samples in different laboratories that employ different SARA techniques can be extremely variable, making it extremely difficult to draw universal conclusions from SARA data from different laboratories [41,49]. Nevertheless, the SARA techniques do provide a relatively complete characterization compared to individual molecular identification of the vacuum residue and are useful for characterizing feedstocks for bottom of the barrel upgrading processes [3,19,24,25].

For more sophisticated SARA separations, Liang et al. [27] proposed an eight group-fraction separation method that further separated aromatics and resins into light, middle, and heavy fractions, respectively [27]. Zhang et al. [23] employed the eight group-fraction SARA separation method to investigate the coking tendency of the eight group-fractions of Iranian vacuum residue. Che et al. [24] employed the eight group-fraction SARA separation method to investigate the pyrolysis behaviors and kinetics of the eight group-fractions, showing that each fraction has individual cracking pathways, which are determined by the chemical nature of the constituents. Zhang et al. [25] investigated the millisecond pyrolysis behavior of the eight group-fractions of Changqing vacuum residue. Their results showed that the eight group-fractions from saturate to asphaltene showed different compositions and structures, which provided valuable, more in-depth information for understanding the structure of heavy oil. Due to this difference in composition and structure, the eight group-fractions showed different cracking behaviors [25]. Within the portfolio of more advanced separations is the Western Research Institute-developed SAR-ADTM separation method [39,40]. In the SAR-AD separation, five distinct maltene fractions (Saturates, Aromatics (Aro-1, Aro-2, Aro-3), and Resins) are obtained by chromatography, and three different asphaltene subfractions are obtained by solubility using three different solvents of increasing solvent power: cyclohexane, toluene, and dichloromethane:methanol (98:2 $vol:vol$) [50,51]. For simplicity, the cyclohexane-soluble asphaltenes are denoted as CyC_6 and the dichloromethane-soluble asphaltenes are denoted CH_2Cl_2. The separation uses an evaporative light scattering detector (ELSD), which provides data similar to gravimetric weight percent, and a variable wavelength detector that measures the concentration of brown colored molecules that absorb light at 500 nm. The Asphaltene Determinator (AD) portion of the separation was initially developed with U.S. Department of Energy and petroleum industry partner funding to quantify and monitor pyrolysis tolerance and coking onsets of heavy oils and bitumen. It was observed that as bitumen undergoes pyrolysis/cracking/visbreaking (thermal bond breaking), the free solvent volume of the asphaltenes decreases. The free solvent volume was found to be directly related to the amount of CyC_6 asphaltenes [52], which systematically decreased with pyrolysis severity. As the CyC_6 asphaltenes decrease, the more polar/less soluble pre-coke CH_2Cl_2 asphaltenes increase. By taking a ratio of these two asphaltene subfractions, a robust Coking Index was developed that is highly sensitive to the pyrolysis history and can predict the onset of coke particle formation [51]. For most bitumen, the Coking Index is between 3 and 16. For visbroken and hydrocracked materials, the Coking Index falls below 3 and can become significantly lower depending upon the severity of the conversion.

In recent studies, we investigated the ebullated bed vacuum residue hydrocracking performance employing the more traditional four-fraction SARA method for feed and hydrocracked vacuum residue characterization [53]. No reports were found in the literature studying ebullated bed vacuum residue hydrocracking performance with feed and hydrocracked vacuum residue characterization by the eight group SARA fractionation methods. Therefore, SAR-AD characterization of different straight-run vacuum residues derived from extra-light, light, medium, heavy, and extra-heavy crude oils from all over the world is included, including hydrocracked vacuum residues obtained at the conversion range of 55–91%. Nineteen individual vacuum residues derived from crude oils from Russia, Saudi Arabia, Iraq, Libya, Tunisia, Kazakhstan, Greece, Italy, Venezuela, Azerbaijan, and Albania, six blended vacuum residues available as feeds for processing in a commercial ebullated bed vacuum residue hydrocracker, and nine hydrocracked vacuum residues were characterized for this work.

The aim of this work is to study the eight SAR-AD fractions during hydrocracking of different vacuum residues and to establish a model for the quantitative relationship between the feedstock SAR-AD fraction contents and other common feed characterization data with relation to the performance of a commercial ebullated bed vacuum residue hydrocracker. A chemical understanding of the types of molecules that report to the various SAR-AD fractions, using various model compounds, helped to explain some of the trends and relationships for the feeds and products.

2. Materials and Methods

The properties of the nineteen studied crude oils and derived vacuum residues were characterized for their bulk density (ASTM D 4052), sulfur content (ASTM D 4294), Conradson carbon content (ASTM D 189), and vacuum residue SARA composition, performed according to the methodology developed in the LUKOIL Neftohim Burgas (LNB) Research Laboratory [36]. These data are summarized in Table 1. The data in Table 1 also includes the content of the vacuum residue fraction of the studied crude oils, determined by the use of a true boiling point (TBP) apparatus operating under the requirements of ASTM D 2892 for the atmospheric part and ASTM D 5236 for the vacuum part. The T50% of the crude oils was determined by the use of high temperature simulated distillation (HTSD) in accordance with the ASTM D 7169 standard.

The determination of softening point, T50% of the VRs, VR molecular weight, and viscosity of blends of the 19 studied vacuum residues (VR) with fluid catalytic cracking heavy cycle oil at a ratio of 70% VR/30% FCC HCO is described in our other recent research [54].

This investigation was performed at the commercial LNB H-Oil vacuum residue hydrocracker. A process diagram of the LNB H-Oil unit and the operating conditions employed at the LNB H-Oil hydrocracker are presented in our earlier studies [53,55,56].

Table 1. Physicochemical properties of studied crude oils and vacuum residue fractions derived thereof.

Nr	1	2	3	4	5	6	7	8	9	10	11	12	13	14	15	16	17	18	19
Crude type	Urals1	Urals2	Arab Med.	Arab Heavy	Basrah L	Basrah H	Kirkuk	El Bouri	CPC	LSCO	Prinos	Boscan	Varandey	Albania	Tempa Rossa	Rhemoura	Arab Light	Azeri Light	Imported AR
Crude D15. g/cm^3	0.877	0.875	0.872	0.889	0.878	0.905	0.873	0.891	0.805	0.854	0.875	1.002	0.85	1.001	0.94	0.865	0.858	0.848	
Crude Sulfur. wt.%	1.53	1.39	2.48	2.91	2.85	3.86	2.65	1.76	0.63	0.57	3.71	5.5	0.63	5.64	5.35	0.75	1.89	0.2	
Crude VR. wt.%	25.2	29	25.2	32	28.3	33.8	24.6	26.2	9.3	18.7	20.3	63.1	14.9	48.2	37.6	20.2	22.9	14.8	
Crude T50%. °C	378	380	376	429	392	418	345	401	238	352	349	571	362	531	428	350	352	321	
VR D15. g/cm^3	0.997	0.995	1.031	1.04	1.052	1.071	1.054	1.05	0.956	0.993	1.108	1.078	0.99	1.094	1.12	1.041	1.029	0.967	1.029
VR CCR. wt.%	17.5	17.0	20.7	23.6	23.8	28.9	25.2	25.5	16	14	32.8	27.8	15.1	31.4	34.3	23.7	18.7	9.5	19.2
VR Sulfur. wt.%	3.0	2.9	5.4	5.8	5.9	7.1	5.9	3.3	2.1	1.58	9.14	6	1.7	8.7	9.3	1.8	4.9	0.5	3.28
VR Sat. wt.%	25.6	22.9	11.8	12.4	12.3	12.3	15.2	12	44.6	25	12.6	15.1	33.5	10	2.2	19.7	15.9	40.2	17.5
VR Aro. wt.%	52.5	66.5	68.3	61.9	64.8	54.1	55.4	57.9	40.8	61.1	50.6	44.5	47.6	52.9	48.4	49.8	64.7	50.1	60.7
VR Res. wt.%	7.8	4.9	5.3	4.4	4.9	5.8	5	12.6	10.3	6.1	6.8	5.3	11.3	6.3	12.6	7.3	7.3	8.4	8.0
VR C$_7$ asp. wt.%	14.1	6.3	14.6	21.3	18	27.7	24.3	17.5	3.4	7.8	30	35.2	7.6	37.7	36.8	23.2	12.1	1.4	13.7
VR C$_5$ asp. wt.%	17.6	13.9	25.5	32.9	27.7	37	33.1	27.3	11	15.5	38.8	41	13.5	49.7	46.8	31.3	18.8	5.4	21.8
VR VIS. mm^2/s *	220.9		338.3	374.6	368.9	731.9	514.1	303	65	149.1	550	1003	103	680	759.5	255	192	77	
VR Softening point. °C	40.1	42.4	44.7	51.2	50.3	68.6	58.1	45	25.2	28.9	69.2	115	43.8	92.2	100	51.1	32.3	30.2	
VR T50%. °C	657	670	709	684	715	676	666	637	631	645	812	621	732	708	642	647	627		
MW. g/mol	808	840	953	877	968	853	827	757	741	760	1330	717	1017	931	766	778	731		

Note: D15 = density at 15 °C; VR = vacuum residue fraction; CCR = Conradson carbon content; Sat. = Saturates; Aro = Aromatics; Res. = Resins; C$_7$ asp. = n-heptane asphaltenes; C$_5$ asp. = n-pentane asphaltenes; VIS = kin. viscosity at 80 °C of the blend 70% VR/30% fluid catalytic cracking heavy cycle oil; Crude T50% = boiling point of 50% of the evaporate from the crude oil; VR T50% = boiling point of 50% of the evaporate from the vacuum residue fraction. * The viscosity values are related to the viscosity at 80 °C of mixtures of vacuum residues with fluid catalytic cracking heavy cycle oil, which has a viscosity at 80 °C of 4.4 mm^2/s.

The SAR-AD method was performed according to the literature [39,40]. The dual-detector SAR-AD chromatograms obtained for a Lloydminster vacuum residue are shown in Figure 1.

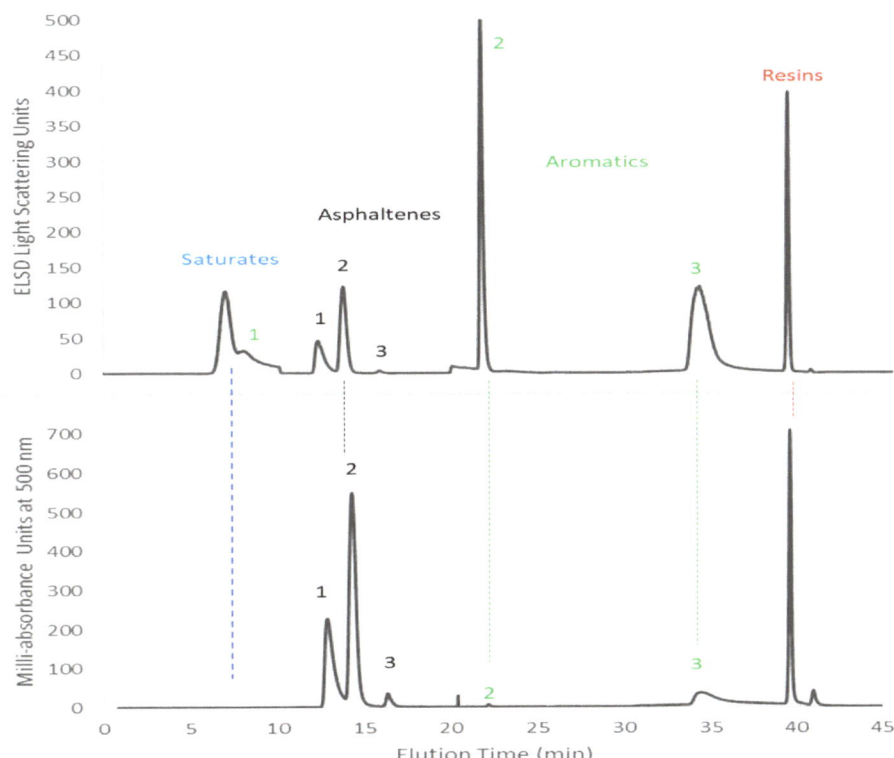

Figure 1. SAR-AD separation profiles for a Lloydminster vacuum residue. Asphaltene 1 = CyC_6, asphaltene 2 = Toluene, and Asphaltene 3 = CH_2Cl_2. (The different colors designate Saturates—blue; Asphaltenes—black; Aromatics—green; Resins—red.)

The top chromatogram in Figure 1 is obtained using an evaporative light scattering detector, which gives an approximate weight percent as long as molecules are heavy enough to remain during the solvent evaporation process. The bottom chromatogram is collected using a variable wavelength or diode array detector set at 500 nm to give the concentration of brown colored material in the sample. The SAR-AD instrument contains both detectors, with the 500 nm detector configured immediately before the ELSD.

The Saturates fraction elutes first in the separation as non-adsorbed molecules flowing through four analytical columns. These molecules include fully saturated alkyl molecules, including cyclic (naphthenic) hydrocarbon molecules. It is the most hydrogen-rich non-polar fraction in the bitumen chemistry spectrum. The Aro-1 fraction contains hydrocarbons with a single isolated aromatic ring with significant amounts of alkyl side chain branching, which may also contain cyclic moieties. Molecules in this fraction are a bit more polar in the solubility/polarity spectrum than those in the Saturates fraction. The Aro-2 fraction generally contains two–three aromatic rings, 4 or 5 ring molecules, and a limited amount of cyclic heteroatom-containing compounds (sulfur, nitrogen, and oxygen). Aro-3 contains primarily molecules with four or more aromatic rings and has increased heteroatom contents, which can consist of heterocyclic N-H, aromatic acyl, NH2, and aliphatic O-H species. The Resins fraction consists of increasingly polar molecules, mainly attributed to polar heteroatom functional groups and fused aromatic ring systems. Resins are the most polar fraction of the maltenes. The CyC_6 asphaltenes consist of alkyl-substituted multi-aromatic core compounds with heteroatoms. Toluene asphaltenes are more polar due to either increased heteroatom polarity, number of heteroatoms, ability to aggregate more efficiently, and/or increased aromaticity. Finally, the CH_2Cl_2 asphaltenes are the most polar of the bitumen fractions, consisting of either the greatest amount of polar functional groups containing highly polar functional groups and/or the least amount of alkyl side chains. During pyrolysis, increasing amounts of CH_2Cl_2 asphaltenes are produced from other molecules and preclude the onset of coke formation, so in this case, they may be considered as highly aromatic pre-coke molecules. CH_2Cl_2 asphaltenes can be chemically different depending on their isolation method (e.g., from emulsion interfaces or from extrography) or petroleum treatment method (e.g., asphaltenes produced upon oxidation of petroleum have a higher amount of oxygen functional groups) from CH_2Cl_2 asphaltenes produced upon pyrolysis.

Model compounds were evaluated to establish some chemical boundaries for the SAR-AD bitumen fractions. Model compounds were purchased from Sigma-Aldrich St. Louis, Missouri, USA or TCI Chemicals, Portland, OR, USA and 1,3-bis-(1-pyrene) propane was purchased from Setareh Biotech, Eugene, OR, USA. For the volatile model compounds, which are not significantly detected in the ELSD and do not absorb at 500 nm, a diode array detector set to 290 nm was used. This allowed for the detection of molecules with at least two fused aromatic rings with virtually no overlap from toluene, which is the mobile phase used to elute two of the fractions. Absorbance at 290 nm was utilized to detect naphthalene; 2,6-diethylnaphthalene; 2,6-diisopropylnaphthalene; 2,6-ditertbutylnaphthalene; acenaphthylene; phenanthrene; 9,10-dihydrophenanthrene; binaphthalene; and indole. Model compound sample solutions were prepared at 2 percent wt/vol in chlorobenzene for injection. All solvents used were HPLC-grade. ELSD or 290 nm data were blank subtracted, and the areas were integrated according to the elution times used to define the fractions, as shown in Figure 1.

A quality control Lloydminster vacuum residue was used at the beginning and end of every sample sequence, and quality control was run after every 5 samples in sample sequences greater than 6 samples to ensure the quality of the separation. The standard deviation for the various fractions of the QC over the course of 10 days was 0.35 for Saturates, 0.50 for Aro-1, 0.69 for Aro-2, 0.90 for Aro-3, 0.58 for Resins, 0.28 for CyC_6 asphaltenes, 0.18 for Toluene asphaltenes, and 0.10 for CH_2Cl_2 asphaltenes.

Reference petroleum porphyrins were isolated from a Peace River bitumen by extracting with acetonitrile and removing the solvent under rotary evaporation. The extracts were then dissolved in heptane and separated chromatographically on activated Davisil 646 grade silica gel (Sigma Aldrich) using toluene as the eluent. The major porphyrin fraction was eluted as a bright red band. The porphyrin signature was determined using UV-Visible spectroscopy, which showed a strong Soret band at 410 nm and Q bands between 500 and 600 nm [57]. Figure 2 shows the elution of the porphyrins, the porphyrins after solvent removal, and the UV-Visible spectrum. Several useful metrics can be calculated from the SAR-AD fractions. The ratio between the CyC_6 and CH_2Cl_2 asphaltenes is a sensitive indicator for pyrolysis severity and is referred to as the Coking Index. It shows the buildup of the least-soluble asphaltenes (the most problematic asphaltenes) relative to the most-soluble asphaltenes and is directly related to how close the residue is to forming coke particles [50,51]. The initial motivation to separate and quantify CyC_6 asphaltenes was to approximate the free solvent volume relative to the total asphaltenes. The free solvent volume represents how much cracking the residue can undergo before forming coke [52,58]. Another useful metric for refinement is the colloidal instability index (CII). This is the ratio of the incompatible phases (Saturates + Aro-1 and Total Asphaltenes [CyC_6 + Toluene + CH_2Cl_2]) to the dissolving/dispersing phase (Aro-2 + Aro-3 + Resins) [38].

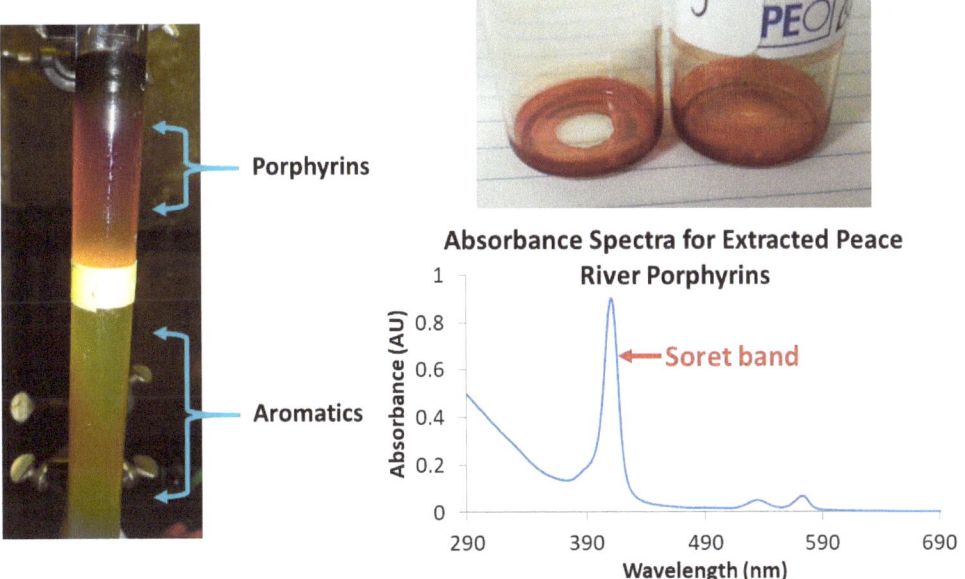

Figure 2. Porphyrins were extracted from Peace River bitumen using column chromatography (**left**), which was dried to give a red-colored porphyrin fraction (**upper right**). This material was analyzed by UV-Visible spectroscopy, which shows the presence of a strong Soret band at 410 nm, confirming the presence of porphyrins. Bands above 500 nm are associated porphyrin Q bands.

For this work, a modification of the CII (MCII) was used because it takes into consideration that the most soluble CyC_6 asphaltenes may be removed from the numerator and placed in the denominator along with the dispersing phase. This is justified because the CyC_6 asphaltenes are consumed during pyrolysis at a similar rate as the Resins fraction, and their association with the free solvent volume indicates that they may be treated separately from the asphaltene nanoaggregate phase. A Maltenes Index (MI) can be calculated to estimate the solvent power of the maltenes phase by omitting the asphaltenes from the CII. Equations for the Coking Index, CII, MCII, and MI are given in Equations (1)–(4):

$$\text{Coking Index} = \frac{CyC_6}{CH_2Cl_2} \tag{1}$$

where:

CyC_6—Cyclohexane asphaltenes;
CH_2Cl_2—Dichloromethane asphaltenes.

$$CII = \frac{(Sat + Aro\ 1 + Total\ Asphaltenes)}{(Aro\ 2 + Aro\ 3 + Resins)} \tag{2}$$

where:

CII—colloidal instability index;
Sat—saturated;
Aro-1, Aro-2, and Aro-3—Aromatic fractions 1, 2, and 3.

$$MCII = \frac{(Sat + Aro\ 1 + Toluene + CH_2Cl_2)}{(Aro\ 2 + Aro\ 3 + Resins + CyC_6)} \tag{3}$$

where:

MCII—Modified colloidal instability index.

$$\text{MI} = \frac{(\text{Sat} + \text{Aro 1})}{(\text{Aro 2} + \text{Aro 3} + \text{Resins})} \quad (4)$$

where:

MI—Maltenes Index.

Changes in SAR-AD fractions as a function of non-catalytic thermal cracking severity were determined by pyrolyzing heavy oil in sealed tubing reactors. Heavy oil (25 g) was loaded into 52 mL capacity Swagelok tubing reactors assembled from 1" stainless steel pipe and 1" VCR weld glands, caps, and gaskets. Reactors were charged with heavy oil (Canadian from Lloydminster or Peace River) and purged with nitrogen. Reactors were sealed and placed in a preheated fluidized sand bath at 400 °C. Pyrolysis was performed under autogenous pressure. Reactors were submerged in the sand bath for a predetermined time and then removed and placed in front of a fan to air cool the reactors so that they were at ambient temperature within 15 min.

Longer reaction times for pyrolysis reactions using FCC slurry oil were performed in a 100 mL high-temperature, high-pressure Series 4590 Micro Reactor system from Parr Instruments Company. The reactor was charged with oil and purged with nitrogen by cycling three times with 300 psi of nitrogen. After the final purge, the reactor was filled with 300 psi of nitrogen. The oil was heated to 430 °C with maximum stirring under autogenous pressure for various residence times. The reaction was cooled to ambient temperature, and the pressure was released. The contents were vacuum distilled to an atmospheric cut point of 240 °C.

A pseudo-delayed coker reaction was performed using a custom 1" stainless steel tubing reactor assembled with Swagelok fittings. The apparatus used a heated nitrogen purge flowing from the bottom of the vertical reactor through a backpressure regulator set to 15 psi, an ambient temperature knockout trap, and finally through two cold traps. The first cold trap was maintained at 0 °C using an ice water bath, and the second trap was maintained at −90 °C using a dry ice/toluene slurry. Lloydminster C_7 asphaltenes (20 g) were placed in the reactor, which was flushed with nitrogen and maintained with a nitrogen flow of 50 mL/min. The reactor was placed in a preheated fluidized sand bath set to 500 °C for 120 min. The coke yield was 45 wt.%, the amount of condensable liquids was 41 wt.%, and the gas was 14 wt.%.

3. Results

3.1. SAR-AD Model Compound Study

To add a chemical meaning to some of the observed processing or behavior phenomena, it is useful to know what kinds of molecules report to the various SAR-AD fractions and obtain some information on the boundaries for those fractions.

From the SAR-AD ELSD chromatogram shown in Figure 1, the first peak (Saturates) is material that ultimately elutes unadsorbed through the silica gel stationary phase with n-heptane as the mobile phase. This material has the weakest interaction with the highly active silica sorbent. This is consistent with saturated hydrocarbons and traditional SARA-type separations. This fraction contains saturated hydrocarbons such as the model compound n-C_{22}, polywax, and natural waxes from crude oils isolated using MEK at −34 °C. For saturated hydrocarbon model compounds, two extremes in structure are abundant in natural hydrocarbons: linear n-alkanes and highly cyclic alkanes. Highly cyclic alkanes are also known as naphthenes or naphthenic hydrocarbons. The elution of highly cyclic alkanes within the saturates fraction was verified by using 5-α-cholestane (Figure 3) as a model compound.

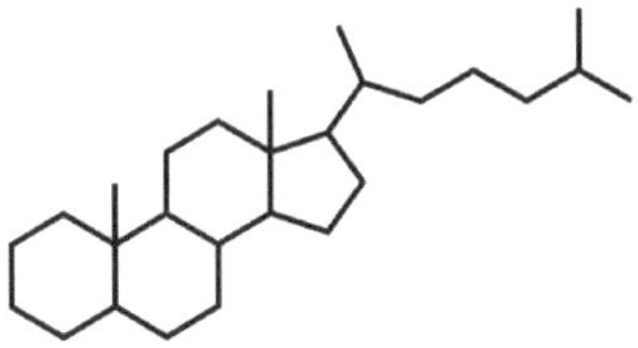

Figure 3. Molecular structure of 5-α-cholestane which reports to the Saturates fraction. Stereochemistry is omitted for clarity.

Shortly after the elution of the Saturates fraction, a second fraction elutes. In most cases, this fraction is not completely chromatographically baseline-resolved from the Saturates fraction. These two closely eluting sets of molecule types are similar except that the material that elutes in the second peak has a stronger interaction with the silica sorbent in the presence of heptane. The enhanced interaction is attributed to the presence of a single aromatic ring, which was confirmed by setting the diode array detector to 180 nm and observing that the Saturates fraction showed no adsorption at this wavelength but that the second peak had a high concentration of molecules that indeed showed absorbance at this wavelength. Using dodecylbenzene (Figure 4) as the model compound, single-ring aromatic compound elution was verified in the second SAR-AD peak. Due to the detection of primarily 1-ring aromatics, this second eluting fraction is termed Aro-1.

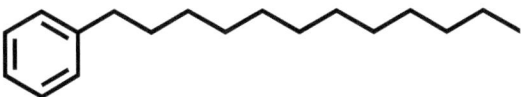

Figure 4. Molecular structure of dodecylbenzene, which reports to the Aro-1 fraction.

In order for single aromatic molecules to be detected in the ELSD, they must be heavily substituted with aliphatic side chains or contain naphthenic structures so that they have a sufficient molecular weight and are not evaporated with the solvent and thus not detected (for example, n-C_{20} is not detected in the ELSD but n-C_{22} is detected). This high degree of substitution causes steric hindrance around the aromatic unit, which prevents it from having a high degree of interaction with the silica gel adsorption sites. This is why this fraction is not completely resolved from the Saturates fraction. Evidence for steric hindrance effects on elution is shown later for the model compounds used for the Aro-2 fraction.

To elute the Aro-2 material, which had previously adsorbed onto the highly active silica gel stationary phase using n-heptane, the mobile phase is switched to toluene. From the model compound evaluated, this fraction was found to contain mostly 2 and 3-ring fused aromatic molecules, the pericondensed 4-ring molecule pyrene, and molecules with 3–5 rings that are not fused, such as o-terphenyl; binaphthyl; and 9,10-diphenylanthracene. Figure 5 shows various aromatic molecules that were eluted in the Aro-2 fraction. From the model compounds shown in Figure 5, it is clear that the presence of small pendent alkyl groups (methyl or ethyl) or naphthenic cyclic structuring (1,2,3,6,7,8-hexahydropyrene) does not significantly affect the elution characteristics of these compounds. It should be noted that most of these exact model compounds do not occur at significant levels in unprocessed petroleum. Instead, most petroleum molecules will contain these aromatic core structures that are substituted with various alkyl groups.

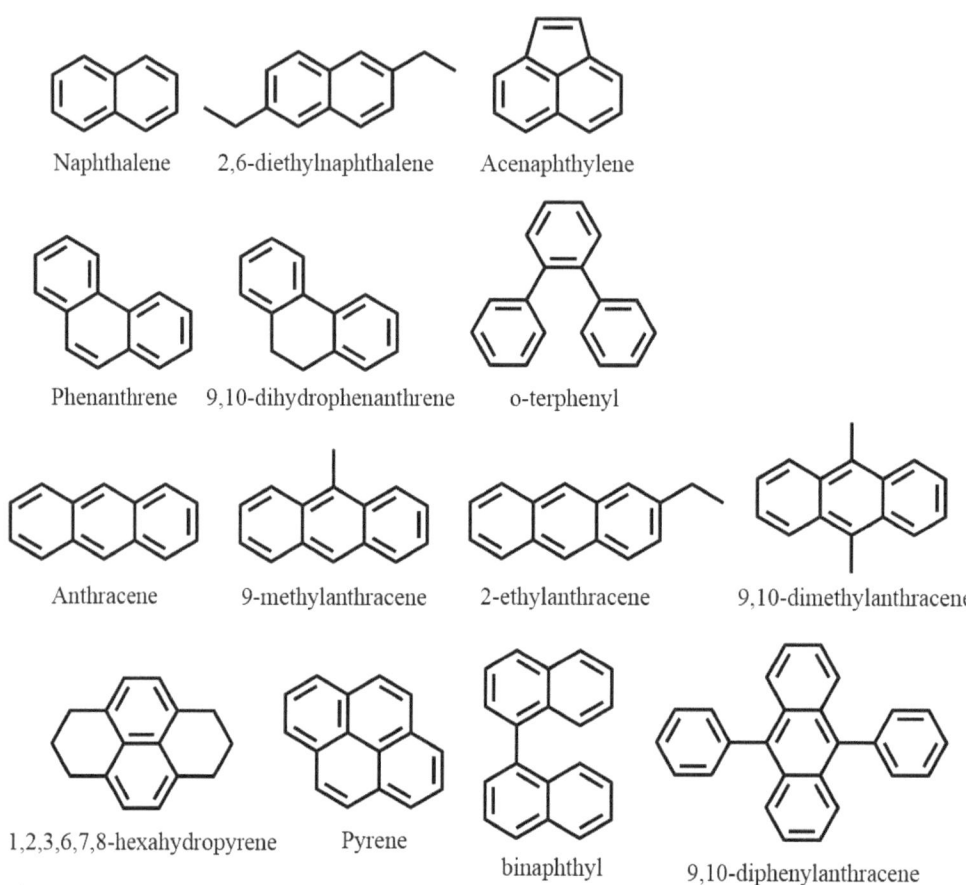

Figure 5. Aromatic model compound molecules that elute in the Aro-2 fraction.

To probe the effect of steric hindrance on elution behavior, naphthalene molecules substituted with alkyl groups of varying steric sizes were analyzed by the SAR-AD. Increasing steric hindrance around the aromatic π-electrons is expected to reduce their interaction with the silica gel sorbent. The model compounds chosen for this study had steric hindrance increasing in the following order: naphthalene; 2,9-diethylnaphthalene; 2,9-diisopropylnaphthalene; and 2,9-ditertbutylnaphthalene (Tolman cone angle for: ethyl = 132°, isopropyl = 160°, and t-butyl = 182° [53]). SAR-AD analysis of these compounds showed that the addition of two ethyl groups provided slight steric bulk to repel the naphthalene core from the sorbent surface, so that about 94% of the compound eluted in Aro-2 (with 6% eluting in Aro-1). The addition of two isopropyl groups significantly altered the elution of the parent naphthalene compound, so that approximately 75% eluted with the Aro-2 fraction. Increasing the steric bulk further by adding the tertbutyl groups slightly affected the elution relative to the isopropyl groups, with 72% eluting with Aro-2. Due to the lack of readily available higher substituted naphthalene compounds, it was not possible to determine the effect of additional isopropyl and tertbutyl groups on the elution behavior of the naphthalene core, but with this limited set of molecules, the trend of steric bulk effects in Aro-1/Aro-2 distribution is evident. Figure 6 shows the molecular structure of the naphthalene model compounds and a visualization of the steric bulk due to the various 2,9-alkyl substituents.

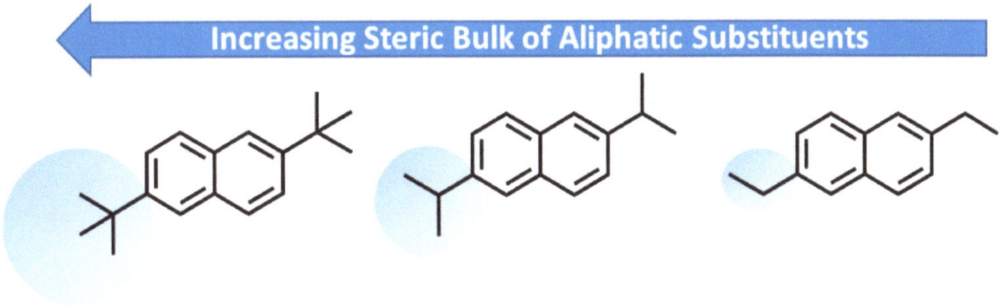

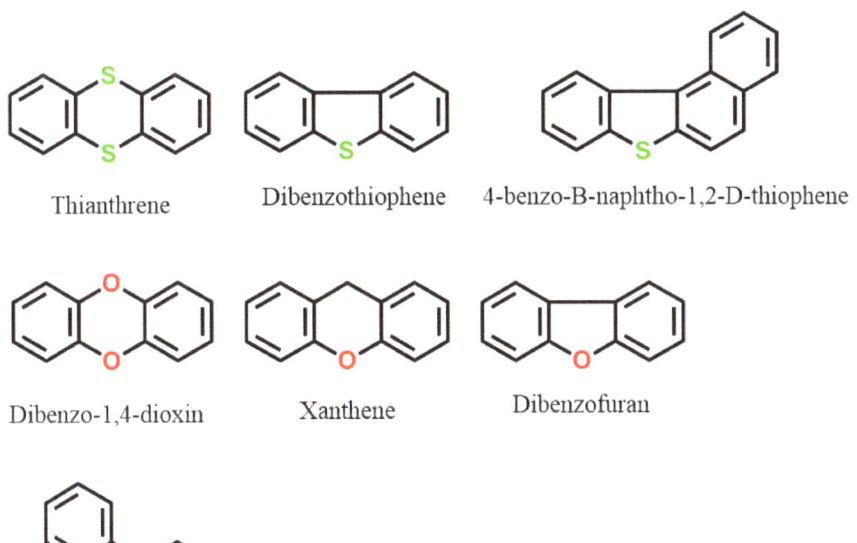

Figure 6. Molecular structures of naphthalene and naphthalene with various 2,9-alkyl substituents and increasing steric bulk. Illustrative steric volumes of pendent alkyl groups are shown in a shaded area. Shaded areas are not to scale. Tolman cone angles are: ethyl = 132°, isopropyl = 160°, and t-butyl = 182° [59].

In common SARA separations, a small number of heteroatoms also begin to appear in the aromatic fraction. Therefore, it was of interest to determine which types of heteroatom functional groups may elute in the Aro-2 fraction. It is not expected that highly polar functional groups such as esters, phenols, carboxylic, thiol, or amines would appear in the aromatics fraction. However, depending on the structure, stearic bulk, and electron distributions, less polar groups such as esters and thioethers (or sulfides) may be expected. Figure 7 shows model compounds containing low-polarity oxygen, sulfur, and nitrogen groups that were also found to elute in the Aro-2 fraction.

Figure 7. Heteroatoms containing three- and four-ring model compounds that eluted in the Aro-2 fraction. (The green color indicates sulfur atoms, red color oxygen atoms and blue color nitrogen).

After elution of the Aro-2 material, a significant amount of material remains adsorbed on the glass beads and aminopropyl silica columns used in the separation. These two chromatography columns, working in tandem, are the stationary phases used for the elution of the Aro-3 and Resins fractions. Some molecules in the Aro-3 fraction absorb light at 500 nm, indicating a small concentration of molecules with larger aromatic chromophores and/or potentially the presence of low-polarity (sulfide, ether, thiophene, pyrrole, and carbazole) heteroatoms. For the non-heteroatom-containing aromatic molecules where all the rings are fused, the 4-membered linear and catacondensed aromatic model compounds elute with this fraction, as do large polycyclic aromatic hydrocarbons (PAHs) like coronene (with seven fused rings). Substitution of some of these PAHs by one or two methyl groups did not affect the elution relative to the parent PAH core. Figure 8 shows the molecular structure of molecules that eluted with the Aro-3 fraction.

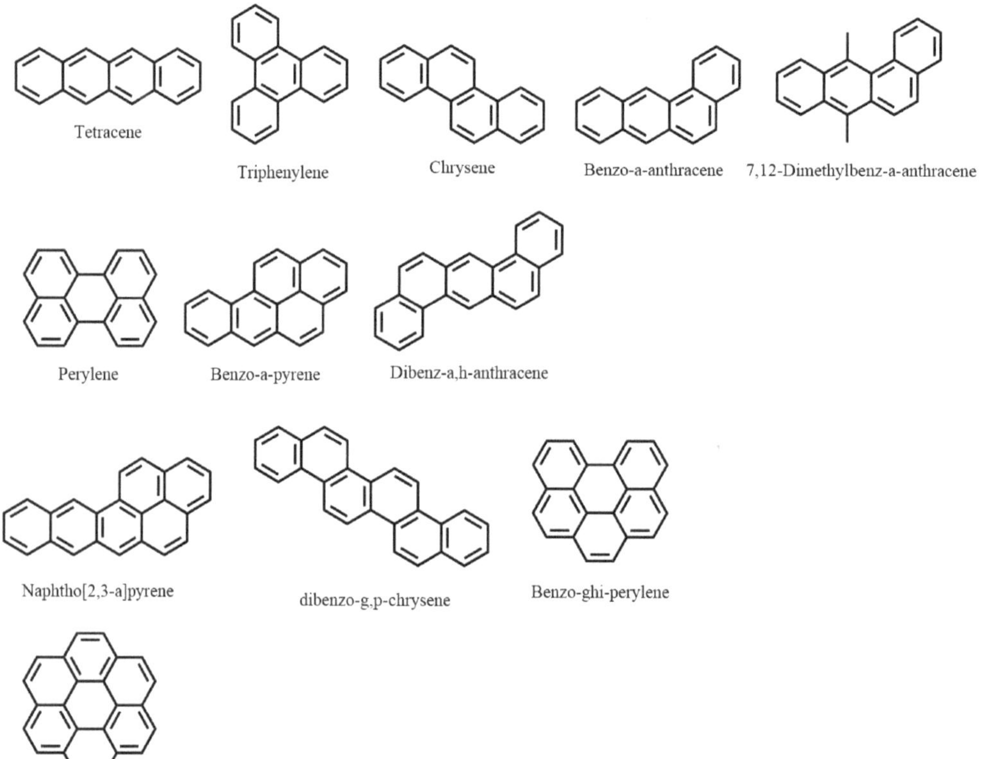

Figure 8. Fused-ring aromatic molecules that eluted to the Aro-3 fraction.

From the model compounds that eluted in the Aro-2 fractions, there were some compounds with additional carbon-carbon bonds (Figure 5) between phenyl or other fused ring units (C_{ar}-C_{ar}) that did not alter the elution characteristics of the largest fused ring subunits (9,10-diphenylanthracene and binaphthyl, respectively). It is expected that the addition of additional phenyl groups to other larger fused ring systems would impact the chromatographic cut point between Aro-2 and Aro-3. It was of interest to probe this further since recent work on scanning tunneling microscopy coupled with atomic force microscopy (STM-AFM) has shown that archipelago types of aromatic structures are present in asphaltenes [60]. The archipelago type of asphaltenes identified by STM-AFM do not show aromatic groups linked by alkyl groups, which was often depicted for archipelago asphaltene structures in early work. Rather, AFM studies generally show direct C_{ar}-C_{ar} bonds linking different aromatic groups to represent archipelago-type molecules. Model compounds analyzed by the non-contact AFM (nc-AFM) method show that aromatic groups connected by long aliphatic linkers are readily detectable and stable with respect to the method, so if they are present in significant amounts they should be readily detected [61]. It should be noted that outside of FCC pitch pyrolysis products [61], to date there has not been evidence for asphaltenes containing significant aliphatic linkages between different aromatic groups, which is why most of the selected model compounds in this work contain aromatic molecules with pendant phenyl or other fused ring groups. For the SAR-AD separation, adding phenyl groups to anthracene did not change its elution from Aro-2, but joining two anthracene molecules together or adding naphthalene to anthracene did increase its interaction with the sorbents, causing it to elute in the Aro-3 fraction. Additionally, large aromatic molecules such as 9,9',10,10'-tetraphenyl-2,2'-bianthracene (MW = 658.84 Daltons), which has a molecular weight similar to asphaltenes, elute exclusively in the Aro-3 fraction. From the non-heteroatom containing aromatic molecules used in this study, no size limit from readily available model compounds was reached, which caused the molecule to elute to more polar fractions, even when using the dye molecule DPB, which has a molecular weight of 804.97 Daltons. However, this does not preclude that other larger, less-soluble, non-heteroatom-containing aromatics, with distinctly different geometries or other combinations of alkyl and aryl substitutions, would prevent these from reporting to the Resins or Asphaltene fractions. It should be noted that substantially larger non-heteroatom aromatics have been identified in asphaltene fractions by nc-AFM55. Figure 9 shows the archipelago-type of model aromatics that eluted with the Aro 3 fraction.

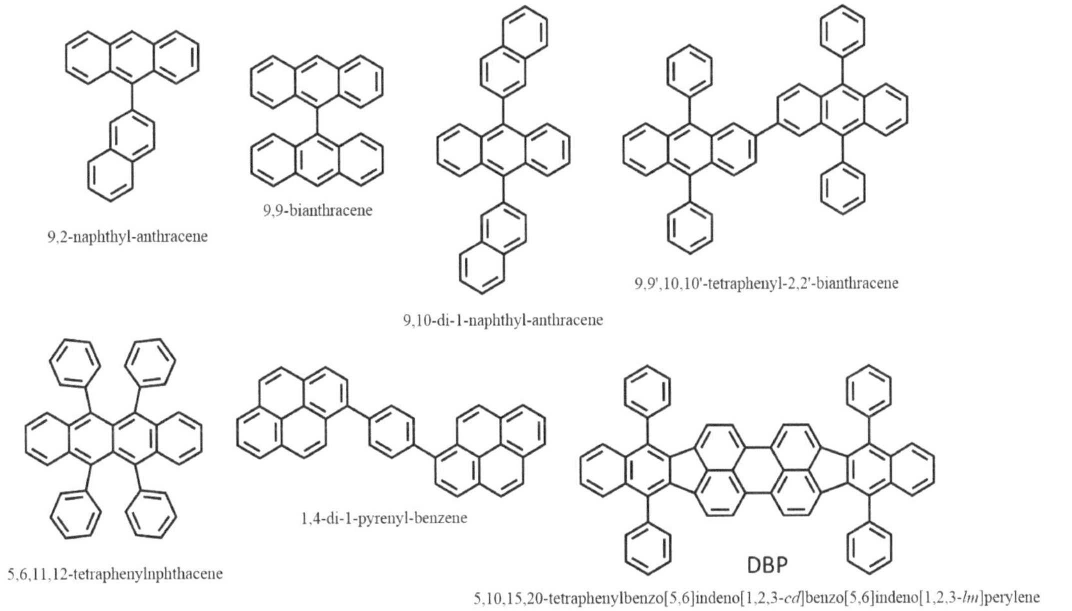

Figure 9. The non-heteroatom contains aromatic molecules, which report to Aro-3 and contain bridging C_{ar}-C_{ar} linkages, with the smaller aromatic cores consisting of three fused aromatic rings (**top row**) and those with four or more fused aromatic rings (**bottom row**).

As mentioned, nc-AFM work on petroleum pitch (M-50, produced through thermal conversion of FCC decant oil to form larger aromatic units for mesophase production and carbon materials) has shown evidence of a minor fraction of molecules with aliphatic carbon-carbon bonds (C_{al}-C_{al}) groups joining aromatic units [62,63]. To study the effect of aliphatic linkages between aromatic units, a model compound with two pyrene groups linked together by a propyl group was analyzed by the SAR-AD. This molecule was shown to elute in the Aro-3 fraction (Figure 10), whereas the single aromatic units that are not linked show up in the Aro-2 fraction. The addition of moderately polar functional groups to small aromatic systems, such as pyrrolic, thiazine, or non-aromatic ring ether, can also cause these molecules to report to the Aro-3 fraction. Figure 11 shows model compounds that eluted in the Aro-3 fraction that would have otherwise eluted in the Aro-2 fraction without their functional groups (it was ambiguous for indene if it would have eluted in the Aro-1 or Aro-2 fraction because it was not able to be detected by ELSD or by absorbance at 290 nm).

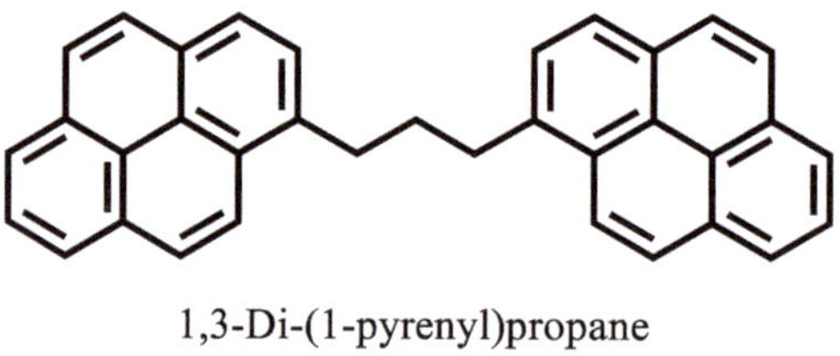

1,3-Di-(1-pyrenyl)propane

Figure 10. Aromatic molecules with bridging C_{al}-C_{al} linkages 1,3-di-(1pyrenyl) propane, which is linked by an aliphatic propyl group. This molecule eluted in the Aro-3 fraction.

Phenothiazine

Benzyl-2-naphtyl ether

Indole

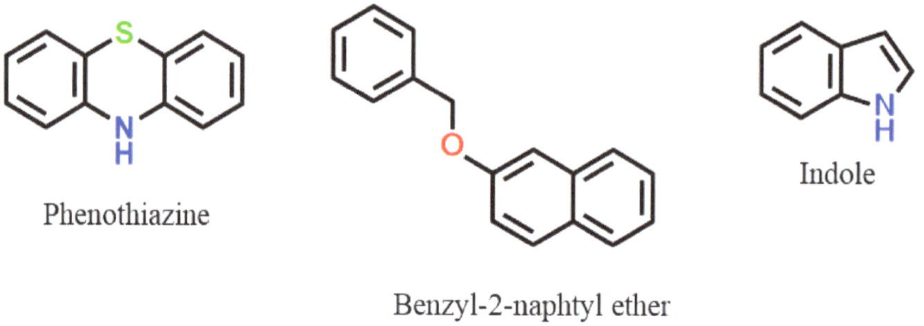

Figure 11. Examples of aromatic molecules that eluted to the Aro-3 fraction that would have otherwise eluted in the Aro-2 fraction if the heteroatoms were replaced by carbon atoms. (The green color designates sulfur atom, the blue color—NH group, and the red color—oxygen atom).

Other functional groups, like carbazole, can cause non-heteroatom parent PAHs that report to Aro-3 to partially elute into the subsequent Resins fraction. For example, tetracene elutes exclusively with the Aro-3 fraction. However, by replacing the aromatic unit with a pyrrolic group, such as in 11H-benzo[a]carbazole, the molecule begins to partition into the Resins fraction (15%). By adding another aromatic unit and also changing the geometry of the molecule from a linear to a "U" shape (7H-dibenzo[c,g] carbazole), a greater net dipole is present, and the pyrrolic molecule contributes even more in the Resins fraction (30%). Figure 12 shows the molecular structures for 11H-benzo[a]carbazole and 7H-dibenzo[c,g] carbazole. In general, the slight shift to the Resins fraction due to the pyrrolic functional groups is not as significant as for other functional groups.

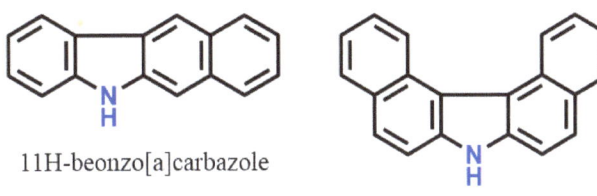

Figure 12. Molecular structures for pyrrolics containing 11H-benzo[a]carbazole and 7H-dibenzo[c,g] carbazole. These molecules belong mostly to the Aro-3 fraction and partially to the Resins fraction. (The blue color indicates the NH group).

More polar ketone and acyl groups connected to Aro-2 parent molecules (like anthracene or pyrene) cause these molecules to report heavily to the Aro-3 fraction with only minor partitioning into the Resins fraction (~<10%). Similar elution patterns were observed with the addition of the amino group in 1-aminopyrene. However, this observation may be more related to the interaction of the amine functional groups with the aminopropyl silica sorbent. Figure 13 shows some examples of model molecules that report mostly to the Aro-3 fraction but would otherwise report to the Aro-2 fraction in the absence of the functional groups.

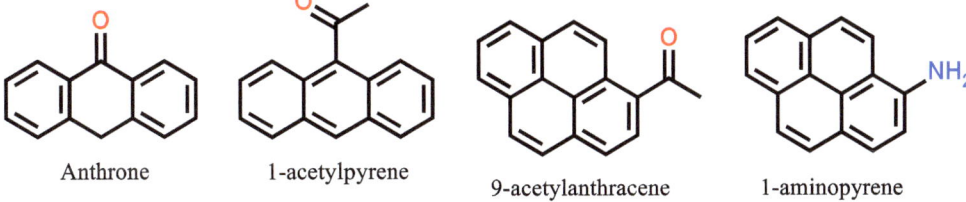

Figure 13. Examples of aromatic molecules that eluted to the Aro-3 fraction that would have otherwise eluted in the Aro-2 fraction if the heteroatoms were replaced by hydrogen atoms. (The red color indicates oxygen atom, and the blue color—the NH_2 group).

Hydroxyl groups are significantly more polar than ketone and acyl groups, and they can participate in strong intermolecular hydrogen-bonding interactions. By placing a hydroxyl group on a highly saturated hydrocarbon, it causes the molecule to report to the Aro-3 fraction with some elution into the Resins fraction (about 10%). This is the case with beta-sitosterol (Figure 14).

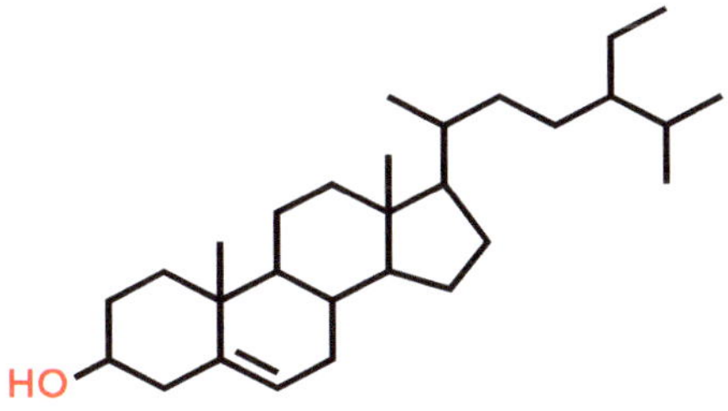

Figure 14. The molecular structure of beta-sitosterol has been attributed mainly to the Aro-3 fraction (~90%) due to the presence of the hydroxyl group. Stereochemistry is omitted for clarity. (The red color indicates OH group).

Phenolic groups are more acidic than aliphatic hydroxyl groups and are expected to produce stronger intermolecular hydrogen bonding. In 4-nonylphenol and 4-dodecylphenol, the phenolic groups and aromatic rings cause these molecules to report exclusively to the Resins fraction. Without the phenolic OH groups, these molecules would normally report to the Aro-1 fraction. Likewise, phenolic groups on anthracene and pyrene cause these molecules to report to the Resins fraction, whereas without the phenolic groups, the parent fused-ring aromatic molecules would report to the Aro-2 fraction. The addition of a less acidic methanolic (CH_2-OH) functional group on fused-ring aromatics, such as 9-anthracenemethanol, also caused the compound to report to the Resins fraction. Other polar functional groups can significantly change the elution of Aro-2 parent fused-ring molecules to report to the Resins fraction. For instance, having two pyridinic nitrogen atoms, as in 1,10′-phenanthroline, allows for a strong chelating effect of the nitrogen groups at active sorbent sites, also causing this molecule to report to the Resins fraction. It is likely that nitrogen substitution at other positions may not have such a strong effect since they would not lend themselves to the chelating effect; for instance, the single nitrogen in phenanthradine still caused the molecule to report to the Aro-2 fraction (Figure 7), like its non-nitrogen-containing analogue phenanthrene. Figure 15 shows various model compound molecules that eluted in the Resins fraction that would otherwise report to less polar aromatic fractions in the absence of their heteroatoms.

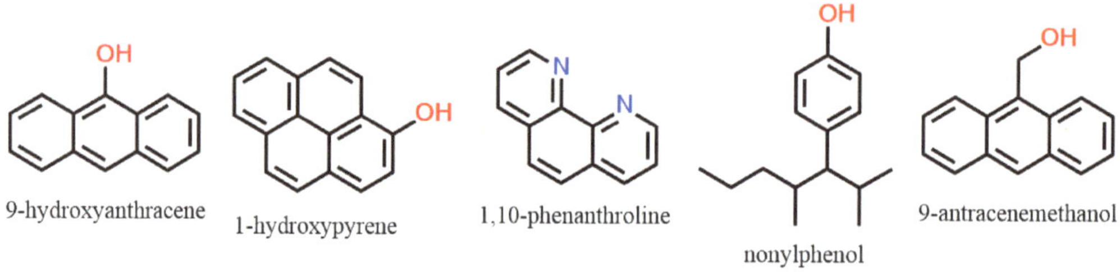

Figure 15. Molecular structures of model compounds that eluted to the Resins fraction. For simplicity, a single isomeric structure for nonylphenol is shown. (The red color indicates OH group, while the blue color designates nitrogen atom).

As shown in Figure 1 and as mentioned previously, elution of asphaltenes occurs in SAR-AD after Aro-1, but will be discussed at this time to preserve continuity of the bitumen solubility/polarity spectrum discussion. Finding reasonable model compounds that report to the three SAR-AD asphaltene subfractions is not trivial. Interestingly, addition of phenyl groups to 1,10-phenathroline, as is the case with bathophenanthroline (Figure 16), caused this compound to elute between the Toluene asphaltenes and the Resins fraction. The split between the two fractions was around 1:1. It should be noted that the SAR-AD separation was not optimized to separate discrete pure compounds but rather to provide a generic and highly repeatable cut point for the separation of complex mixtures of thousands of different compounds. Therefore, it is expected that some model compounds will not cleanly report to a single fraction.

Other types of molecules that were found to report to the asphaltene subfractions were acenaphthenequinone; Coumarin 343; acenaphthenequinone; N,N-bis-2-ethylhexyl-3,4,9,10-perylenetetracarboxylic diimide; and the charged Reichardt's dye molecule. Admittedly, these molecules are not ideal asphaltene models in terms of covering asphaltene average properties for molecular weight, heteroatom content, aromaticity, and functional group type. However, they do provide some insight about the SAR-AD separation and the relationship between molecular size, structure, and functional groups. The molecular structures of the asphaltene model compounds are shown in Figure 17.

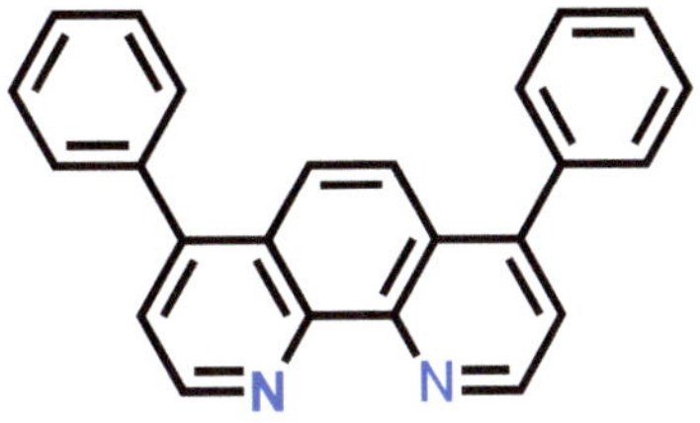

Bathophenanthroline

Figure 16. Molecular structure for bathophenanthroline, which reports to the Resins and Toluene asphaltene fraction (1:1).

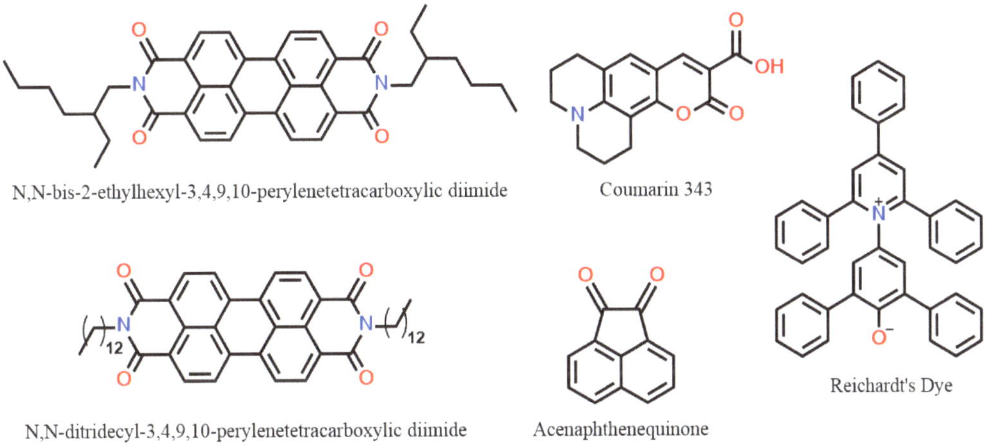

N,N-bis-2-ethylhexyl-3,4,9,10-perylenetetracarboxylic diimide

Coumarin 343

N,N-ditridecyl-3,4,9,10-perylenetetracarboxylic diimide

Acenaphthenequinone

Reichardt's Dye

Figure 17. Molecular structure for model compounds acenaphthenequinone (MW = 182.17 Daltons); Coumarin 343 (MW = 285.29 Daltons); N,N-bis-2-ethylhexyl-3,4,9,10-perylenetetracarboxylic diimide (MW = 614.79 Daltons); and N,N-ditridecyl-3,4,9,10-perylenetetracarboxylic diimide (MW = 755.06 Daltons). Reichardt's dye reports to the CH2Cl2 asphaltenes, while the other molecules elute to the Toluene asphaltenes.

With the exception of Reichardt's dye, all of these molecules consist of polar carbonyl groups, and Coumarin 343 also consists of a carboxylic group. For model compounds to be insoluble in heptane (and thus precipitated on the first analytical column using the SAR-AD technique) but soluble in toluene, there needs to be a balance between the size, polarity (such as the very small but polar acenaphthenequinone), and aromaticity. Coumarin 343 is small and contains a polar carbonyl and carboxylic group, but has two naphthenic cycles, and N,N-bis-2-ethylhexyl-3,4,9,10-perylenetetracarboxylic diimide (MW = 614.79 Daltons) contains four carbonyl groups but two longer branched aliphatic chains. It should be noted that the longer-chain compound N,N-ditridecyl-3,4,9,10-perlenetetracarboxylic diimide (MW = 755.06 Daltons) was also tested and eluted mostly in the Toluene asphaltene fraction, but it was significantly less soluble. Again, with the exception of Reichardt's dye, other asphaltene model compounds showed up primarily in the Toluene asphaltenes, with less than 10% reporting to the CH_2Cl_2 asphaltenes. On the other hand, Reichardt's dye, a charged molecule, reported primarily to the CH_2Cl_2 asphaltene fraction. It would be of interest to determine more realistic model compounds that report to the three different asphaltene subfractions, especially the CyC_6 asphaltenes and CH_2Cl_2 asphaltenes, since these fractions are heavily impacted by the oxidation of asphalt and the pyrolysis of various petroleum feedstocks (the Coking Index for example). It is also important to determine if blends of the various compounds cause interactions that change their co-solubility or elution behavior.

A limited study was performed using porphyrins and their metal complexes. Metalloporphyrins are extremely important since they affect catalyst performance and coke quality. For more aliphatic porphyrins, like octaethylporphyrin, and more aromatic tetraphenylporphyrin, both of these molecules were reported to the Aro-3 fraction. These results are consistent with those of other model compounds in this study, which showed that the pyrrolic group is not highly polar. The metalation of nickel II to etioporphyrin is not expected to change the polarity of the porphyrin system significantly. This was confirmed as the etioporphyrin I nickel complex reported to the Aro-3 fraction. Figure 18 shows the molecular structures for octaethylporphyrin, tetraphenylporphyrin, and etioporphyrin I nickel.

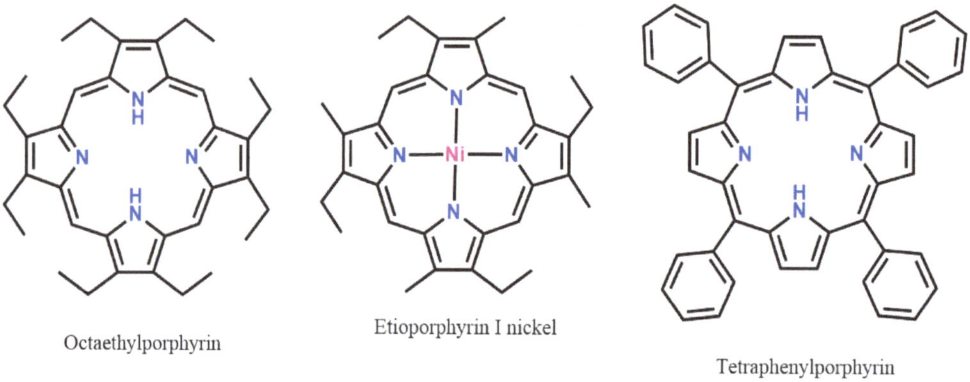

Figure 18. Molecular structures for octaethylporphyrin, tetraphenylporphyrin, and etioporphyrin I nickel, which elute the Aro-3 fraction.

However, vanadium IV oxide porphyrins contain an out-of-plane carbonyl group, which would induce a strong dipole in the complex, causing it to become more polar. This was confirmed as vanadyl octaethylporphyrin eluting in the Resins fraction. Figure 19 shows the molecular structure of vanadyl octaethylporphyrin.

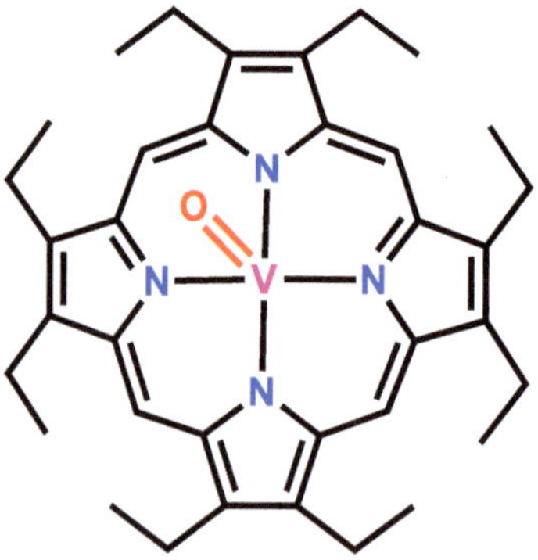

Figure 19. Molecular structure for vanadyl octaethylporphyrin, which elutes to the Resins fraction.

For validation, the petroleum porphyrins concentrated from the Canadian Peace River bitumen (Figure 2) were analyzed by SAR-AD and were found to be concentrated primarily in the Aro-3 and Resins fractions (1.2:1 by ELSD), with less than 10% also showing up in the asphaltenes.

3.2. SAR-AD Hydrocracker Relationships

The primary issue that needs to be overcome with ebullated bed vacuum residues is the formation of coke-like sediments that deposit on the reactor and downstream vessels as well as on the catalyst surface and cause both operability and rapid catalyst deactivation problems [64,65]. Their level in the hydrocracked residual oils determines the hydrocracking reaction severity [66], and it is considered acceptable when the total sediment existent (TSE) in the atmospheric tower bottom (ATB) product is no higher than 0.3–0.4 wt.%. Such a level of ATB TSE guarantees smooth operation and achievement of the planned cycle length between two consecutive cleanings of the commercial ebullated bed vacuum residue hydrocracker unit. In this research, nine cases were investigated where the vacuum residue conversion varied between 55 and 91%. For these cases, the SAR-AD fraction contents, along with reaction temperature, liquid hourly space velocity (LHSV), and bulk properties of the hydrocracked vacuum residues, called vacuum tower bottoms (VTBs), are presented in Table 2.

The data in Table 2 show that the ATB sediment content for the studied cases varied between 0.04 and 2.2 wt.%. Three of the ATB TSE cases are distinguishable because their sediment is greater than 0.4 wt.%. These are higher than the allowable limits, and, as a result, they caused increased fouling in the commercial hydrocracker [54,67].

In order to assess which parameters contribute to the increased ATB sediment content, an intercriteria analysis (ICrA) of the data in Table 2 was performed. The ICrA evaluation determines the degrees of correlation between the criteria, depending on the user's choice of μ and ν. These correlations between the criteria are classified as follows: 'positive consonance', 'negative consonance' or 'dissonance' [68]. The values of μ in the range $0.75 \div 1.00$ and $\nu = 0.00 \div 0.25$ denote a statistically meaningful positive relation. Respectively, the values of negative consonance with $\mu = 0.00 \div 0.25$ and $\nu = 0.75 \div 1.0$ represent a statistically meaningful negative relation. Details of the ICrA application to investigate petroleum property relations are given in our prior publications [61,62].

To visualize the results in the ICrA evaluation for index matrices M^μ and M^ν, we use color scales, which can be achieved with a simple function as the "Conditional Formatting" in Excel, e.g., from green for the results equal to complete intuitionistic fuzzy truth, i.e., the pair $\langle 1,0 \rangle$ to red for the results equal to complete intuitionistic falsity, i.e., the pair $\langle 0,1 \rangle$. This colorization scheme allows for more immediate visual detection and interpretation of the results. Two software packages for ICrA have been developed and are freely available as open source from https://intercriteria.net/software/ (accessed on 21 March 2023); they are described in further detail in [69–72]. Tables 3 and 4 summarize the results for μ and ν values of the ICrA evaluation.

Table 2. Bulk properties and SAR-AD characteristics of hydrocracked vacuum residues (VTB) obtained at the commercial LNB H-Oil hydrocracker.

Cases	Case 1	Case 2	Case 3	Case 4	Case 5	Case 6	Case 7	Case 8	Case 9
Date	22 December 2015	6 November 2015	10 July 2017	21 January 2019	9 May 2017	16 April 2019	12 August 2020	21 February 2022	11 April 2022
Crude slate	100% Urals	100% Urals	85% Ur/15% ME	80% Ur/20% ME	70% Ur/30% ME	14% Ur.36% LSCO/50% ME	61.5% Ur/3% BL/2% AM/19.5% Kirkuk/7.5% LSCO/6.5% Prinos	64% Ur/25% Kirkuk/11% BL	88.6% Ur/5% LSCO/6.5% Kirkuk
FCC slurry, % in H-Oil feed	0.0	0.0	7.6	6.1	8.2	7.5	13.1	0.0	11.5
H-Oil VTB recycle, % of feed	0.0	0.0	0.0	0.0	0.0	0.0	29.4	0.0	0.0
Weight average bed temperature. °C	409	418	426	425	428	426	430.5	429.5	414.5
LHSV. h-1	0.23	0.25	0.21	0.20	0.20	0.17	0.10	0.16	0.14
Atmospheric tower bottom product (ATB) SHFT. wt.%	0.3	2.2	0.4	0.4	0.25	0.04	0.11	0.55	0.46
H-Oil 540 °C + conversion. wt.%	55	65	71.6	73	74.5	76.3	90.8	78	62
Density at 15 °C. g/cm^3	0.985	1.005	1.029	1.033	1.041	1.034	1.093	1.066	1.018
Conradson carbon. wt.%	17.9	20.4	24.4	26	25.5	25.8	35.0	30.5	14.9
Sulfur. wt.%	1.1	1.3	1.38	1.24	1.4	1.3	1.3	1.9	1.3
SAR-AD characteristics									
Saturates, wt.%	27.44	26.98	21.01	21.96	19.76	19.72	13.85	18.66	21.48
Aro-1, wt.%	9.34	8.22	6.85	7.15	6.77	7.48	3.04	5.92	8.41
Aro-2, wt.%	18.76	17.43	16.89	17.82	17.35	18.80	14.75	18.07	20.30
Aro-3, wt.%	33.41	34.59	43.04	40.77	44.09	44.86	60.20	44.74	39.67
Resins, wt.%	6.03	5.93	5.97	6.19	6.01	4.37	2.46	4.42	4.17
CyC$_6$ asphaltenes, wt.%	0.38	0.34	0.23	0.25	0.23	0.17	0.07	0.22	0.14
Toluene asphaltenes, wt.%	4.47	6.12	5.56	5.47	5.47	4.28	4.90	7.00	5.28
CH$_2$Cl$_2$ asphaltenes, wt.%	0.18	0.39	0.46	0.39	0.33	0.32	0.71	0.95	0.53
Total asphaltenes, wt.%	5.03	6.85	6.24	6.11	6.03	4.77	5.68	8.17	5.95
CyC$_6$/CH$_2$Cl$_2$	2.10	0.89	0.49	0.66	0.71	0.55	0.10	0.23	0.27
TPA	16.96	17.96	18.96	19.96	19.96	20.96	11.22	14.24	10.71
Colloidal instability index (CII)	0.718	0.726	0.517	0.544	0.483	0.470	0.292	0.487	0.559
Maltenes Index (MI)	0.632	0.607	0.423	0.449	0.393	0.400	0.218	0.365	0.466
Modified colloidal instability index (MCII)	0.707	0.715	0.512	0.538	0.478	0.466	0.290	0.482	0.555

Table 3. μ-value of the ICrA evaluation of relations between bulk properties, SAR-AD characteristics of H-Oil VTB, and reaction severity. SLO = FCC slurry (% in H-Oil feed), Rec = H-Oil VTB recycle (% of feed), TRX = Weight average bed temperature (°C), LHSV = LHSV (h^{-1}), ATB TSE = Atmospheric tower bottom product (ATB) SHFT (wt.%), Conv. = H-Oil 540 °C + conversion (wt.%), D15 = Density at 15 °C (g/cm³), CCR = Conradson carbon (wt.%), Sul = Sulfur (wt.%).

MU	SLO	Rec	TRX	LHSV	ATB TSE	Conv.	D15	CCR	Sul	Sat	Aro-1	Aro-2	Aro-3	Resins	CyC$_6$	Toluene	CH$_2$Cl$_2$	Total	CyC$_6$/CH$_2$Cl$_2$	TPA	CII	MI	MCII
SLO	1.00	0.31	0.61	0.19	0.28	0.56	0.61	0.47	0.44	0.28	0.31	0.36	0.64	0.28	0.14	0.28	0.58	0.28	0.22	0.42	0.25	0.28	0.25
Rec	0.31	1.00	0.25	0.03	0.06	0.22	0.22	0.22	0.14	0.00	0.00	0.00	0.22	0.00	0.03	0.08	0.22	0.06	0.00	0.06	0.00	0.00	0.00
TRX	0.61	0.25	1.00	0.25	0.36	0.92	0.92	0.83	0.67	0.08	0.03	0.28	0.89	0.36	0.22	0.56	0.64	0.56	0.22	0.50	0.14	0.03	0.14
LHSV	0.19	0.03	0.25	1.00	0.58	0.19	0.19	0.25	0.31	0.81	0.67	0.42	0.22	0.75	0.86	0.64	0.28	0.61	0.83	0.61	0.75	0.75	0.75
ATB TSE	0.28	0.06	0.36	0.58	1.00	0.33	0.33	0.36	0.47	0.64	0.56	0.53	0.28	0.53	0.58	0.78	0.64	0.81	0.47	0.33	0.75	0.64	0.75
Conv.	0.56	0.22	0.92	0.19	0.33	1.00	0.94	0.92	0.61	0.08	0.11	0.36	0.92	0.36	0.22	0.50	0.58	0.50	0.25	0.58	0.14	0.08	0.14
D15	0.61	0.22	0.92	0.19	0.33	0.94	1.00	0.86	0.64	0.08	0.11	0.36	0.92	0.36	0.22	0.50	0.64	0.50	0.25	0.53	0.14	0.03	0.14
CCR	0.47	0.22	0.83	0.25	0.36	0.92	0.86	1.00	0.53	0.17	0.14	0.33	0.83	0.44	0.31	0.50	0.61	0.53	0.28	0.58	0.22	0.17	0.22
Sul	0.44	0.14	0.67	0.31	0.47	0.61	0.64	0.53	1.00	0.17	0.17	0.33	0.61	0.36	0.28	0.61	0.58	0.61	0.25	0.42	0.28	0.17	0.28
Sat	0.28	0.00	0.08	0.81	0.64	0.08	0.08	0.17	0.17	1.00	0.86	0.61	0.06	0.72	0.83	0.50	0.31	0.53	0.83	0.47	0.89	0.94	0.89
Aro-1	0.31	0.00	0.03	0.67	0.56	0.11	0.11	0.14	0.17	0.86	1.00	0.75	0.14	0.58	0.69	0.36	0.28	0.39	0.75	0.50	0.81	0.92	0.81
Aro-2	0.36	0.00	0.28	0.42	0.53	0.36	0.36	0.33	0.33	0.61	0.75	1.00	0.39	0.44	0.47	0.39	0.39	0.42	0.56	0.47	0.61	0.67	0.61
Aro-3	0.64	0.22	0.89	0.22	0.28	0.92	0.92	0.83	0.61	0.06	0.14	0.39	1.00	0.28	0.14	0.47	0.61	0.47	0.22	0.56	0.06	0.06	0.06
Resins	0.28	0.00	0.36	0.75	0.53	0.36	0.36	0.44	0.36	0.72	0.58	0.44	0.28	1.00	0.86	0.50	0.28	0.53	0.78	0.69	0.67	0.67	0.67
CyC$_6$	0.14	0.03	0.22	0.86	0.58	0.22	0.22	0.31	0.28	0.83	0.69	0.47	0.14	0.86	1.00	0.56	0.25	0.58	0.86	0.56	0.78	0.78	0.78
Toluene	0.28	0.08	0.56	0.64	0.78	0.50	0.50	0.50	0.61	0.50	0.36	0.39	0.47	0.50	0.56	1.00	0.64	0.97	0.47	0.42	0.56	0.44	0.56
CH$_2$Cl$_2$	0.58	0.22	0.64	0.28	0.64	0.58	0.64	0.61	0.58	0.31	0.28	0.39	0.61	0.28	0.25	0.64	1.00	0.67	0.14	0.25	0.42	0.31	0.42
Total	0.28	0.06	0.56	0.61	0.81	0.50	0.50	0.53	0.61	0.53	0.39	0.42	0.47	0.53	0.58	0.97	0.67	1.00	0.47	0.39	0.58	0.47	0.58
CyC$_6$/CH$_2$Cl$_2$	0.22	0.00	0.22	0.83	0.47	0.25	0.25	0.28	0.25	0.83	0.75	0.56	0.22	0.78	0.86	0.47	0.14	0.47	1.00	0.61	0.72	0.78	0.72
TPA	0.42	0.06	0.50	0.61	0.33	0.58	0.53	0.58	0.42	0.47	0.50	0.47	0.56	0.69	0.56	0.42	0.25	0.39	0.61	1.00	0.42	0.47	0.42
CII	0.25	0.00	0.14	0.75	0.75	0.14	0.14	0.22	0.28	0.89	0.81	0.61	0.06	0.67	0.78	0.56	0.42	0.58	0.72	0.42	1.00	0.89	1.00
MI	0.28	0.00	0.03	0.75	0.64	0.08	0.03	0.17	0.17	0.94	0.92	0.67	0.06	0.67	0.78	0.44	0.31	0.47	0.78	0.47	0.89	1.00	0.89
MCII	0.25	0.00	0.14	0.75	0.75	0.14	0.14	0.22	0.28	0.89	0.81	0.61	0.06	0.67	0.78	0.56	0.42	0.58	0.72	0.42	1.00	0.89	1.00

Note: Green color denotes statistically meaningful positive relation; red color denotes statistically meaningful negative relation. The intensity of the color designates the strength of the relation. The higher the color intensity, the higher the strength of the relation. Yellow color denotes dissonance.

Table 4. υ-value of the ICrA evaluation of relations between bulk properties, SAR-AD characteristics of H-Oil VTB, and reaction severity. SLO = FCC slurry (% in H-Oil feed), Rec = H-Oil VTB recycle (% of feed), TRX = Weight average bed temperature (°C), LHSV = LHSV (h^{-1}), ATB TSE = Atmospheric tower bottom product (ATB) SHFT (wt.%), Conv. = H-Oil 540 °C + conversion (wt.%), D15 = Density at 15 °C (g/cm^3), CCR = Conradson carbon (wt.%), Sul = Sulfur (wt.%).

Nu	SLO	Rec	TRX	LHSV	ATB TSE	Conv.	D15	CCR	Sul	Sat	Aro-1	Aro-2	Aro-3	Resins	CyC6	Toluene	CH$_2$Cl$_2$	Total	CyC6/CH$_2$Cl$_2$	TPA	CII	MI	MCII
SLO		0.00	0.28	0.69	0.61	0.36	0.31	0.44	0.31	0.64	0.61	0.56	0.28	0.64	0.75	0.61	0.31	0.64	0.69	0.47	0.67	0.64	0.67
Rec	0.00		0.00	0.22	0.19	0.00	0.00	0.00	0.08	0.22	0.22	0.22	0.00	0.22	0.22	0.17	0.03	0.17	0.22	0.19	0.22	0.22	0.22
TRX	0.28	0.00		0.69	0.58	0.06	0.06	0.14	0.14	0.89	0.94	0.69	0.08	0.61	0.72	0.39	0.31	0.42	0.75	0.44	0.83	0.94	0.83
LHSV	0.69	0.22	0.69		0.36	0.78	0.78	0.72	0.50	0.17	0.31	0.56	0.75	0.22	0.08	0.36	0.67	0.36	0.14	0.39	0.22	0.22	0.22
ATB TSE	0.61	0.19	0.58	0.36		0.64	0.64	0.61	0.33	0.33	0.42	0.44	0.69	0.44	0.36	0.17	0.31	0.17	0.50	0.39	0.22	0.33	0.22
Conv.	0.36	0.00	0.06	0.78	0.64		0.06	0.08	0.22	0.92	0.89	0.64	0.08	0.64	0.75	0.47	0.39	0.50	0.75	0.61	0.86	0.92	0.86
D15	0.31	0.00	0.06	0.78	0.64	0.06		0.14	0.19	0.92	0.89	0.64	0.08	0.64	0.75	0.47	0.33	0.50	0.75	0.44	0.86	0.97	0.86
CCR	0.44	0.00	0.14	0.72	0.61	0.08	0.14		0.31	0.83	0.86	0.67	0.17	0.56	0.67	0.47	0.36	0.47	0.72	0.39	0.78	0.83	0.78
Sul	0.31	0.08	0.14	0.50	0.33	0.22	0.19	0.31		0.67	0.67	0.50	0.22	0.47	0.53	0.19	0.22	0.22	0.58	0.39	0.56	0.67	0.56
Sat	0.64	0.22	0.89	0.17	0.33	0.92	0.92	0.83	0.67		0.14	0.39	0.94	0.28	0.14	0.47	0.67	0.47	0.17	0.50	0.11	0.06	0.11
Aro-1	0.61	0.22	0.94	0.31	0.42	0.89	0.89	0.86	0.67	0.14		0.25	0.86	0.42	0.28	0.61	0.69	0.61	0.25	0.47	0.19	0.08	0.19
Aro-2	0.56	0.22	0.69	0.56	0.44	0.64	0.64	0.67	0.50	0.39	0.25		0.61	0.56	0.50	0.58	0.58	0.58	0.44	0.50	0.39	0.33	0.39
Aro-3	0.28	0.00	0.08	0.75	0.69	0.08	0.08	0.17	0.22	0.94	0.86	0.61		0.72	0.83	0.50	0.36	0.53	0.78	0.42	0.94	0.94	0.94
Resins	0.64	0.22	0.61	0.22	0.44	0.64	0.64	0.56	0.47	0.28	0.42	0.56	0.72		0.11	0.47	0.69	0.47	0.22	0.28	0.33	0.33	0.33
CyC6	0.75	0.22	0.72	0.08	0.36	0.75	0.75	0.67	0.53	0.14	0.28	0.50	0.83	0.11		0.39	0.69	0.39	0.11	0.39	0.19	0.19	0.19
Toluene	0.61	0.17	0.39	0.36	0.17	0.47	0.47	0.47	0.19	0.47	0.61	0.58	0.50	0.47	0.39		0.31	0.00	0.50	0.58	0.42	0.53	0.42
CH$_2$Cl$_2$	0.31	0.03	0.31	0.67	0.31	0.39	0.33	0.36	0.22	0.67	0.69	0.58	0.36	0.69	0.69	0.31		0.31	0.83	0.69	0.56	0.67	0.56
Total	0.64	0.17	0.42	0.36	0.17	0.50	0.50	0.47	0.22	0.47	0.61	0.58	0.53	0.47	0.39	0.00	0.31		0.53	0.58	0.42	0.53	0.42
CyC6/CH$_2$Cl$_2$	0.69	0.22	0.75	0.14	0.50	0.75	0.75	0.72	0.58	0.17	0.25	0.44	0.78	0.22	0.11	0.50	0.83	0.53		0.36	0.28	0.22	0.28
TPA	0.47	0.19	0.44	0.39	0.61	0.39	0.44	0.39	0.39	0.50	0.47	0.50	0.42	0.28	0.39	0.58	0.69	0.58	0.36		0.56	0.50	0.56
CII	0.67	0.22	0.83	0.22	0.22	0.86	0.86	0.78	0.56	0.11	0.19	0.39	0.94	0.33	0.19	0.42	0.56	0.42	0.28	0.56		0.11	0.00
MI	0.64	0.22	0.94	0.22	0.33	0.92	0.97	0.83	0.67	0.06	0.08	0.33	0.94	0.33	0.19	0.53	0.67	0.53	0.22	0.50	0.11		0.11
MCII	0.67	0.22	0.83	0.22	0.22	0.86	0.86	0.78	0.56	0.11	0.19	0.39	0.94	0.33	0.19	0.42	0.56	0.42	0.28	0.56	0.00	0.11	

Note: Green color denotes statistically meaningful positive relation; red color denotes statistically meaningful negative relation. The intensity of the color designates the strength of the relation. The higher the color intensity, the higher the strength of the relation. Yellow color denotes dissonance.

Based on the μ and υ values of the ICrA evaluation, one can see that the sediment content in the H-Oil ATB product has statistically meaningful positive relationships with the total asphaltene content ($\mu = 0.81$; $\upsilon = 0.17$); the Toluene asphaltenes ($\mu = 0.78$; $\upsilon = 0.17$); the CII ($\mu = 0.75$; $\upsilon = 0.22$); and the MCII ($\mu = 0.75$; $\upsilon = 0.22$). These results confirm that asphaltenes are primarily responsible for sediment formation during hydrocracking due to their inclination to aggregate, strongly adsorb to surfaces, and promote condensation and crosslinking reactions [73–87]. The data in Tables 3 and 4 suggest that the concentration of Toluene asphaltenes, which are the predominant part of the H-Oil VTB, affects the sediment formation in the H-Oil hydrocracked residual oils. The results also show that CH_2Cl_2 asphaltenes have a stronger influence on the sediment content than CyC_6 asphaltenes. However, the most polar pre-coked CH_2Cl_2 asphaltenes at these low levels in the feeds may not be as polar as the Toluene asphaltenes because they are almost an order of magnitude smaller in amount.

Apart from asphaltene content, sediment formation has been reported to be significantly affected by reaction conditions like LHSV, reaction time, temperature, pressure, and catalytic active site concentration [76,77,80–82,87]. This can explain why the positive consonance of the H-Oil ATB sediment content with the VTB asphaltene content alone, although statistically meaningful, is still weak. This implies that the LHSV, the fresh catalyst addition rate (solid catalyst and liquid nano-dispersed HCAT [53,67] catalyst), and the temperature (pressure is constant) applied at the commercial ebullated bed vacuum residue hydrocracker also have a significant impact on the sediment formation rate.

The data in Tables 3 and 4 indicate that the reaction temperature has strong statistically meaningful consonances with conversion (positive; $\mu = 0.92$; $\upsilon = 0.06$), Saturate content (negative; $\mu = 0.08$; $\upsilon = 0.89$), Aro-1 content (negative; $\mu = 0.03$; $\upsilon = 0.94$), Maltene Index (negative; $\mu = 0.03$; $\upsilon = 0.94$) and intermediate consonances with Aro-3 content (positive; $\mu = 0.89$; $\upsilon = 0.08$), and the colloidal instability index (negative; $\mu = 0.14$; $\upsilon = 0.83$). These findings show that the increase in reaction temperature understandably enhances the conversion of the thermally sensitive Saturates, and Aro-1, with some dependence on Aro-3 components. With increasing temperature, thermal cracking reactions increase more rapidly than their hydrogen addition counterparts [88]. Increasing temperature results in the rapid depletion of VTB Saturates, and Aro-1. These two fractions can continue thermal cracking and conversion, eventually producing gas. However, polyaromatic core structures mostly remain intact, and if they do not become small enough to enter the vapor phase, they can eventually undergo crosslinking and coke formation.

The relationship between polycyclic aromatic molecules in Aro-3 is complex. Cleavage of aliphatic groups, or smaller pendant aromatics, from Aro-3 polyaromatic cores should mostly result in producing smaller Aro-3 core molecular fragments from the parent molecule.

During hydrocracking, some FCC slurry oil is added to the blends. FCC slurry oil is highly aromatic and enriched in predominantly 3–5 aromatic ring systems [89] and is a good control oil to shed some light on the behavior of the aromatic fractions during pyrolysis. Pyrolysis experiments with FCC slurry oil showed that Aro-3 increased due to aromatic addition reactions. This is shown in Table 5. Coincidentally, this experiment also shows the rapid degradation and near-complete conversion of the Saturates fraction, consistent with alkane pyrolysis. In addition to these factors, Aro-3 molecules can be produced by the thermal degradation of asphaltenes. For asphaltenes, both island- and archipelago-type structures have been identified in a wide range of crude sources at varying ratios, which also has a significant impact on various fluid and processing phenomena [90–94]. The amount of Aro-3 produced will be highly dependent on the chemistry of the asphaltenes and whether they are more island- or archipelago-type. In a hydrocracker, hydrogen is intended to cap radicals produced from thermal bond breaking, so it is likely that aromatic addition reactions are somewhat retarded, as in the case of aromatic growth occurring in the FFC slurry oil. In the case of the production of Aro-3 from asphaltenes, this is likely more favored in the presence of hydrogen, as further reactions of heavy molecules and Aro-3 molecular fractions to form coke will be depressed. However, hydrogen is not expected to influence the initial amount of parent Aro-3 molecules fragmenting into cracked Aro-3 molecules. These results suggest that Aro-3 has a distinct and dominant reactivity, especially when compared to Aro-2. Prevailing Aro-3 relationships are likely because the reactivity of this fraction will have a large impact since it is the most abundant of the maltene fractions for the oils surveyed here. The special reaction sensitivity of this fraction may be inferred from oxidation experiments, which show that the Aro-3 fraction is readily consumed in air at 100 °C under a pressure of 2.1 mPa [95]. It is well known that benzyl carbons on aromatic molecules are some of the most reactive compounds in bitumen, so it is reasonable that they are easily reacted during pyrolysis and hydrocracking [96,97].

Table 5. SAR-AD data for FCC slurry oil pyrolyzed at 430 °C at different retention times.

Hours	Saturates	Aro-1	Aro-2	Aro-3	Resins	CyC_6	Toluene	CH_2Cl_2	Total Asp.
0	17.47	0.00	46.19	34.94	0.73	0.00	0.65	0.02	0.67
2	6.63	0.00	40.25	46.68	1.12	0.00	4.56	0.76	5.32
2.5	0.52	0.00	29.10	57.22	0.86	0.00	9.91	2.39	12.30

The LHSV has weak statistically meaningful consonances with conversion (negative; $\mu = 0.19$; $\upsilon = 0.78$), Saturate content (positive; $\mu = 0.81$; $\upsilon = 0.17$), Aro-3 content (negative; $\mu = 0.22$; $\upsilon = 0.75$), Resin content (positive; $\mu = 0.75$; $\upsilon = 0.22$), CyC_6 asphaltene content (positive; $\mu = 0.86$; $\upsilon = 0.08$), CII, and Maltene Index (positive; $\mu = 0.75$; $\upsilon = 0.22$). These findings are in line with expectations, as they show that the increase in LHSV (decrease in reaction time) leads to decreased conversion due to a low level of thermal cracking in the ebullated bed vacuum residue hydrocracking [98,99]. The level of cracking with increased LHSV will be more similar to early thermal cracking since there is less time for interaction with the catalyst and hydrogen. From this analysis, the Saturates content has a strong positive relationship with LHSV, which is likely due to its thermal sensitivity. The decomposition of Saturates relative to Aro-2 and Aro-3 is easily seen in Table 5 for FCC slurry oil, but it is not as easily seen when pyrolyzing heavy oil, as seen in Table 6 and Figure 20. This is because in the case of heavy oil, a significant amount of saturates are also generated from all the other aromatic, resin, and asphaltene fractions while the original Saturates fraction is being cracked (Table 7 shows Saturates generated from pyrolysis of only the asphaltenes). Resins and CyC_6 asphaltenes also have a positive consonance, which is related to their sensitivity to thermal cracking, as shown in Table 6 and Figure 20. It is interesting to note the sensitivity of the Resins and CyC_6 fractions since, if a molecular continuum is assumed, the main difference between these fractions and Aro-3 is largely driven by polar heteroatoms. These heteroatoms may decrease the energy barrier to thermal bond cracking in the aromatic cores, which should be explored in more detail. The Resins and CyC_6 fractions are more soluble than the other asphaltene fractions, which allows them to remain in solution longer and endure a higher level of cracking before phase separation and forming coke.

Table 6. SAR-AD data after 400 °C pyrolysis of Lloydminster vacuum residue at increasing residence time.

min @ 400 °C	Sat	Aro-1	Aro-2	Aro-3	Resins	CyC_6	Toluene	Cl_2Cl_2	Total Asph.
0	14.0	7.5	8.5	36.7	18.8	4.0	10.3	0.1	14.4
10	15.5	8.2	10.1	35.6	16.8	3.6	10.2	0.1	13.8
20	16.3	8.8	10.2	35.4	15.1	2.2	11.9	0.1	14.2
30	17.4	9.3	10.4	35.1	12.6	1.1	13.9	0.2	15.2
40	17.7	9.9	10.7	35.6	9.2	0.8	15.4	0.8	16.9
50	17.6	9.7	10.3	35.1	9.3	0.6	16.3	1.0	17.9
60	17.3	9.4	10.4	35.9	7.9	0.5	16.1	2.4	19.0

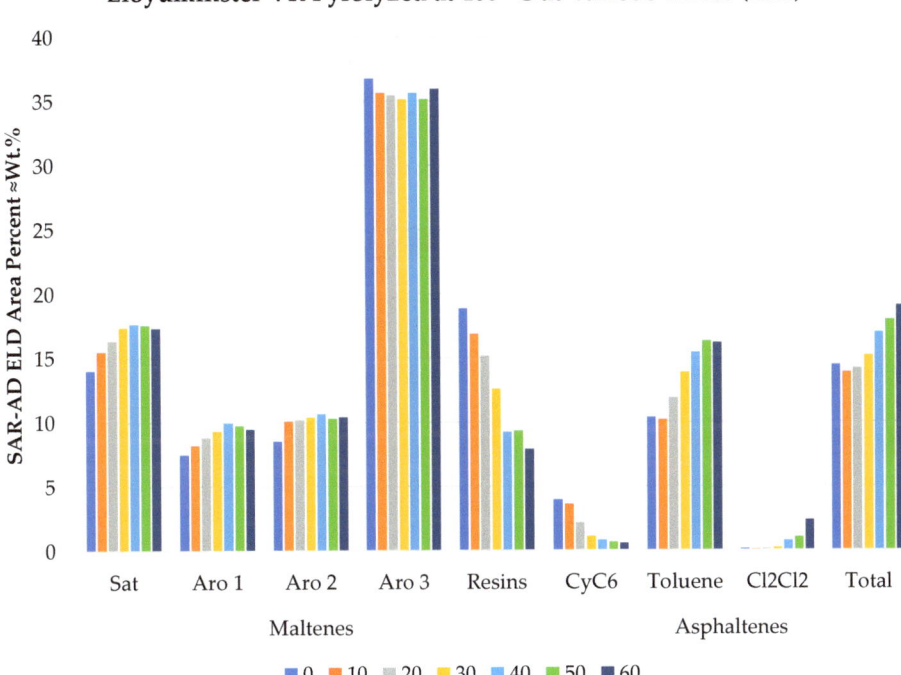

Figure 20. Plot showing the change in SAR-AD fraction from the pyrolysis of Lloydminster vacuum residue in Table 7.

Table 7. SAR-AD data for liquids produced from Lloydminster asphaltenes after heating to 500 °C.

Sample ID	Saturates	Aro-1	Aro-2	Aro-3	Resins	CyC$_6$	Toluene	CH$_2$Cl$_2$	Total Asp.
Coked Lloydminster Asphaltenes	15.62	9.02	47.13	24.55	1.28	0.11	2.09	0.20	2.40

For the various indices, CII, MCII, and MI, the MI had the strongest consonances with the following characterization factors: density at 15 °C (negative; $\mu = 0.03$; $\upsilon = 0.97$), conversion (negative; $\mu = 0.08$; $\upsilon = 0.92$), and CCR (negative; $\mu = 0.17$; $\upsilon = 0.83$). Whereas the CII and MCII were the same for conversion and density at 15 °C (negative; $\mu = 0.14$; $\upsilon = 0.86$) and the CCR had a lower consonance (negative; $\mu = 0.22$; $\upsilon = 0.78$). These relationships are expected since more aliphatic maltenes will result in higher conversion, less density, and lower coke. This is consistent with the results above. However, this does not mean that asphaltenes can be neglected because, for practical applications, they dominate catalyst performance and ATB TSE.

Figures 21 and 22 display plots of variation of Saturates, Aro-1, Aro-2, Aro-3, Resins, CyC$_6$, Toluene, and CH$_2$Cl$_2$ asphaltene fractions in the H-Oil VTBs with conversion severity juxtaposed against these SAR-AD components in the feeds. It is evident from the data in Figure 21 that Saturates increase in the VTB until very high conversion.

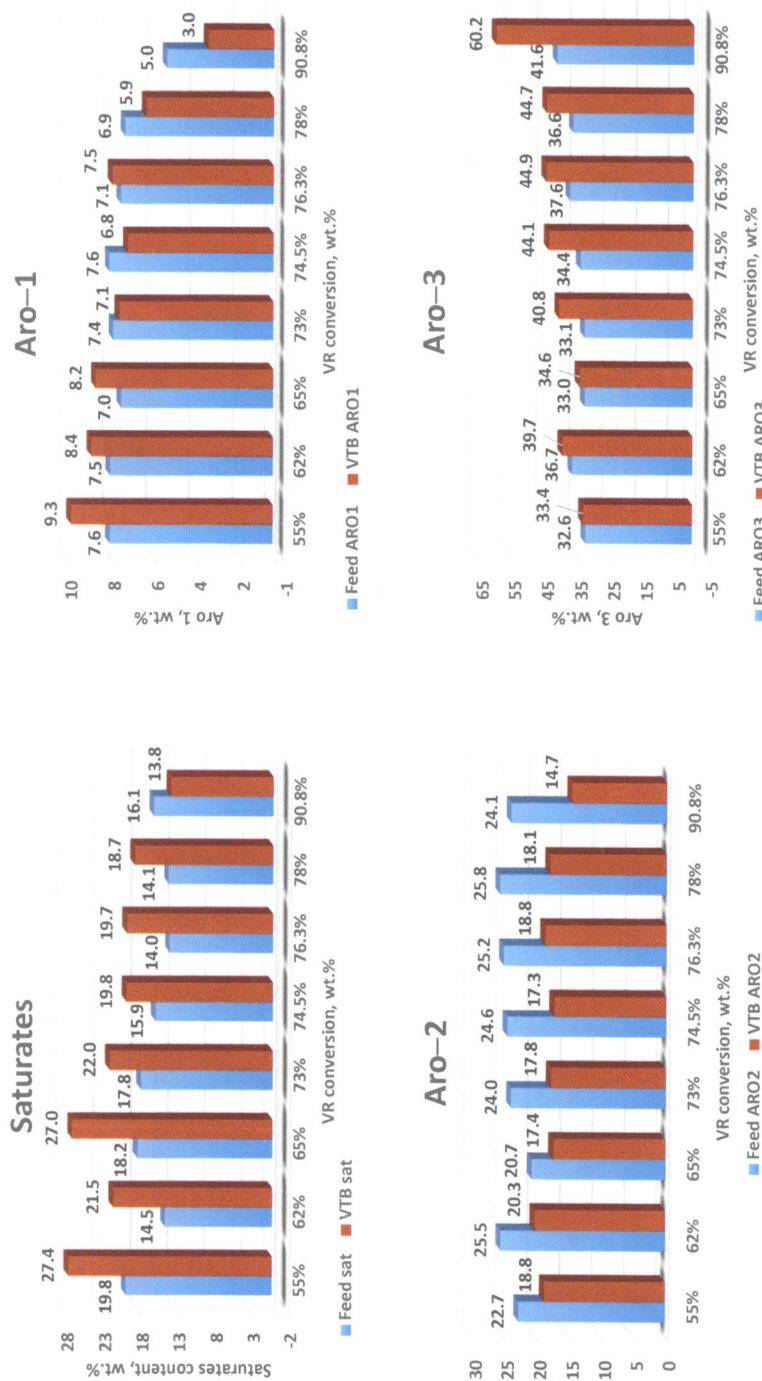

Figure 21. Variation of Saturates, Aro-1, Aro-2, and Aro-3 content in the H-Oil VTBs with conversion alteration, juxtaposed against these SAR-AD components in the feeds.

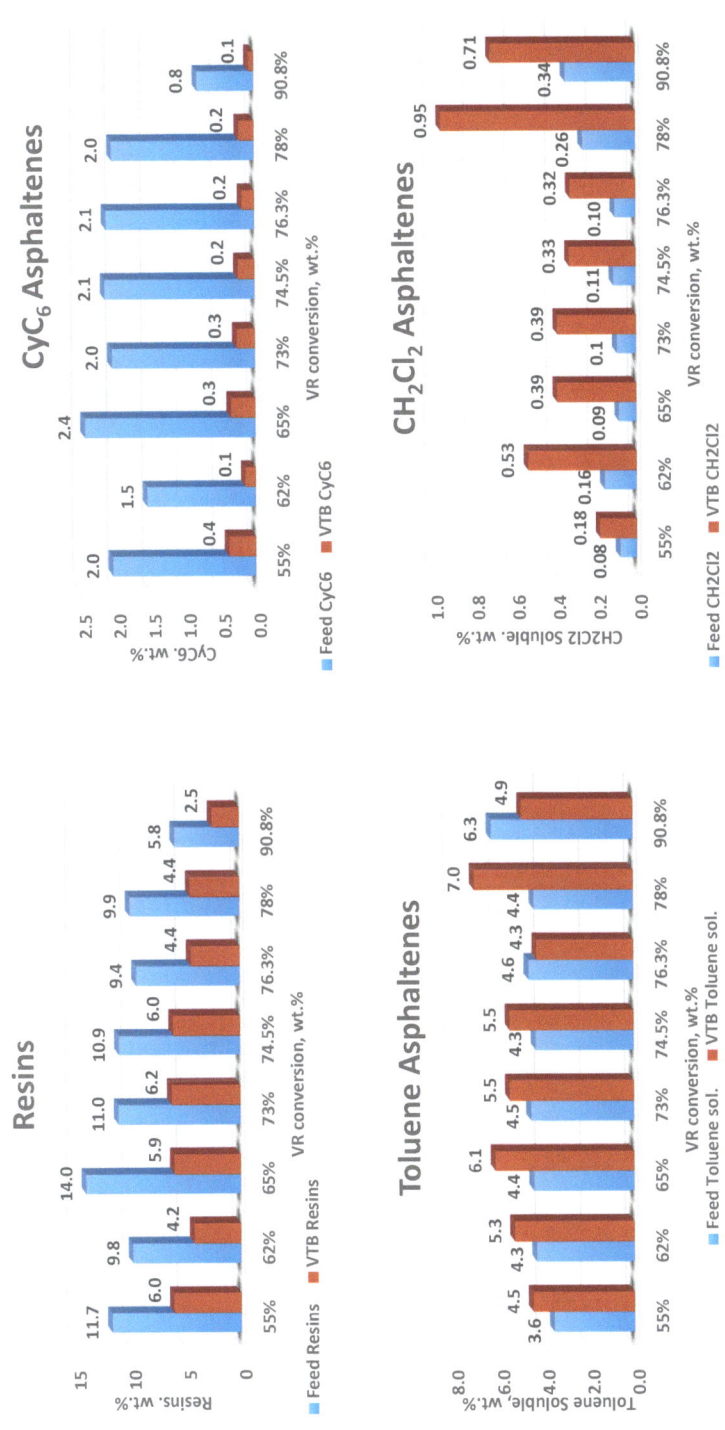

Figure 22. Variation of Resins and CyC$_6$, Toluene, and CH$_2$Cl$_2$ asphaltene content in the H-Oil VTBs with conversion alteration, juxtaposed against these SAR-AD components in the feeds.

This is because aliphatic saturated molecules can be liberated from aromatic cores when cracking asphaltenes and other heavy fractions. This is consistent with observations during thermal cracking without catalyst and hydrogen, as shown in Figure 20. Ultimately, at the highest conversion, the Saturates fraction in the VTB trended lower than the feeds, consistent with further cracking of saturate molecules decreasing in molecular weight with conversion, allowing them to be more easily removed during distillation as lighter fuel fractions. A similar trend was observed for Aro-1, except that the decrease in the VTB with conversion occurred sooner. This is consistent with the fact that Aro-1 is very similar to the Saturates fraction, and this justifies placing the Aro-1 fraction in the numerator for indices such as CII, MCII, and MI.

For the more aromatic fractions—containing fused ring systems—the Aro-2 fraction content initially decreases in the hydrocracked vacuum residue and continues decreasing with amplification of conversion, while that of Aro-3 fraction increases with conversion enhancement. Amounts of Aro-2 decrease because this fraction initially consists of molecules with 2–4 fused rings, and cracking aliphatic groups allows the residual cores to become lighter and more easily distilled. Alternatively, some aromatic ring addition reactions may occur, as in the case of FCC slurry oil (Table 5), to potentially generate Aro-3 and other molecules. Aro-3 molecules have 4+ fused rings, preventing them from becoming significantly volatile, even under severe pyrolysis and complete cracking of pendant groups. Evidence for the production of Aro-3 has also been demonstrated by coking Lloydminster archipelago-type asphaltenes, as previously mentioned (Table 6).

Various models were developed to correlate the SAR-AD data to the ebullated bed VTB hydrocracker conversion level. The dependence of the feed Saturates, Aro-1, Aro-2, and Aro-3 is expressed by the regression Equations (5)–(8). These equations reflect what is observed in the data in Figure 21, indicating that all three fractions—Saturate, Aro-1, and Aro-2—decrease their contents in the hydrocracked vacuum residue, with their contents diminishing in the feed and with enhancement of the conversion. The VTB Aro-3 fraction content also decreases with lower feed Aro-3 content but increases with conversion. As explained, this increase is probably dominated by the breakdown of asphaltene archipelago structures to generate 4+ ring aromatic molecules.

$$VTB_{Saturates} = 33.28 + 0.617046 * Feed_{Saturates} - 0.30778 * Conversion$$
$$R = 0.946; Error = 5.5\%$$
(5)

where:

$VTB_{Saturates}$—Saturate content in the vacuum tower bottom (hydrocracked vacuum residue);

$Feed_{saturates}$—Saturate content in the feed.

$$VTB_{Aro1} = 10.32 + 0.759841 * Feed_{Aro1} - 0.11986 * Conversion$$
$$R = 0.974; Error = 4.7\%$$
(6)

where:

VTB_{Aro1}—Aro-1 fraction content in the VTB;

$Feed_{Aro1}$—Aro-1 fraction content in the feed.

$$VTB_{Aro2} = 13.62 + 0.597046 * Feed_{Aro2} - 0.14038 * Conversion$$
$$R = 0.940; Error = 2.4\%$$
(7)

where:

VTB_{Aro2}—Aro-2 fraction content in the VTB;

$Feed_{Aro2}$—Aro-2 fraction content in the feed.

$$VTB_{Aro3} = -32.84 + 1.233803*Feed_{Aro3} + 0.439633*Conversion$$
$$R = 0.977;\ Error = 3.6\%$$
(8)

where:

VTB_{Aro3}—Aro-3 fraction content in the VTB;

$Feed_{Aro3}$—Aro-3 fraction content in the feed.

The data in Figure 22 show that the contents of Resins and CyC_6 asphaltenes in the VTB are lower than those in the feed, while the content of CH_2Cl_2 asphaltenes in the VTB is higher than that in the feed. The amount of the Toluene asphaltene fraction is higher than that in the feed in six of the nine cases studied. The decrease in Resins and CyC_6 asphaltenes with a corresponding increase in CH_2Cl_2 asphaltenes is consistent with previous observations [51] and thermal cracking data for Lloydminster vacuum residue as shown in Table 7 and Figure 20. When this data in Figure 20 is compared to Figure 22, the observed trends between thermal cracking and hydrocracking are quite similar.

With respect to the Toluene asphaltenes, during thermal cracking, the amount generally increases until 50 min, when it begins to decrease with a substantial increase in the CH_2Cl_2 asphaltenes. This suggests that this fraction is an intermediate fraction in that some molecules form Resins and CyC_6 asphaltenes become new Toluene asphaltenes as they lose their solubilizing aliphatic side chains, while at the same time the indigenous Toluene asphaltenes likewise transform to CH_2Cl_2 asphaltenes due to the loss of aliphatic groups. At higher conversion, the new Toluene asphaltenes also convert to CH_2Cl_2 asphaltenes, and with further conversion, they ultimately become coke [51].

The developed regression Equations (9)–(11) show that the contents of Resins, CyC_6, and CH_2Cl_2 asphaltene fractions in the VTB depend only on the contents of these fractions in the feed.

$$VTB_{Resins} = 0.5026*Feed_{Resins} - 0.233$$
$$R = 0.885;\ Error = 9.8\%$$
(9)

where:

VTB_{resins}—resins content in the VTB;

$Feed_{resins}$—resins content in the feed.

$$VTB_{CyC_6} = 0.10872*Feed_{CyC_6} - 0.00401$$
$$R = 0.864;\ Error = 18.6\%$$
(10)

where:

VTB_{CyC6}—CyC_6 asphaltene content in the VTB;

$Feed_{CyC6}$—CyC_6 asphaltene content in the feed.

$$VTB_{CH2Cl_2} = 3.5294*Feed_{CH_2Cl_2}$$
$$R = 0.960;\ Error = 19.4\%$$
(11)

where:

$VTB_{CH_2Cl_2}$—CH_2Cl_2 asphaltene content in the VTB;

$Feed_{CH_2Cl_2}$—CH_2Cl_2 asphaltene content in the feed.

In order to explore the effect of the SAR-AD eight-fraction composition of the studied straight-run vacuum residual oils processed in the LNB commercial H-Oil hydrocracker, it was necessary to define the conversion level and the sediment formation rate obtained during processing of the individual vacuum residues. Unfortunately, it is common practice at the refinery to process crude oil blends instead of individual crude oils, with the exception of the Urals crude oil, which is still processed individually. Another feature of the commercial ebullated bed vacuum residue hydrocracking is that it operates at an approximately constant sediment level in the ATB product to guarantee fulfillment of the planned cycle length between two consecutive cleanings. Thus, it is not possible to compare the individual vacuum residue hydrocracking behaviors at different sediment formation rates. Therefore, the behavior of the studied individual vacuum residues was compared at the same sediment formation rate. Based on our past experience for distinguishing the effects of the different individual feedstocks processed in blends by fluid catalytic cracking and hydrocracking [99], during the adoption of the approximate linear combination technique [100,101], we determined the conversion levels of 22 feeds whose SAR-AD fraction contents were measured (Table 8). After regression of the data for these 22 individual vacuum residues that were processed in the commercial LNB H-Oil hydrocracker, the following Equation (12) was developed.

$$SRVR_{Conversion} = 65.04 - 0.5659 VR_{Asp} - 0.1051 VR_{Res} + 2.783 VR_{Sul}$$
$$R = 0.983; \text{ Error} = 0.78\%$$
(12)

where:

$SRVR_{Conversion}$—Conversion of the straight-run vacuum residue;
VR_{Asp}—Asphaltene content in the vacuum residue;
VR_{Res}—Resins content in the vacuum residue;
VR_{Sul}—Sulfur content in the vacuum residue.

It is clear from Equation (12), with plotted regression results in Figure 23, that the total asphaltene content, Resin fractions and sulfur contents are the factors controlling the conversion level of the vacuum residues in the commercial ebullated bed vacuum residue hydrocracking operating at the same sediment formation rate.

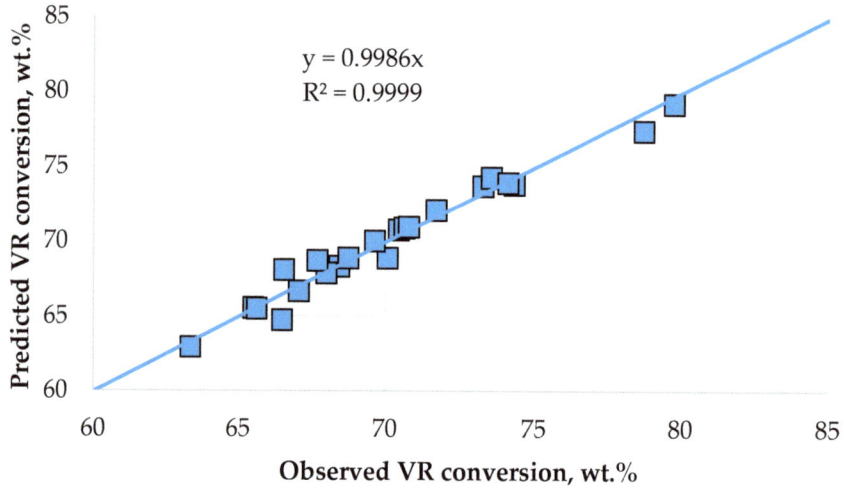

Figure 23. Agreement between observed and predicted by Equation (12) conversion of the straight-run vacuum residues having different SAR-AD fraction compositions.

The effect of sulfur on vacuum residue conversion, as shown in Equation (12), agrees with literature reports. It has been shown that sulfides are some of the most reactive chemical groups and that the rate of cracking is most dependent on their concentration [102], while other studies focus on the total sulfur content of the whole vacuum residue [103,104]. The retardation effect on the conversion of the Resin and total asphaltene content in the vacuum residue during hydrocracking has been previously reported by Guo [9], which showed that the resin and asphaltene fractions are the most refractory components during the thermal cracking of Jinzhou vacuum residue.

Table 8. SAR-AD composition of studied individual straight-run vacuum residues and determined by the use of the approximate linear combination technique conversion levels at the same sediment formation rates observed at the commercial ebullated bed hydrocracker.

Nr	ELSD Data (wt.%)	Sat	Aro-1	Aro-2	Aro-3	Resins	CyC$_6$	Toluene	CH$_2$Cl$_2$	Total Asph.	VR Sulfur	Conversion, wt.%
1	Arab Medium	9.25	8.04	25.37	37.51	11.01	2.43	6.11	0.28	8.82	5.4	73.3
2	Arab Heavy	6.16	6.84	23.51	36.68	13.59	3.34	9.55	0.33	13.21	5.8	71.7
3	Arab Light	11.32	11.07	28.06	34.76	8.98	1.58	4.01	0.22	5.81	4.9	73.6
4	Basra Light	7.92	6.44	22.66	38.30	14.41	2.81	7.18	0.28	10.27	5.9	74.3
5	Basra Heavy	7.40	6.53	23.90	38.88	13.42	2.98	6.60	0.28	9.86	7.1	78.7
6	Kirkuk	9.52	6.61	23.34	39.16	10.20	2.28	8.39	0.49	11.15	5.9	74.1
7	El-Bouri	14.69	8.32	21.38	33.81	10.15	2.33	8.83	0.49	11.64	3.3	67.1
8	Rhemoura	15.69	7.57	18.52	36.03	11.40	1.90	8.45	0.43	10.78	1.8	63.3
9	CPC	39.63	10.55	18.08	22.38	7.02	0.44	1.64	0.24	2.33	2.1	70.1
10	Azeri Light	34.94	6.90	15.67	30.68	10.67	0.25	0.74	0.13	1.12	0.5	66.5
11	Varandey	31.06	7.14	15.83	27.86	13.08	1.60	3.21	0.20	5.01	1.7	65.5
12	Sib Light	21.15	9.45	19.42	32.17	13.38	1.30	2.94	0.14	4.38	1.6	65.6
13	Urals-2	19.77	7.55	22.73	32.60	11.67	2.04	3.56	0.08	5.68	2.8	68.4
14	Urals-1	18.24	7.04	20.75	33.04	13.98	2.43	4.43	0.09	6.95	3.0	68.0
15	Imported AR	7.96	7.34	26.36	39.33	12.06	2.09	4.71	0.15	6.95	3.3	68.8
16	Prinos	4.61	4.64	17.40	44.84	11.14	1.77	14.94	0.61	17.32	9.1	79.8
17	H-Oil Feed blend 1	14.48	7.55	25.52	36.68	9.75	1.54	4.32	0.16	6.02	2.7	66.6
18	H-Oil Feed blend 2	14.12	6.88	25.80	36.61	9.90	2.03	4.39	0.26	6.68	3.8	70.5
19	H-Oil Feed blend 3	16.13	4.96	24.06	41.60	5.81	0.81	6.27	0.34	7.42	3.0	67.7
20	H-Oil Feed blend 4	17.8	7.4	24.0	33.1	11.0	2.0	4.5	0.1	6.7	3.6	69.6
21	H-Oil Feed blend 5	15.90	7.60	24.58	34.39	10.95	2.14	4.33	0.11	6.58	3.9	70.6
22	H-Oil Feed blend 6	13.95	7.07	25.17	37.60	9.35	2.12	4.63	0.10	6.85	3.9	70.8
23	Boscan	1.55	1.89	12.35	26.60	23.39	8.14	25.57	0.50	34.20	6.0	
24	Albanian	1.20	2.01	17.46	41.53	12.88	5.54	18.65	0.64	24.83	8.7	
25	Tempa Rossa	0.75	2.12	18.35	44.24	10.87	4.48	18.40	0.67	23.55	9.3	

The resin and asphaltene vacuum residue fractions contain the majority of vanadium, nickel, and nitrogen impurities [105–107], which are known to have detrimental effects on catalyst activity [108–115] and consequently on sediment formation rate [108,112]. In our previous studies, the dependence on the Resins fraction was not observed [21,53] when using SARA data obtained according to ASTM D4124. This is because ASTM D4124 produces a very large cut for the polar Aromatics/Resins fractions. This lack of resolution masks differences between feeds with respect to a more defined Resins fraction. For the SAR-AD, the Resins fraction is material from the maltenes, which reversibly adsorbs onto glass beads. When eluted, this fraction is highly brown in color, which can be observed in Figure 1 in the 500 nm data. This is different from the Aro-3 fraction, which has a very low concentration of 500 nm-absorbing molecules. The Resins fraction has a high concentration of compounds that absorb at 500 nm, indicating a significant amount of aromatic conjugation, but also polar heteroatoms that change the electronic pi-electron transition of fused aromatic ring systems to make them more colored. Surface activity (polar heteroatoms) in the Resins fraction is confirmed not only by the fact that this material adsorbs to the glass beads column but also by the model compound study, which showed that polar oxygen and nitrogen functional groups report to this fraction. Furthermore, the model compound study shows that metalated polar vanadium oxide porphyrin compounds preferentially report to the Resins fraction as well as isolated petroleum porphyrins. It should be noted that the high concentration of brown material at 500 nm for the Resins fraction does not carry over to how the asphaltene and maltene separations are performed on the first inert column with heptane. This is inferred from the fact that the amount of heptane asphaltenes produced during the SAR-AD separation is in very good agreement with reported gravimetric heptane asphaltene separations performed on well-characterized Strategic Highway Research Program asphalt binders (vacuum residues) [116]. Figure 24 shows the correlation between the heptane SAR-AD asphaltenes and gravimetric asphaltenes.

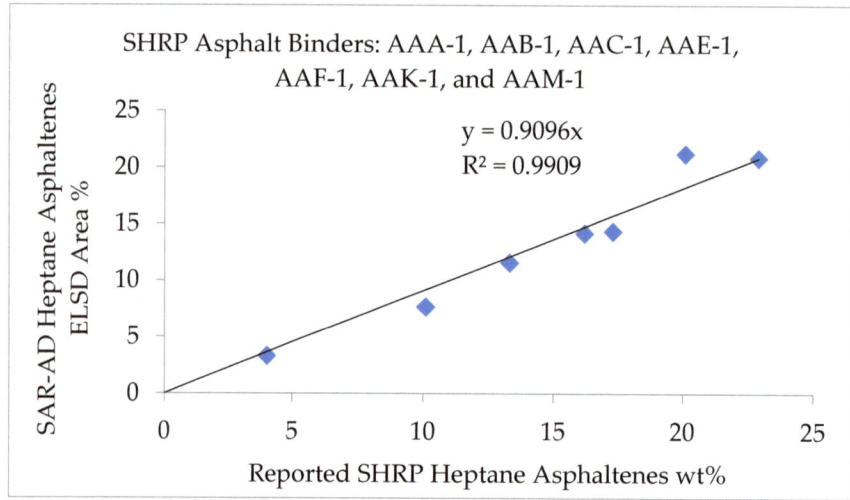

Figure 24. Correlation between SAR-AD heptane asphaltenes and gravimetric heptane asphaltenes for select SHPR core asphalt binders.

Vacuum residues, which are richer in the SAR-AD resins and asphaltene fractions, are expected to exhibit poor performance in the ebullated bed vacuum residue hydrocracking, resulting in a higher sediment formation rate and requiring operation at a lower severity that eventually results in lower conversion.

4. Conclusions

Thirty-four primary and secondary vacuum residual oils were characterized by the Western Research Institute SAR-AD eight-fraction method. On the basis of intercriteria analysis and evaluation, it was shown that the main limitation in the ebullated bed vacuum residue hydrocracking, at a constant sediment formation rate, positively correlates with only two SAR-AD characteristics: toluene asphaltene and total asphaltene content. The content of the Saturates, Aro-1, Aro-2, and Aro-3 fractions in the hydrocracked vacuum residue was found to depend on their contents in the feed and the conversion level. The Resins, CyC_6, and CH_2Cl_2 asphaltene fractions were found to depend only on their content in the ebullated bed vacuum residue feed. The VTB Toluene asphaltene fraction did not show any statistically meaningful relation to its content in the feed or to its conversion level. It seems that the Toluene asphaltene fraction content in the VTB is due to the fraction being an intermediate fraction, produced from the destruction of the Resins fraction and CyC_6 asphaltenes and their subsequent depletion and conversion to CH_2Cl_2 asphaltenes. The Toluene asphaltene content may also depend on the available catalyst active sites, which are governed by the fresh catalyst addition rate. The straight-run vacuum residue conversion at a constant sediment formation rate depends negatively on SAR-AD fractions, resins, and total asphaltenes and positively on the total sulfur content. Non-catalytic coking and mild pyrolysis of Lloydminster asphaltenes and Lloydminster vacuum residue, respectively, show consistency in trends observed with ebullated bed results.

SAR-AD model compound and thermal cracking results helped to explain why the Aro-3 fraction increases with conversion, relative to the other maltene fractions. This is mostly due to the large size and refractory nature of the 4+ fused aromatic ring structures in this fraction. Model compounds also show that polar functional groups and metallated porphyrins are present in the SAR-AD Resins fraction. This explains why the Resins fraction also contributed to lowering conversion levels during hydrocracking despite being good at stabilizing asphaltenes.

The correlations developed in this study can be used to evaluate the effect of the vacuum residues derived from different crude oils on the performance of the ebullated bed hydrocracking in the process of crude oil selection.

Author Contributions: Conceptualization, J.J.A.; methodology, J.F.R. and J.J.A.; software, S.N., S.R. and D.S.; formal analysis, I.S., J.L., A.L. and J.H.; investigation, I.K., D.S., J.J.A., G.P. and J.-P.P.; resources, K.A. and J.J.A.; data curation, D.Y.; writing—original draft preparation, J.J.A.; writing—review and editing, J.J.A.; supervision, K.A.; project administration, J.J.A.; funding acquisition, J.F.R. and J.J.A. All authors have read and agreed to the published version of the manuscript.

Funding: Funding for the SAR-AD model compound study was provided by the University of Wyoming School of Energy Resources through the Carbon Initiative and Carbon Engineering program.

Data Availability Statement: Not applicable.

Acknowledgments: The authors, Krassimir Atanassov and Simeon Ribagin, acknowledge the support from the Bulgarian National Science Fund under Grant Ref. No. KP-06-N22-1/2018 "Theoretical research and applications of InterCriteria Analysis".

Conflicts of Interest: The authors declare no conflict of interest.

Nomenclature:

SAR-AD^{TM}	Saturates, aromatics, and resins—Asphaltene Determinator;
SARA	Saturates, aromatics, resins, and asphaltenes;
TLC/FID	Thin layer chromatography/flame ionization detection;
HPLC	High performance liquid chromatography;
ARO	Aromatics;
ELSD	Evaporative light scattering detector;
AD	Asphaltene Determinator;
CH2Cl2	Dichloromethane;

CyC6	Cyclohexane;
ASTM	American Society for Testing and Materials;
LNB	Lukoil Neftochim Bourgas;
TBP	True boiling point;
HTSD	High temperature simulated distillation;
VR	Vacuum residue;
FCC HCO	Fluid Catalityc Cracking Heavy Cycle Oil;
H-Oil	Ebullated bed hydrocracking;
CII	Colloidal instability index;
MCII	Modified colloidal instability index;
MI	Maltenes Index;
SAT	Saturated;
PAH	Polycyclic aromatic hydrocarbons;
STM-AFM	Scanning tunneling microscopy coupled with atomic force microscopy;
FCC	Fluid Catalityc Cracking;
TSE	Total sediment existent
ATB	Atmospheric tower bottom;
LHSV	Liquid hourly space velocity, h^{-1};
VTB	Vacuum tower bottom;
IcrA	Intercriteria analysis;
D15	Density at 15 °C, g/m^3;
CCR	Conradson carbon content, wt.%;
C7 asp.	n-heptane asphaltenes, wt.%;
C5 asp.	n-pentane asphaltenes, wt.%;
VIS	kin. viscosity at 80 °C of the blend: 70% VR/30% fluid catalytic cracking heavy cycle oil;
Crude T50%	Boiling point of 50% of the evaporate from the crude oil, °C;
VR T50%	Boiling point of 50% of the evaporate from the vacuum residue fraction, °C;
TRX	Weight average bed temperature, °C.

References

1. Stratiev, D.; Shishkova, I.; Marinov, I.; Nikolaychuk, E.; Nedelchev, A.; Ivanova, N.; Yordanov, D.; Tankov, I.; Mitkova, M.; Stanulov, K.; et al. Effect of feedstock origin on conversion and yields of products from the ebullated bed vacuum residue hydrocracker. *Neftepererab. I Neft.* **2017**, *10*, 3–13.
2. Prajapati, R.; Kohli, K.; Maity, S.K. Residue upgradation with slurry phase catalyst: Effect of feedstock properties. *Fuel* **2019**, *239*, 452–460. [CrossRef]
3. Zhou, X.-L.; Chen, S.-Z.; Li, C.A. A predictive kinetic model for delayed coking. *Pet. Sci. Technol.* **2007**, *25*, 1539–1548. [CrossRef]
4. Ghashghaee, M. Thorough assessment of delayed coking correlations against literature data: Development of improved alternative models. *React. Kinet. Mech. Catal.* **2019**, *126*, 83–102. [CrossRef]
5. Muñoz, J.A.D.; Aguilar, R.; Castañeda, L.C.; Ancheyta, J. Comparison of correlations for estimating product yields from delayed coking. *Energy Fuels* **2013**, *27*, 7179–7190. [CrossRef]
6. Redelius, P.; Soenen, H. Relation between bitumen chemistry and performance. *Fuel* **2015**, *27*, 7179–7190. [CrossRef]
7. Stratiev, D.S.; Shishkova, I.K.; Dinkov, R.K.; Petrov, I.P.; Kolev, I.V.; Yordanov, D.; Sotirov, S.; Sotirova, E.; Atanassova, V.; Ribagin, S.; et al. Empirical Models to Characterize the Structural and Physiochemical Properties of Vacuum Gas Oils with Different Saturate Contents. *Resources* **2021**, *10*, 71. [CrossRef]
8. Corbett, L.W. Composition of asphalt based on generic fractionation, using solvent deasphalting, elution-adsorption chromatography, and densimetric characterization. *Anal. Chem.* **1969**, *41*, 576–579. [CrossRef]
9. Guo, A.; Zhang, X.; Wang, Z. Simulated delayed coking characteristics of petroleum residues and fractions by thermogravimetry. *Fuel Process. Technol.* **2008**, *89*, 643–650. [CrossRef]
10. Liu, C.; Zhu, C.; Jin, L.; Shen, R.; Liang, W. Step by step modeling for thermal reactivities and chemical compositions of vacuum residues and their SFEF asphalts. *Fuel Process. Technol.* **1999**, *59*, 51–67. [CrossRef]
11. Schucker, R.C. Thermogravimetric determination of the coking kinetics of Arab Heavy vacuum residuum. *Ind. Eng. Chem. Process Des. Dev.* **1983**, *22*, 615–619. [CrossRef]
12. Russell, C.A.; Crozier, S.; Sharpe, R. Observations from heavy residue pyrolysis: A novel method to characterize fouling potential and assess antifoulant additive performance. *Energy Fuels* **2010**, *24*, 5483–5492. [CrossRef]
13. Yang, C.; Du, F.; Zheng, H.; Keng, H.C. Hydroconversion characteristics and kinetics of residue narrow fractions. *Fuel* **2005**, *84*, 675–684. [CrossRef]

14. Stratiev, D.; Shishkova, I.; Dinkov, R.; Nikolova, R.; Mitkova, M.; Stanulov, K.; Sharpe, R.; Russell, C.A.; Obryvalina, A.; Telyashev, R. Reactivity and stability of vacuum residual oils in their thermal conversion. *Fuel* **2014**, *123*, 133–142. [CrossRef]
15. Félix, G.; Ancheyta, J. Comparison of hydrocracking kinetic models based on SARA fractions obtained in slurry-phase reactor. *Fuel* **2019**, *241*, 495–505. [CrossRef]
16. Xu, C.; Gao, J.; Zhao, S.; Lin, S. Correlation between feedstock SARA components and FCC product yields. *Fuel* **2005**, *84*, 669–674. [CrossRef]
17. Alvarez, E.; Marroquin, G.; Trejo, F.; Centeno, G.; Ancheyta, J.; Diaz, J. Pyrolysis kinetics of atmospheric residue and its SARA fractions. *Fuel* **2011**, *90*, 3602–3607. [CrossRef]
18. Hauser, A.; Alhumaidan, F.; Al-Rabiah, H.; Halabi, M.A. Study on thermal cracking of Kuwaiti heavy oil (vacuum residue) and its SARA fractions by NMR spectroscopy. *Energy Fuels* **2014**, *28*, 4321–4332. [CrossRef]
19. Xia, W.; Xu, T. Thermal characteristics, kinetic models, and volatile constituents during the energy conversion of bituminous SARA Fractions in air. *ACS Omega* **2020**, *5*, 20831–20841. [CrossRef]
20. Alonso-Ramirez, G.; Cuevas-Garcia, R.; Sanchez-Minero, F.; Ramirez, J.; Moreno-Montiel, M.; Ancheyta, J.; Carbajal-Vielman, R. Catalytic hydrocracking of a Mexican heavy oil on a MoS_2/Al_2O_3 catalyst: I. Study of the transformation of isolated saturates fraction obtained from SARA analysis. *Catal. Tod.* **2020**, *353*, 153–162. [CrossRef]
21. Stratiev, D.; Shishkova, I.; Kolev, I.; Yordanov, D.; Toteva, V. Petroleum crude slate effect on H-Oil performance. *Int. J. Oil Gas Coal Technol.* **2021**, *28*, 259–286. [CrossRef]
22. Santos, J.M.; Vetere, A.; Wisniewski, A.; Eberlin, M.N.; Schrader, W. Modified SARA method to unravel the complexity of resin fraction(s) in crude oil. *Energy Fuels* **2020**, *34*, 16006–16013. [CrossRef]
23. Zhang, J.; Tian, Y.; Qiao, Y.; Yang, C.S.H. Structure and reactivity of Iranian vacuum residue and its eight group-fractions. *Energy Fuels* **2017**, *31*, 8072–8086. [CrossRef]
24. Che, Y.; Yang, Z.; Qiao, Y.; Zhang, J.; Tian, Y. Study on pyrolysis characteristics and kinetics of vacuum residue and its eight group-fractions by TG-FTIR. *Thermochim. Acta* **2018**, *669*, 149–155. [CrossRef]
25. Zhang, J.; Niwamanya, N.; Gao, C.; Sekyere, D.T.; Barigye, A.; Tian, Y. Structure and millisecond pyrolysis behavior of heavy oil and its eight group-fractions on solid base catalyst. *Fuel* **2022**, *318*, 123483. [CrossRef]
26. Jiang, C.; Larter, S.R.; Noke, K.J.; Snowdon, L.R. TLC–FID (Iatroscan) analysis of heavy oil and tar sand samples. *Org. Geochem.* **2008**, *39*, 1210–1214. [CrossRef]
27. Liang, W.; Que, G.H.; Chen, Y. Chemical composition and structure of vacuum residues of Chinese crudes I. Chemical composition of vacuum residues. *Acta Pet. Sin. (Pet. Process. Sect.)* **1991**, *7*, 1–7.
28. Masson, J.-F.; Price, T.; Collins, P. Dynamics of bitumen fractions by thin-layer chromatography/flame ionization detection. *Energy Fuels* **2001**, *15*, 955–960. [CrossRef]
29. Schabron, J.F.; Gardner, G.W.; Hart, J.K.; Niss, N.D. The Characterization of Petroleum Residua. *West. Res. Inst. Rep.* **1993**. Report to Mobil Research and Development Corp. and DOE. DOE Report DOE/MC/11076-3539.
30. Woods, J.; Kung, J.; Kingston, D.; Kotlyar, L.; Sparks, B.; McCracken, T. Canadian crudes: A comparative study of SARA fractions from a modified HPLC separation technique. *Oil Gas Sci. Technol.* **2008**, *63*, 151–163. [CrossRef]
31. *ASTM D2007*; Standard Test Method for Characteristic Groups in Rubber Extender and Processing Oils and Other Petroleum-Derived Oils by the Clay-Gel Absorption Chromatographic Method. ASTM: West Conshohocken, PA, USA, 2016.
32. *ASTM D4124-09*; Standard Test Method for Separation of Asphalt into Four Fractions. ASTM: West Conshohocken, PA, USA, 2009.
33. Thenoux, G.; Bell, C.A.; Wilson, J.E.; Eakin, D.; Schroeder, M. Experiences with the Corbett-Swarbrick procedure for separation of asphalt into four generic fractions. *Transp. Res. Rec.* **1988**, *1171*, 66–70.
34. Bissada, K.K.; Tan, J.; Szymczyk, E.; Darnell, M.; Mei, M.; Zhou, J. Group-type characterization of crude oil and bitumen. Part I: Enhanced separation and quantification of saturates, aromatics, resins and asphaltenes (SARA). *Org. Geochem.* **2016**, *95*, 21–28. [CrossRef]
35. Huang, Y.S.; You, H.Q.; Zhou, X.P.; Guitarte, J.; Xian, C.; Liu, W.; Chen, X.; Guo, H. Cased hole formation testing in very challenging operational conditions reveals mystery of reservoir—A case study in South China Sea. In Proceedings of the International Petroleum Technology Conference, Bangkok, Thailand, 7–9 February 2011.
36. Stratiev, D.; Shishkova, I.; Nikolova, R.; Tsaneva, T.; Mitkova, M.; Yordanov, D. Investigation on precision of determination of SARA analysis of vacuum residual oils from different origin. *Pet. Coal.* **2016**, *58*, 109–119.
37. Fuhr, B.J.; Hawrelechko, C.; Holloway, L.R.; Huang, H. Comparison of bitumen fractionation methods. *Energy Fuels* **2005**, *19*, 1327–1329. [CrossRef]
38. Adams, J.; Elwardany, M.; Planche, J.-P.; Boysen, R.; Rovani, J. Diagnostic techniques for various asphalt refining and modification methods. *Energy Fuels* **2019**, *33*, 2680–2698. [CrossRef]
39. Adams, J.J.; Schabron, J.F.; Boysen, R. Quantitative vacuum distillation of crude oils to give residues amenable to the asphaltene determinator coupled with saturates, aromatics, and resins separation characterization. *Energy Fuels* **2015**, *29*, 2774–2784. [CrossRef]
40. Boysen, R.; Schabron, J.F. The automated asphaltene determinator coupled with saturates, aromatics, and resins separation for petroleum residua characterization. *Energy Fuels* **2013**, *27*, 4654–4661. [CrossRef]

41. Kharrat, A.M.; Zacharia, J.; Cherian, V.J.; Anyatonwu, A. Issues with comparing SARA methodologies. *Energy Fuels* **2007**, *21*, 3618–3621. [CrossRef]
42. Todorova-Yankova, L.; Yordanov, D.; Stratiev, D.; Shishkova, I. Investigation of the group hydrocarbon composition of vacuum residues from different types of crude oil, crude oil sands and bitumens. *Ind. Technol.* **2021**, *8*, 51–64.
43. Efimov, I.; Povarov, V.G.; Rudko, V.A. Comparison of UNIFAC and LSER models for calculating partition coefficients in the hexane–acetonitrile system using middle distillate petroleum products as an example. *Ind. Eng. Chem. Res.* **2022**, *61*, 9575–9585. [CrossRef]
44. Efimov, I.; Povarov, V.G.; Rudko, V.A. Use of partition coefficients in a hexane—Acetonitrile system in the GC–MS analysis of polyaromatic hydrocarbons in the example of delayed coking gas oils. *ACS Omega* **2021**, *6*, 9910–9919. [CrossRef] [PubMed]
45. Smyshlyaeva, K.I.; Rudko, V.A.; Kuzmin, K.A.; Vladimir, G.; Povarov, V.G. Asphaltene genesis influence on the low-sulfur residual marine fuel sedimentation stability. *Fuel* **2022**, *328*, 125291. [CrossRef]
46. Ershov, M.A.; Savelenko, V.D.; Makhmudova, A.E.; Rekhletskaya, E.S.; Makhova, U.A.; Kapustin, V.M.; Mukhina, D.Y.; Abdellatief, T.M.M. Technological Potential Analysis and Vacant Technology Forecasting in Properties and Composition of Low-Sulfur Marine Fuel Oil (VLSFO and ULSFO) Bunkered in Key World Ports. *J. Mar. Sci. Eng.* **2022**, *10*, 1828. [CrossRef]
47. Félix, G.; Tirado, A.; Al-Muntaser, A.; Kwofie, M.; Varfolomeev, M.A.; Yuan, C.; Ancheyta, J. SARA-based kinetic model for non-catalytic aquathermolysis of heavy crude oil. *J. Pet. Sci. Eng.* **2022**, *216*, 110845. [CrossRef]
48. Rakhmatullin, I.; Efimov, S.; Tyurin, V.; Gafurov, M.; Al-Muntaser, A.; Varfolomeev, M.; Klochkov, V. Qualitative and quantitative analysis of heavy crude oil samples and their SARA fractions with 13C nuclear magnetic resonance. *Processes* **2020**, *8*, 995. [CrossRef]
49. Stratiev, D.; Shishkova, I.; Tankov, I.; Pavlova, A. Challenges in characterization of residual oils. A review. *J. Petrol. Sci. Eng.* **2019**, *178*, 227–250. [CrossRef]
50. Schabron, J.F.; Rovani, J.F. On-column precipitation and re-dissolution of asphaltenes in petroleum residua. *Fuel* **2008**, *87*, 165–176. [CrossRef]
51. Schabron, J.F.; Rovani, J.F.; Sanderson, M. Asphaltene determinator method for automated on-column precipitation and redissolution of pericondensed aromatic asphaltene components. *Energy Fuels* **2010**, *24*, 5984–5996. [CrossRef]
52. Schabron, J.F.; Pauli, A.T.; Rovani, J.F.J.; Miknis, F.P. Predicting Coke Formation Tendencies. *Fuel* **2001**, *80*, 1435–1446. [CrossRef]
53. Stratiev, D.; Nenov, S.; Shishkova, I.; Georgiev, B.; Argirov, G.; Dinkov, R.; Yordanov, D.; Atanassova, V.; Vassilev, P.; Atanassov, K. Commercial investigation of the ebullated-bed vacuum residue hydrocracking in the conversion range of 55–93%. *ACS Omega* **2020**, *51*, 33290–33304. [CrossRef]
54. Stratiev, D.; Nenov, S.; Nedanovski, D.; Shishkova, I.; Dinkov, R.; Stratiev, D.D.; Sotirov, S.; Sotirova, E.; Atanassova, V.; Ribagin, S.; et al. Empirical modeling of viscosities and softening points of straight-run vacuum residues from different origins and of hydrocracked unconverted vacuum residues obtained in different conversions. *Energies* **2022**, *15*, 1755. [CrossRef]
55. Stratiev, D.; Dinkov, R.; Shishkova, I.; Sharafutdinov, I.; Ivanova, N.; Mitkov, M.; Yordanov, D.; Rudnev, N.; Stanulov, K.; Artemiev, A.; et al. What is behind the high values of hot filtration test of the ebullated bed residue H-Oil hydrocracker residual oils. *Energy Fuels* **2016**, *30*, 7037–7054. [CrossRef]
56. Stratiev, D.S.; Shishkova, I.K.; Dinkov, R.K.; Petrov, I.P.; Kolev, I.V.; Yordanov, D.; Sotirov, S.; Sotirova, E.N.; Atanassova, V.K.; Ribagin, S.; et al. Crude slate, FCC slurry oil, recycle, and operating conditions effects on H-Oil product quality. *Processes* **2021**, *9*, 952. [CrossRef]
57. Zhang, Y.; Schulz, F.B.; Rytting, F.M.; Walters, C.C.; Kaiser, K.; Metz, J.N.; Harper, M.R.; Merchant, S.S.; Mennito, A.S.; Qian, K.J.; et al. Elucidating the geometric substitution of petroporphyrins by spectroscopic analysis and atomic force microscopy molecular imaging. *Energy Fuels* **2019**, *33*, 6088–6097. [CrossRef] [PubMed]
58. Schabron, J.F.; Pauli, A.T., Jr.; Rovani, J.F. Residua Coke Formation Predictability Maps. *Fuel* **2002**, *81*, 2227–2240. [CrossRef]
59. Jover, J.; Cirera, J. Computational assessment on the Tolman cone angles for P-ligands. *Dalton Trans.* **2019**, *48*, 15036. [CrossRef]
60. Schuler, B.; Meyer, G.; Peña, D.; Mullins, O.C.; Gross, L. Unraveling the molecular structures of asphaltenes by atomic force microscopy. *J. Am. Chem. Soc.* **2015**, *137*, 9870–9876. [CrossRef]
61. Zhang, Y.; Schuler, B.; Fatayer, S.; Gross, L.; Harper, M.R.; Kushnerick, J.D. Understanding the effects of sample preparation on the chemical structures of petroleum imaged with non-contact atomic force microscopy. *Ind. Eng. Chem. Res.* **2018**, *57*, 15935–15941. [CrossRef]
62. Chen, P.; Metz, J.N.; Mennito, A.S.; Merchant, S.; Smith, S.E.; Siskin, M.; Ricker, S.P.; Dankworth, D.C.; Kushnerick, J.D.; Yao, N.; et al. Petroleum Pitch: Exploring a 50-year structure puzzle with real-space molecular imaging. *Carbon* **2020**, *161*, 456–465. [CrossRef]
63. Zhang, Y. Applications of Noncontact Atomic Force Microscopy in Petroleum Characterization: Opportunities and Challenges. *Energy Fuels* **2021**, *35*, 14422–14444. [CrossRef]
64. Stanislaus, A.; Hauser, A.; Marafi, M. Investigation of the mechanism of sediment formation in residual oil hydrocracking process through characterization of sediment deposits. *Catal. Today* **2005**, *109*, 167–177. [CrossRef]
65. Pang, W.W.; Kuramae, M.; Kinoshita, Y.; Lee, J.K.; Zhang, Y.Z.; Yoon, S.H.; Mochida, I. Plugging problems observed in severe hydrocracking of vacuum residue. *Fuel* **2009**, *88*, 663–669. [CrossRef]
66. Stratiev, D.; Shishkova, I.; Nikolaychuk, E.; Ilchev, I.; Yordanov, D. Investigation of the effect of severity mode of operation in the H-Oil vacuum residue hydrocracking on sediment formation during processing different feeds. *Pet. Coal* **2020**, *62*, 50–62.

67. Stratiev, D.; Shishkova, I.; Dinkov, R.; Kolev, I.; Argirov, G.; Ivanov, V.; Ribagin, S.; Atanassova, V.; Atanassov, K.; Stratiev, D.D.; et al. Intercriteria analysis to diagnose the reasons for increased fouling in a commercial ebullated bed vacuum residue hydrocracker. *ACS Omega* **2022**, *7*, 30462–30476. [CrossRef]
68. Stratiev, D.; Shishkova, I.; Nedelchev, A.; Kirilov, K.; Nikolaychuk, E.; Ivanov, A.; Sharafutdinov, I.; Veli, A.; Mitkova, M.; Tsaneva, T.; et al. Investigation of relationships between petroleum properties and their impact on crude oil compatibility. *Energy Fuels* **2015**, *29*, 7836–7854. [CrossRef]
69. Mavrov, D. Software for intercriteria analysis: Implementation of the main algorithm. *Notes Intuit. Fuzzy Sets* **2015**, *21*, 77–86.
70. Mavrov, D. Software for intercriteria analysis: Working with the results. *Annu. Inform. Sect. Union Sci. Bulg.* **2015**, *8*, 37–44.
71. Mavrov, D.; Radeva, I.; Atanassov, K.; Doukovska, L.; Kalaykov, I. InterCriteria software design: Graphic interpretation within the intuitionistic fuzzy triangle. In Proceedings of the Fifth International Symposium on Business Modeling and Software Design, Fribourg, Switzerland, 5–7 July 2015; pp. 279–283.
72. Ikonomov, N.; Vassilev, P.; Roeva, O. Software for intercriteria analysis. *Int. J. Bioautomation* **2018**, *22*, 1–10. [CrossRef]
73. Bannayan, M.A.; Lemke, H.K.; Stephenson, W.K. Fouling mechanisms and effect of process conditions on deposit formation in H-Oil. *Stud. Surf. Sci. Catal.* **1996**, *100*, 273–281.
74. Rogel, E.; Ovalles, C.; Moir, M. Asphaltene chemical characterization as a function of solubility: Effects on stability and aggregation. *Energy Fuels* **2012**, *26*, 2655–2662. [CrossRef]
75. Mochida, I.; Zhao, Z.; Sakanishi, K.; Yamamoro, S.; Takashima, H.; Uemura, S.V. Structure and properties of sludges produced in the catalytic hydrocracking of vacuum residue. *Ind. Eng. Chem. Res.* **1989**, *28*, 418–421.
76. Ovalles, C.; Rogel, E.; Moir, M.E.; Brait, A. Hydroprocessing of vacuum residues: Asphaltene characterization and solvent extraction of spent slurry catalysts and the relationships with catalyst deactivation. *Appl. Catal. A Gen.* **2016**, *532*, 57–64. [CrossRef]
77. Manek, E.; Haydary, J. Hydrocracking of vacuum residue with solid and dispersed phase catalyst: Modeling of sediment formation and hydrodesulfurization. *Fuel Process. Technol.* **2017**, *159*, 320–327.
78. Rogel, E.; Ovalles, C.; Pradhan, A.; Leung, P.; Chen, N. Sediment formation in residue hydroconversion processes and its correlation to asphaltene behavior. *Energy Fuels* **2013**, *27*, 6587–6593. [CrossRef]
79. Felix, G.; Ancheyta, J. Using separate kinetic models to predict liquid, gas, and coke yields in heavy oil hydrocracking. *Ind. Eng. Chem. Res.* **2019**, *58*, 7973–7979. [CrossRef]
80. Gaulier, F.; Barbier, J.; Guichard, B.; Levitz, P.; Espinat, D. Asphaltenes transport into catalysts under hydroprocessing conditions. *Energy Fuels* **2015**, *29*, 6250–6258. [CrossRef]
81. Kim, C.H.; Hur, Y.G.; Lee, K.Y. Relationship between surface characteristics and catalytic properties of unsupported nickel-tungsten carbide catalysts for the hydrocracking of vacuum residue. *Fuel* **2022**, *309*, 122103. [CrossRef]
82. Nguyen, N.T.; Kang, K.H.; Pham, H.H.; Go, K.S.; Pham, D.V.; Seo, P.W.; Nho, N.S.; Chul, W.; Sunyoung, P. Catalytic hydrocracking of vacuum residue in a semi-batch reactor: Effect of catalyst concentration on asphaltene conversion and product distribution. *J. Ind. Eng. Chem.* **2021**, *102*, 112–121. [CrossRef]
83. Lim, S.H.; Go, K.S.; Nho, N.S.; Kim, Y.K.; Kwon, E.H.; Kwang, K.; Lee, J. Reaction characteristics and sediment formation of slurry phase hydrocracking with vacuum residue in a bench-scale bubble column reactor. *J. Petrol. Sci. Eng.* **2021**, *196*, 107713. [CrossRef]
84. Lim, S.H.; Go, K.S.; Kwon, E.H.; Nho, N.S.; Lee, J.G. Investigation of asphaltene dispersion stability in slurry-phase hydrocracking reaction. *Fuel* **2020**, *271*, 117509. [CrossRef]
85. Lim, S.H.; Go, K.S.; Nho, N.S.; Lee, J.G. Effect of reaction temperature and time on the products and asphaltene dispersion stability in slurry-phase hydrocracking of vacuum residue. *Fuel* **2018**, *234*, 305–311. [CrossRef]
86. Lim, S.H.; Go, K.S.; Nho, N.S.; Lee, J.G. Effect of aromatic additives on the coke reduction and the asphaltene conversion in a slurry-phase hydrocracking. *Korean Chem. Eng. Res.* **2019**, *57*, 244–252.
87. Du, H.; Liu, D.; Liu, H.; Gao, P.; Lv, R.; Li, M.; Lou, B.; Yang, Y. Role of hydrogen pressure in slurry-phase hydrocracking of Venezuela heavy oil. *Energy Fuels* **2015**, *29*, 2104–2110. [CrossRef]
88. Chabot, J.; Shiflett, W. Residuum hydrocracking: Chemistry and catalysis. *PTQ* **2019**, *Q3*, 1–9.
89. Mochida, I.; Korai, Y.; Hieida, T.; Azuma, A.; Kitajima, E. Detailed analyses of FCC decant oil as a starting feedstock for mesophase pitch. *Fuel Sci. Technol. Int.* **1991**, *9*, 485–504. [CrossRef]
90. Chacón-Patiño, M.L.; Gray, M.R.; Rüger, C.; Smith, D.F.; Glattke, T.J.; Niles, S.F.; Neumann, A.; Weisbrod, C.R.; Yen, A.; McKenna, A.M.; et al. Lessons learned from a decade-long assessment of asphaltenes by ultrahigh-resolution mass spectrometry and implications for complex mixture analysis. *Energy Fuels* **2021**, *35*, 16335–16376. [CrossRef]
91. Chacón-Patiño, M.L.; Rowland, S.M.; Rodgers, R.P. Advances in asphaltene petroleomics. Part 1: Asphaltenes are composed of abundant island and archipelago structural motifs. *Energy Fuels* **2017**, *31*, 13509–13518. [CrossRef]
92. Chacón-Patiño, M.L.; Rowland, S.M.; Rodgers, R.P. Advances in asphaltene petroleomics. Part 2: Selective separation method that reveals fractions enriched in island and archipelago structural motifs by mass spectrometry. *Energy Fuels* **2018**, *32*, 314–328. [CrossRef]
93. Chacón-Patiño, M.L.; Rowland, S.M.; Rodgers, R.P. Advances in asphaltene petroleomics. Part 3. Dominance of island or archipelago structural motif is sample dependent. *Energy Fuels* **2018**, *32*, 9106–9120. [CrossRef]

94. Chacón-Patiño, M.L.; Smith, D.F.; Hendrickson, C.L.; Marshall, A.G.; Rodgers, R.P. Advances in asphaltene petroleomics. Part 4. Compositional trends of solubility subfractions reveal that polyfunctional oxygen-containing compounds drive asphaltene chemistry. *Energy Fuels* **2020**, *34*, 3013–3030. [CrossRef]
95. Adams, J.; Rovani, J.; Boysen, R.; Elwardany, M.; Planche, J.-P. Innovations and developments in bitumen composition analysis. In Proceedings of the 7th Eurasphalt and Eurobitumen Congress, Virtual, Madrid, Spain, 15–17 June 2021.
96. Petersen, J.C. *A Review of the Fundamentals of Asphalt Oxidation: Chemical, Physicochemical, Physical Property and Durability Relationships*; Transportation Research Board: Washington, DC, USA, 2009.
97. Petersen, J.C.; Glaser, R. Asphalt oxidation mechanisms and the role of oxidation products on age hardening revisited. *Road Mater. Pavement Des.* **2011**, *12*, 795–819. [CrossRef]
98. Mitkova, M.; Stratiev, D.; Shishkova, I.; Dobrev, D. *Thermal and Thermo Catalytic Processes for Heavy Oil Conversion*; Professor Marin Drinov Publishing House of Bulgarian Academy of Sciences: Sofia, Bulgaria, 2017.
99. Stratiev, D.; Shishkova, I.; Dinkov, R.; Dobrev, D.; Argirov, G.; Yordanov, D. The Synergy between ebullated bed vacuum residue hydrocracking and fluid catalytic cracking processes in modern refining—Commercial experience. *Profr. Mar. Drinov Publ. House Bulg. Acad. Sci.* **2022**, 1–750.
100. Harding, R.H.; Zhao, X.; Qian, K.; Rajagopalan, K.; Cheng, W.C. The fluid catalytic cracking selectivities of gas oil boiling point and hydrocarbon fractions. *Prep. Am. Chem. Soc. Div. Pet. Chem.* **1995**, *40*, 762–767. [CrossRef]
101. Harding, R.H.; Zhao, X.; Qian, K.; Rajagopalan, K.; Cheng, W.C. The fluid catalytic cracking selectivities of gas oil boiling point and hydrocarbon fractions. *Ind Eng Chem Res.* **1996**, *35*, 2561–2569. [CrossRef]
102. Saxena, A.; Diaz-Goano, C.; Dettman, H. Coking behavior during visbreaking. *J. Can. Petrol. Technol.* **2012**, *51*, 457–463. [CrossRef]
103. Gray, M.; Chacón-Patiño, M.; Rodgers, R. Structure–Reactivity Relationships for petroleum asphaltenes. *Energy Fuels* **2022**, *36*, 4370–4380. [CrossRef]
104. Guitian, J.; Souto, A.; Ramirez, R.; Marzin, R.; Solari, B. Commercial design of a new upgrading process, HDH. In *proceedings international symposium on Heavy Oil and Residue Upgrading and Utilization*; Han, C., Hsi, C., Eds.; International Academic: Beijing, China, 1992; pp. 237–247.
105. Reynolds, J.G. Characterization of heavy residua by application of a modified D 2007 separation and electron paramagnetic resonance. *Liq. Fuels Technol.* **1985**, *3*, 73–105. [CrossRef]
106. Speight, J.G. Petroleum asphaltenes Part 2 The effect of asphaltenes and resin constituents on recovery and refining processes. *Oil Gas Sci. Technol.* **2004**, *59*, 479–488. [CrossRef]
107. Speight, J.G. Petroleum asphaltenes Part 1. Asphaltenes, resins and the structure of petroleum. *Oil Gas Sci. Technol.* **2004**, *59*, 467–477. [CrossRef]
108. Kohli, K.; Prajapati, R.; Maity, S.K.; Sau, M.; Sharma, B.K. Deactivation of a hydrotreating catalyst during hydroprocessing of synthetic crude by metal bearing compounds. *Fuel* **2019**, *243*, 579–589. [CrossRef]
109. Zhou, J.; Zhao, J.; Zhang, J.; Zhang, T.; Ye, M.; Liu, Z. Regeneration of catalysts deactivated by coke deposition: A review. *Chin. J. Catal.* **2020**, *41*, 1048–1061. [CrossRef]
110. Furimsky, E.; Massoth, F.E. Deactivation of hydroprocessing catalysts. *Catal. Today* **1999**, *52*, 381–495. [CrossRef]
111. Gualda, G.; Kasztelan, S. Coke versus metal deactivation of residue hydrodemetallization catalysts. *Stud. Surf. Sci. Catal.* **1994**, *88*, 145–154.
112. Vogelaar, B.M.; Eijsbouts, S.; Bergwerff, J.A.; Heiszwolf, J. Hydroprocessing catalyst deactivation in commercial practice. *Catal. Today* **2010**, *154*, 256–263. [CrossRef]
113. Nguyen, M.T.; Nguyen, D.L.T.; Changlei, X.; Nguyen, T.B.; Shokouhimehr, M.; Sana, S.S.; NirmalaGrace, A.; Aghbashlo, M.; Tabatabaei, M.; Sonne, C.; et al. Recent advances in asphaltene transformation in heavy oil hydroprocessing: Progress, challenges, and future perspectives. *Fuel Proc. Technol.* **2021**, *213*, 106681. [CrossRef]
114. Gawel, I.; Bociarska, D.; Biskupski, P. Effect of asphaltenes on hydroprocessing of heavy oils and residua. *Appl. Catal. A Gen.* **2005**, *295*, 89–94. [CrossRef]
115. Rana, M.S.; Ancheyta, J.; Sahoo, S.K.; Rayo, P. Carbon and metal deposition during the hydroprocessing of Maya crude oil. *Catal. Today* **2014**, *220*, 97–105. [CrossRef]
116. Jones, D.R. *SHRP Materials Reference Library: Asphalt Cements: A Concise Data Compilation*; Report: SHRP-A-645; National Research Council: Washington, DC, USA, 1993.

Disclaimer/Publisher's Note: The statements, opinions and data contained in all publications are solely those of the individual author(s) and contributor(s) and not of MDPI and/or the editor(s). MDPI and/or the editor(s) disclaim responsibility for any injury to people or property resulting from any ideas, methods, instructions or products referred to in the content.

Article

Properties of Selected Alternative Petroleum Fractions and Sustainable Aviation Fuels

Hugo Kittel *, Jiří Horský and Pavel Šimáček

Department of Petroleum Technology and Alternative Fuels, Faculty of Environmental Technology, University of Chemistry and Technology, Technická 1905, 166 28 Prague, Czech Republic
* Correspondence: hugo.kittel@vscht.cz; Tel.: +420-220444236

Abstract: With regard to speed, comfort, and a dense network of destinations, the popularity of air transport is on the rise. For this reason, jet fuel is a commodity with rapidly growing consumption and interesting refinery margins. At the same time, however, it is becoming a focus of attention in terms of reducing negative environmental impacts. As a response to these trends, it will be necessary to coprocess alternative petroleum fractions with sustainable aviation components in oil refineries. Six alternative jet fuel samples of different origin were used to investigate their jet fuel-specific properties, that is, aromatics (from 0 to 59.7 vol%), smoke point (from 12.2 to >50 mm), freezing point (from −49 to <−80 °C) and net specific energy (41.2–43.7 MJ·kg^{-1}), and these properties were compared to standard hydrotreated straight-run Jet A-1 kerosene. The properties of the components studied differed significantly with respect to each other and to the requirements of Jet A-1. Nevertheless, the properties could be well correlated. This provides an opportunity to study possible synergies in blending these components. It was also found that the current methods and instruments used do not always allow a precise determination of the smoke point (>50 mm) and freezing point (<80 °C).

Keywords: jet fuel; density; simulated distillation; carbon number; aromatics; n-alkanes; smoke point; freezing point; net specific energy

Citation: Kittel, H.; Horský, J.; Šimáček, P. Properties of Selected Alternative Petroleum Fractions and Sustainable Aviation Fuels. *Processes* **2023**, *11*, 935. https://doi.org/10.3390/pr11030935

Academic Editors: Dicho Stratiev, Dobromir Yordanov, Aijun Guo and Thomas S.Y. Choong

Received: 1 February 2023
Revised: 5 March 2023
Accepted: 16 March 2023
Published: 19 March 2023

Copyright: © 2023 by the authors. Licensee MDPI, Basel, Switzerland. This article is an open access article distributed under the terms and conditions of the Creative Commons Attribution (CC BY) license (https://creativecommons.org/licenses/by/4.0/).

1. Introduction

Jet fuel is a global strategic commodity with a high potential for growth. Consumption is expected to more than triple by 2050 [1]. Currently, the air transport business is responsible for 2.1% of total carbon dioxide emissions or 12% of carbon dioxide emissions from transport [2]. An overview of the standards applicable to jet fuel is available [3,4]. Jet A-1 [5], produced from crude oil straight-run kerosene refined by oxidation of thiols [6] or hydrotreatment, is the most widely used jet fuel in civil aviation. The properties of typical jet fuels have been reviewed in detail [7–9]. The International Air Transport Association (IATA) estimates that SAF's share of jet fuel consumption will be only 0.1% in 2022 [10]. Therefore, it is entirely legitimate that jet fuel should be part of a general effort to reduce harmful emissions from transport originating from petroleum hydrocarbons. Sustainable aviation fuels (SAFs) are now the subject of extensive research and testing and are an important part of strategic plans for the further development of air transport. It is clear that the future role of SAFs will be much more important in this respect than in car transport, where competing alternatives such as electromobility are now dominating.

Several reviews and strategies have been published on all aspects of SAF implementation [11–29], which together include hundreds of references on this topic. SAFs are part of Task 39 of the International Energy Agency (IEA), and the IEA is very active in this regard [30–32]. The use of various biofeeds and biotechnologies dominates these reviews. Based on these reviews, there are other primary issues associated with the implementation of SAFs: availability, costs [33–37] and different quality [38,39] compared to petroleum jet fuel. It is important to note that the currently applicable jet fuel quality standards were derived from the properties of the petroleum fractions. However, the typical properties of individual SAFs may differ significantly from those of petroleum kerosene. Therefore, SAFs must be qualified for air operations [38]. The drop-in concept plays an important role in overcoming some of the quality problems. The drop-in concept means that SAF can be blended with petroleum-based jet fuel, and the final product does not require changes in infrastructure or equipment. The approved SAF and the maximum concentration in jet fuel are standardized [39]. Jet fuel blends with different compositions have been studied in terms of jet fuel quality [40–42]. Clearly, the most successful SAFs at present are hydrotreated esters and fatty acids (HEFA), which use mainly second-generation feedstocks, especially cooking oils and waste fats [20]. Related technologies were primarily commercialized for the production of hydrotreated vegetable oil (HVO) as a component to diesel fuel [43]— for example, NEXBTL, since 2007 [44,45] in Porvoo, Rotterdam; Singapore oil refineries, and Ecofining, since 2009 [46] in Venice and Gela biorefineries, Livorno; and Sines oil refineries. Each HVO unit can produce from 15 vol% (without additional CAPEX) to 50 vol% (additional CAPEX is required) of HEFA. Moreover, the quality of HEFA is similar to other SAFs based on synthetic i-alkanes produced primarily from the synthesis gas of different origins using Fischer–Tropsch technology followed by the hydrocracking of synthetic crude oil and isomerization of the kerosene fraction [47,48]. Progress in the commercialization of biojet fuel has been discussed [49] and reported [50–54]. From a circular economy point of view, SAFs produced from bulk wastes of petrochemical origin (waste polyolefins [55–60]) and scrapped tires [61] using mature pyrolysis and hydrogenation technologies are very interesting. Regarding the strategy of rapidly increasing jet fuel consumption in a situation of declining crude oil consumption, it is important to address alternative petroleum fractions applicable to this strategy as a basis for the successful implementation of SAFs [62]. These are mainly kerosene from the hydrocracking of vacuum distillates [4,63,64], hydrotreated heavy naphtha from FCC [65], or kerosene obtained instead of the gasoline component by oligomerization and hydrogenation of C_4 hydrocarbons [66,67]. The use of these alternative fractions for jet fuel production can be very interesting; however, it will require specific research on additional CAPEX in oil refineries.

The purpose of the research was to analyze the properties of kerosene samples of different origins, produced by different technologies, and with significantly different properties, all of which provide significant potential for increasing jet fuel production. The quality of standard Jet A-1 produced from hydrotreated straight-run kerosene was compared with alternative kerosene fractions produced by hydrocracking and FCC technologies and with SAFs represented by HEFA and hydrotreated kerosene from the pyrolysis of waste polyolefins and scrapped tires. The focus was mainly on the fractional and group composition of the samples and on jet fuel-specific properties such as aromatic and diaromatics content, smoke point, freezing point, and net specific energy. The samples were selected to be within the possible limits of the physical and chemical properties of the alternative fractions currently being considered, researched, and tested for the production of jet fuel. This is important for assessing synergies when blending fractions. It was also examined whether the methods and analytical instruments currently in use are capable of determining the critical properties of the alternative fractions considered for Jet A-1 and whether these properties of samples of very different origin and composition can be correlated as a function of, for example, mean boiling point, n-alkanes and aromatics content.

2. Materials and Methods

To monitor the properties of the investigated kerosene samples, the following analytical methods and devices were used: Density—EN ISO 12185 and Anton Paar DMA 4000 density analyzer with an oscillating U-tube (Anton Paar GmbH, Graz, Austria). The measurement was carried out at 15 °C. Distillation—ASTM D86 (A) and NDI 440 Monitoring & Control Laboratories automatic distillation unit (Monitoring & Control Laboratories, Frankenwald, South Africa). Exactly 100 mL of sample was consumed for each analysis. Simulated distillation (SimDist)—ASTM D2887 and the Trace GC Ultra gas chromatograph (Thermo Fisher Scientific Inc., Waltham, MA, USA). Primary chromatographic data were also used to calculate the approximate content of n-alkanes and hydrocarbon groups with the same number of carbon atoms. Flash point—ASTM D56 (A) and Tanaka ATG-7 automated instrument (Tanaka Scientific Limited, Tokyo, Japan). Exactly 50 mL of sample was used for each analysis. Aromatics—ASTM D6379 (A) and Shimadzu HPLC-RID automated instrument (Shimadzu Corporation, Tokyo, Japan). Aromatics, diaromatics, and polyaromatics were separated on a liquid chromatograph column. Detection was carried out using a refractive-index detector. Approximately 1 g of sample was consumed for each analysis. Smoke point—ASTM D1322 and ATS Scientific Inc. SP 10 automatic instrument (AD Systems, Saint André sur Orne, France). The result was calculated as an average of three measurements. The instrument measures the smoke point from 0 mm to 50 mm. Exactly 20 mL of the sample was consumed for each analysis. Freezing point—ASTM D5972 and Phase Technology FPA-70X automatic instrument (Phase Technology, Richmond, Canada), which measures the freezing point from 20 °C to −80 °C. Approximately 20 mL of sample was consumed for each analysis. Net specific energy measured—ASTM D4809 and LECO AC-350 automated instrument (LECO Corporation, Sant Joseph, USA). The instrument was calibrated with benzoic acid. Using elemental analysis according to ASTM D5291, the hydrogen and water contents were determined, and these values were entered into the instrument. The results of the elemental analysis were used to calculate the $(H/C)_{at}$ ratio. Approximately 0.5 g of sample was consumed for each analysis. Net specific energy calculated—ASTM D3338 using known aromatic content, mean boiling point from ASTM D86 distillation and density. All test methods were applied in accordance with standard test procedures and uncertainty of measurement was lower than repeatability of the corresponding method.

The redistillation of hydrotreated pyrolysis oil samples was performed on a distillation apparatus from Fischer Technology. The 150–250 °C fraction was taken as kerosene.

The following samples were studied: Jet A-1—the hydrotreated straight-run kerosene distilled from light crude oil. It was a commercial refinery product for which a quality certificate was available. A similar sample can be obtained in a number of oil refineries. Therefore, it was used to validate the measured data. This sample represented a substantial part of the jet fuel currently produced [9]. Jet HC—kerosene produced by deep hydrocracking of vacuum distillates from medium-heavy crude oil, of the quality used in the refinery for Jet A-1 production. A similar sample can only be obtained in some oil refineries since it requires adding stabilization, kerosene fraction additivation and separate storage and distribution of jet fuel to the standard hydrocracker unit. This utilization of kerosene provides an interesting opportunity for hydrocracking-type refineries to increase refinery margins [4]. FCC HN—hydrotreated heavy naphtha obtained by fluid catalytic cracking (FCC) of atmospheric residue from light crude oil, subsequent redistillation of FCC gasoline on a 3-cut splitter and hydrotreating of heavy fraction. FCC hydrotreated heavy naphtha is the standard output of the catalytic cracking process. The fraction is commonly used for the blending of mogas and is currently also used for the production of jet fuel as a drop-in component in units of percent. This represents an opportunity to diversify the products from the FCC. PyrTIR—kerosene from scrapped tires pyrolysis oil from an external pilot unit, hydrotreated in a laboratory scale fixed-bed catalytic unit [68,69] with a capacity of 33 g·h^{-1} under severe conditions (360 °C, 10 MPa, commercial hydrotreating NiMo/γ-Al$_2$O$_3$ catalyst) and redistilled in the laboratory as a fraction with the distillation range of 150–240 °C. PyrPO—kerosene from waste polyolefins pyrolysis oil, treated as described above for the previous sample. Both samples based on pyrolysis oil were prepared specifically for this research. Considering the capacity of the laboratory unit and the yield of kerosene from the hydrotreated product, it was difficult to obtain a sample in the required quantities. Therefore, the focus, in this case, was on the critical and specific properties of jet fuel. Jet fuel from the pyrolysis of waste polyolefins and scrapped tires represents an important opportunity to implement the chemical waste recycling concept and is a major research and development challenge currently. All of the above samples can be considered to be crude oil based. HEFA Cam—biokerosene made from camelina, for which quality data were available from an independent laboratory because this component was previously used to research drop-in components for jet fuel [40]. HEFA 215—biokerosene provided by a partner laboratory from an undisclosed source as an alternative to HEFA from camelina. Both HEFA samples met the quality requirements of ASTM D7566 [39], which was considered essential for their use in research. HEFA, as an alternative jet fuel, is currently the focus of attention of SAF producers, aircraft manufacturers and major airlines.

The authors of this paper do not have permission to mention the manufacturer of the samples used.

The results presented in this paper were part of a master thesis defended at the University of Chemistry and Technology, Prague, in 2022 [70].

3. Results and Discussion

In line with the research objectives described in the introduction, properties important for the evaluation of the studied samples and limiting their yield as jet fuel were summarized and compared with the current Jet A-1 requirements [5] (Table 1). The Table additionally includes the $(H/C)_{at}$ ratio from the elemental analysis (ASTM D5291) and the calculated net energy value (ASTM D3338). Values that did not meet the Jet A-1 requirements are underlined. The data are further discussed in the following figures.

Table 1. Key properties of the samples studied.

Component	JIG Jet A-1 Requirements	Jet A-1	Jet HC	FCC HN	HEFA Cam	HEFA 215	PyrTIR	PyrPO
Density at 15 °C (kg·m^{-3})	775–840	802.3	817.3	858.8	759.5	760.7	850.9	794.8
Distillation (°C)								
10% distilled (°C)	max 205	178.5	181.0	178.2	164.4	180.1	175.8	180.5 [1]
End of distillation (°C)	max 300	234.9	228.6	232.3	279.0	271.0	238.9	240.5 [1]
Distillation residue (vol%)	max 1.5	1.1	1.1	1	1.1	1.4	1.2	[1]
Distillation loss (vol%)	max 1.5	0.3	1	0.3	0.1	0.2	0.8	[1]
$(H/C)_{at}$	-	1.928	1.882	1.550	2.177	2.172	1.708	1.972
Aromatics content (vol%)	max 26.5	19.7	22.7	59.7	0.3	0.0	44.2	15.9
Monoaromatics		18.5	22.6	54.2	0.3	0.0	43.8	15.7
Diaromatics		1.2	0.1	5.5	0.0	0.0	0.4	0.2
Smoke point (mm)	min 18	22.2	18.9	-	>50 [2]	>50 [2]	12.2	26.6
For naphtalenes > 3 vol%	min. 25	-	-	9.3 [3]	-	-	-	-
Freezing point (°C)	max −47	−55.4	<−80	<−80	−57.2	−49.1	−80	−50.1
Flash point (°C)	min 38	50	53	54.5	43.5	43	[1]	[1]
Net specific energy (MJ·kg^{-1})	min 42.8							
measured (ASTM D4809)		42.8	42.7	41.2	43.3	43.7	42.2	43.0
calculated (ASTM D3338)		43.2	43.0	42.0	44.1	44.1	42.3	43.4

[1] Not measured due to lack of sample. ASTM D86 points calculated from SimDist; [2] sample did not smoke; [3] as diaromatics. Values that did not meet the Jet A-1 requirements are underlined.

Distillation is the simplest technology in oil refineries to control product quality. In the case of jet fuel, it is used to control the distillation range, flash point, freezing point in straight-run oil fractions and aromatics in cracking fractions by setting the correct initial and end point of distillation. ASTM D86 is the basis for determining the distillation characteristics of products in oil refineries and was also used for the samples studied (Figure 1).

Since not enough PyrPO sample was available to determine the ASTM D86 distillation, it was substituted in Figure 1 by values calculated from SimDist. The distillation curves of the crude oil-based samples, including PyrTIR and PyrPO, were very similar, the distillation range was relatively narrow (95–5 vol% < 59 °C) and the samples were characterized by a large reserve at 10 vol% distillation temperature and the end of distillation compared to the requirements of JET A-1. The distillation curves of the two HEFA samples differed from the crude oil-based samples and were characterized by a significantly higher range of boiling points (95–5 vol% > 96 °C), therefore, they were steeper.

SimDist (ASTM D2887) provided a more precise distillation characteristic (Figure 2).

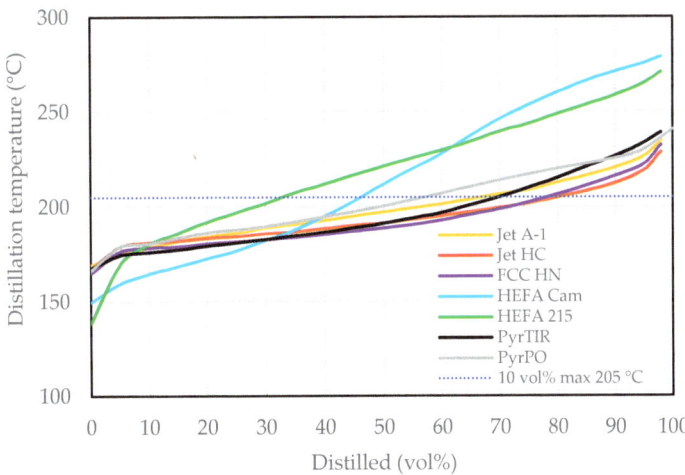

Figure 1. ASTM D86 distillation of the samples studied.

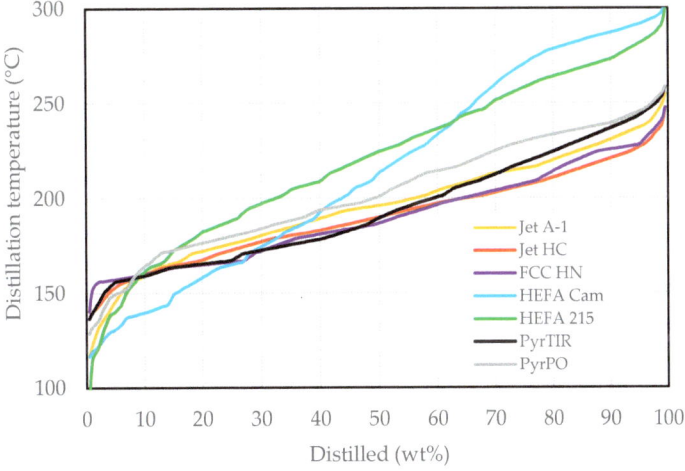

Figure 2. SimDist of the samples studied.

As it results from the nature of the SimDist ASTM D2887 method, which allows a better separation of hydrocarbons by boiling point than the ASTM D86 method, the distillation curves were significantly steeper than those from ASTM D86. However, their relationship was similar to Figure 1, i.e., similar for the oil-based samples and clearly different for the two HEFA samples.

The SimDist results allow us to calculate the ASTM D86 distillation curve. Since the samples studied were of very different origin and composition, it was interesting to compare the experimental ASTM D86 results with these calculated values (Table 2).

Table 2 shows that the SimDist-based calculation can be well used to estimate the ASTM D86 distillation of the kerosene samples of very different quality. The biggest differences were found in IBP. The average absolute deviation of both methods did not exceed 5.1 °C.

The SimDist results allow us to estimate the hydrocarbon distribution (Figure 3) and n-alkanes distribution (Figure 4) by carbon number.

Table 2. Differences between experimental and calculated ASTM D86 results of the samples studied (°C).

Sample	Jet A-1	Jet HC	FCC HN	HEFA Cam	HEFA 215	PyrTIR
IBP	8.8	−4.3	−11.0	−0.9	−10.9	−6.3
5 vol%	1.4	2.2	−1.2	3.1	−3.7	−2.3
10 vol%	2.1	5.3	2.9	3.8	−0.6	0.8
30 vol%	3.3	4.8	5.0	−1.6	−1.3	4.1
50 vol%	2.5	3.1	2.9	−2.8	−1.2	1.8
70 vol%	3.5	5.1	3.3	−1.9	−1.1	1.7
90 vol%	4.4	5.4	6.4	2.4	1.5	5.0
95 vol%	4.3	6.6	8.9	2.8	1.4	5.3
FBP	0.8	3.4	7.4	−1.2	−3.0	−0.4
Average absolute deviation (°C)	3.3	4.2	5.1	2.3	2.7	3.0

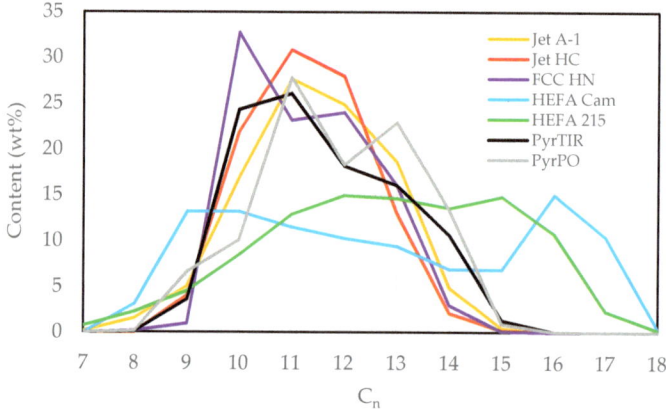

Figure 3. Distribution of hydrocarbons in the samples studied by carbon number.

Each of the samples studied has its characteristic imprint in Figure 3, which differed more significantly than the distillation curves. The high concentration of hydrocarbons C_{10}–C_{13} was typical for crude oil-based samples. The Jet A-1 sample based on the hydrotreated straight-run kerosene had a very similar hydrocarbon distribution to kerosene from hydrocracking (Jet HC). In contrast, in both HEFAs, a wider range of C_9–C_{16} hydrocarbons was present, without a significant maximum. Logically, the narrower the distillation range of the samples studied (Figure 2), the smaller the difference in the carbon numbers of the samples.

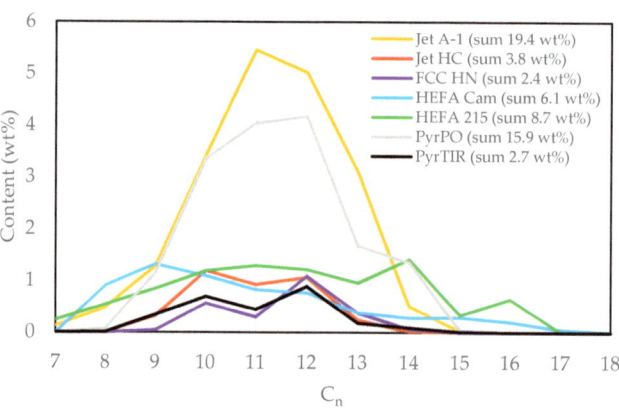

Figure 4. Distribution of n-alkanes in the samples studied by carbon number.

The total n-alkane content of each sample is given in the figure legend. It varied substantially from sample to sample. For samples representing the product of cracking technologies, i.e., hydrocracking (Jet HC, HEFA Cam and HEFA 215), catalytic cracking (FCC HN) and pyrolysis (PyrTIR), the n-alkane content was logically low because n-alkanes crack or isomerize. In the waste polyolefins pyrolysis (PyrPO) sample, n-alkanes were a dominant reaction product mainly for polyethylene cracking. For the Jet A-1 sample, the distribution of n-alkanes corresponded to their presence in straight-run kerosene because n-alkanes are not converted during hydrotreatment, and the concentration was the highest of all samples.

The n-alkane content in kerosene is important due to its direct relationship with the freezing point, which determines the temperature of the formation of the paraffin crystals (Figure 5).

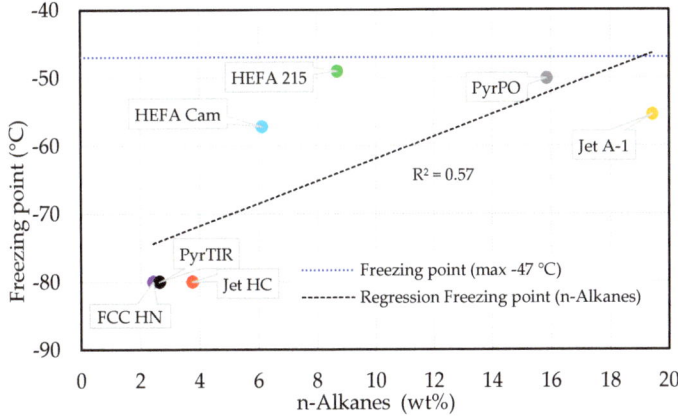

Figure 5. Freezing point relation to the n-alkanes content for the samples studied.

All components met the Jet A-1 freezing point requirements (max -47 °C, see the dotted line in Figure 5). For the three samples studied (Jet HC, FCC HN, and PyrTIR), the freezing point was not measurable by the method used (ASTM D5972); therefore, the value of -80 °C was considered. This may provide an incentive for further development of this method with respect to samples with low concentrations of n-alkanes (<4 wt%) or an extremely low freezing point (<80 °C). On the contrary, both HEFA samples had a relatively high freezing point despite their moderate n-alkane content (<9 wt%). This may be due to the presence of C_{15} and C_{16} n-alkanes in these samples. Although the statement that the freezing point increases with the n-alkane content was generally true for the samples studied, this relationship was not trivial, as shown by the low correlation coefficient $R^2 = 0.57$ for the linear regression in Figure 5. Thus, the n-alkane content was not the only important factor in determining the freezing point of kerosene samples. Aromatics appeared to be another important factor in the behavior of the samples at low temperatures (Figure 6)

The freezing point of the samples decreased with increasing aromatics because the aromatics probably hindered the formation of n-alkane crystals. If aromatics were included as an additional variable in the multivariable linear regression, the value of the correlation coefficient improved significantly ($R^2 = 0.85$). As the alternative components of jet fuel generally represent fractions of very different aromatic contents, this may be a subject of further research.

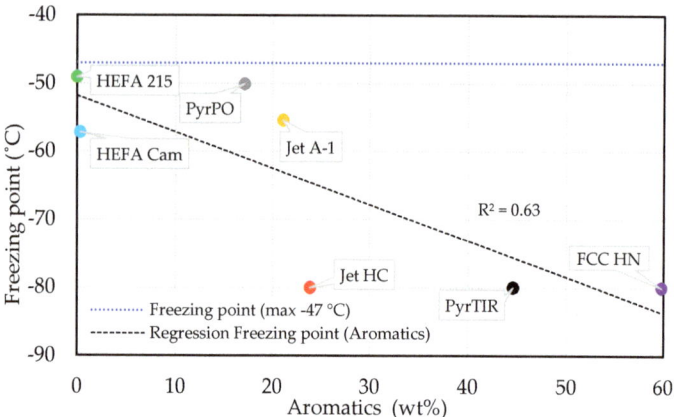

Figure 6. Freezing point relation to the aromatics for the samples studied.

Density is an important characteristic of all petroleum fractions. For jet fuel, density requirements are very liberal, which means that the allowed range is very wide (Table 1). For samples of similar origin, it increases with boiling point. However, for samples of different origin and composition, this relationship is more complex and may even be reversed (Figure 7).

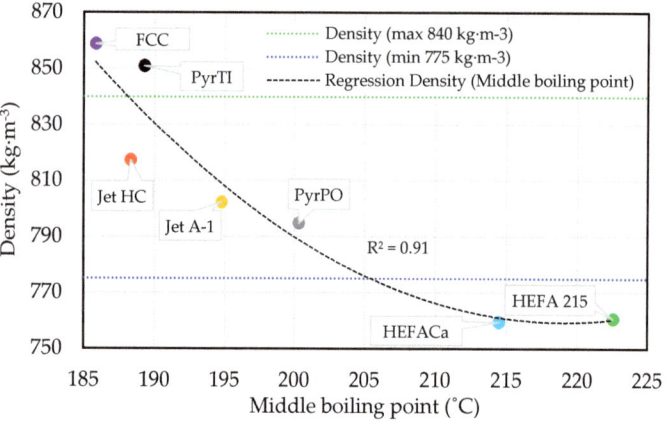

Figure 7. Density relation to the middle boiling point of the samples studied.

Although all of the samples studied met the distillation characteristics and the freezing point required for jet fuel, only three samples met, in principle, the basic density requirement. The density of both HEFA samples was too low due to the almost zero aromatic content, while for the PyrTIR and FCC HC samples, the density was too high, based on their high aromatics (see Table 1). Therefore, for the density of the samples studied, the group composition and aromatics were more important than the distillation characteristic (Figure 8).

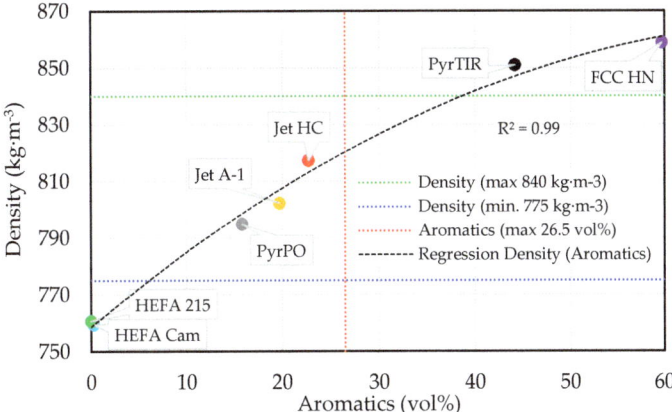

Figure 8. Density relation to the aromatics of the samples studied.

For the samples studied, the density relation to the aromatics was almost linear. The density increased with increasing aromatics. From the samples that did not meet the required density, the PyrTIR and FCC NH samples also did not meet the aromatics requirement. This signals that the use of some samples studied in jet fuel may be problematic because they did not simultaneously meet several critical parameters of jet fuel. However, there might be a possibility of blending samples that are on opposite sides of the density and aromatic spectra, which will be the subject of further research.

The aromatics in jet fuel are closely related to another specific qualitative parameter of this product—the smoke point. In general, the smoke point decreases with increasing aromatics [4]. Which of these characteristics limit the production of jet fuel at the oil refinery first always depends on the specific case. This dependence was investigated for the samples studied (Figure 9).

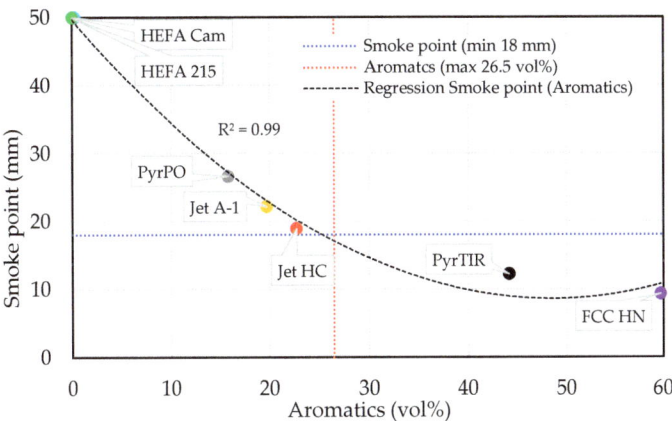

Figure 9. Smoke point relation to the aromatics content for the samples studied.

The dependence of the smoke point on the aromatics was clearly different for samples with a concentration of up to 26.5 vol% and with higher aromatics. For samples with aromatics above the JIG requirement for Jet A-1 max 26.5 vol%, the effect of aromatics on the smoke point was less significant. As far as the two HEFA samples were concerned, the aromatics were so low that the smoke point could not be measured. Therefore, the maximum value of the laboratory instrument used (50 mm) was considered in Figure 9.

Only two samples (PyrTIR and FCC HN) did not meet the smoke point of 18 mm. Furthermore, since the FCC HN sample contained 5.5 vol% diaromatics, it should meet the stricter limit of the smoke point minimum (25 mm), and therefore, this sample was significantly outside the JIG requirement for Jet A-1. Based on Figure 9, it can be concluded that there is a nonlinear relationship between the smoke point and aromatics for components with very different aromatics.

In jet fuel, aromatics represent a chemical structure with the lowest $(H/C)_{at}$ ratio. Since hydrogen generally has the highest net specific energy (NSE) per unit mass of all elements, samples with the highest aromatics should have the lowest value of all samples (Figure 10).

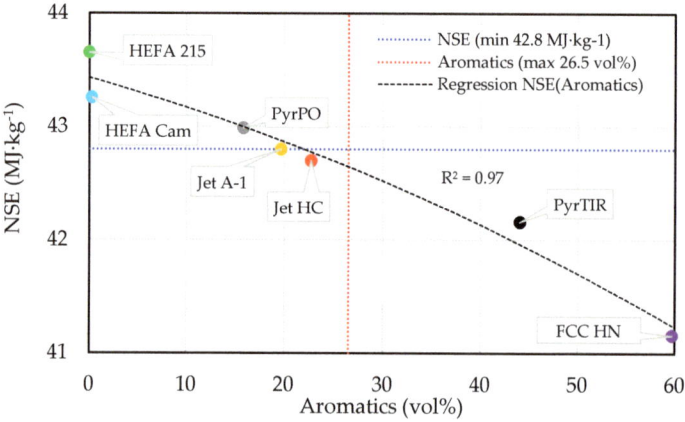

Figure 10. Relationship between measured net specific energy (MJ·kg^{-1}) and aromatics of the samples studied.

The results confirmed the expectations. The two HEFA samples with zero aromatics and the highest $(H/C)_{at}$ ratio (Table 1) had the highest net specific energy, while the two very aromatic samples (PyrTIR and FCC HN) had the lowest value. The Jet A-1 sample, made from hydrotreated straight-run kerosene, had a net specific energy value at the limit of the requirement (42.8 MJ·kg^{-1}).

ASTM D3338 provides a correlation to calculate the net specific energy. It was interesting to see how accurate this calculation is for samples with compositions significantly different from standard jet fuel. A comparison of experimental and calculated values yielded a maximum deviation of 2.1%, indicating that this correlation can be used on a wide range of jet fuel compositions (Table 1).

From the point of view of an airline carrier, the net specific energy in a unit volume of jet fuel, which depends not only on the chemical composition but also on the density of the jet fuel, should be more important than the net specific energy in a unit mass (Figure 11).

This dependence is the opposite of the dependence depicted in Figure 10. Thus, the density has a greater effect on the net specific energy per unit volume of jet fuel than the $(H/C)_{at}$ ratio. For example, a unit volume of the sample of standard jet fuel (Jet A-1, density 802.3 kg·m^{-3}, $(H/C)_{at}$ 1.928) contained 4.3% more energy than the HEF Cam sample (density 759.5 kg·m^{-3}, $(H/C)_{at}$ 2.177).

The experimental results obtained for the Jet A-1 and HEFA Cam samples agree very well with the certificates from the independent laboratories available for these samples, which confirmed the precision of the results obtained.

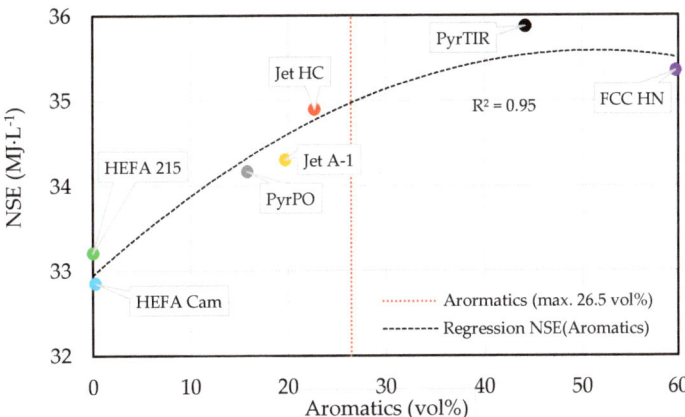

Figure 11. Relationship between measured net specific energy (MJ·L^{-1}) and aromatics of the samples studied.

4. Conclusions

Seven kerosene samples of very different technological origin and composition were studied in terms of Jet A-1 property requirements. The samples represented not only prospective SAFs (HEFA and kerosene from pyrolysis of recycled plastics and scrapped tires) but also interesting crude straight-run kerosene petroleum alternatives, i.e., kerosene produced by deep hydrocracking of vacuum distillates and FCC hydrotreated heavy naphtha. The focus of the study was on the specific and critical properties of these samples related to jet fuel.

Both HEFA samples differed significantly by zero aromatics and non-smoke combustion from the other petroleum-based ones. Four out of the seven samples studied did not meet the current JIG requirements for Jet A-1. These samples were the two HEFA (density < 775 kg·m^{-3}), FCC hydrotreated heavy naphtha and hydrotreated kerosene, from the pyrolysis of scrapped tires (for both density > 840 kg·m^{-3}, aromatics > 26.5 vol%, smoke point < 18 mm and net specific energy < 42.8 MJ·kg^{-1}). Thus, the critical properties of the samples were density, aromatics, smoke point and net specific energy. In contrast to the current prevailing practice of producing jet fuel by simple additivation of a single fraction, it will be necessary to blend the studied alternative components with straight-run kerosene (drop-in concept) or with each other, i.e., similar to the way other motor fuels are now produced. Some of the properties of the samples studied differed significantly from those of the petroleum fractions currently used (freezing point < −80 °C, smoke point > 50 mm, density significantly outside the required range of 775–840 kg·m^3), so it will be necessary to consider modifications to the existing standards and the modification of analytical methods to determine their properties in a wider range (freezing and smoke point). This will be extremely important to properly evaluate the benefits of alternative components in refinery optimization models. The results of the measurements inspired further research aimed at blending alternative petroleum components with SAFs and components that lie on the opposite sides of the spectrum of the properties studied, such as HEFA and FCC hydrotreated heavy naphtha.

Author Contributions: Conceptualization, H.K. and J.H.; methodology, P.Š.; software, P.Š.; validation, H.K., J.H. and P.Š.; formal analysis, H.K. and P.Š.; investigation, P.Š.; resources, H.K. and J.H.; data curation, H.K.; writing—original draft preparation, H.K.; writing—review and editing, J.H. and P.Š.; visualization, H.K.; supervision, P.Š.; project administration, H.K.; funding acquisition, P.Š. All authors have read and agreed to the published version of the manuscript.

Funding: This research was funded by the Ministry of Education, Youth and Sports of the Czech Republic from the institutional support of the research organization (CZ60461373).

Data Availability Statement: The data presented in this study are available on request from the corresponding author.

Conflicts of Interest: The authors declare no conflict of interest.

Nomenclature

ASTM	American Society for Testing and Materials, West Conshohocken, PA, USA
CAPEX	Capital Expenditures
EN	Euro Norm, Office for Official Publications of the European Communities, Luxembourg, Luxembourg
FBP	Final Boiling Point
FCC	Fluid Catalytic Cracking
HEFA	Hydrogenated Esters and Fatty Acids
HN	Heavy Naphtha
HVO	Hydrogenated Vegetable Oil
IATA	International Air Transport Association
IBP	Initial Boiling Point
IEA	International Energy Agency
ISO	International Organization for Standardization, Geneva, Switzerland
JIG	Joint Inspection Group, Cambourne, Great Britain
NSE	Net Specific Energy
SAF	Sustainable Aviation Fuels
UCT	University of Chemistry and Technology Prague

References

1. Hanson, S. EIA Projects Energy Consumption in Air Transportation to Increase through 2050. Available online: https://www.eia.gov/todayinenergy/detail.php?id=41913 (accessed on 15 November 2022).
2. ATAG. ATAG Facts & Figures. Available online: https://www.atag.org/facts-figures.html (accessed on 4 May 2022).
3. Warren, K.A. *World Jet Fuel Specifications with Avgas Supplement*; ExxonMobil Aviation: Brussels, Belgium, 2008.
4. Kittel, H.; Kadleček, D.; Šimáček, P. Factors influencing production of JET fuel by hydrocracking. *Pet. Sci. Technol.* **2021**, *40*, 73–91. [CrossRef]
5. JIG. *The Aviation Fuel Quality Requirements for Jointly Operated Systems (AFQRJOS) Product Specification Bulletin*; Joint Inspection Group: Cambourne, UK, 2022; pp. 1–10.
6. Kolhe, N.S.; Syed, F.; Yadav, S.; Yele, K. Desulphurization of Jet Fuel using Merox Process: A Review. *Int. J. Res.* **2022**, *6*, 3910–3922. [CrossRef]
7. Edwards, J.T. Reference jet fuels for combustion testing. In Proceedings of the 55th AIAA aerospace sciences meeting, Grapevine, TX, USA, 9–13 January 2017; pp. 1–58.
8. Adekitan, A.I.; Shomefun, T.; John, T.M.; Adetokun, B.; Aligbe, A. Dataset on statistical analysis of jet A-1 fuel laboratory properties for on-spec into-plane operations. *Data Brief* **2018**, *19*, 826–834. [CrossRef] [PubMed]
9. Wang, X.; Jia, T.; Pan, L.; Liu, Q.; Fang, Y.; Zou, J.-J.; Zhang, X. Review on the relationship between liquid aerospace fuel composition and their physicochemical properties. *Trans. Tianjin Univ.* **2021**, *27*, 87–109. [CrossRef]
10. IATA. Net Zero 2050: Sustainable Aviation Fuels. Available online: https://www.iata.org/en/iata-repository/pressroom/fact-sheets/fact-sheet---alternative-fuels/ (accessed on 14 January 2023).
11. Liu, G.; Yan, B.; Chen, G. Technical review on jet fuel production. *Renew. Sustain. Energy Rev.* **2013**, *25*, 59–70. [CrossRef]
12. Kandaramath, H.T.; Yaakob, Z.; Binitha, N.N. Aviation biofuel from renewable resources: Routes, opportunities and challenges. *Renew. Sustain. Energy Rev.* **2015**, *42*, 1234–1244. [CrossRef]
13. Ail, S.S.; Dasappa, S. Biomass to liquid transportation fuel via Fischer Tropsch synthesis—Technology review and current scenario. *Renew. Sustain. Energy Rev.* **2016**, *58*, 267–286. [CrossRef]
14. Chuck, C. *Biofuels for Aviation: Feedstocks, Technology and Implementation*; Academic Press: Kidlington, UK, 2016; p. 374.
15. Mawhood, R.; Gazis, E.; de Jong, S.; Hoefnagels, R.; Slade, R. Production pathways for renewable jet fuel: A review of commercialization status and future prospects. *Biofuels Bioprod. Biorefining* **2016**, *10*, 462–484. [CrossRef]
16. Gutiérrez-Antonio, C.; Gómez-Castro, F.; de Lira-Flores, J.; Hernández, S. A review on the production processes of renewable jet fuel. *Renew. Sustain. Energy Rev.* **2017**, *79*, 709–729. [CrossRef]
17. Kaltschmitt, M.; Neuling, U. *Biokerosene: Status and Prospects*; Springer: Berlin/Heidelberg, Germany, 2017; p. 758.

18. Vásquez, M.C.; Silva, E.E.; Castillo, E.F. Hydrotreatment of vegetable oils: A review of the technologies and its developments for jet biofuel production. *Biomass Bioenergy* **2017**, *105*, 197–206. [CrossRef]
19. de Souza, L.M.; Mendes, P.A.; Aranda, D.A. Assessing the current scenario of the Brazilian biojet market. *Renew. Sustain. Energy Rev.* **2018**, *98*, 426–438. [CrossRef]
20. Khan, S.; Kay Lup, A.N.; Qureshi, K.M.; Abnisa, F.; Wan Daud, W.M.A.; Patah, M.F.A. A review on deoxygenation of triglycerides for jet fuel range hydrocarbons. *J. Anal. Appl. Pyrolysis* **2019**, *140*, 1–24. [CrossRef]
21. Bauen, A.; Bitossi, N.; German, L.; Harris, A.; Leow, K. Sustainable Aviation Fuels: Status, challenges and prospects of drop-in liquid fuels, hydrogen and electrification in aviation. *Johns. Matthey Technol. Rev.* **2020**, *64*, 263–278. [CrossRef]
22. Doliente, S.S.; Narayan, A.; Tapia, J.F.D.; Samsatli, N.J.; Zhao, Y.; Samsatli, S. Bio-aviation Fuel: A Comprehensive Review and Analysis of the Supply Chain Components. *Front. Energy Res.* **2020**, *8*, 1–38. [CrossRef]
23. Holladay, J.; Abdullah, Z.; Heyne, J. *Sustainable Aviation Fuel: Review of Technical Pathways*; U.S. Department of Energy: Washington, DC, USA, 2020; p. 67.
24. Dodd, T.; Yengin, D. Deadlock in sustainable aviation fuels: A multi-case analysis of agency. *Transp. Res. Part D Transp. Environ.* **2021**, *94*, 1–14. [CrossRef]
25. Gibbs, A.; Soubly, K.; Calderwood, L.U.; Agnes, C.E.; Delasalle, F.; Moroz, D.; Mugabo, A. Clean Skies for Tomorrow—Sustainable Aviation. In *Clean Skies for Tomorrow: Sustainable Aviation Fuel Policy Toolkit*; World Economic Forum: Geneva, Switzerland, 2021; p. 41.
26. Martinez-Valencia, L.; Garcia-Perez, M.; Wolcott, M.P. Supply chain configuration of sustainable aviation fuel: Review, challenges, and pathways for including environmental and social benefits. *Renew. Sustain. Energy Rev.* **2021**, *152*, 1–21. [CrossRef]
27. Ng, K.S.; Farooq, D.; Yang, A. Global biorenewable development strategies for sustainable aviation fuel production. *Renew. Sustain. Energy Rev.* **2021**, *150*, 1–14. [CrossRef]
28. Mäki-Arvela, P.; Martínez-Klimov, M.; Murzin, D.Y. Hydroconversion of fatty acids and vegetable oils for production of jet fuels. *Fuel* **2021**, *306*, 1–17. [CrossRef]
29. Kittel, H.; Horský, J. The future of Jet fuel as an important refinery product. In Proceedings of the 9th ICCT Conference 2022, Nanjing, China, 11–14 November 2022; Veselý, M., Hrdlička, Z., Hanika, J., Lubojacký, J., Eds.; AMCA Prague: Mikulov, Czech Republic, 2022; pp. 29–36.
30. IEA. The IEA Bioenergy Conference 2021. Available online: https://www.ieabioenergyconference2021.org/ (accessed on 9 December 2022).
31. The IEA Bioenergy Webinar—Sustainable Aviation Fuel/Biojet Technologies—Commercialization Status, Oportunities and Challenges. Available online: https://www.ieabioenergy.com/blog/publications/iea-bioenergy-webinar-sustainable-aviation-fuel-biojet-technologies-commercialisation-status-opportunities-and-challenges/ (accessed on 17 April 2022).
32. IEA. The IEA Bioenergy Task 39—Biofuels to Decarbonize Transport. Available online: https://task39.ieabioenergy.com/ (accessed on 12 April 2022).
33. Seber, G.; Malina, R.; Pearlson, M.N.; Olcay, H.; Hileman, J.I.; Barrett, S.R. Environmental and economic assessment of producing hydroprocessed jet and diesel fuel from waste oils and tallow. *Biomass Bioenergy* **2014**, *67*, 108–118. [CrossRef]
34. Diederichs, G.W.; Ali Mandegari, M.; Farzad, S.; Gorgens, J.F. Techno-economic comparison of biojet fuel production from lignocellulose, vegetable oil and sugar cane juice. *Bioresour. Technol.* **2016**, *216*, 331–339. [CrossRef] [PubMed]
35. Geleynse, S.; Brandt, K.; Garcia-Perez, M.; Wolcott, M.; Zhang, X. The Alcohol-to-Jet Conversion Pathway for Drop-In Biofuels: Techno-Economic Evaluation. *ChemSusChem* **2018**, *11*, 3728–3741. [CrossRef] [PubMed]
36. Dahal, K.; Brynolf, S.; Xisto, C.; Hansson, J.; Grahn, M.; Grönstedt, T.; Lehtveer, M. Techno-economic review of alternative fuels and propulsion systems for the aviation sector. *Renew. Sustain. Energy Rev.* **2021**, *151*, 1–15. [CrossRef]
37. Shahriar, M.F.; Khanal, A. The current techno-economic, environmental, policy status and perspectives of sustainable aviation fuel (SAF). *Fuel* **2022**, *325*, 1–26. [CrossRef]
38. Rumizen, M.A. Qualification of Alternative Jet Fuels. *Front. Energy Res.* **2021**, *9*, 1–8. [CrossRef]
39. *ASTM D7566-22*; Standard Specification for Aviation Turbine Fuel Containing Synthesized Hydrocarbons. American Society for Testing and Materials: West Conshohocken, PA, USA, 2022.
40. Vozka, P.; Šimáček, P.; Kilaz, G. Impact of HEFA Feedstocks on Fuel Composition and Properties in Blends with Jet A. *Energy Fuels* **2018**, *32*, 11595–11606. [CrossRef]
41. Vozka, P.; Vrtiška, D.; Šimáček, P.; Kilaz, G. Impact of Alternative Fuel Blending Components on Fuel Composition and Properties in Blends with Jet A. *Energy Fuels* **2019**, *33*, 3275–3289. [CrossRef]
42. Manigandan, S.; Atabani, A.E.; Ponnusamy, V.K.; Gunasekar, P. Impact of additives in Jet-A fuel blends on combustion, emission and exergetic analysis using a micro-gas turbine engine. *Fuel* **2020**, *276*, 1–9. [CrossRef]
43. Srinivas, D.; Satyarthi, J.K. Challenges and opportunities in biofuels production. *Indian J. Chem.* **2012**, *51*, 174–185.
44. NESTE. Renewable NEXBTL Diesel—Fuel with Many Applications. Available online: https://www.neste.com/renewable-nexbtl-diesel-fuel-many-applications (accessed on 4 May 2022).
45. NESTE. NEXBTL Technology. Available online: https://www.neste.com/about-neste/innovation/nexbtl-technology (accessed on 7 January 2023).
46. HONEYWELL-UOP. Honeywell Introduces Simplified Technology to Produce Renewable Diesel. Available online: https://uop.honeywell.com/en/news-events/2021/january/honeywell-uop-ecofining-single-stage-process (accessed on 12 May 2022).

47. Rytter, E. *Status and Developments in Fischer-Tropsch Synthesis. Issues of Importance to Biomass Conversion and Jetfuel Production*; Norwegian University of Science and Technology: Trondheim, Norway, 2016.
48. Sun, J.; Yang, G.; Peng, X.; Kang, J.; Wu, J.; Liu, G.; Tsubaki, N. Beyond Cars: Fischer-Tropsch Synthesis for Non-Automotive Applications. *ChemCatChem* **2019**, *11*, 1412–1424. [CrossRef]
49. van Dyk, S.; Saddler, J. Progress in Commercialisation of Biojet fuels/SAF: Technologies, potencial and challenges. In Proceedings of the IEA Bioenergy Conference, Online, 29 November–1 December 2021.
50. Chui, S. Flying the Rolls Royce B747 Test Bed—An Experimental Flight with 100% SAF. Available online: https://www.youtube.com/watch?v=4gSKbmODNxI (accessed on 23 March 2022).
51. AIRBUS. First A380 Powered by 100% Sustainable Aviation Fuel Takes to the Skies. Available online: https://www.airbus.com/en/newsroom/press-releases/2022-03-first-a380-powered-by-100-sustainable-aviation-fuel-takes-to-the (accessed on 5 April 2022).
52. AIRBUS. This A380 Is the Latest to Test 100% SAF. Available online: https://www.airbus.com/en/newsroom/news/2022-03-this-a380-is-the-latest-to-test-100-saf (accessed on 24 April 2022).
53. ROLLS ROYCE. Alternative Fuels—Fuelling a Sustainable Future. Available online: https://www.rolls-royce.com/innovation/net-zero/decarbonising-complex-critical-systems/alternative-fuels.aspx (accessed on 9 January 2023).
54. Sieppi, S. Brussels Airlines Starts New Year with a First Delivery of Neste MY Sustainable Aviation Fuel to Brussels Airport via CEPS Pipeline. Available online: https://www.neste.com/releases-and-news/renewable-solutions/brussels-airlines-starts-new-year-first-delivery-neste-my-sustainable-aviation-fuel-brussels-airport (accessed on 7 January 2023).
55. Zhang, X.; Lei, H.; Zhu, L.; Qian, M.; Zhu, X.; Wu, J.; Chen, S. Enhancement of jet fuel range alkanes from co-feeding of lignocellulosic biomass with plastics via tandem catalytic conversions. *Energy* **2016**, *173*, 418–430. [CrossRef]
56. Ragaert, K.; Delva, L.; Van Geem, K. Mechanical and chemical recycling of solid plastic waste. *Waste Manag.* **2017**, *69*, 24–58. [CrossRef]
57. Tomasek, S.; Varga, Z.; Holló, A.; Miskolczi, N.; Hancsók, J. Production of JET fuel containing molecules of high hydrogen content. *Catal. Sustain. Energy* **2017**, *4*, 52–58. [CrossRef]
58. Zhang, Y.; Duan, D.; Lei, H.; Villota, E.; Ruan, R. Jet fuel production from waste plastics via catalytic pyrolysis with activated carbons. *Appl. Energy* **2019**, *251*, 1–17. [CrossRef]
59. Tomasek, S.; Varga, Z.; Hancsók, J. Production of jet fuel from cracked fractions of waste polypropylene and polyethylene. *Fuel Process. Technol.* **2020**, *197*, 1–7. [CrossRef]
60. Qureshi, M.S.; Oasmaa, A.; Pihkola, H.; Deviatkin, I.; Tenhunen, A.; Mannila, J.; Minkkinen, H.; Pohjakallio, M.; Laine-Ylijokid, J. Pyrolysis of plastic waste: Opportunities and challenges. *J. Anal. Appl. Pyrolysis* **2020**, *152*, 1–11. [CrossRef]
61. Suchocki, T.; Witanowski, Ł.; Lampart, P.; Kazimierski, P.; Januszewicz, K.; Gawron, B. Experimental investigation of performance and emission characteristics of a miniature gas turbine supplied by blends of kerosene and waste tyre pyrolysis oil. *Energy* **2021**, *215*, 1–10. [CrossRef]
62. van Dyk, S.; Si, J.; McMillan, J.D.; Saddler, J. *Drop-in: The Key Role that co-Processing Will Play in Its Production*; IEA Bioenergy: Paris, France, 2019.
63. EIA. Hydrocracking Is an Important Source of Diesel and Jet Fuel. Available online: https://www.eia.gov/todayinenergy/detail.php?id=9650 (accessed on 9 February 2023).
64. Peng, C.; Cao, Z.; Du, Y.; Zeng, R.; Guo, R.; Duan, X.; Fang, X. Optimization of a Pilot Hydrocracking Unit to Improve the Yield and Quality of Jet Fuel Together with Heavy Naphtha and Tail Oil. *Ind. Eng. Chem. Res.* **2018**, *57*, 2068–2074. [CrossRef]
65. Larsen, J.L. *Upgrading of FCC Heavy Gasoline to Jet Fuel in a Two-Stage Hydrogenation Process*; American Institute of Chemical Engineers: New York, NY, USA, 1997; p. 21.
66. Kim, H.; Kim, D.; Park, Y.-K.; Jeon, J.-K. Synthesis of jet fuel through the oligomerization of butenes on zeolite catalysts. *Res. Chem. Intermed.* **2018**, *44*, 3823–3833. [CrossRef]
67. Nicholas, C.P. Applications of light olefin oligomerization to the production of fuels and chemicals. *Appl. Catal. A Gen.* **2017**, *543*, 82–97. [CrossRef]
68. Kittel, H.; Straka, P.; Šimáček, P.; Kadleček, D. Kerosene from hydrocracking for JET fuel with reduced aromatic content. *Pet. Sci. Technol.* **2022**, *41*, 507–523. [CrossRef]
69. Straka, P.; Auersvald, M.; Vrtiška, D.; Kittel, H.; Šimáček, P.; Vozka, P. Production of transportation fuels via hydrotreating of scrap tires pyrolysis oil. *Chem. Eng. J.* **2023**, *460*, 141764. [CrossRef]
70. Horský, J. *Study of Synergies in the Production of JET Fuel by Blending Fractions of Different Technological Origin*; UCT Prague: Prague, Czech Republic, 2022.

Disclaimer/Publisher's Note: The statements, opinions and data contained in all publications are solely those of the individual author(s) and contributor(s) and not of MDPI and/or the editor(s). MDPI and/or the editor(s) disclaim responsibility for any injury to people or property resulting from any ideas, methods, instructions or products referred to in the content.

Article

Screening and Investigation on Inhibition of Sediment Formation in a Kuwait Light Crude Oil by Commercial Additives with Some Guidelines for Field Applications

A. Qubian [1], A. S. Abbas [1], N. Al-Khedhair [1], J. F. Peres [1], D. Stratiev [2,3], I. Shishkova [2], R. Nikolova [4], V. Toteva [5] and M. R. Riazi [6,7,*]

1. Innovation and Technology Group, Kuwait Oil Company (KOC), Ahmadi P.O. Box 9758, Ahmadi 61008, Kuwait; aqubian@kockw.com (A.Q.); asabbas@kockw.com (A.S.A.); nkhedhair@kockw.com (N.A.-K.); jperes@kockw.com (J.F.P.)
2. LUKOIL Neftohim Burgas, 8104 Burgas, Bulgaria
3. Institute of Biophysics and Biomedical Engineering, Bulgarian Academy of Sciences, 1113 Sofia, Bulgaria
4. Central Research Laboratory, University Prof. Dr. Assen Zlatarov, 8010 Burgas, Bulgaria
5. Department Chemical Technologies, University of Chemical Technology and Metallurgy, 1756 Sofia, Bulgaria
6. College of Engineering and Petroleum, Kuwait University, Safat P.O. Box 5969, Safat 13060, Kuwait
7. Montreal Oil and Gas Inc., Montreal, QC H2Y 2K9, Canada
* Correspondence: mrriazi@gmail.com

Abstract: The precipitation of asphaltene and waxes occurs when crude oil characteristics change as a consequence of pressure, temperature variations, and/or chemical modifications, etc. The costs associated with the cleaning of deposition on the production equipment and the loss of profit opportunities can go beyond hundreds of millions of USD. Thus, there is a strong incentive to search for ways to mitigate deposit formation during the crude production process. A light crude bottom hole fluid sample from a deep well with an asphaltene deposition problem was analyzed in the laboratory. Basic data on density, viscosity, bubble point, GOR, and asphaltene onset pressure were measured at a PVT laboratory. Asphaltene characterization, as a prescreening for appropriate inhibitors, has been conducted using asphaltene phase diagrams (APD). The APD generated from two developed software programs in both Matlab and Excel codes were favorably compared with the phase behavior of other oil samples available in the literature and has shown to be an excellent match. Various test methods were used to demonstrate the asphaltene instability of the oil samples. Eleven chemical inhibitors from five global companies were screened for testing to inhibit the precipitation. The optimum concentration and the amount of reduction in precipitation were determined for all of these chemicals to identify the most suitable chemicals. Finally, some recommendations are given for the field application of chemicals.

Keywords: crude oil; SARA; asphaltene stability; precipitation; asphaltene inhibitor

1. Introduction

Asphaltene precipitation can negatively affect the oil recovery and refining processes from its early stage in the reservoir and during enhanced oil recovery (EOR), to the flow of produced oil in the production well, as well as surface facilities. Through the adsorption of crude oil polar components onto surfaces, asphaltene can alter wettability. It will also block pore spaces, resulting in reduced local permeability and, therefore, reduce oil production rates. The asphaltene deposition can also occur in the production well where the pressure drop is maximum, and the thickness of deposited asphaltene changes over time. If the crude oil is sensitive to the acids used for well stimulation this may cause a decrease in the production rate due to asphaltene precipitation. Furthermore, it is also reported that an increase in asphaltene precipitation has been observed in sections of the well with increases in turbulence in the flow.

Asphaltenes are complex molecules with molecular weights ranging from 1000 to 5000 g/mol and densities of about 1100–1250 kgm^{-3}. Asphaltene molecules contain some heteroatoms such as nitrogen, sulfur, and oxygen. They are mainly aromatics and may precipitate at certain thermodynamic conditions such as temperature, pressure, and oil composition. Asphaltene colloid formation, flocculation, and precipitation processes have been studied and reported in the literature [1–4].

The presence of resins plays an imperative role in asphaltene precipitation and deposition. During gas injection into a reservoir for enhanced oil recovery processes, the composition of oil changes, and, consequently, precipitation may occur [5]. In addition to the composition of the crude oil, the type and amount of injected gas, temperature, pressure, flow characteristics, and properties of the conduit (pipeline or production well) will affect asphaltene precipitation. A recent review of asphaltene precipitation and associated problems in production processes were made by Mohamed, et al. [6,7].

Due to the complex nature of asphaltene, the phenomenon of asphaltene precipitation was never fully understood by the researchers despite extensive research conducted in this area over the last several decades. The three main questions for the industry regarding asphaltene deposition are: when it happens, how much precipitation occurs, and how to prevent or reduce the amount of precipitation.

It is important to correctly predict the onset of asphaltene precipitation and deposition. Thermodynamic models developed for the prediction of asphaltene precipitation are composition-dependent and they should be optimized for a given crude. We will use some crude oil samples and will develop a suitable thermodynamic model tuned for similar oils and reservoirs. This paper is focused on experimental measurements for a light crude oil sample, the development of an appropriate thermodynamic model for the phase behavior of the oil, and the determination of the regions of instability. The other major objective of this work was to determine a suitable inhibitor or chemical that can be used to minimize the amount of asphaltene precipitation.

2. Materials and Methods

2.1. Crude Oil Samples and Their Characterization

The oil sample was taken by the operating company from an onshore deep well (referred to as sample A). This was the main sample used for experiments, testing, and evaluation. Three samples, each of 500 mL were taken on 5 June 2018 at a depth of 14,000 ft. The bottom hole pressure and temperature were 4063 psi and 242 °F, respectively. This oil sample was used in the petroleum research facility laboratory at Kuwait University to measure the basic PVT data, as given in Table 1. The bubble point was determined from a constant mass experiment (CME) conducted at 242°. The composition of the sample was determined from PVT and a subsequent GC analysis. A summary of the results is given in Table 1.

Some similar basic data on another oil sample (Sample B) from another well located in the same field are given in Table 2. The composition of oil samples for these oils is given in Table 3.

In addition to the live oil sample, 10 L of dead crude oil was collected by the gathering center which was received in November 2020. Basic measured properties for these oil samples are given in this section. Properties such as API, density, viscosity, sulfur, and asphaltene contents were measured at Lukoil Neftochim Burgas and are given in Table 4 and the true boiling point distribution is presented in Figure 1.

Table 1. General Properties for Oil Sample A at 242 °F.

Reservoir Temperature	242
Sample volume used at reservoir T & P, mL	67.5
Flashed Liquid Volume at STP, mL	47.1
GOR, scf/bbl	675.5
Basic Sediment & Water Content, wt.%	0
Reservoir Initial Pressure, psig	9300
Bubble point pressure, psia	2271.6
Asphaltene onset pressure, psia	5200
Density at reservoir condition, g/cm^3	0.640
Density at 60 F, kg/m^3	823.8
Mol. Wt., g/mol	194
API Gravity	40.1
Absolute viscosity, cP	4.91
Kinematic viscosity at 60 F, mm^2/s (cSt.)	4.04
SARA analysis of STO	
Saturates, wt.%	65.5
Aromatics, wt.%	28.3
Resin, wt.%	4.7
Asphaltene, wt.%	1.6

Table 2. SARA Analysis and BP of Oil Sample B.

Reservoir Temperature, F	230
Asphaltene onset pressure, psia	4500
Bubble point pressure, psia	3130
SARA analysis of STO	
Saturates, wt.%	57.3
Aromatics, wt.%	28.5
Resin, wt.%	3.1
Asphaltene, wt.%	1.0

Table 3. Composition of two live oil samples from an oil field in the Middle East.

Component	Sample A mol %	Sample B mol %
CO_2	2.03	0.90
N_2	0.12	0.03
H_2S	1.91	0.03
C_1	27.47	41.95
C_2	12.68	10.68
C_3	8.23	7.11
nC_4	3.10	3.48
iC_4	0.90	0.96
nC_5	3.41	2.10
iC_5	2.95	1.22
C_6	5.36	2.89
C_{7+}	31.84	28.65
MW_{7+}	212	211
SG_{7+}	0824	0.843

The densities at two different temperatures were measured according to the ASTM D4052 test method. The sulfur for each cut was measured according to the ISO 8754 test method. These data are given in Table 5 and presented in Figures 2–4. Simulated Distillation (GC) by ASTM D 7196 is presented in Figures 5 and 6.

Table 4. Basic properties of dead crude oil sample.

Property	Value
Density at 15 °C, g/cm^3	0.8313
Density at 20 °C, g/cm^3	0.8277
API Gravity, 60 °F/60 °F	39.29
Sulfur content, wt.%	1.049
C_5 asphaltenes, wt.%	2.6
C_7 asphaltenes, wt.%	1.6
Kin. Viscosity at 40 °C, mm^2/s	9.4

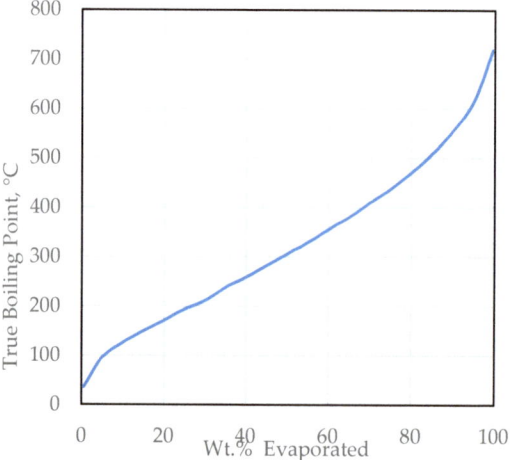

Figure 1. TBP Distribution for the crude oil sample. Test Methods: ASTM D2892 and ASTM D 5236.

Table 5. Density and sulfur contents of narrow cuts. Test Methods: Density: ASTM D4052. Sulfur: ISO 8754.

| Narrow Cuts BP, °C | Density g/cm^3 | | Content of Sulfur, wt.% |
	at 15 °C	at 20 °C	
IBP-70 °C	0.6496	0.6447	0.060
70–100 °C	0.6949	0.6902	0.048
100–110 °C	0.7170	0.7124	0.061
110–130 °C	0.7302	0.7256	0.058
130–150 °C	0.7503	0.7458	0.063
150–170 °C	0.7675	0.7630	0.073
170–180 °C	0.7775	0.7733	0.070
180–200 °C	0.7857	0.7819	0.073
200–220 °C	0.7952	0.7914	0.077
220–240 °C	0.8029	0.799	0.107
240–260 °C	0.8160	0.8123	0.224
260–280 °C	0.8307	0.8271	0.466
280–300 °C	0.8442	0.8406	0.677
300–320 °C	0.8482	0.8446	0.787
320–340 °C	0.8638	0.8602	1.252
340–360 °C	0.8820	0.8784	1.831
>360 °C			
360–380 °C	0.8885	0.8812	1.824
380–390 °C	0.8949	0.8916	1.815
390–430 °C	0.9000	0.8967	1.716
430–470 °C	0.9163	0.9132	1.876
470–490 °C	0.9291	0.9261	2.047
490–500 °C	0.9377	0.9347	2.248
>500 °C	0.9828	0.9802	3.025

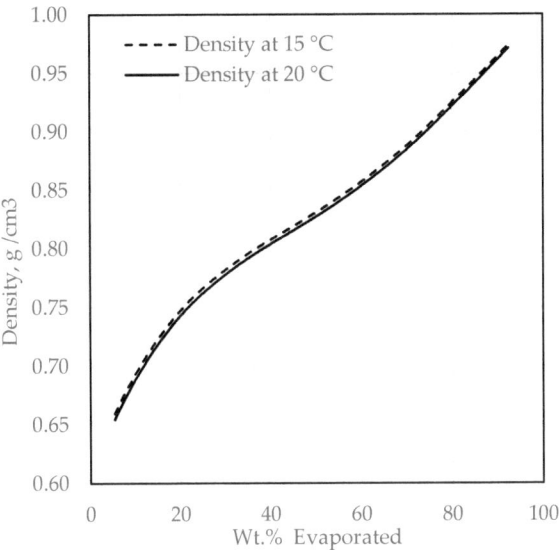

Figure 2. Density of crude cuts at 15 °C and 20 °C.

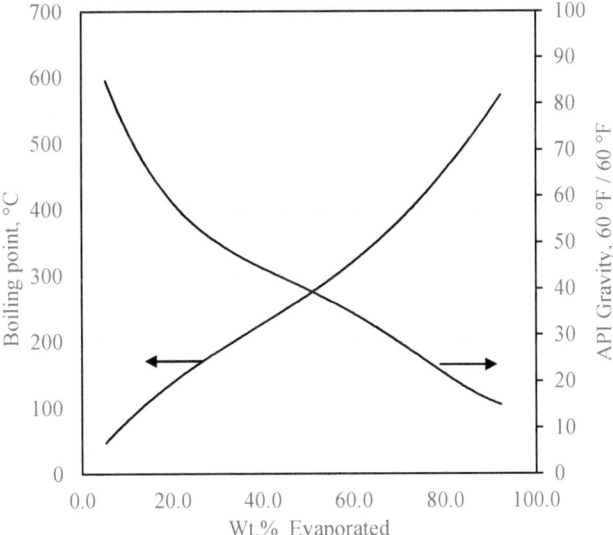

Figure 3. API gravity and boiling point of narrow cuts.

2.2. *Asphaltene Stability Test Methods*

The asphaltene stability test methods employed in this study are itemized below:
- Method I: asphaltene/resin ratio deduced from a SARA analysis as described by Yen et al. [8];
- Method II: colloidal instability index (CII) defined based on SARA analysis as explained in [8] and shown by Equation (1):

$$\text{CII} = \frac{\text{Saturates (wt.\%)} + \text{Asphaltenes (wt.\%)}}{\text{Aromatics (wt.\%)} + \text{Resins (wt.\%)}} \qquad (1)$$

- Method III: asphaltene stability test by the Stankiewicz method explained in detail in [9];
- Method IV: based on the method suggested by Yen et al. [8] based on SARA analysis, where the graph of the Y-X diagram is prepared with Y = Asphaltenes + Saturates; and X = Aromatics + Resins;
- Method V: based on the method suggested by de Boer et al. [10]. It employs the difference between initial pressure and bubble point pressure and the density of reservoir fluid under reservoir conditions.

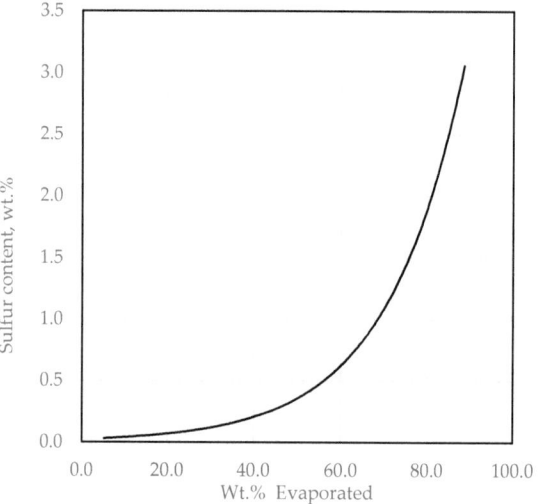

Figure 4. Sulfur content of narrow cuts, wt.%.

Figure 5. Simulated Distillation (GC) by ASTM D7196 for Crude Sample A.

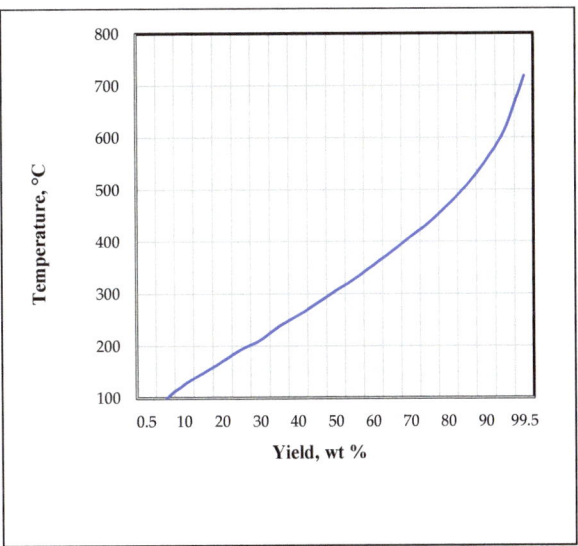

Figure 6. Simulated Distillation (GC) Graph for the Crude Oil Sample A.

2.3. Regions of Asphaltene Instability

Once it has been determined that an oil sample is unstable, based on the methods discussed in the previous section, it is important to determine the region in the phase diagram where asphaltene precipitation can occur. This can be done through an asphaltene phase diagram (APD). Generation of an APD is the key to determining under what conditions asphaltene formation occurs. Perturbed chain statistical associating fluid theory (PC-SAFT) is a rather advanced approach to the estimation of the behavior of a complex mixture originally proposed by Chapman et al. [11], and later modified by Gross and Sadowsky [12]. Cubic-plus-association equation of state (CPA-EOS) is also another class of EOS, which takes into account the association between the molecules. Chapman and his group at Rice University over the last two decades showed that PC-SAFT is quite suitable for estimating the asphaltene–crude oil PVT behavior [13–17]. They particularly proposed a thermodynamic framework based on PC-SAFT EOS to predict asphaltene phase behavior and named the tool the asphaltene deposition tool (ADEPT) [13]. According to Gross and Sadowsky, the total compressibility factor can be calculated as the sum of the ideal gas, hard chain, and dispersion contributions, as follows [12]: $Z = Z^{id} + Z^{hc} + Z^{disp}$. In the PC-SAFT framework, three parameters of segment number in a chain (m), the segment diameter (σ), and segment energy (ϵ/k) are used to differentiate components. So far, researchers have proposed different methods for the estimation of these parameters [11]. There exist a few correlations that are mostly used for asphaltene precipitation modeling, as reported by Gonzalez et al. [15] which can be used for calculating the PC-SAFT parameters of petroleum cuts and fractions.

In this work, the PC-SAFT approach of neglecting the association term was used to develop software for the asphaltene phase equilibria calculation of some Kuwaiti oil samples. Two software were developed, one with Matlab and one fully with Excel VBA code. The Matlab version is faster as it uses its internal optimization tool while for Excel, we developed our own optimization in the VBA codes. The input data for each oil sample is fluid composition, SARA analysis, bubble point, and or onset pressure at least at the reservoir or bottom hole temperature (BHT). For gas injection processes, an option for the amount of injected gas is provided. Experimental data on bubble point and/or upper asphaltene onset pressure (UAOP) can be used to get optimized values for the aromaticity and molecular weight of the asphaltene component of the oil sample. These parameters need to be determined only once for each crude sample, and for all subsequent calculations, there is no need for this optimization step. When optimized parameters are used, the calculations in Excel are quite fast (similar to Matlab) and calculations are performed in less than 30 seconds. A schematic of the flow diagram for the calculation of asphaltene onset and bubble point pressures is shown in Figure 7.

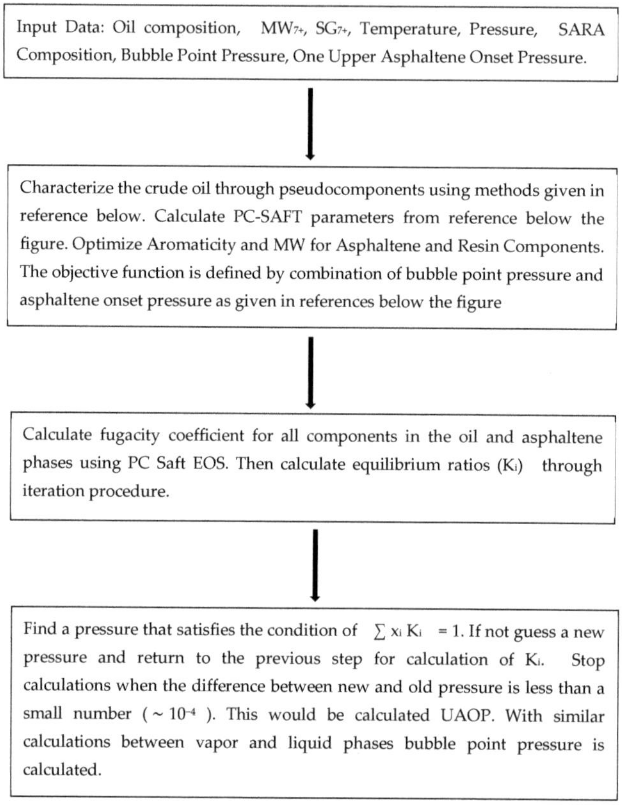

Input Data: Oil composition, MW$_{7+}$, SG$_{7+}$, Temperature, Pressure, SARA Composition, Bubble Point Pressure, One Upper Asphaltene Onset Pressure.

↓

Characterize the crude oil through pseudocomponents using methods given in reference below. Calculate PC-SAFT parameters from reference below the figure. Optimize Aromaticity and MW for Asphaltene and Resin Components. The objective function is defined by combination of bubble point pressure and asphaltene onset pressure as given in references below the figure

↓

Calculate fugacity coefficient for all components in the oil and asphaltene phases using PC Saft EOS. Then calculate equilibrium ratios (K$_i$) through iteration procedure.

↓

Find a pressure that satisfies the condition of $\sum x_i K_i = 1$. If not guess a new pressure and return to the previous step for calculation of K$_i$. Stop calculations when the difference between new and old pressure is less than a small number ($\sim 10^{-4}$). This would be calculated UAOP. With similar calculations between vapor and liquid phases bubble point pressure is calculated.

Figure 7. A summary of calculation procedure for the bubble point and upper asphaltene onset pressures. Characterization method taken from Reference [1], PC-SAFT parameters from [15], optimization procedure from [13,16–18].

2.4. Screening of Chemical Inhibitors for Retardation of Asphaltene Precipitation

The asphaltene flow assurance problem can be handled in three different ways: (one) to prevent it from happening, (two) to reduce the extent of precipitation, and (three) to dissolve deposited asphaltene. It is interesting to know that if the asphaltenes in the produced fluid are in the stable dispersion form, they will not harm the production through permeability reduction, although they will increase the oil–solid mixture viscosity. The extent of asphaltene precipitation can be controlled by not allowing the size of the asphaltene aggregate to grow. For example, the adsorption of nonionic dispersants onto the surface of an asphaltene particle can avoid its growth and, therefore, will limit the size of the aggregate, which in turn will allow the asphaltene to be carried along the oil phase [19].

There are clearly two groups of chemical additives that can prevent asphaltene deposition. They are ADs (asphaltene dispersants) and asphaltene inhibitors (AIs). Examples of nonpolymeric ADs are the very low polarity alkylaromatics or the alkylaryl sulfonic acids. Examples of AIs are the alkylphenol/aldehyde resins and similar sulfonated resins, polyolefin esters, amides or imides with alkyl, alkylenephenyl or alkylenepyridyl functional groups, and alkenyl/vinyl pyrrolidone copolymers. AIs are not effective in formations but are mainly used in wellbores and surface equipment. AIs increase the asphaltene stability under wider operation conditions while ADs reduce the particle size and keep particles in suspension form in the oil. These chemicals are oil-specific. For example, the presence of nitrogen in asphaltene can interact with the polymeric inhibitors containing H+ atoms such as hydroxyl groups. In general, AIs are polymeric-type chemicals and to be effective we must reach a certain critical concentration while ADs act almost proportionately to concentration. AIs can be best applied upstream of the bubble point pressure which is commonly downhole to prevent asphaltene flocculation. It is recommended to use either an AI or an AD, but not both. The use of live oils and dead oils in testing AIs and ADs may give different results, however, tests with dead oil can be used for general screening of AIs or ADs since the trends of effectiveness are similar to those with live oils. More specific information about the properties and effectiveness of these chemical additives is given by Kelland [19].

When an inhibitor is used to reduce asphaltene deposition, we need to determine its performance by measuring the amount of deposit before and after a dispersant is used. Methods of deposit test level are fully described in the literature [20–35]. The asphaltene dispersant test (ADT) method has been used in this study to determine the effectiveness of an inhibitor in reducing asphaltene deposition as described in our earlier study [26] and adopted from [27]. Once the mass of asphaltene before and after the addition of an inhibitor is measured, the efficiency can be calculated from the following equation:

$$\text{Efficiency (\%)} = \frac{\text{Volume of asphalteen deposit before inhibitor} - \text{Volume of Asphalteen deposit after inhibitor}}{\text{Volume of asphalteen deposit before inhibitor}} \times 100 \quad (2)$$

The effect of the use of inhibitors to suppress sediment formation was examined by employing an asphaltene dispersant test (ADT), as described in [27]. The oil sample is mixed with large amounts of heptane to obtain a clear sample that allows sediment observation through it. During this study, the crude oil sample A and the H-Oil ATB samples were mixed with n-heptane in an amount of 93%. The blend of 7% oil/93% n-heptane was placed in a graduated centrifuge tube and then centrifuged at 5000 rpm for 30 min. A sample of the oils with no dispersant was used as a control. The commercial additives were mixed with the studied oils and then homogenized in a closed beaker for a period of one hour using a magnetic stirrer at 700 rpm. Then, three grams of crude oil sample A (0.5 grams of H-Oil VTB samples) with the additive were placed in a graduated centrifuge tube and mixed with 40 grams of n-heptane, and after that centrifuged at 5000 rpm for 30 min. Reading the volume of the sediment from the graduated centrifuge represents the amount of the sediment formed at the conditions studied. The sediment volume of the pure crude oil sample A was 0.12 mL, while those of the pure H-Oil ATB samples were 0.40, and 0.45 mL. The relative error of the measurement of the sediment volume was found to be 11.0%.

3. Results

3.1. Results from Asphaltene Stability Test Methods

One simple method to judge the oil colloidal stability is to calculate the ratio of saturates/aromatics from SARA analysis. This ratio is an indirect measure of the solvating power of an oil sample for asphaltenes (a high ratio implies poor solvating power). The asphaltene/resin ratio, on the other hand (Method I), relates to the measure of colloidal stability of the asphaltenes (ratio of asphaltene/resin implies good colloidal stabilization). Oils with higher resin content are more stable with the addition of a solvent such as n-C_5 or n-C_7. Another simple method is to determine a parameter known as the colloidal instability index (CII) defined based on SARA analysis as described by Yen et al. [8]. If CII is less than 0.7, the oil is stable and if greater than 0.9, it is unstable. If CII is between 0.7 and 0.9, the oil is mildly unstable (Method II). In addition to these methods, there are three other graphical methods. Method III was proposed by Stankiewizc, et al. [9] and Method V is based on the difference between the initial pressure and the bubble point pressure applied to crude oil sample A, as shown in Figure 8a,b, respectively. Another method proposed by Yen et al. [8] shows three regions of unstable, mildly stable, and stable regions from the correlation of SARA data (Method IV). Results obtained from all these methods are consistent with each other. For example, as shown in Figure 9a,b, when Methods III and IV were used to test oil sample B, both methods showed that the crude oil sample is unstable. For the oil in sample B (Table 2), the ratio of asphaltenes/resins is 0.337, which is greater than 0.3, and based on Method I, the oil is unstable. Similarly, the colloidal instability index (CII) based on Method II was calculated for this oil as 2.03, which is greater than 0.9, and, thus, the oil is unstable. As a result, both crude oil samples were unstable according to all these five stability test methods.

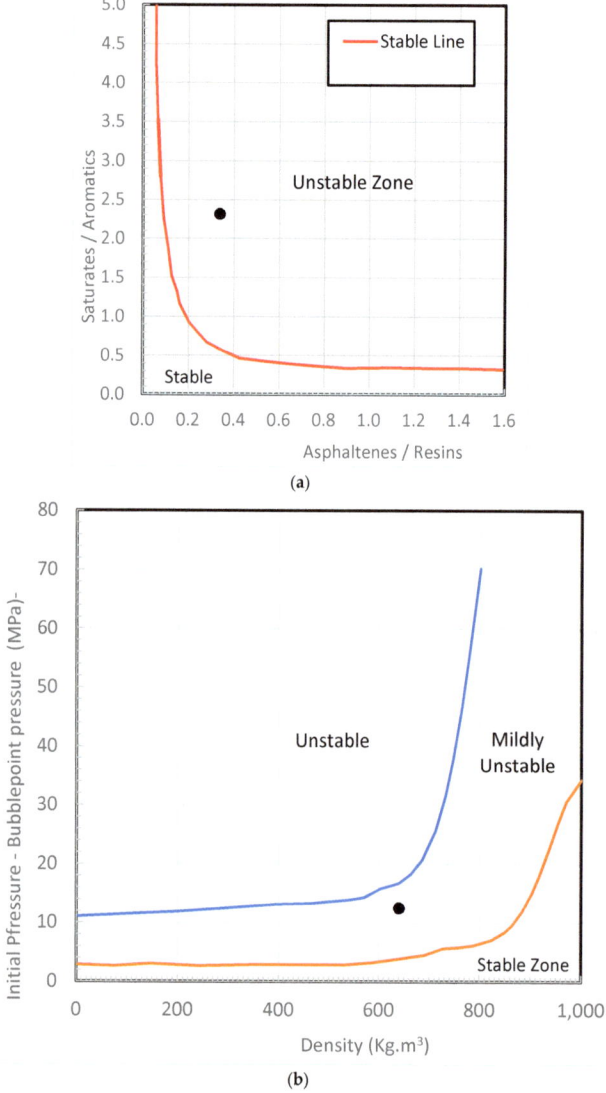

Figure 8. (**a**). Asphaltene Stability Test Method III Applied to Oil Sample A. (**b**). Asphaltene Stability Test Method V Applied to Oil Sample A.

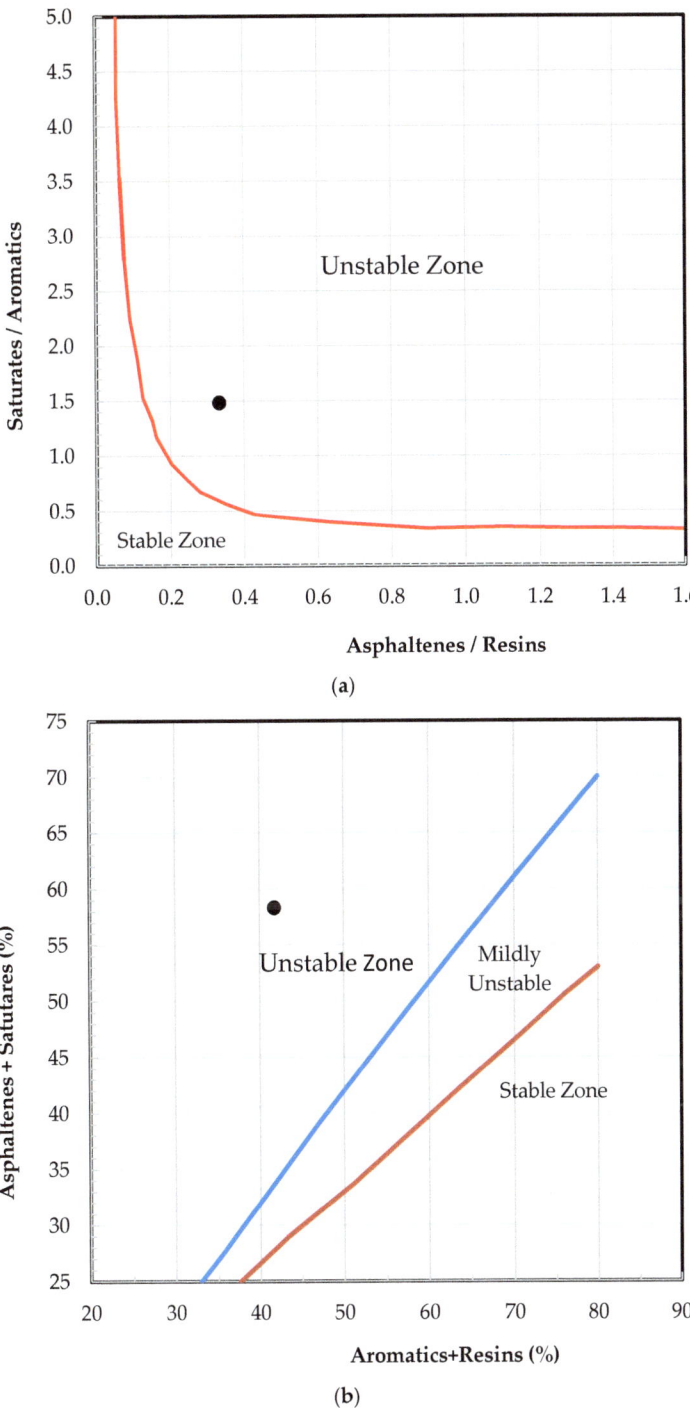

Figure 9. (**a**) Asphaltene Stability Test by Stankiewicz et al. [9] method (Method III) for the Oil Sample B (Table 2). (**b**) Asphaltene Stability Test by Yen's Method (Method IV) for the Oil Sample B.

3.2. Determination of Regions of Asphaltene Instability for the Studied Crude Oil Samples

To evaluate our program, described in Section 2.3 in this work, we used ADEPT [13] of the Chapman group at Rice University with several oil samples, and a good agreement was observed, as shown in Figure 10. A similar agreement was observed when tested with other oil samples in which the ADEPT results were available in the literature.

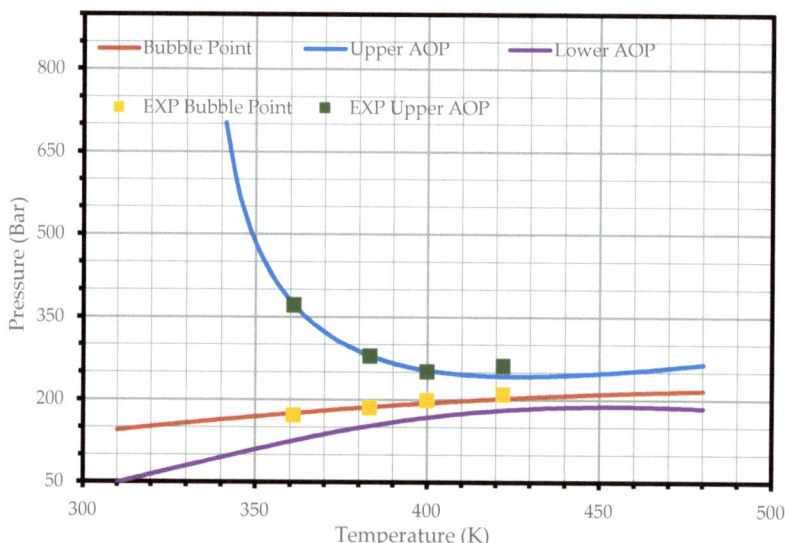

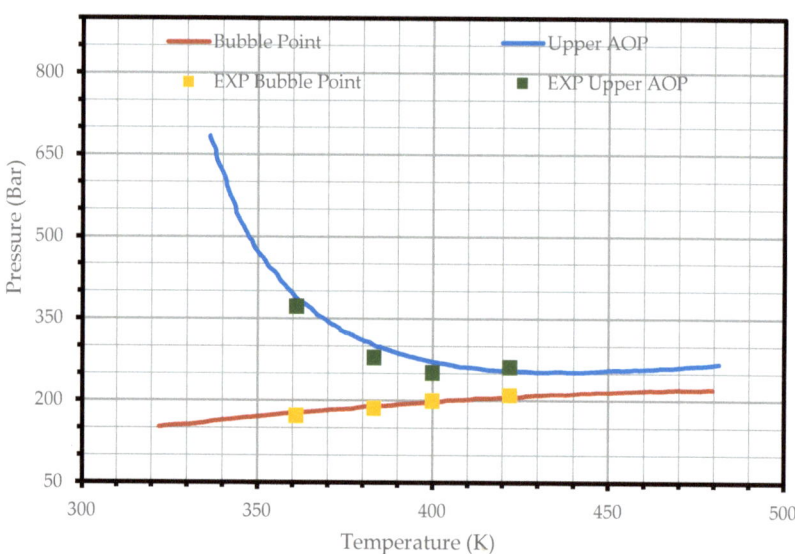

Figure 10. Evaluation of APD program (**a**) with ADEPT model (**b**) using oil data from Jamaluddin et al. [29].

An asphaltene phase diagram for oil sample A is given in Figure 11 and for oil sample B in Figure 12. The impact of injecting CO_2 gas on APD for oil sample A is shown in Figure 13 for 20% CO_2 injection. By comparing Figures 11 and 13, one can see that by adding CO_2 to the oil, the unstable region increases to a wider condition.

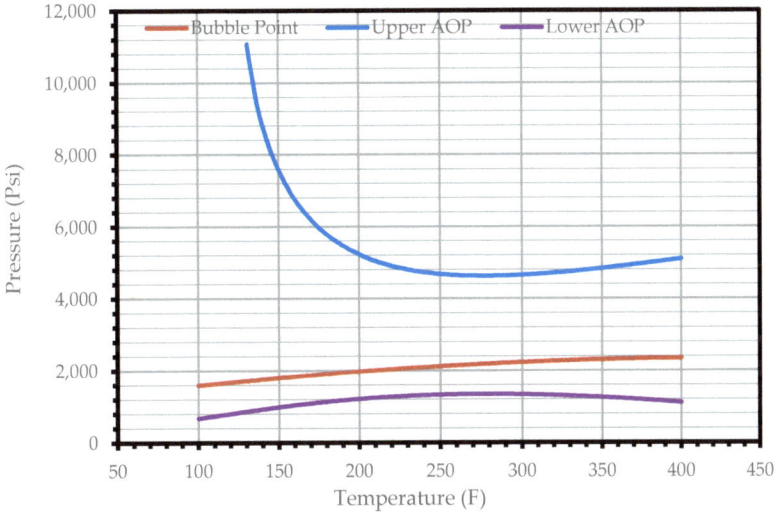

Figure 11. Asphaltene phase diagram (APD) for oil Sample A (in Table 3).

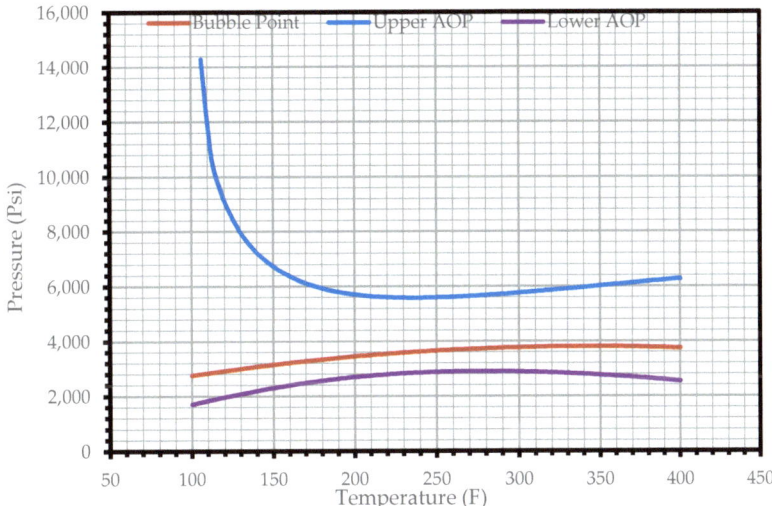

Figure 12. Asphaltene phase diagram (APD) for oil Sample B (in Table 3).

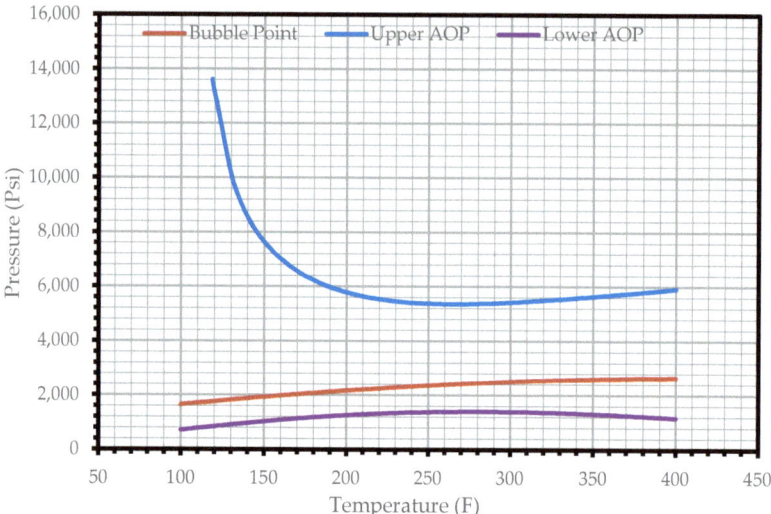

Figure 13. Asphaltene phase diagram (APD) for oil Sample A with 20% CO2 (see Figure 11 for no CO_2).

3.3. Retardation of Asphaltene Precipitation by the Use of Chemical Additives

Eleven chemical additives employed to retard sediment formation, manufactured and supplied by five major companies around the world, were selected to be used in this study. These chemicals and additives are used for the inhibition, dispersion, and dissolving (dissolution) of asphaltene as well as other types of solid deposition from petroleum fluids with applications in production fields.

The scarce information provided by the supplier indicates that the 11 chemical additives may contain amines in the aromatic solvent, poly-iso-buthylene succinimide, polymer in an aromatic solvent, phosponothioc acid, poly-isobutenyl derivatives, esters with penta-erythritol, alkenyl thio phosphorous ester, formaldehyde, polymers with branched 4 nonylphenol,ethylene-diamine, phosphoric acid, 2-ehyl-hexyl ester, C24-36 alkene, alpha-polymers with maleic anhydride, organic acid derivative, and 1,2,4 trimethylbenzene. The individual additives present a blend of the chemical substances mentioned above in a proprietary and confidential ratio. They are labeled as A1, A2, A3, A4, A5, A6, A7, A8, A9, A10, A11. In order to get some insight into the chemical nature of these 11 additives, infrared (IR) analysis was performed. The IR spectra of the 11 additives are presented in Figures S1–S13. The data from Figures S1–S7 suggest that the additives A1, A2, A3, A4, A5, and A6 pertain to the group of organic acid derivatives. The additives A1, A2, A3, A4, A5, and A6 have the same valence oscillations, however, in different ratios, suggesting a different ratio of the active components in the distinct additives. Figure 14 presents graphs of precipitate volume versus inhibitor concentration for the additives A1–A6 treatment of the crude oil in sample A.

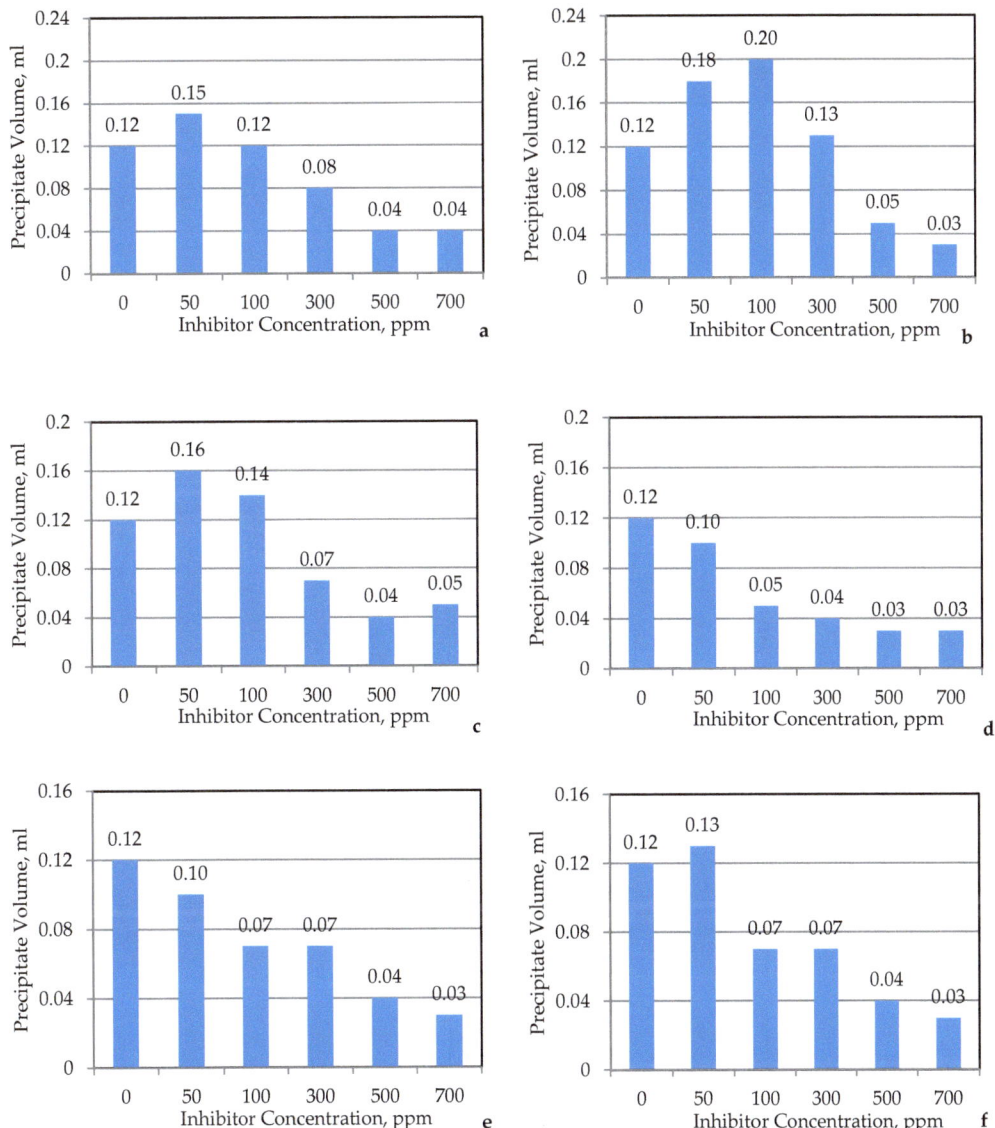

Figure 14. Amount of deposit versus treating rate of inhibitors A1 (**a**). A2 (**b**), A3 (**c**), A4 (**d**), A5 (**e**), and A6 (**f**) (treated crude oil sample A).

Figure 15 presents graphs of precipitate volume versus inhibitor concentration for the additives A7–A11 treating the crude oil in sample A.

Figure 16 presents graphs of precipitate volume versus inhibitor concentration for the additives A2 (a), A3 (b), A4 (c), A5 (d), A7 (e), and A8 (f) with H-Oil hydrocracked atmospheric residue (H-Oil ATB)—sample 1 was treated with additives A2, A3, A4, and H-Oil ATB. Sample 2 was treated with additives A5, A7, and A8—Table 6.

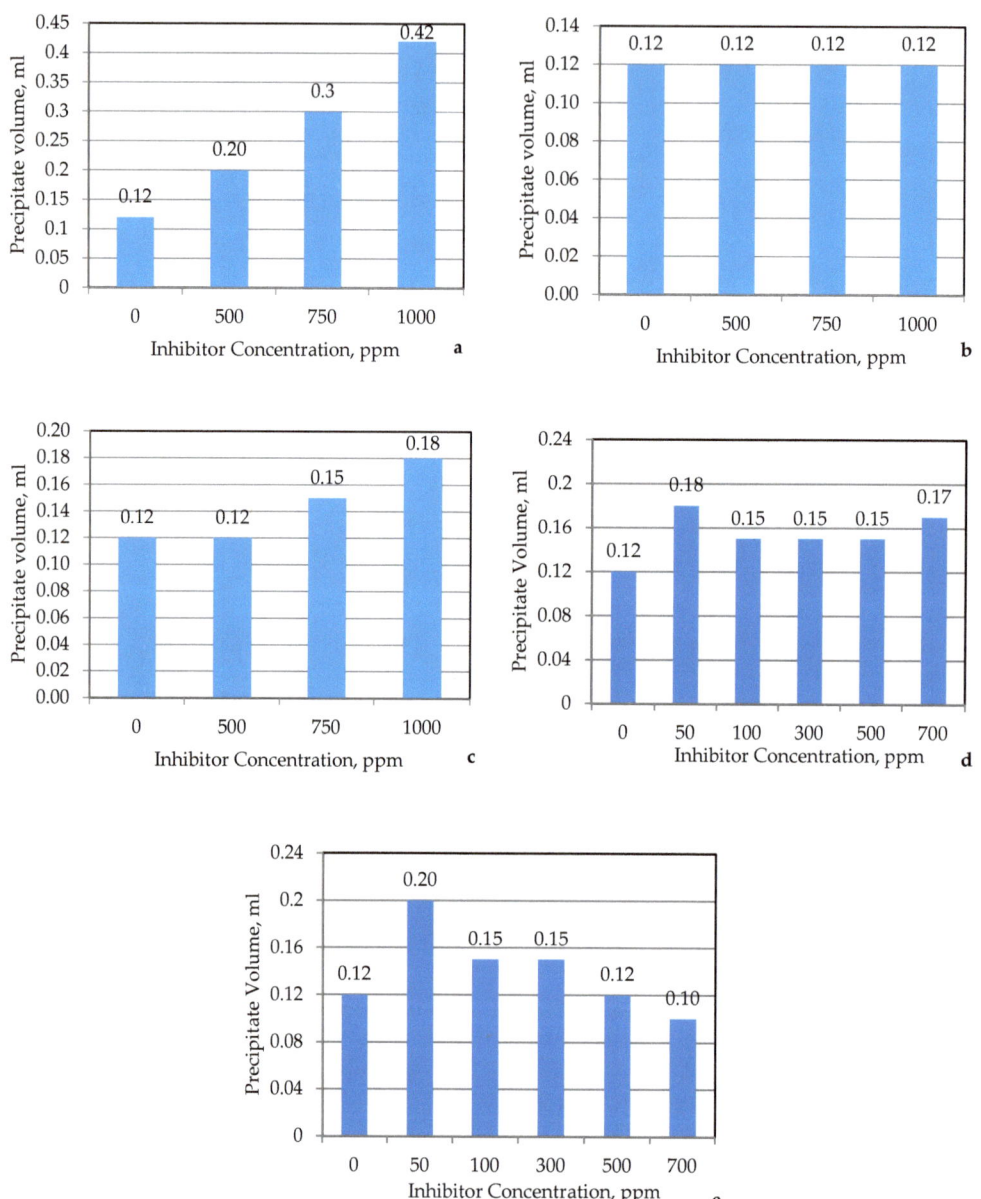

Figure 15. Amount of deposit versus treating rate of inhibitors A7 (**a**). A8 (**b**), A9 (**c**), A10 (**d**), and A11 (**e**) (treated crude oil sample A).

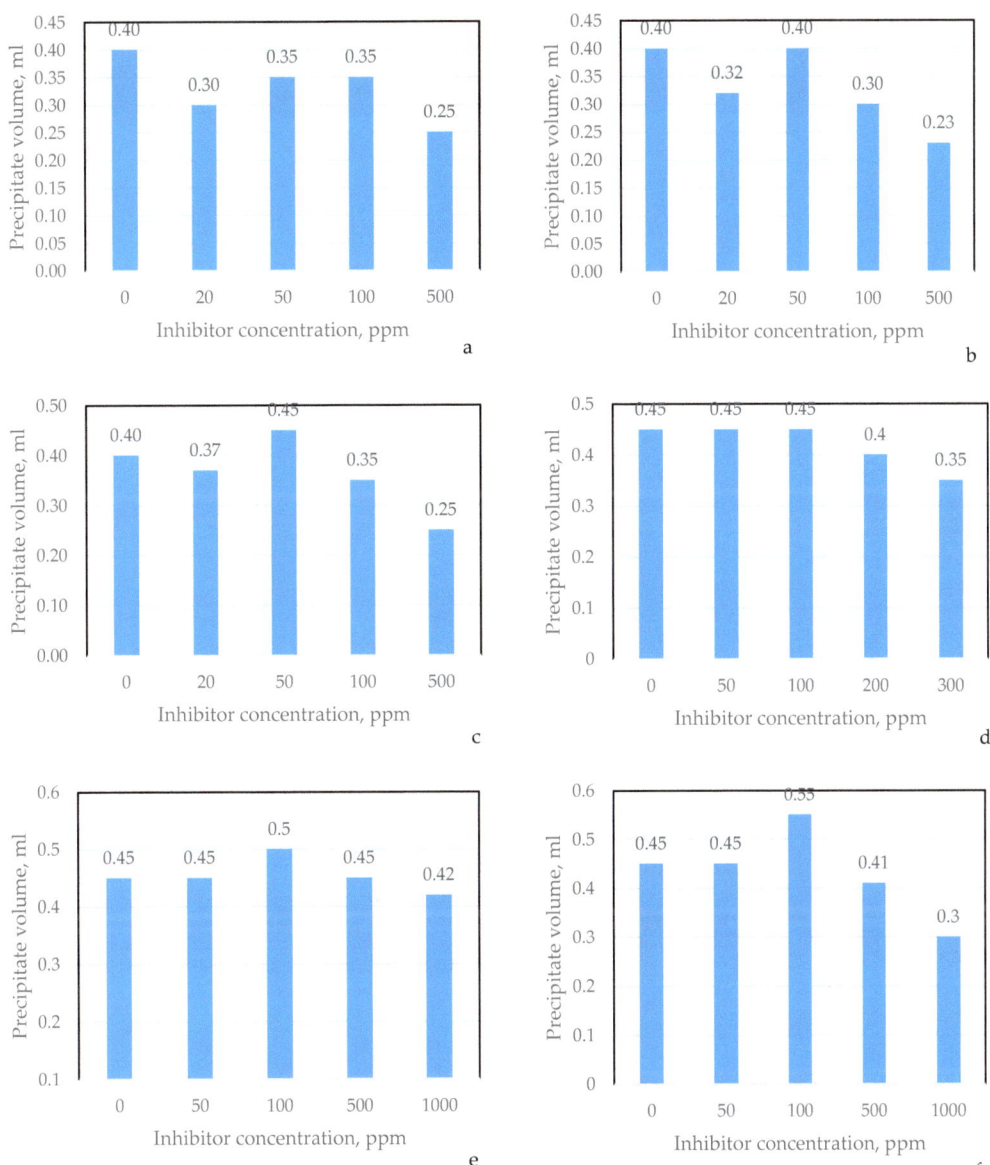

Figure 16. Amount of deposit versus the treating rate of the inhibitors A2 (**a**). A3 (**b**), A4 (**c**), A5 (**d**), A7 (**e**), and A8 (**f**) with H-Oil hydrocracked atmospheric residue (ATB)—sample 1 treated with additives A2, A3, A4, and ATB. Sample 2 treated with additives A5, A7, and A8—Table 6.

The optimum concentration and amount of reduction in a solid deposition for the tested chemicals with crude oil sample A are given in Table 7.

Table 6. SARA Analysis and BP of Oil Sample C.

Properties	H-Oil ATB (68%Urals/32BL) 15.10.2018 Sample-1	H-Oil ATB (80%Urals/20BL) 15.10.2018 Sample-2
H-Oil VR conversion, wt.%	73.6	72.9
Specific gravity SG_4^{20}	1.027	1.012
SARA analysis		
Saturates, wt.%	28.9	31.4
Aromatics, wt.%	59.4	56.8
Resin, wt.%	3.7	4.5
Asphaltene, wt.%	8.0	7.3
Colloidal instability index	0.58	0.62

Table 7. Ranking of the commercial Inhibitors for crude oil Sample A.

Performance Ranking Order	Inhibitor ID	Figure No. for Performance Test	Optimum Concentration ppm	Optimum %Reduction in Precipitate
1	A4	Figure 13d	500 ppm	75%
2	A5	Figure 13e	700 ppm	75%
3	A6	Figure 13f	700 ppm	75%
4	A2	Figure 13b	700 ppm	75%
5	A3	Figure 13c	500 ppm	67%
6	A1	Figure 13a	500 ppm	67%
7	A11	Figure 14e	700 ppm	17%
8	A8	Figure 14b	500 ppm	0% (no effect)
9	A10	Figure 14d	700 ppm	+42% (increasing precipitation)
10	A9	Figure 14c	700 ppm	+50% (increasing precipitation)
11	A7	Figure 14a	1000 ppm	+250% (increasing precipitation)

The optimum concentration and amount of reduction in a solid deposition for the tested chemicals with the H-Oil ATB samples are given in Table 8.

Table 8. Ranking of the commercial inhibitors for H-Oil ATB samples.

Performance Ranking Order	Inhibitor ID	Figure No. for Performance Test	Optimum Concentration ppm	Optimum %Reduction in Precipitate
1	A3	Figure 15b	500 ppm	42%
2	A2	Figure 15a	500 ppm	38%
3	A4	Figure 15c	500 ppm	38%
4	A8	Figure 15f	1000 ppm	33%
5	A5	Figure 15d	300 ppm	22%
6	A7	Figure 15e	1000 ppm	4%

It is interesting to note here that while with the crude oil sample A, additive A8 had no effect on the reduction of the precipitation volume. For the case of H-Oil ATB sample-2, the precipitated volume was reduced by 33%. Additive A7 showed a promotion effect on the precipitation volume of crude oil sample A, whereas, with H-Oil, ATB sample-2 exhibited no effect. The findings in our study are in line with the reports of Mahdi et al. [22], Melendez-Alvarez et al. [27], and Barsenas et al. [30] that the asphaltene dispersants can promote sediment formation depending on the oil treated, chemistry of the additive, medium, and the concentrating range. Barsenas et al. [30] showed in their study that the same asphaltene aggregation inhibitors at lower concentrations inhibited the asphaltene agglomeration while increasing their treatment rate and their efficacy diminished significantly. They found that the same inhibitor during the changing of the medium (from toluene at 50 °C to o-dichlorobenzene at 90 °C) the asphaltene inhibitor turned into an asphaltene aggregation promoter [30]. They suggested that the inhibitor molecules (i) significantly self-associated in the more polar solvent (o-dichlorobenzene), which could be a reason for the asphaltene adsorption (and enhanced agglomeration) on the surface of such inhibitors and (ii) self-associate occulting their head polar part in the less polar solvent (toluene), which might be a reason for the reduction in inhibitor adsorption on the asphaltene surface and worsening of the inhibition efficiency [30].

3.4. Optimum Inhibitor Concentration at the Field and Impact of Water Cut

The optimum concentrations reported in Table 7 were obtained from laboratory tests conducted at room conditions and with a dead crude oil sample. The conditions at the field are quite different, specifically with the following parameters:

- Temperature;
- Pressure;
- Fluid composition (presence of lighter components);
- Flow rate;
- Water (water cut);
- Concentration of salt and metals in the brine such as Al^{3+} and Fe^{3+} in water.

The temperature of the fluid in the well is higher than the lab temperature. At higher temperatures, the solubility of asphaltene in the oil increases, and this will result in less precipitation and deposition at the field. Furthermore, at higher pressures, the asphaltene stability in the oil increases, as is demonstrated in the APD of Figure 11. Another important factor is the amount of water cut in the wellbore. Generally, as the percentage of water cut increases, the amount of deposition decreases. With a high water cut, the oil is emulsified in water. A high amount of water may turn the wellbore to become water wet and asphaltene deposition may significantly be reduced. However, for the case of well A, the water cut is low at 5%. Furthermore, the flow of oil can cause a reduction in asphaltene precipitation and, as shown by Kor and Kharrat [31], with an increase in oil velocity, asphaltene deposition on the wall decreases. All these factors contribute to a reduction in the amount of inhibitor when applied in a production well. As a rule of thumb, it is believed that the amount of asphaltene deposition in the wellbore is about 30% less than those given in Table 7. Therefore, the optimized dosage in the field is expected to be in the range of 200–300 ppm for recommended chemicals.

Another contributing factor to the rate of asphaltene deposition is the composition of water in the wellbore. Salts contribute to the promotion of asphaltene deposition. Furthermore, the presence of Al^{3+} and Fe^{3+} ions in the water also causes an increase in the amount of deposition. For these reasons, although laboratory tests are helpful to identify suitable chemicals, the best method to determine the optimum concentration is field testing. It is also a good idea to test the chemicals over a period of time (a few days or more) to evaluate their performance and compare it with the incumbent chemical's performance. The best chemical is the one that minimizes the amount of asphaltene deposition at the lowest possible cost per unit barrel of crude. At higher water-cut fields use of a demulsifier that produces the fastest and cleanest separation of oil and water at the lowest possible cost per unit barrel of crude is recommended.

The water associated with oil sample A was separated and analyzed for metal elements that may affect the amount of asphaltene precipitation. The instrument used for the water analysis was the Sequential Wavelength Dispersive X-Ray Fluorescence Spectrometer or SWD XRF–ZSX available in the Chemical Engineering Laboratory which is capable of analyzing elements from Be to U with a microanalysis to analyze samples as small as 500 μm. The instrument is recommended for an elemental analysis of solids, liquids, powders, alloys, and thin films. The results are given in Table 9. The water weight is 81.18% and the remaining is total dissolved solid.

Table 9. Test results (in both ppm and wt.%) for water associated with oil sample A collected on 28 February 2021.

Comp.	Na	Mg	Al	Si	S	Cl	K	Ca	Br	Sr	Ba	W	H_2O
Unit	mass%	mass%	mass%	mass%	mass%	mass%	mass%	mass%	mass%	mass%	mass%	mass%	mass%
Result	5.205	0.243	0	0.001	0.019	11.42	0.241	1.530	0.082	0.062	0.021	0.001	81.18
Unit	ppm	ppm	Ppm	ppm	ppm	ppm	ppm	ppm	ppm	ppm	ppm	ppm	ppm
Result	52046	2432	<29	15	192	114169	2406	15291	822	618	214	11	52046

The water was also analyzed for Al^{3+} and Fe^{3+} ions by another instrument microwave plasma (Agilent model—4100 MP-AES) and the result indicated that the Al content was 0.4 ppm and the Fe content of the water was 3.29 ppmw. The total amount of dissolved solids (TDS), as determined by a simple evaporation and drying method (without the use of any instrument), was determined to be about 21 wt.%, which is just slightly above 19 wt.% determined by the XRF instrument given in the above table.

3.5. Calculation of the Required Amount of Inhibitor, Cost Analysis, and Final Recommendations

The volume rate of the inhibitor required to be injected for a certain oil production rate and ppm can be calculated from one of the following simple relations in gallon, liter, or kg:

Required Inhibitor Rate, Gallon/day = $(4.2 \times 10^{-5}) \times$ (Oil Rate, BPSD) $\times$ (ppm);

Required Inhibitor Rate, Liters/day = $(1.59 \times 10^{-4}) \times$ (Oil Rate, BPSD) $\times$ (ppm);

Required Inhibitor Rate, Kg/day = $(1.431 \times 10^{-4}) \times$ (Oil Rate, BPSD) $\times$ (ppm);

where:

Required Inhibitor Rate, Gallon/d = Required Inhibitor Rate in Gallons per day;
Required Inhibitor Rate, Liter/d = Required Inhibitor Rate in Liters per day
ppm = Desired concentration of inhibitor in oil in ppm;
Required Inhibitor Rate, Kg/d = Required Inhibitor Rate in kilogram per day;
Oil Rate (BPSD) = Oil Production Rate (after separator and excluding water cut and associated gas) in BPSD (barrel per service day);
Unit Conversion Factors: 1 US Gallon = 3.785 liters, 1 barrel = 42 US Gallons, 1 ppm = 1 part per million = 1×10^{-6} v/v or g/g. Approximate density of the inhibitor ≈ 900 kg/m^3 (0.9 g/mL).

For example, for each 1000 bbl of oil to have an inhibitor concentration of 300 ppm, a volume of 47.7 L (12.6 US Gallons) or about 43 kg of inhibitor should be injected into the wellbore. If the inhibitor price is taken at 5 EUR/kg, the chemical injection cost would be about 200 EUR for each 1000 bbl of crude oil produced. The above relations show that the inhibitor rate is directly proportional to the oil flow rate or desired concentration in oil in ppm.

Any selected chemical, when used over a period of time, must be economically attractive and contribute to the overall return on investment (ROI). Cost analysis can be gauged through ROI, which can be calculated as:

ROI = (Incremental Revenue-Incremental Cost of Treatment)/(Incremental Cost of Treatment) $\times 100$

where:

Incremental Revenue in USD = (oil production after treatment, BPSD − oil production before treatment, BPSD) $\times$ (oil price, $/bbl);

Incremental Cost of Treatment in USD = (Rate of inhibitor injected in Gallons per day) $\times$ (unit price of inhibitor, $/gallon);

It is very important that a chemical is injected at the right and optimized dose. An overdose or a low dosage may cause adverse effects resulting in an increased amount of asphaltene deposition. One way to avoid this is a regular monitoring plan and testing in the field more often.

4. Discussion

The employed methods to determine the asphaltene stability of studied crude oil samples denoted that crude oil samples A and B are unstable (or mildly unstable) (Figures 8 and 9). Thus, one may expect that they would be prone to precipitate asphaltenes and form sediments in the process of crude oil production. In order to minimize the probability of asphaltene precipitation 11 commercial chemical additives designed to inhibit the sediment formation process were examined. It was found that six of these additives were capable of asphaltene precipitation minimization (Figure 14, Table 7). The IR-spectra (Figures S1–S7) of these six additives showed the presence of valence oscillations in the region 3000–2800 cm^{-1}, typical for the presence of aliphatic groups, with bands at about 2960and 2870 cm^{-1} corresponding to the symmetric and asymmetric oscillation of CH_3 groups, whilst those at 2860 cm^{-1} corresponding to the symmetric oscillation of CH_2 groups, with bands at around 1600 and 1500 cm^{-1} which are probably a result from the oscillation of C-C bonds in the aromatic ring. There is a maximum at around 1770 cm^{-1} which is an indicator of the presence of C=O ester and cyclic ester. The band at around 1700 cm^{-1} is probably a result of the oscillation of the C=O bond participating in the carboxylic group. There is a band at about 1460 cm^{-1} characterizing the asymmetric oscillation of CH_3 groups. Therefore, the additives A1-A6 could be considered to be composed of aliphatic, aromatic, and organic acid derivative components. However, the ratio between these components seems to be different for the distinct additives judging from the different areas of the peaks responsible for the diverse component structures.

The additives A9, A10, and A11 exhibit the same valence oscillations as those of additives A1-A6, however with different intensities (Figures S10–S12). This suggests a different ratio between the aliphatic, aromatic, and organic acid derivative components. The additives A9, A10, and A11 exhibited either a very small inhibiting effect or the promotion of asphaltene precipitation (Figure 15, Table 7). Therefore, the ratio between the component structures seems to be crucial for the performance of the chemical additive. Barsenas et al. [30] showed that the same inhibitor during the changing of the medium (from toluene at 50 °C to o-dichlorobenzene at 90 °C) turned from an asphaltene inhibitor into an asphaltene aggregation promoter. Thus, the ratio between the aliphatic, aromatic, and organic acid derivative components seems to control the efficiency of the additive as an asphaltene precipitation inhibitor. The IR spectra of the additive A7 (Figure S8) showed that it contains bands in the region of 3000–2800 cm^{-1} at 1463 and 1380 cm^{-1}, which is typical for the presence of aliphatic groups. Three broad bands at about 2700–2500 cm^{-1}, 2400–2100 cm^{-1}, and 1800–1600 cm^{-1} are due to the presence of hydroxyl groups that are strongly involved in hydrogen bonding to phosphoryl oxygen atoms in acidic organophosphorus acids. The very strong and broad band at 1213 cm^{-1} is due to the P=O stretching vibration. The strongest and also very broad absorption at ~1024 cm^{-1} is attributed to the P-O stretching vibrations. Several weak bands between 881–650 cm^{-1} are characteristic of the ethylhexyl groups. The absorption intensities at 1607 cm^{-1} and 1505 cm^{-1} correspond to carbon–carbon stretching vibrations in the aromatic ring, indicating the presence of aromatic compounds. Obviously, the existent ratio between the component structures in additive A7 is unfavorable for asphaltene precipitation in crude oil sample A, making it an asphaltene precipitation promoter instead of an inhibitor. This component structure ratio in A7, however, as evident from the data in Figure 15e (Table 8) which does not make it an asphaltene precipitation promoter when H-Oil ATB is treated, which confirms again that the additive performance is oil specific, as reported in another research [23]. A more informative view of the functional groups identified to be present in the 11 studied additives by the use of FTIR is presented in Table 10.

Table 10. Assignments of IR absorption bands in the spectra of all tested additives (A1–A11).

A1	A2	A3	A4	A5	A6	A7	A8	A9	A10	A11	Functional Group/ Assignments
				Group Frequency, Wavenumbers (cm^{-1})							
3450	3449	3483		3448	3447	3400	3426		3386		–OH; –NH stretch
						3002		3017			=C–H stretch
2963	2957	2963	2959	2956	2956	2961	2953	2964	2953	2958	C–H asymmetric stretch
2931	2926	2933	2926	2926	2927	2930	2925	2925	2925	2925	C–H asymmetric stretch
2873	2872	2872	2872	2871	2873	2873				2871	C–H symmetric stretch
	2856			2855	2858		2854	2855	2855	2856	C–H asymmetric stretch
1736	1770	1736	1735		1772			1780	1735		C=O stretch
						1717		1711			
	1706			1701	1702				1702		
1607	1608	1607	1607	1602	1602	1607		1607		1607	carbon-carbon stretching vibrations in the aromatic ring
								1516	1577		
1505	1506	1505	1505	1505	1505	1505		1505			
1462	1464	1461	1462	1464	1466	1463	1459	1455	1466	1462	C–H bend:CH$_2$
1386/1366		1385/1366		1389/1366					1377/1366		CH(CH$_3$)$_2$
			1366		1380	1377	1377				C–H bend: CH$_3$
	1388/1377/1366		1385/1377/1366						1389/1377/1366		C(CH$_3$)$_3$
					1213						P=O stretch
					1024						P–O stretch
900–700	900–700	900–700	900–700	900–700	900–700			900–700		900–700	C–H out-of-plane bend
							750–400				Metal—oxygen stretch

The data in Table 8 (Figure 15) displays that additives A2, A3, and A4 demonstrated good performance as asphaltene precipitation inhibitors also when H-Oil ATB was treated. The efficiency of the asphaltene precipitation reduction, however, was almost double as low as that of the crude oil sample A (Table 7) implying that the efficiency of asphaltene inhibition is also oil specific. The additive A5 being Nr.2 in the ranking of asphaltene inhibitors for crude oil sample A (Table 7) also showed precipitation reduction when H-Oil ATB sample 2 was treated (Figure 15d). However, with the H-Oil ATB, the ranking of A5 is number five indicating again that the efficiency of asphaltene inhibitor performance is oil specific. Therefore, the selection of a chemical additive to inhibit deposit formation during oil production or during refining operations is a subtle matter.

The proper selection can provide an opportunity to improve profitability by increasing the cycle length of the operation equipment, reducing maintenance costs, and creating higher reliability in crude oil production and oil refining facilities to overcome chemical costs. The improper selection, however, can have a deleterious effect on the economics of both crude oil production and refining.

5. Conclusions

Two crude oil samples (A, and B) from the same deep reservoir located in Kuwait were analyzed for asphaltene instability. A simulator was developed to construct asphaltene phase diagrams and to show regions of instability. The crude oil samples were qualified as unstable or mildly unstable based on the five methods applied to assess crude oil stability. Eleven commercial chemical inhibitors were examined to reduce asphaltene precipitation by the use of an asphaltene dispersion test. IR spectra of the inhibitors revealed that they were composed of aliphatic, aromatic, and organic acid derivative components in different ratios. Six of the inhibitors were ranked as suitable for field application, reducing the asphaltene precipitation between 67 and 75%. The other five chemical additives were considered inappropriate since they either had no effect or promoted asphaltene precipitation.

Aside from crude oil sample two, H-Oil ATB samples were also tested with six commercial chemical inhibitors. It was found that four of the inhibitors reduced the asphaltene precipitation in the H-Oil ATBs as they did when the crude oil sample was treated. However, their efficiency was lower than that observed during the crude oil treatment. An inefficient additive for the crude oil sample was found efficient when the H-Oil ATBs were treated. An additive that promoted asphaltene precipitation during crude oil treatment did not show the same promoting effect when the H-Oil ATBs were treated. This confirms the conclusion made by other researchers that additive performance is oil specific. The paper concluded with some recommendations for the field application of chemical inhibitors.

Supplementary Materials: The following supporting information can be downloaded at: https://www.mdpi.com/article/10.3390/pr11030818/s1, Figure S1: IR-spectra of additive A1; Figure S2: IR-spectra of additive A2; Figure S3: IR-spectra of additive A3; Figure S4: IR-spectra of additive A4; Figure S5: IR-spectra of additive A5; Figure S6: IR-spectra of additive A6; Figure S7: Combined IR-spectra of the additives A1, A2, A3, A4, A5, and A6.; Figure S8: IR-spectra of additive A7; Figure S9: IR-spectra of additive A8; Figure S10: IR-spectra of additive A9; Figure S11: IR-spectra of additive A10; Figure S12: IR-spectra of additive A11; Figure S13: Combined IR-spectra of the additives A7, A8, A9, A10, and A11.

Author Contributions: Conceptualization, M.R.R. and A.Q.; Data curation; Formal analysis, J.F.P.; Funding acquisition, N.A.-K.; Investigation, D.S., I.S., R.N. and V.T.; Project administration, A.S.A.; Resources, N.A.-K. and J.F.P.; Software, M.R.R., A.S.A. and J.F.P.; Supervision, M.R.R.; Validation, A.Q., A.S.A. and N.A.-K.; Visualization, A.Q.; Writing—original draft, M.R.R. and D.S.; Writing—review & editing, M.R.R. and D.S. All authors have read and agreed to the published version of the manuscript.

Funding: Kuwait Oil Company.

Data Availability Statement: Not applicable.

Acknowledgments: Part of this manuscript was presented orally at the session: Advances in Petroleum Production and Processing at the 2022 AIChE Annual Meeting, 13–18 November 2022, Phoenix, AZ, USA. Funding received from KOC to conduct the work is greatly appreciated. The author Radoslava Nikolova acknowledges the support from Bulgarian Ministry of Education and Science under the National Program "Young Scientist and Postdoctoral Students-2".

Conflicts of Interest: The authors declare no conflict of interest.

Nomenclature

ADEPT	Asphaltene Deposition Tool
ADs	Asphaltene Dispersants
ADT	Asphaltene Dispersant Test
AIs	Asphaltene Inhibitors
APD	Asphaltene Phase Diagrams
APDD	Asphaltene Phase Diagram and Deposition
API Gravity	The American Petroleum Institute gravity
ATB	H-Oil hydrocracked atmospheric residue
BHT	bottom hole temperature
BP	Bubble point
BPSD	Barrel Per Stream Day
CII	Colloidal Instability Index
CME	Constant Mass Experiment

cP	Centipoise
CPA-EOS	Cubic-plus-association equation of state
cSt	Centistokes
EOR	Enhanced Oil Recovery
GC	Gas chromatography
GOR, scf/bbl	Gas Oil Ratio, standard cubic feet of gas per barrel of oil
H-Oil ATB	H-Oil hydrocracked atmospheric residue
IBP	Initial Boiling Point, °C
ID	Identity
IR	Infrared
KOC	Kuwait Oil Company
Mol. Wt.	Molecular weight
MW_{7+}	Molecular weight of C7+
PC-SAFT	Perturbed chain statistical associating fluid theory
Psia	Pounds per square inch absolute
Psig	Pounds per square in gauge
PVT	pressure–volume temperature
ROI	return on investment
SWD XRF–ZSX	Sequential Wavelength Dispersive X-ray Fluorescene Spectrometer
UAOP	Upper asphaltene onset pressure
VBA codes	Visual Basic for Applications
XRF	X-ray fluorescence

References

1. Riazi, M.R. *Characterization and Properties of Petroleum Fractions*; ASTM International: Conshohocken, PA, USA, 2005.
2. Mousavi-Dehghani, S.A.; Riazi, M.R.; Vafaie-Sefti, M.; Mansoori, G.A. An Analysis of methods for determination of onsets of asphaltene phase separations. *J. Pet. Sci. Eng.* **2004**, *42*, 145–156. [CrossRef]
3. Riazi, M.R. *Characteristics of Asphaltenic and Waxy Oils*; Annual AIChE Meeting, Session on Heavy Oil and Flow Assurance: San Francisco, CA, USA, 2013.
4. Akbarzadeh, K.; Dhillon, A.; Svrcek, W.Y.; Yarranton, H.W. Methodology for the characterization and modeling of asphaltene precipitation from heavy oils diluted with n-alkanes. *Energy Fuels* **2004**, *18*, 1434–1441. [CrossRef]
5. Fakher, S.; Ahdaya, M.; Elturki, M.; Imqam, A. An experimental investigation of asphaltene stability in heavy crude oil during carbon dioxide injection. *J. Pet. Explor. Prod. Technol.* **2020**, *10*, 919–931. [CrossRef]
6. Mohammed, I.; Mahmoud, M.; Al Shehri, D.; El-Husseiny, A.; Alade, O. Asphaltene precipitation and deposition: A critical review. *J. Pet. Sci. Eng.* **2021**, *2*, 107956. [CrossRef]
7. Pereira, V.J.; Setaro, L.L.O.; Costa, G.M.N.; de Melo, S.A.B. Evaluation and improvement of screening methods applied to asphaltene precipitation. *Energy Fuels* **2016**, *31*, 3380–3391. [CrossRef]
8. Yen, A.; Yin, Y.R.; Asomaning, S. *Evaluating Asphaltene Inhibitors: Laboratory Tests and Field Studies*; SPE International Symposium on Oilfield Chemistry: Houston, TX, USA, 2001; Paper Number: SPE-65376-MS. [CrossRef]
9. Stankiewicz, A.B.; Flannery, M.D.; Fuex, N.A.; Broze, G.; Couch, J.L.; Dubey, S.T.; Iyer, S.D.; Ratulowski, J.; Westerich, J.T. Prediction of asphaltene deposition risk in E&P operations. In Proceedings of the 3rd International Symposium on Mechanisms and Mitigation of Fouling in Petroleum and Natural Gas Production, AIChE 2002 Spring National Meeting, New Orleans, LA, USA, 10–14 March 2002; paper 47C. pp. 410–416.
10. De Boer, R.B.; Leelooyer, K.; Eigner, M.R.P.; van Bergen, A.R.D. 1995, Screening of crude oils for asphalt precipitation: Theory, practice, and the selection of inhibitors. *SPE Prod. Oper.* **1995**, *10*, 55–61. [CrossRef]
11. Chapman, W.G.; Gubbins, K.E.; Jackson, G.; Radosz, M. SAFT: Equation of state solution model for associating fluids. *Fluid Ph. Equilibria* **1989**, *52*, 31–38. [CrossRef]
12. Gross, J.; Sadowski, G. Perturbed chain SAFT: An equation of state on a perturbed theory for chain molecules. *Ind. Eng. Chem. Res.* **2001**, *40*, 1244–1260. [CrossRef]
13. Kurup, A.S.; Wang, J.; Subramani, H.J.; Buckley, J.; Creek, J.L.; Chapman, W.G. Revisiting asphaltene deposition tool (ADEPT): Field application. *Energy Fuels* **2012**, *26*, 5702–5710. [CrossRef]
14. Kurup, A.S.; Vargas, F.M.; Wang, J.; Buckley, J.; Creek, J.L.; Subramani, H.J.; Chapman, W.G. Development and application of an asphaltene deposition tool (ADEPT) for well bores. *Energy Fuels* **2011**, *25*, 4506–4516. [CrossRef]
15. Gonzalez, D.L.; Ting, P.D.; Hirasaki, G.J.; Chapman, W.G. Prediction of asphaltene instability under gas injection with the PC-SAFT equation of state. *Energy Fuels* **2005**, *19*, 1230–1234. [CrossRef]
16. Ting, P.D.; Gonzalez, D.L.; Hirasaki, G.J.; Chapman, W.G. *Application of the of PC-SAFT Equation of State to Asphaltene Phase Behavior, Asphaltene, Heavy Oils, and Petroleomics*; Springer: Berlin/Heidelberg, Germany, 2007; pp. 301–327.
17. Panuganti, S.R.; Tavakkoli, M.; Vargas, F.M.; Gonzalez, D.L.; Chapman, W.G. SAFT Model for upstream asphaltene applications. *Fluid Ph. Equilibria* **2013**, *359*, 2–16. [CrossRef]

18. Nazari, F.; Asssareh, M. An effective asphaltene modeling approach using PC-SAFT with detailed description for gas injection conditions. *Fluid Phase Equi.* **2021**, *532*, 112937. [CrossRef]
19. Kelland, M.A. *Production Chemicals for the Oil and Gas Industry*; Taylor & Francis, CRC Press: New York, NY, USA, 2009.
20. Da Silva, R.; Haraguchi, A.C.; Notrispe, L.; Loh, F.R.; Mohamed, W.R.S. Interfacial and colloidal behavior of asphaltenes obtained from Brazilian crude oils. *J. Pet. Sci. Eng.* **2001**, *32*, 201–216.
21. Ramdass, K.K.; Chakrabarti, D.P. Effectiveness of Biodiesel as an Alternative Solvent for the Remediation of Asphaltene Deposits. Available online: https://www.researchgate.net/publication/324128907_Effectiveness_of_Biodiesel_as_an_Alternative_Solvent_for_the_Remediation_of_Asphaltene_Deposits (accessed on 11 January 2023).
22. Mahdi, M.; Kharrat, R.; Hamoule, T. 2018, Screening of inhibitors for remediation of asphaltene deposits: Experimental and modeling study. *Petroleum* **2018**, *4*, 168–177.
23. Abrahamsen, E.L. Organic Flow Assurance: Asphaltene Dispersant/Inhibitor Formulation Development through Experimental Design. Ph.D. Thesis, University of Stavanger, Stavanger, Norway, 2012.
24. Stratiev, D.; Dinkov, R.; Shishkova, I.; Sharafutdinov, I.; Ivanova, N.; Mitkova, M.; Yordanov, D.; Rudnev, N.; Stanulov, K.; Artemiev, A.; et al. What is behind the high values of hot filtration test of the ebullated bed residue H-Oil hydrocracker residual oils? *Energy Fuels* **2016**, *30*, 7037–7054. [CrossRef]
25. Schermer, W.E.M.; Melein, P.M.J.; van den Berg, F.G.A. Simple techniques for evaluation of crude oil compatibility. *Pet Sci Technol.* **2004**, *22*, 7–8, 1045–1054. [CrossRef]
26. Stratiev, D.; Shishkova, I.; Tavlieva, M.; Kirilov, K.; Dinkov, R.; Yordanov, D.; Yankova, L.; Toteva, V.; Nikolova, R. Inhibiting sediment formation in an extra light crude oil and in a hydrocracked atmospheric residue by commercial chemical additives. *J. Chem. Technol. Metall.* **2022**, *57*, 63–75.
27. Melendez-Alvarez, A.A.; Garcia-Bermudes, M.; Tavakkoli, M.; Doherty, R.H.; Meng, S.; Abdallah, D.S.; Vargas, F.M. On the evaluation of the performance of asphaltene dispersants. *Fuel* **2016**, *179*, 210–220. [CrossRef]
28. Ghloum, E.F.; Al-Qahtani, M.; Al-Rashid, A. Effect of inhibitors on asphaltene precipitation for Marrat Kuwaiti reservoirs. *J. Petrol. Sci. Eng.* **2010**, *70*, 99–106. [CrossRef]
29. Jamaluddin, A.K.M.; Creek, J.; Kabir, C.S.; McFadden, J.D.; D'Cruz, D.; Manakalathil, J.; Joshi, N.; Ross, B. Laboratory techniques to measure thermodynamic asphaltene instability. *J. Can. Pet. Technol.* **2002**, *41*, 44–52. [CrossRef]
30. Barcenas, M.; Orea, P.; Buenrostro-González, E.; Zamudio-Rivera, L.S.; Duda, Y. Study of medium effect on asphaltene agglomeration inhibitor efficiency. *Energy Fuels* **2008**, *22*, 1917–1922. [CrossRef]
31. Kor, P.; Kharrat, R. 2016, Modeling of asphaltene particle deposition from turbulent oil flow in tubing: Model validation and a parametric study. *Petroleum* **2016**, *2*, 393–398. [CrossRef]
32. Amiri, R.; Khamehchi, E.; Ghaffarzadeh, M.; Kardani, N. Static and dynamic evaluation of a novel solution path on asphaltene deposition and drag reduction in flowlines: An experimental study. *J. Pet. Sci. Eng.* **2021**, *205*, 108833. [CrossRef]
33. Nezhad, S.R.; Kiomarsiyan, A.; Darvish, H. A novel experimental study on inhibition of asphaltene deposition. *Pet Sci Technol.* **2022**, 1–9. [CrossRef]
34. Ali, S.I.; Lalji, S.M.; Haneef, J.; Tariq, S.M.; Zaidi, S.F.; Anjum, M. Performance evaluation of asphaltene inhibitors using integrated method—ADT coupled with spot test. *Arab. J. Geosci.* **2022**, *15*, 674. [CrossRef]
35. Khormali, A.; Moghadasi, R.; Kazemzadeh, Y.; Struchkov, I. Development of a new chemical solvent package for increasing the asphaltene removal performance under static and dynamic conditions. *J. Pet. Sci. Eng.* **2021**, *206*, 109066. [CrossRef]

Disclaimer/Publisher's Note: The statements, opinions and data contained in all publications are solely those of the individual author(s) and contributor(s) and not of MDPI and/or the editor(s). MDPI and/or the editor(s) disclaim responsibility for any injury to people or property resulting from any ideas, methods, instructions or products referred to in the content.

Article

Analysis of Asphaltene Precipitation Models from Solubility and Thermodynamic-Colloidal Theories

Esaú A. Hernández, Carlos Lira-Galeana and Jorge Ancheyta *

Instituto Mexicano del Petróleo, Eje Central Lázaro Cárdenas Norte 152, Col. San Bartolo Atepehuacan, Mexico City 07730, Mexico
* Correspondence: jancheyt@imp.mx

Abstract: Asphaltenes are known to cause problems related to flocculation, precipitation, and plugging, either in the formation, production lines, and processing equipment. Different models have been proposed to predict the thermodynamic conditions under which asphaltenes precipitate over the past years. This work analyses the performance of various models on their capability to match the literature experimental data of precipitated asphaltene mass fractions. Twenty-five different models based on equation-of-state (EoS), polymer solution, and thermodynamic-colloidal theories were identified. The performance/test datasets were collected and classified according to their pressure/temperature conditions, CO_2, n-C_5/n-C_7 gas, and liquid titrations. Statistical analysis, including residuals, parity plots, and average absolute relative deviation (AARD, %), were used to compare the adequacy of selected models. Results confirmed the need for further model development for general applications over wide pressure, temperature, and composition intervals.

Keywords: asphaltene precipitation modeling; EoS; polymer solutions; colloidal theories; model evaluation

1. Introduction

The growing production of heavy crude oil as reservoirs continue to deplete has motivated the search for methods to improve their extraction, transportation, and refinement. One of the natural properties of these oils is their high amount of asphaltenes, which causes high viscosity and difficulties in producing and refining them.

Asphaltenes are a solubility class of compounds with high aromaticity, high molecular weight, and an undefined boiling point. Asphaltenes are soluble in aromatic compounds, such benzene or toluene, and insoluble in low-molecular-weight alkanes, such as n-pentane or n-heptane. Asphaltenes are considered the most polarizable and aromatic fraction of crude oil. They are rich in heteroatoms (nitrogen, oxygen, and sulfur) and metals (nickel and vanadium) [1]. Asphaltenes mainly exist as monomers in bulk crude oil, while they behave as a polymer upon association and precipitation [2]. In both refinery and production operations, asphaltene dispersion with chemicals is preferred to avoid their aggregation and subsequent precipitation. It is generally accepted that resins, which are absorbed on the surface of asphaltenes, are natural peptizing agents of asphaltenes [3]. Asphaltenes are known to be the main precursor of sediment formation, with major difficulties in oil production, transportation, and processing equipment [4]. Several investigations have revealed that asphaltene behavior is influenced by pressure, temperature, crude oil properties, type and amount of precipitant, and characteristics of porous media (oil wells). Solid formation inducted by asphaltene precipitation causes major effects on production systems, in both upstream and downstream operations. [5].

Asphaltene precipitation is influenced by the nature of the medium in which they are hosted [6]. Changes in composition (in-field mixing with different crude oils, addition of solvent, dispersant, CO_2 injection, etc.) can modify the stable-to-unstable conditions in the medium, leading heavy organics to flocculate, precipitate, and deposit [4]. Asphaltene adsorption onto surfaces is a phenomenon that can be used to predict and avoid asphaltene precipitation from reservoir production and downstream operations. Asphaltene adsorption could be an efficient method to assist enhanced oil recovery efforts [7].

Rheological properties of the oil are important for the study of precipitation of asphaltenes in different stages of the oil production chain. Asphaltene flow behavior in diverse media, including waxy matrix, polymer matrix, and oil/water emulsions, represents interactions at the interface between asphaltene-asphaltene, asphaltene-maltenes, and asphaltene-water. Because the amount of asphaltene and resins tends to increase as a result of oil well decline, rheological properties of oil changes and asphaltene behavior is more complex and tends to precipitate onto reservoir and production facilities [8].

Therefore, the study of asphaltenes is of great importance for anticipating the problems that they may cause, particularly when dealing with unstable, asphaltenic crude oils. In previous works, our group reviewed methods based on SARA (saturates, aromatics, resins asphaltenes) analysis to determine the stability of crude oils [9]. We applied them to a wide range of Mexican crude oils [10]. Apart from SARA-analysis-based methods, there are other more sophisticated models which use a solubility approach or a colloidal approach to predict precipitation.

In this work, we perform a comprehensive review of the literature models used to calculate asphaltene precipitation, either as a function of pressure and temperature, or from gas and liquid titration data, using their reported data-matching accuracy and statistical tests. Conclusions on the most appropriate models are given, based on the above tests.

2. Description of Models for Asphaltene Precipitation

To estimate asphaltene precipitation, various studies have been carried out using different approaches, and these can be classified into two different approaches: solubility approach models and colloidal approaches models [11].

2.1. Solubility Approach Models

It is common to quantitatively describe asphaltene precipitation via parameters of solubility. The solubility parameter indicates the relative solvency behavior of a specific solvent, and the relationship among solubility, van der Waals forces, and the cohesive energy density. Hildebrand defined the solubility parameter as the square root of the cohesive energy density (Vargas and Tavakkoli 2018).

The solubility approach is classified into four different theories: regular solution theory models (RST), cubic equation of state models (C-EoS), cubic plus association equation of state models (CPA-EoS), statistical association fluid theory equation of state models (SAFT-EoS), Scott-Magat theory models (SMT), and Flory-Huggins theory models (FHT). Table 1 summarizes the RST models, while C-EoS, CPA-EoS, SAFT-EoS, SMT, and FHT are reported in Tables 2 and 3.

Table 1. Models to calculate asphaltene precipitation based on solubility approach (RST).

Regular Solution Theory Author	Equation	Author	Equation
(1) Hirschberg et al.	$(x_{va})_{max} = exp\left\{\frac{V_a}{V_L}\left[1 - \frac{V_a}{V_a} - \frac{V_a}{RT}(\delta_a - \delta_L)^2\right]\right\}$	(6) Chung	$x_a^L = exp\left[-\frac{\Delta H_f^i}{RT}\left(1 - \frac{T}{T_f^i}\right) - \frac{V_a^L}{RT}(\delta_m^L - \delta_a^L)^2 - \ln\frac{V_a^L}{V_m^L} - 1 + \frac{V_a^L}{V_m^L}\right]$
(2) Burke et al.	$x_{va} = exp\left\{\frac{V_a}{V_L}\left[1 - \frac{V_a}{V_a} - \frac{V_a}{RT}(\delta_a - \delta_L)^2\right]\right\}$	(7) Cimino et al.	$\ln(1 - x_{va}^*) + \left(1 - \frac{V_s}{V_a}\right)x_{va}^* + \frac{V_s}{RT}(\delta_a - \delta_L)^2 x_{va}^{*2} = 0$
(3) Novosad and Constain	$v_i^{(k)} = exp\left[1 - \frac{V_i}{V^{(k)}} - \frac{V_i}{RT}(\delta_i - \delta^{(k)})^2\right]$	(8) de Boer et al.	$S = exp\left\{-1 + V_a\left[\frac{1}{V_o} - \frac{(\delta_a - \delta_o)^2}{RT}\right]\right\}C$
(4) Rassamdana et al.	$x_{va}^L = x_{va}^S exp\left[\frac{V_a^L}{V_a^L} - 1 - \frac{V_a^L}{RT}(\delta_a - \delta_L)^2\right]$	(9) Alboudwarej et al.	$K_i = \gamma_i^{L_1} = exp\left\{\ln\frac{V_i^{L_1}}{V_m^{L_1}} + 1 - \frac{V_i^{L_1}}{V_m^{L_1}} + \frac{V_i^{L_1}}{RT}(\delta_i - \delta_m)^2\right\}$
(5) Buckley et al.	$\delta = \left(\frac{\sqrt{3}\pi}{384}\frac{hV_a}{\sigma^3}\right)^{1/2}\frac{\sigma^3}{V/N_A}\frac{n^2-1}{(n^2+2)^{3/4}}$	(10) Yarranton and Masliyah	$K_i = exp\left\{\frac{\Delta H_f^i}{RT}\left(1 - \frac{T}{T_f^i}\right) + 1 - \frac{V_i^L}{V_m^L} + \ln\left(\frac{V_i^L}{V_m^L}\right) + \frac{V_i^L}{RT}(\delta_m - \delta_i^L)^2\right\}$
(11) Thomas et al.	$K_i^S = \frac{x_i^s}{x_i^L} = exp\left\{\frac{V_i}{RT}\left[(\delta - \delta_i)_L^2 - (\delta - \delta_i)_S^2\right] + \frac{\Delta H_f^i}{RT}\left[1 - \frac{T}{T_f^i} + \ln\frac{T_f^i}{T}\right] + \frac{\Delta C_P}{R}\left[1 - \frac{T}{T_f} - \frac{T_f}{T} + \ln\frac{T_f}{T}\right] + \int_0^P\left(\frac{V^L - V^S}{RT}\right)dP\right\}$		
(12) Wang and Buckley	$\ln(1 - x_{va}^L) + \left(1 - \frac{V_m}{V_{va}^L}\right)x_{va}^L + \mathcal{X}(x_{va}^L)^2 = \ln(1 - x_{va}^H) + \left(1 - \frac{V_a}{V_a}\right)x_{va}^H + \mathcal{X}(x_{va}^H)^2$ $\ln x_{va}^L + (1 - x_{va}^L)\left(1 - \frac{V_a}{V_m}\right) + (1 - x_{va}^L)^2\frac{V_a}{V_m}\mathcal{X} = \ln x_{va}^H + (1 - x_{va}^H)\left(1 - \frac{V_a}{V_m}\right) + (1 - x_{va}^H)^2\frac{V_a}{V_m}\mathcal{X}$ $\mathcal{X} = \frac{V_m}{RT}(\delta_a - \delta_m)^2$		

Table 2. Models to calculate asphaltene precipitation based on solubility approach (EoS, SAFT, SAFT-HS, and SAFT-VR).

Equation of State (EoS)			
Author	Equation	Author	Equation
(13) Nghiem et al.	$\ln f_a = \ln f_a^* + \frac{V_a(P-P^*)}{RT}$	(14) Sabbagh et al.	$C_i = 0.3796 + 1.485\omega_i - 0.1644\omega_i^2 + 0.01667\omega_i^3$

Statistical Association Fluid Theory (SAFT)		Statistical Association Fluid Theory-Hard Sphere (SAFT-HS)	
Author	Equation	Author	Equation
(15) Ting et al.	$\frac{A^{res}}{RT} = \frac{A^{seg}}{RT} + \frac{A^{chain}}{RT} = m\left(\frac{A_0^{hs}}{RT} + \frac{A_0^{disp}}{RT}\right) + \frac{A^{chain}}{RT}$ $\frac{A_0^{hs}}{RT} = \frac{6}{\pi\rho}\left[\frac{\zeta_2^3 + 3\zeta_1\zeta_2\zeta_3 - 3\zeta_1\zeta_2\zeta_3^2}{\zeta_3(1-\zeta_3)^2} - \left(\zeta_0 - \frac{\zeta_2^3}{\zeta_3^2}\right)\ln(1-\zeta_3)\right]$ $\frac{A_0^{disp}}{RT} = \frac{A_1}{RT} + \frac{A_2}{RT^2}$ $\frac{A^{chain}}{RT} = \sum x_i(1-m_i)\ln g_{ii}^{hs}(d_{ii})$	(16) Wu et al.	$A = A^{id} + A^{hs} + A^{vdw} + A^{assoc} + A^{chain}$ $\frac{A^{id}}{KT} = \sum_{i=1}^{2} N\ln(\rho_i\Lambda_i^3) - N_t$ $\frac{A^{hs}}{KT} = N_t\left\{\left[\frac{\zeta_2^3}{\zeta_0\zeta_3^2} - 1\right]\ln(1-\zeta_3) + \frac{3\zeta_1\zeta_2}{\zeta_0(1-\zeta_3)} + \frac{\zeta_2^3}{\zeta_3\zeta_0(1-\zeta_3)^2}\right\}$ $\frac{A^{vdw}}{KT} = \frac{V}{2}\sum_{i=1}^{2}\sum_{j=1}^{2}\rho_i\rho_j\frac{u_{ij}}{KT}$ $\frac{A^{assoc}}{KT} = 2N_A\left(\ln x_\alpha + \frac{1-x_\alpha}{2}\right) + N_R\left(\ln x_\beta + \frac{1-x_\beta}{2}\right)$ $\frac{A^{chain}}{KT} = N_R(1-l_R)\ln g_{22}^{hs}(\sigma_{22})$

Statistical Association Fluid Theory-Variable Range (SAFT-VR)	
Author	Equation
(17) Buenrostro et al.	$\frac{A}{NKT} = \frac{A^{ideal}}{NKT} + \frac{A^{mono}}{NKT} + \frac{A^{chain}}{NKT} + \frac{A^{assoc}}{NKT}$ $\frac{A^{ideal}}{NKT} = \left(\sum_{i=1}^{n} x_i \ln \rho_i \Lambda_i^3\right) - 1$ $\frac{A^{mono}}{NKT} = \left(\sum_{i=1}^{n} x_i m_i\right)\frac{A^M}{N_S KT} = \left(\sum_{i=1}^{n} x_i m_i\right)a^M$ $\frac{A^{chain}}{NKT} = -\sum_{i=1}^{n} x_i(m_i-1)\ln y_{ii}^M(\sigma_{ii})$ $\frac{A^{assoc}}{NKT} = \sum_{i=1}^{n} x_i\left[\sum_{a=1}^{S_i}\left(\ln X_{\alpha,i} - \frac{x_{\alpha,i}}{2}\right) + \frac{S_i}{2}\right]$

Table 3. Models to calculate asphaltene precipitation based on solubility approach (CPA-EoS, SMT, and FHT).

Cubic Plus Association Equation of State		
Author	Equation	
(18) Li and Firoozabadi	$\frac{A_{ph}^{cs}}{nRT} = -\ln(1-b\rho) - \frac{a}{2\sqrt{2}bRT}\ln\left(\frac{1+(1+\sqrt{2})b\rho}{1+(1-\sqrt{2})b\rho}\right)$ $\frac{A_{assoc.}^{cs}}{nRT} = N_a\mathcal{X}_a\left(\ln\mathcal{X}_a + \frac{1-\mathcal{X}_a}{2}\right) + N_R\mathcal{X}_R\left(\ln\mathcal{X}_R + \frac{1-\mathcal{X}_R}{2}\right)$	Author	Equation
		(19) Shirani et al.	$Z = Z^{ph} + Z^{assoc.}$ $Z^{assoc.} = -\frac{1}{2}\left(1 + \frac{1}{V}\frac{\partial \ln g}{\partial\left(\frac{1}{V}\right)}\right)\sum_i x_i \sum_{A_i}(1 - x_{a_i})$

Scott-Magat theory	
Author	Equation
(20) Kawanaka et al.	$V_{f_a}^L = \int dV_{f_{a_i}}^L = \int_0^\infty \left\{ \frac{\left(\frac{M_{a_i}}{M_a}\right)V_a^c}{V^L + V^S exp(-N_{sa_i}\theta)} \right\} F(M_{a_i}) dM_{a_i}$

Flory-Huggins theory	
Author	Equation
(21) Flory-Huggins	$\frac{\Delta G_m^m}{RT} = x_a \ln x_{va} + x_b \ln x_{vb} + x_a x_{vb} \mathcal{X}_{ab}$ $\mathcal{X}_{ab} = \frac{V_r}{RT}(\delta_a - \delta_b)^2$
(22) Flory-Huggins-Zuo equation of state (FHZ EoS)	$\Delta A(h) = \Delta A_{entropy}(h) + \Delta A_{sol}(h) + \Delta A_{grav}(h)$ $\Delta A_{entropy}(h) = kT \sum_i n_i \ln \varphi_i$

2.1.1. Regular Solution Theory

The regular solution theory was originally developed by Scatchard, Hildebrand, and Wood to describe the thermodynamics of solutions [12]. Models developed by this theory provide semiquantitative estimates of solubility parameters for solutions of nonpolar liquids. The models based on RST identified in this work are the following:

(1) Hirschberg et al., model [13]. This model was developed to describe the behavior of asphalt and asphaltenes in crude oil reservoir upon changes in pressure, temperature, or composition. The model appears to be well applicable to conditions at which asphaltenes are associated with resins, and may be used to identify field conditions where asphalt or asphaltene precipitation would occur. The model overestimates the solubility of asphaltenes at very high dilution ratios [11].

(2) Burke et al., model [14]. The model describes the precipitation mechanism as a polymer solution theory. The overall model depends on two types of fluid equilibria: V/L equilibrium of the total fluid and L/L equilibrium between liquid oil and pseudo-liquid asphaltene phases. The agglomeration of asphaltenes may hinder the quantitative performance of the model. Data generated by the model can be used to determine critical properties of the solvent/oil system. The model can also be used to estimate the probability of precipitates formation as the composition and properties of the reservoir fluid change.

(3) Novosad and Costain model [15]. Hirschberg's model with asphaltene-asphaltene and asphaltene-resin association was used to correlate asphaltene precipitation data. The Peng-Robinson EoS was used to determine the V/L equilibrium data on oil-CO_2 mixtures. The model has a large number of fitting parameters. More data on physical properties of asphaltenes and resins are needed to predict asphaltene stability and the extent of their precipitation with confidence. All asphaltene precipitation data were successfully correlated using a molecular thermodynamic model with association. Model calculations indicated that asphaltene destabilization may be minimized by producing wells at high wellhead flowing pressures.

(4) Rassamdana et al., model [16]. The model employs a scaling function, somewhat like those encountered in aggregation and gelation phenomena. The scaling function has a very simple form, and its predictions agree well with the experimental data. This scaling equation provides a particularly simple, and apparently universal, prediction for the onset of asphaltene (or asphalt) precipitation.

(5) Buckley et al., model [17]. The model assumes that the dominant intermolecular interaction energy governing asphaltene precipitation is the London dispersion contribution to the van der Waals forces. The interaction energy is a function of the differences between the squares of the refractive indices of the asphaltene and solvent. Solubility parameters of the asphaltene and solvent are related to their refractive indices. The refractive index is a function of the composition and density. Refractive indices were extrapolated to zero frequency as a parameter into the model.

(6) Chung model [18]. The model is based on thermodynamic principles for solid-liquid phase equilibrium and assumes that asphaltenes are dissolved in oil in a true liquid-solid state, not in a colloidal suspension. The model considers the effects of temperature, composition, and activity coefficient on the solubility of wax and asphaltenes in organic solutions, and can predict the solubility of asphaltene in crude oil systems.

(7) Cimino et al., model [19]. The model based on polymer solution thermodynamics and was developed using experimental phase behavior data. The model allows for the prediction of asphaltene stability with few experimental data, and considers that on phase separation, asphaltenes contain a fraction of the solvent.

(8) de Boer et al., model [20]. The model is based on the solubility of the oil and the asphaltenes and their molar volumes (similar to the Hirschberg model). The author found that all crude oil properties were correlated with the density of the crude at in situ conditions. The model assumes that the asphaltene precipitation depends on the degree of saturation of the asphaltene phase due to the pressure drop during production.

(9) Alboudwarej et al., model [21]. The model is based on the liquid-liquid equilibrium regular solution theory. The input parameters of the model are the mole fraction, molar volume, and solubility parameters of each component. During the model development, asphaltenes were divided into fractions with different associated molar mass according to the Schultz-Zimm molar mass distribution. The effect of the solvent type and the onset and amount of asphaltene precipitation can be calculated with the model.

(10) Yarranton and Masliyah model [22]. The model describes the asphaltene solubility using a solid-liquid equilibrium through the calculation of K-values derived from Scatchard-Hildebrand solubility theory and Flory-Huggins entropy of mixing. Asphaltenes were considered as a series of polyaromatic hydrocarbons with randomly distributed associated functional groups. The model calculates asphaltene precipitation onset and the amount of precipitated asphaltenes.

(11) Thomas et al., model [23]. The model relates the fugacities of the liquid/solid components. The model's main contribution is the correlation of the required properties: enthalpy change of fusion, fusion temperature, solubility parameters, and liquid partial molar volumes.

(12) Wang and Buckley model [24,25]. This asphaltene solubility model (ASM) was developed to predict the phase behavior of asphaltenes in crude oil. The thermodynamic model was derived from Flory-Huggins polymer theory and reproduces a wide range of experimental data for the onset of asphaltene precipitation. The better prediction of the model over others arises by the estimation of solubility parameters based on refractive indices measurements, the solution of the thermodynamic equations to obtain compositions of both asphaltene poor and asphaltene rich phases, and the use of the Gibbs free energy curve to define onset conditions.

2.1.2. Cubic Equation-of-State (C-EoS)

Equations of state are useful to describe properties of fluids, mixtures, and solids. In the oil industry, the most widely used EoS are Soave-Redlich-Kwong (SRK) and Peng-Robinson (PR). Equations of state are not limited to describing the liquid-vapor equilibrium, but they can also describe liquid-liquid and liquid-solid equilibria. Models developed from equations of state include the following.

(13) Nghiem et al., model [26]. The model is based on the division of the heaviest component in the oil into a non-precipitating and a precipitating component. Model can make quantitative calculations of experimental data from the literature, as well as additional data from industry. Asphaltenes are considered a pure dense phase, and are referred to as the asphalt phase and can either be liquid or solid. The model can calculate a decrease in asphaltene precipitation at high solvent concentrations.

(14) Sabbagh et al., model [27]. The model is an adaptation of the Peng-Robinson equation of state using group contribution methods for the fitting and prediction of the onset and amount of asphaltene precipitation from both asphaltenes/toluene/n-alkane and bitumen/n-alkane systems. A liquid-liquid equilibrium is assumed with only asphaltenes partitioning to the dense phase, while saturates, aromatics, and resins are considered as single pseudo-components. The model matches asphaltene yields for n-alkane diluted bitumen. However, it fails to fit yields from n-pentane-diluted bitumen at high dilution ratios.

2.1.3. Statistical Association Fluid Theory Equation of State (SAFT-EoS)

SAFT-EoS is the most widely used for the prediction of asphaltene phase behavior by applying Wertheim's theory. SAFT is an equation of state where the molecules are modeled in the form of chains composed of bonded spherical segments. This equation of state describes the residual Helmholtz free energy (A^{res}) of a mixture of associating fluids. The PC-SAFT equation of state is organized into different types of intermolecular interactions, such as the hard chain reference, dispersion, association, polar interaction, and ions.

(15) Ting et al., model [28]. The SAFT equation of state was used to model asphaltene phase behavior in live oil (mixture of n-C7 insoluble asphaltenes, toluene, and methane)

and a recombined oil (stock tank oil with its separator gas). The refractive index of the mixture at onset of asphaltene precipitation was used to characterize SAFT parameters of the asphaltenes. With this data, the densities for stock tank oil and the recombined oil were predicted very well with experimental measurements.

(16) Wu et al., model [29,30]. The author considered that asphaltenes are represented by attractive hard spheres that can associate with themselves. The Helmholtz energy of hard spheres (A^{hs}) was included in the SAFT equation (SAFT-HS). The author concludes that the effect of the oil medium on asphaltene precipitation is only determined by its Hamaker constant (obtained from oil´s density and concentration of light compounds in the oil).

(17) Buenrostro et al., model [31]. The author includes intermolecular interactions in SAFT EoS with variable-ranged potentials (SAFT-VR). SAFT-VR approach exploits that molecular parameter to model real effects in fluids. SAFT-VR approach resulted in a promising ability to predict phase equilibria of asphaltene precipitation due to changing conditions (P, T, and composition), as well as for pressure depletion at reservoir conditions in live oil samples.

2.1.4. Cubic Plus Association Equation of State (CPA-EoS)

The cubic plus association equation of state is a combination of the classical cubic equation of state and chemical contribution (association). Classical EoS describes the physical part of attraction and repulsion, and the chemical contribution is related to Chapman's association term originally developed for statistical association fluid theory (SAFT). The CPA equation of state has been successfully applied to a variety of complex phase equilibria, including mixtures containing alcohols, glycols, organic acids, water, and hydrocarbons. The following models are based on this approach:

(18) Li and Firoozabadi model [32]. It is applied to model the effects of temperature, pressure, and composition on asphaltene precipitation in live crude oils. A liquid-liquid equilibrium between the upper onset and bubble point pressures, and a gas-liquid-liquid equilibrium between the bubble point and lower onset pressures were considered to develop the model. The model's advantage is based on the existing fluid characterization, which can be readily implemented in compositional reservoir simulators. It was able to reproduce the amount and onset pressures of asphaltene precipitation in several live oils over a broad range of composition, temperature, and pressure conditions.

(19) Shirani et al., model [33]. The model is based on a combination of a physical part and an association term. The model combines a cubic EoS and association (chemical) terms from Wertheim theory. The interactions between molecules are considered in the physical and association parts. The model is expressed in terms of the compressibility factor, Z. The physical contribution of the compressibility factor was obtained using Peng-Robinson and Soave-Redlich-Kwong equations of state. For the physical part, SRK EoS gives more accurate results than the PR EoS for predicting the asphaltene phase behavior. The model showed good accuracy with experimental data from three live oil samples.

2.1.5. Scott-Magat Theory

The Scott-Magat theory assumes that polymers have a heterogeneous structure, and polydispersity plays an important role in the molecular weight of polymers. This assumption is applicable when using the following model.

(20) Kawanaka et al., model [34]. This statistical thermodynamic model is used to predict the onset point and amount of asphaltene deposition of crude oils. Asphaltene is assumed to consist of many components of similar polymeric molecules. The model is used to predict the phase behavior in CO_2/oil mixtures, and is applicable to estimate organic deposition (asphaltene, wax, diamantine, etc.) from reservoir fluids under the influence of a miscible solvent at various temperatures, pressures, and compositions.

2.1.6. Flory-Huggins Theory

The Flory-Huggins theory was originally developed by Flory and Huggins to describe the Gibbs free energy mixing of polymer solutions [35,36]. The theory assumes that asphaltenes have a homogeneous structure and properties. Models based on this theory are the following.

(21) Flory-Huggins model [35,36]. It assumes that the polymer has the form of a flexible chain of segments and that each segment is equal in size to a solvent molecule. Several models are based on this theory.

(22) Flory-Huggins-Zuo equation of state (FHZ EoS) [37]. Flory-Huggins-Zuo EoS assumed that a reservoir fluid is treated as a mixture with two pseudo-components: non-asphaltene (or maltene) and asphaltene components. It also describes the equilibrium concentration distribution of heavy ends in the oil column. The FHZ EoS includes gravitational forces on the existing Flory-Huggins regular solution model, which has been used to model asphaltene precipitation in the oil and gas industry. It has been successfully employed to estimate asphaltene concentrations in different crude oil columns around the world, incorporating the size of asphaltene molecules, asphaltene nanoaggregates, and asphaltene clusters. Downhole fluid analysis (DFA) has been used to measure continuous fluid profiles and properties of discontinuous fluids in reservoir connectivity [38]. DFA measurements are related to all parameters of the FHZ EoS, like composition, the gas-oil ratio, and the density of heavy components.

2.2. Colloidal Approach Models

The colloidal approach assumes that asphaltenes exist in the oil medium as solid particles suspended and stabilized by resins. The short-range intermolecular repulsions between resin molecules adsorbed on neighboring asphaltene particles and the long-range repulsions between asphaltene particles are the conditions for keeping asphaltenes stable in solution. On the other hand, the precipitation of asphaltenes is assumed to be an irreversible process, and a certain quantity of resins is necessary to completely peptize the asphaltenes in crude oil. The colloidal approach has three different paths to describe asphaltenes precipitation: chemical potential, micellization, and reverse micellization. Table 4 summarizes the models based on the colloidal approach.

Table 4. Models to calculate asphaltene precipitation based on the colloidal approach (Chemical Potential, Micellization, and Reverse Micellization).

Chemical Potential Author	Equation	Micellization Author	Equation
(23) Leontaritis and Mansoori	$\mu^A_{resin} = \mu^o_{resin}$ $\frac{\Delta \mu_R}{RT} = \frac{\mu_R - (\mu_R)_{reference}}{RT} = \ln(x_{vR}) + 1 - \frac{v_R}{v_m} + X_R$	(24) Victorov and Firozoobadi	$x_M = x^{n1}_{a1} x^{n2}_{r1} exp\left\{\frac{\Delta G^{00}_M}{RT}\right\}$ $\Delta G^{00}_M = n_1 \mu^*_{a1} + n_2 \mu^*_{r1} - \mu^{00}_M$
Reverse Micellization Author	Equation		
(25) Pan and Firoozabadi	$\Delta G^{00}_m = $ $\sum_{i=1}^{N_a} \left[\left(\Delta G^0_a\right)_{Tr} + \left(\Delta G^0_a\right)_{Def}\right] + \left(\Delta G^0_m\right)_{Inf} + \left(\Delta G^0_r\right)_{Tr} + \left(\Delta G^0_r\right)_{Adp} + \left(\Delta G^0_r\right)_{Def}$		

2.2.1. Chemical Potential

Chemical equilibrium between two phases is related to the chemical potential and is equal in both phases for each component. Since resins act in the peptizing of asphaltenes, its chemical potential is equal to the resins in the asphaltene and oil phases. The next model was developed according to this thermodynamic concept.

(23) Leontaritis and Mansoori model [39]. The model is based on the thermodynamic-colloidal approach and is capable of predicting the onset of flocculation of colloidal asphaltenes in oil mixtures, either due to changes in composition (solvent addition) or electrical phenomena (streaming potential generation due to flow of asphaltenes containing

oil in conduits or porous media). The model can make predictions regarding the velocity ranges where colloidal asphaltene flocculation can be avoided.

2.2.2. Micellization

Micellization is a self-association phenomenon that occurs on the surface of active materials in aqueous systems. An asphaltene colloidal particle has a core of asphaltene molecules surrounded by resin molecules on its surface. The following model is based on this approach.

(24) Victorov and Firoozabadi model [40]. The model describes asphaltene molecules in crude oils as micelles, and the solubilization of asphaltene polar species by resin polar molecules in the micelles. The model describes the change in precipitation power of different alkane precipitants and the effect of pressure on asphaltene precipitation. The amount and the onset of predicted asphaltene precipitation are sensitive to the quantity of resins in the crude oil. The authors concluded that, at high solvent ratios, the asphaltene material does not precipitate, and when precipitation does take place, most of the asphaltene material remains in the crude oil.

2.2.3. Reverse Micellization

Reverse micellization assumes that asphaltenes can be redissolved into the oil phase when conditions are favorable for redissolution, and the asphaltene precipitation process is reversible. The following model is based on this approach.

(25) Pan and Firoozabadi model [41,42]. The model was developed using a liquid-liquid equilibrium to obtain a thermodynamic micellization model. The heavy phase is assumed to be in the liquid state and to consist of only asphaltene and resin. The model is used to calculate asphaltene precipitation and shows good accuracy. The effect of pressure, temperature, and composition on precipitation is calculated by the model. The model can calculate resin precipitation at high propane concentrations and asphaltene precipitation at high concentrations of CO_2 and injected gasses. The model shows that an increase in resin concentration could inhibit asphaltene precipitation.

3. Results and Discussion

Following a consecutive description of the various models mentioned in the preceding section, we use the numbers 1 to 25 to refer to model features and results. The results of statistical analysis refer to the literature experimental data of precipitated asphaltene mass fraction of the reported models.

3.1. Experimental Titrations

Liquid titrations are used to determine the amount of asphaltenes for a particular n-alkane titrant/test crude oil system in the laboratory. Calculation of the entire titration curve (i.e., asphaltene weight % vs. volume of n-alkane titrant added/g of test crude oil) is an important calculation test for any asphaltene model. Table 5 shows the type of test crude oils, solvents used, and the type of titration data (liquid/gas) used in the works where a particular model has been reported in the literature. Some models were developed from a set of self-measured experiments, and others have used data reported elsewhere in the literature. As can be seen, the set of experimental data measured by Hirschberg et al. and Burke et al. were used in the development of models 13, 19, 20, 23, 24, and 25.

Table 5. Samples, solvents, and methods for experimental titrations for asphaltene precipitation.

Model	Samples	Solvent	Method	Range of Asphaltene Content (wt%)
1	Two crude oils (30.54–34.97 °API)	C_1, C_3, n-C_5, n-C_7, n-C_{10}, CO_2	IP 143	0.60 to 3.90
2	Six crude oils (19.0–48.0 °API)	n-C_7	ASTM D893-80 with n-C_7	0.40 to 16.80
3	Crude oil (29.0 °API)	n-C_6, n-C_{10}, CO_2	n-C_6, n-C_{10}, CO_2 precipitations	5.50
4	Light tank crude oil (29.7 °API)	n-C_5 to n-C_{10}	IP 143 and Thin Layer Chromatography	2.20
5	Crude oils (19.0–41.0 °API)	n-C_7	n-C_7 precipitation and Refractive Index measurements	1.20 to 10.90
6	From the bottom-hole of a production well in San Andres Unit of Seminole oilfield (TX)	n-C_5	n-C_5 precipitation	–
7	Villafortuna-Trecate oil (41.2 °API) and crude oil (35.6 °API)	n-C_5	IP 143	0.10 to 1.40
8	Light crude oils (40° API)	n-C_7	n-C_7 precipitation	0.30
9	Athabasca Bitumen, Cold Lake, Lloydminster	n-C_5, n-C_7, n-C_{10}	ASTM D2007M	14.60 to 15.30
10	Syncrude coker feed Athabasca bitumen	n-C_7	n-C_7 precipitation	14.50
11	Keg river crude oil, Nisku crude oil	C_2, C_3, n-C_4	C_2, C_3, and n-C_4 precipitations	–
12	Mars-Pink crude oil	n-C_5 to n-C_{15}	n-C_5, n-C_{15} precipitations and Refractive Index measurements	4.40
13	Crude oils (19.0–48.0 °API)	C_1, C_3, n-C_5, n-C_7, n-C_{10}, CO_2	IP 143, ASTM D893-80 with n-C_7	1.90 to 7.80
14	Athabasca Bitumen, Cold Lake, Lloydminster, Venezuelan 1 and 2, Russian, Indonesian	n-C_5, n-C_6, n-C_7, n-C_8 n-C_{10}	ASTM D2007M	4.70 to 21.80
18	Crude oils (24.6–44.2 °API)	n-C_7, CO_2	n-C_7, CO_2 precipitations	0.40 to 4.90
19	Crude oil (19 °API), Iranian oil field, crude oil (29 °API)	CO_2	CO_2 precipitation	–
20	Crude oils (30.54 °API)	n-C_5, n-C_7, and n-C_{10}	IP 143	4.02
23	Two crude oils (30.54–34.97 °API)	C_1, C_3, n-C_5, n-C_7, n-C_{10}, CO_2	IP 143	0.60 to 3.90
24	Crude oils (19.0–48.0 °API)	C_1, C_3, n-C_5, n-C_7, n-C_{10}, CO_2	IP 143, ASTM D893-80 with n-C_7	0.40 to 16.80
25	Crude oil (34.97 °API), North Sea reservoir, Weyburn reservoir	C_3, CO_2	IP 143	0.60 to 8.90

From Table 5, it can be seen that most of the models were developed with crude oils with API gravity ranging from 19 to 48, and only a few used Athabasca bitumen samples. The asphaltene content ranged from 0.1 to 21.8 wt%. Interestingly, the method of choice used to precipitate asphaltenes was IP-143. Some models were developed with precipitated asphaltenes with only one solvent (n-C_5, n-C_7 or CO_2), while others used up to six different solvents.

3.2. Pressure and Temperature Conditions for Each Model

Since each model was developed with different types of crude oil and solvent, the pressure and temperature conditions for asphaltene precipitation were different, and the applicability of each model depends on all of these conditions. Figure 1 depicts the pressure and temperature conditions used to develop each model. Not all of the models reported the experimental conditions. In general, temperatures ranged from −20 to 250 °C, while pressure ranged from 0 to 105.5 MPa. Only model 11 used a wide range of temperatures, i.e., −20 °C to 250 °C, being the one with the widest temperature range. Models 7 and 19 were second in terms of wider temperature ranges (25–177 °C), and the widest pressure range (0–105 MPa for model 7, and 5–50 MPa for model 19). The model with the narrowest pressure and temperature ranges was model 4 (21 to 38 °C, and 0.1 to 1.0 MPa).

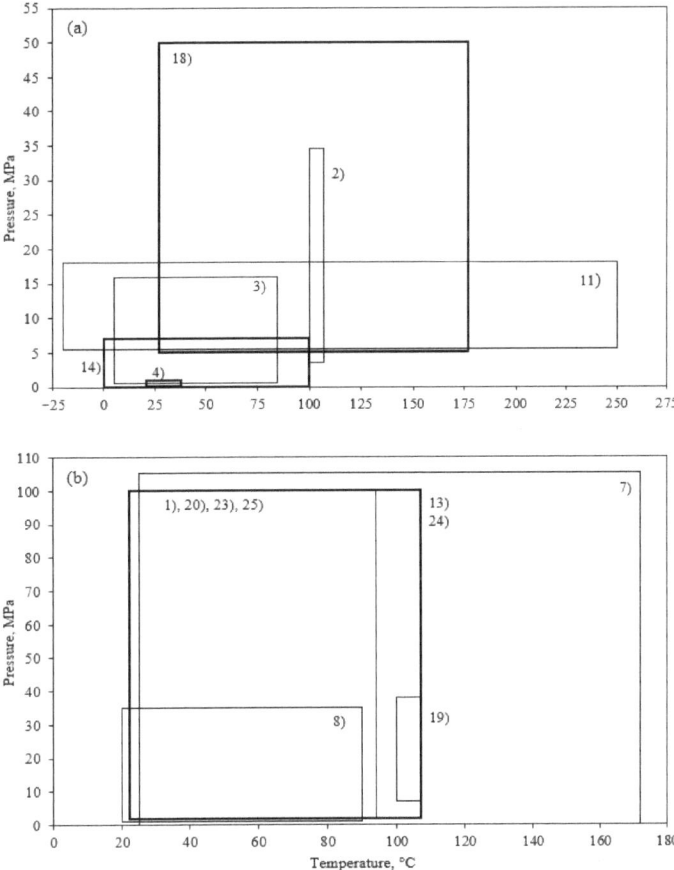

Figure 1. Pressure and temperature conditions for different models. (**a**) models: 2, 3, 4, 11, 14, and 18. (**b**) models: 1, 7, 8, 13, 19, 20, 23, 24, and 25.

3.3. Models Excluded from the Analysis

Some models did not report information to validate their accuracy in calculating asphaltene precipitation (models 5, 8, 10, 12, 21, and 23), and others only reported limited information (models 2, 3, 6, 7, 9, 11, 13, and 22). For later models, the limited information provided was considered insufficient to carry out a statistical analysis. Only 11 out of the 25 models (i.e., 1, 4, 13, 14, 16, 17, 18, 19, 20, 24, and 25) reported information on the precipitated asphaltene mass fraction to perform the statistical analysis. Models excluded from the analysis were: 2, 3, 5, 6, 7, 8, 9, 10, 11, 12, 15, 21, 22, and 23. The few calculation properties reported by the models excluded were: solubility parameters for asphaltenes and solvents (Burke et al., Chung et al., and de Boer et al. models), refractive index of asphaltenes and solvents (Buckley et al., Ting et al., and Wang and Buckley models). Furthermore, a comparison between experimental and calculated asphaltene precipitation data was not reported by these models.

3.4. Analysis of Models

Asphaltenes are dispersed in crude oil in equilibrium with saturates, aromatics, and resins fractions, constituting a colloidal system. Asphaltene precipitation is caused due to changes in pressure, temperature, composition, flow, etc., which alter this colloidal system equilibrium, and then induce aggregation and precipitation.

3.4.1. Effects of Pressure and Temperature

Hirschberg et al. and Pan and Firoozabadi reported comparisons of calculated values from their models against experimental data from Hirschberg et al., (tank oil 1 and propane weight ratio 1:7, at 93 °C) as depicted in Figure 2a. In general, models calculated the trend of asphaltenes precipitation with changes in pressure well; i.e., when pressure decreases, asphaltene precipitation increases. Shirani et al., Ngheim et al., and Victorov and Firoozabadi reported comparisons of calculated values from their models against experimental data from Burke et al., (live crude oil 3 at 100 °C) as depicted in Figure 2b. The model by Shirani et al. could calculate asphaltene precipitation with higher accuracy than the models by Nghiem et al. and Victorov and Firoozabadi. It exhibited a slight error at pressures between 13 and 15 MPa.

At 30 °C, Figure 3 shows that Li and Firoozabadi's model was not able to calculate asphaltene precipitation from the experimental data from Szewczyk et al. [43,44]. At low pressures (<10 MPa), the model then overestimated the experimental data from 10 to 15 MPa for oil X2. For pressures higher than 25 MPa, it calculated the experimental data quite well, with a slight underestimation. For oil X3, the model was not able to calculate asphaltene precipitation at P <20 MPa, and it overestimated the experimental data from pressures 20 to 25 MPa. Above 30 MPa, the model showed a slight underestimation.

3.4.2. Effects of Injected CO_2

Injection of CO_2 is one of the techniques used for oil recovery, but sometimes it can lead to significant problems of asphaltene precipitation in the reservoir. Figure 4 shows that Li and Firoozabadi, Pan and Firoozabadi, Wu et al., and Shirani et al. models calculated that, as CO_2 concentration increases, asphaltene precipitation also increases. Experimental data from Weyburn crude oil with 4.9 wt% of asphaltenes [45] were used by these models to obtain asphaltene precipitation in the presence of CO_2. The models by Pan and Firoozabadi and Li and Firoozabadi exhibited a tendency to underestimate the experimental data from 0.41 to 0.6 fractions of CO_2 and overestimated the experimental data up to 0.65 to 0.75 fractions of CO_2 with a maximum error of 29%. Pan and Firoozabadi were not able to calculate asphaltene precipitation at <0.51 mole fraction of CO_2. It exhibited a maximum error of almost 15%. The model by Shirani et al. exhibited good accuracy in reproducing experimental data quite well from 0.46 to 0.53 mole fractions of CO_2, then underestimated the experimental data from 0.54 to 0.65 mole fractions of CO_2. It exhibited a maximum error of 17%. The model by Wu et al. overestimated the experimental data up to 0.38 to 0.54 fractions of CO_2 and underestimated the experimental data from 0.55 to 0.65 with a maximum error of 23%.

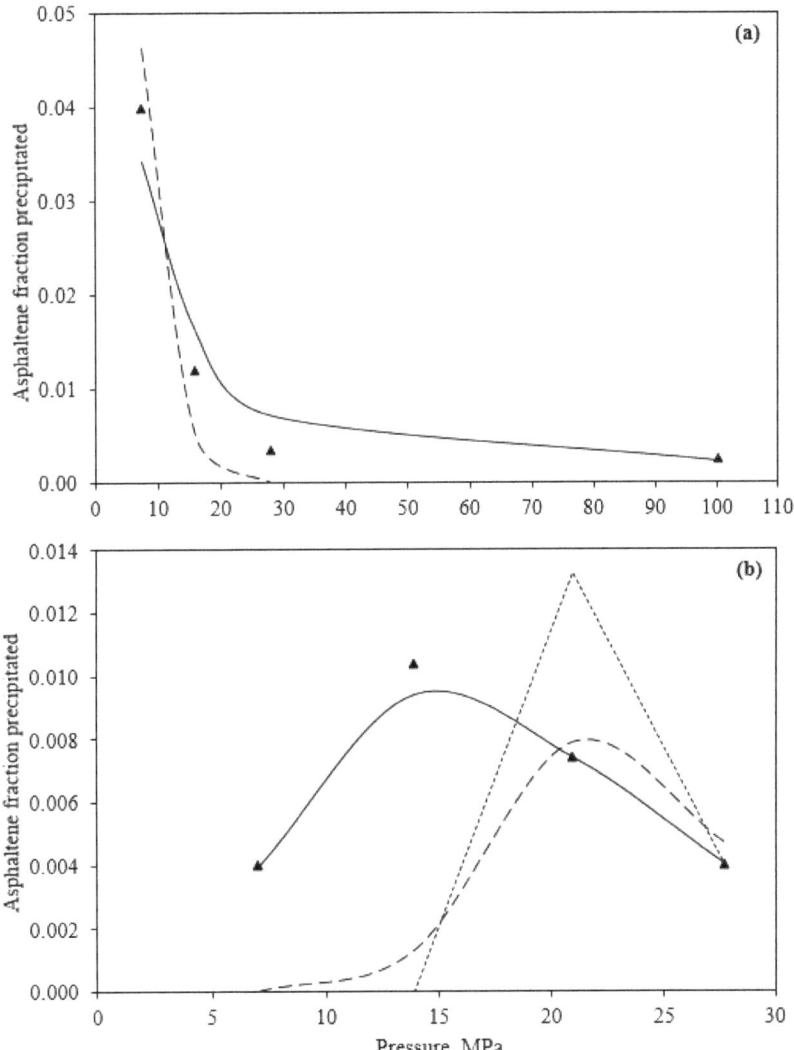

Figure 2. Pressure and temperature effects on precipitated asphaltene fraction calculated by different models. (**a**) Experimental data (▲) by Hirschberg et al., at 93 °C, (—) calculated by Pan and Firoozabadi) and (— —) calculated by Hirschberg et al.). (**b**) Experimental data (▲) by Burke et al., at 100 °C, (—) calculated by Shirani, (— — —) calculated by Victorov and Firoozabadi) and (— —) calculated by Nghiem.

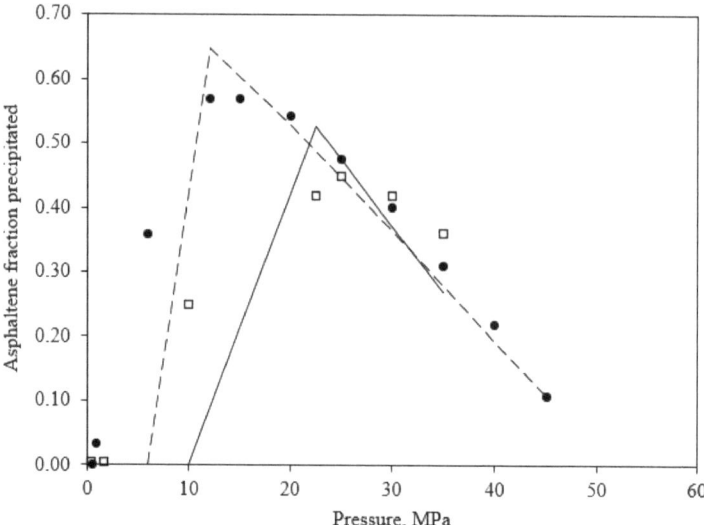

Figure 3. Pressure and temperature effects on precipitated asphaltene fraction calculated by Li and Firoozabadi. Experimental data (•) by Szewczyk et al., at 30 °C for oil X2, (— —) calculated. Experimental data (□) by Szewczyk et al., at 30 °C for oil X3 (—) calculated.

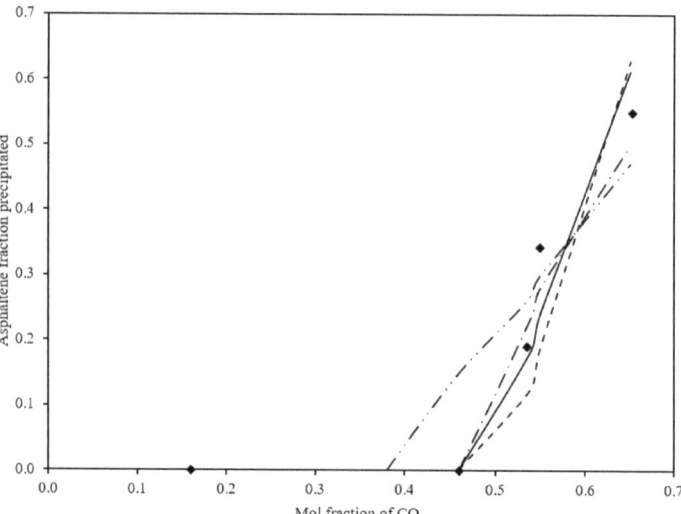

Figure 4. Effect of CO_2 injection (in Weyburn oil) on precipitated asphaltene fraction. Experimental data (♦), (— ·· —) calculated by Wu et al., (— · —) calculated by Shirani et al., (—) calculated by Pan and Firoozabadi, and (— —) calculated by Li and Firoozabadi.

3.4.3. Effects of the Addition of n-Alkanes as Solvents

The models by Kawanaka et al., Sabbagh et al., Rassamdana et al., Wu et al., Buenrostro et al., and Victorov and Firoozabadi reported asphaltene precipitation by adding n-C5 and n-C7 as solvents. Figures 5 and 6 depict the experimental data versus the calculated results for these models. The models show an increase in asphaltenes precipitation due to an increase in solvents (n-C5 and n-C7). Figure 5a,b shows the results of asphaltene precipitation in five models with n-C5 as solvent. The model by Kawanaka et al. used the experimental data of crude oil with a 1.9 wt% asphaltene content. Initially, the model overestimated the experimental data from 0.60 to 0.80 mass fraction of the solvent, then calculations exhibited good accuracy in the range of 0.85 to 0.97 mass fraction of the solvent. It exhibited a maximum error of 3%. Sabbagh et al. calculated asphaltene precipitation from Athabasca bitumen and Cold Lake bitumen with contents of 14.60 and 15.30 wt% of asphaltenes, respectively. For both samples, the model underestimated the experimental data, and presented a maximum error of 51% for Athabasca bitumen and 27% for Cold Lake bitumen. Rassamdana et al. and Victorov and Firoozabadi could calculate experimental data with a maximum error of 42 and 29%, respectively. Wu et al. could calculate asphaltene precipitation quite well for Suffield oil. For Lindberg oil, the model exhibited a considerable deviation from 0.6 to 0.94 mass fraction of n-C5. In general, the model showed a maximum error of 14%. Buenrostro et al. were able to reproduce experimental data quite well for both Mexican oils (C1 and Y3). The model exhibited a slight underestimation at 0.97 mass fraction of n-C5.

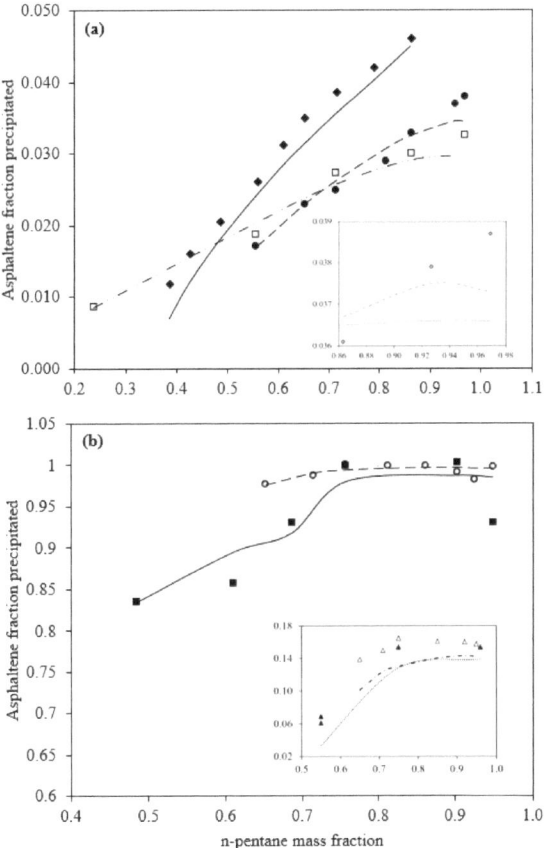

Figure 5. Effect of adding n-pentane solvent on precipitated asphaltene fraction. (**a**) Rassamdana et al., (♦ experimental, — calculated), Buenrostro et al., (for oil Y3: □ experimental, — ·· — calculated, and for oil C1: • experimental, — — calculated), plot inside refers to: Experimental data (▲) by Hirschberg et al., at 60 °C, (••••) calculated by Victorov and Firoozabadi, and (— · —) calculated by Kawanaka et al., (**b**) Wu et al., (for oil Lindberg: ■ experimental, — calculated, and for oil Suffield: ○ experimental, — — calculated), plot inside refers to Sabbagh et al., (for Athabasca bitumen: ▲ experimental, •••• calculated, and for Cold lake bitumen: △ experimental, — · — calculated).

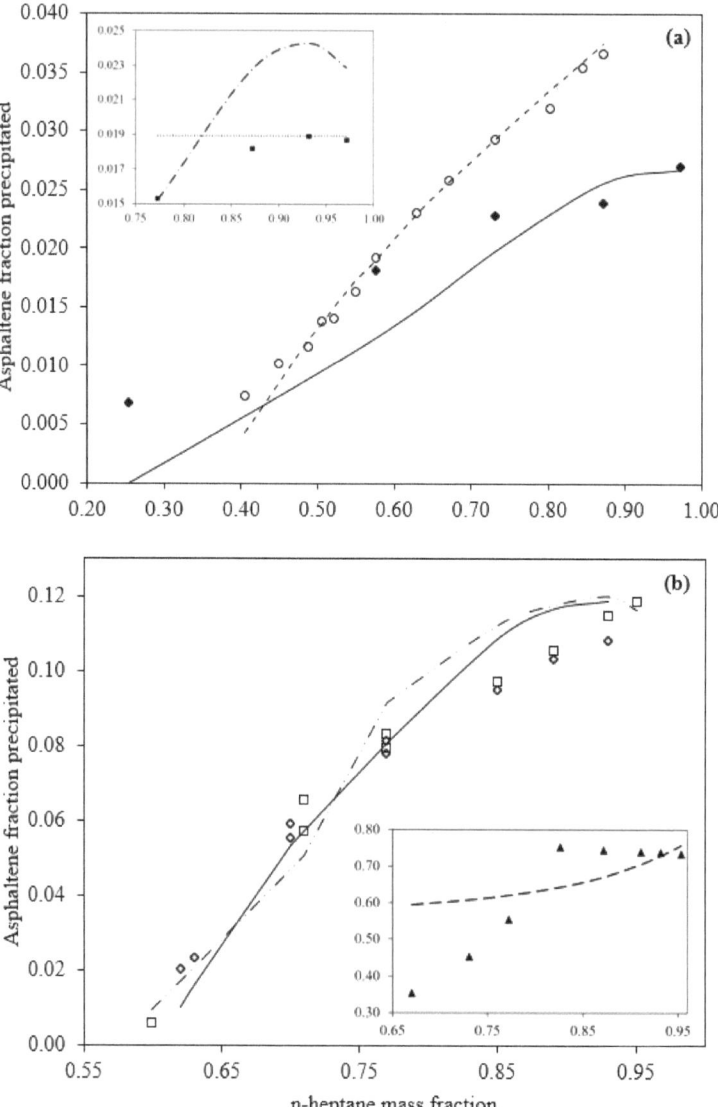

Figure 6. Effect of adding n-heptane solvent on precipitated asphaltene fraction. (**a**) Buenrostro et al., (for oil Y3: ◆ experimental, —— calculated), Rassamdana et al., (○ experimental, – – calculated), plot inside refers to: Experimental data (■) by Hirschberg et al., at 60 °C, (●●●●) calculated by Victorov and Firoozabadi, and (– · –) calculated by Kawanaka et al., (**b**) Sabbagh et al., (for Athabasca bitumen: □ experimental, –··– calculated, and for Cold lake bitumen: ◇ experimental, —— calculated), plot inside refers to: Wu et al., (for Suffield oil: ▲ experimental, – – calculated).

Figure 6a,b shows the results of asphaltene precipitation by five models with n-C_7 as a solvent. The model by Kawanaka et al. calculated the experimental data quite well from 0.60 to 0.80 mass fraction of n-C_7, then overestimated the experimental data above 0.80 mass fraction of n-C_7. The model by Sabbagh et al. initially exhibited good accuracy from 0.60 to 0.71 mass fraction of n-C_7, then, for both samples, the model overestimated the experimental data from 0.71 to 0.95 mass fraction of n-C_7. The model exhibited a maximum error of 51% for Athabasca bitumen, and 50% for Cold Lake bitumen. The model by Rassamdana et al. calculated the experimental data with a certain accuracy in all ranges of mass fraction of n-C_7, and exhibited a maximum error of 42%. The model by Victorov and Firoozabadi presented a constant amount of precipitated asphaltene (0.019 wt% of asphaltene) from 0.78 to 0.98 mass fraction of n-C_7. The model by Wu et al. was capable of calculating asphaltene precipitation quite well for Suffield oil. In general, the model showed a maximum error of 14%. The model by Buenrostro et al. underestimated experimental data from 0.25 to 073 mass fraction of n-C_7 and exhibited a slight overestimation at 0.87 mass fraction of n-C_7.

3.5. Statistical Analysis

The experimental data sets on the precipitated asphaltene mass fraction reported by some models were used to perform a statistical analysis to determine which model is the most accurate to calculate asphaltene precipitation according to the effect of pressure, CO_2 injection, and addition of n-alkanes (n-C_5 and n-C_7). To evaluate the accuracy of each model, the following parameters were used:

$$\text{Residual } (R): R = x_{wa}^{exp} - x_{wa}^{calc} \tag{1}$$

$$\text{Error } (E): E = \left(\frac{x_{wa}^{exp} - x_{wa}^{calc}}{x_{wa}^{exp}} \right) \times 100 \tag{2}$$

$$\text{Average absolute relative deviation } (AARD): AARD_i = \frac{100}{n} \sum \left| \frac{x_{wa}^{exp} - x_{wa}^{calc}}{x_{wa}^{exp}} \right| \tag{3}$$

Tables 6–8 show the results of the statistical analysis of the models.

Table 6. Statistical analysis for models to calculate asphaltene precipitation by effects of pressure and temperature.

Model	Hirschberg et al. 1	Nghiem et al. 13	Li and Firoozabadi 18	Shirani et al. 19	Victorov and Firoozabadi 24	Pan and Firoozabadi 25
AARD, %	74.8564	52.6946	40.3938	7.3951	70.0516	40.8937
(+) Residuals	4	2	13	8	3	3
(−) Residuals	1	2	4	7	1	5
Highest positive residual	0.0070	0.0091	0.3588	0.0093	0.0104	0.0057
Lowest negative residual	−0.0064	−0.0007	−0.1058	−0.0034	−0.0058	−0.0044
Range	0.0134	0.0097	0.4646	0.0127	0.0162	0.0101
R^2	0.9817	0.0014	0.7902	0.9857	0.0028	0.9532
Slope	1.2743	0.0434	1.0470	0.9714	0.1092	0.8243
Intercept	−0.0057	0.0032	−0.0522	0.0000	0.0036	0.0025

Statistical Analysis for the Best Model to Calculate Asphaltene Precipitation

(a) For pressure and temperature effects. The models by Hirschberg et al., Nghiem et al., Li and Firoozabadi, Shirani et al., Victorov and Firoozabadi, and Pan and Firoozabadi were analyzed. The statistical analysis for the models evaluated are presented in Table 6. The model by Shirani et al. exhibited the best AARD% value (7.39%) and a good balance of residuals with eight positive residuals and seven negative residuals, and values of R2, slope, and intercept of 0.985, 0.9714, and 0.00, respectively. The model by Hirschberg et al. showed a tendency to underestimate the experimental data, as it presented four positive residuals and only one negative residual, and an AARD% value of 74.85%. According to the parameters of R2, slope, and intercept, Victorov and Firoozabadi´s model exhibited values of 0.0028, 0.1092, and 0.0036, being the worst model to calculate asphaltene precipitation due to changes in pressure and temperature.

Table 7. Statistical analysis for models to calculate asphaltene precipitation by effects of CO_2 injection.

Model	Wu et al. 16	Li and Firoozabadi 18	Shirani et al. 19	Pan and Firoozabadi 25
AARD, %	23.5848	29.4782	17.2113	14.5783
(+) Residuals	2	2	2	2
(−) Residuals	1	1	1	1
Highest positive residual	0.0800	0.1492	0.0622	0.1017
Lowest negative residual	−0.0800	−0.0741	−0.0463	−0.0624
Range	0.1600	0.2233	0.1085	0.1642
R^2	0.9312	0.9036	0.9237	0.9030
Slope	0.5799	1.3970	0.7508	1.2222
Intercept	0.1365	−0.1863	0.0679	−0.0949

Table 8. Statistical analysis for models to calculate asphaltene precipitation by effects of adding n-alkanes (n-C_5 and n-C_7), as precipitants.

Model	Rassamdana et al. 4	Sabbagh et al. 14	Wu et al. 16	Buenrostro et al. 17	Kawanaka et al. 20	Victorov and Firoozabadi 24
AARD, %	9.5662	18.0057	7.5443	13.0570	13.8824	15.4236
(+) Residuals	15	18	11	11	3	6
(−) Residuals	7	10	9	5	4	1
Highest positive residual	0.0048	0.0371	0.1099	0.0069	0.0014	0.0056
Lowest negative residual	−0.0025	−0.0151	−0.2413	−0.0018	−0.0054	−0.0005
Range	0.0073	0.0522	0.3512	0.0086	0.0068	0.0061
R^2	0.9728	0.8745	0.8743	0.9307	0.3049	0.9815
Slope	1.0417	0.8781	0.7686	1.0427	0.3458	1.1614
Intercept	−0.0020	0.0043	0.2098	−0.0023	0.0208	−0.0072

(b) For CO_2 injection effect. The models by Wu et al., Li and Firoozabadi, Shirani et al., and Pan and Firoozabadi were analyzed. Table 7 exhibits statistical analyses realized for these models. The model by Pan and Firoozabadi et al. exhibited the best AARD% value, with 14.578%, and a good balance of residuals with two positive residuals and one negative residuals. This means that the model does not tend to over or underestimate the experimental data. The model that exhibited the highest value of AARD% was the model by Li and Firoozabadi, with a value of 29.478%. According to the parameters of R2, slope, and intercept, the model by Wu et al. exhibited the best values (0.931, 0.579, and 0.136, respectively). The model by Shirani et al. exhibited the best performance to calculate asphaltene precipitation with pressure, as well as temperature changes. The model by Pan and Firoozabadi exhibited the best performance to calculate asphaltene precipitation with an injection of CO_2 effects.

(c) For n-C_5 and n-C_7 titration tests. The models by Rassamdana et al., Sabbagh et al., Wu et al., Buenrostro et al., Kawanaka et al., and Victorov and Firoozabadi were analyzed. According to residual balance, the model by Rassamdana et al. did not over or underestimate the experimental data. It exhibited a residual balance of fifteen positive residuals and seven negative residuals. The model by Sabbagh et al. exhibited 18 positive residuals and 10 negative residuals, indicating that the model did not tend to over or underestimate the experimental data when n-C_5 or n-C_7 were added. The few experimental data reported by Kawanaka et al. and Victorov and Firoozabadi were not sufficient (seven experimental data were reported for both models) to determine their accuracy. The model by Kawanaka et al. exhibited a residual balance of three and four positive and negative residuals, while the model by Victorov and Firoozabadi showed six and one positive and negative residuals, respectively. The models by Wu et al. and Buenrostro et al. exhibited the best residual balance, with eleven positive residuals and nine negative residuals, and eleven positive residuals and five negative residuals, respectively. According to AARD%, the model by Wu et al. was the best, with 7.54%. The model by Rassamdana et al. was second with an AARD% value of 9.56%, and the model by Victorov and Firoozabadi exhibited an AARD% value of 15.42%, the highest value in this analysis. For parameters R^2, slope, and intercept, the models by Rassamdana et al. and Buenrostro et al. exhibited similar values (0.972, 1.041 and −0.002 for Rassamdana, 0.930, 1.042 and −0.002 for Buenrostro), being the models with best performance to calculate asphaltene precipitation due to the addition of n-alkanes (n-C_5 and n-C_7).

In order to determine which model was the best in calculating asphaltene precipitation among all models analyzed, we used the average absolute relative error (AARD, %). Tables 6–8 and Figure 7 depict values of AARD for each model analyzed. The model by Shirani et al. exhibited the lowest values, with 7.395% for pressure and temperature changes. The model by Pan and Firoozabadi exhibited the lowest value, with 14.578% for the injection of CO_2. The model by Wu et al. exhibited the lowest value, with 7.544% for the addition of n-C_5/n-C_7. The model by Hirschberg et al. exhibited the highest value (74.856%) for pressure and temperature changes. The model by Li and Firoozabadi exhibited the highest values (29.478%) for CO_2 injection effect. The model by Sabbagh et al. exhibited the highest values (18.005%) for the addition of n-C_5/n-C_7 effect. For R^2, slope, and intercept, the model by Shirani et al. exhibited the best values (0.985, 0.971, and 0.0003, respectively) for pressure and temperature changes. The model by Wu et al. exhibited the best values (0.931, 0.579, and 0.136, respectively) for the injection of CO_2 effect. The model by Victorov and Firoozabadi exhibited the best values (0.981, 1.161, and −0.007, respectively) for addition of n-C_5/n-C_7 effect.

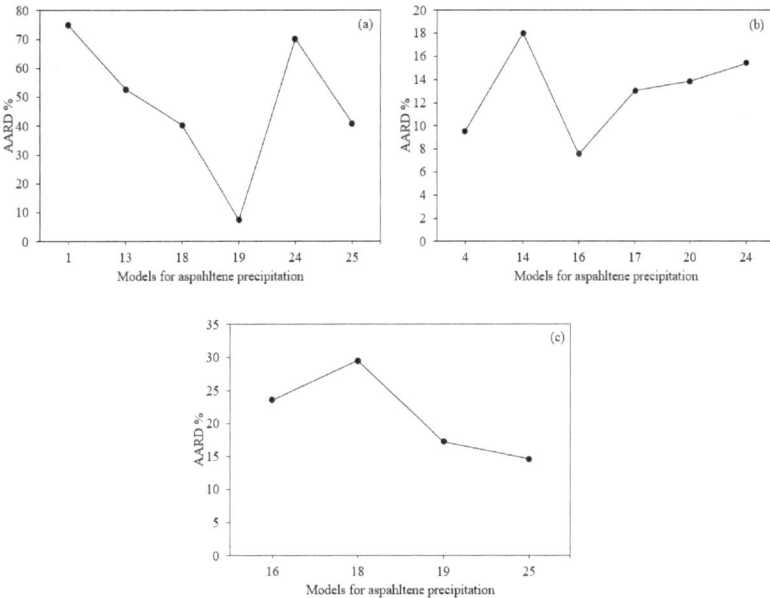

Figure 7. AARD% for different models to calculate asphaltene precipitation. (**a**) by effect of pressure and temperature changes. (**b**) by effect of addition of n-C_5/nC_7. (**c**) by effect of CO_2 injection.

4. Discussion

In this work, a study of the calculation capabilities of eleven published models of asphaltene precipitation was carried out, using statistical analysis from their reported calculation results in the literature. Model accuracies were compiled and used to perform a statistical analysis to determine which model could calculate asphaltene precipitation with good accuracy. It was observed that when the pressure is reduced in a system, the precipitation of asphaltenes is favored; the temperature also increases the amount of asphaltenes to precipitate decreases.

In the case of CO_2 and $n\text{-}C_5$ and $n\text{-}C_7$ titrations, the precipitation of asphaltenes increases when the addition of these compounds increases. This is due to the low or no solubility of asphaltenes with saturated compounds (n-alkanes). Unlike other models, the model by Sabbagh et al. explicitly addresses heavy crude oils (Athabasca and Cold Lake bitumen). This model only covers the addition of $n\text{-}C_5$ and $n\text{-}C_7$ as solvents.

Table 5 shows the types of crude oils used for the development of each model, as well as the solvent used in its development and the amount of asphaltenes present in the sample. On the other hand, Figure 1 shows the pressure and temperature conditions for each model.

As seen in Table 5, previous studies have focused on experiments with blends of crude oils with aromatic solvents (i.e., toluene) and precipitants (i.e., $n\text{-}C_5$, $n\text{-}C_7$, and CO_2). Blending crude oils with different chemical natures may cause asphaltene precipitation, so there is still a need to improve some of the models so that their applicability is extended to heavier crude oils, as well as for mixtures between different types of crude oils.

To achieve these goals, it is important to obtain accurate and exhaustive experimental data so that the parameters included in the models can be properly predicted to allow for better predictions of the behavior of hydrocarbons under different conditions. Experiments with different crude oils and asphaltenes are also necessary to establish a dependence of model parameters on feed properties.

5. Conclusions

From the literature reports, it is observed that the solubility approach has a greater impact on the study of asphaltene precipitation, with 18 models developed under this method. Most of the models in the literature have used $n\text{-}C_5$ and $n\text{-}C_7$ titration data to determine the model's performance and accuracy. Since the solubility and colloidal approaches require the calculation of thermodynamic properties, such as solubility parameters, molar volumes and molecular weight, equations-of-state, such as Soave-Redlich-Kwong and Peng-Robinson (Hirschberg et al., Novosad and Costain, Rassamdana et al., Cimino et al., Nghiem et al., Sabbagh et al., Li and Firoozabadi, Shirani et al., Ting et al., Wu et al., Buenrostro et al.), are typically used to determine these thermodynamic parameters for crude oils and solvents. According to the statistical analysis of the precipitated asphaltene mass fraction by different procedures and approaches, the model by Shirani et al. exhibited the best values for R^2, slope, and intercept (0.985, 0.971, and 0.0003, respectively), as well as an AARD value of 7.395% when this model was applied to calculate the amount of precipitated asphaltenes as functions of pressure and temperature changes. The model by Victorov and Firoozabadi exhibited values for R_2, slope, and intercept of 0.981, 1.161, and -0.007 when this model was applied to calculate the amount of precipitated asphaltenes due to the addition of n-alkanes. The model by Wu et al. exhibited values for R^2, slope, and intercept of 0.931, 0.5799, and 0.136 when this model was applied to calculate the amount of precipitated asphaltenes due to the injection of CO_2. As per the AARD analysis, models that exhibited the worst values of AARD were those by Hirschberg et al., with 74.85%, and Victorov and Firoozabadi, with 70.05% for pressure and temperature changes. The models by Li and Firoozabadi, with 29.47%, and Wu et al., with 23.58%, had the worst values for CO_2 injection effect. The models by Sabbagh et al., with 18.00%, and Victorov and Firoozabadi, with 15.42%, had the worst values for the addition of $n\text{-}C_5/n\text{-}C_7$ effect. From these results, it is evident that it is necessary to develop a model that addresses the precipitation of asphaltenes when dilutions are made between crude oils with different characteristics.

Author Contributions: E.A.H.: Conceptualization; Formal analysis; Investigation; Methodology; Validation; Writing—original draft; Writing—review & editing; C.L.-G.: Investigation; Methodology; Validation; Writing—original draft; J.A.: Methodology; Validation; Writing—original draft; Writing—review & editing. All authors have read and agreed to the published version of the manuscript.

Funding: This research received no external funding.

Data Availability Statement: Data sharing not applicable. No new data were created or analyzed in this study. Data sharing is not applicable to this article.

Acknowledgments: E.A.H. thanks to Consejo Nacional de Ciencia y Tecnología (CONACyT) for the Ph.D. scholarship. The authors also thank the Mexican Institute of Petroleum and CONACyT for the financial support (Project Y.61057).

Conflicts of Interest: The authors declare that they have no known competing financial interests or personal relationships that could have appeared to influence the work reported in this paper.

References

1. Rodríguez, S.; Ancheyta, J.; Guzmán, R.; Trejo, F. Experimental setups for studying the compatibility of crude oil blends under dynamic conditions. *Energy Fuels* **2016**, *30*, 8216–8225. [CrossRef]
2. Du, J.L.; Zhang, D.A. Thermodynamic model for the prediction of asphaltene precipitation. *Pet. Sci. Technol.* **2004**, *22*, 1023–1033. [CrossRef]
3. Vargas, F.M.; Gonzalez, D.L.; Creek, J.L.; Wang, J.; Buckley, J.; Hirasaki, G.J.; Chapman, W.G. Development of a general method for modeling asphaltene stability. *Energy Fuels* **2009**, *23*, 1147–1154. [CrossRef]
4. Vafaie-Sefti, M.; Mousavi-Dehghani, S.A.; Mohammad-Zadeh, M. A simple model for asphaltene deposition in petroleum mixtures. *Fluid Phase Equilibria* **2003**, *206*, 1–11. [CrossRef]
5. Alimohamadi, S.; Zendehboudi, S.; James, L. A comprehensive review of asphaltene deposition in petroleum reservoirs: Theory, challenges, and tips. *Fuel* **2019**, *252*, 753–791. [CrossRef]
6. Ancheyta, J.; Trejo, F.; Rana, M.S. *Asphaltenes: Chemical Transformations during Hydroprocessing of Heavy Oils*, 1st ed.; CRC Press, Taylor and Francis Group: Abingdon-on-Thames, UK, 2009. [CrossRef]
7. Adams, J.J. Asphaltene Adsorption, a Literature Review. *Energy Fuels* **2014**, *28*, 2831–2856. [CrossRef]
8. Moud, A.A. Asphaltene induced changes in rheological properties: A review. *Fuel* **2022**, *316*, 123372. [CrossRef]
9. Guzmán, R.; Ancheyta, J.; Trejo, F.; Rodríguez, S. Methods for determining asphaltene stability in crude oils. *Fuel* **2017**, *188*, 530–543. [CrossRef]
10. Guzmán, R.; Rodríguez, S.; Torres-Mancera, P.; Ancheyta, J. Evaluation of asphaltene stability of a wide range of Mexican crude oils. *Energy Fuels* **2021**, *35*, 408–418. [CrossRef]
11. Rashid, Z.; Wilfred, C.D.; Gnanasundaram, N.; Arunagiri, A.; Murugesan, T. A comprehensive review on the recent advances on the petroleum asphaltene aggregation. *J. Pet. Sci. Eng.* **2019**, *176*, 249–268. [CrossRef]
12. Vargas, F.M.; Tavakkoli, M. *Asphaltene Deposition: Fundamentals, Prediction, Prevention, and Remediation*, 1st ed.; CRC Press, Taylor and Francis Group: Abingdon-on-Thames, UK, 2018. [CrossRef]
13. Hirschberg, A.; de Jong, L.N.J.; Schipper, B.A.; Meijer, J.G. Influence of temperature and pressure on asphaltene flocculation. *Soc. Pet. Eng.* **1984**, *24*, 283–293. [CrossRef]
14. Burke, N.E.; Hobbs, R.E.; Kashou, S.F. Measurement and modeling of asphaltene precipitation. *JPT J. Pet. Technol.* **1990**, *42*, 1440–1446. [CrossRef]
15. Novosad, Z.; Costain, T.G. Experimental and modeling studies of asphaltene equilibria for a reservoir under CO_2 injection. In Proceedings of the SPE Annual Technical Conference and Exhibition, Gamma, New Orleans, LA, USA, 23–26 September 1990; pp. 599–607. [CrossRef]
16. Rassamdana, H.; Dabir, B.; Nematy, M.; Farhani, M.; Sahimi, M. Asphalt flocculation and deposition: I. The onset of precipitation. *AIChE J.* **1996**, *42*, 10–22. [CrossRef]
17. Buckley, J.S.; Hirasaki, G.J.; Liu, Y.; Von Drasek, S.; Wang, J.X.; Gill, B.S. Asphaltene precipitation and solvent properties of crude oils. *Pet. Sci. Technol.* **1998**, *16*, 251–285. [CrossRef]
18. Chung, T.H. Thermodynamic modeling for organic solid precipitation. In Proceedings of the SPE Annual Technical Conference and Exhibition, Washington, DC, USA, 4–7 October 1992. [CrossRef]
19. Cimino, R.; Correra, S.; Sacomani, P.A.; Carniani, C. Thermodynamic modelling for prediction of asphaltene deposition in live oils. In Proceedings of the SPE International Symposium on Oilfield Chemistry, San Antonio, TX, USA, 14–17 February 1995. [CrossRef]

20. De Boer, R.B.; Leerlooyer, K.; Eigner, M.R.P.; van Bergen, A.R.D. Screening of crude oils for asphalt precipitation: Theory, practice, and the selection of inhibitors. *SPE Prod. Facil.* **1995**, *10*, 55–61. [CrossRef]
21. Alboudwarej, H.; Akbarzadeh, K.; Beck, J.; Svrcek, W.Y.; Yarranton, H.W. Regular solution model for asphaltene precipitation from bitumens and solvents. *AIChE J.* **2010**, *49*, 2948–2956. [CrossRef]
22. Yarranton, H.W.; Masliyah, J.H. Molar mass distribution and solubility modeling of asphaltenes. *AIChE J.* **1996**, *42*, 3533–3543. [CrossRef]
23. Thomas, F.B.; Bennion, D.B.; Bennion, D.W.; Hunter, B.E. Experimental and theoretical studies of solids precipitation from reservoir fluid. *J. Can. Pet. Technol.* **1992**, *31*. [CrossRef]
24. Wang, J.X.; Buckley, J.S. An experimental approach to prediction of asphaltene flocculation. In Proceedings of the SPE International Symposium on Oilfield Chemistry, Houston, TX, USA, 13–16 February 2001; pp. 179–187. [CrossRef]
25. Wang, J.X.; Buckley, J.S. A two-component solubility model of the onset of asphaltene flocculation in crude oils. *Energy Fuels* **2001**, *15*, 1004–1012. [CrossRef]
26. Nghiem, L.X.; Hassam, M.S.; Nutakki, R.; George, A.E.D. Efficient modelling of asphaltene precipitation. In Proceedings of the SPE Annual Technical Conference and Exhibition, Sigma, Houston, TX, USA, 3–6 October 1993; pp. 375–384. [CrossRef]
27. Sabbagh, O.; Akbarzadeh, K.; Badamchi-Zadeh, A.; Svrcek, W.Y.; Yarranton, H.W. Applying the PR-EoS to asphaltene precipitation from n-alkane diluted heavy oils and bitumens. *Energy Fuels* **2006**, *20*, 625–634. [CrossRef]
28. Ting, P.D.; Hirasaki, G.J.; Chapman, W.G. Modeling of asphaltene phase behavior with the SAFT equation of state. *Pet. Sci. Technol.* **2003**, *21*, 647–661. [CrossRef]
29. Wu, J.; Prausnitz, J.M.; Prausnitz, J.M. Molecular-thermodynamic framework for asphaltene-oil equilibria. *AIChE J.* **1998**, *44*, 1188–1199. [CrossRef]
30. Wu, J.; Prausnitz, J.M.; Firoozabadi, A. Molecular thermodynamics of asphaltene precipitation in reservoir fluids. *AIChE J.* **2000**, *46*, 197–209. [CrossRef]
31. Buenrostro-Gonzalez, E.; Lira-Galeana, C.; Gil-Villegas, A.; Wu, J. Asphaltene precipitation in crude oils: Theory and experiments. *AIChE J.* **2004**, *50*, 2552–2570. [CrossRef]
32. Li, Z.; Firoozabadi, A. Cubic-plus-association equation of state for asphaltene precipitation in live oils. *Energy Fuels* **2010**, *24*, 2956–2963. [CrossRef]
33. Shirani, B.; Nikazar, M.; Naseri, A.; Mousavi-Dehghani, S.A. Modeling of asphaltene precipitation utilizing Association Equation of State. *Fuel* **2012**, *93*, 59–66. [CrossRef]
34. Kawanaka, S.; Park, S.J.; Mansoori, G.A. Organic deposition from reservoir fluids: A thermodynamic predictive technique. *SPE Reserv. Eng.* **1991**, *6*, 185–192. [CrossRef]
35. Huggins, M.L. Solutions of long chain compounds. *J. Chem. Phys.* **1941**, *9*, 440. [CrossRef]
36. Flory, P.J. Thermodynamics of high polymer solutions. *J. Chem. Phys.* **1942**, *10*, 51–61. [CrossRef]
37. Zuo, J.Y.; Mullins, O.C.; Freed, D.; Elshahawi, H.; Dong, C.; Seifert, D.J. Advances in the Flory-Huggins-Zuo equation of state for asphaltene gradients and formation evaluation. *Energy Fuels* **2013**, *27*, 1722–1735. [CrossRef]
38. Zuo, J.Y.; Mullins, O.C.; Dong, C.; Zhang, D. Modeling of Asphaltene Grading in Oil Reservoirs. *Nat. Resour.* **2010**, *1*, 19–27. [CrossRef]
39. Leontaritis, K.J.; Mansoori, G.A. Asphaltene flocculation during oil production and processing: A thermodynamic colloidal model. In Proceedings of the Society of Petroleum Engineers of AIME, San Antonio, TX, USA, 8 February 1987; pp. 149–158.
40. Victorov, A.I.; Firoozabadi, A. Thermodynamic micellization model of asphaltene precipitation from petroleum fluids. *AIChE J.* **1996**, *42*, 1753–1764. [CrossRef]
41. Pan, H.Q.; Firoozabadi, A. Thermodynamic micellization model for asphaltene precipitation from reservoir crudes at high pressures and temperatures. In Proceedings of the SPE Annual Technical Conference and Exhibition, San Antonio, TX, USA, 5–8 October 1997. [CrossRef]
42. Pan, H.Q.; Firoozabadi, A. Thermodynamic micellization model for asphaltene precipitation inhibition. *AIChE J.* **2000**, *46*, 416–426. [CrossRef]
43. Szewczyk, V.; Thomas, M.; Behar, E. Prediction of volumetric properties and (multi-) phase behavior of asphaltenic crudes. *Rev. Inst. Fr. Pet.* **1998**, *53*, 51–58. [CrossRef]
44. Szewczyk, V.; Behar, E. Compositional model for predicting asphaltenes flocculation. *Fluid Phase Equilibria* **1999**, *158–160*, 459–469. [CrossRef]
45. Srivastava, R.K.; Huang, S.S.; Dong, M. Asphaltene deposition during CO_2 flooding. *SPE Prod. Facil.* **1999**, *14*, 235–245. [CrossRef]

Disclaimer/Publisher's Note: The statements, opinions and data contained in all publications are solely those of the individual author(s) and contributor(s) and not of MDPI and/or the editor(s). MDPI and/or the editor(s) disclaim responsibility for any injury to people or property resulting from any ideas, methods, instructions or products referred to in the content.

Article

Prediction of Molecular Weight of Petroleum Fluids by Empirical Correlations and Artificial Neuron Networks

Dicho Stratiev [1,2,*], Sotir Sotirov [3], Evdokia Sotirova [3], Svetoslav Nenov [4], Rosen Dinkov [1], Ivelina Shishkova [1], Iliyan Venkov Kolev [1,2], Dobromir Yordanov [3], Svetlin Vasilev [3], Krassimir Atanassov [2,3], Stanislav Simeonov [3] and Georgi Nikolov Palichev [2]

[1] LUKOIL Neftohim Burgas, 8104 Burgas, Bulgaria
[2] Institute of Biophysics and Biomedical Engineering, Bulgarian Academy of Sciences, Georgi Bonchev 105, 1113 Sofia, Bulgaria
[3] Intelligent Systems Laboratory, Department Industrial Technologies and Management, University Prof. Dr. Assen Zlatarov, 8010 Burgas, Bulgaria
[4] Department of Mathematics, University of Chemical Technology and Metallurgy, Kliment Ohridski 8, 1756 Sofia, Bulgaria
* Correspondence: stratiev.dicho@neftochim.bg

Abstract: The exactitude of petroleum fluid molecular weight correlations affects significantly the precision of petroleum engineering calculations and can make process design and trouble-shooting inaccurate. Some of the methods in the literature to predict petroleum fluid molecular weight are used in commercial software process simulators. According to statements made in the literature, the correlations of Lee–Kesler and Twu are the most used in petroleum engineering, and the other methods do not exhibit any significant advantages over the Lee–Kesler and Twu correlations. In order to verify which of the proposed in the literature correlations are the most appropriate for petroleum fluids with molecular weight variation between 70 and 1685 g/mol, 430 data points for boiling point, specific gravity, and molecular weight of petroleum fluids and individual hydrocarbons were extracted from 17 literature sources. Besides the existing correlations in the literature, two different techniques, nonlinear regression and artificial neural network (ANN), were employed to model the molecular weight of the 430 petroleum fluid samples. It was found that the ANN model demonstrated the best accuracy of prediction with a relative standard error (RSE) of 7.2%, followed by the newly developed nonlinear regression correlation with an RSE of 10.9%. The best available molecular weight correlations in the literature were those of API (RSE = 12.4%), Goosens (RSE = 13.9%); and Riazi and Daubert (RSE = 15.2%). The well known molecular weight correlations of Lee–Kesler, and Twu, for the data set of 430 data points, exhibited RSEs of 26.5, and 30.3% respectively.

Keywords: petroleum; molecular weight; modeling; artificial neural network; nonlinear regression; empirical correlation

1. Introduction

In petroleum engineering simulations to design new equipment or rate the existing one the molecular weight of the petroleum fluids is one of the most important characterization parameters [1–5]. It affects thermodynamic phase equilibrium, reaction kinetics, and vapor density calculations [5]. The measurement of petroleum fluid molecular weight is not a simple job, and, depending on the method used, either vapor pressure osmometry or freezing point depression, some discrepancies may arise [6]. For example, Powers et al. [7] reported repeatability of 15% for molecular weight measurement of asphaltenes, while Yarranton et al. [8] reported repeatability of 12% for saturates/aromatics/resins (SAR), and Lemus et al. [2] reported repeatability of ±15% for the bitumen and its distillation cuts. All these studies [2,7,8] employed vapor pressure osmometry. Thus, petroleum fluid molecular weight has the highest measurement uncertainty of the three main physical properties: boiling point, specific gravity, and molecular weight [1]. Considering the higher precision of measurement of boiling point and specific gravity, several empirical correlations were developed to predict petroleum fluid molecular weight from boiling point and specific gravity (density) [1,2,6–23]. Schneider [6] summarized the petroleum fluid molecular weight correlations, which appeared in the period 1964–1984. He concluded that the molecular weight correlation selected impacts engineering calculations to a significant degree [6]. During simulation of a crude distillation column for Bachaquero crude feed constant side-draw product rates, constant barrels per day (bpsd) overflash, constant column bottoms true boiling point (TBP) 5% point flash zone temperature variations of 10 to 30 °F, and heater duty differences of 5 to 10%, were obtained when different molecular weight correlations were employed [6]. Such large variations, he concluded, would make the process design and troubleshooting inaccurate. Unfortunately, he did not point out which of the studied molecular weight correlations were most appropriate. Instead he deduced that a molecular weight correlation used for any purpose should not be extended beyond the limits for which it is valid without caution. Goosens [9] announced in his research that a major oil company had reviewed 37 different methods and their marked deviations beyond molecular weights of 300 g/mol. A major reason for the abundance of still less satisfactory correlations, he underlined, is the fact that the principal independent variable for the prediction of the molecular weight, being some average boiling point, is often ill-defined. Lemus in her PhD thesis [1] summarized the petroleum fluid molecular weight correlations, which appeared in the period 1989–2010. She reported average absolute relative deviation for the molecular weight prediction of bitumen and heavy oils ranging between 7.6 and 30.7% for the different literature correlations [1]. The new molecular weight correlation proposed in her PhD thesis shows an average absolute relative deviation of 5.3%. Since 2016, no reports have appeared in the literature to summarize the available information about the molecular weight correlations of petroleum fluids. Moreover, in 2021 Hosseinifar, and Shahverdi [10] proposed a new petroleum fluid molecular weight correlation suggesting that it should be superior to others. Considering the importance of the molecular weight in petroleum engineering calculations, we decided to make a generalization of the correlations published in the literature for the period 1969–2021. Table 1 summarizes 13 published in the literature petroleum fluid molecular weight correlations for the period 1969–2021. Nine of these correlations (Hariu and Sage [21], Kesler and Lee [13], Riazi and Daubert (1980) [15], Twu [20], Rao and Bardon [19], Soreide [12], Goosens [9], Riazi and Daubert for MW $\leq$ 300 [18], Riazi and Daubert for MW $\leq$ 700 [15]) and their applications have been already discussed in the PhD thesis of Lemus [1]. The additional four correlations included in Table 1 (Liñan et al. [23], Liñan et al. (API) [23], Lemus et al. [2], and Hosseinifar, and Shahverdi [10]) have not been examined with a great number of data points, and can be considered relatively new because the last assessment of molecular weight correlations was reported in 2016 [2]. The correlation of Liñan et al. [23] has been developed to predict molecular weight of petroleum residues and cuts. The correlation of Lemus et al. [2] has been developed to predict molecular weight of heavy oil distillation cuts. The correlation of Hosseinifar, and Shahverdi [10] has been developed for petroleum fluids having a specific gravity from 0.68 to 0.92, boiling points from 340 to 722 K, and molecular weight from 84 to 414 g/mol.

There is no consent in the literature about which correlation can be deemed most appropriate to predict the molecular weight of petroleum fluids. For example, Liu et al. [24] argue that the developed correlations after those of Lee–Kesler correlation [13,14], and the Twu correlation [20], described by Riazi [18] do not have a significant advantage over the Lee–Kesler or Twu correlations. Liu at al. [24] reported that Aspen HYSYS uses the Twu correlation to calculate the molecular weight of petroleum fluids.

Table 1. Summary of correlations available in the literature to estimate molecular weight.

Source (Year of Publication)	Correlation	Range of Applicability	Eq.
Hariu, and Sage [21] (1969)	$MW = 0.6670202 \ +0.1552531 Kw \ -0.005378496 Kw^2 \ \times 0.004583705 T_b Kw \ +0.00002500584 T_b Kw^2 \ +0.000002698693 T_b^2 \ +0.00003875957 T_b^2 Kw \ -0.00000001566228 T_b^2 \times Kw^2$	$30 < T_b < 800$	(1)
Kesler and Lee [13] (1976)	$MW = [D] + \frac{[A]}{T_b} + \frac{[B]}{T_b^3}$ $D = -12272.6 + 9486.4 \times SG + (4.6523 - 3.3287 \times SG) \times T_b$ $A = (1 - 0.77084 \times SG - 0.02058 \times SG^2) \times \left(1.3437 - \frac{720.79}{T_b}\right) \times 10^7$ $B = (1 - 0.80882 \times SG + 0.02226 \times SG^2) \times \left(1.8828 - \frac{181.92}{T_b}\right) \times 10^{12}$	$T_b < 750$	(2)
Riazi and Daubert [15] (1980)	$MW = 0.000045673 \times T_b^{2.1962} \times SG^{-1.0164}$	$300 < T_b < 610$	(3)
Twu [20] (1984)	$\ln(M) = \ln M° [(1 + 2f_M)/(1 - 2f_M)]^2$ $f_M = \Delta SG_M \left[\chi + \left(-0.0175691 + \frac{0.143979}{T_b^{1/2}}\right)\Delta SG_M\right]$ $\chi = \left|0.012342 - 0.2445541/T_b^{1/2}\right|$ $\Delta SG_M = exp\left[5\left(SG° - SG\right)\right] - 1$ $SG° = 0.843593 - 0.128624\alpha - 3.36159\alpha^3 - 13749.5\alpha^{12}$ $\alpha = 1 - T_b/T_b°$	$MW < 600$	(4)
Rao and Bardon [19] (1985)	$\ln MW = (1.27 + 0.071 K_w) \ln\left(\frac{1.8 T_b}{22.31 + 1.68 K_W}\right)$	$361 < T_b < 830$	(5)
Soreide [12] (1989)	$T_b = [1928.3 - 169500 \times MW^{-0.03522} \times SG^{3.266} D]/1.8$ $D = EXP(0.004922 \times MW - 4.7685 \times SG + 0.003462 * MW * SG)$	$361 < T_b < 830$	(6)
Goosens [9], (1996)	$MW = 0.010770 T_b^{[1.52869 + 0.06486 \ln\left(\frac{T_b}{1078 - T_b}\right)]}/d$	$306 < T_b < 1012$	(7)
Riazi and Daubert for $MW \leq 300$ g/mol [18] (2005)	$M = 1.6607 \times 10^{-4} T_b^{2.1962} SG^{-1.0164}$	$300 < T_b < 610$	(8)
Riazi and Daubert for $MW \leq 700$ g/mol [18], (2005)	$M = 42.965 [exp(2.097 \times 10^{-4} T_b - 7.78712 SG + 2.08476 \ \times 10^{-3} T_b SG)] T_b^{1.26007} SG^{4.98308}$	$300 < T_b < 900$	(9)
Liñan et al. [23] (2011)	$M_{WadC} = 284.75 [exp(0.00322(t_{VABP} + 273.15))][exp(-2.52 SG)] \times (t_{VABP} + 273.15)^{0.083} SG^{2.44}$	$673 < T_b < 1235$	(10)
Liñan et al. [23] (2011) (API)	$M_{WAPI} = 219.05 [exp(0.0039(t_b + 273.15))][exp(-3.07 SG)] \times (t_b + 273.15)^{0.118} SG^{1.88}$		(11)
Lemus et al. [2] (2016)	$T_b = [1805 - 21131 \times MW^{-0.049} \times SG^{1.5258} D]/1.8$ $D = EXP(-0.005 \times MW - 2.675 \times SG + 0.003 \times MW \times SG)$	$300 < T_b < 900$	(12)
Hosseinifar, and Shahverdi [10] (2021)	$M_w(T_b, SG) = \left\| d_1 \times T_b^{d_2} \left(\frac{3+2SG}{3-SG}\right)^{\frac{d_3}{2}} + d_4 \times T_b^{d_5} \left(\frac{3+2SG}{3-SG}\right)^{\frac{d_6}{2}} \right\|^{d_7}$	$340 < T_b < 722$	(13)

Goosens [9] stated that the correlation developed in his work was superior to that of API procedure 2B2.1 imposed as a standard that was limited to molecular weights of 700. The correlation of Goosens covers the full practical range of molecular weights of 75–1700 [9]. Hosseinifar and Shahverdi [10] have developed recently a new petroleum fluid molecular weight correlation, which is suggested to have advantage over the published (until 2021) other molecular weight correlations. In addition, Hosseinifar and Shahverdi [25] developed a method to generate TBP distillation data from molecular weight, or $T_{50\%}$ and density, that allowed us, in our recent study, to employ artificial neural network (ANN) to predict petroleum viscosity [26]. The same approach could be applied to predict petroleum fluid molecular weight from boiling point and density using the method of Hosseinifar and Shahverdi [25] to generate more than two (density and boiling point) inlet parameters to allow the employment of the ANN method. In our recent research, the ANN method using the approach discussed above demonstrated the best prediction of petroleum viscosity [26]. In order to evaluate the molecular weight prediction ability of the available empirical correlations in the literature, data from 430 petroleum fluids and individual hydrocarbons with molecular weight variation between 70 and 1685 g/mol were selected from 21 literature sources [1,2,9,22,23,27–42] and shown in Table S1. The data generated by the use of the Hosseinifar and Shahverdi [25] method, described in our recent research [26], along with specific gravity, boiling point, and the corresponding molecular weight of the 430 petroleum fluids to be used for molecular weight modeling by the ANN method, are presented Supplementary Table S2. The wide range of variation of molecular weight, boiling points, and density of the 430 petroleum fluids and individual hydrocarbons allows us to explore the capabilities of two commonly used techniques to model petroleum properties: the nonlinear regression and the ANN. This can give a notion as to which method is better to model petroleum fluid molecular weight. Comparisons between capabilities of the nonlinear regression and the metaheuristic methods to model oil properties have been reported in several studies [43–48]. However, no such study has been reported yet, to the best of our knowledge, for modelling of petroleum fluid molecular weight by the use of ANN. That was the reason for us to conduct this research.

The aim of this investigation is to develop two new methods to predict petroleum fluid molecular weight using two different techniques, nonlinear regression and ANN, and contrast them with the empirical correlations available in the literature.

2. Materials and Methods

The petroleum fluids, whose measured density, boiling point, and molecular weight were extracted from the literature, vary between light naphtha and vacuum residue. The carbon number of the individual hydrocarbons, extracted from the literature, and used in this study, varies between C_6 and C_{52}. The boiling point of the 430 petroleum fluids and individual hydrocarbons varies between 30 (303K) and 739 °C (1012K), and specific gravity at 15.6 °C varies between 0.631 and 1.527. The boiling point, specific gravity, and measured molecular weight of the 430 oils are summarized in Table S1.

The method of Hosseinifar and Shahverdi [25] and its use to generate TBP boiling point at 5, 10, 30, 50, 70, and 90 vol.% and its application for making more inlet parameters required by the ANN method is detailed in our recent research [26]. The equations used to generate TBP boiling point at 5, 10, 30, 50, 70, and 90 vol.% are shown below:

$$T50 = 1.037003 * Tb - 16.0825 \tag{14}$$

$$T70 = -1.06487 * Tb + 18.49267 \tag{15}$$

$$T30 = \left[(1.679547 * Tb - 31.7009)^3 - T50^3 - 2T70^3 \right]^{1/3} \tag{16}$$

$$T10 = \frac{\left[Abs\left((-0.94473 * Exp(SG) + 3.178959) * Kw^{-1.52054} \right) \right]^{1.011152}}{T50^{-1.58808}} \tag{17}$$

$$T90 = \frac{[-1.01857 * 0.5 * (Tb + T70) + 11.24528]^2}{0.5 * (T50 + T10)} \tag{18}$$

$$T5 = Abs\left((1.42946 * Tb * T50)^{0.5} - 7.25905 \right)^3 - T70^3 - T90^3)^{0.343176} \tag{19}$$

where,

T50–TBP boiling point at 50% evaporate, °C;
T70–TBP boiling point at 70% evaporate, °C;
T30–TBP boiling point at 30% evaporate, °C;
T10–TBP boiling point at 10% evaporate, °C;
T90–TBP boiling point at 90% evaporate, °C;
T5–TBP boiling point at 5% evaporate, °C;

It is worth mentioning here that the use of the method of Hosseinifar and Shahverdi [25] has not been made to construct the real TBP curve, but instead to make more than two inlet parameters (specific gravity, and boiling point) to apply for ANN modeling purposes. Kw-characterization factor of the studied oils was estimated as shown in our recent article [26]. Table S2 summarizes the data employed for ANN modeling that includes nine inlet characterizing parameters: specific gravity, boiling point (K), $T_{5\%}$, $T_{10\%}$, $T_{30\%}$, $T_{50\%}$, $T_{70\%}$, $T_{90\%}$, and Kw. The Kw-characterization factor for the studied oils varies between 7.4 and 14.5.

The computer algebra system (CAS) Maple and NLPSolve with Modified Newton Iterative Method as described in [43] was employed to develop a new empirical correlation predicting molecular weight of petroleum fluids using the data extracted from the literature and discussed above.

The artificial neural network (ANN) modeling approach used in this investigation is described in our earlier research [26].

The accuracy of petroleum fluid molecular weight prediction has been evaluated by the statistical parameters shown as Equations (20)–(25).

$$Error\ (E): E = \left(\frac{MW_{exp} - MW_{calc}}{MW_{exp}}\right) \times 100 \qquad (20)$$

$$Standard\ error\ (SE): SE_i = \left(\sum\left(\frac{(MW_{exp} - MW_{calc})^2}{N-2}\right)\right)^{\frac{1}{2}} \qquad (21)$$

$$Relative\ standard\ error\ (RSE): RSE_i = \frac{SE}{mean\ of\ the\ sample} \times 100 \qquad (22)$$

$$Sum\ of\ square\ errors\ (SSE): SSE = \sum \frac{1}{MW_{exp}^2}(MW_{exp} - MW_{calc})^2 \qquad (23)$$

$$Average\ absolute\ deviation\ (\%AAD): \%AAD = \frac{1}{N}\frac{\sum|MW_{exp} - MW_{calc}|}{MW_{exp}} \times 100 \qquad (24)$$

$$Sum\ of\ relative\ errors\ (SRE): SRE = \sum\left(\frac{MW_{exp} - MW_{calc}}{MW_{exp}}\right) \times 100 \qquad (25)$$

3. Results

Goosens [9] mentioned in his work that a great number of petroleum fluid molecular weight correlations exhibited marked deviations beyond molecular weights of 300 g/mol. That was the reason for us to select a data base with a very wide range of variation of molecular weight, boiling points, and specific gravity. Figure 1 shows a graph of dependence of molecular weight on boiling point for the selected data base of 430 petroleum fluids and individual hydrocarbons. It is evident from this data that molecular weight exponentially increases with boiling point augmentation. It can be also seen that some individual polynuclear aromatic hydrocarbons deviate from the general exponential dependence, displaying lower molecular weight at the same boiling point.

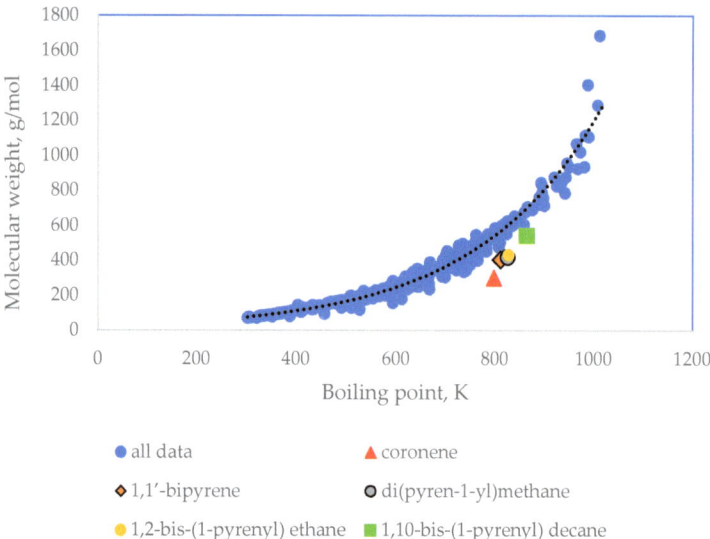

Figure 1. Dependence of molecular weight on boiling point for petroleum fluids and individual hydrocarbons.

The specific gravity, which well reflects the aromatic structure content [45], accounts for this deviation of the polynuclear aromatic compounds from the general exponential dependence of molecular weight on boiling point. By the use of CAS Maple and NLPSolve with Modified Newton Iterative Method and 306 points (the data with numbers from 1 to 306 from Table S1) out of 430, the following new empirical correlation was developed:

$$MW = -552.982 + 453.095 * EXP(0.19239 * EXP\left(0.000421163 * \frac{BP^{1.22097}}{SG^{0.297075}}\right)) \quad (26)$$

where,

BP = boiling point of the petroleum fluid or individual hydrocarbon, K;
SG = specific gravity at 15.6 °C.

The remaining 124 data points were used to test the validity of Equation (26). For the development of the artificial neural network, a 3-layer deep learning neural network with a structure of 9 inputs (SG, BP, $T_{5\%}$, $T_{10\%}$, $T_{30\%}$, $T_{50\%}$, $T_{70\%}$, $T_{90\%}$, and Kw), 12 neurons in the first layer, 1 neuron in the output layer, and 1 output was used. Figure 2 presents the structure of the neural network employed in this study.

The entire training process took 18 iterations, and the performance was 0.0031481. The training process is shown in the Figure 3.

The regression coefficients of the artificial neural network are: Training—0.99705, Testing—0.99118, Validation—0.99638, All—0.99615 (Figure 4).

It is worth mentioning here that, during ANN modeling, the logarithm of molecular weight was modeled and the output of the ANN model was converted in molecular weight by the use of exponential function.

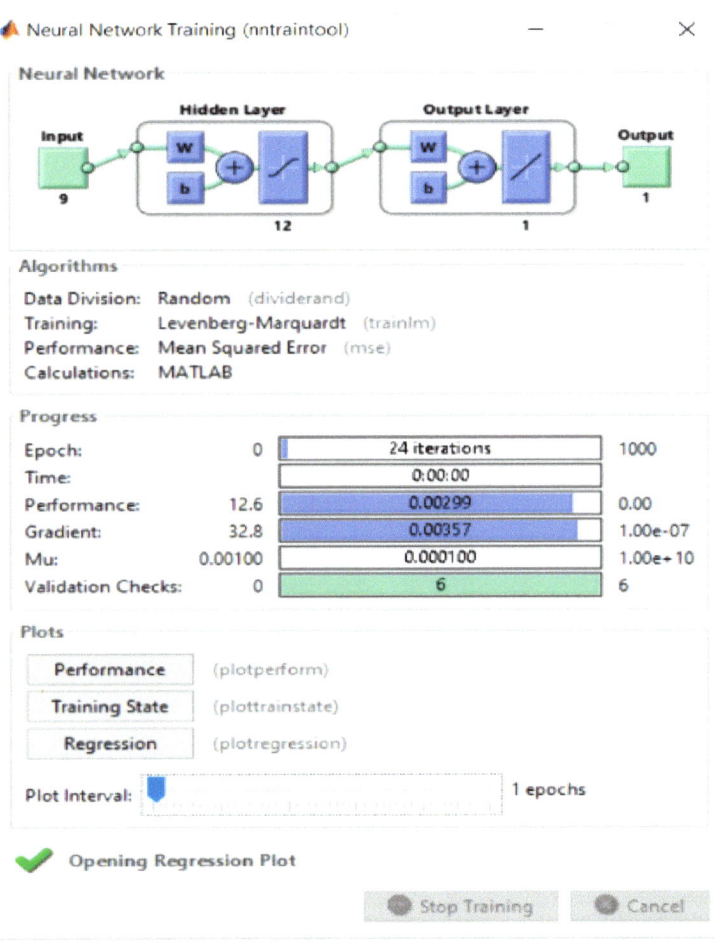

Figure 2. Structure of the neural network employed in this study.

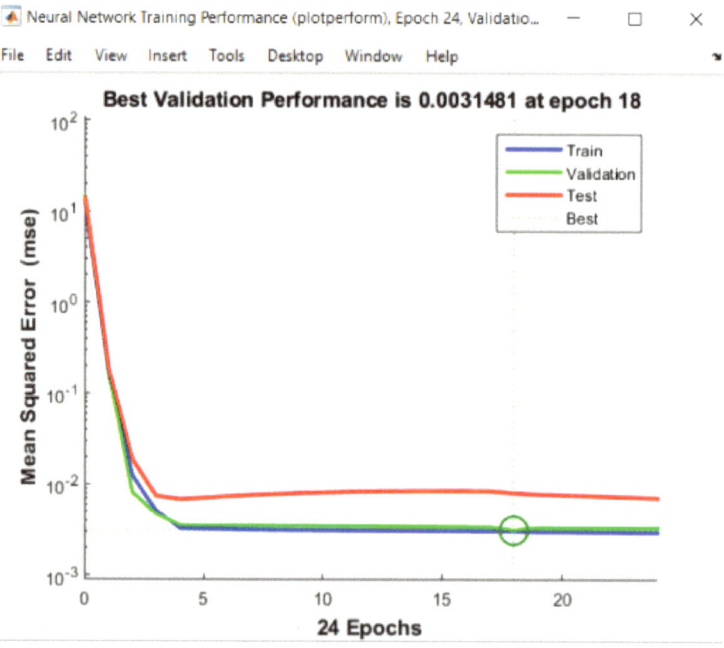

Figure 3. Training process of the neural network.

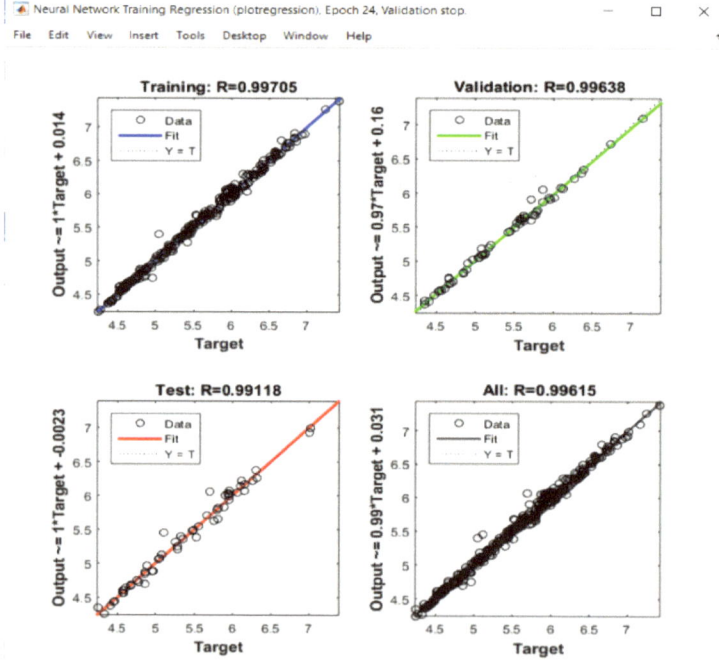

Figure 4. Regression coefficients of the learning process of the ANN.

Figure 5 presents parity graphs for both new methods to predict molecular weight of petroleum fluids using nonlinear regression (Figure 5a) and ANN (Figure 5b).

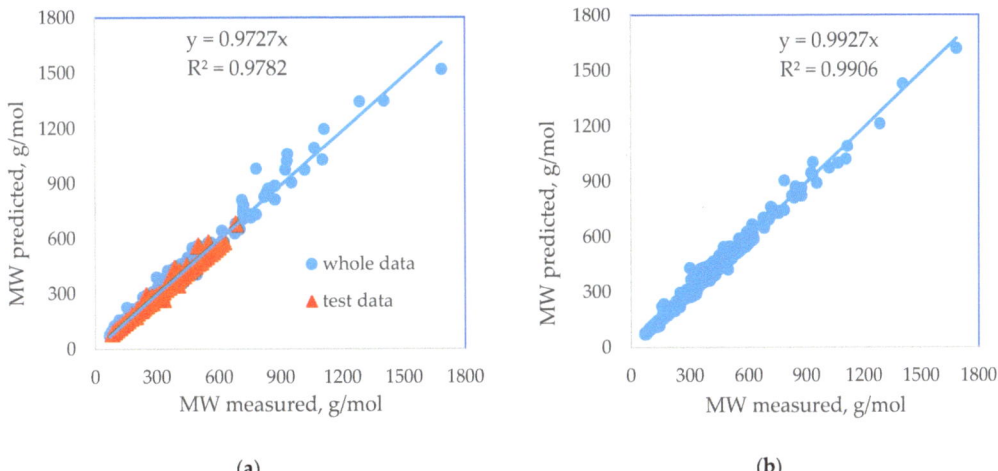

(a)   (b)

Figure 5. Parity graph for predicted versus measured molecular weight by Equation (20) (**a**) and by the ANN model (**b**).

Figures 6–9 presents parity graphs of predicted versus measured molecular weight by the empirical correlations of Goosens (Figure 6a), the API method reported in [23], Riazi and Daubert correlations for MW $\leq$ 300 (Figure 7b) and 700 g/mol (Figure 7a), Kesler and Lee [14] (Figure 8a), Twu (Figure 8b), Liñan et al. [23] (Figure 9 a), and Hosseinifar and Shahverdi [10] (Figure 9b).

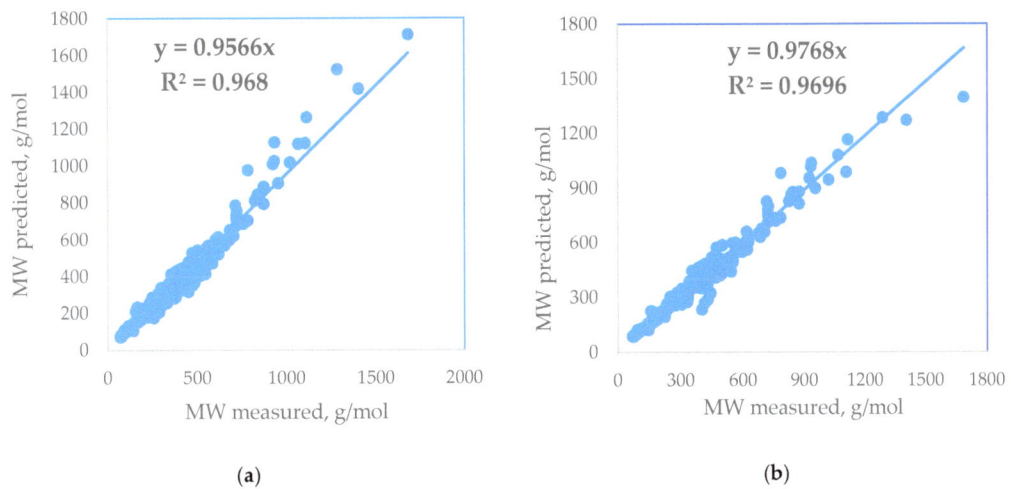

(a)   (b)

Figure 6. Parity graph for predicted versus measured molecular weight by Equation (7) (Goosens correlation) (**a**) and by Equation (11) (API method, 2011) (**b**).

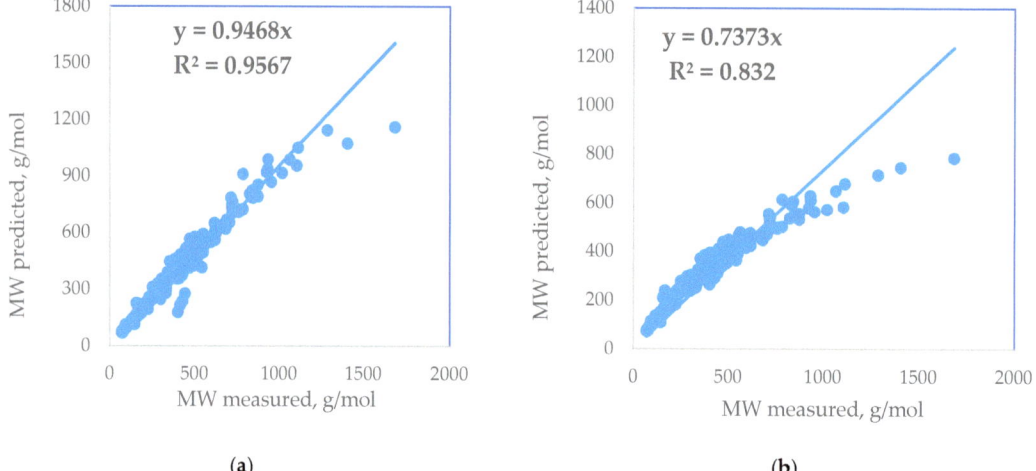

Figure 7. Parity graph for predicted versus measured molecular weight by Equation (9) (Riazi and Daubert correlation up to MW $\leq$ 700 g/mol) (**a**) and by Equation (8) (Riazi and Daubert correlation up to MW $\leq$ 300 g/mol) (**b**).

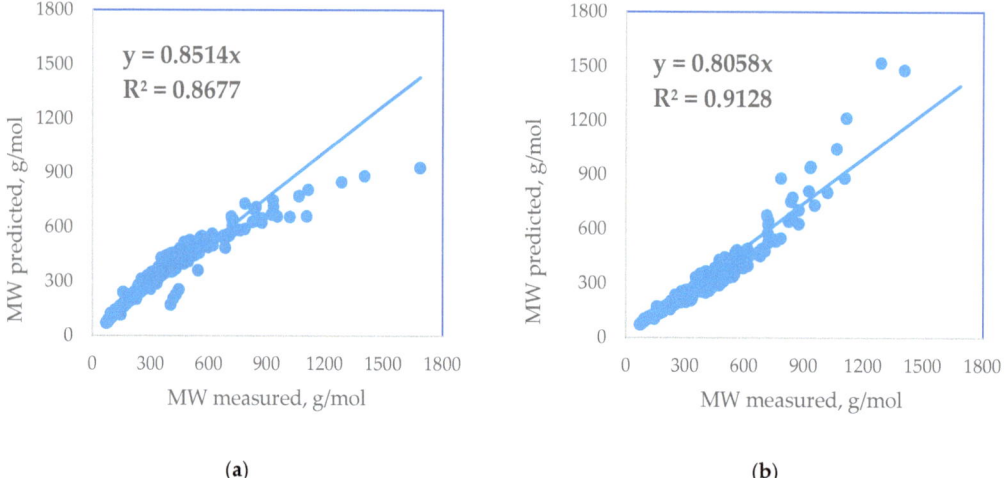

Figure 8. Parity graph for predicted versus measured molecular weight by Equation (2) (Kesler and Lee) (**a**) and by Equation (4) (Twu) (**b**).

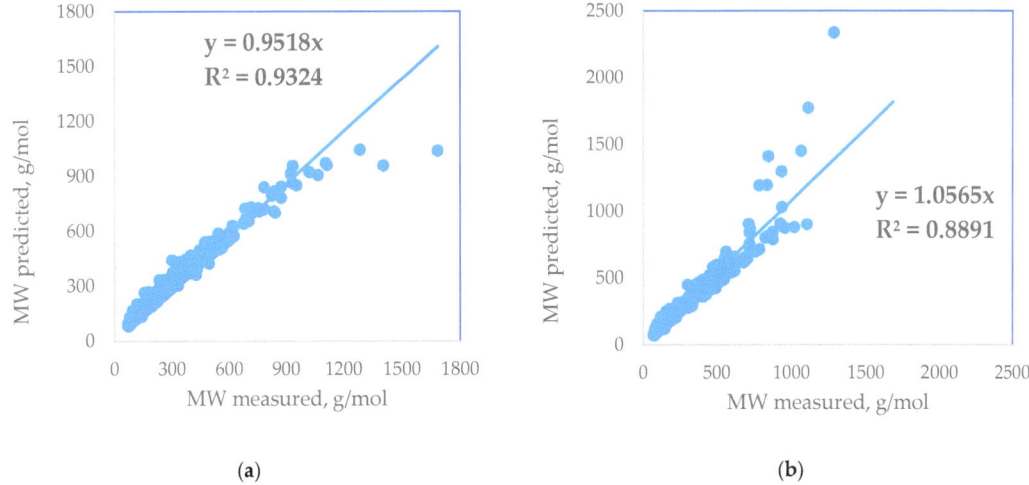

Figure 9. Parity graph for predicted versus measured molecular weight by Equation (11) (Liñan et al.) (**a**) and by Equation (13) (Hosseinifar, and Shahverdi) (**b**).

Table 2 summarizes the statistical analyses for the new empirical correlation, the ANN model, and the ten studied empirical correlations available from the literature.

Table 2. Statistical analysis of studied methods to predict petroleum fluid molecular weight for the whole range of studied molecular weights.

	Standard Error	Rel. St. Error	Sum of Squarred Errors	%AAD	SRE
ANN	23.0	7.2	1.6	4.3	−126.8
New empirical correlation (this work)	34.8	10.9	3.4	6.4	695.5
Hosseinifar (2021) [10]	84.4	26.6	8.6	9.4	−1851.7
Goosens (1996) [9]	44.1	13.9	4.5	7.6	1970.2
Riazi and Daubert MW ≤ 700 g/mol (2005) [18]	48.3	15.2	3.9	6.3	358.2
API (2011) [23]	39.3	12.4	5.1	8.6	−999.1
Liñan (2011) [23]	54.4	17.1	10.2	11.3	−2973.1
Twu (1984) [20]	96.4	30.3	20.6	18.7	7840.0
Lee–Kesler (1976) [14]	84.2	26.5	7.1	9.7	345.9
Riazi and Daubert ≤ 300 g/mol (2005) [18]	117.3	36.9	12.4	12.5	4155.7
Lemus et al. (2016) [2]	103.0	32.4	14.0	10.8	864.9
Soreide (1989) [12]	84.1	26.5	12.2	9.4	−598

The data in Table 2 indubitably indicates that the ANN method provides the best accuracy of molecular weight prediction of petroleum fluids, following by the new empirical correlation developed in this work. If one compares the data for accuracy of molecular weight prediction of the methods tested in this work with the 430 petroleum fluid sample points with those reported by the authors who have developed the correlations, some discrepancies will be seen. For example, Goosens [9] reported standard deviation for his method of about 2%, while the relative standard error, that can be assumed equivalent to the standard deviation shown in Table 2, is 13.9%. The %AAD of Riazi and Daubert MW ≤ 700 g/mol was reported as 4.7 [18], while that shown in Table 2 for this method is 6.3%. Liñan et al. [23] reported %AAD of 2.2, while that shown in Table 2 for this method is 11.3. Lemus et al. [2] reported %AAD of 5.3, while that shown in Table 2 for this method is 10.8. The reason for these discrepancies may lie in the range for which the discussed correlations were developed, confirming again the statement of Schneider [6] that any molecular weight correlation should not be extended beyond the limits for which it is valid. Considering that some of the tested correlations were developed for a narrower range of boiling point and molecular weight variations, a statistical analysis of the studied methods was performed for the petroleum fluids whose molecular weight is ≤300 g/mol.

Table 3 presents data of standard error, relative standard error, and %AAD for the predictive methods employing only these petroleum fluid data whose molecular weight is ≤300 g/mol.

Table 3. Statistical analysis of studied methods to predict molecular weight for petroleum fluids and individual components whose molecular weight ≤ 300 g/mol.

	Standard Error	Rel. St. Error	%AAD
ANN	13.4	7.9	3.6
New empirical correlation (this work)	16.5	9.7	5.1
Hosseinifar (2021) [10]	18.1	10.7	8.1
Goosens (1996) [9]	17.8	10.5	5.4
Riazi and Daubert MW ≤ 700 g/mol (2005) [18]	16.0	9.4	4.0
API (2011) [23]	17.0	10.0	5.4
Twu (1984) [20]	38.8	22.9	13.0
Lee–Kesler (1976) [14]	18.3	10.8	7.3
Riazi and Daubert MW ≤ 300 g/mol (2005) [18]	11.5	6.8	4.6
Lemus et al. (2016) [2]	29.4	17.3	8.0
Soreide (1989) [12]	32.0	18.8	7.6

The data in Table 3 indicates that the correlation of Riazi and Daubert MW ≤ 300 g/mol and the ANN model demonstrate the highest accuracy in molecular weight prediction, followed by the new correlation developed in this work. It is worth mentioning here that a great part of the data points in Table S1 which have molecular weight ≤ 300 g/mol 83 points out of 240 (35%), is taken from Riazi's work [27]. Therefore, the highest accuracy of the correlation of Riazi and Daubert MW ≤ 300 g/mol may be attributed to this fact. It is also worth noting here that the accuracy of prediction of the lower molecular weight petroleum fluids (MW ≤ 300 g/mol) is understandably higher than that of the higher molecular weight petroleum fluids (MW ≥ 300 g/mol), because the heavy oil molecular weight is measured with a lower exactitude. Nevertheless, the correlations developed on the basis of extended molecular weight range also exhibit a satisfactory prediction for the lower molecular weight petroleum fluids (see, for example, the data for the ANN model, the new correlation, and Riazi and Daubert MW ≤ 700 g/mol from Table 3).

4. Discussion

Artificial neural networks are a mathematical model inspired by biological neural networks [49]. They are a class of artificial intelligence algorithms addressing different aspects or elements of learning, such as how to learn, how to induce, and how to deduce [50]. In our study, a classical three-layered neural network, as depicted in Figure 10, was availed.

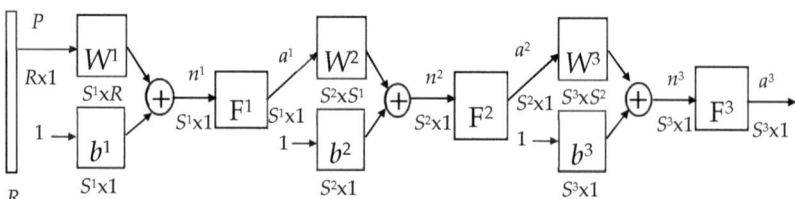

Figure 10. Flow chart of the multylaer neural network.

where

- P is an entry network's vector;
- am is the exit of the m-th layer of the neural network, where;
- wm is a matrix of the coefficients of all inputs;
- bm is neuron's input bias;
- Fm is the transfer function of the m-th layer exit.

In multilayer networks, the outputs of the previous (or first) layer become inputs to the next. In tutored learning (supervised learning), the neural network must achieve a result that is labeled as a goal and is predefined. Weighting factors are accordingly calculated to target values. After training, the neural network is tested—only input signals are given, without the one to be received. The main algorithm for training neural networks with a teacher is back-propagation. It is designed for multilayer networks with direct transfer.

The ANN molecular weight model developed in this research, as shown in the data in Figure 5b and Tables 2 and 3, distinguishes with the highest accuracy of prediction among all investigated empirical correlations. These findings support the opinion of Hadavimoghaddam et al. [51] that the artificial intelligence models provide the lowest average absolute relative error of petroleum property prediction. The use of Hossenifar and Shahverdi [25] method to generate seven additional inputs for the ANN showed again that it is a successful approach to model not only viscosity, as reported in our recent research [26], but also molecular weight of petroleum fluids.

The data in Table 2 and in Figures 5–9 and Figure 11 indicates that the new empirical correlation (Equation (26)) demonstrates the best accuracy among the other empirical correlations available in the literature when the whole data base of 430 points is concerned. Then the correlations of Goosens (Equation (7)), Riazi and Daubert (Equation (9)), and that of API (Equation (11)) distinguish with better accuracy in molecular weight prediction than the remaining seven correlations. However, the new correlation (Equation (26)) and those of Goosens and Riazi and Daubert have been developed based on a great amount of data in Table S1. That is why their comparison with data not included in their development may give a better indication of their molecular weight prediction ability. This was performed with 124 data points, and the statistical analysis of this comparison is summarized in Table 4.

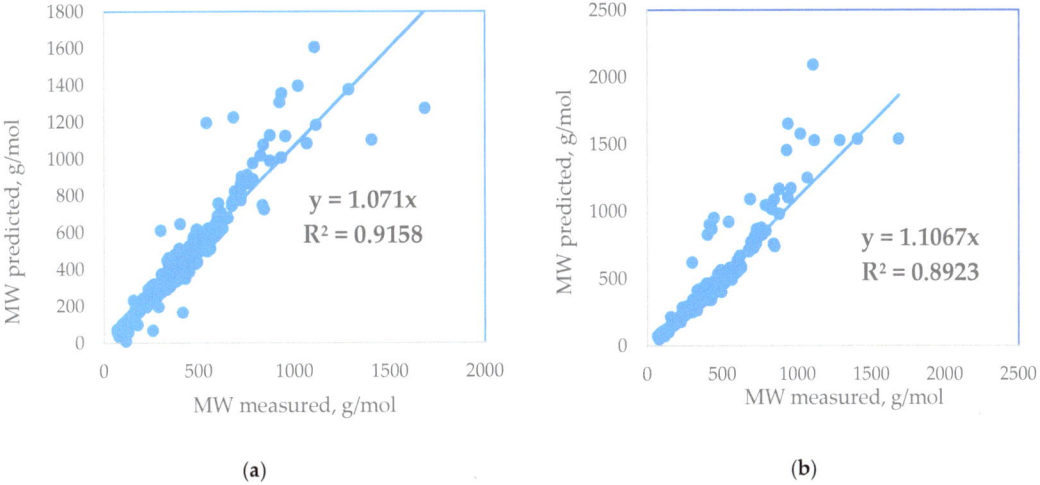

Figure 11. Parity graph for predicted versus measured molecular weight by Equation (6) (Soreide) (**a**) and by Equation (12) (Lemus et al.) (**b**).

Table 4. Statistical analysis of the new empirical correlation developed in this work, and of the correlations of Goosens, Riazi and Daubert, and API with 124 data points not used in their development.

	Standard Error	Rel. St. Error	%AAD
New empirical correlation (this work, test data)	42.1	11.6	8.8
Goosens (1996) [9]	56.7	15.6	12.1
Riazi and Daubert MW $\leq$ 700 g/mol (2005) [18]	52.7	14.5	8.7
API (2011) [23]	47.1	13.0	9.0

The data in Table 4 again confirms the best performance of Equation (20) among the empirical correlations. It deserves mentioning here that 52 data points (42%) (the data pints with numbers from 379 to 430 from Table S1) of all tested 124 data points (the data pints with numbers from 307 to 430 from Table S1) were reported to be measured with repeatability of 15% [1]. This could explain the higher inaccuracy of molecular weight prediction for this test data set compared with that observed for the whole 430 data points and shown in Table 2.

5. Conclusions

The measurement of molecular weight of heavy oils is a difficult task associated with an error of about 15%. Thus, the correlations which satisfactorily predict molecular weight of various petroleum fluids can be an appropriate substitute for measurement. Among the correlations existing in the literature examined in this work, three distinguished with a better precision of prediction: Goosens, Riazi and Daubert, and API. The new correlation developed in this work using a nonlinear regression technique demonstrated a higher accuracy of molecular weight prediction than that of the three correlations mentioned above. However, the molecular weight prediction by the ANN three-layered neural network with a back-propagation teacher model exhibited much better exactitude than the new nonlinear regression correlation. This observation confirms again that the ANN method can predict petroleum properties with a higher accuracy than the regression correlations. In opposite of some statements in the literature that the other correlations developed after those of Lee–Kesler and Twu are not superior, the results of this research showed that the correlations of Goosens, Riazi and Daubert, API, and the new correlation predicted the molecular weight with a higher accuracy.

Supplementary Materials: The following supporting information can be downloaded at: https://www.mdpi.com/article/10.3390/pr11020426/s1, Table S1: 430 data points for boiling point, specific gravity, and molecular weight of petroleum fluids, and individual hydrocarbons to be used for nonlinear regression modeling; Table S2: 430 data points for boiling point, specific gravity, Kw-factor, and TBP distillation characteristics and molecular weight of petroleum fluids, and individual hydrocarbons to be used for ANN modeling.

Author Contributions: Conceptualization, D.S.; methodology, E.S.; software, S.N. and S.S. (Sotir Sotirov); validation, S.S. (Stanislav Simeonov), R.D. and D.Y.; formal analysis, G.N.P.; investigation, I.V.K. and S.V.; data curation, I.S.; writing, D.S.; supervision, K.A. All authors have read and agreed to the published version of the manuscript.

Funding: This research was funded by Asen Zlatarov University—Burgas, Project: Center of Excellence UNITE BG05M2OP001-1.001-0004 /28.02.2018 (2018–2023).

Conflicts of Interest: The authors declare no conflict of interest.

Nomenclature

ANN	Artificial neural network
%AAD	% Average absolute deviation
E	Error
Kw	Kw-characterization factor of petroleum fluids
MW	Molecular weight
RSE	Relative standard error
SE	Standard error
SRE	Sum of relative errors
SSE	Sum of squared errors
RSE	Dichloromethane
Tb	Boiling point

References

1. Lemus, M.C.S. Extended Distillation and Property Correlations for Heavy Oil. Ph.D. Thesis, University of Calgary, Calgary, AB, Canada, December 2015.
2. Lemus, M.C.S.; Schoeggl, F.; Taylor, S.D.; Yarranton, H.W. Physical properties of heavy oil distillation cuts. *Fuel* **2016**, *180*, 457–472. [CrossRef]
3. Nji, G.N. Characterization of heavy oils and bitumens. Ph.D. Thesis, University of Calgary, Calgary, AB, Canada, January 2010.
4. Al-Mhanna, N.M. Simulation of High Pressure Separator Used in Crude Oil Processing. *Processes* **2018**, *6*, 219. [CrossRef]
5. Aladwani, H.A.; Riazi, M.R. Some guidelines for choosing a characterization method for petroleum fractions in process simulators. *Trans IChemE Part A Chem. Eng. Res. Des.* **2005**, *83*, 160–166. [CrossRef]
6. Schneider, D.F. Select the Right Hydrocracbon Molecular Weight Correlation. Available online: https://www.stratusengr.com/Articles/MoleWt.pdf (accessed on 17 November 2022).
7. Powers, D.P.; Sadeghi, H.; Yarranton, H.W.; van den Berg, F.G.A. Regular solution based approach to modeling asphaltene precipitation from native and reacted oils: Part 1, molecular weight, density, and solubility parameter distributions of asphaltenes. *Fuel* **2016**, *178*, 218–233. [CrossRef]
8. Yarranton, H.W.; Powers, D.P.; Okafor, J.C.; van den Berg, F.G.A. Regular solution based approach to modeling asphaltene precipitation from native and reacted oils: Part 2, molecular weight, density, and solubility parameter of saturates, aromatics, and resins. *Fuel* **2018**, *215*, 766–777. [CrossRef]
9. Goosens, A.G. Prediction of molecular weight of petroleum fractions. *Ind. Eng.Chem. Res.* **1996**, *35*, 985–988. [CrossRef]
10. Hosseinifar, P.; Shahverdi, H. A predictive method for constructing the distillation curve of petroleum fluids using their physical bulk properties. *J. Petrol. Sci. Eng.* **2021**, *200*, 108403. [CrossRef]
11. Altgelt, K.H.; Boduszynski, M.M. *Composition and Analysis of Heavy Petroleum Fractions*; Marcel Dekker: New York, NY, USA, 1994; pp. 1–495.
12. Soreide, I. Improved Phase Behavior Predictions of Petroleum Reservoir Fluids from a Cubic Equation of State. Ph.D. Thesis, Norwegian Institute of Technology, Department of Petroleum Technology and Applied Geophysics, Trondheim, Norway, 1989.
13. Lee, B.I.; Kesler, M.G. A Generalized thermodynamic correlation based on the three-parameter corresponding states. *AIChE J.* **1975**, *21*, 510–527. [CrossRef]
14. Kesler, M.G.; Lee, B.I. Improve prediction of enthalpy of fractions. *Hydrocarb. Process* **1976**, *55*, 153–158.
15. Riazi, M.R.; Daubert, T.E. Simplify property predictions. *Hydrocarb. Process* **1980**, *59*, 115–116.
16. Riazi, M.R.; Daubert, T.E. Analytical correlations interconvert distillation-curve types. *Oil Gas J.* **1986**, *84*, 50–57.
17. Riazi, M.R.; Daubert, T.E. Characterization parameters for petroleum fractions. *Ind. Eng. Chem. Res.* **1987**, *26*, 755–759. [CrossRef]
18. Riazi, M.R. *Characterization and Properties of Petroleum Fractions*, 1st ed; ASTM International: West Conshohocken, PA, USA, 2005; pp. 1–407.
19. Rao, V.K.; Bardon, M.F. Estimating the molecular weight of petroleum fractions. *Ind. Eng. Chem. Proc. Des. Dev.* **1985**, *24*, 498. [CrossRef]
20. Twu, C.H. An internally consistent correlation for predicting the critical properties and molecular weight of petroleum and coal-tar liquids. *Fluid Phase Equilibria* **1984**, *16*, 137–150. [CrossRef]
21. Hariu, O.H.; Sage, R.C. Crude split figured by computer. *Hydrocarb. Process* **1969**, *4*, 143–148.
22. Katz, D.L.; Firoozabadi, B. Predicting phase behavior of condensate/crude oil systems using methane interaction coefficients. *J. Pet. Tech.* **1978**, *228*, 1649–1655. [CrossRef]
23. Liñan, L.Z.; Lima, N.M.N.; Maciel, M.R.W.; Filho, R.M.; Medina, L.C.; Embiruçu, M. Correlation for predicting the molecular weight of Brazilian petroleum residues and cuts: An application for the simulation of a molecular distillation process. *J. Pet. Sci. Eng.* **2011**, *78*, 78–85. [CrossRef]
24. Liu, Y.A.; Chang, A.-F.; Kiran, P. Chapter 1: Characterization, physical and thermodynamic properties of oil fractions. In *Petroleum Refinery Process Modeling: Integrated Optimization Tools and Applications*; Wiley-VCH Verlag GmbH & Co. KGaA: Weinheim, Germany, 2018; pp. 1–58.

25. Hosseinifar, P.; Shahverdi, H. Prediction of the ASTM and TBP distillation curves and specific gravity distribution curve for fuels and petroleum fluids. *Can. J. Chem. Eng.* **2022**, *100*, 3288–3310. [CrossRef]
26. Stratiev, D.; Shishkova, I.; Dinkov, R.; Nenov, S.; Sotirov, S.; Sotirova, E.; Kolev, I.; Ivanov, V.; Ribagin, S.; Atanassov, K.; et al. Prediction of petroleum viscosity from molecular weight and density. *Fuel* **2023**, *331*, 125679. [CrossRef]
27. Riazi, M.R.; Daubert, T.E. Prediction of molecular-type analysis of petroleum fractions and coal liquids. *Ind. Eng. Chem. Res.* **1986**, *25*, 1009–1015. [CrossRef]
28. Riazi, M.R.; Daubert, T.E. Improved characterization of wide boiling range undefined petroleum fractions. *Ind. Eng. Chem. Res.* **1987**, *26*, 629–632. [CrossRef]
29. White, C.M.; Perry, M.B.; Schmidt, C.E.; Douglas, L.J. Relationship between refractive indices and other properties of coal hydrogenation distillates. *Energy Fuels* **1987**, *1*, 99–105. [CrossRef]
30. Bollas, G.M.; Vasalos, I.A.; Lappas, A.A.; Iatridis, D.K.; Tsioni, G.K. Bulk molecular characterization approach for the simulation of FCC feedstocks. *Ind. Eng. Chem. Res.* **2004**, *43*, 3270–3281. [CrossRef]
31. Vargas, F.M.; Chapman, W.G. Application of the one-third rule in hydrocarbon and crude oil systems. *Fluid Phase Equilib.* **2010**, *290*, 103–108. [CrossRef]
32. Yarranton, H.W.; Okafor, J.C.; Ortiz, D.P.; van den Berg, F.G.A. Density and refractive index of petroleum, cuts, and mixtures. *Energy Fuels* **2015**, *29*, 5723–5736. [CrossRef]
33. Carbognani, L.; Díaz-Gómez, L.; Oldenburg, T.B.P.; Pereira-Almao, P. Determination of molecular masses for petroleum distillates by simulated distillation. *Cienc. Tecnol. Futuro* **2012**, *4*, 43–55.
34. Wang, S.; Dong, X.; Sun, R. Predicting saturates of sour vacuum gas oil using artificial neural networks and genetic algorithms. *Expert Syst. Appl.* **2010**, *37*, 4768–4771.
35. Wang, G.; Liu, Y.; Wang, X.; Xu, C.; Gao, J. Studies on the catalytic cracking performance of coker gas oil. *Energy Fuels* **2009**, *23*, 1942–1949. [CrossRef]
36. Pitault, I.; Nevicato, D.; Forissier, M.; Bernard, J.-R. Kinetic model based on a molecular description for catalytic cracking of vacuum gas oil. *Chem.Eng.Sci.* **1994**, *49*, 4249–4262. [CrossRef]
37. Sheng, Q.; Wang, G.; Duan, M.; Ren, A.; Yao, L.; Hu, M.; Gao, J. Determination of the hydrogen-donating ability of industrial distillate narrow fractions. *Energy Fuels* **2016**, *30*, 10314–10321. [CrossRef]
38. Altgelt, K.H.; Boduszynski, M.M. Composition of heavy petroleums. 3. An improved boiling point-molecular weight relation. *Energy Fuels* **1992**, *6*, 68–72. [CrossRef]
39. Dominguez, M. FCC feed fractionation. *Pet. Coal* **2003**, *45*, 113–118.
40. Van Camp, C.E.; Van Damme, P.S.; Froment, G.F. Thermal cracking of kerosene. *Ind. Eng. Chem. Process Des. Dev.* **1984**, *23*, 155–162. [CrossRef]
41. Nace, D.M.; Voltz, S.E.; Weekman, V.W., Jr. Application of a kinetic model for catalytic cracking. Effects of charge stocks. *Ind. Eng. Chem. Process Des. Develop.* **1971**, *10*, 530–538. [CrossRef]
42. Zhang, Y.; Schuler, B.; Fatayer, S.; Gross, L.; Harper, M.R.; Kushnerick, J.D. Understanding the effects of sample preparation on the chemical structures of petroleum imaged with non-contact atomic force microscopy. *Ind. Eng. Chem. Res.* **2018**, *57*, 15935–15941. [CrossRef]
43. Stratiev, D.; Nenov, S.; Nedanovski, D.; Shishkova, I.; Dinkov, R.; Stratiev, D.D.; Stratiev, D.D.; Sotirov, S.; Sotirova, E.; Atanassova, V.; et al. Different Nonlinear Regression Techniques and Sensitivity Analysis as Tools to Optimize Oil Viscosity Modeling. *Resources* **2021**, *10*, 99. [CrossRef]
44. Stratiev, D.; Nenov, S.; Sotirov, S.; Shishkova, I.; Palichev, G.; Sotirova, E.; Ivanov, V.; Atanassov, K.; Ribagin, S.; Angelova, N. Petroleum viscosity modeling using least squares and ANN methods. *J. Pet. Sci. Eng.* **2022**, *212*, 110306. [CrossRef]
45. Sinha, U.; Dindoruk, B.; Soliman, M. Machine learning augmented dead oil viscosity model for all oil types. *J. Pet. Sci. Eng.* **2020**, *195*, 107603. [CrossRef]
46. Sinha, U.; Dindoruk, B.; Soliman, M.Y. Physics augmented correlations and machine learning methods to accurately calculate dead oil viscosity based on the available inputs. *SPE J.* **2022**, *27*, 3240–3253. [CrossRef]
47. Stratiev, D.; Marinov, I.; Dinkov, R.; Shishkova, I.; Velkov, I.; Sharafutdinov, I.; Nenov, S.; Tsvetkov, T.; Sotirov, S.; Mitkova, M.; et al. Opportunity to improve diesel fuel cetane number prediction from easy available physical properties and application of the least squares method and the artificial neural networks. *Energy Fuels* **2015**, *29*, 1520–1533. [CrossRef]
48. Shishkova, I.; Stratiev, D.; Kolev, I.V.; Nenov, S.; Nedanovski, D.; Atanassov, K.; Ivanov, V.; Ribagin, S. Challenges in Petroleum Characterization—A Review. *Energies* **2022**, *15*, 7765. [CrossRef]
49. D'Addona, D.M. Neural Network. In *CIRP Encyclopedia of Production Engineering*; Laperrière, L., Reinhart, G., Eds.; Springer: Berlin/Heidelberg, Germany, 2014. [CrossRef]
50. Yang, Z.R.; Yang, Z. 6.01—Artificial Neural Networks. *Compr. Biomed. Phys.* **2014**, *6*, 1–17. [CrossRef]
51. Hadavimoghaddam, F.; Ostadhassan, M.; Heidaryan, E.; Sadri, M.A.; Chapanova, I.; Popov, E.; Cheremisin, A.; Rafieepour, S. Prediction of dead oil viscosity: Machine learning vs. classical correlations. *Energies* **2021**, *14*, 930. [CrossRef]

Disclaimer/Publisher's Note: The statements, opinions and data contained in all publications are solely those of the individual author(s) and contributor(s) and not of MDPI and/or the editor(s). MDPI and/or the editor(s) disclaim responsibility for any injury to people or property resulting from any ideas, methods, instructions or products referred to in the content.

Article

Correlations of HTSD to TBP and Bulk Properties to Saturate Content of a Wide Variety of Crude Oils

Dicho Stratiev [1,2,*], Rosen Dinkov [1], Mariana Tavlieva [1], Ivelina Shishkova [1], Georgi Nikolov Palichev [2], Simeon Ribagin [2,3], Krassimir Atanassov [2,3], Danail D. Stratiev [2], Svetoslav Nenov [4], Dimitar Pilev [4], Sotir Sotirov [3], Evdokia Sotirova [3], Stanislav Simeonov [3] and Viktoria Boyadzhieva [5]

[1] LUKOIL Neftohim Burgas, 8104 Burgas, Bulgaria
[2] Institute of Biophysics and Biomedical Engineering, Bulgarian Academy of Sciences, Georgi Bonchev 105, 1113 Sofia, Bulgaria
[3] Intelligent Systems Laboratory, University Prof. Dr. Assen Zlatarov, Professor Yakimov 1 St., 8010 Burgas, Bulgaria
[4] Department of Mathematics, University of Chemical Technology and Metallurgy, Kliment Ohridski 8, 1756 Sofia, Bulgaria
[5] Department of Chemical Engineering, The University of Manchester, Oxford Rd, Manchester M13 9PL, UK
* Correspondence: stratiev.dicho@neftochim.bg

Citation: Stratiev, D.; Dinkov, R.; Tavlieva, M.; Shishkova, I.; Nikolov Palichev, G.; Ribagin, S.; Atanassov, K.; Stratiev, D.D.; Nenov, S.; Pilev, D.; et al. Correlations of HTSD to TBP and Bulk Properties to Saturate Content of a Wide Variety of Crude Oils. *Processes* **2023**, *11*, 420. https://doi.org/10.3390/pr11020420

Academic Editor: Qingbang Meng

Received: 6 January 2023
Revised: 18 January 2023
Accepted: 27 January 2023
Published: 30 January 2023

Copyright: © 2023 by the authors. Licensee MDPI, Basel, Switzerland. This article is an open access article distributed under the terms and conditions of the Creative Commons Attribution (CC BY) license (https://creativecommons.org/licenses/by/4.0/).

Abstract: Forty-eight crude oils with variations in specific gravity ($0.782 \leq SG \leq 1.002$), sulphur content ($0.03 \leq S \leq 5.6$ wt.%), saturate content ($23.5 \leq Sat. \leq 92.9$ wt.%), asphaltene content ($0.1 \leq As \leq 22.2$ wt.%), and vacuum residue content ($1.4 \leq VR \leq 60.7$ wt.%) were characterized with HTSD, TBP, and SARA analyses. A modified SARA analysis of petroleum that allows for the attainment of a mass balance ≥ 97 wt.% for light crude oils was proposed, a procedure for the simulation of petroleum TBP curves from HTSD data using nonlinear regression and Riazi's distribution model was developed, and a new correlation to predict petroleum saturate content from specific gravity and pour point with an average absolute deviation of 2.5 wt.%, maximum absolute deviation of 6.6 wt.%, and bias of 0.01 wt.% was developed. Intercriteria analysis was employed to evaluate the presence of statistically meaningful relations between the different petroleum properties and to evaluate the extent of similarity between the studied petroleum crudes. It was found that the extent of similarity between the crude oils based on HTSD analysis data could be discerned from data on the Kw characterization factor of narrow crude oil fractions. The results from this study showed that contrary to the generally accepted concept of the constant Kw characterization factor, the Kw factors of narrow fractions differ from that of crude oil. Moreover, the distributions of Kw factors of the different crudes were different.

Keywords: petroleum; crude oil; characterization; HTSD; TBP; SARA; correlation; regression; intercriteria analysis

1. Introduction

The characterization of petroleum is undoubtedly the most crucial element in petroleum engineering and processing. It provides information required by petroleum engineers to assess the behavior of petroleum during exploration operations and by oil-refining engineers to evaluate the performance of refining units while processing particular crude oils or crude oil blends [1–4]. True boiling point (TBP) distillation analysis and the measurement of specific gravity of narrow crude oil cuts are considered necessary for the petroleum engineering calculations of petroleum engineering and processing [5,6]. Unfortunately, TBP distillation analysis is tedious, time-consuming and costly, so other less expensive and faster methods to convert data into TBP information are desired. Some methods have been developed to convert American Society for Testing and Materials (ASTM) methods into TBP methods used for oil fractions [7,8]. Simulated distillation was found to be equivalent to the TBP of oil fractions boiled up to 360 °C [9]. Villalanti and Raia [10] showed an excellent agreement between high-temperature simulated distillation (HTSD) and ASTM D2892 [11] (TBP) and D 5236 [12] for reference oil boiled at 10% of 231 °C and at 90% of 495 °C. We also showed in our recent study [13] that HTSD (ASTM D7169) is equivalent to TBP for gas oil fractions boiled between 231 and 655 °C. Durand et al. [14] also reported a very good agreement between conventional simulated distillation, with the TBP for gas oils having aromatic content of between 2 and 75%. The agreement between HTSD and TBP for deasphalted oils with saturate contents of 8.5% and 45%, a vacuum distillate with a saturate content of 31.2%, and atmospheric residue with a saturate content of 59% was also very good [14]. Different studies in the literature have dealt with the simulated distillation and TBP analysis of petroleum fluids [15–22]. To the best of our knowledge, however, no reports have compared the HTSD and TBP of a wide variety of crude oils in the five main crude oil groups: extra light, light, medium, heavy, and extra heavy. In our previous research [23], we concluded that additional investigations for the development of a reliable method that allows for the conversion of simulated distillation data into TBP data for all crude oil types are still required. The current research compares HTSD and TBP distillation data for a wide range of crude oils in to the main five groups originating from all over the world.

Another important petroleum characterization method that is used in a number of state equations, forming the basis of thermodynamic models predicting sediment formation in the process of petroleum extraction and refining the saturates/aromatics/resins/asphaltenes (SARA) analyses [24–36]. However, the mass balance closure of the SARA analysis of crude oils with a specific gravity of less than 0.92, as reported in our previous paper [23], is an issue. Due to the higher content of highly volatile components, lighter crude oils are lost during the process of solvent recovery following column SAR (saturates, aromatics, and resins) separation. To avoid this loss, 48 crude oils in to the five main groups were distilled in a TBP apparatus to separate the naphtha fraction from the crude oil. Then, the naphtha fraction was analyzed with gas chromatography to determine the PIANO (paraffins, iso-paraffins, aromatics, naphthenes, and olefins) composition. The reduced crudes were analyzed for saturates, aromatics, resins and asphaltenes. Then, the results from both analyses were combined to obtain the whole crude oil SARA composition. In this way, we achieved a mass balance closure no lower than 97 wt.% and a saturate content of 92.2 wt.%. The higher saturate content reported in our earlier research [23] based on literature data was 88.9 wt.%. In this study, we investigated the possibility of predicting the saturate content in petroleum crudes from other easier, faster, and less expensive methods than SARA analysis.

The aims of this work were to research a procedure to simulate the TBP curves of all kinds of crude oils from HTSD data, to develop a method to predict the saturate content of all kinds of petroleum, and to evaluate the possibility of obtaining the specific gravity curves of the crude oils from HTSD and the bulk petroleum specific gravity.

2. Materials and Methods

Petroleum crudes from all over the world (Albania, Australia, Azerbaijan, Brunei, Egypt, Equatorial Guinea, Greece, Indonesia, Iraq, Italy, Kazakhstan, Kuwait, Libya, Mexico, Nigeria, the Netherlands, Russia, Saudi Arabia, Tunisia, Turkmenistan, the UK, the USA, and Venezuela) in the five main groups—extra light (API > 40), light (30 < API < 40), medium (20 < API < 30), heavy (10 < API < 20) and extra heavy crude oils (API ≈ 10)—were investigated in this research. They were analyzed in terms of their bulk properties: specific gravity in accordance with ASTM D4052 [37], sulphur content following ASTM D4294 [38] requirements, pour point according to ASTM D97 [39], and kinematic viscosity according to ASTM D445 [40].

The crude oils were analyzed for their true boiling point (TBP) distribution with the Euro Dist System from ROFA Deutschland GmbH, designed to perform according to ASTM D2892 [11] requirements at pressure drop from 760 to 2 mmHg. Its fractionation column is equipped with packing equivalent to 15 theoretical plates, and a condenser provides the standard mandatory reflux ratio of 5:1. The atmospheric residue from the TBP column was fractionated under vacuum from 1 to 0.2 mmHg in Potstill Euro Dist System from ROFA Deutschland GmbH according to ASTM D5236 [12] requirements.

In addition to the TBP analysis of the investigated crude oils, their distillation characteristics were also analyzed with gas chromatographic high-temperature simulated distillation (HTSD) according to ASTM D7169 requirements. The HTSD analyses were carried out with the Agilent Technologies GC System 7890B, which was equipped with a FID (flame ionization detector). Liquid nitrogen was used as a coolant. The carrier gas was helium of 99.9999% purity (14 mL/min), and the inlet pressure was 1.2 psi (8.27 kPa) with a total flow equal to 87 mL/min. Hydrogen was used as a fuel gas (40 mL/min) and nitrogen was used as a makeup gas (15 mL/min), both with high purity (99.999%). The installed column was 5 m long and 530 µm in diameter, and the film thickness was 0.15 µm. The oven operated under a program from −20 °C to 430 °C at a ramp rate of 15 °C/min and a 4 min hold time at the maximum temperature. The injector was programmed to operate from 50 °C to 450 °C at a rate of 15 °C/min, and the injected sample volume was 4 µL. Before the simulated distillation analyses, the studied oil samples were preliminarily stirred and accurately weighted to obtain 2 weight percent of the studied oils dissolved in carbon disulphide (0.03 g of each sample dissolved in 1.5 mL of CS_2 (99.9%)). All prepared samples were stored at a temperature around 4 °C prior to analyses. The simulated distillation characteristics were automatically calculated with SIMDIS software, and the distillation curve boiling point in °C versus evaporate in wt. % was obtained. The minor intervention of the operator took place during the chromatogram processing. The HTSD GC was calibrated with a blend of normal paraffins with a carbon number between C_5 and C_{120}. The software (GC OpenLab CDS with Simdis program for ASTM D7169) used in this application of HTSD allowed for the estimation of the final boiling point of the residual oils higher than 750 °C.

The SARA (saturates, aromatics, resins, asphaltenes) analysis of the reduced crude oils (the crude oil fraction boiling above 220 °C) was performed following the procedure described in our earlier research [41]. Considering that the content of asphaltenes in crude oil is not an additive value, as reported in our recent study [23], it was determined for the whole not fractionated crude oil following the procedure described in our earlier research [42].

The PIANO (paraffins, iso-paraffins, aromatics, naphthenes olefins) analysis of the crude oil fraction boiled below 220 °C (naphtha fraction) was carried out with a gas chromatograph equipped with a flame ionization detector. To identify the compounds in the naphtha fraction, gas chromatography/mass spectrometry was utilized. The gas chromatograph with flame ionization detector was a model 5890 series II Hewlett Packard (Agilent Technologies, Inc., Santa Clara, CA, USA). An HP PONA capillary column (50 m length × 0.20 mm id × 0.5 µm film thickness) was used with a split injector. The instrument parameters were as follows: The initial oven column temperature was 35 °C, and then it increased at increments of 2 °C/min to 200 °C and held for 30 min at 200 °C; helium was used as a carrier gas at a flow rate of 0.5 mL/min; the injector and detector temperatures were 200 °C and 250 °C, respectively; and the volume that was injected and analyzed was 0.1 µL. Data acquisition parameters, instrument operation information, and chromatographic data were collected and recorded by means of Clarity 2.6. Gas chromatography/mass spectrometry analysis was performed with a 7890A GC System equipped with an HP PONA capillary column (50 length m × 0.2 mm id × 0.5 µm film thickness) and a 5975C Inert XL EI/CI mass selective detector (Agilent Technologies, Inc., Santa Clara, CA, USA). The oven column temperature conditions were identical to those used with the gas chromatograph with flame ionization detector. High-purity helium was used as the carrier gas at a flow rate of 0.8 mL/min. The injection port was held at 200 °C, and the injection volume was 0.1 µL of the sample. The mass selective detector was operated in the electron impact ionization mode (70 eV) with continuous scan acquisition from 15 to 250 m/z at a cycling rate of approximately 1.5 scan/s. The parameters were as follows: the electron multiplier was set to 1224 V, the source temperature was set to 230 °C, and the transfer line temperature was set to 150 °C. System control and data acquisition were achieved with HP G1033A D.05.01 MSD ChemStation revision E.02.00.493. The compounds were identified with the NIST MS Search version 2.0 library of mass spectra.

The Kw characterization factor of the studied crude oils and their narrow fractions was estimated with Equation (1).

$$Kw = \frac{\sqrt[3]{1.8[T_{50\%} + 273.15]}}{SG} \qquad (1)$$

where $T_{50\%}$ = boiling point of 50% of evaporate according to the TBP (ASTM D292/D5236), °C, and SG = specific gravity at 15 °C.

The computer algebra system Maple and NLPSolve with the Modified Newton Iterative Method was used to develop nonlinear regression equations to transform the HTSD data into TBP data for the studied crude oils. Riazi's distribution model, shown as Equation (2), was used to build the TBP curve from the HTSD data transformed into TBP data.

$$\frac{T_i - T_0}{T_0} = \frac{A}{B}\left[Ln\left(\frac{1}{1-x_i}\right)\right]^{\frac{1}{B}} \qquad (2)$$

where T_i = boiling point of i-weight fraction of distillation curve, K; T_0 = initial boiling point, K; and x_i = weight fraction of i-component.

Intercriteria analysis (ICrA) evaluation was employed to determine the degree of similarity between the studied crude oils based on distillation characteristics, Kw characterization factor variation through the whole crude oil distillation range, and sulphur variation through the whole crude oil distillation range. It was also used to determine the statistically meaningful relations between the different crude oil characteristics. The intercriteria analysis (ICrA) was developed in the Institute for Biophysics and Biomedical Engineering, Bulgarian Academy of Sciences (BAS) as a tool to support decision making in multi-object multicriteria problems [43–45]. It has been successfully applied in the fields of medicine, biology, economics, and physics, among others, and it can be considered a component of the artificial intelligence toolkit [43]. It was also successfully applied in several studies in the field of petroleum chemistry and technology [46–48]. A detailed explanation of the essence of ICrA applied in the field of petroleum processing can be found in [49]. $\mu = 0.75 \div 1.00$ and $\upsilon = 0 \div 0.25$ denote a statistically meaningful significant positive relation, where the strong positive consonance exhibits values of $\mu = 0.95 \div 1.00$ and $\upsilon = 0 \div 0.05$ and the weak positive consonance exhibits values of $\mu = 0.75 \div 0.85$ and $\upsilon = 0.2515 \div 0.1525$. The values of negative consonance with $\mu = 0.00 \div 0.25$ and $\upsilon = 0.75 \div 1.00$ indicate a statistically meaningful negative relation, where the strong negative consonance exhibits values of $\mu = 0.00 \div 0.05$ and $\upsilon = 0.95 \div 1.00$, and the weak negative consonance exhibits values of $\mu = 0.15 \div 0.25$ and $\upsilon = 0.75 \div 0.85$. All other cases are considered dissonance.

3. Results

3.1. HTSD and TBP of Crude Oils

The high-temperature simulated distillation data of extra light, light medium, heavy, and extra heavy 30 crude oils (boiling point at 1%) are presented in Table S1.

The same crude oil HTSD data in the TBP analysis format (evaporates at 70, 110, 130, 150, 170, 180, 200, 220, 240, 260, 280, 300, 320, 340, 360, 380, 390, 430, 470, 490, and 540 °C) are presented in Table S2.

The true boiling point distillation (TBP) data of the extra light, light medium, heavy, and extra heavy 29 crude oils are summarized in Table S3.

TBP data of 21 crude oils extracted from [47] are presented in Table S4.

HTSD data of 21 crude oils extracted from [47] are presented in Table S5.

Figure 1 shows the TBP and HTSD distillation curves of the extra light, light, medium, and heavy crude oils. These data clearly show that both distillation curves do not coincide and that equations to convert HTSD into TBP are needed.

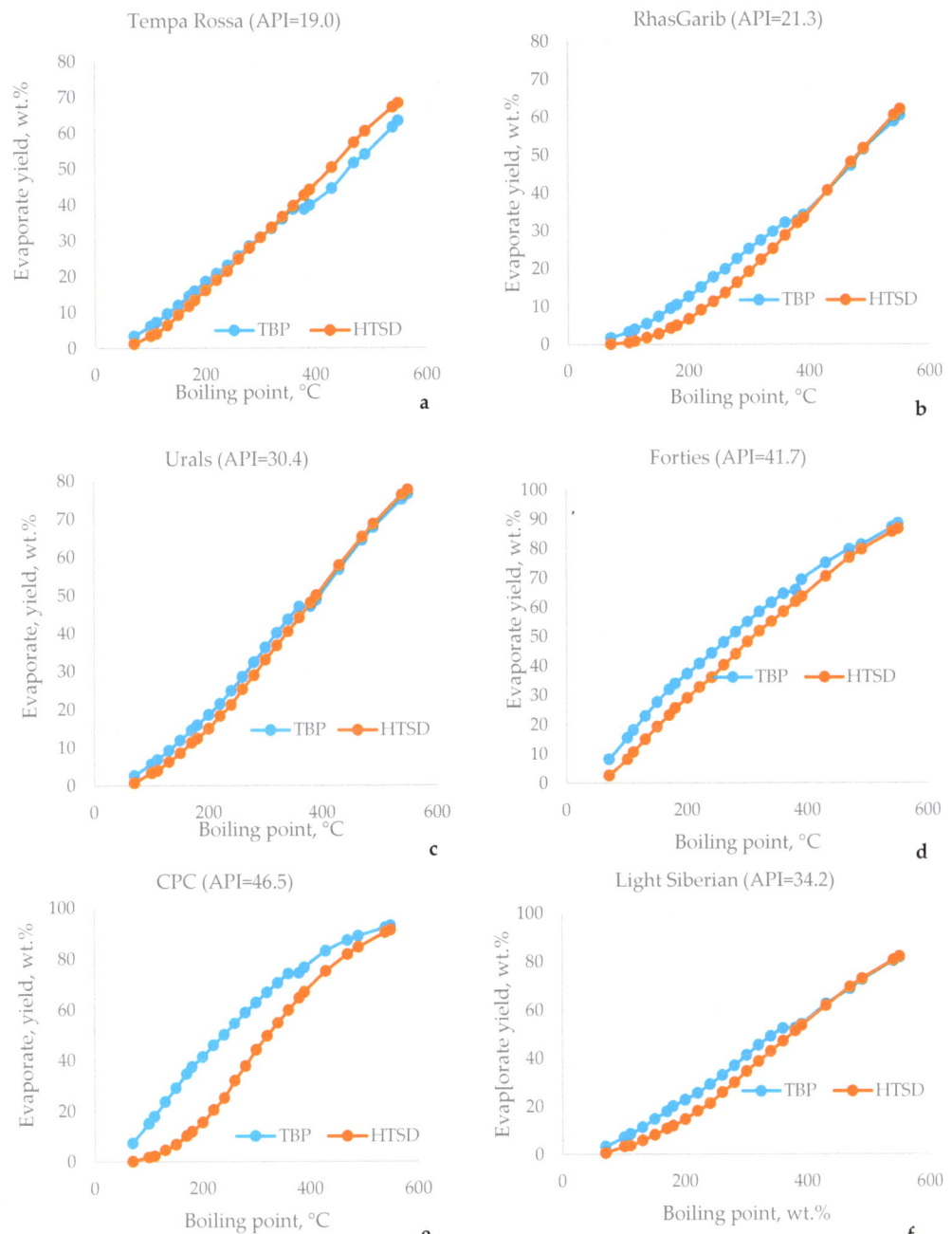

Figure 1. TBP and HTSD curves of extra light (**d**,**e**), light (**f**), medium (**b**,**c**), and heavy (**a**) crude oils.

Crude oil specific gravity and HTSD data for the 110–180 °C; 180–240 °C; 240–360 °C; IBP—360 °C; IBP—540 °C; and $T_{50\%}$ fractions were employed to develop conversion equations. With nonlinear regression and the computer algebra system Maple (and Global Optimization Toolbox), the following conversion equations were developed:

$$\begin{aligned}\text{TBP}_{110-180} =\ & 3592.34 \times 8\text{SG} - 1.071599 \times \text{HTSD}_{110-180} - 4541.274 + 256.8781 \times \text{SG}^2 + \\ & 14.0653\text{SG} \times \text{HTSD}_{110-180} - 0.313177 \times \text{HTSD}^2_{110-180} - 13.06334 \times \text{SG}^2 \times \text{HTSD}_{110-180} + \\ & 0.310779 \times \text{SG} \times \text{HTSD}^2_{110-180} - 860.6919 \times \text{SG}^3 + 0.000738 \times \text{HTSD}^3_{110-180} + \frac{1557.6812}{\text{SG}} - \frac{5.286048}{\text{HTSD}_{110-180}}\end{aligned} \quad (3)$$

where $\text{TBP}_{110-180}$ = TBP yield of crude oil fraction 110–180 °C, wt.%; $\text{HTSD}_{110-180}$ = HTSD yield of crude oil fraction 110–180 °C, wt.%; and SG = specific gravity of crude oil at 15 °C.

$$\begin{aligned}\text{TBP}_{180-240} =\ & -22042.5019 \times \text{SG} - 307.7052 \times \text{HTSD}_{180-240} + 10231.8034 + 18132.809451 \times \text{SG}^2 + \\ & 558.8987\text{SG} \times \text{HTSD}_{180-240} + 6.5239 \times \text{HTSD}^2_{180-240} - 261.4616 \times \text{SG}^2 \times \text{HTSD}_{180-240} - \\ & 5.32183 \times \text{SG} \times \text{HTSD}^2_{180-240} - 5209.1464 \times \text{SG}^3 - 0.061063 \times \text{HTSD}^3_{180-240} - \frac{1362.90998}{\text{SG}} - \frac{75.10173}{\text{HTSD}_{180-240}}\end{aligned} \quad (4)$$

where $\text{TBP}_{180-240}$ = TBP yield of crude oil fraction 180–240 °C, wt.%, and $\text{HTSD}_{180-240}$ = HTSD yield of crude oil fraction 180–240 °C, wt.%.

$$\begin{aligned}\text{TBP}_{240-360} =\ & -124049.5808 \times \text{SG} + 118.857 \times \text{HTSD}_{240-360} + 84179.95766 + 80735.579 \times \text{SG}^2 \\ & -261.2551 \times \text{SG} \times \text{HTSD}_{240-360} + 0.02985 \times \text{HTSD}^2_{240-360} \\ & +166.7441 \times \text{SG}^2 \times \text{HTSD}_{240-360} - 0.503125 \times \text{SG} \times \text{HTSD}^2_{240-360} - 19873.07896 \times \text{SG}^3 \\ & +0.0037714 \times \text{HTSD}^3_{240-360} - \frac{21395.469}{\text{SG}} + \frac{2207.4797}{\text{HTSD}_{240-360}}\end{aligned} \quad (5)$$

where $\text{TBP}_{240-360}$ = TBP yield of crude oil fraction 240–360 °C, wt.%, and $\text{HTSD}_{240-360}$ = HTSD yield of crude oil fraction 240–360 °C, wt.%.

$$\begin{aligned}\text{TBP}_{\text{IBP-360}} =\ & -1486302.4 \times \text{SG} + 706.3558 \times \text{HTSD}_{\text{IBP-360}} - 816751.6624 - 1177897.12 \times \text{SG}^2 \\ & -1308.126\text{SG} \times \text{HTSD}_{\text{IBP-360}} + 2.3461 \times \text{HTSD}^2_{\text{IBP-360}} + 674.042 \times \text{SG}^2 \times \text{HTSD}_{\text{IBP-360}} \\ & +1.41365\text{SG} \times \text{HTSD}^2_{\text{IBP-360}} + 343817.1466 \times \text{SG}^3 + 0.0059531 \times \text{HTSD}^3_{\text{IBP-360}} \\ & +\frac{162215.444}{\text{SG}} + \frac{26821.6259}{\text{HTSD}_{\text{IBP-360}}}\end{aligned} \quad (6)$$

where $\text{TBP}_{\text{IBP}-360}$ = TBP yield of crude oil fraction IBP—360 °C, wt.% (IBP = initial boiling point), and $\text{HTSD}_{\text{IBP}-360}$ = HTSD yield of crude oil fraction IBP—360 °C, wt.%.

$$\begin{aligned}\text{TBP}_{\text{IBP-540}} =\ & -2232.1983 \times \text{SG} - 655.3758 \times \text{HTSD}_{\text{IBP-540}} - 31682.394 + 18264.286 \times \text{SG}^2 + \\ & 1125.409 \times \text{SG} \times \text{HTSD}_{\text{IBP-540}} + 1.9522 \times \text{HTSD}^2_{\text{IBP-540}} + 495.3427 \times \text{SG}^2 \times \text{HTSD}_{\text{IBP-540}} - \\ & 1.66488 \times \text{SG} \times \text{HTSD}^2_{\text{IBP-540}} - 4936.8613 \times \text{SG}^3 - 0.001997 \times \text{HTSD}^3_{\text{IBP-540}} + \frac{21798.8637}{\text{SG}} - \frac{23085.8313}{\text{HTSD}_{\text{IBP-540}}}\end{aligned} \quad (7)$$

where $\text{TBP}_{\text{IBP}-540}$ = TBP yield of crude oil fraction IBP—540 °C, wt.%, and $\text{HTSD}_{\text{IBP}-540}$ = HTSD yield of crude oil fraction IBP—540 °C, wt.%.

$$\begin{aligned}\text{TBP}_{50\%} =\ & -936589.633 \times \text{SG} + 116.4095 \times \text{HTSD}_{50\%} + 533529.969 + 738502.444 \times \text{SG}^2 - \\ & 195.3968 \times \text{SG} \times \text{HTSD}_{50\%} + 0.0007634 \times \text{HTSD}^2_{50\%} + 205.4164 \times \text{SG}^2 \times \text{HTSD} - 0.227388 \times \text{SG} \times \\ & \text{HTSD}^2_{50\%} - 238553.77 \times \text{SG}^3 + 0.00014461 \times \text{HTSD}^3_{50\%} - \frac{124986.531}{\text{SG}} + \frac{1.993594}{\text{HTSD}_{50\%}}\end{aligned} \quad (8)$$

where $\text{TBP}_{50\%}$ = TBP boiling point at 50 wt.% evaporate, °C, and $\text{HTSD}_{\text{IBP}-540}$ = HTSD TBP boiling point at 50 wt.% evaporate, °C.

Figures 2 and 3 juxtapose the TBP with HTSD yields for the 110–180 °C, 180–240 °C, 240–360 °C, IBP—360 °C, and IBP—540 °C, $T_{50\%}$ fractions of TBP versus HTSD.

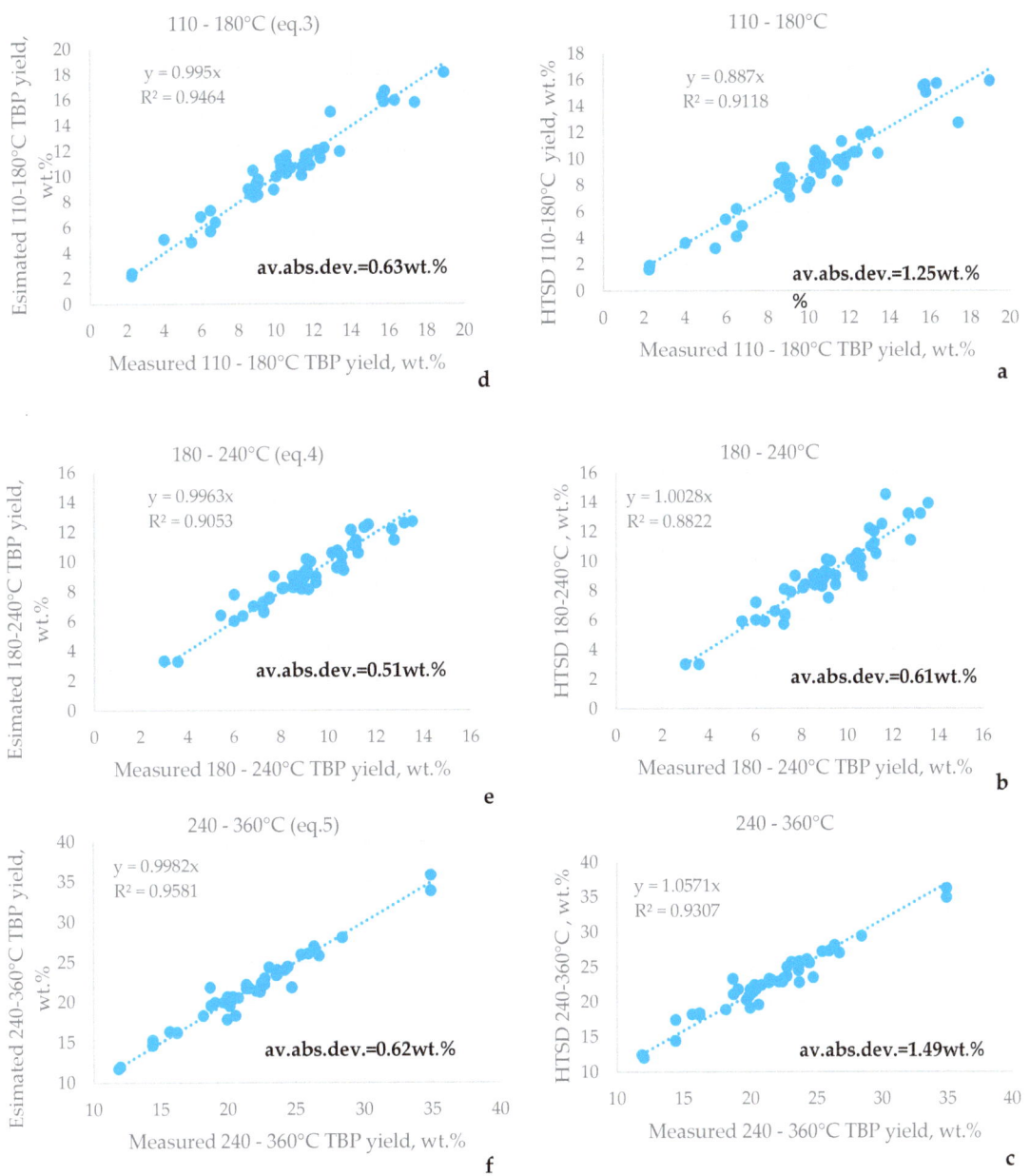

Figure 2. Juxtaposition of the TBP with HTSD yields of the 110–180 °C (**a**), 180–240 °C (**b**), and 240–360 °C (**c**) fractions; the estimated TBP yields according to Equation (3) (**d**), Equation (4) (**e**), and Equation (5) (**f**).

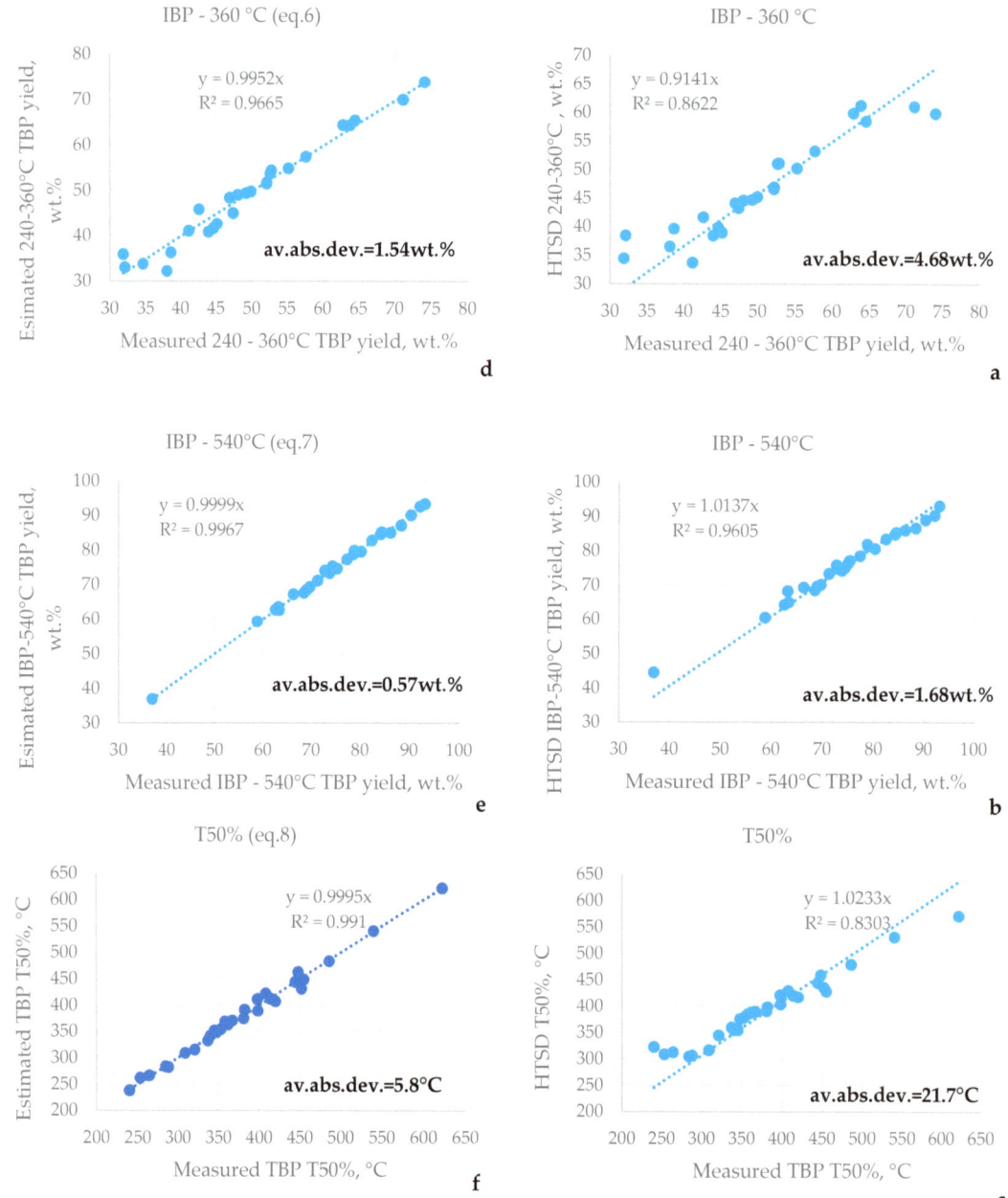

Figure 3. Juxtaposition of the TBP with the HTSD yields of the IBP—360 °C (**a**), IBP—540 °C (**b**), and $T_{50\%}$ (TBP versus HTSD) (**c**) fractions; the estimated TBP yields according to Equation (6) (**d**) and Equation (7) (**e**); the estimated TBP $T_{50\%}$ according to Equation (8) (**f**).

These data clearly show that the equations developed in this work provided a better match to the TBP data than the HTSD data themselves. Using Equations (3)–(8) and employing Riazi's distribution model (Equation (2)), a full TBP curve could be established, as shown in Figure 4. The values of the A and B parameters from Equation (2) estimated with the distillation data of the studied crude oils are presented in Table S6. The studied crude oils enabled the satisfactory prediction of TBP data from HTSD and specific gravity data (deviation in predicted yields of lower than 1.4 wt.%, as required by ASTM D2892 [11]), except for two crude oils: Oryx (deviation = 3.5 wt.%) and South Green Canyon (deviation = 3.0 wt.%), whose simulated and actual TBP data are shown in Figure 5. The reason for the bigger deviations in TBP yield predictions for these crude oils lies in the poor forecast of the IBP—360 °C fraction yield that resulted in the inadequate prognosis of the lighter part of TBP curve. This is understandable for HTSD, which underpredicts the lighter ends of TBP because of the co-elution of C_4–C_8 crude oil hydrocarbons with the CS_2 solvent, as stated in the ASTM D7169 standard [50]. Although the employment of Equations (3)–(8) and Riazi's distribution model (Equation (2)) enabled the satisfactory prediction of TBP data from HTSD and specific gravity data for some crude oils, the deviations in predictions of the lighter part of the TBP curve were larger than the reproducibility of the ASTM D2892 method. Thus, as reported in [51], a combination of ASTM D7169 and ASTM D7900 can provide the accurate representation of full TBP curves for crude oils for minutes instead of the three days required to complete ASTM D2892 and ASTM D5236 analyses. Moreover, HTSD can more accurately represents the content of hydrocarbon fractions in heavy oils than the ASTM D5236 and ASTM D1160 physical distillation methods [13,52–54].

3.2. Kw Characterization Factor, and Sulphur Distributions of Narrow Fractions in the Crude Oils

The TBP analysis of crude oil allowed us to measure the density (specific gravity) and sulphur content of the narrow crude oil fractions. Based on the middle boiling point of the narrow fractions (which in our study was assumed to be equal to $T_{50\%}$) and the specific gravity, the Kw characterization factor of each fraction and of the whole crude oil could be calculated using Equation (1). The Kw characterization factor of the narrow fractions of the 30 studied crude oils is shown in Table S7. It is evident from the data in Figure 6 that the distribution of the narrow fraction Kw characterization factor had different shapes for each crude oil and that the whole crude oil Kw factor could be derived from that of the narrow fractions. This is opposite to the generally accepted concept of the constant Kw factor of petroleum fluids [55–57]. According to this concept, the density of the narrow fractions can be calculated with Equation (9).

$$SG = \frac{\sqrt[3]{1.8[T_{50\%} + 273.15]}}{Kw} \quad (9)$$

The data in Table S7 and Figure 6, however, indicate that the Kw factor varied depending on the boiling point range of the crude oil. For example, the Varandey crude oil exhibited a Kw factor of 12.50 of the lightest narrow fraction ($T_{50\%}$ = 47.5 °C), then dropped to 11.67 for the narrow fraction with $T_{50\%}$ = 85 °C, and started increasing to reach 12.49 for the narrow fraction with $T_{50\%}$ = 545 °C. On the other hand, the Kw factor of the whole Varandey crude oil was 11.88. Considering Tempa Rossa crude oil, the Kw factor of the narrow fractions continually decreased from 12.78 for the lightest narrow fraction ($T_{50\%}$ = 47.5 °C) to 11.24 for the heaviest narrow fraction with $T_{50\%}$ = 545 °C. On the other hand, the whole Tempa Rossa crude oil Kw factor was 11.62. Using intercriteria analysis evaluation allowed us to quantify the extent of similarity in the pattern of Kw factor variation through the whole crude oil boiling range. Table 1 shows the degree of similarity quantified with ICrA evaluation on the basis of Kw factor variation through the whole boiling range of the crude oils. Normally in ICrA, the final matrix is nxn, where n is the number of objects being compared, but here, due to the large size of the matrix, only the part containing the most significant elements is shown. The data in Table 1 indicate that there was no strong statistically meaningful consonance ($\mu \geq 0.95$) between any of the studied crude oils, confirming the statement made by Abdel-

AalMohammed and Alsahlawi [58] and Gary et al. [59] that no two crude oils are the same. These data also indicate that the patterns of Kw factor variation through the whole boiling range of the crude oils may be very different, as also indicated by the data shown in Figure 6. Therefore, the concept of a constant Kw factor may lead to the reporting of wrong values for the specific gravity curves of crude oils.

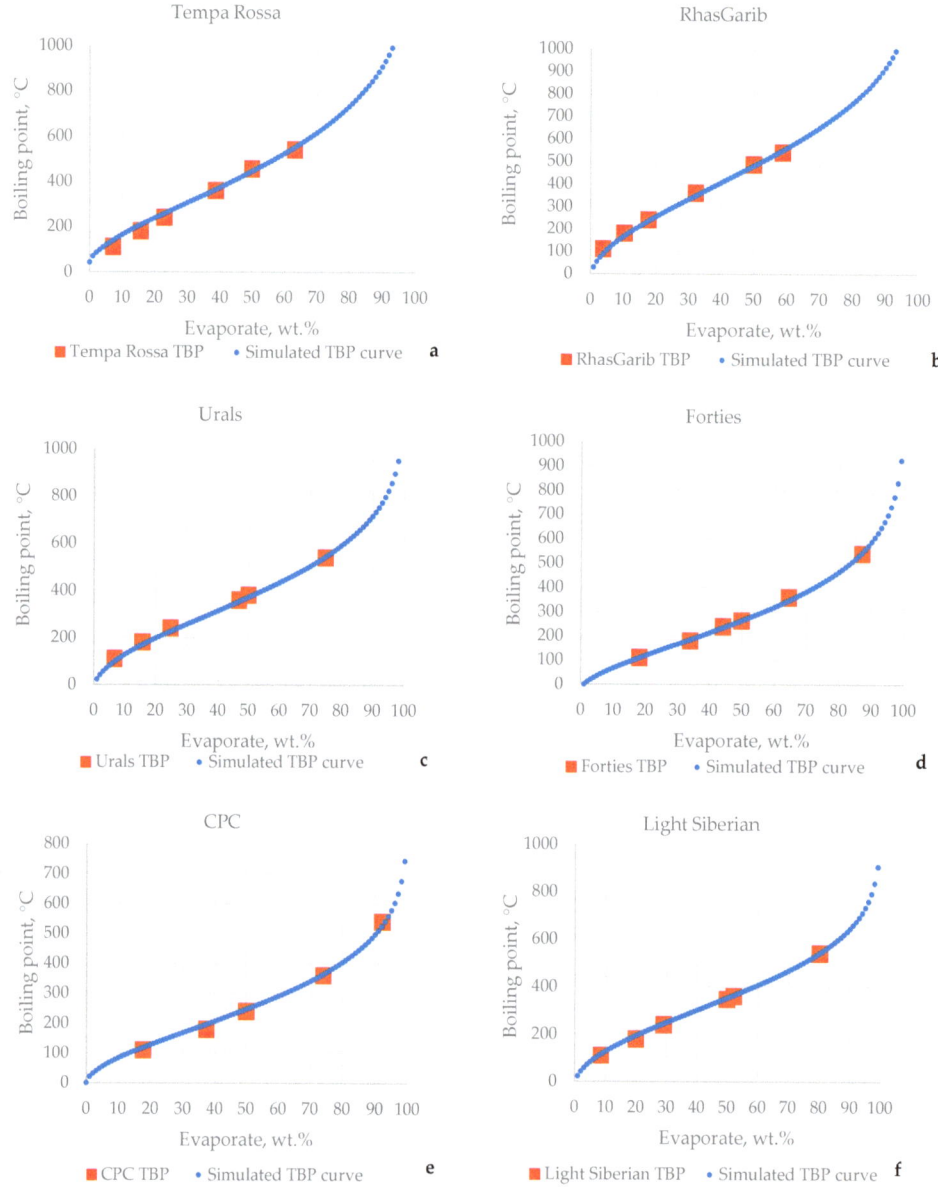

Figure 4. TBP curves of extra light (**d**,**e**), light (**f**), medium (**b**,**c**), and heavy (**a**) crude oils simulated with Equations (3)–(8) and Riazi's distribution model (Equation (2)).

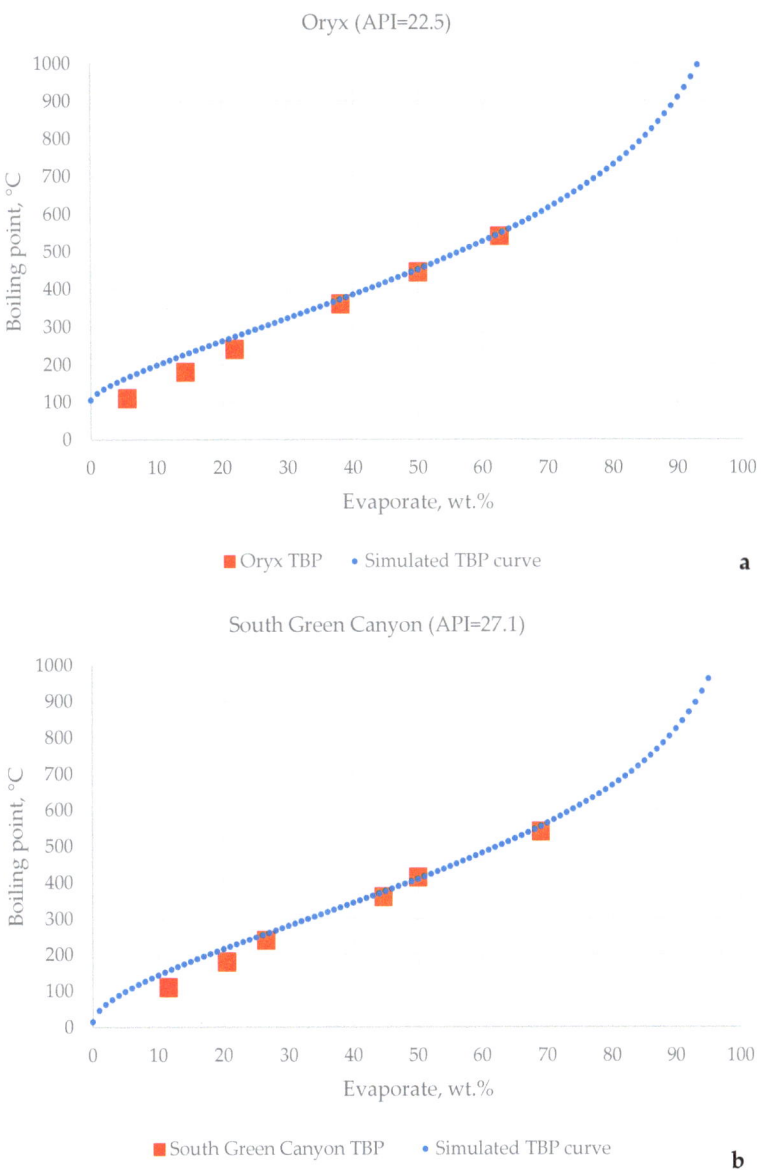

Figure 5. TBP curves of Oryx (**a**) and South Green Canyon (**b**) crude oils simulated with Equations (3)–(8) and Riazi's distribution model (Equation (2)).

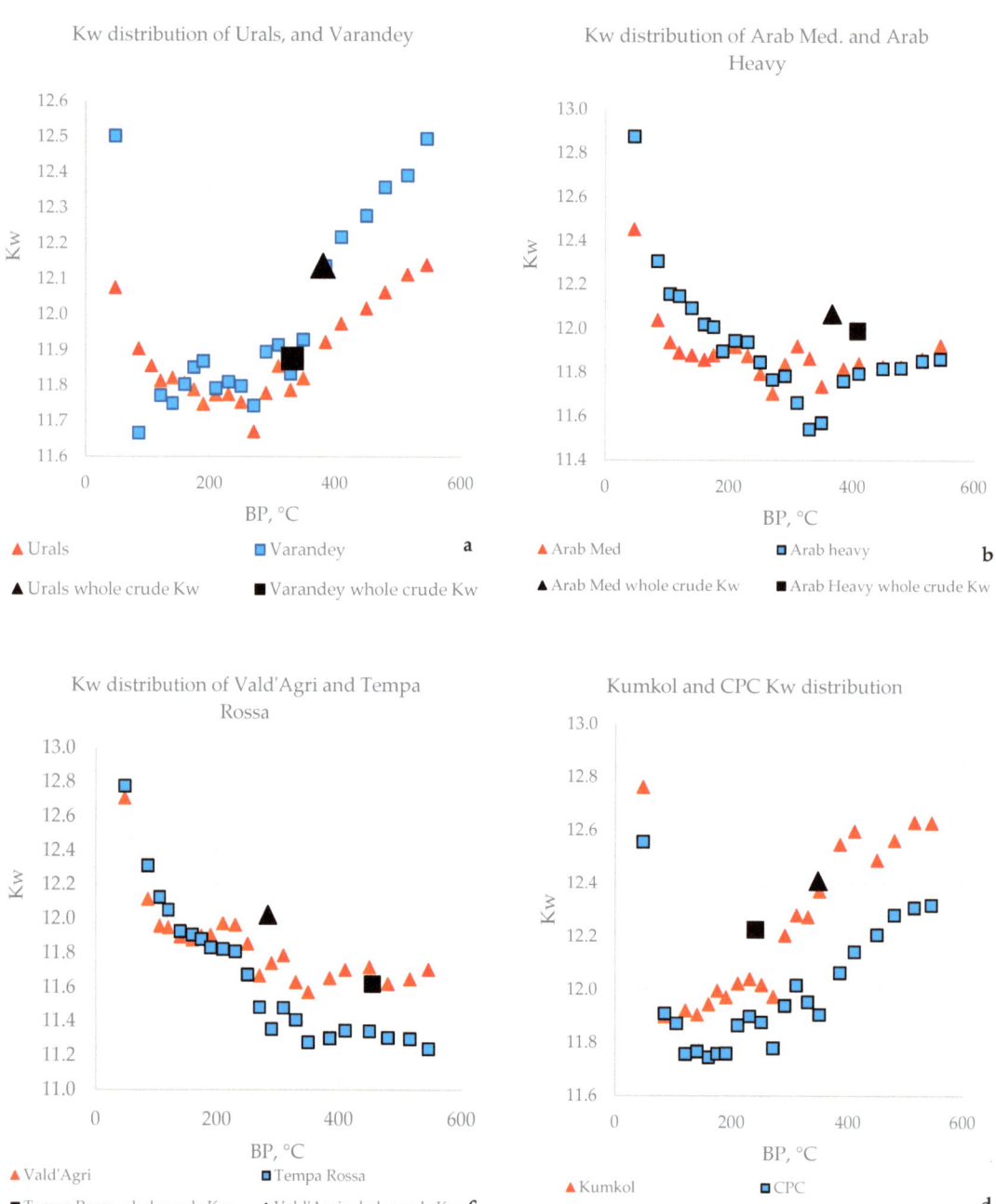

Figure 6. Kw characterization factor of narrow fraction distributions and the whole crude oil Kw characterization factor for the different crude oils studied in this work (**a**–**d**).

Table 1. Degree of similarity between some of the investigated crude oils determined based on the application of intercriteria analysis and Kw factor variation through the whole boiling range of the crude oils.

μ	Urals	Arab M	Arab H	Vald'Agri	Basrah L	Basrah H	Kirkuk	Iranian H	KEB	El Bouri
Urals	1	0.5628	0.5714	0.4372	0.5411	0.4502	0.6017	0.7489	0.5541	0.8398
Arab M	0.5628	1	0.71	0.7619	0.7965	0.7013	0.8268	0.7056	0.7619	0.5671
Arab H	0.5714	0.71	1	0.8052	0.8485	0.8658	0.7879	0.6104	0.7359	0.5628
Vald'Agri	0.4372	0.7619	0.8052	1	0.8701	0.8312	0.7965	0.6061	0.697	0.4632
Basrah L	0.5411	0.7965	0.8485	0.8701	1	0.8095	0.8701	0.658	0.7749	0.5455
Basrah H	0.4502	0.7013	0.8658	0.8312	0.8095	1	0.7576	0.5498	0.7446	0.4719
Kirkuk	0.6017	0.8268	0.7879	0.7965	0.8701	0.7576	1	0.7273	0.7835	0.5844
Iranian H	0.7489	0.7056	0.6104	0.6061	0.658	0.5498	0.7273	1	0.6797	0.7619
KEB	0.5541	0.7619	0.7359	0.697	0.7749	0.7446	0.7835	0.6797	1	0.5671
El Bouri	0.8398	0.5671	0.5628	0.4632	0.5455	0.4719	0.5844	0.7619	0.5671	1
Kazakh	0.8961	0.5584	0.5758	0.4545	0.5498	0.4719	0.6061	0.7489	0.6104	0.7965
CPC	0.7835	0.5065	0.4242	0.3939	0.4978	0.355	0.5238	0.6883	0.5325	0.7532
LSCO	0.8701	0.5195	0.4719	0.3896	0.4978	0.3766	0.5455	0.6883	0.5152	0.7922
Rhem.	0.7576	0.4286	0.3896	0.3203	0.4286	0.3074	0.4719	0.6061	0.4805	0.7013
Prinos	0.5541	0.5974	0.5455	0.6277	0.6537	0.5974	0.6364	0.6364	0.5931	0.5411
Azeri L	0.7186	0.4113	0.329	0.29	0.3896	0.2597	0.4199	0.6277	0.4372	0.7056
SGC	0.697	0.5368	0.5411	0.4935	0.5931	0.4545	0.619	0.7273	0.5455	0.71
Oryx	0.4199	0.6883	0.7922	0.8398	0.7706	0.8658	0.7229	0.5152	0.684	0.4242
Okwuib	0.6537	0.6883	0.8268	0.658	0.7359	0.7186	0.7273	0.6667	0.7403	0.6494
RasGharib	0.8355	0.6147	0.632	0.5152	0.5974	0.5368	0.6537	0.7273	0.645	0.8139
Varandey	0.7403	0.4762	0.3939	0.3463	0.4242	0.2857	0.4632	0.6667	0.4762	0.7446
Arab L	0.5498	0.7446	0.8442	0.8182	0.8442	0.8139	0.8268	0.645	0.7619	0.5541
Tempa Rossa	0.3853	0.671	0.7835	0.8182	0.7143	0.8485	0.6667	0.4762	0.645	0.3896

Note: Green color denotes statistically meaningful positive relation; red color denotes statistically meaningful negative relation. The intensity of the color designates the strength of the relation. The higher the color intensity, the higher the strength of the relation. Yellow color denotes dissonance.

Just for comparison, Table 2 presents the degree of similarity between some of the investigated crude oils determined based on the application of intercriteria analysis and HTSD data, total sulphur content, and crude oil specific gravity. These data indicate the presence of strong positive consonance ($\mu \geq 0.95$) between, for example, the Tempa Rossa, Arab Heavy, Albanian, Arab Medium, Basrah Light, Oryx, and South Green Canyon crude oils that implies that these crude oils are similar in terms of their distillation characteristics, total sulphur content, and bulk specific gravity. The data in Tables 1 and 2 suggest that the distillation characteristics of the crude oils cannot be used as an indicator of the Kw factor variation through the whole crude oil boiling range. Thus, while the TBP simulated with a gas chromatographic could be used to predict distillation, specific gravity curve simulation cannot be accurate applied the concept of a constant Kw factor. Additional investigations are needed to develop an appropriate procedure to simulate crude oil specific gravity curves.

The sulphur content data of 23 narrow fractions of the 34 studied crude oils are presented in Table S8. Figure 7 shows the distribution of sulphur among the boiling point range of some of the studied crude oils. These data show that the sulphur content generally increased with boiling point increases. However, the shape of the curve and the slope of increase were different for each crude oil. For the dataset in Table S8, ICrA evaluation was performed to assess the similarity of sulphur content variation through the whole boiling range of the studied crude oils. Table 3 presents the degree of similarity between some of the investigated crude oils determined based on the application of intercriteria analysis and sulphur content variation through the whole crude oil boiling range. The data in Table 3 indicate the presence of a higher degree of similarity between the studied crude oils than that observed in Table 1, where the Kw factor distribution was evaluated with ICrA. For example, the Iranian Heavy crude oil had a positive consonance $\mu = 0.9407$ with Arab Medium crude oil. Although this value was higher than the highest positive consonance of $\mu = 0.9177$ (between Bonga and RasGharib) observed in the ICrA evaluation of Kw factor distribution, it was much lower than the $\mu = 0.9863$ (between Tempa Rossa and Oryx) observed in the ICrA evaluation of boiling point distribution.

Table 2. Degree of similarity between some of the investigated crude oils determined based on the application of intercriteria analysis and HTSD data, total sulphur content, and crude oil specific gravity.

μ	Tempa Rossa	Forties	Kuwait Light	Arabian light	Kumkol	Arabian Heavy	Alban Crude	Ras Gharib
Tempa Rossa	1	0.8261	0.3852	0.916	0.6025	0.9683	0.9717	0.9076
Forties	0.8261	1	0.4168	0.7899	0.4725	0.8255	0.805	0.7588
Kuwait Light	0.3852	0.4168	1	0.4401	0.5745	0.3854	0.3908	0.3908
Arabian light	0.916	0.7899	0.4401	1	0.656	0.923	0.9115	0.8863
Kumkol	0.6025	0.4725	0.5745	0.656	1	0.6221	0.6112	0.6711
Arabian heavy	0.9683	0.8255	0.3854	0.923	0.6221	1	0.9507	0.9092
Alban crude	0.9717	0.805	0.3908	0.9115	0.6112	0.9507	1	0.8992
Ras Gharib	0.9076	0.7588	0.3908	0.8863	0.6711	0.9092	0.8992	1
Boscan	0.0034	0.1006	0.012	0.0104	0.021	0.0157	0.0008	0.0381
Aseng	0.2297	0.1448	0.5605	0.3	0.5499	0.2443	0.2389	0.2793
El Sharara	0.4126	0.3485	0.7759	0.4849	0.6994	0.428	0.4202	0.4619
Helm C.O.	0.5165	0.4667	0.7916	0.5874	0.6661	0.5277	0.523	0.5759
Arab Medium	0.9683	0.8255	0.3966	0.9272	0.6087	0.9636	0.9549	0.9028
Azeri light	0.5011	0.4322	0.7952	0.5524	0.7375	0.4983	0.5028	0.5095
Basrah Light	0.9549	0.8277	0.3905	0.9137	0.6157	0.9588	0.9465	0.9017
Bozachi	0.4555	0.4583	0.8165	0.5325	0.6249	0.4745	0.4667	0.523
Cheleken	0.2521	0.2686	0.7941	0.3218	0.5899	0.2644	0.2569	0.3112
CPC	0.1403	0.188	0.7246	0.2084	0.4936	0.1532	0.1437	0.2034
El Bouri	0.8591	0.7325	0.4675	0.8731	0.709	0.8675	0.851	0.851
Kazakh	0.2992	0.2123	0.6669	0.3725	0.6555	0.3157	0.3123	0.3745
Kirkuk	0.9669	0.8305	0.4	0.9258	0.6039	0.9594	0.949	0.8947
Kuwait Export Blend	0.9695	0.8322	0.3815	0.9151	0.6031	0.963	0.9476	0.9039
Okwibome	0.1006	0.0933	0.6053	0.1616	0.419	0.1014	0.1112	0.1367
Oryx	0.9863	0.83	0.3784	0.9216	0.6059	0.9756	0.9664	0.9134
Urals	0.8605	0.7387	0.4672	0.8874	0.6762	0.8695	0.8588	0.8454
Rhemoura	0.9014	0.8062	0.4297	0.8863	0.5941	0.8936	0.898	0.8723
Sib. Light	0.5476	0.4585	0.7073	0.6185	0.8216	0.5627	0.5501	0.6123
South Green Canyon	0.97	0.8185	0.3672	0.9109	0.6168	0.9737	0.9485	0.9283
Prinos	0.9597	0.8028	0.4064	0.9221	0.6246	0.9443	0.9574	0.9154
ValD'Agri	0.5966	0.5695	0.6919	0.6199	0.5053	0.5835	0.5983	0.5745

Note: Green color denotes statistically meaningful positive relation; red color denotes statistically meaningful negative relation. The intensity of the color designates the strength of the relation. The higher the color intensity, the higher the strength of the relation. Yellow color denotes dissonance.

Table 3. Degree of similarity between some of the investigated crude oils determined based on the application of intercriteria analysis and sulphur content variation through the whole crude oil boiling range.

μ	Urals	Arab M	Arab H	ValD'Agri	Basrah L	Basrah H	Kirkuk	Iranian H	KEB	El Bouri
Urals	1	0.6324	0.498	0.5573	0.5138	0.4585	0.5613	0.6047	0.5494	0.4269
Arab M	0.6324	1	0.8498	0.9091	0.834	0.7787	0.8893	0.9407	0.9091	0.7628
Arab H	0.498	0.8498	1	0.8854	0.834	0.8735	0.8735	0.8617	0.917	0.8656
ValD'Agri	0.5573	0.9091	0.8854	1	0.8696	0.8221	0.8933	0.9051	0.9289	0.7826
Basrah L	0.5138	0.834	0.834	0.8696	1	0.8972	0.9209	0.8458	0.8538	0.7549
Basrah H	0.4585	0.7787	0.8735	0.8221	0.8972	1	0.8577	0.7984	0.8379	0.7945
Kirkuk	0.5613	0.8893	0.8735	0.8933	0.9209	0.8577	1	0.917	0.9091	0.7708
Iranian H	0.6047	0.9407	0.8617	0.9051	0.8458	0.7984	0.917	1	0.9051	0.751
KEB	0.5494	0.9091	0.917	0.9289	0.8538	0.8379	0.9091	0.9051	1	0.8063
El Bouri	0.4269	0.7628	0.8656	0.7826	0.7549	0.7945	0.7708	0.751	0.8063	1
Kazakh	0.6838	0.7115	0.6245	0.6561	0.6206	0.5534	0.664	0.7036	0.6798	0.5455
CPC	0.8063	0.4545	0.3439	0.3953	0.3992	0.3597	0.4229	0.4506	0.3874	0.3281
LSCO	0.8142	0.7154	0.6206	0.664	0.6285	0.5494	0.6917	0.7115	0.664	0.5099
Rhem.	0.7549	0.7747	0.664	0.7154	0.6561	0.5929	0.7273	0.7708	0.7312	0.5613
Prinos	0.8261	0.5692	0.4625	0.5178	0.4783	0.4308	0.5494	0.585	0.5178	0.4032
Azeri L	0.6285	0.3004	0.1818	0.2332	0.1818	0.1265	0.2451	0.2964	0.249	0.2055
SGC	0.6957	0.8735	0.7945	0.8142	0.7549	0.7233	0.834	0.8696	0.8221	0.6838
Oryx	0.419	0.7628	0.8972	0.8142	0.8538	0.8933	0.8379	0.7787	0.8379	0.7866
Okwuib	0.5652	0.2292	0.1107	0.1621	0.1265	0.0791	0.166	0.2174	0.17	0.2055
RasGharib	0.3004	0.3202	0.4071	0.3557	0.3913	0.4625	0.3676	0.3241	0.3557	0.4941
Varandey	0.6838	0.5138	0.4032	0.4466	0.4664	0.4506	0.498	0.4862	0.4466	0.4506
Arab L	0.7075	0.8617	0.7352	0.8182	0.7352	0.6561	0.7905	0.8419	0.7866	0.6245
KBT	0.5652	0.8458	0.8063	0.8577	0.8854	0.7984	0.9249	0.8577	0.8498	0.7036
Tempa Rossa	0.0158	0.2213	0.3241	0.2727	0.3202	0.3676	0.2885	0.2332	0.2727	0.3281

Note: Green color denotes statistically meaningful positive relation; red color denotes statistically meaningful negative relation. The intensity of the color designates the strength of the relation. The higher the color intensity, the higher the strength of the relation. Yellow color denotes dissonance.

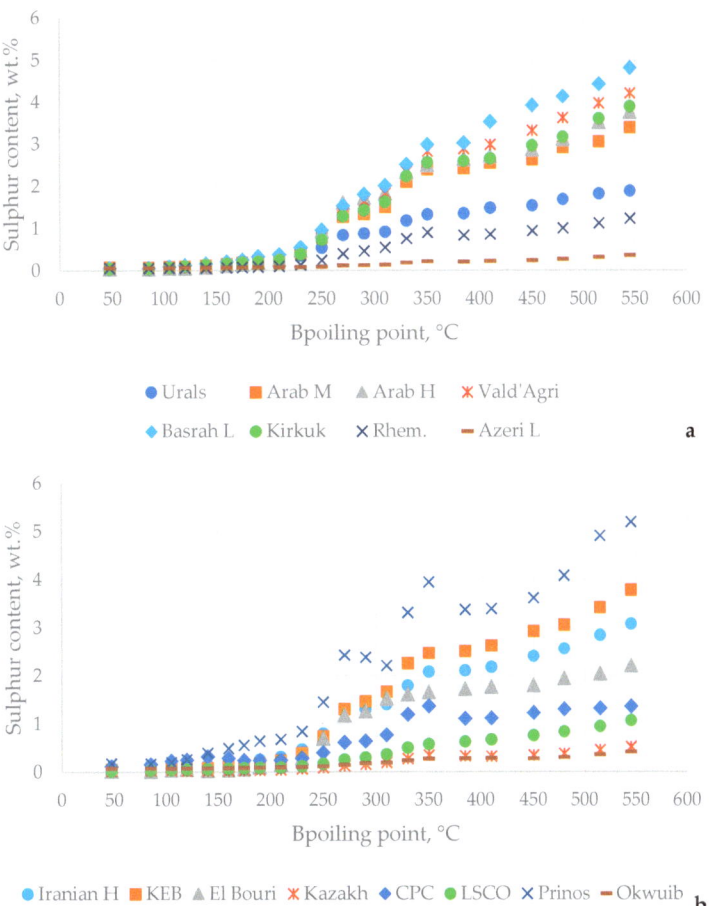

Figure 7. Distribution of sulphur in the boiling point range of some of the studied crude oils (**a**,**b**).

This may imply that the crude oil boiling point distribution cannot be considered reliable enough for use it as a tool to predict specific gravity and sulphur distribution curves, which is in contrast with the conclusion of Swafford and McCarthy [60] that specific gravity, total sulphur content, and simulated distillation can be used to simulate a complete comprehensive assay of a crude oil. Indeed, some relations between the different crude oil properties may be found, as reported in our earlier study [47], but the limit of uncertainty for the prediction of density, for example, can be broad for some crude oils. This statement is completely in line with the conclusions reached by Abdel-AalMohammed and Alsahlawi [58] and Gary et al. [59] that no two crude oils are the same.

3.3. SARA Composition and Bulk Properties of Studied Crude Oils

The SARA analysis data and bulk properties of 48 extra light, light medium, heavy, and extra heavy crude oils are summarized in Table S9. Table 4 summarizes the range of variations in the SARA composition and crude oil bulk properties

Table 4. Range of variations in the SARA composition and bulk properties of the studied crude oils.

	Sat, wt.%	Aro, wt.%	Resins, wt.%	As, wt.%	SG	Sulphur, wt.%	VR Yield, wt.%	Pour Point, °C	VIS at 40 °C, mm²/s	Slope	Kw
min	23.5	7.1	0.0	0.1	0.782	0.03	1.4	−45.6	0.9	2.9	11.33
max	92.9	62.1	7.7	22.2	1.002	5.64	60.7	37.8	19430.0	5.2	12.67

Tables 5 and 6 present the results of ICrA evaluation used for the determination of statistically meaningful relations between the SARA composition data and the bulk crude oil properties.

Table 5. µ-value of the ICrA evaluation of relations between crude oil SARA composition data and bulk properties.

µ	Sat	Aro	Resins	As	SG	Sulphur	VR Yield	PP	VIS
Sat	1	0.1687	0.1404	0.1727	0.0677	0.1525	0.101	0.4667	0.1283
Aro	0.1687	1	0.7535	0.7566	0.7727	0.7707	0.7626	0.4515	0.7646
Resins	0.1404	0.7535	1	0.8202	0.797	0.8394	0.8212	0.4566	0.7889
As	0.1727	0.7566	0.8202	1	0.7828	0.8273	0.8081	0.4596	0.7475
SG	0.0677	0.7727	0.797	0.7828	1	0.7919	0.9	0.4879	0.8626
Sulphur	0.1525	0.7707	0.8394	0.8273	0.7919	1	0.8242	0.404	0.7778
VR yield	0.101	0.7626	0.8212	0.8081	0.9	0.8242	1	0.5081	0.9091
PP	0.4667	0.4515	0.4566	0.4596	0.4879	0.404	0.5081	1	0.5141
VIS	0.1283	0.7646	0.7889	0.7475	0.8626	0.7778	0.9091	0.5141	1

Note: Green color denotes statistically meaningful positive relation; red color denotes statistically meaningful negative relation. The intensity of the color designates the strength of the relation. The higher the color intensity, the higher the strength of the relation. Yellow color denotes dissonance.

Table 6. υ-value of the ICrA evaluation of relations between crude oil SARA composition data and bulk properties.

υ	Sat	Aro	Resins	As	SG	Sulphur	VR Yield	PP	VIS
Sat	0	0.8273	0.8394	0.8192	0.9202	0.8394	0.897	0.4737	0.8677
Aro	0.8273	0	0.2263	0.2354	0.2131	0.2212	0.2354	0.4889	0.2313
Resins	0.8394	0.2263	0	0.1556	0.1727	0.1364	0.1606	0.4717	0.1909
As	0.8192	0.2354	0.1556	0	0.199	0.1606	0.1859	0.4768	0.2444
SG	0.9202	0.2131	0.1727	0.199	0	0.1899	0.0879	0.4424	0.1232
Sulphur	0.8394	0.2212	0.1364	0.1606	0.1899	0	0.1697	0.5323	0.2141
VR yield	0.897	0.2354	0.1606	0.1859	0.0879	0.1697	0	0.4343	0.0889
PP	0.4737	0.4889	0.4717	0.4768	0.4424	0.5323	0.4343	0	0.4263
VIS	0.8677	0.2313	0.1909	0.2444	0.1232	0.2141	0.0889	0.4263	0

Note: Green color denotes statistically meaningful positive relation; red color denotes statistically meaningful negative relation. The intensity of the color designates the strength of the relation. The higher the color intensity, the higher the strength of the relation. Yellow color denotes dissonance.

The data in Tables 5 and 6 show similar relations as those observed for the vacuum residues from our recent study [61], with the specific gravity being the crude oil characteristic most related to saturate content. Based on the data of SARA composition for 308 crude oil samples measured in accordance with ASTM D2007, modified ASTM D4124, HPLC, TLC-FID (Iatroscan), and liquid chromatography in our recent research [23], a relation (Equation (10)) between crude oil saturate content and crude oil specific gravity was developed.

$$Crude\ oil\ saturates\ (\text{wt.\%}) = 100 - \left(\frac{100}{0.2748 + 5.198e^{-4.787SG}} - 239\right) \quad (10)$$

Figure 8 shows the relation of crude oil density to the saturate content estimated with Equation (10). The average absolute deviation of Equation (10) was found to be 3.3 wt.%. The maximum absolute deviation was 13.3 wt.%. The bias was −0.7 wt.%.

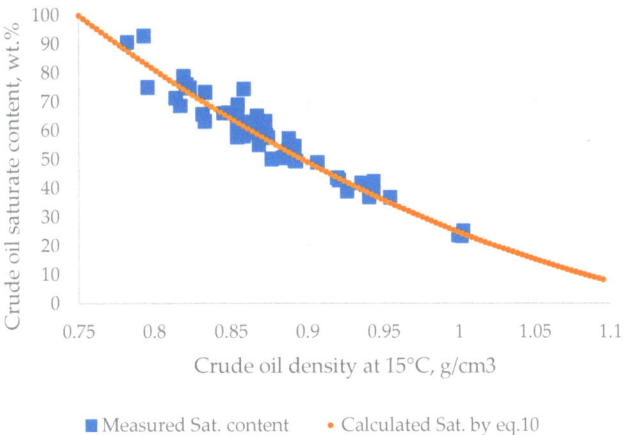

Figure 8. Relation of crude oil saturate content to specific gravity.

A more accurate prediction of crude saturate content was obtained by using nonlinear regression and employing the data generated with Equation (10), which relates saturate content to crude oil specific gravity and pour point. The new regression designated as Equation (11) is shown below.

$$\begin{aligned}
\text{Crude oil saturates (wt.\%)} = {} & 0.30283 \times Sat(SG) - 0.25515 \times PP + \\
& 31.45053 + 0.0052145 \times Sat(SG)^2 + 0.0028855 \times Sat(SG) \times PP - \\
& 0.0067996 \times PP^2 + 0.00006159 \times Sat(SG)^2 \times PP + 0.000152899 \times \\
& Sat(SG) \times PP^2 - \tfrac{441.77259}{Sat(SG)}
\end{aligned} \quad (11)$$

where Sat(SG) = crude oil saturate content calculated with Equation (10) from SG, wt.%.

The average absolute deviation of Equation (11) was found to be 2.5 wt.%. The maximum absolute deviation was 6.6 wt.%. The bias was −0.01 wt.%. Figure 9 shows parity graphs of measured crude oil saturate content versus crude oil saturate content estimated with Equation (10) (Figure 9a) and Equation (11) (Figure 9b). The data in Figure 9 show that the new Equation (11) provided a lower prediction dispersion.

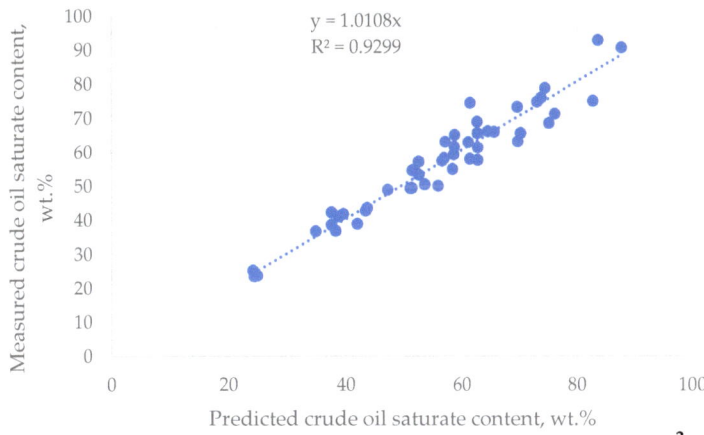

Figure 9. Cont.

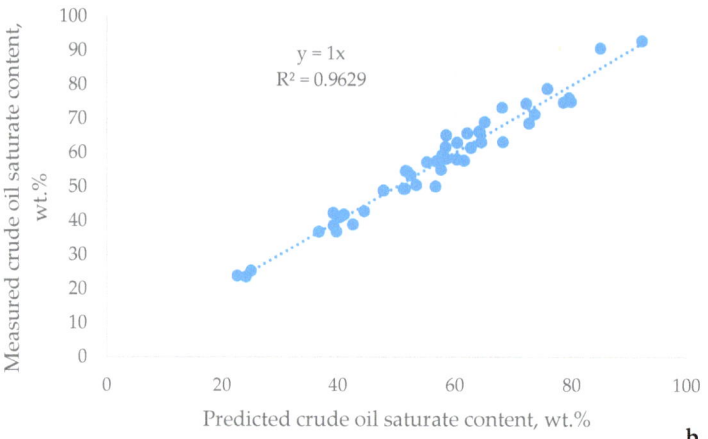

Figure 9. Parity graphs of measured crude oil saturate content versus crude oil saturate content predicted with Equation (10) (**a**) and Equation (11) (**b**).

4. Discussion

The developed equations (Equations (3)–(8)) used to convert HTSD to TBP, as shown in Figures 2 and 3, reasonably well-predicted the TBP yields and $T_{50\%}$. The data they generated were very well-described by the Riazi's distribution model that allowed us to construct a full TBP curve from the HTSD data and specific gravity of each crude oil.

The direct juxtaposition of HTSD to TBP did not provide the satisfactory matching of HTSD with TBP. Despite the relatively good prediction of TBP curves via the simultaneously employment of Equations (3)–(8) with Equation (2) (Riazi's distribution model), some crudes did not allow for the very accurate prediction of the lighter part of the TBP curve, as shown in Figure 5. This shortcoming could be overcome by simultaneously employing ASTM D7169 and ASTM D7900, as reported in [51]. HTSD was shown to be superior to physical vacuum distillation in our recent study [13], and it can be used to predict the TBP for heavy oils. HTSD is carried out over 40 min, while TBP analysis requires three days. However, the TBP analysis allows for the measurement of the specific gravity and sulphur content of narrow crude oil fractions, which (as shown in the previous section) are difficult to accurately predict from crude boiling point distributions. Therefore, the method developed in this work to build crude oil TBP curves from HTSD and crude specific gravity data can be used to control the quality of cargoes of known crude oils via a controlled crude assay. However, for crude oils that are not known, the use of TBP analysis along with specific gravity and sulphur content measurements of narrow fractions should be applied. The specific gravity of narrow fractions is a very useful characteristic that correlates with aromatic content, which is important for the evaluation of the cetane index of the middle distillates, and the crackability of heavy oil fractions. Thus, its correct determination affects the proper planning of yields in the conversion of oil-refining units. The sulphur content of narrow fractions is also an important characteristic when evaluations of HDS and sulphur recovery unit performance are performed. This can explain why TBP analysis is the best choice to characterize a new crude oil.

Regarding crude oil SARA analysis, the prediction of saturates was described by Yarranton [62] as a very important step in obtaining a full crude oil SARA composition. By predicting the saturate and asphaltene content of a vacuum residue with the method described in our recent research [63] and employing the relationship of vacuum residue asphaltene to crude oil asphaltene content determined in our previous study [23] and the relation between C_5 and C_7 asphaltenes established in [23], it is possible to simulate full crude oil SARA composition. Equation (11) (newly developed in this work), Equation (10), and the data of crude oil specific gravity and pour point can be used to obtain an average absolute deviation of 2.5 wt.%, maximum average deviation of 6.6 wt.%, and bias of −0.01 wt.% for 48 crude oils, while the method proposed by Yarranton showed an average absolute deviation of 2.7 wt.%, a maximum average deviation of 8.0 wt.%, and bias of −0.5 wt.% for 25 crude oils [62]. Therefore, our new method can be considered superior to the method of Yarranton [62]. The measurement of C_5 and C_7 asphaltenes enables the determination of C_5 resins via the subtraction of C_7 asphaltenes from C_5 asphaltenes, and the aromatic content can be determined via the subtraction of saturate contents, C_5 resins, and C_7 asphaltenes from 100 wt.%.

The data in Tables 5 and 6 indicate that viscosity was found to be significantly negatively related to saturates and positively related to specific gravity and vacuum residue content. These findings are in line with those observed in our recent studies on crude oil viscosity modelling [64,65].

5. Conclusions

HTSD, specific gravity, and the Riazi's distribution model can be used to simulate the TBP of crude oils. For most studied crude oils, the TBP simulation from HTSD data, the correlations developed in this work, and Riazi's distribution model showed satisfactory deviations within the uncertainty of TBP yield measurements according to the ASTM D2892 standard. For some crude oils, however, the lighter part of the TBP curve was predicted with a lower accuracy than that reported by the ASTM D2892 standard. This finding suggests that a combination of the ASTM D7169 and ASTM D7900 gas chromatographic methods could correctly simulate a whole crude oil TBP curve.

The concept of a constant Kw characterization factor was disproved in this study. The diverse crude oils exhibited distinct Kw factor distributions of narrow fractions that were difficult to predict from boiling point distribution and crude oil bulk properties. The same was found to be valid for the sulphur distribution of the narrow fractions of the different crude oils. While the degree of similarity of crude oils evaluated with ICrA based on the distillation characteristics could be high for some crude oils, those evaluated on the basis of the Kw characterization factor and sulphur distributions were not so high. The degree of similarity of the crude oils evaluated using ICrA based on the distillation characteristics differed from that evaluated on the basis of the Kw characterization factor and sulphur distributions. This suggests that the Kw characterization factor and sulphur distributions cannot be accurately predicted from distillation distribution data and crude oil bulk properties. Therefore, when accurate information about the density (Kw factor) and sulphur distribution of crude oil is needed, a TBP analysis is required.

Furthermore, crude oil saturate content can be predicted with a satisfactory accuracy with information about the density and pour point of crude oil.

Supplementary Materials: The following supporting information can be downloaded at: https://www.mdpi.com/article/10.3390/pr11020420/s1, Table S1: High-temperature simulated distillation of extra light, light medium, heavy, and extra heavy crude oils (boiling point at 1%); Table S2: High-temperature simulated distillation of extra light, light medium, heavy, and extra heavy crude oils (evaporates at 70, 110, 130, 150, 170, 180, 200, 220, 240, 260, 280, 300, 320, 340, 360, 380, 390, 430, 470, 490, and 540 °C); Table S3: True boiling point distillation of extra light, light medium, heavy, and extra heavy crude oils (evaporates at 70, 110, 130, 150, 170, 180, 200, 220, 240, 260, 280, 300, 320, 340, 360, 380, 390, 430, 470, 490, and 540 °C); Table S4: True boiling point distillation of extra light, light medium, heavy, and extra heavy crude oils (evaporates at 70, 110, 130, 150, 170, 180, 200, 220, 240, 260, 280, 300, 320, 340, 360, 380, 390, 430, 470, 490, and 540 °C) extracted from [48]; Table S5: High-temperature simulated distillation of extra light, light medium, heavy, and extra heavy crude oils (evaporates at 70, 110, 130, 150, 170, 180, 200, 220, 240, 260, 280, 300, 320, 340, 360, 380, 390, 430, 470, 490, and 540 °C) extracted from [37]; Table S6: Values of the parameters A and B from Riazi's distribution model (Equation (2)) for the studied crude oils estimated using the distillation data; Table S7: Kw characterization factor of narrow fractions of 30 studied crude oils; Table S8: Sulphur content of TBP crude fractions of extra light, light, medium, and heavy crude oils; Table S9: SARA analysis data and bulk properties of extra light, light medium, heavy, and extra heavy crude oils.

Author Contributions: Conceptualization, D.S. and I.S.; methodology, R.D.; software, S.N., D.D.S. and S.R.; validation, S.S. (Sotir Sotirov), E.S. and S.S. (Stanislav Simeonov); formal analysis, D.P.; investigation, M.T., G.N.P. and V.B.; resources, K.A.; data curation, R.D.; writing—original draft preparation, D.S.; writing—review and editing, D.S.; visualization, G.N.P.; supervision, K.A.; project administration, K.A.; funding acquisition, S.S. (Sotir Sotirov). All authors have read and agreed to the published version of the manuscript.

Funding: This research received no external funding.

Data Availability Statement: Not applicable.

Acknowledgments: The authors Krassimir Atanassov and Simeon Ribagin acknowledge support from the Bulgarian National Science Fund under Grant Ref. No. KP-06-N22-1/2018 "Theoretical research and applications of InterCriteria Analysis".

Conflicts of Interest: The authors declare no conflict of interest.

Nomenclature

API	American Petroleum Institute gravity
Aro	Aromatics
As	Asphaltenes
ASTM	American Society for Testing and Materials
FID	Flame ionization detector
GC	Gas chromatography
HP	Hewlett Packard
HPLC	High-performance liquid chromatography
HTSD	High-temperature simulated distillation
IBP	Initial boiling point
ICrA	Intercriteria analysis
Kw	Watson characterization factor
PIANO	Paraffins, iso-paraffins, aromatics, naphthenes, and olefins
PONA	Paraffins, olefins, naphthenes, and aromatics
PP	Pour point
SARA	Saturates, aromatics, resins, asphaltenes
Sat.	saturates
SG	Specific gravity
Slope	Slope in Walther equation [65] for double logarithm dependence on logarithm of temperature
T_0	Boiling point at zero yield of distillate
TBP	True boiling point
T_i	Boiling point of i-weight fraction of distillation curve
TLC	Thin-layer chromatography
VIS	Kinematic viscosity
VR	Vacuum residue
x_i	Weight fraction of i-component.

References

1. Liu, Y.; Chang, A.; Pashikanti, K. *Petroleum Refinery Process Modeling: Integrated Optimization Tools and Applications*; Wiley-VCH Verlag & Co. KGaA: Weinheim, Germany, 2018.
2. Gao, C. *Petroleum Production Technology*; Science Press: Beijing, China, 2017.
3. Hsu, C.S.; Robinson, P.R. *Petroleum Science and Technology*; Springer: Berlin/Heidelberg, Germany, 2019.
4. Kaiser, M.J.; De Klerk, A.; Gary, J.H.; Handwerk, G.E. *Petroleum Refining. Technology, Economics, and Markets*, 6th ed.; CRC Press: Boca Raton, FL, USA, 2020.
5. Lopes, M.S.; Savioli Lopes, M.; Maciel Filho, R.; Wolf Maciel, M.R.; Medina, L.C. Extension of the TBP curve of petroleum using the correlation DESTMOL. *Procedia Eng.* **2012**, *42*, 726–732. [CrossRef]
6. Chapter 5. Heptanes Plus Characterization. Available online: http://www.ipt.ntnu.no/~{}curtis/courses/PVT-Flow/Plus-Characterization/Molar-Distribution/SPE-Phase-Behavior-Monograph-Ch-5.pdf (accessed on 23 December 2022).
7. Riazi, M.R. *Characterization and Properties of Petroleum Fractions*; ASTM International: West Conshohocken, PA, USA, 2007.
8. Speight, J. *Rules of Thumb for Petroleum Engineers*; John Wiley & Sons, Inc.: Hoboken, NJ, USA, 2017.
9. Stratiev, D.S.; Marinov, I.; Nedelchev, A.; Velkov, I.; Stratiev, D.D.; Veli, A.; Mitkova, M.; Stanulov, K. Evaluation of approaches for conversion of ASTM into TBP distillation data of oil fractions. *OGEM* **2014**, *40*, 216–221.

10. Villalanti, D.C.; Raia, J.C.; Maynard, J.B. High-temperature simulated distillation applications in petroleum characterization. In *Encyclopedia of Analytical Chemistry*; John Wiley & Sons, Ltd.: Hoboken, NJ, USA, 2006.
11. *ASTM D2892-20*; Standard Test Method for Distillation of Crude Petroleum (15-Theoretical Plate Column). ASTM International: West Conshohocken, PA, USA, 2020.
12. *ASTM D5236-18a*; Standard Test Method for Distillation of Heavy Hydrocarbon Mixtures (Vacuum Potstill Method). ASTM International: West Conshohocken, PA, USA, 2018.
13. Stratiev, D.; Shishkova, I.; Ivanov, M.; Dinkov, R.; Argirov, G.; Vasilev, S.; Yordanov, D. Validation of diesel fraction content in heavy oils measured by high temperature simulated distillation and physical vacuum distillation by performance of commercial distillation test and process simulation. *Appl. Sci.* **2022**, *12*, 11824. [CrossRef]
14. Durand, J.-P.; Bré, A.; Béboulène, J.-J.; Ducrozet, A.; Carbonneaux, S. Improvement of simulated distillation methods by gas chromatography in routine analysis. *Oil Gas Sci. Technol.* **1999**, *54*, 431–438. [CrossRef]
15. Characterization of Crude Oil by Simulated Distillation. Patent WO2016111965A1, 14 July 2016.
16. Diaz, O.C.; Yarranton, H.W. Applicability of simulated distillation for heavy Oils. *Energy Fuels* **2019**, *33*, 6083–6087. [CrossRef]
17. Villalanti, D.C.; Raia, J.C.; Subramanian, M.; Williams, B. Application of high-temperature simulated distillation to the residuum oil supercritical extraction process in petroleum refining. *J. Chromatogr. Sci.* **2000**, *38*, 1–5.
18. Jennerwein, M.K.; Eschner, M.S.; Wilharm, T.; Zimmermann, R.; Gröger, T.M. Proof of concept of high-temperature comprehensive two-dimensional gas chromatography time-of-flight mass spectrometry for two-dimensional simulated distillation of crude oils. *Energy Fuels* **2017**, *31*, 11651–11659. [CrossRef]
19. Espinosa-Pena, M.; Figueroa-Gomez, Y.; Jimenez-Cruz, F. Simulated distillation yield curves in heavy crude oils: A comparison of precision between ASTM D-5307 and ASTM D-2892 physical distillation. *Energy Fuels* **2004**, *18*, 1832–1840. [CrossRef]
20. Rodrigues, E.V.A.; Silva, S.R.C.; Romão, W.; Castro, E.V.R.; Filgueiras, P.R. Determination of crude oil physicochemical properties by high-temperature gas chromatography associated with multivariate calibration. *Fuel* **2018**, *220*, 389–395. [CrossRef]
21. Coutinho, D.M.; França, D.; Vanini, G.; Gomes, A.O.; Azevedo, D.A. Understanding the molecular composition of petroleum and its distillation cuts. *Fuel* **2022**, *311*, 122594. [CrossRef]
22. Azinfar, B.; Zirrahi, M.; Hassanzadeh, H.; Abedi, J. Characterization of heavy crude oils and residues using combined Gel Permeation Chromatography and simulated distillation. *Fuel* **2018**, *233*, 885–893. [CrossRef]
23. Shishkova, I.; Stratiev, D.; Kolev, I.V.; Nenov, S.; Nedanovski, D.; Atanassov, K.; Ivanov, V.; Ribagin, S. Challenges in petroleum characterization—A review. *Energies* **2022**, *15*, 7765. [CrossRef]
24. Abutaqiya, M.I.L.; Sisco, C.J.; Khemka, Y.; Safa, M.A.; Ghloum, E.F.; Rashed, A.M.; Gharbi, R.; Santhanagopalan, S.; Al-Qahtani, M.; Al-Kandari, E.; et al. Accurate Modeling of Asphaltene Onset Pressure in Crude Oils Under Gas Injection Using Peng–Robinson Equation of State. *Energy Fuels* **2020**, *34*, 4055–4070. [CrossRef]
25. David Ting, P.; Hirasaki, G.J.; Chapman, W.G. Modeling of Asphaltene Phase Behavior with the SAFT Equation of State. *Pet. Sci. Technol.* **2003**, *21*, 647–661. [CrossRef]
26. Panuganti, S.R.; Vargas, F.M.; Gonzalez, D.L.; Kurup, A.S.; Chapman, W.G. PC-SAFT characterization of crude oils and modeling of asphaltene phase behavior. *Fuel* **2012**, *93*, 658–669. [CrossRef]
27. Punnapala, S.; Vargas, F.M. Revisiting the PC-SAFT characterization procedure for an improved asphaltene precipitation prediction. *Fuel* **2013**, *108*, 417–429. [CrossRef]
28. Abutaqiya, M.I.L.; Sisco, C.J.; Wang, J.; Vargas, F.M. Systematic Investigation of Asphaltene Deposition in the Wellbore and Near-Wellbore Region of a Deepwater Oil Reservoir Under Gas Injection. Part 1: Thermodynamic Modeling of the Phase Behavior of Polydisperse Asphaltenes. *Energy Fuels* **2019**, *33*, 3632–3644. [CrossRef]
29. Sisco, C.J.; Abutaqiya, M.I.L.; Wang, F.; Zhang, J.; Tavakkoli, M.; Vargas, F.M. Asphaltene Precipitation Modeling. In *Asphaltene Deposition: Fundamentals, Prediction, Prevention, and Remediation*, 1st ed.; CRC Press: Boca Raton, FL, USA, 2018; pp. 111–159.
30. Klein, G.C.; Angström, A.; Rodgers, R.P.; Marshall, A.G. Use of saturates/aromatics/resins/asphaltenes (SARA) fractionation to determine matrix effects in crude oil analysis by electrospray ionization fourier transform ion cyclotron resonance mass spectrometry. *Energy Fuels* **2006**, *20*, 668–672. [CrossRef]
31. Efimov, I.; Povarov, V.G.; Rudko, V.A. Comparison of UNIFAC and LSER models for calculating partition coefficients in the hexane–acetonitrile system using middle distillate petroleum products as an example. *Ind. Eng. Chem. Res.* **2022**, *61*, 9575–9585. [CrossRef]
32. Efimov, I.; Povarov, V.G.; Rudko, V.A. Use of partition coefficients in a hexane–acetonitrile system in the GC–MS analysis of polyaromatic hydrocarbons in the example of delayed coking gas oils. *ACS Omega* **2021**, *6*, 9910–9919. [CrossRef]
33. Benassi, M.; Berisha, A.; Romão, W.; Babayev, E.; Römpp, A.; Spengler, B. Petroleum crude oil analysis using low-temperature plasma mass spectrometry. *Rapid Commun. Mass Spectrom.* **2013**, *27*, 825–834. [CrossRef]
34. Rakhmatullin, I.; Efimov, S.; Tyurin, V.; Gafurov, M.; Al-Muntaser, A.; Varfolomeev, M.; Klochkov, V. Qualitative and quantitative analysis of heavy crude oil samples and their sara fractions with 13C nuclear magnetic resonance. *Processes* **2020**, *8*, 995. [CrossRef]
35. Afanasjeva, N.; González-Córdoba, A.; Palencia, M. Mechanistic approach to thermal production of new materials from asphaltenes of Castilla crude oil. *Processes* **2020**, *8*, 1644. [CrossRef]
36. Zheng, F.; Shi, Q.; Vallverdu, G.S.; Giusti, P.; Bouyssiere, B. Fractionation and characterization of petroleum asphaltene: Focus on metalopetroleomics. *Processes* **2020**, *8*, 1504. [CrossRef]

37. *ASTM D4052-18a*; Standard Test Method for Density, Relative Density, and API Gravity of Liquids by Digital Density Meter. ASTM International: West Conshohocken, PA, USA, 2018.
38. *ASTM D4294-21*; Standard Test Method for Sulfur in Petroleum and Petroleum Products by Energy Dispersive X-ray Fluorescence Spectrometr. ASTM International: West Conshohocken, PA, USA, 2021.
39. *ASTM D97-12*; Standard Test Method for Pour Point of Petroleum Products. ASTM International: West Conshohocken, PA, USA, 2015.
40. *ASTM D445-21e2*; Standard Test Method for Kinematic Viscosity of Transparent and Opaque Liquids (and Calculation of Dynamic Viscosity). ASTM International: West Conshohocken, PA, USA, 2021.
41. Stratiev, D.; Shishkova, I.; Nikolova, R.; Tsaneva, T.; Mitkova, M.; Yordanov, D. Investigation on precision of determination of SARA analysis of vacuum residual oils from different origin. *Pet Coal.* **2016**, *58*, 109–119.
42. Stratiev, D.; Shishkova, I.; Tsaneva, T.; Mitkova, M.; Yordanov, D. Investigation of relations between properties of vacuum residual oils from different origin, and of their deasphalted and asphaltene fractions. *Fuel* **2016**, *170*, 115–129. [CrossRef]
43. Atanassov, K.; Mavrov, D.; Atanassova, V. Intercriteria decision making: A new approach for multicriteria decision making, based on index matrices and intuitionistic fuzzy sets. *Issues Intuit. Fuzzy Sets Gen. Nets* **2014**, *11*, 1–8.
44. Atanassov, K.; Atanassova, V.; Gluhchev, G. Intercriteria analysis: Ideas and problems. *Notes Intuit. Fuzzy Sets* **2015**, *21*, 81–88.
45. Atanassov, K. *Index Matrices: Towards an Augmented Matrix Calculus*; Springer: Berlin/Heidelberg, Germany, 2014.
46. Stratiev, D.S.; Sotirov, S.; Shishkova, I.; Nedelchev, A.; Sharafutdinov, I.; Anife, V.; Mitkova, M.; Yordanov, D.; Sotirova, E.; Atanassova, K.; et al. Investigation of relationships between bulk properties and fraction properties of crude oils by application of the Intercriteria analysis. *Petrol. Sci. Technol.* **2016**, *34*, 1113–1120. [CrossRef]
47. Stratiev, D.; Shishkova, I.; Nedelchev, A.; Kirilov, K.; Nikolaychuk, E.; Ivanov, A.; Sharafutdinov, I.; Veli, A.; Mitkova, M.; Tsaneva, T.; et al. Investigation of relationships between petroleum properties and their impact on crude oil compatibility. *Energy Fuels* **2015**, *29*, 7836–7854. [CrossRef]
48. Stratiev, D.; Nenov, S.; Shishkova, I.; Georgiev, B.; Argirov, G.; Dinkov, R.; Yordanov, D.; Atanassova, V.; Vassilev, P.; Atanassov, K. Commercial investigation of the ebullated-bed vacuum residue hydrocracking in the conversion range of 55–93%. *ACS Omega* **2020**, *51*, 33290. [CrossRef] [PubMed]
49. Stratiev, D.; Shishkova, I.; Dinkov, R.; Kolev, I.; Argirov, G.; Ivanov, V.; Ribagin, S.; Atanassova, V.; Atanassov, K.; Stratiev, D.D.; et al. Intercriteria analysis to diagnose the reasons for increased fouling in a commercial ebullated bed vacuum residue hydrocracker. *ACS Omega* **2022**, *7*, 30462–30476. [CrossRef] [PubMed]
50. *ASTM D7169-20*; Standard Test Method for Boiling Point Distribution of Samples with Residues Such as Crude Oils and Atmospheric and Vacuum Residues by High Temperature Gas Chromatography. ASTM International: West Conshohocken, PA, USA, 2020.
51. Combining Simulated Distillation (ASTM D7169) and Detailed Hydrocarbon Analysis (ASTM D7900) for the Full Boiling Point Distribution of Crude Oils. Available online: https://www.petro-online.com/article/analytical-instrumentation/11/scion-instruments/combining-simulated-distillation-astm-d7169-and-detailed-hydrocarbon-analysis-astm-d7900-for-the-full-boiling-point-distribution-of-crude-oils/2943 (accessed on 4 January 2023).
52. Golden, S.; Barletta, T.; White, S. Vacuum unit performance. *Sour Heavy* **2012**, 11–15. Available online: www.digitalrefining.com/article/1000565 (accessed on 5 January 2023).
53. Golden, S.; Barletta, T. Designing vacuum units. *PTQ* **2006**, *Q2*, 105–110.
54. Golden, S.; Villalanti, D.C.; Martin, G.R. Feed characterization and deep cut vacuum columns: Simulation and design. In Proceedings of the AIChE 1994, Spring National Meeting, Atlanta, GA, USA, 17–21 April 1994.
55. He, P.; Ghoniem, A.F. A Group contribution pseudocomponent method for phase equilibrium modeling of mixtures of petroleum fluids and a solvent. *Ind. Eng. Chem. Res.* **2015**, *54*, 8809–8820. [CrossRef]
56. Mlquel, J.; Hernandez, J.; Castells, F. A New method for petroleum fractions and crude oil characterization. *SPE Reserv. Eng.* **1992**, *7*, 265–270.
57. Wauquier, J.-P. *Crude Oil Petroleum Products. Process Flowsheets*; Editions Technip: Paris, France, 1995.
58. Abdel-AalMohammed, H.K.; Alsahlawi, A. *Petroleum Economics and Engineering*, 3rd ed.; Taylor & Francis Group: Abingdon, UK, 2014.
59. Gary, J.H.; Handwerk, G.E.; Kaiser, M.J. *Petroleum Refining Technology and Economics*, 5th ed.; CRC Press: Boca Raton, FL, USA; Taylor & Francis Group: Abingdon, UK, 2007.
60. Swafford, P.; McCarthy, R. Improving crude oil selection. *PTQ* **2008**, *Q3*, 125–129.
61. Stratiev, D.; Shishkova, I.; Palichev, G.N.; Atanassov, K.; Ribagin, S.; Nenov, S.; Nedanovski, D.; Ivanov, V. Study of bulk properties relations to SARA Composition data of various vacuum residues employing intercriteria analysis. *Energies* **2022**, *15*, 9042. [CrossRef]
62. Yarranton, H. Prediction of crude oil saturate content from a simdist assay. *Energy Fuels* **2022**, *36*, 8809–8817. [CrossRef]
63. Stratiev, D.; Nenov, S.; Nedanovski, D.; Shishkova, I.; Dinkov, R.; Stratiev, D.D.; Stratiev, D.D.; Sotirov, S.; Sotirova, E.; Atanassova, V.; et al. Empirical modeling of viscosities and softening points of straight-run vacuum residues from different origins and of hydrocracked unconverted vacuum residues obtained in different conversions. *Energies* **2022**, *15*, 1755. [CrossRef]

64. Stratiev, D.; Nenov, S.; Sotirov, S.; Shishkova, I.; Palichev, G.; Sotirova, E.; Ivanov, V.; Atanassov, K.; Ribagin, S.; Angelova, N. Petroleum viscosity modeling using least squares and ANN methods. *J. Pet. Sci. Eng.* **2022**, *212*, 110306. [CrossRef]
65. Stratiev, D.; Shishkova, I.; Dinkov, R.; Nenov, S.; Sotirov, S.; Sotirova, E.; Kolev, I.; Ivanov, V.; Ribagin, S.; Atanassov, K.; et al. Prediction of petroleum viscosity from molecular weight and density. *Fuel* **2023**, *331*, 125679. [CrossRef]

Disclaimer/Publisher's Note: The statements, opinions and data contained in all publications are solely those of the individual author(s) and contributor(s) and not of MDPI and/or the editor(s). MDPI and/or the editor(s) disclaim responsibility for any injury to people or property resulting from any ideas, methods, instructions or products referred to in the content.

MDPI AG
Grosspeteranlage 5
4052 Basel
Switzerland
Tel.: +41 61 683 77 34

Processes Editorial Office
E-mail: processes@mdpi.com
www.mdpi.com/journal/processes

Disclaimer/Publisher's Note: The title and front matter of this reprint are at the discretion of the Guest Editors. The publisher is not responsible for their content or any associated concerns. The statements, opinions and data contained in all individual articles are solely those of the individual Editors and contributors and not of MDPI. MDPI disclaims responsibility for any injury to people or property resulting from any ideas, methods, instructions or products referred to in the content.

www.ingramcontent.com/pod-product-compliance
Lightning Source LLC
LaVergne TN
LVHW072315090526
838202LV00019B/2288